THE OXFOR
HISTORY OF ENGLIS

❧

VOLUME II

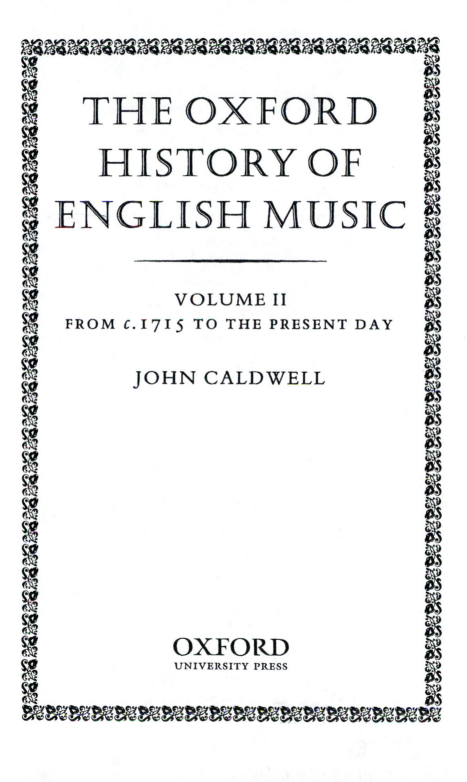

THE OXFORD
HISTORY OF
ENGLISH MUSIC

VOLUME II
FROM c.1715 TO THE PRESENT DAY

JOHN CALDWELL

OXFORD
UNIVERSITY PRESS

*This book has been printed digitally and produced in a standard specification
in order to ensure its continuing availability*

OXFORD
UNIVERSITY PRESS

Great Clarendon Street, Oxford OX2 6DP

Oxford University Press is a department of the University of Oxford.
It furthers the University's objective of excellence in research, scholarship,
and education by publishing worldwide in

Oxford New York

Auckland Bangkok Buenos Aires Cape Town Chennai
Dar es Salaam Delhi Hong Kong Istanbul Karachi Kolkata
Kuala Lumpur Madrid Melbourne Mexico City Mumbai Nairobi
São Paulo Shanghai Singapore Taipei Tokyo Toronto
with an associated company in Berlin

Oxford is a registered trade mark of Oxford University Press
in the UK and in certain other countries

Published in the United States
by Oxford University Press Inc., New York

ISBN 0-19-816288-X

Cover illustration: Lyceum Theatre (interior), London.
Engraving from *Illustrated London News*, 19 April 1856.
Copyright of The Royal College of Music, London

Preface

⚜

THIS second volume of *The Oxford History of English Music* carries the
story forward from the early eighteenth century to as close to the
present day as is consistent with a balanced and historical approach.

In general the method of treatment is similar to that of the previous
volume. The main subdivisions in the first four chapters are according to
genre; composers are discussed in relation to their contributions to a genre
rather than in their own right, as they would be in a monograph or
encyclopaedia. But in Chapter 5, dealing with the period 1914–45, when
the importance of genre is beginning to recede, I have offered thumbnail
sketches of the principal composers as well. In the next two chapters the
contributions of individual composers form the basis of the discussion. A
chapter on folk and popular music follows, and a conclusion.

A number of difficult questions of principle have arisen in the course of
writing this volume, though they were predictable from the outset. One is
how to handle the issue of quality. To overpraise the English music of the
eighteenth and nineteenth centuries would be as damaging as its previous
denigration has been. A reviewer of Volume I threw down the gauntlet over
my attempt to link England's musical fame abroad with the political alliances
of the late sixteenth and early seventeenth centuries: how would the argument apply, he asked, to the late nineteenth century, when the British
Empire was at its height? My answer is that, fortunately perhaps for
England, music was no longer a currency in diplomatic relations. I have
simply tried to allocate praise and blame as fairly as I can—praise of
composers who coped successfully with the problems with which they
were faced, and criticism when they failed to lift their level above the
commonplace. (I stress, lest I be misunderstood, that I do not intend this
in a moral sense: I am concerned simply with the lasting value of their music
from a present-day perspective.)

The final chapter explains and attempts to justify the rationale of the
treatment in the two volumes as a whole, and it has also given me the
opportunity of handling the further question of the relation between
England and its close neighbours—Scotland, Ireland, and Wales. The

truth is that, while the term 'English' cannot be held to imply the inclusion of these countries, their total exclusion from the narrative would be equally misleading. Scottish, Irish, and Welsh composers (as defined by birth and a certain retained identity) are discussed in the main narrative if they became English by adoption, so to speak: one thinks for example of the Irishmen Balfe and Stanford. Some others not so considered are mentioned more briefly in the last chapter, where this relationship is treated as the middle term in a series dealing with England and the wider world on the one hand and London and the provinces on the other.

A final question, the one most frequently asked of me while I was engaged on the book, was where to call a halt. It was clear that I ought to be as up-to-date as possible on the output of major composers. In the event I decided not to discuss on an individual basis the music of any composer born after 1960 (if an occasional mention has slipped through the net, I apologize). Although the oldest of them will reach the age of 40 in the year 2000, it is difficult to be confident about their lasting place in English musical history. Certainly there is an enormous variety of talent amongst composers of that age and younger, but quite apart from the strains put upon one's critical faculties in making a choice from among them, there was the danger of producing no more than an annotated list of personal preferences.

I do not claim to have eliminated personal preferences from the book as a whole, however: it would hardly have been possible, and in my view would have been undesirable, to do so. The reader will quickly become aware of my enthusiasms and blind spots. Nor do I intend an encyclopaedic completeness. From time to time I have discussed and even illustrated music of decidedly inferior quality, not in order to make fun of it but because it is characteristic of its period. If at times these examples appear to have crowded out worthier specimens that is partly because a great deal of the best of English music is now available in excellent editions.

It remains for me to thank those who have helped in the writing of this book. So many friends have contributed to my understanding through casual conversation and chance remarks that it would be impossible to name them all; they may well find that they recognize as their own some unacknowledged insight of which I have forgotten the origin. Both this volume and its predecessor owe much to the friendly disposition of Brian Trowell, always ready to discuss points of detail over an astonishingly wide chronological range. Those who have answered individual questions include Robert Bruce and Peter Ward Jones at the Bodleian Library, and my colleague Harry Johnstone. For help of various kinds I am much indebted to Barry Griffiths, John Manger, David Maw, and Mark Taylor. I should also like to acknowledge a general indebtedness to the *Blackwell* (originally *Athlone*) *History of Music in Britain*; it has been a particular convenience that each of the well-researched volumes devoted to the period covered by this book has appeared before its completion. I am grateful to the reviewers of Volume I, some of whose more general concerns I have tried to address in writing this one. My thanks also to those who read the typescript, in full or in part: Harry Johnstone, Peter Evans, Michael Hurd, and Stephen Banfield. Their contribution has been enormously helpful, though they are not to be impugned with those errors of fact or of judgement that remain, for which I take the entire responsibility. To Bruce Phillips of Oxford University Press I owe a great debt for his long-standing confidence in the whole enterprise as well as for his constant encouragement and support. To Helen Foster and her colleagues at the Press, too, I offer my warmest thanks; to the expert copy-editor, Bonnie Blackburn; to Humaira Erfan-Ahmed; and to successive secretaries at the Music Faculty who have typed the bulk of the book. Finally I acknowledge with gratitude the continued support of my wife, Janet, and family; she, too, has contributed much by way of typing, editing, and other forms of practical help while remaining, as always, my most persistent encourager when things appeared to be going more slowly than they should.

J.C.

Oxford
June 1997

Acknowledgements

The author and publisher are grateful to the following for permission to reproduce musical examples from works in their copyright ownership. While every effort has been made to trace copyright owners, any inadvertent omission will be repaired in a future edition.

The Basil Harwood Estate

Basil Harwood, Communion Service in A flat

Boosey and Hawkes Music Publishers Ltd.

Peter Maxwell Davies, Symphony No. 1. © 1978 Boosey & Hawkes Music Publishers Ltd.

Peter Maxwell Davies, Symphony No. 2. © 1978 Boosey & Hawkes Music Publishers Ltd.

Frederick Delius, *A Village Romeo and Juliet*. © 1910 Hawkes & Son (London) Ltd.

John Ireland, Fantasy-Sonata in E flat for clarinet and piano. © 1945 Hawkes & Son (London) Ltd.

Nicholas Maw, *Scenes and Arias*. © 1971 Boosey & Hawkes Music Publishers Ltd.

Vaughan Williams, *On Wenlock Edge*. © 1911 by Ralph Vaughan Williams. Revised edition © 1946 Boosey & Co. Ltd.

Chester Music Ltd.

Lennox Berkeley, Violin Concerto, Op. 59. Reproduced by permission of Chester Music Ltd., 8/9 Frith Street, London W1V 5TZ

Vaughan Williams, 'Silent Noon'. Reproduced by permission of Edwin Ashdown Ltd., 8/9 Frith Street, London W1V 5TZ

Vaughan Williams, *Sancta Civitas* (for territories except the UK, Republic of Ireland, Canada, Australia, New Zealand, Israel, Jamaica, and South Africa). Reproduced by permission of J. Curwen & Sons Ltd., 8/9 Frith Street, London W1V 5TZ

EMI Music

Elisabeth Lutyens, *O saisons, ô châteaux*

Faber Music Ltd.

Vaughan Williams, *Sancta Civitas* (for the UK, Republic of Ireland, Canada, Australia, New Zealand, Israel, Jamaica, and South Africa)

Novello & Co. Ltd.

Malcolm Arnold, Divertimento for Wind Trio, Op. 37; Symphony No. 2, Op. 40. Reproduced by permission of Peterson's Publications Ltd.

Edward Elgar, *The Black Knight*, Op. 25; *Caractacus*, Op. 35; 'Pleading', Op. 48 No. 1; Variations on an Original Theme, Op. 36; Symphony No. 1 in A flat, Op. 55; Quintet in A minor for piano and strings, Op. 84; Quartet in E minor, Op. 83; Cello Concerto, Op. 85. Reproduced by permission of Novello & Co., Ltd., 8/9 Frith Street, London W1V 5TZ

Gustav Holst, *The Mystic Trumpeter; Egdon Heath*. Reproduced by permission of Novello & Co., Ltd., 8/9 Frith Street, London W1V 5TZ

Oxford University Press

John Buller, *Proença*, © Oxford University Press 1985
Ivor Gurney, *Brown is my Love*. © Oxford University Press 1959
M. Karpeles (ed.), four folk songs from *Cecil Sharp's Collection of English Folk Songs*. © Oxford University Press 1974
Alan Rawsthorne, String Quartet No. 1. © Oxford University Press 1946
William Walton, Symphony No. 1. © Oxford University Press 1936
Vaughan Williams, *Riders to the Sea*. © Oxford University Press 1936

Schott & Co. Ltd., London; Alfred A. Kalmus Ltd.

Alexander Goehr, *Das Gesetz der Quadrille*, Op. 41. © 1983 Schott & Co. Ltd., London. Reproduced by permission

Alexander Goehr, '. . . *a musical offering (J.S.B. 1985)* . . .', Op. 46. © 1985 Schott & Co. Ltd. London. Reproduced by permission

Cyril Scott, *Rainbow Trout*. © 1916 B. Schotts Söhne, Mainz. Reproduced by permission

Michael Tippett, *Boyhood's End*. © 1945 Schott & Co. Ltd., London. Reproduced by permission

Michael Tippett, Symphony No. 2. © 1958 Schott & Co. Ltd., London. Reproduced by permission

Ethel Smyth, *The Wreckers*. © 1911 Ethel Smyth. Reproduced by permission of Alfred A. Kalmus Ltd.

Stainer & Bell Ltd.

Basil Harwood, *Dithyramb*. Reproduced by permission of Stainer & Bell Ltd., © 1892

Herbert Howells, Rhapsodic Quintet. Reproduced by permission of Stainer & Bell Ltd., © 1921

E. J. Moeran, String Trio. Reproduced by permission of Stainer & Bell, Ltd., © 1936

Vaughan Williams, *Phantasy Quintet*. Reproduced by permission of Stainer & Bell Ltd.

Contents

List of Plates

The author and publisher are grateful to those named below for permission to reproduce illustrations in their possession, and to their copyright owners.

   I. (*a*) John Christopher Pepusch (1667–1752). Portrait by an unknown artist. Faculty of Music, Oxford; (*b*) Carl Friedrich Abel (1723–87). Portrait by an unknown artist. Faculty of Music, Oxford; (*c*) Ticket for a Bach–Abel concert season. Royal College of Music.

  II. (*a*) *The Bohemian Girl* at Drury Lane. *Illustrated London News*, 23 December 1843. Royal College of Music; (*b*) Lyceum Theatre, interior, 1856. *Illustrated London News*. Royal College of Music

 III. (*a*) Charles Dibdin (1745–1814). Watercolour by Robert Dighton. Royal College of Music; (*b*) Thomas Attwood (1765–1838). Portrait by an unknown artist, *c.* 1815. Royal College of Music; (*c*) Samuel Sebastian Wesley (1810–76). Portrait by William Keighley Briggs, 1849. Royal College of Music

  IV. (*a*) Louis Jullien conducting at Covent Garden. *Illustrated London News*, 7 November 1846. Royal College of Music; (*b*) The former Colston Hall, Bristol (from a postcard, *c.* 1940). Royal College of Music

   V. (*a*) Granville Bantock, Barry Jackson, Edward Elgar, H. K. Ayliff, Cedric Hardwicke, Edith Evans, and G.B. Shaw, Malvern, *c.*1930. Royal College of Music; (*b*) Herbert Howells (1892–1983). Drawing by William Rothenstein, 1919; (*c*) Ethyl Smyth (1858–1944). Portrait by Neville Lytton, 1936

  VI. (*a*) Arthur Sullivan (1842–1900). Marble bust by W. G. John, 1902. Royal College of Music; (*b*) George Grove (1820–1900). Bronze bust by Alfred Gilbert, 1895. Royal College of Music

 VII. A rehearsal for *The Rape of Lucretia* at Glyndebourne: Ernest Ansermet (directing Nancy Evans and Flora Nielsen, out of sight), Benjamin Britten (at the piano), and Reginald Goodall, who conducted some of the performances. *Picture Post*, 13 July 1946. Hulton–Getty

VIII. Peter Maxwell Davies (b. 1934). Portrait by Fred Schley, 1997. Royal College of Music, reproduced by permission of the artist

List of Tables

List of Musical Examples

Abbreviations

THE following, in addition to those in common use, are employed in the footnotes and bibliography. Where full details are given here the item is not repeated in the bibliography; nor are details given of easily found journals and some other series. Publishers' names are included only for editions of music.

AcM	*Acta Musicologica*
AIM	American Institute of Musicology
BHMB	*The Blackwell History of Music in Britain*, ed. I. Spink (London, 1981, and Oxford, 1988–)
EBM	*Early Bodleian Music*, 3 vols., ed. Sir J. Stainer (vols. i–ii) and E. W. B. Nicholson (vol. iii) (London: Novello, 1901–13)
EECM	Early English Church Music, ed. F. Ll. Harrison and others (London: Stainer and Bell, 1963–)
FMJ	*Folk Music Journal* (1965–)
HG	*G. F. Händels Werke: Ausgabe der deutschen Händelgesellschaft*, ed. F. W. Chrysander (Leipzig and Bergedorf bei Hamburg: Breitkopf und Härtel, 1858–94, 1902)
HHA	*Hallische Händel-Ausgabe im Auftrage der Georg Friedrich Händel-Gesellschaft*, ed. M. Schneider, R. Steglich, and others (Kassel, etc.: Bärenreiter, 1955–)
JAMS	*Journal of the American Musicological Society*
JEFDS	*Journal of the English Folk Dance Society* (London, 1914–15, 1927–31)
JEFDSS	*Journal of the English Folk Dance and Song Society* (London, 1932–64)
JFSS	*Journal of the Folk-Song Society* (London, 1899–1931)
LPS	The London Pianoforte School 1766–1860 (facs.), ed. N. Temperley, 20 vols. (New York and London: Garland, 1984–7)
LS	*The London Stage 1660–1800: A Calendar of Plays, Entertainments and Afterpieces*, 5 pts. in 11 vols., ed. W. Van Lennep, E. L.

	Avery, A. H. Scouten, G. W. Stone, and C. B. Hogan (Carbondale, Ill., 1960–8)
LSJ	*Lute Society Journal*
MB	Musica Britannica (London: Stainer and Bell, 1951–)
MC	Musica da Camera, ed. J. Caldwell (London: Oxford University Press, 1972–)
ML	*Music and Letters*
MLE	Music in London Entertainment 1660–1800 (Tunbridge Wells: Richard McNutt, 1983–7; London: Stainer and Bell, 1988–)
MQ	*Musical Quarterly*
MR	*Music Review*
MT	*Musical Times*
NGD	*The New Grove Dictionary of Music and Musicians*, ed. S. Sadie, 20 vols. (London, 1981)
NOBC	*The New Oxford Book of Carols*, ed. A. Parrott and H. Keyte (Oxford, 1992)
NOHM	*The New Oxford History of Music*, ed. J. A. Westrup *et al.*, 10 vols. (London and Oxford, 1954–90)
PMFC	Polyphonic Music of the Fourteenth Century
PRMA	*Proceedings of the Royal Musical Association*
RECM	*Records of English Court Music*, 9 vols., ed. A. Ashbee (Snodland and Aldershot, 1986–96)
RMARC	*Royal Musical Association Research Chronicle*
RRMBE	Recent Researches in Music of the Baroque Era
STC	*A Short-Title Catalogue of Books Printed in England, Scotland, and Ireland . . . 1475–1640*, 2nd edn., 3 vols., ed W. A. Jackson, F. S. Ferguson, and K. F. Pantzer (London, 1976–90)
TECM	*The Treasury of English Church Music*, 5 vols., ed. G. H. Knight and W. L. Reed (London: Blandford, 1965)

Author's Note

MUSICAL examples have where possible been transcribed from primary sources. In a few cases an evidently reliable secondary source, such as a manuscript copy or a posthumous print, has been used. Sources are in full score unless otherwise noted, and are generally compressed without special mention being made of the fact. For large-scale vocal works, I have usually availed myself of a contemporary vocal score; in such cases I have followed the copy literally except where noted. Where additional material has been imported from the full score, or where other changes of layout have been made, the word 'adapted' is used in the captions.

In a work covering so large a period complete consistency in editorial procedure is scarcely attainable, though every effort has been made to represent the sources faithfully. Bass figuring has been placed below the stave whatever the practice of the original. The orthography of the texts has not been normalized, though word-division has been supplemented. Accidentals are as in the source; elements in square brackets are editorial, while those in round brackets are to be inferred from information given elsewhere in the source.

1

HANDEL AND HIS ENGLISH CONTEMPORARIES, *c.1715–c.1760*

THE career of Handel in England in many ways anticipates that of a composer such as Mozart in youth or Haydn in his later years in its jettisoning of the constraints of service for the sake of independence and the risks and rewards of catering for the public taste. In this respect Handel's own predilections coincided with the imperatives of English musical life, where the social and political structure did not allow of congenial long-term employment outside the increasingly humdrum routine of the royal court and chapel and that of the major churches. Handel had experienced a mixture of enterprise and short-term employment (with the marquis Francesco Ruspoli) in Italy, and had subsequently become Kapellmeister to the elector of Hanover, later George I of England. On his first visit to England Handel achieved enormous musical and social success,[1] and this must have encouraged him to return, ostensibly for a second short visit, in 1712. Encouraged by his ready acceptance (he was given a pension by Queen Anne and commissioned to write a Te Deum and Jubilate to commemorate the Treaty of Utrecht),[2] he stayed on, only to be confronted, as we have seen, by the accession of George I. But any embarrassment this may have caused was soon dissipated, and Handel came to enjoy the highest official favour as well as considerable public esteem.[3] His professional life was by no means without vicissitudes, but as a whole it represented a highly successful manipulation of social and financial opportunity. Handel did not reject paid employment; rather, he combined it with risk-bearing enterprise in such a way as to keep himself before the public eye and maximize his gains.

[1] See Vol. I, p. 588.
[2] In 1713. His birthday ode for Queen Anne, 'Eternal source of light divine', dates from the same year.
[3] He retained his Hanover Kapellmeistership for a time, and his pension was increased first to £400, later to £600, an income which he enjoyed for life (*NGD*).

All this would be of little interest were it not for Handel's towering genius. His English contemporaries were given the posts that carried the greatest prestige, but they could not match, even the best of them, the extraordinary vitality of his music. Although English audiences later came to admire Handel for the wrong reasons, there was in many respects an excellent match between their expectations and his propensities. What is more, he found himself well able to adapt his style to changes of taste. It is true that he pursued the cultivation of Italian opera long after realistic hopes that his achievements would be widely appreciated had evaporated. But he was here grappling with a deeper current, and he eventually came to realize that English oratorio, accidentally invented and its artistic potential not immediately grasped, could indeed restore the desired symbiosis between the composer and a wide audience.

The current just mentioned was a shift from the libertinism of post-Restoration England (and especially London) towards a more censorious and puritanical society.[4] In some quarters the highest ethical standards had always been proclaimed, but the rift between public aspirations and their fulfilment in practice had been widely tolerated. In some ways it was a move from a 'Catholic' attitude, with its understanding of and ready pardon for sin, to a 'Protestant' one with its emphasis on predestination. It led in due course to Methodism (which penetrated where earlier forms of dissent had not) and ultimately to the entrenchment of evangelical or 'low church' opinion in the fabric of the Anglican Church.

Handel had been brought up in a tradition of liberal Protestantism; he had explored Italian opera while earning his living in the Hamburg orchestra, and was thoroughly at home in the musical ambience of Catholic Italy, where he wrote two more operas, solo cantatas, Latin church music, and the oratorios *Il trionfo del Tempo* and *La resurrezione*. By the end of his Italian sojourn early in 1710 he had mastered that idiom of elevated courtliness, suited alike to theatre and church, which is the hallmark of the late Baroque. That was what he brought to London, and that was what London in the reign of Queen Anne, with its newly fashionable Italian opera and a not yet obsolete tradition of ecclesiastical pomp, was ready to welcome.

But from the outset conditions differed from those that Handel had previously experienced. Italian opera had put down only shallow roots, and for eminently predictable social and cultural reasons it remained a tender plant on British soil. The Church, even in the shape of the Chapel Royal, had ceased to provide a worthwhile challenge for creative genius, and required elaborate music only for special occasions. In the second decade of the eighteenth century, however, these inherent differences lay below the surface. The Chapel Royal maintained high standards under

---

[4] W. Dean, *Handel's Dramatic Oratorios and Masques* (London, 1959), 130–2, 136.

William Croft (whose death, and succession as organist and composer by Maurice Greene, in 1727 coincided with the accession of the second George); the court put a premium on public magnificence; and in the hurly-burly of London's theatrical life the Italian opera seemed to have a promising future.

In such a world, with no serious living English rival, Handel could not but quickly reach the position of dominance which he never relinquished. Lacking a regular church or court post, he was spared the tedium of routine work while being available to compose for the most spectacular occasions. In the midst of a frenetic burst of new composition, and the re-arrangement and adaptation of earlier works of all kinds, however, it is clear that it was Italian opera which engaged his attention at the deepest level and seemed to hold out the promise of becoming the most profitable and satisfying of his ventures. Although this was the sphere to which English-born composers were least drawn, either by ability or by natural inclination, a discussion of its role in English musical life, and of Handel's remarkable contribution to it, forms an essential backdrop to the native achievement in the period covered by this chapter.

Handel's Operas

Handel was arguably the greatest of all composers of *opera seria*, as well as being happy to contribute to the lighter genres of pastoral and comedy. *Opera seria* (literally 'serious opera') in the eighteenth century was a tightly circumscribed form, governed essentially by the alternation between recitative, in which the action was carried on, and arias, in which individual characters expressed the emotions to which their situation gave rise. This convention grew out of an understandable desire to exploit the opportunities afforded by music both for the dramatic heightening of actual speech and for the portrayal of mood; but the resulting polarization became all too predictable, and the arias a vehicle for vocal display—not solely of agility, but of any of the qualities required for the effective delivery of a particular type of vocal line. The da capo convention allowed for a contrast of mood but necessitated a return to the original one, masked, however, by the vocal ornamentation that was considered obligatory on the repeat. Audiences tended to value *opera seria* more as an exhibition of vocal prowess, enhanced by scenery, costume, and stage effects, than for any dramatic or even purely musical qualities it may have had. The librettos themselves (as 'reformed' by Apostolo Zeno and his successor Pietro Metastasio) eschewed comedy and all but the most conventional deployment of situation and motive; plots were complex webs of intrigue and mistaken identity, carried on in the palaces of ancient or mythological heroes and brought to a conclusion by some improbable act of regal clemency.

The *opera seria* convention, however, despite its encouragement of thoughtless conformity in both words and music, had its advantages. In the hands of a tolerably competent composer, it could be guaranteed to express the emotions called for at key moments of the dramatic action. More importantly, perhaps, it sanitized the discourse by channelling the emotional content into predictable formulae. *Opera seria* depended for its impact on a type of restraint that can legitimately be called 'classical'; it adopted (like other forms of classicism) an ethical standpoint related to Christian values, but expressed almost exclusively in terms of mythology or ancient history. The ethical stance was too generalized to be a matter for religious contention, and the subject-matter too closely bound up with the fabric of European education to be dismissed out of hand, however trivialized it might seem to the more austere moralists.

But Handel's operas transcend their genre. Small variations on established convention were sufficient to give dramatic impetus to unpromising situations, while episodes of sorcery, madness, or comedy entailed a wider expressive range. He did not set unaltered librettos by Metastasio or Zeno; his books were either adaptations or, occasionally, newly written dramas by such men as Giacomo Rossi, Nicola Francesco Haym, and Paolo Rolli, all of them resident in London at various periods.[5] Conditions in the second decade of the eighteenth century, however, did not encourage the full flowering of the form's potential. Rossi, Handel's collaborator for the strikingly successful *Rinaldo* as well as for the much less spectacular *Pastor fido* and for *Silla*, which vanished almost without trace, was a mediocre dramatist; while Handel, who had composed *Rinaldo* in haste by drawing extensively on existing music, seems not to have been fired by the two other librettos. *Teseo* and *Amadigi di Gaula*, however, derived by Haym from five-act French librettos, are another matter:[6] the strains of adaptation show in the omission of the typically French chorus parts and the failure of the singers to exit after their arias in the manner required by Italian convention, but their more sympathetically portrayed characters drew from Handel an inexhaustible flow of expressive melody, and together they mark a further stage in his progress towards full operatic maturity.

Despite the initial success of *Teseo* (thirteen performances in 1713), the continued popularity of *Amadigi* (seventeen performances between 1715 and 1717), and a revival of *Rinaldo*, which had ten performances in 1716–17, and despite all attempts to woo audiences with pasticcios and operas by other composers, the fortunes of Italian opera in the King's Theatre waned rapidly, and after the 1716–17 season performances ceased altogether. During this period Handel was much occupied with other music of various

[5] On Handel's librettists, see W. Dean and J. M. Knapp, *Handel's Operas 1704–1726* (Oxford, 1987), 16–17. This book is the principal modern source for the period covered.

[6] For Haym's probable authorship of *Amadigi*, see Dean and Knapp, 274.

kinds (including three suites of 'Water Music', some or all of which presumably accompanied a famous royal barge party on the Thames on 17–18 July 1717), and resided for a time (1713–16) at Burlington House, the earl of Burlington's palatial residence in Piccadilly (it is possible that *Silla* was given its one and only performance there). After the collapse of the Italian opera, however, he took the post of resident composer to the earl of Carnarvon, later duke of Chandos, living mainly (it seems) at the earl's country mansion at Cannons, near Edgware.[7] Here he wrote amongst other things the eleven Chandos anthems and the 'masques' *Acis and Galatea* and *Hamon and Mordecai* (or *Esther*), to which we shall return.

Italian opera, then, had failed as an ordinary commercial enterprise. In assessing the reasons for this we should bear in mind that serious English musical drama was even less successful; nevertheless, the language barrier was certainly one of the obstacles to a more general appreciation, and together with use of castrati and the integration of musical display into the dramatic action contributed to its later perception as 'an exotick and irrational entertainment'.[8] What is more surprising is that a group of influential noblemen and other enthusiasts should feel sufficiently concerned to mount a rescue operation. The result of their enterprise was known as 'The Royal Academy of Musick'. This took the form of a joint stock company: there were to be fifty shares of £200 each, to be paid for in instalments, and the rather unrealistic expectation was that subscribers would eventually see a return on their money from the sale of tickets, though they were themselves expected to pay for admission. An annual subsidy of £1,000 was granted by George I. Handel became musical director and the Swiss impresario J. J. Heidegger manager. Despite these preparations, the operas lost money, and from the third season (1721/2) an annual subscription scheme, guaranteeing fifty performances for 20 guineas, was introduced. This worked well to begin with, but after this season the opera company again started losing money, and the last season in which operas were given was that of 1727/8, though the company was not formally wound up until early in 1729.[9]

For this company Handel wrote his finest operas, culminating in a splendid series of collaborations with Haym: *Ottone* (12 January 1723), *Flavio* (14 May 1723), *Giulio Cesare in Egitto* (20 February 1724), *Tamerlano* (31 October 1724), and *Rodelinda* (13 February 1725).[10] His earlier and later collaborations with Haym, and those with Rolli, are on the whole less convincing dramatically, though all contain fine music and were not

---

[7] The earl's Master of Music was John Christopher Pepusch (see below, pp. 9–10).

[8] Samuel Johnson, Life of John Hughes, in his *Lives of the Poets* (1781). For Hughes see below, p. 49.

[9] E. Gibson, *The Royal Academy of Music 1719–1728* (New York and London, 1989) gives full details of the fortunes of this enterprise.

[10] Dates are those of first performance: seasons ran from September to June. Dean and Knapp make a good case for the underrated *Flavio*.

necessarily less appealing to the audiences of the day. *Radamisto* in particular, Handel's own first contribution to the Academy (27 April 1720), set the pattern of heroic opera, with its story of illicit and virtuous love in conflict. In *Giulio Cesare*, which for consistency of style and dramatic aptness must be accounted Handel's masterpiece in the genre, Caesar's passion for Cleopatra becomes the focus of the action, and his victory over Ptolemy the occasion of its ultimate triumph. The employment of a historical framework to sanction the amoral treatment of sexual behaviour recalls the plot of Monteverdi's *L'Incoronazione di Poppea* and foreshadows the preoccupations of Romantic opera. Handel's music is not Romantic in a stylistic sense, but it employs a wide range of instrumentation, much *recitativo accompagnato*, and a compelling rhetorical treatment of the vocal line in the arias. Handel's musical language did indeed develop beyond this point, but he never again equalled that combination of piercing intensity and icy detachment that makes this work so compelling a theatrical experience.

The Academy's seasons also included operas by Giovanni Porta, Domenico Scarlatti (*Narciso*, arranged by Thomas Roseingrave), Giovanni Bononcini, Attilio Ariosti, and others, together with masquerades (to which the Bishop of London objected) and concerts.[11] After its collapse, the King's Theatre was leased for five years to Handel and Heidegger personally, and the so-called 'Second Academy' was born. Between December 1729 and July 1734 they mounted new operas by Handel himself, together with revivals and pasticcios. Amongst the revivals were performances of *Acis* and *Esther*; the 'new' oratorio *Deborah*, itself based largely on old material, was produced on 17 March 1733. The artistic summit of this venture was the opera *Orlando* (27 January 1733), in which Handel displayed a richer variety of resource than hitherto, not least in the vivid depiction of the eponymous hero's madness. Though Handel's personal standing was as high as ever, his difficulties with his singers, and in particular with the castrato Senesino, led to resentment of his monopoly on the part of his principal patrons. The rival 'Opera of the Nobility' opened at Lincoln's Inn Fields with Porpora's *Arianna in Nasso* (2 December 1733), while Handel produced his own *Arianna in Creta* at the King's Theatre (26 January 1734, with seventeen performances altogether).

After the 1733/4 season Heidegger resumed sole control of the King's Theatre under noble patronage, while Handel moved to Covent Garden, which had opened in 1732 under the management of John Rich.[12] London

---

[11] For the masquerades see Gibson, 130.

[12] John Rich (1691 or 1692–1761) was the son of Christopher Rich, manager of the Drury Lane Theatre from 1690 to 1709 and hence during the initial phase of Italianate opera there. John Rich had been manager of Lincoln's Inn Fields when *The Beggar's Opera* was produced there (see below, p. 12). For further light on the vicissitudes of Handel's operatic career at this period see R. D. Hume, 'Handel and Opera Management in London in the 1730s', *ML* 67 (1986), 347–62.

was to experience Italian opera intermittently throughout the eighteenth century, but in the 1730s and 1740s neither Handel nor his rivals enjoyed more than an occasional temporary success. Handel's last successful operatic season, that of 1734–5, saw, in addition to a revival of *Arianna* and the pasticcio *Oreste*, the production of *Ariodante* (8 January 1735, with eleven performances) and *Alcina* (16 April, with eighteen performances), both based like *Orlando* on episodes from Ariosto's *Orlando furioso*. These modest successes were by no means sufficient to turn the tide of his fortunes. Despite his commercial difficulties, however, and despite a stroke brought on by overwork, he continued to struggle with opera: he returned to the King's Theatre under Heidegger in 1738 with *Faramondo* (3 January) and *Serse* (15 April). In 1739/40 and 1740/1 he leased Lincoln's Inn Fields, where his last two operas, *Imeneo* (22 November 1740) and *Deidamia* (10 January 1741) were given. They received two and three performances respectively, and Handel finally acknowledged defeat.

Handel was not merely a composer of Italian opera but an administrator and impresario, sometimes as a salaried employee and sometimes on a freelance basis. As a non-Italian working in England, his preoccupation with the form must have stemmed partly at least from his optimistic view of its artistic viability and its rightness for him personally. Its commercial potential was founded on the public's desire to hear great singers in the medium for which they were trained and in which alone they could or would perform. The early successes of the Royal Academy were due to its ability to engage the finest singers: castrati such as Senesino and Berselli, the sopranos Francesca Cuzzoni and Faustina Bordoni, and the tenor Francesco Borosini. Although Cuzzoni enjoyed a spectacular debut in Handel's *Ottone*, it was in the musically more straightforward operas of Bononcini that the attractions of great singing were most appreciated at first. The 'Opera of the Nobility' owed its initial success to its engagement of the great castrato Carlo Broschi, known as Farinelli, who had earlier declined to sing for Handel.[13] Eventually Handel came to rely more and more on English singers, who alone were capable of doing justice to his oratorios, and so to play his own vital part in developing a native tradition of fine solo singing.

Musical Theatre in English

We shall return to Handel and his oratorios, but first something needs to be said about other forms of musical theatre in England. Music was an essential adornment of all types of theatre throughout the eighteenth century, though it gradually ceased to play more than a marginal role in most 'straight' plays. But serious spoken drama was in decline in any case, and while a new

---

[13] Gibson, 282–3.

respect for the text came to be adopted in revivals of Shakespeare, a degree of musical elaboration was invariably maintained; and in a few cases, as with *Macbeth*, the seventeenth-century tradition of 'operatic' treatment persisted. These special cases apart, and with the exception of Italian opera, the London musical theatre extended from serious attempts at all-sung English opera on the one hand to pantomimes and burlesques on the other. In between came a variety of types of entertainment: 'masques', semi-operas, ballad operas, and more sophisticated types of comic opera with spoken dialogue. To devise a rigid typology of musical theatre in eighteenth-century England would be a pointless exercise, but some attempt should be made to define the principal genres.

All-sung opera in English could take either the form of a direct imitation of the Italian model, or else that of the masque, a term which by now usually referred to a lighter dramatic piece with continuous music. Of the various attempts to introduce full-scale opera in English during the first decade of the eighteenth century only one, Clayton's and Addison's *Rosamond*, had an entirely original libretto set to newly written music by an English composer, and it was a decisive failure. Two further experiments followed in the second decade, both with music by J. E. Galliard, a German composer who had settled in England: these were *Calypso and Telemachus*, to a libretto by John Hughes (Queen's Theatre, 17 May 1712, with five performances in all, and three more subsequently at Lincoln's Inn Fields), and *Circe*, to an old libretto of Davenant's (Lincoln's Inn Fields, 1719), the music of which is lost. *Calypso and Telemachus* was published in full score without the recitatives, and reveals the minor talent of a worthy but unimaginative composer.

The masque would seem at first to have held out more promise for future development. The masque at this period (1670–1720) was usually a short dramatic action in one or more acts, sung throughout—an opera in all but name, in fact. It could be self-standing, if it were long enough (as with Blow's *Venus and Adonis*, performed at court around 1682), or it could take the form of one or more interludes between the acts of a spoken play (as with Locke's *Orpheus*, performed within Settle's *Empress of Morocco* in 1674). Purcell's *Dido* was adapted as a multi-interlude masque in 1700, and subsequently given as a unified afterpiece in 1704. The host play might also have its own incidental music (not always by the same composer), and the so-called semi-operas or 'dramatic operas' of this period are really spoken plays with both incidental music and one or more masques: only rarely is the main dramatic action itself sung in such cases. Paradoxically, the masques in the most elaborate and best-integrated semi-operas tended to be less truly dramatic than those imported quite adventitiously into the host play.

The real problem with the independently conceived masque was one of length: it was usually too short for a complete evening but (by 1700 at least) too long to comprise a single interlude. The multiple interlude, though still popular in Italy and elsewhere in Europe, dissipated any sense of dramatic continuity, while performance at the end of a spoken play (as an 'afterpiece') was less likely to be listened to attentively. The four 'prize' settings of Congreve's *Judgment of Paris* (1701) were performed independently of any play, but the circumstances in that case were rather different. Nevertheless these four works (or at any rate those of John Weldon, John Eccles, and Daniel Purcell) raised the profile of the form considerably, and more might have been expected to follow from it. Eccles's setting of Peter Motteux's *Acis and Galatea*, the music of which is lost, soon left the protection of its host drama and enjoyed considerable success as an afterpiece from late 1702 on. On the other hand his setting of Congreve's *Semele* (c.1706), the score of which does survive and is of considerable merit, was never performed. There is then a gap in the production of this kind of drama until 1715, when Pepusch started putting on masques at Drury Lane.[14]

John Christopher Pepusch (1667–1752) was, like Galliard, of north German origin, and lived in London from about 1700, earning his living at first from orchestral playing. Despite a rather pedantic turn of mind he made a not inconsiderable contribution to English musical life in the second and third decades of the new century. He was director of music at Cannons from about 1716 until about 1730, where he wrote a number of anthems. But masques, odes, and cantatas, together with a fair body of instrumental music (some of which probably predates his settlement in England) were more in his line. His first masque, *Venus and Adonis*, to a text by Colley Cibber, has survived in full and is an agreeable piece.[15] It was produced at Drury Lane (12 March 1715), for which Pepusch wrote three further masques, of which *Apollo and Daphne*, with words by Hughes (12 January 1716), again survives complete.[16] Pepusch and most of his singers transferred to Lincoln's Inn Fields in late 1716 or early 1717, where under John Rich's management *Thomyris* and *Camilla* were revived and, less successfully, Galliard's *Calypso and Telemachus*. Galliard also wrote two masques for the company, *Pan and Syrinx* and *Decius and Paulina*, to texts by Lewis Theobald, as well as the opera *Circe* mentioned above.[17] *Pan and Syrinx* survives in the composer's

[14] For full details of these and all later masques see M. Burden, 'The Independent Masque in Britain in the Eighteenth Century: A Catalogue', *RMARC* 28 (1995), 59–159, listing 117 items in all; and id., 'The British Masque 1690–1800', Ph.D. diss. (University of Edinburgh, 1991).

[15] It was published, without recitatives or the final chorus, in full score; a manuscript score and set of parts, which include the missing items, survive in the Royal College of Music Library, MS 975. R. Fiske, *English Theatre Music in the Eighteenth Century* (2nd edn., Oxford, 1986), 56–8; see also D. F. Cook, 'The Life and Works of Johann Christoph Pepusch (1667–1752), with Special Reference to his Dramatic Works and Cantatas' (Ph.D. thesis, University of London, 1983).

[16] Royal College of Music, MS 976. The other two were *Myrtillo* (5 Nov. 1715, complete in Royal Academy of Music, MS 88), and *The Death of Dido* (17 Apr. 1716, full score in RAM, MS 85). Leveridge's *Pyramus and Thisbe* was also given during that season at Drury Lane (11 Apr. 1716, music lost). Fiske, 56–9.

[17] *Decius and Paulina* was an insertion in Settle's play *The Lady's Triumph* (music lost). Fiske, 59–60.

autograph and is not without a certain picturesque charm: one of Pan's arias is scored for viola solo and 2 treble recorders, with a bass recorder doubling the *basso continuo*.

The other traditional 'serious' genre, the semi-opera, was kept going with revivals of Purcell's *Dioclesian* and other works, together with the Shakespearean 'operas' *Macbeth* (with music by Richard Leveridge) and *The Tempest* (mainly, it seems, by Weldon), and such novelties as Pepusch's own version of *Dioclesian*, the music of which is lost.[18] But with the passing of the generation of Eccles, Jeremiah Clarke, Daniel Purcell, and Weldon, there was no steam left in the movement to preserve the semi-opera and masque, and the latter term came to be applied so loosely as to deprive it of any real significance. But a word must be said about Handel's two essays in masque form, having as they did a very different (and quite unforeseen) progeny.

Acis and Galatea and *Esther*, though privately produced at Cannons, should be seen in the general context of enthusiastic cultivation of the masque by Pepusch and others in the half-decade 1715–19. Pepusch was, after all, master of the music at Cannons at the time, and the cultivation of an appropriate masque style can be seen as a connecting link between the two composers, despite the manifestly lesser talents of the one. The libretto of *Acis* was attributed to John Gay only after the author's death; it includes an aria by Hughes and some passages adapted from Pope, both of whose contributions may have been still more extensive. Its potential for comic characterization within a framework of Arcadian pathos made it an ideal vehicle for a composer with the imagination to exploit the contrast, and Handel here showed himself a master in judging the level at which the emotions might most effectively be engaged and the extent to which they might be relieved by musical humour. The work is best heard with the small forces for which it was originally conceived and without an interval.[19]

Esther is an altogether less interesting work, and it is not even certain that it was originally conceived as a masque rather than as an oratorio. Handel's autograph now lacks the first page, which might have resolved the matter; and while an early copy apparently read *Haman and Mordecai. A Masque*,[20] other evidence seems to indicate that the title *Esther* and the designation 'oratorio' (or some such word) were in use prior to Handel's 1732 revival.

[18] Lincoln's Inn Fields, 28 Nov. 1724.

[19] The chapter on *Acis* in Dean, *Handel's Dramatic Oratorios and Masques*, 153–90, is the principal secondary source. His suggested date of 1718 has been confirmed; an ample review of the work done since is contained in B. Trowell, 'Acis, Galatea and Polyphemus: A "*Serenata a tre voci*"?', in *Music and Theatre: Essays in Honour of Winton Dean*, ed. N. Fortune (Cambridge, 1987), 31–93. Trowell believes that *Acis* was originally conceived as a three-voiced *serenata*, though revised and eventually produced, without full theatrical illusion, in a version for five solo singers (who also sang the 'choral' parts).

[20] Ed. Chrysander, vol. xl; Dean, 192 (but he does not describe Chrysander's MS, which perhaps no longer survives).

On the other hand it seems unlikely that 'masque' would have replaced 'oratorio' at any stage if the more familiar designation had been in use from the outset. The question is of only secondary importance, since it is almost certain that *Esther* was first presented in a manner similar to that of *Acis*, most probably in the summer of 1720.

Esther is in any case derived ultimately from the Bible by way of Racine and a close English imitation of Racine by one Thomas Brereton of Brasenose College, Oxford. Handel's librettist, whose identity is unknown, paraphrased Brereton extensively but dissipated the opportunities for effective drama that are inherent in the biblical narrative.[21] Handel's music includes numerous borrowings amid some powerful new choral writing (in five parts, originally one voice to a part, as in *Acis*). There is also some striking orchestration, including a difficult harp solo in one of the airs. But the work's dramatic weaknesses were no impediment to its effective revival, twelve years on, as a concert-oratorio, and it is in that form that *Esther* is primarily remembered nowadays.

Burlesque and The Beggar's Opera

The serious potential of English musical drama was not much in evidence, as we have seen, during the 1720s; instead, the public was regaled with a diet of burlesques and other kinds of light theatrical entertainment. The tradition of operatic burlesque— which is not an easy form to define—goes back to Thomas D'Urfey's *Wonders in the Sun* (Queen's Theatre, 5 April 1706), the music of which was drawn from a variety of sources. It was also an element in the various pantomimes that grew up in the second decade of the century and reached their peak in the period 1723–8. These were given at Drury Lane and Lincoln's Inn Fields in close rivalry: they combined elements of the harlequinade with a 'serious' mythological element told in dancing and song, and were normally given as afterpieces.[22] Their prototypes were the harlequinade itself (usually just a short dance in the middle of a longer entertainment) and the true 'pantomime', a mythological story told in mime and dance. John Weaver's *Loves of Mars and Venus*, produced at Drury Lane on 2 March 1717, was perhaps the only pure example of the latter;[23] all later examples included song and a comic element based on the characters of the *commedia dell'arte*, separate from or integrated with the main plot. There are

---

[21] Dean, 196; but one should make allowance for assumed knowledge of the Bible, greater then than now.

[22] E. W. White, *The Rise of English Opera* (London, 1951), 172; Fiske, 67–93.

[23] Cf. J. Weaver, *A History of the Mimes and Pantomimes* (London, 1728), and the Preface to the published 'Description', both cited by Fiske, 69–72. But even in its 'true' sense the word 'pantomime' is based on a misapprehension, derived from the staging of *ballets-pantomimes* at Sceaux by the Duchesse du Maine (1676–1753), who imagined that she was reviving an ancient art of dramatic mime. Normally the word *pantomimus*, in the ancient theatre, meant an actor who played all the parts, and the purely mythological pantomime of the early 18th c. is really a species of *ballet d'action*.

extant some examples of the 'comic tunes' associated with the harlequinade, and a number of songs, but the music seems on the whole tame compared with the extravagance of the scenic effects which were no doubt the main attraction of these curious entertainments. Galliard was the chief composer at Lincoln's Inn Fields, Henry Carey and Richard Jones at Drury Lane. Lewis Theobald's efforts as librettist and deviser of such things at the former house were much derided by Pope in *The Dunciad*, but their financial success must have helped to make more serious ventures possible.

Some of the ideas behind *The Beggar's Opera*, written by John Gay and incorporating popular airs of his own choice, had been discussed in his circle for some time, but the timing of its production at Lincoln's Inn Fields on 29 January 1728 was impeccable. The second phase of Italian opera in London, that of the Royal Academy of Musick, was foundering in the seas of financial instability, the serious English semi-opera and masque were dying a natural death, and the pantomime craze had temporarily exhausted itself. *The Beggar's Opera* did not hasten the demise of these forms—least of all that of Italian opera, which was to remain a feature of upper-class entertainment for long afterwards—but it offered the prospect of a genuinely new and indigenous form of musical theatre, one which the English middle classes could enjoy without feeling out of their depth. The fact that the music consisted entirely of well-known tunes, though it doubtless contributed to the success of the piece, is in a sense an incidental factor. The songs are not mere insertions but an integral part of the dramatic structure. This was not entirely unprecedented in England, but the procedure, when combined with Gay's tragi-comedy of low life, lent an air of mocking detachment that kept seriousness at bay without detracting from the realism of the characterization. Pepusch wrote a lively overture and harmonized the tunes, though the exact details of his orchestral methods can be inferred only indirectly.

The complete integration of spoken and sung drama in *The Beggar's Opera* put to rest a long-standing English inhibition about combining the two in a single dramatic action. It led to a plethora of imitations: Gay's own sequel, *Polly*, was suppressed, but there were about fifty successors between 1728 and 1735.[24] But it also gave rise to two related forms: the comedy-pasticcio, which used pre-existing art-music, and true comic opera, in which the music was newly composed. With the revival of burlesque and pantomime, the scene was set for the establishment of a healthy popular musical theatre, with which serious all-sung opera in English or Italian, together with the dialogue-masque (a late descendant of semi-opera), found it difficult to compete.

---

[24] White, 178; Fiske, 103–26. There is a good scholarly edn. of *The Beggar's Opera* by J. Barlow (Oxford, 1990).

The Beggar's Opera is both in general intent and in some of its detail a satire on serious, especially Italian, opera. But it also contained an element of political satire, no less pointed for its restrained expression, and it was this tendency of the genre, as later exploited by Henry Fielding and others, which led to the Stage Licensing Act of 1737. This put a stop to the uninhibited criticism of the Government in the theatre, but in any case the artistic potential of ballad opera could be realized only through musical expansion and a lessening of the importance of the spoken text. In the meantime, however, one of the most successful of subsequent ballad operas, *The Devil to Pay, or, The Wives Metamorphos'd*, with a libretto by Charles Coffey and John Mottley (Drury Lane Theatre, 6 August 1731), had embarked on the career which led to its production in Berlin in 1743 and a succession of Continental imitations thereafter. Despite a wealth of other precedents stretching back to medieval times, *The Devil to Pay* was in a very real sense the ancestor of *Fidelio* and even *Carmen*.

Musical Theatre, 1730–1760

Other forms of theatre music in the period 1730–60 developed along lines already laid down. In the first place there was Italian opera, a more pervasive influence than is sometimes realized. Although from the point of view of popular taste it was a specialized and largely incomprehensible entertainment, it provided a constantly evolving stylistic model and was the subject of both serious and burlesque imitations. Italian opera itself, though normally of the 'serious' variety, could be comic: 'comic interludes', i.e. intermezzi, were given in London in 1737–8, and full-scale comic operas in 1748–50 and 1760–1.[25]

As has been mentioned, Handel in partnership with Heidegger had a monopoly of Italian opera in London from 1729 until 1733, when the rival 'Opera of the Nobility' was set up in Lincoln's Inn Fields (1733–4) and in the King's Theatre (the three seasons of 1734–7). Handel's continued competition, mostly at Covent Garden, led to a deterioration in his health, and in 1737 he suffered a stroke. But Farinelli abandoned the Nobility and left the country; early in 1738 Handel was back on the scene with two new operas.

The chief composers at the Nobility were Nicola Porpora, himself a singer, Francesco Maria Veracini, and Johann Adolf Hasse. Although Farinelli's departure left the company in disarray, noble patronage, in the shape of the earl of Middlesex, was eventually able to rescue the venture. Baldassare Galuppi was brought over from Venice in 1741, and his easy-going music remained popular in London for many years. Giovanni Battista

---

[25] The primary source of information about Italian opera in London is the fourth volume of Charles Burney's *General History of Music*, published in 1789.

Lampugnani became the composer in residence in 1743, and Gluck for the 1745–6 season, though because of the Jacobite rebellion performances in 1745 were held over.[26] After the comic operas of 1748–50 there were three seasons without Italian opera; then *opera seria* was resumed in 1753–4. The repertory was undistinguished, but the orchestral playing improved under Felice Giardini. Not until the arrival of J. C. Bach in 1762, however, were any new operas of genuine merit introduced. The real significance of this phase of Italian opera in London lay in its adoption of a more relaxed, 'post-Baroque' idiom. Italian composers such as G. B. Sammartini (whose brother Giuseppe worked in London as an orchestral oboist and as musical director to Frederick, Prince of Wales) were at the forefront of what became the 'pre-classical' or *galant* idiom in Europe, while Porpora, Pescetti, Veracini, Lampugnani and Galuppi, together with the Germans Hasse and Gluck, popularized it in the sphere of Italian opera. Indeed it was in opera sooner than in any other form, through the orchestral *sinfonia* as well as the aria, that the transition from a 'learned' Baroque idiom to a light proto-classical style was accomplished.

We may consider English-language musical theatre, apart from mere incidental music, in terms of the two broad categories of all-sung opera and opera with spoken dialogue. The first embraces both serious and comic forms, including even pantomime, while the latter ranges from ballad opera on the one hand to serious masques with dialogue on the other. Contemporary terminology will not help much, for the terms 'opera' and 'masque' were applicable to both genres, and a single work might be known by either. We shall also have to distinguish between staged and concert performances of dramatic works, and between dramatic and non-dramatic concert works. Terms such as masque and pastoral were designedly vague in just that sphere.

There was to begin with, in this period as so often since, a renewed attempt to establish full-length opera in English as a going concern. Thomas Arne senior's season of 'English opera' in 1732–3 was one of the most ambitious of all such endeavours: to be precise, it was a season-and-a-half, opening at the Little Theatre in the Haymarket in March 1732, and later continuing both there and at Lincoln's Inn Fields, which was vacated when John Rich moved to the new Covent Garden in the autumn of 1732. An odder feature was the inexperience of the composers and performers, and the fact that of the former only Arne junior was English-born. J. F. Lampe, with three operas, was German, and J. C. Smith, the son of Handel's copyist, had been brought over from Germany in 1720 at the age of 8: two of the operas were his. The season also included an unauthorized production of Handel's *Acis*, T. A. Arne's *Rosamond*, and, in a different

---

[26] Gluck's offering was *La caduta de' giganti*, produced on 7 Jan. 1746 in honour of the duke of Cumberland. No doubt it inspired the duke to victory at Culloden on 16 Apr. of that year.

category, his adaptation of Fielding's burlesque tragedy *Tom Thumb* under the title *The Opera of Operas*.

Probably the whole venture was too ambitious to have any real chance of success: only Lampe's *Amelia*, despite the absurdities of Henry Carey's libretto, and Arne's *Opera of Operas* reached as many as ten performances. Hardly any of Lampe's music for these operas has survived, but there exist full scores of Smith's *Ulysses*; this has moments of real promise, which was destined, alas, to remain unfulfilled. Arne's *Rosamond*, a re-setting of the Addison libretto so catastrophically mishandled by Clayton in 1705, received six performances, but only one song from this version survives (he later rewrote the opera as an afterpiece, and of that a manuscript full score exists).[27]

Rosamond launched the young Arne on a career of musical theatre that was to last nearly half a century. His contributions ranged from pantomime to the grandest of opera; he knew abject failure and brilliant success, and was regularly at odds with his theatrical managers, not least David Garrick, who was manager at Drury Lane from 1747 (initially with John Lacy) until 1763, and again from 1765 until 1776. What is perhaps surprising is his constant willingness to salvage and improve on his pieces, or at least to make them more attractive to the public. His most famous stage work, *Alfred*, began life as a masque with dialogue, became a full-length opera, and underwent successive transformations for close on forty years.[28] Arne was a remarkably uneven composer, but at his best he achieved an admirable synthesis of the new operatic *galant* manner and a wholly English turn of melody. He wore his technique more lightly than (say) Greene or William Boyce, but he was no less a craftsman than they and a far more natural man of the theatre.

Arne's second offering, and the final production in the 'English opera' season, was *The Opera of Operas*, a transposition to the operatic sphere of Fielding's burlesque *The Tragedy of Tragedies, or The Life and Death of Tom Thumb the Great*. It received eleven performances in its original version and must be accounted a success, but it is hard to judge of its effect as burlesque from the single surviving song. Later it was cut (like *Rosamond*) to make an afterpiece (as Fielding's play had originally been), and in this form it remained in the repertory for some time. Oddly enough, owing to a dispute that resulted in an exchange of actors between the Little Theatre and Drury Lane, a second setting of the original libretto was composed by Lampe for the 1733–4 season at the latter house, where it had only three performances.[29]

[27] A detailed account of the whole season, with a sober assessment of its achievement in commercial terms, appeared in J. Milhous and R. D. Hume, 'J. F. Lampe and English Opera at the Little Haymarket in 1732–3', *ML* 78 (1997), 502–31.

[28] The modern edition in MB 47, a snapshot of its 1753 state, describes most of the work's vicissitudes.

[29] But it later became popular in Dublin: Fiske, 159 and (for the complex interrelationships of the works of Fielding, Arne, and Lampe) 147–8. The sixteen songs published anonymously, once attributed to Arne, are now believed to be by Lampe.

The most successful of all the burlesques was Lampe's *The Dragon of Wantley*, which survives complete in a manuscript full score.[30] Carey's libretto, based on a popular song originally published by D'Urfey,[31] features a singularly unsaintly dragon-slayer and a far from pure maiden. Lampe's music is on the whole rather ordinary, and much of the humorous effect must have been realized (as Fiske has pointed out) in the manner of performance. But popular entertainment though it may have been, it is hard to credit it with much effect on the fortunes of Italian opera in England. The latter appealed to an audience unlikely to be influenced by burlesque, and the temporary gap in opera performances at the King's Theatre from 1738 to 1741 was due to a multiplicity of causes, amongst them the departure of a favourite singer and a surfeit of the traditional operatic fare. A renewal of noble patronage and a slight change of diet were sufficient to re-establish the appetite of the fashionable elite, and Italian opera continued once more to co-exist with everything that the native theatre could supply as an antidote.

Lampe and Carey wrote a sequel, *Margery, or a Worse Plague than the Dragon*, but it was less successful despite some arresting features in the music.[32] Lampe composed several further short burlesques—the music of his *Pyramus and Thisbe* (Covent Garden, 25 January 1745), based on a version of Shakespeare earlier used by Leveridge, survives[33]—and it seems to have been the form in which he was most at home. His was a strange career in which considerable gifts were sacrificed to a taste for whimsicality.

Many of the most satisfying English operas of this period were intended not for the public theatres but for private performance, with or without action. Greene's *Florimel*, a setting of a 'dramatic pastoral' by John Hoadly, son of Benjamin Hoadly, bishop of Winchester, survives in no fewer than six manuscripts,[34] and is one of the foremost works by a native Englishman to have been produced during the 1730s. Yet the circumstances of its first and subsequent performances are obscure: it seems to have been given in 1734 at Farnham Castle, the bishop's country seat, and at the Three Choirs Festival in Gloucester in 1745. There is also a copy of a libretto of 1737 with the names of two different casts written in by hand, so the work can hardly be said to have been neglected.[35] But it was never staged in a public theatre, and it is fairly clear that some of its performances were not staged at all.

---

[30] Royal College of Music, MS 927.

[31] *Wit and Mirth: Or Pills to Purge Melancholy*, iii. 10–15 (1959 reprint of 1719 edn.)

[32] Fiske, 155; the full score (minus the recitatives as usual) was published.

[33] Fasc. of the edn. by Walsh (1745, without recitatives) in MLE, C/3; for Leveridge see n. 16 above.

[34] In two versions: the first, in which the part of Myrtillo is scored for soprano, in Brit. Lib., R.M. 22 d. 14 (facs. in MLE, C/6) and Royal College of Music, MS 226 (full scores), and MS 227 (vocal score with a set of string parts); and the second, with the part of Myrtillo written for alto, in Brit. Lib., Add. 15980 (Part II only, in the hand of Boyce), Add. 5325, and Royal Academy of Music, MS 109.

[35] In the Royal College of Music; one of the casts was entirely male. Another copy, with the same cast-lists, survives in Otago, NZ (see K. Maslen in 'Dr Hoadly's "Poems Set to Music by Dr. Greene"',

The case of *Florimel* is in fact typical of a situation in which such admirable composers as Greene and Boyce, though standing high in professional esteem, failed to win acceptance in the London theatrical world—until indeed Boyce's comic afterpiece *The Chaplet* achieved popularity on its first production in 1749. Maurice Greene (1696–1755), who had been organist of St Paul's cathedral since 1718, became organist and composer to the Chapel Royal in 1727, Professor of Music at Cambridge in 1730, and Master of the King's Musick in 1735; neither of the last two appointments necessitated his relinquishing the others, for the Cambridge chair was a sinecure and the obligations of the Master of the King's Musick, mainly the composition of a biannual court ode, were easily compatible with his duties at St Paul's and the Chapel Royal. But he seems to have lacked the kind of business acumen which Handel possessed and which gave many a nonentity a foothold in the theatrical world.

Works such as *Florimel* provided a convenient opportunity for such a composer to exercise his musico–dramatic skills away from the limelight of the London stage. In this case Hoadly's pastoral, originally called *Love's Revenge*, has the simplest of plots and scarcely needs a staged performance to make its effect. Greene's music is not dramatic in any obvious sense, but it is unfailingly apposite and stylish.

Other works of this kind include Greene's *The Judgment of Hercules* (music lost, libretto published in 1740) and *Phoebe* (1747), this latter an ambitious three-act work intended probably for the Apollo Society.[36] After a spritely overture, the hunting ambience is suggested by rollicking horns in the same key of F major, to which the opera returns at the end. Amongst a wealth of entertaining music we may instance a comic duet in which Celia, a shepherdess, tries to fend off the advances of the boorish Linco (see Ex. 1.1).

William Boyce's *Peleus and Thetis*, based on a free handling of the subject of Aeschylus's lost play *Prometheus Unbound*, is an excellent example of a shorter dramatic work on a mythological theme. The libretto is a masque inserted in *The Jew of Venice*, a Shakespearean adaptation by George Granville, Lord Lansdowne (1701: the original music is lost and its composer unknown). Boyce's setting had been composed by 1740, probably for the Apollo Society, though its earliest documented performance took place in 1747.[37] The opening recitative is remarkable for its tonal range. Peleus and

Studies in Bibliography, 48 (1995), 85–94; and further H. D. Johnstone, 'More on Dr. Hoadly's "Poems Set to Music by Dr. Greene"', ibid. 50 (1997), 262–71.

[36] Oxford, Bod. Lib., Mus. d. 53 (autograph); Brit. Lib., Add. 5324. There was a later performance in Soho, 16 Jan. 1755: *BHMB*, iv. 148–50. The Apollo Society was founded around 1732 by Greene and Michael Christian Festing; it usually met in The Devil Tavern near Temple Bar.

[37] At the Swan Tavern on 29 Apr. The setting is ascribed to Boyce in a *Miscellany of Lyric Poems* published for the Apollo Society in 1740. The overture is printed in MB 13 (Boyce, *Overtures*), 131–8. The autograph score is in Bod. Lib., Mus. d. 24; there is another score and a set of parts, Mus. Sch. c. 113a–c.

Ex. 1.1

Ex. 1.1, continued

continued

Ex. 1.1, continued

Ex. 1.1, continued

Maurice Greene, duet 'Thou'rt a clown' from *Phoebe*, Act I: Oxford, Bod. Lib., Mus.d.53, fos. 43ʳ–46ʳ

Prometheus are vying for supremacy as to the acuteness of their agony; in an unstaged performance it would not immediately be obvious that Peleus is addressing Prometheus, whose liver is being gnawed by a vulture as he lies chained to the summit of the Caucasus (Ex. 1.2). Peleus is in love with Thetis, a sea-nymph desired by Jupiter, who is eventually persuaded to release her, and Prometheus too. There is a good deal of comic bluster from Jupiter (there are echoes of Polyphemus in *Acis* here), but the tenderer moments are equally arresting (Ex. 1.3), and as a whole the score shows a

Ex. 1.2

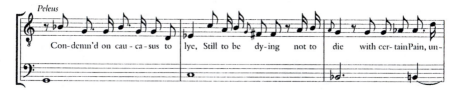

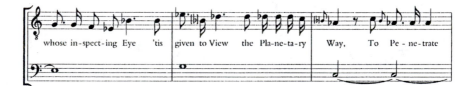

Ex. 1.2, continued

Prometheus

- plain   and Bring a   Heart as full of pain.   From

Ju - pi-ter   spring all our   Woes,   The - tis is   Jove's who once was thine;   'Tis

vain,   O   Pe - lus to op - pose   thy Tor - tu-rer and   mine.   Con -

- ten-ted   with De-spair   O___   wretch-ed Man!   re - sign whom you a - dore   or else pre-

- pare for Change of Tor-ments, great as   mine.   'Tis vain   O   Pe - leus   to op-pose thy

continued

Ex. 1.2, continued

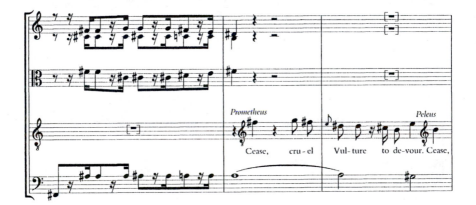

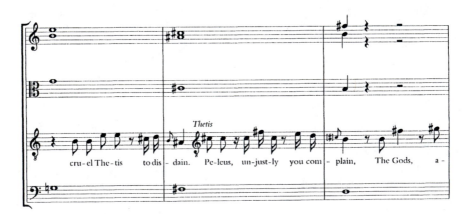

Ex. 1.2, continued

William Boyce, recitative 'Condemn'd on Caucasus to lie' from *Peleus and Thetis*: Oxford, Bod. Lib., Mus.d.24, fos. 6ᵛ–9ʳ

high level of invention and technique. Boyce also wrote a setting of Dryden's *Secular Masque* around 1745, but this may not have been heard until his Cambridge visit of 1749 (see below).

Meanwhile, however, a more public type of 'masque' continued to exist. Arne had set the libretto of Pepusch's 1716 *Death of Dido* for performance at Drury Lane early in 1734, and had followed this with the first of his many patriotic effusions, *Britannia, or Love and Glory* (Drury Lane, 21 March 1734). The music of both is lost, and the latter, with only three performances, was a failure. Arne's breakthrough came in 1738 with his setting of John Dalton's adaptation of Milton's *Comus*, first given at Drury Lane on 4 March of that year. Like the original masque this has a good deal of spoken dialogue, most of it taken unaltered from Milton, and it may be that the combination of a revered literary classic with agreeable new music suited public taste better than any other type of serious musico-dramatic work. The published full score and a somewhat later manuscript give us virtually all the music,[38] and it must be said that something of the Miltonic spirit survives in this eighteenth-century concoction and that it could still give pleasure today.

It is now known that Arne's *Alfred*, originally a similar combination of dialogue and song to a libretto by James Thomson, was initially intended for

---

[38] Modern edn. in MB 3. The MS is London, Brit. Lib., Add. 11518.

Ex. 1.3

Ex. 1.3, continued

William Boyce, aria 'But to gaze on thy face' from *Peleus and Thetis*: Oxford, Bod. Lib., Mus.d.24, fo. 31^{r-v}

Drury Lane, no doubt as a follow-up to the success of *Comus*.[39] The first performance, however, was at Cliveden, the seat of Frederick, Prince of Wales, on his daughter's birthday (1 August 1740); Giuseppe Sammartini provided a setting of Congreve's *Judgment of Paris* for the same occasion. The stage history of *Alfred* is complex. Arne himself refashioned the libretto and made the piece into an all-sung opera, and this was given in various forms in 1745 (Drury Lane), 1753 (King's Theatre), and 1759 (Covent Garden), not to speak of still later versions. Meanwhile Charles Burney, under the pseudonym of 'The Society of the Temple of Apollo', had written the music for a mainly spoken adaptation by David Mallet, given by Garrick at Drury Lane in 1751 after Arne's dismissal.[40]

Little is known of the original *Alfred* beyond its most famous number, the concluding 'ode' 'When Britain first at heaven's command', which remained a constant feature through all its transformations both by Arne and by others. The fullest surviving version is that of 1753, for which there exists a libretto (referring to it as a 'masque') and a full score (describing it as an 'English opera' and omitting the recitatives and most of the choral music). It is a brave venture to stage such a work today, but it is full of fine music and makes for an enjoyable concert.

The terminological confusion exhibited in the printed libretto and full score of this work reveal the futility of trying to separate the genres of opera and masque at this date. But Arne continued during the 1740s and 1750s to write shorter 'masques' with continuous music: the first, and the only one for which the music survives, was his own setting of *The Judgment of Paris* (Drury Lane, 12 March 1742). This is probably the most appealing of all Arne's fully extant, or almost fully extant, stage works: again the *secco* recitatives and most of the choral movements are missing, but they can be (and have been expertly) reconstructed,[41] and the small scale of the work contributes to the atmosphere of civilized entertainment. When Arne was trying he could be very good indeed: a symptom of this lies in the length and complexity of his ritornelli, which like Handel's are often full of surprises and far from being a perfunctory introduction to a song (Ex. 1.4).

Arne was commissioned by Garrick to celebrate the Peace of Aix-la-Chapelle with *The Triumph of Peace* (Drury Lane, 21 February 1749, ten performances), the music of which is lost. Apart from a couple of unsuccessful comic operas and the 1753 version of *Alfred*, his next effort was another full-length national opera, *Eliza* (Little Theatre, 29 May—Oakapple Day—1754), to a libretto by the 'amiable hack' Richard Rolt.[42] This contains fine

---

[39] Modern edn. in MB 47, from which these and the following details are drawn.
[40] See Fiske, *English Theatre Music*, 222–9, for full details of both the Arne/Thomson and the Burney/Mallet versions.
[41] MB 42, ed. I. Spink.
[42] Fiske, 239.

Ex. 1.4

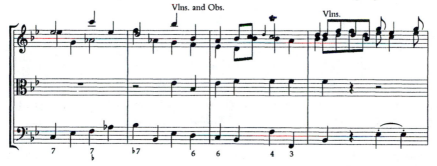

continued

Ex. 1.4, continued

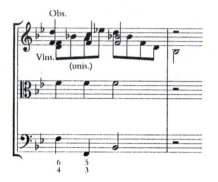

T. A. Arne, ritornello from aria 'Happy I of human race' from *The Judgment of Paris* (London, *c.*1745), pp. 14–15

music to an irredeemably tedious (not to say jingoistic) plot: no doubt, however, it was safer in Hanoverian England to celebrate the defeat of the Armada than the restoration of the Stuart dynasty. In 1755, moreover, came *Britannia*, to a libretto by Mallet—Arne's second work of that title and his final patriotic fling. Mercifully only a few of the songs survive.[43]

Arne's theatrical career had received a setback when his all-sung comic opera *Don Saverio* (Drury Lane, 15 February 1750) had only three perform- ances. In the absence of the music it is impossible to say why exactly this was so, but like his equally unsuccessful *Henry and Emma* at Covent Garden (31 March 1749) it marked a fresh attempt to set a more or less contemporary story to continuous music.[44] This contrasts oddly with the unexpected success of Boyce's pastoral comedy *The Chaplet*, an Arcadian soufflé by one Moses Mendez, 'a popular and very wealthy young Jewish stockbroker whose grandfather had come over from Portugal as medical attendant to Queen Catherine of Braganza'.[45] Boyce's music is good, but nothing like as consistently so as in his earlier *Peleus and Thetis*.

The production of *The Chaplet* on 2 December 1749 at Drury Lane crowned an eventful year for Boyce. In the summer he had received the doctorate of Music at Cambridge, and the festivities there had outdone by a considerable margin those attendant on the similar award to his master Greene in 1730. In Boyce's case the celebrations amounted to an entire

[43] Published as No. X in the series begun with the four books of *Vocal Melody* (*c.*1746–52) and continued with *The Agreeable Musical Choice* (four books, 1753–8) and other titles.

[44] The prototype was Carey's *Nancy*, first given at Covent Garden in 1739 and subsequently enlarged. For the complex history of this very slight piece see Fiske, 155–6.

[45] Ibid. 213.

one-man festival, the new works being an orchestral anthem, 'O be joyful in God', and an ode for the installation of the Duke of Newcastle as Chancellor, while the retrospective part comprised performances of his ode 'Gentle lyre begin the strain' (after Pindar), *The Secular Masque, Peleus and Thetis*, and *Solomon*, all necessarily in concert performances.[46] His later theatrical works were a self-sufficient 'burletta' within Mrs Clive's play *The Rehearsal* (Drury Lane, 15 March 1750), *The Shepherds' Lottery* (another pastoral confection by Mendez, produced at Drury Lane, 19 November 1751), and the masque in *The Tempest* (1757) as well as a share in the pantomime *Harlequin's Invasion* (1759) and a certain amount of incidental music.[47]

Pantomime production, mainly at Drury Lane, continued unabated in the 1730s, 1740s, and 1750s. The set of six medley overtures by Arne, Lampe, Richard Charke, Samuel Howard, and (probably) Peter Prelleur published in 1763 reveal one aspect of their musical character; the 'comic tunes', usually anonymous, another; and the surviving songs yet another. In the hands of such composers as Arne, Boyce, and Burney, these entertainments cannot have been wholly contemptible; yet, their music being largely lost and the style of performance recoverable only by a strong effort of the imagination, these are the most mysterious of all eighteenth-century theatrical forms.[48]

Comic opera with dialogue may be passed over here as not yet having realized its full potential, but a combination of spoken dialogue and song was familiar not only in plays with incidental music but in the continuing vogue for more elaborate Shakespearean adaptions. *The Tempest* was given with Arne's music at Drury Lane in 1746; when Garrick took over in 1747 he reverted to Weldon's score, but later mounted versions with music by

---

[46] See *BHMB*, iv. 94. 'Gentle lyre' (a version by the Revd Walter Harte of Pindar's first Pythian Ode) is in Bod. Lib., Mus. Sch. c. 111 (score).

[47] For *The Rehearsal* and *The Shepherd's Lottery* see Fiske, 216, 218–21; there is a facsimile of the published full score of the latter in MLE, C/4. *The Tempest* is in the Royal College of Music, MS 92, and Bod. Lib., Mus. d. 14; a different section of the latter gives (in a different hand) the music for the animation of the 'statue' in *The Winter's Tale*, and a third section the 'ode' 'Arise immortal Shakespear' (as it stands this is hardly a coherent work, however, and may represent parts of a theatre piece composed about 1759). A quite different Shakespearean ode is 'Titles and ermine fall behind' (William Havard), the autograph of which is in Birmingham, University Library, MS 5008 (the opening section has been restored to the manuscript since the publication of the catalogue, which cites it as 'Oracle! Or one yet more divine') and a copy in the Bodleian Library, MS Mus. Sch. c. 114 a–b. This latter work was first performed at Drury Lane on 1 Apr. 1756. (I am grateful to Mr R. J. Bruce for information on the two Shakespearean pieces, and to Dr. A. Trowles for the date of 'Titles and ermine'.) Boyce's dirge for *Romeo and Juliet*, 'Rise, rise, heartbreaking sighs' (Garrick) is in MS Mus. c. 3 in the Bodleian (see R. J. Bruce, 'William Boyce: Some Manuscript Recoveries', *ML* 55 (1974), 437–43; Arne's music for Barry's rival production in 1750 was later published in full score).

[48] Fiske, 160–70. The overture to Howard's music for *The Amorous Goddess* (Drury Lane, 1 Feb. 1744) was published in parts, and the whole of the music on two staves, in 1744; the two-stave version was reprinted by Harrison, c.1784, as no. 95 of *The Monthly Musical Magazine*. The music consists of a four-movement overture, ten short binary dances or comic tunes, an accompanied recitative, 'Amid these melancholy shades', an aria, and a final aria, 'Happy while with sportive pleasure'.

J. C. Smith jun. (1756) and Boyce (1757). Smith's work was in fact sung throughout, like *The Fairies* (1755), also a Shakespearean adaption. It should not be forgotten that there are scores extant (but without recitatives) of two Italian operas by Smith: *Issipile* (1743) and *Il Ciro riconosciuto* (1745); he also wrote *Dario* (1746) and left unfinished a setting of Metastasio's *Artaserse*. The last two, at least, were written abroad, and no performances of any of them have been traced.

One is inevitably struck by the number and variety of the attempts at opera in English in the period 1730–60. But English opera on the Italian model was bound to fail, partly at least because the model itself had run into an artistic cul-de-sac (and notwithstanding the success that Arne was about to achieve with his *Artaxerxes*). Italian opera continued because it was fashionable, and because its absurdities were less evident in a language foreign to its audiences. Opera in English enjoyed no such protection, irrespective of the quality of its music and its performance. So composers fell back on the tradition of the masque, adding to the repertory of ancient mythology the inanities of pseudo-historical patriotism. In both cases a tendency towards static and simple (not to say simplistic) plots led to a situation in which the actual staging and enactment of such works came to seem a superfluous gloss on a dramatic experience readily apprehensible without them. Already by 1732 Handel had taken a momentous decision that effectively precluded the establishment of an English national opera for the foreseeable future.

Handel's Oratorios and Related Works

The unstaged (or perhaps more accurately unacted) performance of dramatic works has a complex history. The oratorio and cantata in Italy, Germany, and France were sometimes wholly dramatic, sometimes not, and were given in a wide variety of locations and in diverse manners of performance. At one extreme are those works which are none other than sacred operas, presented in a theatre with all the trappings of an opera; at the other are religious works performed in church and only marginally dramatic if at all. In the secular dramatic sphere, anything from a short solo cantata to a large-scale opera might, for one reason or another, be presented without action. It should be remembered that performance in a theatre, with the chorus and protagonists on stage and perhaps also an allegorical backdrop and scenery, could seem very little different from a genuine enaction: the real difference lay between that and a performance in a church such as was accorded to the Passions and cantatas of Bach.

The reasons for performing a dramatic work without action were various. Apart from convenience, economy, and smallness of scale, the most commonly cited are the prohibition of the performance of sacred subjects on the public stage, and the prohibition of acting during Lent, more particularly on Wednesdays and Fridays. But the precise circumstances under which unacted public performances were established in London are not entirely clear, and it should be remembered that the tradition was widespread and of long standing.

It was a revival of interest in *Acis* and in *Esther* that led indirectly to the establishment of both secular and sacred drama without action in the London theatres.[49] *Acis* was produced, apparently with action, at Lincoln's Inn Fields on 26 March 1731 for the benefit of Philip Rochetti, who sang the part of *Acis*. Handel did not challenge this, but he reacted sharply to the two performances of *Acis* in Arne's season of 'English operas' by mounting an enlarged version of his own, with 'no Action on the Stage' but with appropriate scenery and costumes. Four performances took place at the King's Theatre in June 1732, and four more in December of that year as part of Handel's new opera season there (see Table 1).

In the meantime a similar tale was unfolding in regard to *Esther*. Bernard Gates, the master of the Chapel Royal choristers, had put on three performances at the Crown and Anchor Tavern in February and March 1732, staged and apparently with real action.[50] In April a pirated performance took place at York Buildings, and again it was this second production to which Handel took exception. An inflated version was quickly put together and performed six times at the King's Theatre in May 1732, overlapping with Arne's *Acis* and preceding Handel's new version of the latter. *Esther* was given this time (like *Acis*) with 'no Action on the Stage', and (unlike *Acis*) without scenery or costume either. This was therefore the earlier and more radical of Handel's revivals without action and, given the later preponderance of sacred over secular English dramas in his output, the more significant historically of the two. While the Italian singers had difficulty with their English texts, these performances did not reach the absurdities of the bilingual *Acis*, in which arias from the 1708 'serenata' *Aci, Galatea e Polifemo* were incorporated.

Handel's decision not to stage *Esther*, despite its being given in the King's Theatre, has been ascribed to the interference of the bishop of London, Edmund Gibson. Gibson, who was also *ex officio* Dean of the Chapel Royal, had apparently put his foot down about the children's taking part in a performance there, 'even with books in [their] hands',[51] but the decision not to stage it at all must have been a quid pro quo to ensure a relaxation of the veto. From this development arose the most striking feature of all Handel's oratorios and similar works, namely a chorus drawn from the

---

[49] For a useful and well-illustrated account of this development see *NOHM* vi. 23–96.

[50] Dean, *Handel's Dramatic Oratorios*, 204. Much of what follows is based on this authoritative work.

[51] Burney, cited Dean, 205. Gates's performances had been technically private.

singers of the main London churches: the Chapel Royal, which provided the boys, St Paul's, and Westminster Abbey.

TABLE 1. *Performances of Handel's* Acis, Esther, Deborah, *and* Athalia, *1731–1733*

Year	Opera	Venue	Date	Comments
1731	*Acis*	Lincoln's Inn Fields	26 Mar.	For the benefit of Philip Rochetti. Described as a Pastoral and presumably staged. No further performances.
1732	*Esther*	Crown and Anchor Tavern	23 Feb., 1 Mar. 3 Mar.	For the 'Philharmonic Society'. For the Academy of Ancient Musick. Conducted by Bernard Gates with singers of the Chapel Royal and additional voices, played by members of the 'Philharmonic Society'. Staged.
		York Buildings ('Great Room')	20 Apr.	Pirated, possibly by Arne sen., and probably staged.
		King's Theatre	2, 6, 9, 13, 16, 20 May	Under Handel with Chapel Royal singers; 'no Action on the stage'.
	Acis	Little Theatre (Haymarket)	17 and 19 May	Under Arne sen., in 3 acts. Unauthorized.
		King's Theatre	10, 13, 17, 20 June; also 5, 9, 12, 16 Dec.	As a 'serenata', 3 acts, bilingual. Under Handel. 'There will be no Action on the Stage, but the Scene will represent . . . a Rural Prospect.'
1733	*Deborah*	King's Theatre	17, 27, 31 Mar.; 3, 7, 10 Apr.	
	Esther	King's Theatre	14, 17 Apr.	
		Oxford, Sheldonian Theatre	5, 7 July	
	Athalia	Oxford, Christ Church Hall	11 July	
	Acis	Oxford, Christ Church Hall	11 July	
	Deborah	Oxford Sheldonian Theatre	12 July	

Principal source: Dean, *Handel's Dramatic Oratorios and Masques*, 171–5 (*Acis*), 203–7, 210 (*Esther*), 236–7 (*Deborah*), 258–9 (*Athalia*).

Note. Easter Day in the three years was on 18 April, 9 April, and 25 March respectively, the dominical letter of each being C, BA (leap year), and G. Thus Handel's performances at the King's Theatre were all on Tuesdays and Saturdays, and after or before Easter as the case may be. There are convenient chronological tables in *The Oxford Companion to English Literature* (various edns.).

It is harder to understand Handel's decision not to enact *Acis*, but he may have been influenced by the success of *Esther* and by an instinct that made him cautious about the potential of genuine English opera. Whatever the reason, his failure to put his weight behind a movement that had arrived at a historically opportune moment put paid to the chances of establishing a native tradition for a long time to come.[52] But perhaps Handel was right. The broader English public was ripe for edification through the medium of serious music, but not for giving serious attention to its musical entertainment. Opera in English demanded more than that public was prepared to give, and Handel, despite his continuing efforts with the Italian form, began to bend his attention towards the development of an indigenous genre which would satisfy both his own dramatic flair and the public mood.

In assessing Handel's somewhat erratic progress in the sphere of dramatic oratorio it is important to bear in mind the priority for him of Italian opera over the new form at this period. Nevertheless, anxious to capitalize on the success of *Esther*, he quickly assembled *Deborah*, largely from his own earlier music. The choice of subject may have been suggested by Greene's recent *Song of Deborah and Barak*, which had been given a private performance in the autumn of 1732. This latter is a narrative rather than a truly dramatic work, and seems to demonstrate the influence of the softer *bel canto* idiom of Porpora and Hasse as well as of Handel himself. Another recent production was of *Judith* by William De Fesch, performed at Lincoln's Inn Fields on 16 February 1733. It is hardly conceivable that Handel felt threatened by these unfashionable precedents; indeed, so secure was he that he doubled his prices for the first night of *Deborah* on 17 March. Later performances, of which there were five, were given as part of the normal opera subscription season. The principal parts were taken by Italians, all of whom except Anna Strada, who took the part of Deborah, were subsequently purloined by the Opera of the Nobility. Although Handel was to soldier on for another year at the King's Theatre, he cannot have been entirely happy with the turn events had taken. In the meantime, however, he had other plans in mind.

The summer of 1733 was the occasion in Oxford for an orgy of academic posturing in the form of a revived 'publick Act', a ceremony formerly associated with the annual Encaenia or commemoration of departed members and originating in the 'inception' or admission of Doctors and of Masters of Arts to their teaching duties by a formal test. By the early eighteenth century this had degenerated into a riotous assembly, spread over two or three days and punctuated by speeches and musical odes in

---

[52] Aaron Hill, who had prepared the scenario for *Rinaldo* in 1710 or 1711, wrote a famous letter to Handel dated 5 Dec. 1732, suggesting that he turn his attention to the development of opera in English; the reply, if any, is lost. Dean, *Handel's Dramatic Oratorios*, 266; Fiske, 142–3.

the Sheldonian Theatre.[53] The 1733 revival provided an appropriate context for an attempt to outdo Cambridge in its honouring of Greene in 1730 by offering a Doctorate of Music to Handel and the opportunity for a festival of his music. *Athalia* was the new work provided by Handel as his academic offering (though a formal exercise was not required), and it is quite the grandest work ever produced for such an occasion.[54] It was performed in the Sheldonian Theatre on 10 July and repeated on the 11th; within a period of eight days (5–12 July) Oxford experienced in addition two performances of *Esther* and one each of *Acis* and *Deborah*. Not everyone was pleased: Thomas Hearne referred to 'Handel and (his lowsy Crew) a great number of forreign fidlers', and another worthy objected 'that the Theater was erected for other-guise Purposes, than to be prostituted to a Company of squeeking, bawling, out-landish Singsters'.[55] But the appreciation of the public at large is uncontested.

Athalia is however a great deal more than a successful public-relations exercise. It is in Dean's words 'the first great English oratorio', and it set the standards by which Handel's later such works should be judged. Like *Esther* it was based on a play by Racine; the libretto was by Samuel Humphreys, who had revised *Esther* for the 1732 revival, but it is far stronger dramatically than *Esther* in any of its forms. The scenario (in which Queen Athalia, who has deserted Jehovah for Baal, receives her just deserts) observes the unities of time, place, and action, while the chorus of Jewish people is, in the manner of ancient tragedy, both commentator and protagonist. But it is the richness of Handel's music that gives life to the plan, and in this work we can see for the first time the wholesale exploitation of those techniques (such as elaborate choral writing and instrumentation) which were at that date impracticable in opera but an invaluable resource in the cause of dramatic truth in oratorio.

Athalia was not given in Handel's London season of 1733–4,[56] but he mounted it at Covent Garden in April 1735, where *Esther* and *Deborah* were also revived in March of that year.[57] A pattern of oratorio performances on Wednesdays and Fridays in Lent was now beginning to emerge; *Esther* was repeated in early April in 1736 and 1737, but Handel did not write another new oratorio until the season of 1738–9, when *Saul* was given several performances at the King's Theatre in January, February, March, and

---

[53] The immediately preceding Act, in 1713, had been the occasion for odes by Croft (two) and Pepusch (see n. 73 below)

[54] Handel was not offered an honorary degree in the modern sense, as no such distinction had yet been invented. He never 'supplicated' for the degree, and it was consequently never conferred.

[55] Dean, 133 (from Hearne's Diary), 259 (from an anonymous pamphlet).

[56] *Il Parnasso in Festa*, however, based on *Athalia*, and *Deborah* were given at the King's Theatre in Apr. 1734, followed by *Acis* on 7 May.

[57] *Athalia* was followed in the King's Theatre by *Alcina* (16 Apr., with 18 performances altogether).

TABLE 2.   *Handel at the King's Theatre, 1739 (1738–9 season)*

Date[a]	Oratorio and comment[b]
Monday, 8 Jan.	*Saul* rehearsed in public
Tuesday, 16 Jan.	*Saul* (King, Duke, and Princesses present)
Tuesday, 23 Jan.	*Saul* 'With several new Concertos on the Organ'
Saturday, 3 Feb.	*Saul* 'With several Concertos on the Organ'
Saturday, 10 Feb.	*Saul* 'With several Concertos on the Organ'
Saturday, 17 Feb.	*Alexander's Feast* 'With several concertos on the Organ, and other Instruments'
Saturday, 24 Feb.	*Alexander's Feast* 'With several Concertos...' (etc. as above)
Saturday, 3 Mar.	*Il trionfo del tempo & della verità* (as above)
Tuesday, 20 Mar.	*Alexander's Feast* (as above; then:) 'Particularly a New Concerto on the Organ by Mr Handel, on purpose for this Occasion'
Tuesday, 27 Mar.	*Saul* 'With several Concertos on the Organ'
Wednesday, 4 Apr.	*Israel in Egypt* 'With several Concertos on the Organ, and particularly a new one'
Wednesday, 11 Apr.	*Israel in Egypt* 'Which will be shortned and Intermix'd with Songs. And the two last new Concertos on the Organ'
Saturday, 14 Apr.	*Love and Folly* 'A New Serenata' by Galliard. 'Intermix'd with the Choruses to the Tragedy of Julius Caesar'
Tuesday, 17 Apr.	*Israel in Egypt*
Thursday, 19 Apr.	*Saul* 'With a Concerto on the Organ by Mr Handel. And another on the Violin, by the famous Sig Plantanida, who is just arrived from Abroad'
Tuesday, 1 May	*Jupiter in Argos* (i.e. *Giove in Argo*, semi-staged). 'Intermix'd with Choruses, and two Concertos on the Organ'
Saturday, 5 May	*Jupiter in Argos*

Source: LS, iii/2. *Daily Advertiser*, 29 Dec. 1738: 'Mr Handel has hir'd the Opera-House in the Hay-Market for the Season, and intends to entertain the Town twice every week with Oratorios, &c.' There were no other performances during the season at this theatre.

[a] Easter Day 22 Apr.; dominical letter G.
[b] Comments are from playbills or advertisements.

April (see Table 2).[58] By then the outlook for Handelian opera was looking gloomier than ever, but once more Handel misread the signals and turned his attention to non-dramatic religious works in addition to his last operas.

Saul is a great work by any standards, and Handel's failure to follow it up with further dramatic oratorios, at least in the short term, has puzzled and distressed his modern commentators. He had found in Charles Jennens an

---

[58] But *Alexander's Feast* was given in 1736, and *Il trionfo del tempo e della verità*, an expanded version of *Il trionfo del tempo e del disinganno* (Naples or Rome, 1707) in 1737: see Dean, 267 ff., for other activities in these years.

ideal collaborator, a fluent versifier and one who well understood the dramatic potential of the form. Yet Handel went on to write *Israel in Egypt* (possibly with Jennens), a setting of Dryden's *Ode for St Cecilia's Day*, *L'Allegro* (Milton, adapted by Jennens), and *Messiah* (to biblical texts selected by Jennens) in a variety of circumstances. Again, however, we must beware of attributing to Handel and his collaborators the aesthetic priorities of the twentieth century. *Israel in Egypt* may have been intended originally as a *Song of Moses*,[59] and only later extended into what was at that time a unique example of a biblical narrative setting occupying a whole evening's entertainment. But its first performance at the King's Theatre on 4 April 1739 (between the last two performances of *Saul*) was a failure; and though it has been popular since then it is a makeshift affair, relying extensively on music borrowed from other composers and confused in its aims.[60]

The *Ode for St Cecilia's Day* was first given at Lincoln's Inn Fields on 22 November 1739 together with *Alexander's Feast*;[61] *L'Allegro* followed early in 1740. This last is a fine and coherently structured work based on an alternating series of passages from Milton's *L'Allegro* and *Il Penseroso*, in two parts, to which Jennens had added, in typically eighteenth-century fashion, a third part entitled *Il Moderato*. The 1740–1 season, also at Lincoln's Inn Fields, saw the final collapse of Handel's operatic hopes, and there were rumours of his impending return to Europe, possibly for good.[62] But then came his visit to Dublin (at the invitation of the Lord Lieutenant of Ireland), for which Handel composed *Messiah* in great haste, completing it on 14 September 1741 before leaving for Dublin in November. He stayed until the following August; *Messiah* was given its first performance on 13 April at the Fishamble Street Music Hall, where there were also revivals of *Acis*, *Esther*, and *Saul*. The artistic and financial success of the visit must have contributed greatly to Handel's confidence; and while his next dramatic oratorio, *Samson*, had been drafted before he set out, the quantity and quality of his output in that form thereafter is surely the outcome of this period of renewal.

Messiah is wholly untypical of its composer's normal methods, and an objective evaluation is difficult in view of the place it has subsequently taken

---

[59] Cf. Greene's *Song of Deborah and Barak*, referred to above. The completed work was preceded in its early performances by the funeral anthem for Queen Caroline (d. 1737), 'The ways of Zion do mourn'.

[60] Borrowing from the works of other composers first occurred in *Saul*; for a discussion and complete list (as regards the dramatic oratorios), including self-borrowings, see Dean 50–7, 641–8. Recent criticism of the oratorios has emphasized their religious content as a response to the concerns of contemporary society in contradistinction to their dramatic and theatrical context: see A. H. Shapiro, '"Drama of an Infinitely Superior Nature": Handel's Early English Oratorios and the Religious Sublime', *ML* 74 (1993), 215–45; more generally, R. Smith, *Handel's Oratorios and 18th-Century Thought* (Cambridge, 1995). While this is certainly a considerable factor to be borne in mind in the study of their creation and reception, it is not unreasonable to judge works that are dramatic in form by the standard of musico–dramatic truth—which is not necessarily the same thing as theatrical effectiveness.

[61] For the first performance of this, a setting of Dryden's second St Cecilia ode (1697), see n. 58 above.

[62] Dean, 314–15.

in British social and musical life. Its musical idiom draws on such precedents as the German Passion and English anthem as well as on the long-established usages of Italianate musical drama. But it also further develops the exploitation by Handel, already begun in his later operas, of the simpler melodic outlines of the newer *opera seria*, the style cultivated by Leonardo Leo and Leonardo Vinci as well as Porpora and Hasse. It is this more recent acquisition, as much as the dramatic excitement of the accompanied recitative and the stunning power of the choral writing, that contributes to the ethos of the work and was mainly responsible for Handel's vocabulary of religious meditation.

The whole of Handel's later oratorio and secular dramatic production may be said to rest on the stylistic precedents of the three masterpieces of 1738–41. *Saul* provided the language of dramatic confrontation, *L'Allegro* that of natural imagery, and *Messiah* that of spiritual perception. This is of course a simplification, and the elements are mixed in all three works as in their successors; but amongst the latter one can point to *Belshazzar* as obviously indebted to *Saul* for its dramatic methods, *Semele* and *Susanna* as embodying the natural element, and *Samson* and *Jephtha* as drawing on Handel's ability to explore the deepest recesses of the human soul. The conventionalized rejoicing of the Jewish people, too often an overt symbol of Hanoverian prosperity and righteousness, is usually a weaker element, though in the case of *Solomon* its grandeur is so essential to the pageantry of the work's conception that we cannot but submit to the spell.

All these later works have their weaknesses and longueurs, and a few—*Joseph and his Brethren*, *Judas Maccabaeus* (despite its popularity), *Alexander Balus*, and *Joshua*—come close to failure, at least in dramatic terms. In *Samson*—skilfully adapted by Newburgh Hamilton from Milton's *Samson Agonistes*—the spiritual desolation symbolized by Samson's humiliation and blindness is tellingly depicted in phrases that resemble those of 'He was despised and rejected' in *Messiah*, while Micah's 'Return, O God of Hosts' exhibits Handel's ability to project a collaboration between spokesman and chorus in a daring but perfectly controlled adaptation of da capo form.

The more sparing use of literal da capo was a development of the period 1738–41 which Handel was able to put to good dramatic use in his later works. The simple substitution of a chorus for the da capo is a common device, found for example at the end of *Samson*. But in Handel's next dramatic work, *Semele*, the proportion of da capo airs is increased, perhaps because of the work's more 'operatic' nature. The pagan scenario, in which Jupiter is tricked by Juno into destroying the current object of his affections, scandalized all but his most robust supporters, and the piece received only six performances in Handel's lifetime, four in February and two in December 1744. Only in recent times have its dramatic and musical qualities come to be fully appreciated. *Joseph* followed *Semele* at Covent Garden in March

1744, also with four performances, together with a few more in later revivals.[63]

The popularity of Handel's later oratorios and comparable works was in inverse proportion to their merits. *Hercules*, which has a strong claim to be the finest of all eighteenth-century dramatic works to an English text with continuous music, was produced at the King's Theatre in January 1745; it enjoyed two performances then, and four more in Handel's later life. *Belshazzar*, marking a return to collaboration with Jennens and featuring the dramatic confrontation of choruses representing Jews, Persians, and Babylonians, followed it in March with three performances, with a further three at Covent Garden in 1751 and 1758. *Judas Maccabaeus*, on the other hand, achieved an astonishing total of fifty-four performances between April 1747 and 1759; *Joshua* (1748) had fourteen in all, and of the second-rate ones only *Alexander Balus* shared the obscurity of its peers.

The failure of *Hercules* and *Belshazzar*—for their few performances were played to half-empty houses, a fact which could not be compensated for by successful revivals of his earlier oratorios—led to Handel's final break with the King's Theatre, where he had spent the better part of his career since his debut with *Rinaldo* in 1711. His health was affected, and it is understandable that a recouping of his financial losses was a priority. The *Occasional Oratorio*, a setting of texts from the Bible, appeared at Covent Garden in February 1746; the words may have been selected by the Reverend Thomas Morell, who in any case was his collaborator for *Judas*, *Alexander Balus*, and *Joshua*. Morell was an easy-going divine whose platitudinous temperament quite failed to produce the sparks needed to ignite Handel's genius. There is fine music in all these oratorios, but as wholes they are unconvincing. *Judas* is too obviously a celebration of Hanoverian dominance after the rebellion of 1745 and the victory of Culloden in April 1746. *Joshua* and *Alexander Balus* (composed in reverse order) followed in the spring of 1748, and the former at least, so similar in mood to *Judas*, became a success in Handel's lifetime.

There the story would have ended but for a remarkable revival of Handel's powers in the last decade of his life. *Susanna* and *Solomon* were produced in 1749, *Theodora* in 1750, *The Choice of Hercules* in 1751, and *Jephtha* in 1752. It is their variety as much as their individual qualities that is impressive: the 'rural comedy' and 'pageantry' of *Susanna* and *Solomon* respectively, and the 'philosophical approach' of *Theodora* and *Jephtha*.[64] *The Choice of Hercules* is based largely on the music of an abandoned semi-opera, *Alceste*, and is a short allegorical piece in one act.[65] Dean attributes to *Theodora* and *Jephtha* a spiritual depth that transcends the limitations of Morell's librettos, and sees in *Jephtha* a 'damning indictment' of the very

---

[63] e.g. in Mar. 1745, while De Fesch's *Joseph* was going on at Covent Garden (Dean, 407).
[64] The epithets are Dean's, 556.
[65] The libretto for *Alceste* was by Smollett after Euripides.

providence that the poet had contrived, by his distortion of the biblical narrative, to present in a favourable light. This need not imply a rejection by Handel of Judaeo-Christian theism, however. The language of protest and incomprehension prior to submission is by no means alien to religious experience, and we may justifiably see in the great chorus 'How dark, O Lord, are thy decrees', with its concluding 'Whatever is, is right',[66] the 'central core of the oratorio' and an epitome of Handel's own spiritual journey towards blindness and death.

Handel's sacred and secular dramas in English were essentially works of the theatre, despite the lack of action on the stage. At the King's Theatre and Covent Garden they contributed to seasons which also included Italian operas and, at Covent Garden, many other kinds of theatrical production. Even a few non-dramatic works were introduced in both, while conversely some of the dramatic works received later performances in a variety of locations, both suitable and unsuitable. Of the major works only *Athalia* (Oxford) and *Messiah* (Dublin) were first heard outside that context, and of the two it was of course *Messiah* which paved the way for the later non-theatrical, non-dramatic concept of the oratorio. At the same time the co-operation of the London ecclesiastical choirs in all Handel's oratorios gave them a flavour different from that of contemporary opera. The blend was unique, and proved to be inimitable.

Oratorios and Similar Works by Handel's Contemporaries

The number of oratorios by other composers and produced in public theatres in this period can be counted on the fingers of one hand. De Fesch's *Judith* (1733) and *Joseph* (1745) have already been mentioned: to these may be added Arne's *Abel* (Smock Alley Theatre, Dublin, 18 February 1744, and Drury Lane, 12 March 1755), J. C. Smith's *Paradise Lost* (Covent Garden, 29 February, 1760) and John Stanley's *Zimri* (Covent Garden, 12 March 1760). Stanley's *Jephtha*, though it survives in two manuscripts, seems not to have been publicly performed.[67] More characteristic were performances given to private bodies such as Greene's Apollo Society and the Academy of Ancient Music, or to the public in concert halls. Amongst these were Greene's *Deborah and Barak* (1732), Boyce's setting of John Lockman's *David's Lamentation over Saul and Jonathan* (Apollo Society, 16 April 1736), J. C. Smith's setting of an expanded version of the same text (Hickford's Rooms, 22 February 1740), Greene's *Jephtha* (Apollo Society, 1737), Boyce's 'serenata' *Solomon* (Ruckholt House, Essex, 22 August 1743), and Greene's *The Force of*

---

[66] Cf. Pope's *Essay on Man*, i. 293–4: 'And, spite of pride, in erring reason's spite, / One truth is clear, Whatever is, is right'.

[67] London, Royal College of Music, MS 1021, and in Hamburg, Staats-and Universitätsbibliothek. For the dating of this work see A. G. Williams, 'The Life and Works of John Stanley (1712–86)', Ph.D. thesis (University of Reading, 1977), i. 180; *BHMB*, iv. 80, 432 (n. 84).

Truth (Apollo Society, 1744). The Apollo Society met at the Devil Tavern in Temple Bar, and while this may seem an odd venue for such performances, the large rooms of inns and taverns made them convenient for the purpose. Gates's revival of *Esther*, as mentioned, took place at the Crown and Anchor in the Strand, the home of the Academy of Ancient Music, and even *Messiah* was performed there in 1744 and 1747.[68] But except for Boyce's *Solomon* and Arne's *Abel*, these homespun creations did not attract the following outside London that attended Handel's more popular works.[69]

Greene's *Jephtha* and Boyce's *Solomon* are amongst the more ambitious and successful of these pieces. *Solomon*, which is only nominally a sacred work,[70] adopts the pastoral manner of *Acis*; despite its stylistic mastery, it can hardly be said to break new ground. *Jephtha*, on the other hand, while it did not lack for stylistic models, was a bold attempt at telling a tragic and morally uncomfortable tale in music. The biblical story, which is analogous to the Greek myth of Iphigenia, was retained in its essentials by Greene's librettist, John Hoadly; the result has been thought static, but its uncompromising approach is a strong point, and the simplicity of the action is fully in the spirit of ancient drama as seen through Augustan eyes. Greene does not approach the moral grandeur of Handel's later treatment, but he has some affecting moments which Handel's librettist did not allow for, such as Jephtha's personal encounter with his daughter on his return from victory in battle. Jephtha's horror and his daughter's bewilderment are finely represented in dramatic recitative, and this is followed by a pathetic air whose tortured lines seem to recall Carissimi's treatment of Jephtha's daughter and her companions 'bewailing their virginity' (Ex. 1.5). Greene later rewrote the part of the daughter for an alto, casting this aria, for example, a major sixth lower. The variants are interspersed amongst the original versions in the autograph score,[71] giving its two volumes the superficial appearance of a more substantial work than it actually is. In fact its relative modesty of scale and effect give it a flavour quite unlike that of Handel's larger works.

Secular dramatic works (in addition to those by Handel) were also not infrequently given in unacted performances. This may well be true of some of those already mentioned, such as Boyce's *Peleus and Thetis* and Greene's *Phoebe*; J. C. Smith's *Rosalinda* was performed at Hickford's Rooms on 4 January 1740 (the music is lost) as part of the season in which his setting of

---

[68] Dean, 83.

[69] To the list of provincial oratorios from this period should be added at any rate William Hayes's one-act, non-dramatic *The Fall of Jericho* (? Oxford, 1749): see S. J. Heighes, *The Life and Works of William and Philip Hayes* (New York and London), 198–204.

[70] The libretto, by Edward Moore, is based on *The Song of Songs*. In addition to the published full score, an autograph (RCM, MS 4109) survives; modern edn. in MB 68 (1996). See also I. Bartlett and R. J. Bruce, 'William Boyce's "Solomon"', *ML* 61 (1980), 28–49.

[71] Oxford, Bodleian Library, MS Mus. d. 54–5. Further examples are quoted in *NOHM*, vi. 74–7, and *BHMB*, iv. 78–9, 81.

Ex. 1.5

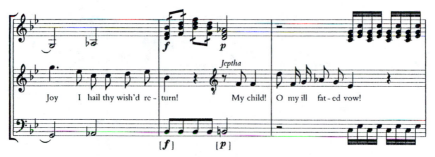

continued

Ex. 1.5, continued

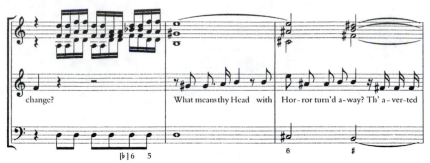

change?   What means thy Head with Hor-ror turn'd a-way? Th' a-ver-ted

Eye fill'd with sad ____ Tears,   fix'd mo-tion-less on   Earth?   Is this my

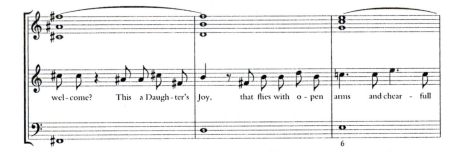

wel-come?   This a Daugh-ter's Joy,   that flies with o-pen arms   and chear-full

Smiles   to meet a dear be-lov'd   vic-to-rious Fa-ther?   Ah!

Ex. 1.5, continued

Air

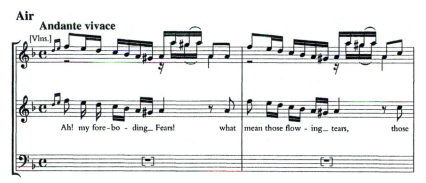

Ah! my fore-bo-ding_ Fears! what mean those flow - ing_ tears, those

flow - - ing_ tears, what mean those flow - ing_ tears, those

sor - rows, those sor - rows, that weigh _____ down, that

continued

Ex. 1.5, continued

Maurice Greene, recitative 'What do I see' and aria 'Ah! my foreboding fears' from *Jephtha*: Oxford, Bod. Lib., Mus.d.55, fos. 23ᵛ–26ʳ

David's Lamentation (see above) was performed. Smith also wrote *The Seasons*, and a setting of Pope's early dramatic pastoral *Daphne*: the scores of both of these, dated 1740 and 1744 respectively, have survived in Hamburg, but no performances have been traced. Two masques by William Hayes, *Circe* (published in 1742) and *Peleus and Thetis*, have also come down to us, in the latter case in both score and parts; again no performances are known, but it is probable that they were intended for Oxford in the first instance.[72]

It would be possible to extend this investigation of unacted secular music-drama into the sphere of the chamber cantata; but the cantata in England was by no means always dramatic in form and is best considered in the context of solo song. But we should certainly look here at some of the numerous examples of non-dramatic works for chorus and orchestra. These were as popular with audiences as dramatic works when given in the public theatres, as was the case with Handel's *Alexander's Feast*, the *Ode for St Cecilia's Day*, and *L'Allegro*. The first two of these are similar in genre, being

[72] The two scores and the set of parts for *Peleus and Thetis* are in the Bodleian Library, Mus. d. 79–80 and Mus. d. 125–6 respectively, mistakenly indexed under Boyce in the *Summary Catalogue*. For a discussion of both *Circe* and *Peleus* see Heighes, *Life and Works*, i. 263–72. Other extended dramatic works surviving in MS but for which no definite performances are recorded include Stanley's *Pan and Syrinx* and *The Choice of Hercules* (Cambridge, King's College, Rowe Music Library MS 7; the latter also in London, British Library, Add. MS 5328). The Rowe MS also includes *The Power of Music*, Stanley's B.Mus. exercise (Oxford, 1729), but this is an ode rather than a dramatic work. See A. G. Williams, 'Life and Works', i. 149–50; R. Goodall, *18th-Century English Secular Cantatas* (New York and London, 1989), 193.

settings of words by Dryden in praise of music, and were first performed in 1736 and 1739 respectively. The continuous tradition of writing Cecilian odes for performance on 22 November had lapsed after 1703, but it was revived occasionally thereafter. As usual, English-born composers lacked the opportunity to put such works before the theatre-going public, but the well-known poems of Dryden and Pope, together with some more recent efforts by Lockman and others, were pressed into service for academic ceremonies and exercises.[73] Greene wrote a fine setting of Pope's *Ode for Musick on St Cecilia's Day*, altered for the purpose by Pope himself and performed on 6 July 1730 at the opening of the new Senate House in Cambridge.[74] Boyce wrote two such odes, to poems by Vidal and Lockman respectively; the second of these is exceptionally long and elaborate.[75]

Some of Boyce's other miscellaneous odes have already been mentioned,[76] and there are numerous examples by his lesser contemporaries, many of them written for academic and similar occasions. Those of William Hayes, ranging from his Bachelor of Music exercise in 1735 ('When the fair consort') to an Encaenia ode in 1773, are typical of their era: Hayes was Professor of Music at Oxford from 1741 until his death in 1777 (and he had been organist of Magdalen College since 1734), presiding over something of a renaissance in the musical activities of the university and spreading its reputation through his contacts in London and at the Three Choirs Festival.[77] Then there are the numerous court odes, provided in this period by Eccles, Greene, and Boyce as successive Masters of the King's Musick. These were usually given twice a year, on New Year's Day and on the monarch's birthday, but with an occasional omission owing, for example, to the death or illness of a member of the royal family. Eccles had been the main composer since about 1700, when he became 'Master of the Musick' on the death of Nicholas Staggins, but in 1710 he retired from London life to devote himself to the rod and line.[78] He seems to have continued to provide the annual ode until his death in 1735, however, and is indeed the only composer named in that connection from 1715 on.[79] Only a few of these odes survive, together with some extracts in his *Collection of Songs* (1704),

[73] The odes by Pepusch and Croft performed at the 1713 'Act' (see above at n. 53) were doctoral exercises. Pepusch's ode is lost; the two by Croft, 'Laurus cruentas' and 'With noise of Cannons' on the Peace of Utrecht, were published in 1715 under the title *Musicus Apparatus Academicus*. For Stanley's *Power of Music* see n. 72.

[74] MB 58, ed. H. D. Johnstone.

[75] Bod. Lib., MSS Mus. Sch. c. 110 and d. 266 respectively.

[76] See above, nn. 46, 47. Full list in *NGD* s.v. 'Boyce'.

[77] Heighes, *The Life and Works of William and Philip Hayes*, 3–44 (life of William Hayes), 215–29 (odes of William and Philip Hayes), 340–1 (catalogue of odes by William Hayes). For Philip Hayes see below, Ch. 2.

[78] *The King's Musick*, ed. H. C. de Lafontaine (London, 1909); *RECM*, ii. 67; Goodall, 107 (based on an assertion of Hawkins).

[79] R. McGuinness, *English Court Odes 1660–1820* (Oxford, 1971), 23–31.

and none at all for the period 1715–35. Greene wrote thirty-five court odes between 1735 and 1755, thirteen of which remain;[80] because of their sycophantic and pedestrian texts (it was Greene's misfortune that Colley Cibber was poet laureate throughout this period) they are usually regarded as unperformable nowadays, though they contain some admirable music. Then in 1755 William Boyce, who succeeded Greene as Master, embarked on his immense series of forty-four odes: their survival *in toto* presents British musicology with a challenge which it has not yet addressed.[81]

The court odes were usually rehearsed in public a few days before their performance before the monarch and his family, so their audience was not as restricted as might be imagined. The same may be said of the various orchestrally accompanied anthems and services composed for great royal occasions: coronations, weddings, funerals, and days of national thanksgiving. Here again Handel stole the limelight from his English competitors, most notably perhaps in the four coronation anthems (including *Zadok the Priest*) for 1727, but also in the 'Utrecht' and 'Dettingen' Te Deum settings[82] and in the fine funeral anthem, 'The ways of Zion do mourn', for the death of Queen Caroline (1737). The eleven Chandos anthems, on the other hand, are a quite exceptional instance of orchestrally accompanied works for a private chapel. Croft, Greene, Boyce, and others contributed to the orchestrally accompanied genre, for example as degree exercises or for academic ceremonies as well as for royal occasions. Croft's Te Deum and Jubilate is a fine example of the post-Purcellian type,[83] while Greene's 'Hearken unto me, ye holy children', performed in Cambridge in March or April 1728, perhaps owes something of its conception if not the details of its execution to Handel's anthems of 1727.[84] One of the best of all eighteenth-

[80] Nine are preserved in MSS Mus. d. 33–40 in the Bodleian Library; another, 'In vain the muse', for New Year 1745, is in London, RCM 229, and three more are in the Royal Academy of Music, in Tokyo, Nanki Music Library, and in the Britten–Pears Library, Aldeburgh, respectively.

[81] The principal series is in Bod. Lib., MSS Mus. Sch. d. 298–340, all in score and parts; another copy of 'Pierian sisters' (Birthday, 1755) and of 'When Caesar's fatal day' (Birthday, 1756) is in MS Mus. d. 11. A set of three birthday odes for Prince George, grandson of George II, is in Mus. Sch. c. 106, c. 105, and d. 264 respectively (fac. in MLE, F/4). George became Prince of Wales after the death of his father Prince Frederick on 20 Mar. 1751 and succeeded to the throne as George III in 1760; these three odes were composed for his 11th or 12th, 13th, and 14th birthdays in 1749 or 1750–2, the first performed at Cliveden as a commission by Frederick, the other two, after Frederick's death, at Ranelagh Gardens.

[82] The first of these, with Jubilate, was composed early in 1713 to celebrate the Treaty of Utrecht; there was a public rehearsal of the music on 19 Mar. and an official thanksgiving service at St Paul's on 7 July. The Te Deum for the Dettingen victory was performed at the Chapel Royal on 27 Nov. 1743. Three other settings (the 'Caroline', 1714, the 'Chandos' *c*.1718, and one in A, the last being based on the 'Chandos' work, are known (*NGD*).

[83] The Te Deum was composed in 1709 for a victory celebration; it was revised, and the Jubilate added, in time for a performance at St Paul's on 20 Jan. 1715 (see the short score edition of the Te Deum by W. Shaw, Oxford, 1979, and the note by P. Holman for the Hyperion recording). Four orchestral anthems by Croft are known, two of them printed in his *Musica sacra* (see below).

[84] Edited, with the *Ode on St Cecilia's Day*, by H. D. Johnstone (MB 58). Altogether 20 orchestral anthems by Greene survive, and 7 settings of the Te Deum with orchestra, two of them also with Jubilate (*NGD*).

century orchestral anthems is Boyce's 'O be joyful in God'; it was performed on 2 July 1749 at Great St Mary's, Cambridge, as his doctoral exercise and as part of the 'festival' of his music there already mentioned.[85]

Chamber Cantatas

The enormous repertory of solo song may be thought of under three main headings: popular songs and ballads (nearly always strophic and for voice and bass alone); art-songs (strophic or through-composed, sometimes multipartite, or in some combination of these, often with one or more obbligato instruments, sometimes even with full strings); and chamber cantatas, sometimes dramatic and initially modelled on the Italian form but gradually acquiring a distinctively English identity. These categories tend to merge into each other (and the last into the dramatic pastoral or ode), but they are sufficiently distinct to warrant separate treatment. Here we shall consider them in reverse order.

Although the eighteenth-century English cantata, so called, was indeed dependent initially on the Italian model, there are native antecedents.[86] Whether described as 'songs', 'dialogues', or 'cantatas', they are generally multipartite in structure; they may be for two or more voices or require one or more obbligato instruments.

Purcell's immediate successors in the field of the multipartite song were such men as Weldon, Eccles, Daniel Purcell, and Croft. Their songs of this type were often in the form of a dramatic monologue, and intended for professional performance in a public theatre or concert-room—not (usually) within a spoken play, but as a self-contained act.[87] Some of Weldon's songs are vocally very demanding and represent the farthest limits of the post-Purcellian style. A potential cul-de-sac was avoided with the cultivation of the Italian cantata idiom by Daniel Purcell, Eccles, Galliard, and above all Pepusch, whose Six English Cantatas (1710) are settings of poems by John Hughes. Hughes was a minor poet whose enthusiasms included the fostering of Italianate opera to English texts, and the cantata offered a convenient opportunity for experiment in this vein and for the education of the public taste. The cantatas proved to be of little use in the furtherance of English opera, but they introduced a lasting vogue for the new form itself. Daniel Purcell produced his Six Cantatas in 1713, Galliard a

[85] There are eight orchestral anthems by Boyce extant, three of them for the coronation of George III in 1761. For a recent study see M. Atkinson, 'The Orchestral Anthem in England, 1700–1775', DMA thesis (University of Illinois, 1991).

[86] M. Boyd, 'English Secular Cantatas in the Eighteenth Century', MR 30 (1969), 85–97; Goodall, Eighteenth-Century English Secular Cantatas, 84–111. The latter, which deals also with art-song, though less comprehensively, is the standard authority and will be cited frequently hereafter; see also Cook, 'The Life and Works of Johann Christoph Pepusch'.

[87] Goodall, 22.

similar set in 1716, George Hayden a set of three in 1717, and Pepusch a second collection in 1720, while around that year the publisher John Walsh brought out a miscellaneous set of *XII Cantatas*.[88]

Somewhat surprisingly these cantatas, like many of their successors, are more often narrative than dramatic in form. Their underlying ethos is that of the pastoral, inspired by Theocritus and Virgil and imitated by poets such as Pope, Hughes, Carey, Prior, and many a lesser figure. Their poetry often included couplets and quatrains and longer passages in direct speech, but these were usually placed in a narrative framework rather than being left to speak for themselves. Even the examples of continuous monologue are rarely assigned with precision (explicitly or by implication) to an imagined character, and sometimes (as in Prior's 'Let 'em censure', later set by Maurice Greene) it is all too obviously the poet himself who speaks. Most often, however, the identity of the protagonist is simply left vague.

Almost all chamber cantatas in this period are for solo soprano voice, but the accompaniments vary from basso continuo (harpsichord with or without violoncello) alone to basso continuo with one or more obbligato instruments or full strings (two violins, viola, and violoncello), to which additional instruments might be added for colouristic effect. Pepusch was already using strings and two oboes in the last cantata ('Cloe') of his first book, and trumpet and strings in the fifth and sixth of his second book, and anything very much beyond that would have exceeded the bounds of what was still an inherently intimate form. Separate instrumental parts were not printed, but they were presumably copied by hand when the ensemble was too large for all to read from the harpsichordist's copy.

In form, too, the early eighteenth-century cantata was fairly stereotyped. Recitative, air, recitative, and air is standard, though the first recitative is sometimes omitted. There is almost always unity of key (allowing for change of mode), but the first air may be in a contrasting key if there is a preceding recitative. There are occasional examples of 'accompanied' recitative, and this becomes more frequent as the century progresses.

The opening of the third cantata from Pepusch's second collection, an unusual example for him of a semi-dramatic monologue (the poet here tells us what he himself said),[89] will illustrate something of the style which served later English composers as a model. The original Italian idiom is mediated through a Germanic control of form, and Pepusch's manner is indeed not far inferior to that of Handel at this period. His ability to write convincing recitative in English is shown in the expressive treatment of the word

---

[88] This included cantatas by Abiell Whichello (two, to words by Henry Carey), Anthony Young, John Sheeles, Pepusch, Galliard, and Italian composers. Many more survive in manuscript, and individually in Walsh's serial publication *The Monthly Mask of Vocal Music* from 1708 onwards (Goodall, 118).

[89] The words are by James Blackley. The other poets represented in this collection are John Hughes, John Slaughter, 'Mr Gee', Lewis Theobald, and Colley Cibber.

'scorn', while the musically parallel leap of a seventh on 'streams' is softened by the retention of the underlying harmony. The following air is less constrained by the need to adapt to the exigencies of the English language, but its careful craftsmanship is characteristic of a composer whose influence should not be underrated (Ex. 1.6).

A number of later composers—Carey, Hayes, Stanley, and Arne, for instance—published similar collections, while they and others also produced mixed volumes of cantatas and songs, the distinction in some cases being rather fine. Already in 1724, with his *Cantatas for a Voice with Accompanyment; Together with Songs on Various Subjects*, Carey had introduced both serious and burlesque cantatas, the burlesque example in this collection, 'Unhappy me', being described as 'The Tragical Story of the Mare, Compos'd in the High Stile by Sig^r Carini'; it is the dramatic lament of a rider whose mare has lost her shoe and who has suffered various other indignities. Carey never lost his taste for the burlesque. In 1740 he published *Three burlesque cantatas* under the same Italianate pseudonym: its first item was a reprint of 'Unhappy me', while the other two were reprinted from *The Musical Century* (2 vols., 1737–40). The first of these mocks the composition of court odes; the second is *The Musical Hodge Podge*, beginning 'An Old Woman cloathed in grey', and incorporates burlesque imitations of several castrati, ending with 'But of all the Songsters in the Land, there's none like Farinelli', one of several parodies of his famous ballad 'Sally in our alley'.[90] Carey's more serious extended work is of less account, but there is real dramatic power in 'I go to the Elisian Shade', from the 1724 collection, a monologue in which the swiftly changing moods of a despairing lover are given apt expression.[91]

Apart from these works of Carey and a few examples by Leveridge, there was little in the way of English cantata publication between 1720 and 1735, when a vogue for the extended serious type re-emerged. The intervening years, however, saw the publication in London of numerous sets of Italian cantatas by such composers as Giovanni Bononcini, Attilio Ariosti, and Porpora; there was also published a set by Thomas Roseingrave (1735), and there is a large manuscript collection (eleven cantatas and five duets) by Maurice Greene.[92] It is against this background that the subsequent history of the English cantata should be set.

Of its later practitioners John Stanley, with sixteen published cantatas, was the most prolific if not perhaps the most interesting.[93] His musical

---

[90] Of this ballad, first published singly around 1715, *The Musical Century* contains both the original (ii. 32) and a parody, 'Of all ye Toasts that Brittain boasts' (i. 31, with a superior bass).

[91] Carey's serious side is better shown in his *Six Cantatas* (1732); his cantatas as a whole are ably discussed by Goodall, 162–72.

[92] Oxford, Bod. Lib., Mus. d. 52. A twelfth cantata and several other Italian secular works are known (information kindly supplied by Dr H. D. Johnstone).

[93] His cantata publications were *Six Cantatas* (Op. 3, c.1742, repr. 1760), *Six Cantatas* (Op. 8, 1748), and *Three Cantatas and Three Songs* (Op. 9, 1751); also a single cantata, *The Redbreast* (1784). The dates and

Ex. 1.6

J. C. Pepusch, recitative 'When love's soft passion' and aria 'O love thou know'st my anguish' from Cantata III: *Six Cantatas*, Bk. II (London, 1720), pp. 14–15

idiom, though impeccably crafted, was somewhat stereotyped and his choice of texts (apparently by John Hawkins) conventional.[94] His recitatives are stilted and the arias, though some of them have splendid ritornellos, tend to be somewhat instrumentally conceived. In spite of this they enjoyed a certain popularity both in the pleasure gardens and in the theatres. Maurice Greene cultivated the English cantata far less extensively, but his three published examples all have distinctive features.[95] The earliest, 'Beneath a beach [sic] as Strephon laid', is one of the few intended for more than one voice (if one excludes strophic dialogues). The second, a setting of Prior's 'Let 'em censure, what care I', is a curious affair, inspired (it has been suggested) by the critical reception accorded to his *Forty Select Anthems* in 1743. The third, a setting of Hughes's 'Fair rival to the God of Day', is noteworthy for its richly scored first air, almost Bachian in its handling of a motivically complex accompaniment (see Ex. 1.7).[96] But for sustained interest throughout a set, few composers approached William Hayes, who poured into this smaller form, as into the more extended pastoral, something of the originality which circumstances prevented him, working professor and provincial organist that he was, from exhibiting on the public stages of the metropolis. The violoncello obbligato that opens the third cantata of the set published in 1743 admirably evokes the courtly nostalgia of the high Baroque (Ex. 1.8), while for picturesqueness the recitative 'Listen, nymph divine' and the following air, with its plucked strings and harpsichord solo, could hardly be outdone (Ex. 1.9).[97]

Yet another branch of the cantata tradition is found in Arne and Boyce, for whom the form was in many ways a projection of their stage *personae* and whose settings lay at the upper end of the pleasure-garden market. In this respect Arne was the more prolific and successful of the two. He was not unduly troubled by a desire for formal regularity or tonal unity: few of his longer works, in fact, begin and end in the same key. *Colin and Phoebe* and *Damon and Cloe*, from the first two books respectively of *Lyric Harmony* (c.1745–6), are simple strophic dialogues, with a concluding 'chorus' in

opus-numbers of the three collections are inferential. See J. Wilson, 'John Stanley: Some Opus Numbers and Editions', *ML* 39 (1958), 359–62; T. Frost, 'The Cantatas of John Stanley (1713–86)', *ML* 53 (1972), 284–92; Goodall, 193–205; A. G. Williams, 'The Life and Works of John Stanley'.

[94] The Preface to Op. 3 is unsigned and seems to imply that both it and the texts are by Stanley; but there is some evidence to suggest that Hawkins wrote the preface and the texts of all but one cantata of Op. 3, all of those of Op. 8, and possibly the three of Op. 9 as well (Goodall, 195).

[95] Goodall, 175–84, with details of sources. Greene's Italian cantatas (see n. 92) remain virtually unknown.

[96] *A Cantata and English Songs . . .* [Book II] (London, [1746]), pp. 6–7. Later issued as *A Cantata and English Songs . . . Book II*: the cantata comes last in both cases, but part of it was re-engraved for the second issue, with a supplementary pagination 1–10, the preceding songs being paginated 11–15 as well as the original 1–5. Presumably the intention, not carried out, was to reverse the order of cantata and songs in this second issue.

[97] From the sixth cantata, 'Daughter sweet voice and air'. Goodall, 184–92.

Ex. 1.7

Fair Ri - val to the God of Day, Beau - ty, Beau - ty to

thy Ce-les-tial Ray   A thou - sand spright-ly Fruits we   owe: Gay Wit,

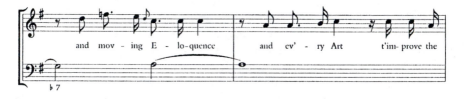

and mov - ing E - lo-quence   and ev' - ry Art   t'im- prove the

Sense,   and ev'-ry Grace, ev' - ry   grace_____ that shines be - low.

Air

Largo e cantabile

Ex. 1.7, continued

Maurice Greene, recitative 'Fair rival to the God of Day' and aria 'Not Phoebus does our songs inspire' from Cantata II: *A Cantata and Four English Songs*, [Bk. II], (London, [1746]), pp. 6–7

Ex. 1.8

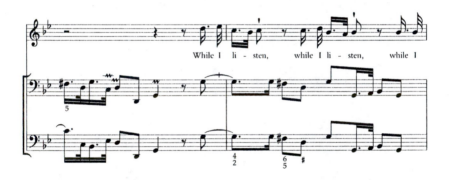

Note: ᰡ = notes cued in for harpsichordist

William Hayes, aria 'While I listen' from Cantata III: *Six Cantatas* (London, 1743), p. 18

Ex. 1.9

(1) This instruction probably means that 2 sopranino recorders are to double here, sounding an octave higher.

continued

Ex. 1.9, continued

William Hayes, recitative 'Listen, nymph divine' from Cantata VI: *Six Cantatas* (London, 1743), pp. 40–2

which a bass voice joins in. The first two volumes of *Vocal Melody* (*c*.1746) contain a cantata each, while his most popular cantata, *Cymon and Iphigenia*, was published separately around 1749 and often reprinted. The *Six Cantatas* of 1755 illustrate his sense of colour and variety to perfection: all call for full strings, generally with pairs of oboes and horns, the former sometimes alternating with two transverse flutes. In the second cantata, 'Beneath this sad and silent gloom', obbligato bassoons are specified. The opening of *The Morning*, 'The glitt'ring sun begins to rise' is a piece of tone-painting worthy of the future Haydn (Ex. 1.10).[98]

Boyce's more ambitious cantatas are preserved in manuscript, while those printed amongst the songs of his six-volume *Lyra Britannica* generally display simple forms and the characteristically tuneful lyricism that is one of his hallmarks as a composer.[99] Here are a Scots Cantata, 'Blate Jonny faintly teld fair Jean', and even a Lapland Cantata, 'Thou rising sun', each of them presaging that wider appeal to popular taste that was to dominate the genre in the succeeding epoch.

Solo Song

Solo song no less than cantata covered an enormous formal and expressive range. The more elaborate songs might consist of two or more separate (though short) airs, usually in binary form and without connecting recitative, while another type of elaboration might attach the idiom of recitative to an otherwise strophic structure, perhaps with additional instruments. But the greatest bulk of song-setting took a simple strophic form for voice and bass, with the second and subsequent stanzas written out below the music. It was a common practice to add below that a version for 'flute' in a convenient key, either the treble recorder or, later, the 'German' or transverse flute.

Amongst those who published their own collections of songs in the first two decades of the eighteenth century were John Weldon, Vaughan Richardson, John Abell, John Eccles, Anthony Young, John Reading, and James Graves.[100] But the real popularity of the genre is revealed by the serial publications that were issued, such as John Walsh's *Monthly Mask of Vocal Music* (1702–11, and 1717–24), and, a little later, George Bickham's *Musical Entertainer* (1737–9).[101] Publishers also compiled anthologies derived

---

[98] Goodall, 220–31, and, for cantatas written after 1760, pp. 232–6.

[99] London, Royal College of Music, MS 782, with three cantatas and other secular works, and Oxford, Bod. Lib., MS Mus. c. 3, with two cantatas and other works (see n. 47 above). Goodall, 212–19. Facs. of *Lyra Britannica* in MLE.

[100] For James Graves, whose *Twenty New Songs* were published in 1717, see Goodall, 110.

[101] *The Monthly Mask of Vocal Music* is the title of the first issue in Nov. 1702; that of the annual collective volumes was *The Whole Volume Compleat Intituled The Monthly Masks of Vocal Musick*. See W. C. Smith, *A Bibliography of the Musical Works Published by John Walsh 1695–1720* (London, 1968), nos. 140, 160, 188, 223, 258, 282a, 331, 370, 382, and, for the resumed series, 517. *The Musical Entertainer* was issued fortnightly in instalments consisting of four songs each from Jan. 1737 to Dec. 1739 and

Ex. 1.10

T. A. Arne, opening of Cantata V, 'The glitt'ring sun': *Six Cantatas* (London, 1755), p. 47

from the innumerable 'single sheet' publications of the early eighteenth century: Walsh's *Collection of the Choicest Songs and Dialogues* (*c.*1715), Watts's *Musical Miscellany* (6 vols., 1729–31) and the like. Popular composers like Leveridge and Carey issued extensive collections of their own songs, and somewhat later we find Boyce and Arne doing the same thing. Much of their output was, of course, originally sung in the theatre. It would be impossible to review all this material adequately in a general survey: attention will be focused on what seems to be representative and, in the first instance, on the more ambitious undertakings.

While Leveridge and Carey clearly aimed at a wide public even when writing cantatas and other multipartite songs, Maurice Greene wrote for a more discerning audience. His collection of *Spensers Amoretti*, published in 1739, is perhaps the first, apart from settings of Shakespeare, to draw on the poetry of the (by then) distant past, and certainly the first to use an Elizabethan sonnet-sequence as the basis of a quasi-cyclic collection. The emphasis here is on the 'quasi'; Greene chose twenty-five out of the original eighty-nine sonnets, keeping to Spenser's order except by starting with sonnet 80, 'After so long a race', which refers to his being half way through *The Faerie Queene* at the time. It is not altogether clear what governed the composer's choice of poems, and there is no sense of musical progression through the collection.[102] Nor does he reveal any sensitivity to the ethos of the sonnet: his settings are in two, three, or four short self-contained (usually binary) sections, with much verbal repetition. Although the melodic line is carefully wrought, it lacks the fluidity normally engendered by the more familiar phraseology of Augustan poetry, and its conciseness occasionally seems forced. A single complete setting will illustrate some of these points (Ex. 1.11).[103]

We find Greene in more relaxed vein in other published songs, both in the 'double-aria' form and in the strophic kind. It is interesting to compare his setting of Shakespeare's 'Orpheus with his lute' with his approach to Spenser as exemplified just now. The two stanzas of the poem are given contrasted binary airs, the second in a moderately quick 3/8 time. The first of these airs will show how, despite some anachronistic verbal repetition, the essentially lyrical quality of the poem translates into a more spontaneous flow of melody. This is accomplished song-writing (Ex. 1.12).[104]

subsequently issued in two volumes. See C. Humphries and W. C. Smith, *Music Publishing in the British Isles* (2nd edn., Oxford, 1970), 71 and pl. 216.

[102] The order of songs differs slightly in two MS versions: Greene's draft in the Royal College of Music, MS 812, and a fair copy by his pupil Martin Smith (London, Brit. Lib., Add. MS 31626). Greene's draft already places sonnet 80 at the head: it is hard to see why it should come third from the end in Smith's copy, which otherwise preserves the order of the printed edition. Goodall gives a comparative table, p. 255.

[103] *Spensers Amoretti set to Music by Dr. Green*, no. 11.

[104] Greene, *A Cantata and Four English Songs [1745]*, p. 9.

Ex. 1.11

Ex. 1.11, continued

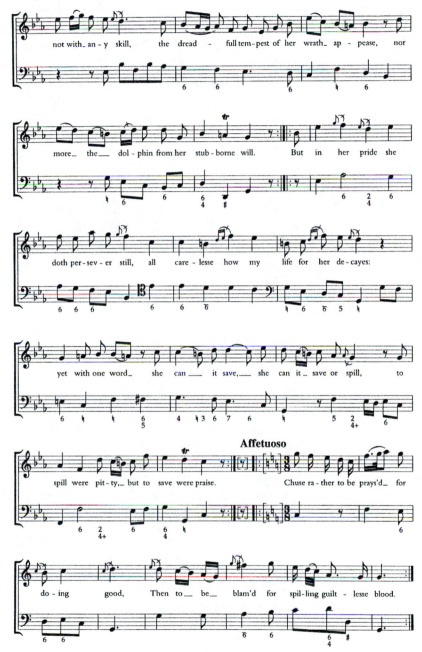

not with an-y skill, the dread - full tem-pest of her wrath ap-pease, nor

more the dol-phin from her stub-borne will. But in her pride she

doth per-sev-er still, all care-lesse how my life for her de-cayes:

yet with one word she can it save, she can it save or spill, to

Affetuoso

spill were pit-ty, but to save were praise. Chuse ra-ther to be prays'd for

do-ing good, Then to be blam'd for spil-ling guilt-lesse blood.

continued

Ex. 1.11, continued

Maurice Greene, Sonnet XI, 'Arion, when through tempest's cruell wrack': *Spensers Amoretti* (London, 1739), pp. 22–3

Stanley's three published songs are simply da capo arias requiring an obbligato instrument (unspecified, but by implication the violin). But most composers of songs exploited a wide range of forms, styles, and types of instrumental accompaniment. Greene himself wrote a number of strophic songs accompanied only by basso continuo, as did Arne, Boyce, and many lesser composers. At their simplest these are no more than popular ballads, and there was obviously a limit to their emotional potential. In seeking to overcome this composers often fell back on the methods of the cantata and the older multipartite song. Carey's cantata 'I go to the Elisian shade', which has already been mentioned, is a good example of a song that breaks out of the conventional formal mould to achieve a strong emotional effect through rapid changes of pace and with basso continuo accompaniment alone. But it was also possible to enhance the strophic principle through more elaborate instrumentation and varied repetition. Amongst a large number of lesser composers, William Jackson 'of Exeter', whose first collection of *Twelve Songs* was published in 1755, shows a heartening taste for experiment. The second of the set, 'Blest as th' immortal Gods', with full string accompaniment, has two lengthy stanzas in binary form with repeated sections, the second being a subtle variation of the first. The sixth song, 'The merchant to secure his Treasure', is similar in form and instrumentation (though without viola) but begins with an accompanied recitative (Ex. 1.13).[105] The whole

[105] Jackson, *Twelve Songs* [Op. 1]; also set by Greene.

Ex. 1.12

(1) *sic* (no slur, no hyphen); the composer may have intended to set 'Showers' as one syllable, like 'Flow'rs',
or as two, as on repetition.

Maurice Greene, 'Orpheus with his lute': *A Cantata and Four English Songs*, [Bk.I] (London,
1745), p. 9

Ex. 1.13

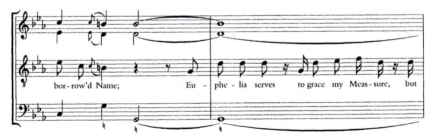

Ex. 1.13, continued

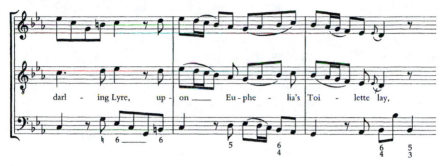

darl - ing Lyre, up - on ___ Eu - phe - lia's Toi - lette lay,

William Jackson, 'The merchant to secure his treasure': *Twelve Songs* (London, 1755), no. 6, pp. 18–19

collection is refreshingly varied in form and style and is altogether free of musical triviality, though the same can hardly be said of the verbal texts.

Apart from strophic settings, the succession of two binary arias was the commonest type of art-song; but in reality a wide variety of formal techniques, involving various combinations of recitative, aria (both binary and da capo), and a strophic element, was available. These, together with more elaborate and sophisticated instrumentation, became more common in the 1740s and 1750s with the development of musical entertainment in the pleasure gardens, where musical gestures needed to be bolder to make their effect. The distinction between cantata and elaborated solo song became less clear-cut; in both cases the expansion of their expressive potential is really only a development of the earlier traditions of the concert or theatrical solo 'act'. The vocal collections of Arne and Boyce reflect the variety of their theatrical experience as well as the opportunities afforded by the pleasure gardens, while for Michael Festing and Joseph Baildon these provided the sole raison d'être.[106] After about 1760 there was a decline into mere vocal effect in this type of entertainment, but during the previous two decades it had been of positive benefit to the development of English art-song.

The simplest and most directly appealing songs can be thought of as ballads, though the term was not often employed to denote a straightforward accompanied song until a later period. It appears in the subtitle of Henry Carey's *Musical Century, in One Hundred English Ballads* (2 vols., 1737–40), which as we have seen included two mock cantatas, and from this use alone we may adopt it to denote a wide range of sentimental,

[106] Goodall, 260–1; he discusses Festing's cantatas on pp. 206–8.

nostalgic, rumbustious, and burlesque songs.[107] Even a strophic musical form is not absolutely de rigueur, though it is by far the most usual. The interest of the genre lies as much in its social significance as in any musical qualities it may possess. The ballad was essentially a form of popular entertainment that could be successfully reproduced in the home; but while that could be said of a good deal of much earlier music, the new terminology draws attention to and coincides with a broadening of the appeal through musical simplicity and the cultivation of homely sentiment.

The further development of a distinctive type of song with such attributes will be considered in later chapters; for the moment it is sufficient to note the appearance in the first half of the eighteenth century of a genre that was beginning to diverge in quality from earlier types of popular song and had considerable potential.

Orchestral Music

The instrumental repertories of the period, though hardly less voluminous than the vocal, may be discussed more economically. It is convenient to distinguish between orchestral and chamber music, though a fixed boundary is not in evidence and their functions as well as their stylistic parameters overlap. Orchestral music is essentially 'public' in character; it is associated with the theatre, with concerts of vocal and instrumental music intermixed, and with the less formalized entertainment of the pleasure gardens.[108] Chamber music (including solo harpsichord music) was intended primarily for domestic consumption. But it could be performed effectively in smaller public venues (and outside the theatres most such venues were indeed small by modern standards); while a large household could enjoy what we should call orchestral music, much as it could sponsor private theatrical events.[109]

Two forms in particular predominated in the orchestral sphere: the concerto and the overture or symphony. The development of the latter as an independent concert form took place mainly in the second half of the eighteenth century, at least in the British Isles. Here it is necessary only to draw attention to the distinction between the characteristically French type of *ouverture*—with a moderately paced but rhythmically vigorous introduction, a fast fugal section, with a reprise of the introductory material, and

---

[107] The earliest use in this sense appears to be in J. F. Lampe's *Wit Musically Embellish'd . . . A Collection of Forty New English Ballads* (1731): *BHMB*, iv. 164. There seems to be no direct link either with the earlier literary use (which certainly referred to singable strophic poetry) or to the music of the narrative ballad, though there is a semantic overlap in both cases. The 'ballad operas', or at any rate the earliest ones, were not originally so called, but the term was used in *The Gentleman's Magazine* for Feb. 1731: cited V. Schoelcher, *The Life of Handel* (London, 1857), 82 (I owe this reference to Professor B. L. Trowell).

[108] For concerts, see *BHMB*, iv. 32–43; for pleasure gardens, ibid. 70–4.

[109] See e.g. above, p. 28, with regard to Prince Frederick.

sometimes one or more dance-like movements to conclude—and the Italianate *sinfonia*, normally in a tripartite fast–slow–fast form. Both types came to enjoy independent concert life, but it was the latter, with its intrinsically more coherent structure, that ultimately prevailed.[110]

The other main form, the concerto, also had theatrical associations, but in some of its guises at least had long had an independent history. The so-called concerto grosso for strings had come to England in the shape of Arcangelo Corelli's twelve concertos, Op. 6; the set became enormously popular and subsequently achieved the accolade of an edition in score (1732), said to have been 'revis'd by Dr Pepusch'.[111] Pepusch himself composed a number of similar concertos, and amongst other composers of foreign origin who contributed to the genre in the 1730s were Francesco Geminiani, Pietro Castrucci, Michael Christian Festing, and not least Handel.[112] Most of their concertos were composed for and published in the standard 'seven parts', allotted normally to the two violins and violoncello which constituted the 'concertino' or solo group, and the two violins, viola, and bass of the 'ripieno' or 'concerto grosso'. It is this latter term, used by Corelli to denote the 'tutti' group, that was later adopted by scholars to denote the genre itself. Corelli had indicated that in his concertos the 'concerto grosso' section was optional, and also that if used the parts might be doubled or not at pleasure.[113] His concertino group was musically self-sufficient, its cello part provided with figures for a harpsichordist; and, since the violin and bass parts of the 'concerto grosso' mostly doubled those of the concertino in the tutti sections, a tutti effect was achieved even without recourse to further doubling.

Most subsequent string concertos were more ambitious than this in their deployment of resources, however, and Geminiani (Opp. 2 and 3, 1732) actually transferred the viola to the concertino section, an expedient which was in any case temporarily available to any composer simply by marking

[110] John Walsh published numerous sets of parts of the overtures of Handel's operas and oratorios, together with a large collection in score and arrangements for harpsichord, in the period up to 1760; he also published various sets and arrangements of overtures by other composers (see W. C. Smith, *Handel: A Descriptive Catalogue of the Early Editions* (2nd edn., Oxford, 1970), 280–302; Smith and Humphries, *A Bibliography of . . . John Walsh . . . 1721–1766*, 256–7). The most important individual sets by English-born composers in this period were those of Greene (*Six Overtures*, 1745, also for harpsichord), Arne (*Eight Overtures*, 1751), and Boyce (*Eight Symphonies*, 1760). The vast majority of all these works are in French overture style, though some of those of Arne and Boyce are Italianate *sinfonie*, and some of Greene's are hybrid (as pointed out to me by Dr H. D. Johnstone).

[111] Corelli's concertos were first published posthumously by Roger and Le Cène (Amsterdam, 1714), and by Walsh and Hare in London, 1715. The edition by Pepusch in score was published by Benjamin Cooke, 1732, with a first volume devoted to the trio sonatas, and reprinted by John Walsh in that form, 1735.

[112] The concerto repertory of this period is described in *BHMB*, iv. 473–68.

[113] 'e duoi altri Violini, Viola e Basso di Concerto Grosso ad arbitrio che si potranno radoppiare'. It is likely, however, that if these works were played as trio sonatas the keyboard player would have used the basso part rather than the violoncello.

the relevant passage 'soli' in the part.[114] The popularity of the genre no doubt owed much to its inherent technical simplicity, and something perhaps to the appeal to publishers of a relatively stereotyped genre. Some of Handel's concertos Op. 6 have oboe parts added in the autographs, but the collection was issued for strings alone and in this form presumably enshrines Handel's intentions. Most of them had previously been heard in the theatre, but their publication in standardized format ensured a wider dissemination and provided the basis of an amateur repertory.[115]

The concerto idiom could be employed in works which did not employ a concertino at all—in other words, in pieces for string orchestra—which was the form taken in the first such publication by a British-born composer, namely the three books of William Corbett's *Le bizzarie universali, a quatro* (c.1728).[116] An alternative way of playing these pieces was as trio sonatas for pairs of oboes, recorders, or flutes and continuo: such transferences of medium were commonplace in the eighteenth century, and some music seems to have been devised especially to allow for an almost infinite series of permutations. By 1760 about a dozen more sets of concertos had appeared, including those of Michael Christian Festing (Op. 3, 1734, Op. 5, 1739, and Op. 9, 1756), John Humphries (Op. 2, c.1740, Op. 3, 1741), Stanley (Op. 2, 1742), John Hebden (1745), Richard Mudge (1749), John Alcock (1750), Pieter Hellendaal (c.1758), and the remarkable series issued by Charles Avison in Newcastle and London (Op. 2, 1740, Op. 3, 1751, Op. 4, 1755, and Op. 6, 1758; Op. 9 was to follow in 1766, and Op. 10 in 1769); and there are in addition Avison's Scarlatti arrangements, published as a set of twelve concertos in 1744.[117]

Of all these concertos those of Stanley, much influenced by Handel though they may be, are the most consistently inventive. Even here, nevertheless, the idioms have a certain predictability, and striking ideas (such as the violoncello solo in the second movement of no. 2) are counter-balanced by lightweight binary dances and lengthy episodes for solo violin and basso continuo. It is for immaculate workmanship that we can admire these works, and nowhere more so than in their robust fugal movements.

[114] e.g. Festing, Op. 3 no. 11 (MC 6); Stanley, Op. 2 no. 1 (MC 106). (The masculine plural form of the word was normally used irrespective of the number of players or the grammatical gender of the part-name.)

[115] As we shall see, however, many published collections of the time did include works with optional or compulsory (solo) wind parts. Handel's Op. 3, a botched set first issued by Walsh in 1734, includes oboe, flute, recorder, and bassoon parts, the first two also as solo instruments, and there is even a borrowed organ concerto movement in no. 6. Walsh published four collections of *Select Harmony* 'for Violins and other Instruments', devoted to concertos by Vivaldi, Albinoni, Geminiani and other Italians; the fourth collection (1741) included Handel's 'Alexander's Feast' concerto in C, which has inessential ripieno oboe parts, and two other short works of his with solo oboe (*HG*, xxi. 63–97).

[116] Reissued in 1742 as *Concerto's or Universal Bizzaries*.

[117] Of those mentioned the collections of Festing, Humphries, Mudge, and Alcock include works for other solo instruments (see below).

Avison deserves a special word if only because of the sheer volume of his concerto writing. In addition to the collections cited above he brought out an edition of *Twenty Six Concertos ... in Score* (1758), modelled on Geminiani's revised edition in score of his Opp. 2 and 3 (*c.* 1755) and representing a definitive version of his own Opp. 3, 4, and 6 (the six concertos of Op. 2 having been subsumed into the twelve of Op. 6 in their revised versions). With the twelve of Op. 9 and the six of Op. 10 the total number of original concertos for strings comes to forty-four, and, with the Scarlatti arrangements added, to fifty-six. It was a remarkable achievement, no less so for the composer's occasional lapses into cliché. He is rarely ineffective, and not infrequently displays considerable originality. The rather touching garrulity displayed in his prefaces may indicate a lack of self-confidence, but nevertheless represents the mind of a clear-thinking practical musician in the best traditions of native common sense, a character most fully evident in his remarkable *Essay on Musical Expression* (1752).[118]

Of the others mentioned, Hebden and Mudge—the latter a Warwickshire clergyman of whom little else is known—are the most reliable technically. One should add to the tally of string concertos the unpublished and little known works of Boyce and William Hayes, and the published sets of foreigners such as the brothers Sammartini.

Many sets published in the standard seven-part format included works for solo instruments other than the concertino strings, in some cases as an optional alternative. All of William Babell's posthumously published concertos (*c.*1730) are for one or two recorders and strings, while those of Festing, Humphries, Mudge, and Alcock include works for solo recorders, flutes, trumpet, and organ. Those of John Garth's set (1760) are all for solo violoncello. The range of possibilities was in fact very wide, and not at all inhibited by the apparent uniformity of publishing convention.

The solo concerto in England has a complex pedigree, since it was based on long-standing British precedent as well as on newer Italian models. The 'trumpet sonata' tradition (involving solo trumpet and strings) was well established by 1700, both inside and outside the theatre: Humphries's concerto Op. 2 no. 12, and Mudge's first, are as much a development of that tradition as of newer Italianate practice. The latter was represented by Vivaldi's Op. 3 (*L'Estro armonico*), published in London in 1715 as was Corelli's Op. 6, and also by Albinoni (Op. 2, 1709, 1717) and Torelli (1718),[119] and was largely responsible for the subsequent cultivation of three-movement concerto form by English composers in whatever medium. But apart from the keyboard, solo concertos and concerti grossi for

---

[118] See below, p. 89.

[119] Torelli's concertos were made available by Walsh and Hare in an Amsterdam publication containing works by him, Albinoni, and Martino Bitti (Smith, *Bibliography... 1695–1720*, p. 157; Smith and Humphries, *Bibliography... 1721–1766*, p. 324).

instruments other than strings made little permanent headway in England.[120] Even the solo violin failed to become a magnet for virtuosity in
this context and so to assist in the transformation from the Baroque to the
Classical concerto.

Keyboard concertos did indeed flourish, partly because of Handel's
example and partly because of their domestic usefulness—they could usually
be played straight through as keyboard solos, tutti passages being invariably
included in the published solo part. Handel's organ concertos were intended
for performance between the acts of his oratorios, and were a simpler way of
providing for this need than the writing of string concertos, since he could
(and often did) improvise the solo sections 'on the night'. Indeed, some of
the published movements consisted entirely of orchestral ritornelli with solo
sections indicated by the words *ad libitum*. His Op. 4 was published in 1738
and a *Second Set*, consisting mostly of arrangements from Op. 6, in 1740.[121]
The first two concertos of the *Second Set*, however, are original works and
are amongst his finest: Walsh published no orchestral parts for them (having
otherwise relied on the ripieno parts of Op. 6), but fortunately both concertos survive in autograph and various manuscript copies.[122] A third set,
once more of original works, was published posthumously in 1761 as Op. 7.

Handel's concertos were published as for organ or harpsichord, and the
formula was repeated in those of his imitators. As in Handel's sets, the
keyboard parts are normally a continuous amalgam of solo and tutti material; numerous such parts survive, but their accompanying orchestral parts are
not always so readily located. Stanley and Avison also published keyboard
versions of their string concertos, the accompanying parts in such cases
being identical with those of the model. Although the more interesting
examples of English keyboard concertos belong to the period covered by
the next chapter, there are attractive original works by Henry Burgess the
younger (two sets), Thomas Chilcot of Bath (two sets, published in 1756
and 1765 respectively), and William Felton (five sets, Opp. 1, 2, 5, and 7,
containing altogether thirty-two concertos published between 1744 and
1762),[123] and isolated works in printed and manuscript form by Charles
Avison (1742), William Hayes, and others.[124] Johann Adolph Hasse, who

[120] Apart from the composers already mentioned we may instance Pepusch (Amsterdam, c.1717 and
in MS), Robert Woodcock (*XII Concertos*, 1727), and John Baston (*Six Concertos*, 1729, though probably
composed rather earlier) as composers of solo and other concertos for a variety of instruments.

[121] Op. 4 no. 6 is for solo harp. The most comprehensive source of information on the concertos of
Handel and his English followers is P. Lynan, 'The English Keyboard Concerto in the Eighteenth
Century', 2 vols. (D.Phil. thesis, University of Oxford, 1997).

[122] The first two concertos are very similar to Op. 6 nos. 9 and 11, but are apparently original in this
form. Parts for these two alone were eventually published c.1761. Modern editions in MC 104, 105.

[123] There were six concertos in each set, but Op. 7 (c.1760) was reissued in 1762 with two additional
concertos.

[124] The work by Hayes (Bod. Lib., Mus. d. 82) is a lively three-movement piece with an 8-bar slow
introduction, as if the composer could not quite bring himself to abandon the four-movement pattern.

was in London in 1738–9, had a set of six concertos published by Walsh; they are somewhat more advanced in style than those of Handel, being in fast–slow–fast form (except for no. 5, which has a minuet added) with *galant* features. English composers frequently adopted this form, but the degree of *galanterie* varied: Felton, for example, was more adventurous than Chilcot, who remained resolutely Handelian in spirit.

Chamber Music

The larger forms of chamber music with basso continuo sometimes resembled the concerto in character and seem to straddle the divide between chamber and orchestral music.[125] The tendency in the eighteenth century, however, was towards a greater differentiation, and the larger ensemble works of Croft are closer to his trio sonatas, to which they are joined in a set of six unpublished works altogether. (Even trio sonatas, however, were sometimes played 'orchestrally'). Another tendency, though not one attributable to Croft, was to rely on Corelli rather than on Purcell as a model for the classic trio-sonata style: his Opp. 1–4 became well known in England through foreign editions and manuscript copies, and were eventually published in score in the same collection as the concertos Op. 6.[126] Though Corelli himself scored these works only for violins (with an accompaniment rather curiously designated as being 'for violone or arch-lute'), his English imitators, including Handel, were more adventurous in their choice of melodic instruments—and their publishers anxious to capitalize on viable alternatives. Nor on the whole did they espouse the Corellian distinction between chamber and church sonatas, any more than they had in the concerto. Yet another foreign model for both solo and trio sonatas were the numerous publications of Jean-Baptiste Loeillet and his cousin J. B. Loeillet 'de Gant', of whom the former came to live in London in 1705.[127] Their fluent, resourceful, easy-going music, variously scored, was much emulated.

Handel himself, of course, transformed whatever he imitated, and his Op. 2 sonatas for violins, oboes, or flutes, once they had appeared around 1730,[128] were themselves as influential as any earlier set. Much of the repertory—by such composers as Pepusch, Corbett, Humphries, Festing, and J. G. Freake—is of little intrinsic worth, but the twelve sonatas published by Boyce in 1747 (and three more in manuscript) are excellent

---

[125] See Vol. I, pp. 610–11. The word 'sonata' was often used for works employing a full complement of strings, as in Godfrey Keller's sonatas for trumpet (or oboe) and strings, published in Amsterdam in 1699 or 1700 with an English title-page. See MC, lxxiii. Keller lived in England from c.1694 until his death in 1704.

[126] See above, n. 111.

[127] See Vol. I, p. 609.

[128] For the date see T. Best, 'Handel's Chamber Music: Sources, Chronology and Authenticity', *Early Music*, 12 (1985), 476–99, esp. p. 492.

examples of the sturdy native idiom, an impeccably crafted amalgam of Corelli, Handel, and his own fund of melodic originality. Arne's seven sonatas (1757) are more modern and incipiently *galant* in outlook.[129]

The solo sonata repertory was considerably larger than that of the trio sonata, but the musical interest is less consistently maintained, perhaps because the larger market encouraged facile overproduction. Again Corelli, whose Op. 5 violin sonatas provided the primary model, overshadowed earlier memories of Nicola Matteis and the Purcellian tradition preserved by Croft and Daniel Purcell.[130] His sonatas were played in public early on by Gasparo Visconti (known as Gasparini); and the Italian style was further promoted by Geminiani, whose sonatas Op. 1 (1716, revised 1739) considerably extended the level of technical demands on the player and are in fact amongst the most difficult to be published in England. Geminiani was a strong influence on Festing, who published no fewer than four sets, and on Festing's teacher Richard Jones, an obscure London player whose violin suites are surprisingly original.[131] Even more rewarding are the eight sonatas of Joseph Gibbs (1699–1788), an east Anglian organist with a penchant for striking harmony.[132]

The oboe, flute, and recorder were the most popular of the other solo instruments, with the transverse flute largely replacing the recorder in solo sonatas after the 1720s. Handel's so-called Op. 1—a miscellany compiled by the publisher John Walsh— contained works for each of these instruments, together with three for the violin, and other composers sometimes included works for different instruments in the same publication or even, like Stanley, suggested performance of any of them on more than one instrument.[133] Babell's twelve sonatas, published soon after his tragically early death in 1723, are designated 'for a violin or hautboy', but the complete absence of idiomatic violin writing, and above all the character of the elaborate ornamentation in the slow movements, strongly suggest the oboe as the intended instrument. Few later sets, indeed, are anything like so well suited to any one wind instrument, though those of Thomas Vincent (1720–83) 'for a Hautboy, German Flute, Violin, or Harpsicord' are worth an airing on the first-named instrument (Vincent was himself an oboist in

[129] For two sonatas by the little-known F. E. Fisher (from his 2nd set, Op. 2, c.1760), see MC 49, 50. There is also a repertory of works for a pair of instruments without bass (see below).

[130] Croft, three for violin in *Six Sonatas or Solos ... by Mr. Wm. Crofts & an Italian Mr.* (1700); D. Purcell, *Six Sonata's or Solos, three for a Violin, and three for the Flute* [i.e. recorder] (1698: mod. edn. by P. Everitt, London: European Music Archive, 1980).

[131] Op. 2, c.1735, and Op. 3, c.1740; editions of one of the former by L. Salter in *18th-Century Violin Sonatas*, Bk. 2 (London: Associated Board, 1975) and of the first four of the latter by G. Beechey, MC 27–30.

[132] No. 1 ed. Salter, ibid., Bk. 1; nos. 3 and 5 ed. D. Stone (London: Schott, 1974); nos. 3 and 5 ed. D. Stone and R. Platt, MC 77, 78 (1990). See further in *BHMB*, iv. 184–8, and below for Handel.

[133] There is a thorough account of Handel's solo sonatas in Best, 'Handel's Chamber Music': for editions, in addition to those in *HHA* (iv/3, 4, 18), see Bibliography.

the King's Band). Thomas Roseingrave's *XII Solos for a German Flute* (1728) are not particularly idiomatic, though their occasionally tortured lines provide a compensating interest;[134] neither for that matter are those of Handel, and it comes as no surprise to discover that one of those published by Walsh as for the flute was originally written for the violin, and another (in all probability) for the recorder. In fact Handel's recorder sonatas are amongst the most attractive in the player's repertory.

For really idiomatic flute music we must again turn to John Stanley, whose eight solos Op. 1 (1740) and six solos Op. 4 (1745) 'for German flute, Violin, or Harpsicord' are among the most accomplished of their kind.[135] John Hebden's less well known *Six Solos* (*c.*1745) are also accomplished, notwithstanding his own career as a bassoonist and cellist; another unduly neglected composer is Charles Frederick Weideman, whose set of twelve 'sonatas or solos' (1737) reflects the interest of a professional flautist.[136] Weideman also contributed to the genre of sonatas for two or more flutes without bass. Earlier English examples of this (for example by Croft, 1704) are for recorders rather than transverse flutes; the popularity of the latter medium may have been enhanced by the republication by Walsh in 1728 of the six sonatas for two flutes by J. B. Loeillet 'de Gant', first issued by Roger of Amsterdam in 1717. The very widespread cultivation of the transverse flute amongst amateur musicians is an interesting social phenomenon; whatever the reasons, it gave rise to a huge number of arrangements, far more than original works, for one or two flutes with or without bass, with and without other instruments, mainly of vocal music of all kinds.

To return to sonatas with bass, we should mention for completeness the six sonatas for bassoon or cello by J. E. Galliard (1733); Walsh published Benedetto Marcello's six for cello in 1732, and the duet sonata for two cellos—not quite the same thing as a sonata for cello with basso continuo—also enjoyed a certain vogue. It is perhaps surprising that the enthusiasm of Prince Frederick for the cello did not give rise to a more distinguished repertoire, but like some of the other sonata genres just discussed, that for cello and bass blossomed more freely in the following period.

Solo Keyboard Music

As mentioned above, the solo harpsichordist had at his (or her) disposal the whole of the published keyboard concerto repertory in addition to original works and other kinds of transcription. Amongst the latter were numerous arrangements of orchestral music such as theatre overtures, together with

[134] Selections of works by Babell are in MC 51, 52; by Vincent in MC 98, 99; and by Roseingrave in MC 21, 54 (and see Bibliography).

[135] MC 15–18, 61–6, and other edns. cited in Bibliography.

[136] MC 74 (Hebden), 71, 72 (Weideman).

much of the solo sonata repertory published on two staves, excluding only the more idiomatic solo violin music and that for bassoon or cello. Virtually the entire repertory of published organ music, moreover, was available, nearly all of it with the harpsichord specified as an alternative instrument; and while some of this, like the orchestral arrangements, would sound best on a large two-manual instrument of the kind being made from about 1730, there was very little that could not be managed on the more traditional English single-manual harpsichord or spinet. Since the bulk of the organ repertory was in any case devoid of specific liturgical significance it is best considered here as part of an overall 'keyboard' genre.

The traditional domestic form was the suite, a category that could embrace varying degrees of formal coherence. In the early eighteenth century, following late seventeenth-century precedent, the majority of published collections were devoted to several composers and included miscellaneous pieces ('lessons') as well as suites or 'sets'; and it is not always clear how many consecutive movements in a single key actually belong to a particular 'set'. No doubt players simply performed as many pieces together as they wished, irrespective of the composer's actual intentions. After Purcell (1696) and Blow (1698) only Philip Hart (1704), Jeremiah Clarke (1711, posthumously), and Anthony Young (1719) published individual collections before 1720; there are, moreover, very few coherent 'sets' in the anthologies after 1700. On the other hand, a considerable quantity of valuable music by Blow and Croft was never published at all. Much of the published and manuscript music of this period consists of arrangements of theatre music, both vocal and instrumental, and even the most rewarding of the original works are not particularly demanding technically.

In this and in other respects Handel's *Suites de pièces de clavecin . . . Premier volume* (J. Walsh 'for the author', 1720) as usual signal a change of outlook.[137] Despite the fact that the collection is a somewhat belated issue of pieces that in some cases had been in existence in some form or another for quite a while, it consists solely of eight coherent and weighty multi-movement works of considerable polish and sophistication. (His collection of 1733 more obviously scrapes the barrel and has no such coherence.) Such elaborate fugal and variation writing, with its massive and sparkling treatment of the harpsichord, was quite new in England at the time. Although the set had few imitators—Thomas Chilcot's *Six Suites of Lessons* (c.1734) are the most obviously derivative—it influenced the repertory in more general ways, primarily by enlarging the acceptable range of technical demands and their associated sonorities. This was as much in evidence in orchestral transcriptions as in original works.

---

[137] Ed. A. Hicks (Munich: Henle, 1983). The Roger publication of c.1721 contains fewer than half of the same pieces.

Another liberating influence was that of Domenico Scarlatti, whose *Essercizi* (a set of thirty single-movement sonatas) were published in London in 1739, and again in an enlarged collection of forty-two edited by Thomas Roseingrave, published in two volumes in the same year. It appears already in Roseingrave's own *Eight suits of lessons* (1728 and two later editions) and to a greater extent in Greene's *Collection of Lessons* (1750). Greene had previously suffered an unauthorized publication (in 1733) of some rather immature suites, but the 1750 set offers an individual amalgam of Scarlattian features and a surprisingly *galant* idiom in general.[138] Despite a number of other such publications, such as those of Richard Jones (1732), James Nares (1747), and Thomas Arne (1756),[139] Greene's collection represents the high point in this sphere. The cultivation of a more consistently proto-Classical idiom by such figures as Joseph Kelway and John Burton belongs largely to the following epoch.

The numerous organ voluntaries of the period owe rather less to Continental models, though we may see Vivaldian concerto-like traits in some such works by Greene and Stanley. The eighteenth-century voluntary, a form designed as it were to lubricate the performance of the Anglican liturgy, grew out of the post-Restoration types cultivated by Locke, Blow, Purcell, and later Croft, John Reading, Philip Hart, and numerous minor figures of the early eighteenth century. Their occasionally rather extravagant efforts to get more out of the contemporary church organ than it was designed to give were superseded by a more 'classical' approach to texture, one governed by line rather than by sonority. The formal design, moreover, became more systematized. A slow introduction would be followed by a fast movement—either a fugue or a concerto-like piece using a solo stop such as flute, 'cornet', or trumpet.[140] Some voluntaries consisted of two such pairs, in which case the fugue would normally come second and the 'solo' movement last. There are also examples of a three-movement Vivaldian structure, including a very effective one by John Stanley (Op. 5 no. 8).

While Stanley's thirty published voluntaries, together with those of Greene and Boyce, are the best known to organists today, it would be wrong to discount the contribution of such figures as Croft, Roseingrave,

---

[138] Facs. edn. D. Moroney (London: Stainer and Bell, 1977). It is difficult to account for Burney's description of the suites as 'a boarding-school book... produced for idle pupils at different times, with whom facility was the first recommendation' (*History*, ii. 492): the music is not at all easy to play well.

[139] Arne's *VIII Sonatas* are ed. C. Hogwood (Oxford, 1983), and in facs. by G. Beechey and T. Dart (London: Stainer and Bell, 1969). Their reputation may be due more to their title than to their intrinsic merits. Jones's very individual works may owe something to Rameau, though Rameau's solo keyboard music (nearly all of it in print by 1728) was not published in England until the 1760s.

[140] The cornet stop was a multi-rank register, usually available only from c♯ upwards. Very few English organs at this time possessed pedals, but solo stops such as those named, with vox humana, oboe, horn, 'cremona' (all reed stops), and the like, began to appear, sometimes as part of an enclosed division with a shuttered swell (see below).

Travers, Walond, and Bennett. Roseingrave in his first set (1728) experi-
mented with strange harmonic progressions. His *Six Double Fugues* (1750)
were presumably influenced by Handel's *Six Fugues* (published in 1735 but
based on earlier materials), which in any case helped to raise the general
level of fugal writing by English composers. John Travers (*c.*1703–58)
adopted a popular, easy-going style: his twelve voluntaries were published
posthumously in 1769. William Walond (1719–68), a rather obscure Oxford
organist, seems to have been the first to specify *crescendo* and *diminuendo* in
organ music, while John Bennett (*c.*1725–84), who succeeded Charles
Burney as organist of St Dionis Backchurch in 1752, was an admired
exponent whose early promise remained largely unfulfilled.[141]

Church Music

The church music which we are now to consider is to be distinguished fairly
sharply from the occasional elaborately accompanied cantata-like anthems
discussed earlier in this chapter. The more modest requirements for the
regular Chapel Royal music, though anticipated in the reigns of William
and Mary and of Queen Anne, were entrenched in the Hanoverian system
and mean that from henceforth it is possible to think in terms of a 'cathedral
music' that is fairly uniform over the whole range of cathedral and collegiate
churches including the Chapel Royal itself, a situation that is in many
respects unchanged today. From now on the musical forms of anthem and
service, except on special occasions of national rejoicing or mourning, came
to occupy a less significant place in the repertory, not only for us today but
also, one suspects, in the minds of contemporary followers of musical
fashion. Nevertheless, the best church music of the eighteenth century
attained a high standard, and the lack of excessive virtuosity in what was
now being written for the Chapel Royal helped to create more realistic and
achievable targets elsewhere. The published anthems and service-music of
Croft, Greene, and Boyce, therefore, together with the preserved 'canon' of
pre-Hanoverian music for general use, form the measure by which the
general level may be judged, even if this was not always and everywhere
attained.[142]

In the late Stuart and early Hanoverian Chapel Royal tradition, most
eloquently represented in Croft's *Musica sacra* (1724), the organ is not only a

[141] Walond's two sets appeared *c.*1752 and in 1758; those of Bennett in the latter year. Modern
editions of this repertory, where they exist, are cited in the Bibliography: note also *English Organ Music*,
ed. R. Langley (London: Novello, 1987–8), vols. iii–v.

[142] On the formation of this canon, which stems ultimately from Tudway's manuscript collections
(London, Brit. Lib., Harl. 7337–42) and from copies of older music by John Alcock and Maurice Greene,
whose plans for a published Collection were eventually carried out by Boyce (*Cathedral Music*, 3 vols.,
1760–73), see W. Weber, *The Rise of Musical Classics in 18th-Century England* (Oxford, 1992), 36–46. See
also H. D. Johnstone, 'The Genesis of Boyce's "Cathedral Music"', *ML* 56 (1975), 26–40. For some
comments on liturgical requirements in this period and the next, see Ch. 2 n. 123.

continuo instrument but frequently acts as a substitute for the disbanded string ensemble by supplying the tuneful upper part of the ritornelli or 'symphonies' and as much of the inner harmony as the player could manage to encompass. In a 'full' anthem or service, indeed, there were no such ritornelli, and the idiom varied from a grave *prima pratica* to something more up-to-date and 'Handelian', such as Croft attempted in his not very exciting 'God is gone up with a merry noise' and which Greene essayed rather more successfully in his 'O clap your hands together all ye people' for five voices.[143] The concept of the 'full' anthem permitted the inclusion of short 'verse' sections, often for the familiar grouping of alto, tenor, and bass soloists, and without ritornelli or much if any independent writing for the organ continuo. Croft's 'O Lord rebuke me not', for six voices in the 'full' sections, is a fine example,[144] but the majority of his works are 'verse' anthems for various solo groups with one or more sections for chorus: the organ continuo part is inevitably independent for much of the time and there is often some obbligato writing for the right hand. The openings of two unpublished anthems will illustrate the variety of approach that was possible within the idiom. In the first, from 'Hear my crying, O God', an essentially contrapuntal idea is treated with considerable freedom and eventually yields to a mellifluous idea in parallel thirds (Ex. 1.14), while 'I waited patiently for the Lord' (Ex. 1.15) opens with a small-scale aria for treble, the whole work being for solo voice with short choral sections after each of the three 'verses'.[145]

About eighty anthems by Croft survive, four of them with orchestra, together with three services (in addition to the orchestral Te Deum and Jubilate already mentioned) and the Burial Service, in which he retained Purcell's 'Thou knowest, Lord, the secrets of our hearts'. They breathe the spirit of quiet yet confident Anglicanism that characterized the reign of Anne and somehow survived the trauma of a Hanoverian succession. Croft tended to write longer sections than his stylistic mentors, Purcell and Blow, and he laid the foundations of the multi-movement anthem cultivated by Greene, Boyce, Travers, Nares, and others.

Greene was Croft's natural artistic successor and a fine composer of church music. Nearly a hundred anthems of his survive, twenty of them the orchestral anthems for special occasions already mentioned. The great

---

[143] Both in *TECM*, iii, 140, 171. 'God is gone up' is not in *Musica sacra* but is e.g. in Bod. Lib. MS Mus. d. 28, p. 1; 'O clap your hands' is in Greene's *Forty Select Anthems* (1743).

[144] *TECM*, iii. 124, from *Musica sacra*. Burney remarks in a note (*History*, ii. 484): 'The two octaves in the last line of the chorus, between the second treble and the tenor, will be easily pardoned, in so many parts, by a good contrapuntist, for the sake of the imitations.' His tolerance in this instance does not redeem a thoroughly Beckmesserish examination of the anthems of Croft and Greene in particular, ibid. 480–92.

[145] Bod. Lib., Mus. d. 29, p. 55, and Mus. d. 28, p. 102. Several works from this collection (Mus. d. 27–31) have been overlooked in *NGD*.

Ex. 1.14

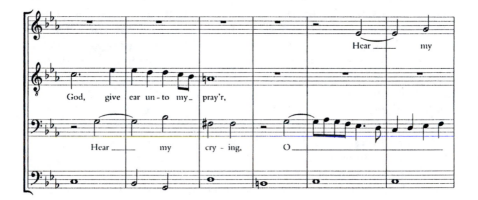

Ex. 1.14, continued

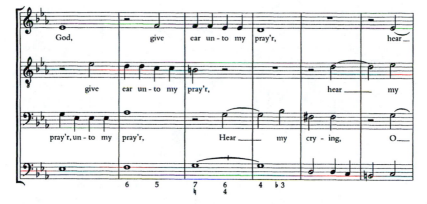

continued

Ex. 1.14, continued

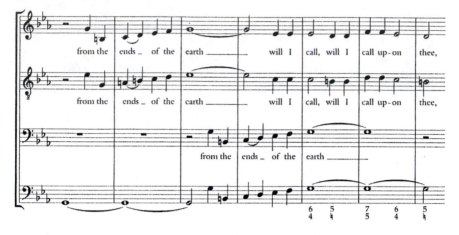

William Croft, 'Hear my crying': Oxford, Bod. Lib., Mus.d.29, pp. 155–7

majority of the remainder, sixty-five out of seventy-nine, are solo or verse anthems with choral sections; many of these have an obbligato organ part as opposed to a mere basso continuo, though this too is naturally essential in such works and often fulfils a ritornello function on its own. He expanded the scale of the anthem by enlarging the musical structure of the individual movements; and while not every 'verse' section can count as an independent entity, the majority of the solo and choral sections are broadly laid out. In this way the organ-accompanied verse or solo anthem came not infrequently to resemble the cantata-like works with orchestral accompaniment, a development which inevitably led to some trivial note-spinning in some of Greene's less gifted followers. At its best, however, this type of anthem achieved the brilliance, pathos, and delicacy called for by the texts without loss of underlying dignity. It provided the climax of a morning or evening service in which the musical element also included the intoned versicles and prayers of the celebrant, the chanted responses and psalms (usually though not invariably harmonized) of the choir, and the 'full' writing which normally characterized the settings of the canticles.[146] Greene himself wrote a finely varied setting of the morning and evening canticles with Sanctus and Gloria for the Communion service, rising from four to eight voices in full style and interspersed with verses. He also wrote a set of six five-part anthems in each of the 'modes'—Dorian, Phrygian, Lydian,

---

[146] Greene's 'Arise, shine, O Zion' is in *TECM*, iii. 152. For responses and psalms see R. M. Wilson, *Anglican Chant and Chanting in England, Scotland, and America 1660–1820* (Oxford, 1996).

Ex. 1.15

continued

Ex. 1.15, continued

William Croft, 'I waited patiently for the Lord': Oxford, Bod. Lib., Mus.d.28, pp. 102–3

Mixolydian, Aeolian, and Ionian—an interesting example of a kind of antiquarianism that seems to have been in the air just then.[147]

Boyce was perhaps less successful in his anthems than one might have expected. Many are ambitious and lengthy works, but their ideas are often feeble and their tonal scope limited. Several lesser figures, amongst them Travers and James Nares (1715–83), a later Master of the Children of the Chapel Royal whose anthems were published in 1778, were sometimes able to impart a picturesqueness that Boyce might well have thought inappropriate.[148] By the 1760s, in fact, composers were finding it increasingly difficult to steer a course between the Scylla of dullness and the Charybdis of meretricious ornament.

Parochial music was dominated by metrical psalmody, which could be sung in unison unaccompanied, or accompanied by the organ, or in vocal harmony, in which case the tune was normally placed in the tenor. A number of handbooks for organists, with examples of 'givings out', harmonizations, and interludes between the lines or stanzas, were published for the use of urban parishes in which an organ could be afforded. But the most interesting developments took the form of harmonized settings by country musicians, whose publications often exhibit a technically unconventional but resourceful use of the vocal medium. They also contributed to the large body of new tunes for which the eighteenth century was especially notable and which permanently enriched the tradition of English hymnody.

---

[147] It is possible that they were intended for performance by the Academy of Ancient Music, but their 'pure' modality distinguishes them from ordinary examples of the contrapuntal tradition that the Academy valued. There are 'modal' exercises in counterpoint by Pepusch and Travers, and by Handel in Cambridge, Fitzwilliam Museum, MS MU 260, pp. 55–8, 63–6 (facs. in HHA Suppl., i. 53–62). (The old distinction between authentic and plagal modes was not maintained in this genre.)

[148] See *TECM*, iii. 184–235 for a representative selection of works by Travers, Boyce, and Nares.

But their achievement reached its climax in the following period and will be considered more fully in the next chapter.[149]

Psalm-tunes are nowadays thought of as hymns, but the eighteenth-century 'hymn' was more akin to a continuo song, like the Lieder and 'arias' of contemporary Lutheranism. Some of them have survived into modern congregational hymnody, but only after much adaptation. The three tunes written by Handel to hymns by Charles Wesley are a good example of the type: two of them are scarcely known today, while the third has remained popular ever since (Ex. 1.16).[150] It was but a short step from the continuo hymn to the 'parochial anthem', a genre that again reached the limits of its potential in the subsequent epoch.

Musical Thought and Scholarship

The eighteenth century was an age of technical and historical enquiry, of criticism and controversy, and of provision for practical self-help. A consideration of each of these in turn will enable some of the more significant writings of the period to be brought under review.

Technical and historical musicology, as we should now call them, were closely associated, largely because a purely academic interest in the music of antiquity necessarily embraced the study of ancient Greek mathematics and acoustics. The tradition of technical investigation was well established in the seventeenth century, when the speculative and practical study of acoustics gained added impetus from the founding of the Royal Society in 1660.[151] The publication in 1682 of Ptolemy's *Harmonics* by John Wallis, himself a prominent mathematician, was a landmark because it showed how the Greeks themselves were able to build on Pythagorean theory in order to account for musical refinement.[152] We now find English musical scientists going over some of the ground already covered by sixteenth-century Italian theorists such as Zarlino, but with the benefit of a more favourable climate for experimental observation. The study of intervals and scale-forms had a

[149] The standard account is that of N. Temperley, *The Music of the English Parish Church*, 2 vols. (Cambridge, 1979).

[150] Cambridge, Fitz. Mus., MS MU 262, p. 9; facs. in *HHA Suppl.*, i. 84. The 1st edn., from this MS, was by S. Wesley, c.1825.

[151] P. Gouk, 'Music in the Natural Philosophy of the Early Royal Society', Ph.D. diss. (London, Warburg Institute, 1982); L. Miller and A. Cohen, *Music in the Early Royal Society of London 1660–1806* (Detroit, 1987); J. C. Kassler, *The Science of Music in Britain, 1714–1830*, 2 vols. (New York and London, 1979); P. M. Gouk, 'Music', *Seventeenth-Century Oxford*, ed. N. Tyacke (Oxford, 1997), 621–40.

[152] See Vol. I, p. 612: the *Harmonics* was reprinted, with Porphyry's *Commentary*, in vol. iii of Wallis's *Opera mathematica* (Oxford, 1699). The main source of knowledge of ancient theory before that was of course Boethius, but the *De musica* was available only in rare 15th- and 16th-c. editions of the complete works. Some scholars may have had access to Marcus Meibom's *Antiquae musicae auctores septem* (1652), which included the works of Aristoxenus, Aristides Quintilianus, and the ninth book of Martianus Capella's *De nuptiis Philologiae et Mercurii* (a Latin offshoot of Aristides) with other less important Greek writings.

Ex. 1.16

Ex. 1.16, continued

(c)

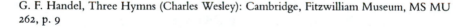

G. F. Handel, Three Hymns (Charles Wesley): Cambridge, Fitzwilliam Museum, MS MU 262, p. 9

bearing on the tuning and temperament of keyboard instruments, and inventions such as that described in Ambrose Warren's *Tonometer* (1725) were intended to permit the more accurate verification of small intervals. Perhaps the most influential consequence of mathematical acoustics was the harmonic theory of Jean-Philippe Rameau, which was enthusiastically adopted by John Frederick Lampe and others.[153] Although based in part on acoustical misunderstanding, the appeal of the theory lay in its application of mathematical principles to the practice of harmony in the modern

---

[153] Rameau's *Traité de l'harmonie* was first published in 1722; an English translation of Book III, *Principes de Composition*, was published in 1752 under the misleading title *A Treatise of Musick, Containing the Principles of Composition*. J. F. Lampe's *The Art of Musick* (1740) is heavily influenced by the *Traité* and quotes verbatim from it.

sense of the word. The physical nature of sound and its reception by the ear were less well understood than the mathematics of pitch–relationships, and were to remain so until the scientific advances of the nineteenth century.

The study of classical literature, above all that of ancient Greece in its original language, led not only to an interest in the nature and behaviour of sound but also to the consideration of music's ethical properties and its role in education and society. It also served as the starting-point for the study of musical history in its own right, though there is little sign of a comprehensive approach prior to the appearance of the substantial works of Burney and Hawkins later in the century. Nevertheless, it is evident from the writings of Roger North, as of Henry Aldrich and James Talbot before him, that the spirit of historical enquiry had been born.[154] North's writings were not published, but the range of his knowledge and his particular view of musical development were not peculiar to him: the assumptions on which they were based underlay much of what other musically educated writers had to say. Briefly, these are that the music of the ancients was valued by the philosophers for the sake of its ethical force and judged accordingly, though as it cannot be recovered we have to rely on the descriptions of ancient writers as evidence. With the collapse of classical civilization music experienced a reverse from which it only gradually recovered through the plainchant of the Roman church, through plainchant-based polyphony from Guido of Arezzo to the Renaissance masters, and from that point to the present perfect union of melody and harmony.[155]

This pattern of history led to the question—by no means a new one—whether the ancient or the modern music was superior: a question that could not be answered on the evidence available but which nevertheless generated a good deal of controversy. But the matter is complicated by the various senses in which the term 'ancient' came to be used. When the Academy of Vocal Music (founded in 1726) changed its name to the Academy of Ancient Music in 1731, the term 'ancient' was understood to refer to the music of the sixteenth century.[156] But the frequent inclusion of

---

[154] For Talbot and Aldrich, see Vol. I, p. 612 n. 122. North's fullest historical summary is in *The Musicall Grammarian 1728*, ed. M. Chan and J. C. Kassler (Cambridge, 1990), 221–73. Tudway also attached a history of music to his collection of church music (see above, n. 142): see C. Hogwood, 'Thomas Tudway's History of Music', in *Music in Eighteenth-Century England*, ed. C. Hogwood and R. Luckett (Cambridge, 1983), 19–47.

[155] On the disappearance of ancient music, see North, *Musicall Grammarian*, 221; C. Avison, *Essay on Musical Expression* (2nd edn., London, 1753), 71–2 n. North's recollections of the old consort music and his admiration (not uncritical) for Locke and Jenkins has sometimes been thought to indicate conservatism; yet for him the perfection of musical style was represented by his close contemporary Corelli, and the last pages of the *Musicall Grammarian* suggest no disapproval of the current state of the art, only admiration for its diversity.

[156] Weber, *The Rise of Musical Classics*, 56, 169 n. Yet another sense of 'ancient' (to which Weber gives insufficient weight, 30 n.) refers to the history, literature, and (by extension) music of Britain in former times: see Ch. 8 below.

seventeenth-century compositions in its programmes meant that the boundaries of the ancient were in practice being gradually extended, until in due
course the word came to refer to anything not less than twenty years old.

The comparison between the new and the not-so-new led to a lively
controversy and to the development of a cult of 'ancient' music that was
unique in Europe at that time. In that age, however, almost any musical
issue—aesthetic, social, or moral—was capable of generating a war of
words. Aesthetic issues were often focused on the criticism of currently
fashionable entertainment, such as that of Italian opera by Richard Steele,
John Dennis, Joseph Addison, and (reputedly) J. E. Galliard early in the
century. Italian opera found a defender in the anonymous author of *The
Touchstone: or . . . Essays on the Reigning Diversions of the Town* (1728), who
considered it a legitimate manifestation of the principles of classical
drama.[157] Both sides of the debate relied ultimately on Aristotle for their
view of dramatic propriety.

Aristotle was also the basis of eighteenth-century views of the arts as
modes of imitation (*mimesis*). Although Aristotle appeared to embrace
instrumental music in his account of *mimesis* (*Poetics*, ch. 1), he did not
pursue the connection, and the more thoughtful commentators perceived
its limitations. James Harris in the second of his *Three Treatises* (1744), the
'Discourse on Music, Painting, and Poetry', noted the inadequacy of the
theory of imitation as applied to music and concluded that its 'charm' lay
elsewhere, and principally in 'raising *Affections*'.[158] His point was developed
in the most notable contribution of the period to musical aesthetics, Charles
Avison's *Essay on Musical Expression* (1752). The imitation of sounds or
motions is of very limited use to a composer, whose task rather is 'to
blend such an happy Mixture of Air and Harmony, as will affect us most
strongly with the Passions or Affections which the Poet intends to raise'.[159]
He is not very clear how this applies to instrumental music, but there is the
implication that the idioms appropriate to word-setting, and even the
sonorous attributes of verse itself, were transferable to the instrumental
medium:

The Power of Music is . . . parallel to the Power of Eloquence: if it works at all, it
must work in a secret and unsuspected Manner . . . And I don't know, whether the
same Propriety, in regard to the Part of Expression in *Poetry*, may not as well be

---

[157] See I. Lowens, 'The *Touch-stone*: A Neglected View of London Opera', *MQ* 45 (1959), 325–42;
BHMB, iv. 401; L. Lindgren, 'Another Critic Named Samber', in *Festa Musicologica: Essays in Honor of
George J. Buelow*, ed. T. J. Mathiesen and B. V. Rivera (Stuyvesant, NY, 1995), 407–34 (attributes the
tract to Robert Samber). Arbuthnot's letter in defence of *The Beggar's Opera* (Gibson, *The Royal Academy
of Music*, 398) may have been intended as a reply to this tract.

[158] Cf. already Francis Hutcheson in his 'Inquiry into the Original of our Ideas of Beauty and Virtue'
(1725), p. 99: the 'charm' of music is that of 'raising the agreeable Passions' (cited McGeary in *BHMB*, iv.
419; cf. Kassler, *Musical Science*, 451–3).

[159] Avison, *Essay* (2nd edn., 1753), 69.

applied to *Musical Expression*; since there are discordant and harmonious Inflections of musical Sounds when united, and various Modes, or Keys, (besides the various Instruments themselves) which, like particular Words, or Sentences in Writing, are very expressive of the different Passions, which are so powerfully excited by the Numbers of Poetry.[160]

Avison recommended the study of the best contemporary models, whom he names as Marcello for vocal music and Geminiani for instrumental. The strength of the *Essay* is that it presents the plain good sense of a genuine if minor composer; but its criticisms of other and better composers, amongst them Vivaldi, Palestrina, and even (by implication) Handel, as subordinating harmony to melody or vice versa,[161] enraged some of his contemporaries and brought a furious reaction from William Hayes, whose anonymously published pamphlet attacked Avison the composer as lacking the skill to justify his credentials as a theorist. Avison replied with dignity to his 'virulent, though, I flatter myself, not formidable, Antagonist', countering his criticisms of specific passages with reasoned defences and the citation of parallels in generally admired composers.[162]

Discussion of the ethical and social functions of music was frequently based on propositions deriving ultimately from Plato and Aristotle. For Plato music was to be judged according to its ethical effect, and only the good made available and taught to the young.[163] Mathematical studies, including harmonics, are recommended as a prelude to the study of dialectic.[164] Aristotle had a more relaxed attitude to the enjoyment of music, which he recommended as being 'not useful or essential but elevated and gentlemanly'. Even so, its chief purpose was to inspire virtue, and as such should form a part of a child's education. Moreover, 'since ... actual performance is needed to make a good critic, [children] should while young do much playing and singing, and then, when they are older, give up performing; they will then, thanks to what they have learned in their youth, be able to enjoy music aright and give good judgements'.[165]

[160] *Essay*, 70, 72–3, reinforced by a quotation from Pope's *Essay on Criticism*, ll. 366–82: 'Soft is the strain when Zephyr gently blows, / And the smooth stream in smoother numbers flows; . . .'.

[161] Vivaldi is included in the 'first and lowest Class [of those] whose Compositions being equally defective in various Harmony, and true Invention, are only a fit Amusement for Children' (*Essay*, 39). There may here be an ironic reference to the title of Vivaldi's Op. 8, *Il Cimento dell'armonia e dell'inventione*.

[162] Avison's *riposte* was first published separately and then included in the 2nd edn. of the *Essay*. He defends the upward resolution of a 9th by a quotation from the end of Croft's 'O Lord rebuke me not', a passage containing those parallel octaves on which we have noted Burney's comment (above, n. 144).

[163] *Republic*, 398–401A, translated in O. Strunk, *Source Readings in Music History* (New York, 1950, repr. in 5 vols., 1965), i. 4–7; *Laws*, 812B–E. For these and other relevant passages see A. Barker, *Greek Musical Writings I* (Cambridge, 1984), 124–63.

[164] *Republic*, 530C–531C: Barker, *Greek Musical Writings II* (Cambridge, 1989), 55–6.

[165] Aristotle, *Politics*, 1338[a], 1340[b] (transl. T. A. Sinclair, Harmondsworth, 1962, 303, 310–11); cf. Barker, *Greek Musical Writings I*, 170–82.

The influence of this line of thought on many writers of the period is clear. The Earl of Chesterfield wrote to his natural son in Italy: 'if you love music, hear it; go to operas, concerts, and pay fiddlers to play to you; but I insist on your neither piping nor fiddling yourself'. He offered advice in a similar vein to his godson fifteen years later, adding: 'Musick though generally reckoned among the liberal Arts, is in my mind a very illiberal occupation for a Gentleman.'[166] Chesterfield's confusion was understandable enough, for Aristotle's 'liberal sciences', or subjects of study fit for a gentleman, had become the 'liberal arts' of the medieval academic tradition. These were no more than speculative disciplines, but the inclusion of 'music' amongst them, and the ambiguity of its status in the universities, not unnaturally led to the assumption that the practice as well as the study of music was implied. In the circles in which Chesterfield moved, music was very much the Cinderella of gentlemanly pursuits, even on a non-participating level; yet he was himself a director of the Italian Opera in London from 1720 until 1744 at least, and many of his colleagues must have been far more positive in their attitude. Their objections, if any, would have been to the adoption of music as a profession rather than to its active pursuit as an amateur.

Yet another type of polemic is represented by Arthur Bedford's *The Great Abuse of Musick* (1711), which combines a desire to rescue music from its trivialization in the theatre with an effort to promote its advancement in the church. The 'High Church' movement to which he adhered gave rise to numerous sermons on the appropriateness of music in divine worship as a counterblast to the increasingly influential evangelical opinion that would restrict it to unaccompanied unison psalmody, while Bedford himself was an active figure in the early cult of 'ancient music'.[167]

An obvious connecting link between 'practical' and 'technical' theory is provided by those approaches to harmony that were supposedly based on natural acoustic laws. J. F. Lampe tried rather unsuccessfully to teach 'thorough bass' in the light of Rameau's theory of the 'fundamental bass', his view being that the mere mechanics of interpreting the figures were insufficient for an understanding of the compositional process.[168] He took his ideas further in a short pamphlet, *The Art of Musick* (1740), in which

---

[166] Cited by Gibson, *The Royal Academy of Music*, 46–8, from B. Dobrée's edn. of the letters (London, 1932), iv. 1330–1, and S. L. Gulick, *Some Unpublished Letters of Lord Chesterfield* (Berkeley, 1937), 76–81. Chesterfield's letters to his son Philip were first published posthumously (by the son's widow) in 1774.

[167] Weber, *The Rise of Musical Classics*, 47–56. A number of published sermons on music are listed in the bibliography to N. Temperley's *Music of the English Parish Church*; cf. Weber, 115–16, with special reference to Thomas Bisse's 'Three Choirs' sermon of 1726, *Musick the Delight of the Sons of Men* (London, 1726). Bedford himself preached a sermon on *The Excellency of Divine Musick* (1733).

[168] *A Plain and Compendious Method of Teaching Thorough Bass* (London, 1737); cf. B. Cooper, 'Englische Musiktheorie im 17. und 18. Jahrhundert', in *Geschichte der Musiktheorie*, ix (Darmstadt, 1986), 177–8; Kassler, *The Science of Music*, ii. 674–6.

Rameau's *Traité* of 1722 is quoted. The third book of the *Traité* itself was published in English translation in 1752,[169] though the whole work must have been known before then to others besides Lampe. Rather more conventional treatises on harmony and thorough-bass were published with attributions to Pepusch,[170] while other works on harmony and composition included those of Geminiani (*Guida armonica... Opera X, c.*1752, and a supplement published shortly after) and Giorgio Antoniotto (*L'Arte Armonica or a Treatise on the Composition of Musick*, 1760). Another type of writing was exemplified by Geminiani's two treatises on taste (*Rules for playing in a true Taste,... Opera VIII, c.*1748, and *A Treatise of Good Taste in the Art of Musick*, 1749),[171] and yet another by William Tans'ur's *New Musical Grammar*, first published in 1746 and running to seven editions by 1829. Vocal and instrumental tutors had existed for some time, often in the form of brief introductions to anthologies of tunes.[172] The early eighteenth century saw an expansion of this trade and the publication of a more comprehensive work, *The Compleat Musick-master*, which came out in three editions in 1704, 1707, and 1722. Peter Prelleur's *Modern Musick-Master*, in six sections respectively for voice, recorder, flute, oboe, violin, and harpsichord, appeared in 1730,[173] and there were numerous such publications for single instruments thereafter. Among the more original and unusual works were Galliard's translation of Tosi's *Observations on the Florid Song* (1743) and Geminiani's *Art of Playing on the Violin* (1751).[174] It is difficult to imagine that Tosi's *obiter dicta*, first published in 1723, could have been as 'useful for all performers, instrumental as well as vocal' in the England of the 1740s as the translator claimed on the title-page; but they

---

[169] See above, n. 153.

[170] *A Short Treatise on Harmony*, publ. anonymously (London, 1730), repr. under Pepusch's name as *A Treatise on Harmony* (1731); *Rules, or A Short and Compleat Method for Attaining to Play a Thorough Bass on the Harpsichord or Organ, by an Eminent Master* (London, *c.*1730); see Kassler, *The Science of Music*, ii. 822–30.

[171] Kassler, *The Science of Music*, i. 379–86, gives earlier dates for some of Geminiani's treatises; but these conflict with the evidence of the opus numbers. The dates given above are those established in E. Careri, *Francesco Geminiani* (Oxford, 1993), 274–87, where all the treatises are fully described.

[172] A rather incomplete list is given by A. Simpson, 'A Short-Title List of Printed English Instrumental Tutors up to 1800, Held in British Libraries', *RMARC* 6 (1966), 24–50. It may be supplemented by T. E. Warner, *An Annotated Bibliography of Woodwind Instruction Books, 1600–1830* (Detroit, 1967) and, for the violin, by D. Boyden, 'A Postscript to "Geminiani and the First Violin Tutor"', *AcM* 32 (1960), 40–7; cf. J. M. Pickering, *Music in the British Isles 1700–1800: A Bibliography of Literature* (Edinburgh, 1990), 341–59.

[173] The collective title-page bears the date November 1730, but the earliest copies of the constituent parts are dated 1731: see Warner, *An Annotated Bibliography*, 14. Kassler, *Musical Science*, ii. 853–5, and Pickering, 341, assume a substantive edition of 1730 and a reissue of 1731. There were several further issues, both of the work as a whole and of the various parts separately. Prelleur's authorship is vouched for by Hawkins, though in fact the work is no more than a compilation of existing material.

[174] Tosi is published in facs. (Geneva, 1978), and Geminiani also in facs., ed. D. Boyden (London, 1952). Geminiani's treatise is fully discussed in D. Boyden, *The History of Violin Playing from its Origins to 1761* (London, 1965; 3rd impr., 1974, repr. Oxford, 1990), esp. 356–390.

will have been of some use to teachers and are of interest today for the light they throw on contemporary attitudes to performance. Geminiani's treatise is a far more practical work for the advanced learner, with its numerous examples (including twelve complete works) and its insistence on an expressive style of performance. It is in fact, with those of Leopold Mozart (1756) and L'Abbé le fils (1761), one of the three major works of the mid-century, though it represents the culmination of Baroque style rather than the stirrings of the Classical. As the work of a leading composer and performer, however, it carries at least as much weight as the other two and must have had a profound effect on the development of London as a leading performance venue in the second half of the century.

2

THE LATER EIGHTEENTH AND EARLY NINETEENTH CENTURIES, 1760–1815

ANY chronological subdivision of the long period that separates the death of Handel from the first stirrings of what is generally called the English musical renaissance is bound to be somewhat artificial. There are few clear landmarks by which one might chart the calamitous decline that occurred between (say) the productions of Arne's *Artaxerxes* in 1762 and of Sullivan's *Ivanhoe* in 1891, to name the most ambitious operatic efforts of two highly talented men of the theatre. The solution adopted here, the last thirty years of the nineteenth century having been marked out as the arena for the conflict between high Victorian cultural values and those of its challengers, is to divide the remaining 110 years, 1760–1870, into two approximately equal halves. In this analysis the third chapter chronicles a gradual change in the threat to musical values from one of aristocratic trivialization to those of commercialism and puritanism in a bourgeois ascendancy.

The making of these strictures on taste and attitudes is not to imply that the period from 1760 to 1870 was a cultural desert. Quite the reverse is the case, even in music, let alone in literature and the fine arts. While we are not to look for 'greatness' in English composers in the sense that one can legitimately apply the term to the Viennese Classical composers and the European Romantics, there is a very tolerable level of achievement throughout. English audiences, moreover, enjoyed without intermission a varied diet of well-performed music by Continental masters, demonstrating by their attendances a considerable degree of discrimination. The result was that to a certain extent English composers were sidelined into providing either the ephemeral or the merely worthy, and their efforts to overcome this became increasingly subject to failure. We shall encounter dozens of exceptions in the shape of minor talents whose real achievements were widely appreciated in their day and in some cases still are, but it is only with the young Elgar and some of his near contemporaries that a permanent change in this landscape begins to emerge.

Theatre Music

The pattern of theatrical entertainment in London conformed to the mould set by convention and legislation earlier in the century. Only two theatres, Drury Lane and Covent Garden, were allowed to present plays, in effect any performance with spoken dialogue. There was nothing to stop either of them from offering all-sung (or all-mimed) performances, and they often did so. In 1766, however, the Little Theatre in the Haymarket received a royal patent, so becoming the third Theatre Royal in the capital, and was allowed to put on spoken plays during the summer, when the other two licensed theatres were in theory shut.[1] Otherwise, here and elsewhere (at the pleasure gardens and Sadler's Wells, for example), continuous music was de rigueur. At the King's Theatre, the usual fare was Italian opera, serious or (more and more often) comic, with English or Italian oratorios in Lent, though the principal venue for oratorio remained Covent Garden.[2] When the King's Theatre was destroyed by fire in June 1789, Italian operas were put on first at Covent Garden (for the end of the 1789 season), at the Little Theatre, and (in 1791) at the Pantheon in Oxford Street—a rotunda modelled on Hagia Sophia in Constantinople—opened in January 1772 and used hitherto for concerts. When the new King's Theatre opened in February 1791 Italian opera was at first not allowed, the King having transferred his patronage to the Pantheon; one of the casualties of this policy was Haydn's *L'anima del filosofo*, commissioned for the new theatre and in the event never produced.[3] But the Pantheon itself was burnt in January 1792, and although rebuilt, staged opera only rarely thereafter. The King's Theatre reverted to Italian opera on 16 January 1793 with Paisiello's *Il barbiere di Siviglia*. As for the two other major theatres, Drury Lane, which had been extensively renovated in 1775, was pulled down in 1791 and greatly enlarged, reopening in March 1794; it was burnt down in 1809 and a new theatre, the fourth on the site, opened in 1812. Meanwhile Covent Garden had also been destroyed in 1808 (on 19 September); its

---

[1] The Theatre Royal, Haymarket, stands on the east side of the street, on a site adjacent to the original one and opposite Her Majesty's, formerly the King's Theatre. It is often referred to simply as 'the Haymarket'.

[2] At the King's Theatre comic operas were usually performed on Tuesdays, serious operas on Saturdays; oratorios, if at all, on Thursdays (C. S. Terry, *John Christian Bach* (2nd edn., Oxford, 1967), 64, 120; *LS, passim*). J. C. Bach produced Jomelli's *La passione* and his own *Gioas, rè di Giuda*, in Lent 1770 (Terry, 120); Burney, *History*, ii. 877). At Covent Garden J. C. Smith the younger had been put in charge of oratorio performances from 1754; he was joined by John Stanley after Handel's death in 1759, and in 1770 they moved to Drury Lane. See further below, pp. 108–9.

[3] Instead the King's Theatre was used by the Drury Lane company during the rebuilding of their own theatre (see below, n. 22).

successor opened in 1809. Apart from the disruption to entrepreneurial management, these two fires resulted in the loss of an immense quantity of performing material, the outcome being that very few of the enormous number of English operas and comparable works performed in the second half of the eighteenth century and the first few years of the nineteenth can now be reconstructed in full.

The major foreign presence in London during the 1760s and 1770s was that of J. C. Bach, who was invited over as resident opera composer at the King's Theatre in 1762. Five of his eleven operas were written for London; he also contributed to various pasticcios, and was responsible for the first London performance of Gluck's *Orfeo ed Euridice* in 1770.[4] But the initial enthusiasm soon waned, and three of his later operas were produced in Mannheim and Paris. He had, however, achieved social recognition with his appointment as music master to Queen Charlotte and became prominent in London's concert life from 1764, until the series that he ran with C. F. Abel also began to suffer from changes in musical fashion and the competition of newer and more vigorous enterprises.

As Bach's operatic fortunes declined, comic opera by such composers as Baldassare Galuppi and Niccolò Piccinni became more popular at the King's Theatre, while in the 1770s the repertory was dominated by Antonio Sacchini and Tommaso Traetta. Thomas Arne's Metastasian opera *L'Olimpiade* was produced there in April 1765, though it was unsuccessful and its music is lost. Burney maliciously ascribed its failure to the composer's adoption of an idiom not native to him, but he made the same strictures on the highly successful *Artaxerxes* (at Covent Garden) three years earlier, an opera Italianate in everything but its language. Bach's last London opera, *La Clemenza di Scipione* (4 April 1778) was well received, but the composer died in poverty on 1 January 1782 and the fortunes of the King's Theatre began to suffer a marked deterioration. In 1785, after a further revival of Gluck's *Orfeo*, to quote Burney, 'the whole opera machine came to pieces, and all its springs, disordered by law suits, warfare, and factions, were not collected and regulated, till the next year'.[5] In the later 1780s we begin to encounter the operas of a rising new generation, that of Giovanni Paisiello (1740–1816) and Domenico Cimarosa (1749–1801), and of the gifted young Englishman Stephen Storace (1762–96). Very little of Storace's music for the King's Theatre has survived, and we are left with the paradox of a reputation sustained mainly by the two early comic operas written for Vienna; the

---

[4] Terry, *J. C. Bach*, 117–19. Several new musical numbers were added by Bach, though the work was revived in Mar. 1773 in its original (Viennese) form (ibid. 145); see also E. Warburton, 'J. C. Bach's Operas', *PRMA* 92 (1965–6), 95–105.

[5] *History*, ii. 897. More detailed information is now available in C. Price, J. Milhous, and R. D. Hume, *Italian Opera in Late Eighteenth-Century London: The King's Theatre, Haymarket, 1778–1791* (Oxford, 1995).

second of these, *Gli equivoci* (1786), to a libretto by Lorenzo Da Ponte, is a minor masterpiece. Storace wrote two comic operas, one Italian and one English, and a serious opera with English text, *Dido, Queen of Carthage* (1792), for the King's Theatre, but the main survival from his short theatrical career in England is the comic opera with dialogue, *No Song, no Supper*.[6]

The pattern of English operatic life was beginning to change radically, and would have done so even if fire and rebuilding had not disrupted it. After the resumption of Italian opera at the King's Theatre in 1793, the emphasis was still more on the importation of Italian operas already well known abroad; the repertoire lost the consistency of style imposed by a resident composer, and while a broader appeal was sought, the standing of the Opera as an arbiter of taste diminished. The true impact of Italian opera in London on English music in the eighteenth century has still not been properly assessed, and will not be until much more of the repertory becomes available for study; but it can be deduced that its influence was profound, and remained so until the rapid development of orchestral concert-music in the 1770s and 1780s at first challenged its hegemony and finally usurped its role altogether.

The main venues for the performance of opera in English were Covent Garden and Drury Lane. Although, as has been mentioned, they did over the years put on a number of all-sung operas, their monopoly of spoken drama enabled them to mount stage productions of all kinds, including of course ordinary plays. There was in fact much less enthusiasm for serious all-sung opera in this period than previously:[7] the all-sung masque had died a natural death, and the times were no longer propitious (if indeed they ever had been) for an offensive like that of the elder Arne in 1732–3. What the previous epoch had achieved, starting with *The Beggar's Opera*, was a general acceptance that song and spoken dialogue might contribute on equal terms to the same dramatic action. This tradition, which, as we have seen, helped in the establishment of similar forms in Germany and France, remained the favoured one in England, and if it were not for the wholesale destruction of performing materials there would be a great deal more to be said about the age of Arnold, Dibdin, and Shield. Opportunist though they and their collaborators were, with their resort to pasticcio and their espousal of pantomime, they represent a native tradition that enjoyed a vitality difficult to recapture even in the imagination.

In the circumstances it is somewhat surprising that two of Thomas Arne's successes in the early 1760s were in the realm of all-sung opera.

[6] An edition of *Gli equivoci* is planned in MB (see also n. 23 below). The works in English for the King's Theatre were performed by the Drury Lane company (see n. 22); further on Storace's English operas see below, pp. 106–7.

[7] This generalization does not apply to the genres of burletta and pantomime, which remained extremely popular.

With *Thomas and Sally* (Covent Garden, 28 November 1760) he finally achieved what he had earlier attempted in *Don Saverio* and *Henry and Emma*:[8] an all-sung comic opera of wide appeal. No doubt its success was due as much to its librettist Isaac Bickerstaffe, an Irish playwright who became a familiar figure on the London theatrical scene until he was forced to flee the country in 1772. Arne's second all-sung effort was even more striking: a setting of his own translation of Metastasio's *Artaserse* (*Artaxerxes*, Covent Garden, 2 February 1762). Here Arne proved himself a complete master of the Italian style, and the rare opportunity of hearing fine singing— including that of the castrato Tenducci—in its own language was welcomed by the bourgeois public. The work was often revived, even in the early nineteenth century, but it failed to establish a tradition. It was published in full score, an increasingly rare luxury, but as usual without the *secco* recitatives; these have never been recovered, although they may well survive in a shortened form, with the figured bass replaced by full strings, in the version made by Henry Bishop for Covent Garden in 1814. Derivative the work may be, as Burney implied, but it has a vitality not often associated with the grand operatic manner in the hands of an English composer.[9]

Early in the next season Arne established another important precedent with *Love in a Village* (Bickerstaffe; Covent Garden, 8 December 1762). This is what has become known as a 'comedy pasticcio', a dialogue-opera with songs adapted from various sources. In this case Arne himself composed only five numbers for the opera out of a total of forty-two; but the others were mostly substantial pieces of music, unlike the thinly harmonized airs of the ballad operas. Newly composed or not, the comic opera with dialogue quickly became the most popular form of operatic entertainment in England and long remained so.[10]

Of Arne's theatrical successors it was Samuel Arnold (1740–1802) who achieved the greatest prominence. A man of unusually wide gifts, he was not only the outstanding impresario of the late eighteenth century but also a church musician and scholar, trained in the Chapel Royal, where he became composer and organist in 1783. In 1789 he was appointed director

[8] *Henry and Emma* was subsequently reset as a dialogue-opera (CG, 13 Apr. 1774); the music for this version too is lost.

[9] For *Artaxerxes*, including a discussion of its stage history and sources, see Fiske, *English Theatre Music*, 305–10. Jommelli had set *Artaserse* in 1749, and J. C. Bach in 1760, but neither had been heard in London. Another Metastasian opera in English was *The Royal Shepherd*, by the little-known composer George Rush: this adaptation of Metastasio's *Il re pastore* was put on at Drury Lane (24 Feb. 1764) as the company's response to *Artaxerxes*. It was published in vocal score, but only the overture, additionally published in full score, achieved a lasting success (modern edn. in *The Symphony 1720–1840*, ed. B. S. Brook (New York, 1979–86), vol. E1, no. 10).

[10] The earliest comic dialogue-opera with music entirely newly composed was Arne's *Guardian Outwitted* (CG, 12 Dec. 1764); but composers for long afterwards commonly inserted at least a few items from current popular favourites into their comic operas.

of the Academy of Ancient Music, and in 1787 initiated a collected edition of Handel's music, a short-lived but prophetic venture.[11] Such a man could, perhaps, have left a monument of fine music, but he devoted his creative talents to productions that have proved ephemeral.

The Maid of the Mill (produced at Covent Garden, 31 January 1765) was Arnold's first theatrical success, and indeed it was continually revived even into the nineteenth century. Again the librettist was Isaac Bickerstaffe, who drew this time on Richardson's novel *Pamela*; again the opera was a pasticcio with dialogue, only four of the numbers being by Arnold himself. One of the others was contributed (rather surprisingly) by J. C. Bach; the remaining items are mainly adaptations of Italian arias by such composers as Galuppi, Gioacchino Cocchi, and Hasse, together with a few items from French operas by Pierre-Alexandre Monsigny, Philidor, and Egidio Duni. The primary source is a printed vocal score, though like most others of the period it shows some of the instrumental detail.

Arnold became manager of Marylebone Gardens—where he lost a good deal of money—in 1769, and composer and musical director at the Little Theatre Royal in 1777. Here his talent for burletta and pantomime, as well as for more conventional dialogue-opera, found full scope. Very little of this music survives in full score, but on the whole, to judge from the extant vocal scores, this hardly seems a crushing loss. Like his contemporaries Arnold set out to entertain, and he did so with whatever materials lay most conveniently to hand. In the three-act afterpiece *Two to One* (Little Theatre, 19 June 1784), for example, the overture and eleven vocal numbers are by Arnold, one is by Philip Hayes, and no fewer than ten are based on popular ballads (one of which is identified as 'Yankee Doodle'). But at least Arnold provided an appropriate musical setting for such things, writing proper introductions and interludes, and even in the simplest pieces demonstrating his practical craftsmanship. His last stage works, all for the Little Theatre, were the ballets *Obi, or Three-fingered Jack* (2 February 1800), *The Corsair* (29 July 1800), and *Fairies' Revels* (14 August 1802). On 22 October of that year he died as a result of a fall in his library.

Arnold's reign at the Little Theatre enabled the talents of Dibdin, Shield, Hook, the Linleys, Storace, and Attwood to flourish at Covent Garden, Drury Lane, and elsewhere. Charles Dibdin (1745–1814) was a racy character, a singer and actor, a debtor on an impressive scale, and in the end an independent entertainer. His technique of composition was in some ways rather rough and ready, but there is a theatrical appositeness about his music that often compensates for the simplicity of his procedures. Very little

[11] Thirty-six volumes appeared from 1787 to 1797. Arnold became organist of Westminster Abbey in 1793, and edited three volumes (with an organ part) of *Cathedral Music* (1799). For the last word on this composer see R. H. B. Hoskins, 'Dr Samuel Arnold (1740–1802); An Historical Assessment', Ph.D. diss. (University of Auckland, 1981).

survives orchestrally, but what there is shows a competent hand.[12] In Dibdin's works, slightly pretentious music, with an emphasis on vocal bravura, rubs shoulders with sentimental or humorous ballads, the latter predominating as time went on.

Dibdin's major early success was a comic afterpiece, *The Padlock* (Drury Lane, 3 October 1768), with a libretto by Bickerstaffe based on a story by Cervantes. Dibdin's best operatic music is often to be found, as here, in his ensembles, for which he had a marked penchant. The finale to Act I, for example, responds vividly by means of rapid changes of tempo and metre to the comedy of a forced entrance to the padlocked home; but we are not to expect the subtlety of characterization or the structural strength of a Mozartian finale in such lightweight entertainment. The second version of Dibdin's *Lionel and Clarissa*, revived in 1770 as *The School for Fathers*,[13] is regarded as his operatic masterpiece; but he continued to write successful stage works until 1778, when his all-sung 'burletto' *Poor Vulcan* was given at Covent Garden on 4 February. After quarrelling with the management he attempted to establish his own theatre, was imprisoned for debt, and devoted the rest of his life to the one-man shows he called 'Table Entertainments.'[14]

The elder Thomas Linley (1733–95) was another prolific contributor to the London stage. He had grown up in Bath and was a well-known director of concerts and oratorios there from the later 1750s to the early 1770s. He wrote a successful opera for Covent Garden (*The Royal Merchant*, 14 December 1767) and was invited in 1775 by his newly acquired son-in-law Richard Brinsley Sheridan to prepare the music for his opera *The Duenna*.[15] In the event the opera was a pasticcio, about half the music being by Linley and his gifted son, also named Thomas. When Garrick retired in 1776, the elder Linley became joint director of Drury Lane with Sheridan, composing several mostly trivial works—dialogue and ballad operas, pantomimes, and farces—for that theatre.[16] The death of his son Thomas, born in 1756 and one of twelve children, at the age of 22 in a boating accident at Grimsthorpe Park, was a tragic loss. Thomas the younger's afterpiece *The Lady of Bagdad* (Drury Lane, 19 February 1778) was not a success, but something of his potential as a theatre composer can be seen from his music for *The Tempest* (1777) and from the splendid *Shakespeare*

[12] The main item is the overture to *The Padlock* (see below), which was published in parts by John Johnston (c.1770).

[13] DL, 8 Feb. 1770.

[14] Dibdin was a voluminous writer as well as a composer. He produced an enormous number of lyrics (collected in 1842 by George Hogarth), and amongst several substantial prose works two entertaining autobiographical books: *Observations on a Tour through almost the Whole of England and a Considerable Part of Scotland* (1801–2) and *The Professional Life of Mr Dibdin* (1803, enlarged edn. 1809).

[15] Produced CG, 21 Nov. 1775.

[16] The most successful of these was the first, *Selima and Azor* (5 Dec. 1776). *The Beggar's Opera* was revived under their management on 29 Jan. 1777; another very successful production at Drury Lane was William Jackson's *The Lord of the Manor* (27 Dec. 1780).

Ode (1776).[17] He had met Mozart in Florence in 1770 while studying with Pietro Nardini and when both composers were 14 years old; but whatever he may have picked up from that early friendship, he must subsequently have kept in touch with Mozart's deepening idiom, since his own later development seems in many ways to parallel it.

William Shield (1748–1829), Dibdin's principal successor, became house composer at Covent Garden, where nearly all his stage works were produced, in 1782. He had studied with Avison in Newcastle and was a violinist in Scarborough before coming to London as a string-player at the King's Theatre. He was a versatile musician with a serious scholarly interest in folk song, and not at all averse to the composition of popular ballads.[18] He composed about forty stage works together with five string quartets and other instrumental pieces.

Rosina, produced at Covent Garden on 31 December 1782, was a highly successful pasticcio and is the only one of Shield's operas to survive with its orchestral accompaniment.[19] While it would not do to overstate his claims as a composer, he was well acquainted with the current Italian operatic style and sometimes wrote difficult arias for those of his soloists (such as Mrs Billington) who were up to the challenge. The alternation of these slightly pretentious pieces with homely ballads was one of the attractions of the musical theatre in the late eighteenth century.

Much of the same can be said of James Hook (1746–1827), two years senior to Shield. Hook is best known for his contribution to the summer entertainments at Marylebone Gardens (1768–74) and Vauxhall Gardens (from 1774), for which he composed numerous organ concertos and some 2,000 songs. But he also wrote about thirty dialogue-operas and other works for the conventional stage, one of the most successful being *The Double Disguise* (Drury Lane, 8 March 1784) to a libretto by his wife. Something of his gifts can be seen from the published vocal score of this work: there is a genuine feeling, if in attenuated form, for the contribution that extended structures, imaginative orchestration, bold modulations, and vocal virtuosity can make to theatrical comedy in music. The elaborate soprano aria (in C major), 'Amidst a thousand sighing swains', is scored for oboe and bassoon ('Fagotti') obbligati, presumably with strings, and opens with a 31-bar ritornello in concertante style similar to that of J. C. Bach in the aria 'Infelice, in van m'affanno' from *La Clemenza di Scipione* (see Ex. 2.1), while the later modulatory passage seems to look forward to Haydn (Ex. 2.2). The scoring of the 'Glee' that ends the first act (Ex. 2.3) reflects a

---

[17] MB 30, ed. G. B. Beechey (1970), who has provided a detailed biographical note.

[18] He has been credited with the composition of the tune used (though not originally) for 'Auld lang syne'. Something like it appears in the overture to *Rosina*, but even in that form it is unlikely to have originated with Shield.

[19] Brit. Lib., Add. 22815 is a set of orchestral parts. Mod edn. by J. Drummond (MB, 72).

Ex. 2.1

Con spirito

[Strings]

Oboe solo

p

[Vlc.]

Fagotti solo [*sic.*]

[Fagotti]

[Vlc.]

Ex. 2.1, continued

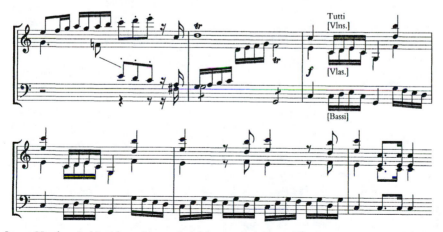

James Hook, aria 'Amidst a thousand sighing swains' (ritornello) from *The Double Disguise*: compressed from vocal score (London, *c.*1784), pp. 34–5

Ex. 2.2

James Hook, aria 'Amidst a thousand sighing swains' (middle section) from *The Double Disguise*: vocal score (London, *c.*1784), pp. 36–7

Ex. 2.3

James Hook, glee (ritornello) from *The Double Disguise*: compressed from vocal score (London, *c*.1784), p. 20

command of the Viennese orchestral palette that is amply confirmed by indications elsewhere in the score, and for that matter in much of Hook's other work.[20]

Stephen Storace (1762–96), though his father was an Italian immigrant, was born in London, and of an English mother. He was sent to Naples for

[20] It is always difficult to assess the exact pedigree where stylistic influence is concerned. J. C. Bach's aria may have influenced Mozart when writing 'Martern aller Arten' in *Die Entführung aus dem Serail* (produced 16 July 1782), and Hook's aria is in the key of this latter; but could he have been directly acquainted with it? Haydn's instrumental music (together with a few vocal works such as the 'Stabat mater') was published in considerable quantities in London from *c*.1780 on; very little of Mozart's appeared there before the 1790s, for the most part in *Storace's Collection of Original Harpsichord Music* (1787–9: this includes violin sonatas and piano trios).

his musical training, while his sister Nancy became the prima donna of the Viennese court theatre, where she created the role of Susanna in Mozart's *Figaro*. Stephen, as we have seen, wrote two comic operas for Vienna before he and Nancy, together with Michael Kelly, an Irish tenor who had sung Basilio and Curzio in *Figaro*, returned to England in the spring of 1787.[21] The King's Theatre proved unwilling to put on Storace's Viennese operas (let alone *Figaro*), but he quickly settled down to writing new works both for that theatre and for Drury Lane. *La cameriera astuta* (King's Theatre, 4 March 1788) was criticized for noisy orchestration, but Storace scored some notable successes after he and Nancy had transferred to Drury Lane. Almost all his later operas included spoken dialogue, but this did not preclude a sophisticated approach to musical form, particularly when it came to organizing effective finales. Unfortunately most of them survive only in vocal score, if at all.

Of Storace's full-length operas to English texts the most important are *The Haunted Tower* (Drury Lane, 24 November 1789) and *The Pirates* (King's Theatre, 21 November 1792).[22] *The Siege of Belgrade* and *Lodoiska* drew extensively on music by others, while *Dido, Queen of Carthage* (King's Theatre, 23 May 1792), which had no dialogue, was a failure. Its music was not published and is now lost. Storace completed two more full-length operas, *The Cherokee* and *The Iron Chest*, and was at work on a third, *Mahmoud*, when he died: it was completed from his other scores by his sister and Michael Kelly and is also lost.

In addition to these eight operas there were another eight short afterpiece operas (some of them pasticcios); Storace also directed the 1793 and 1794 Italian opera seasons at The King's Theatre with Michael Kelly, when he introduced Paisiello's *Il barbiere di Seviglia* and his own ballet *Venus and Adonis* (26 February 1793). It is hardly surprising that overwork brought its toll. Storace is now best known for his afterpiece *No Song, no Supper* (Drury Lane, 16 April 1790), the only one to survive orchestrally, possibly because a new score was made when it was transferred to The Little Theatre in 1793–4. The slender but well-crafted and amusing libretto by Prince Hoare is matched by an equally well-written score in which the sentimentality as well as the humour of the situations is pointed up.[23] As usual in

---

[21] Michael Kelly's *Reminiscences* (1826) are a valuable source of information on the musical life of Vienna in the 1780s, as well as on the activities of the King's Theatre and Drury Lane in the late 18th and early 19th cc. Kelly was stage manager of the King's Theatre from 1793, and wrote or compiled numerous works for the London theatre (*NGD* lists over sixty). For Storace see now J. Girdham, *English Opera in Late Eighteenth-Century London: Stephen Storace at Drury Lane* (Oxford, 1997).

[22] The Drury Lane company used the King's Theatre from Sept. 1791 to Mar. 1794, and also the Haymarket from Jan. 1793, when the King's was in use for Italian opera.

[23] MB 16, ed. R. Fiske. Prince Hoare was the son of a Bath painter. The scene in which a peasant couple quarrel about who should shut the door is probably derived from a poem in Herder's *Scottish Songs* (1769).

works of this type, some numbers are borrowed, and Storace also reworked some of his own earlier music; but whatever its limitations this is still a performable operetta in the best manner of the native theatre of its day.

Thomas Attwood (1765–1838) wrote, or contributed to, over thirty stage works, mostly in the last decade of the eighteenth century. A Chapel Royal chorister under Nares, he studied first at Naples and then in Vienna with Mozart (1783–5); an exceptionally full record of his lessons with Mozart has survived, but it speaks more for Mozart's patience and his capacity for turning dross into gold than for any great talent on the part of his pupil. His best work was not for the theatre; he contributed far more to the early nineteenth-century revival of church music and by no means negligibly to early Romantic song in England.[24]

It was Henry Rowley Bishop (1786–1855) who dominated the London musical stage in the first half of the nineteenth century: the works which he is known to have written or adapted by 1840 (after which he became respectable) amount to about 150, and although few of them can claim to be artistic wholes from his own pen, they contain a surprising quantity of genuinely worthwhile music. The main part of his career, from his appointment as musical director at Covent Garden in 1810, will be considered in the next chapter. Even by then he had enjoyed a major success at Drury Lane with *The Circassian Bride* (23 February 1809); the theatre was burnt down on the following day and the performing material destroyed, though the composer subsequently reconstructed the score. *The Maniac* (with a libretto by Samuel Arnold's son, S. J. Arnold) was given by the Drury Lane company at the Lyceum Theatre (13 March 1810) and had twenty-six performances; its success led to his position at Covent Garden, which he held until 1824.[25]

Another precocious theatrical talent of the early nineteenth century was that of Charles Edward Horn (1786–1849), son of the organist Karl Friedrich Horn (1762–1830), who had settled in England in 1782. His later career will be recounted in the next chapter, but like Bishop he achieved theatrical success in early life, notably with *The Devil's Bridge* (Lyceum Theatre, 6 May 1812).[26]

While London cannot be compared with such cities as Vienna, Paris, Prague, Milan, or Naples as a centre of operatic innovation at this period,

---

[24] See below, pp. 231, 238. *The Castle of Sorrento* (LT, 13 July 1799) has a truly dreadful overture (a trivial march followed by a tedious and prolonged trumpet solo), a duet by Paisiello, an 'Irish tune', and half a dozen numbers by Attwood himself.

[25] These details are from *NGD* (Temperley); there is an excerpt from *The Maniac* in B. Carr, 'Theatre Music: 1800–1834', *BHMB*, v. 288–306, on pp. 297–300. This is part of a glee (from the finale to Act I), illustrating a more developed and elaborate type than that represented by Ex. 2.3 above.

[26] This was a collaboration with John Braham, the famous English tenor (1774–1856) and M. P. Corri (c.1784–1849), again to a libretto by S. J. Arnold. There is a published vocal score, and manuscript material in the Royal College of Music.

one's estimate of its achievements depends a good deal on the point of view. Granted that the indigenous forms never blossomed into a full flowering of compelling musical dramaturgy, the musico-theatrical life of the capital enjoyed a vigorous development at many levels. But this was a period of transition, in which a many-layered culture, ranging from aristocratic opera in Italian at the top to pantomime and burlesque at the bottom, gave way to one in which a variety of imported attractions competed with an almost equal range of home-produced entertainment. Amongst the former in the early nineteenth century were most of Mozart's major operas, always in Italian, at the King's Theatre. There was still an element of élitism, but for the first time since the days of Handel the house proved willing and able to put on operas of universal musical and dramatic appeal. London began to play its part, as it was already doing in its concert life and publishing ventures, in the formation of the internationally recognized 'canon' of Viennese Classical and European Romantic musical works.[27] The rift between this canon and the products of homegrown enterprise grew steadily deeper, but the efforts to close it in the field of opera made for a lively battle of conflicting interests for the remainder of the century.

The Oratorio and Kindred Forms

Not even the most persuasive advocates have been able to make a convincing case in favour of English oratorio in the half century after the death of Handel. Even in Handel's lifetime, audiences had spurned some of his finest dramatic achievements in favour of those which were either not dramatic at all (*Messiah*) or were content with a merely conventional response to dramatic potential (*Judas Maccabaeus, Joshua*). Although oratorios were usually performed in theatres and were originally supposed to be a form of dramatic entertainment appropriate for Wednesdays and Fridays in Lent, audiences had tended to think of them more as sacred concerts, as occasions for edification rather than entertainment. A dramatic form of libretto was merely one possibility among others, and at its lowest an 'oratorio' was indeed nothing more than a string of loosely connected pieces of diverse origin. If Handel himself had been obliged to dilute his concept to attract audiences, it could hardly be expected that a more stringent definition would apply after his death.

In the circumstances it is perhaps surprising that a quasi-Handelian tradition was maintained at all. But something was needed by the managements of Covent Garden and Drury Lane to occupy their theatres during

---

[27] Weber, *The Rise of Musical Classics*, traces the concept of 'canon' to the cult of 'ancient music' in the 18th c. (cf. pp. 88–9 above). It seems to me to be much more due to the sort of developments just mentioned, together with the advent of modern musical criticism at much the same time, both in England and abroad.

Wednesdays and Fridays in Lent, for even ordinary stage plays, of which they had a virtual monopoly in London, could not be performed on those days. J. C. Smith had been responsible for Handel's oratorio seasons at Covent Garden from 1753; now he and Stanley took over and attempted to supply new works of their own. Smith's *Paradise Lost* and Stanley's *Zimri* were performed in Lent 1760 but are hamstrung by feeble librettos and, in the case of *Zimri*, by a choice of subject hardly capable of arousing religious or for that matter patriotic fervour.[28] In 1770 they moved to Drury Lane, where Arne and others had been giving Lenten oratorios and concerts for some time. Arne's *Judith* (Drury Lane, 27 February 1761) is much the most considerable oratorio of this period and would merit an occasional revival.[29] The oratorio seasons at Drury Lane were maintained by Smith and Stanley until 1774, then by Stanley and the elder Linley until 1786, and then by Arnold and Linley until 1791.[30]

There had been occasional series at the Haymarket since the early 1760s, organized at first by Charles Barbandt, whose *David and Jonathan* was given there on 28 January 1761. There were also oratorios given at the King's Theatre, both English and Italian, usually on Thursdays in Lent, and at the Lock Hospital, where such works as John Worgan's *Manasseh* and Felice Giardini's *Ruth* were heard.[31] But many oratorios consisted of pasticcio arrangements, often of music by Handel alone, and wholly original works became the exception rather than the rule. Arnold wrote both pasticcios and original works, but in most cases the music was unpublished and is now lost. Amongst the more noteworthy pieces of the 1770s were Arnold's *The Prodigal Son* (Haymarket, 5 March 1773) and Stanley's *The Fall of Egypt* (Drury Lane, 23 March 1774). In that year, too, Samuel Wesley, then aged 8, completed an oratorio, *Ruth*, which he followed up six years later with *The Death of Abel* (1779).[32]

[28] Zimri reigned in Israel for eight days after assassinating his predecessor. The libretto is a tale of guilty love.

[29] This work is discussed extensively by H. Smither, *The Oratorio in the Classical Era* (Oxford, 1987), 257–90, and in *BHMB*, iv. 215–18.

[30] There is a useful list of London oratorio seasons from 1750 to 1800 in S. W. McVeigh, *Concert Life in London from Mozart to Haydn* (Cambridge, 1993), 238–41. It should be borne in mind that secular music continued to be heard on 'oratorio' evenings at the playhouses—both in the form of complete works (invariably the popular masterpieces of Handel) and of selections (again largely but not entirely drawn from music by Handel). Concertos, moreover, continued to be played during intervals.

[31] *Ruth* was given in most years from 1763 until 1780 at the (Methodist) Lock Hospital chapel: the music in 1763 was partly by Avison (parts 1 and 3) and again in 1765 (part 1 only); from 1768 the music was wholly by Giardini. The music is lost. The oratorio in 1764 was Arne's *Judith*; in 1766 and 1767 it was Worgan's *Manasseh*. For an account of the Hospital's charitable concerts from 1748 to 1780, see S. W. McVeigh, 'Music and Lock Hospital in the 18th Century', *MT* 129 (1988), 235–40 (see also ibid. 385): see also N. Temperley, 'The Lock Hospital Chapel and its Music', *JRMA* 118 (1993), 44–72.

[32] London, Brit. Lib., Add. 34997 (*Ruth*); Add. 34999 (*The Death of Abel*). The latter was presumably performed at one of the subscription concerts given regularly from 1779 to 1785 at the Marylebone house of Charles Wesley sen., father of Charles and Samuel.

The theatrical associations of oratorio were lost sight of when the form was transferred to the provinces. Handel's short summer season in 1733 at Oxford set the pattern, while his production of *Messiah* in Dublin was followed in London, after a series of not very successful performances in the theatres, by annual performances at the Foundling Hospital from 1750 to 1775. It was perhaps the growing popularity of *Messiah*, a wholly non-dramatic conception, that contributed most to the weakening of the form as a dramatic entertainment. In London not only the charitable hospitals (Lock, Foundling, and Middlesex) but also Westminster Abbey came to be used for oratorio performances, through the Handel Commemoration of 1784 and subsequent years (1785, 1786, and 1791). This is often said to mark the beginning of the tradition of performing Handel with inappropriately large forces; but it must be emphasized that though the forces were indeed large on those occasions, no actual reorchestration was involved at this stage.[33]

Messiah, with a few other popular oratorios and a large diet of selections from these and other works, was also the mainstay of the provincial festivals: those of the Three Choirs at Hereford, Worcester, and Gloucester in turn, Salisbury, Winchester, Norwich, Bristol, Birmingham, and Derby, to name no others. Lenten seasons of oratorio were organized at Bath by the elder Linley (from the mid-1750s until *c*.1775), and they were also an occasional feature of life at Oxford and Cambridge. At Oxford the tradition established by William Hayes was continued by his son Philip, who succeeded him as Professor and also composed oratorios.[34] It was at Trinity Hall, Cambridge, that the 14-year-old Crotch had part of his oratorio *The Captivity of Judah* performed in 1789.

William Crotch (1775–1847) was perhaps the most precociously gifted musician of a generation copiously endowed with infant prodigies; unlike some of the others he not only survived into relatively old age but retained his inventiveness and (unlike Samuel Wesley) his enjoyment of life. Although it is as a musician that he displayed his astonishing gifts as a young child, he became a painter of distinction and interested himself in

---

[33] The primary source for the 1784 commemoration (the year having been mistaken for the centenary of Handel's birth) is Burney's *Account* (London, 1785). There were 251 players (including the organist and conductor, Joah Bates) and 274 singers (Burney, 17–21). The soprano line was supplemented by women, as had been the case at Covent Garden since 1773, and earlier in the provinces (McVeigh, *Concert Life*, 206). Not all the instruments (e.g. horns, trombones) will have played in all the works performed, and of course the majority will have participated only in the choruses.

[34] Heighes, *The Lives and Works of William and Philip Hayes*. A. Boden, *Gloucester, Hereford, Worcester* (Stroud, 1992); T. Fawcett, *Music in Eighteenth-Century Norwich and Norfolk* (Norwich, 1979); S. Wollenberg, 'Music in 18th-Century Oxford', *PRMA* 108 (1981–2), 69–99; J. Burchell, *Polite or Commercial Concerts? Concert Management and Orchestral Repertoire in Edinburgh, Bath, Oxford, Manchester, and Newcastle, 1730–1799* (New York and London, 1996); Weber, *The Rise of Musical Classics*, esp. 103–42; B. W. Pritchard, 'The Music Festival and the Choral Society in England in the 18th and 19th Centuries: A Social History', Ph.D. thesis (University of Birmingham, 1968); and his articles, with D. J. Reid, in *RMARC* 5 (1965), 6 (1966), 7 (1967), and 8 (1970).

the natural sciences—not to speak of his pioneering studies of musical history and aesthetics. To these last we shall return; but his successful combination of composition and musicology in one career was unusual in his day and has remained so since.

Although Crotch was by early training and instinct a somewhat conservative musician—as is exemplified by his recommendation of the archaic 'true sublime' idiom as the only suitable one for church music—he nevertheless absorbed a good deal of the constantly developing late Classical and early Romantic style into his musical thought. He wrote several smaller works for voices and orchestra after the oratorio just mentioned, amongst them a setting of *Part of* Messiah, *a Sacred Eclogue by Pope* (1790), and his doctoral exercise for Oxford, a setting of Warton's *Ode to Fancy* (1799).[35] These are conventional in many respects, the former through immaturity, the latter no doubt because of the occasion of its composition. The *Ode* is however quite fully scored, with a clarinet obbligato in one number, and is noteworthy for its indication of speeds by means of the length of a pendulum. This is an entirely scientific procedure, explained by Crotch himself in an article published in 1800, and it can be adopted today by attaching a weight to the end of a tape measure (to which the equivalents in terms of half-cycles per minute—the familiar metronome marks—are easily added if desired).[36] The actual speeds indicated in this way are not without interest, as we shall see, and are probably a good deal more trustworthy than those worked out by the deaf Beethoven with the aid of a clockwork metronome a little later on.

Though he later wrote several other cantatas and odes, Crotch's large-scale masterpiece is the oratorio *Palestine*, a fine work despite some moments of tedium and the hindrance of a stilted libretto.[37] This is an entirely non-dramatic evocation of Israelite history in a Christian context: the first part tells of the desolation of Jerusalem following the captivity and the eventual rebuilding of the Temple, while the second part tells of the coming of the Messiah, his reception by the gentiles ('Lo, star-led chiefs') and (very

---

[35] *Part of* Messiah is in London, Brit. Lib., Add. 30392, fos. 5^v–17^v: a photocopy of a handwritten edition by R. G. Boulton (1988) is in Oxford, Bod. Lib., Mus. 51 c.165. The original MS of the *Ode to Fancy* is in Bod. Lib., Mus. Sch. Ex. b.4, dated 28 Oct. 1799; it was published in the following year. See J. Rennert, *William Crotch* (London, 1975) for an authoritative account.

[36] A supplementary footnote in the MS of the *Ode to Fancy*, found also in the printed score, refers us to the *Monthly Magazine* for Jan. 1800. The laws of pendulum motion and the logarithmic ratio of length to speed had been discovered by Galileo, but the information was made very little use of by musicians as a means of indicating tempo, and hardly at all (if at all) by composers before the end of the 18th c. Thomas Wright published a piano concerto c.1795 with indications related to the width of a specified number of keys (*BHMB*, iv. 258, 453–4). J. Clarke-Whitfeld also adopted Crotch's system in some of his publications.

[37] The work was first performed in London on 21 Apr. 1812 and frequently repeated in London and the provinces, always with Crotch as conductor and supplier of the MS parts (*NGD*, 'Crotch'). The libretto is a prize poem by Reginald Heber.

abruptly) his passion, death, resurrection, and ascension. The music is by no means lacking in vivid characterization, however. The overture is a vigorous introduction and fugue, while the best of the vocal music has some of the imaginative qualities we associate with Haydn—somewhat unexpectedly in the light of Crotch's earlier very lukewarm appreciation of *The Creation*.[38] The orchestration represents a major advance for an English composer of this period: the work is scored for double woodwind (except that there is only one flute part), two horns, two trumpets, three trombones, kettledrums, cymbal, and strings, with a solo harp in two numbers. While the scoring is at times merely conventional, it is at its best highly evocative, as may be seen from the opening of the chorus 'Let Sinai tell' (Part I, no. 8), where the contemporary vocal score (by Crotch himself) does scant justice to the colouring (Ex. 2.4). The aria and semichorus 'In frantic converse' (Part I, no. 17) is similarly mysterious, in harmony as well as in orchestration (Ex. 2.5); here the tempo indication offers a salutary warning against too slow a speed in a Larghetto movement of this type. Finally one may draw attention to the exquisite colouring of the solo sextet 'Lo cherub bands', in E major (Part II, no. 20), perhaps the most Haydnesque section of the work (Ex. 2.6).

Crotch's *Palestine* is a splendid achievement by a relatively young composer at the height of his inventive powers. Even the sub-Handelian movements, like the treble air 'Triumphant race' (Part I, no. 12) with its jaunty ritornello (Ex. 2.7), are of considerable merit. Yet despite the continued popularity of certain numbers, the work failed to join the repertory of established classics. Perhaps that is because despite its inventiveness it was an attempt to revive an outmoded tradition rather than to fashion a new one. One could say as much of *The Creation*;[39] but of course Haydn outshines Crotch at every point. This mattered not only to contemporary audiences: just as important is the fact that when amateur choralism became well established towards the middle of the century it was only those older works with a continuous performing tradition and an unassailable critical

[38] The first English performance of *The Creation* took place at Covent Garden on 28 Mar. 1800 (N. Temperley, *Haydn: The Creation* (Cambridge, 1991), 39). Crotch's lecture on *The Creation*, given first in Oxford in Nov. 1800 and later in London, has been recovered and edited by Howard Irving: see his article 'William Crotch on "The Creation"', *ML* 75 (1994), 548–60. The exchange of letters between Burney and Crotch following the delivery of a version of the lecture to the Royal Institution in Jan. 1805 (which Burney did not attend) was first printed in the edition of Burney's *History* by F. Mercer (London, 1935).

Exx. 2.4 and 2.7 are taken from the full-score copy in Bod. Lib., Ten. 1207, with additional indications from the printed vocal score in round brackets. Exx. 2.5 and 2.6 are taken from the printed vocal score, but adapted to represent the instrumentation more fully. There are autograph full scores in the Brit. Lib., Add. 30390 (draft), 30391 (fair copy), and an autograph vocal score in Bod. Lib., Mus. c. 15.

[39] *The Creation* has a German libretto adapted by Gottfried van Swieten from an English text (largely retained in the score as first published) that seems originally to have been prepared for Handel (Temperley, *Haydn*, 19–24). There is no doubt that Haydn considered his work to be in the Handelian oratorio tradition as he understood it.

Ex. 2.4

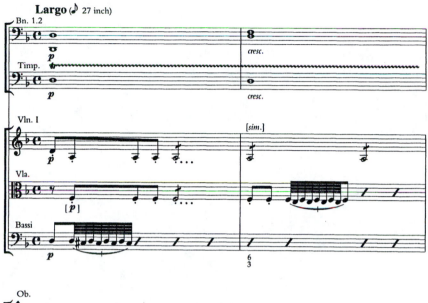

continued

Ex. 2.4, continued

Ex. 2.4, continued

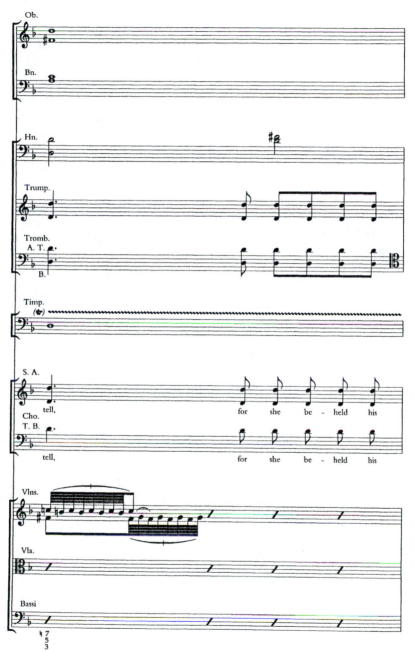

continued

Ex. 2.4, continued

Ex. 2.4, continued

continued

Ex. 2.4, continued

William Crotch, chorus 'Let Sion tell' from *Palestine*: Oxford, Bod. Lib., Tenbury 1207, pp. 85–8

Ex. 2.5

William Crotch, aria 'In frantic converse' (ritornello) from *Palestine*: adapted from vocal score (London, *c.*1812), p. 8; cf. Oxford, Bod. Lib., Tenbury 1207, p. 110

reception that had a chance of being taken up. Choral societies performed plenty of up-to-date rubbish, but in their selection of the older repertory there was little besides *The Creation* that could be put alongside the great warhorses of Handel. A marked preference in such quarters for sacred subjects, moreover, eliminated even *The Seasons* from widespread apprecia-tion.[40]

The oratorio was not the only moribund form at this period.[41] The great series of court odes came to an end in 1810; but they had in any case for a

[40] *The Seasons* is of course a less fine work, while the English version of its libretto (by van Swieten) owes little to Thomson's original poem and is of poor quality (Smither, *The Oratorio*, iii. 512).

[41] Crotch's second version of *The Captivity of Judah*, though composed in 1812–15, was not performed until 1834: cf. Ch. 3, p. 213.

Ex. 2.6

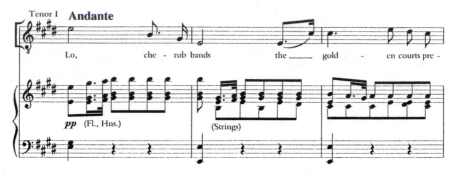

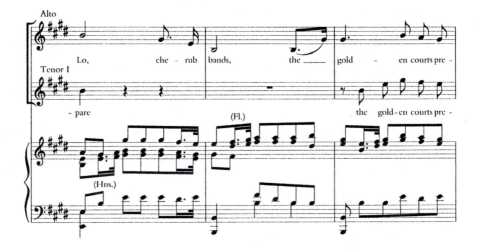

Ex. 2.6, continued

William Crotch, sextet 'Lo cherub bands' from *Palestine*: adapted from vocal score (London, *c.*1812), p. 154; cf. Oxford, Bod. Lib., Tenbury 1207, pp. 265–6

long time consisted of nothing more than adaptations by Sir William Parsons of music by Handel. Fiske has noted an ode by Shield to words by Southey, dated 1818; and Crotch himself wrote an ode for the accession of George IV in May 1820. Odes were written, and continued for some time after 1815 to be written, for academic occasions such as the installation of chancellors at Oxford and Cambridge; it was also a popular form of 'exercise' for degrees in Music then and later. The annual celebrations in honour of St Cecilia had long since ceased to take place, but the existing poetic 'odes' for this and similar functions were reset from time to time. Secular occasions such as the celebrations in honour of Shakespeare or his birthday called for odes, now as previously; in this period the younger Linley's *Ode on the Spirits of Shakespeare*, performed at Drury Lane in 1776, is a striking manifestation of his precocious talent and his major surviving achievement.[42]

[42] MB 30 (1970), ed. G. Beechey.

Ex. 2.7

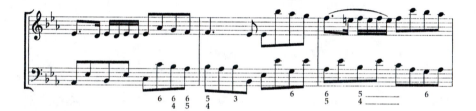

William Crotch, aria 'Triumphant race' (ritornello): Oxford, Bod. Lib., Tenbury 1207, p. 97

At a more modest level are the orchestrally accompanied cantatas and songs which were a mainstay of the repertory of the London gardens and provincial watering places. Here we are on the borderlines of vocal chamber music, since most such works are for a solo voice and since the accompaniment was usually very light; in any case the concert repertory of the period did not make a clear distinction between orchestral (or orchestrally accompanied) music and chamber music.[43] Nevertheless the performing context can be brought to bear on the question even though the scores themselves may be unhelpful. As Goodall points out, 'in the majority of post-1760 cantatas the intimate chamber quality is abandoned in favour of a more public style, conceived quite clearly with al fresco performance in mind'.[44] On the other hand, many of the simpler songs and ballads must have been performed with an accompaniment that could under no circumstances be called 'orchestral'. In a sense the distinction is a rather pointless one—it would not be an issue in the context of opera or oratorio, for example—and it will be sufficient here to say a few words about the cantata as such.

Thomas Arne continued to write cantatas for the pleasure gardens until his death in 1778, and these were published mostly in his miscellaneous collections of vocal music. James Hook began publishing such collections as early as 1767, while he was still employed at Marylebone, and continued to do so on an annual basis until around 1807; he also published a number of cantatas separately. Most of this enormous amount of music has never been examined in detail and it is impossible to generalize about its quality. It is generally assumed that because of its sheer quantity it must mostly be trivial; yet Hook was more than capable of rising above the level of mere professional competence, and it would be rash to consign it all to oblivion on the grounds that it must have been turned out very quickly.

The cantata was, however, virtually extinct by about 1790, notwithstanding a renewed vogue for burlesque forms in the tradition established by Henry Carey.[45] A posthumous collection in two volumes of the vocal music of the two Linleys came out around 1800; it includes six cantatas in score, though their allocation as between father and son is uncertain.[46] They are in any case amongst the best of their kind in this period and, to the extent that they are the work of the son, a further testimony to the unfulfilled promise of this remarkable young man.

Orchestral Music

Our discussion of oratorio and kindred repertory has led us away from the theatre to other venues—to the concert, in fact, a concept of great elasticity. An unstaged performance in a theatre is itself a concert, though in the eighteenth century even a non-dramatic oratorio in such surroundings was

[43] For a discussion of this repertory see Goodall, *Eighteenth-Century English Secular Cantatas*, 232–45.
[44] Ibid. 211–12.
[45] By such composers as James Oswald, J. H. Moze, and Samuel Arnold. There were also numerous cantatas by provincial composers such as Richard Langdon of Exeter (collections published c.1754 and 1769), Christopher Dixon of York (*Two English Cantatas and Four Songs*, c.1760), John Pixell of Birmingham (*Odes, Cantatas, Songs, etc.*, 1775), and Robert Barber of Newcastle (*Four Songs Two Cantatas...*, c.1775). Goodall, 241–3.
[46] G. Beechey, 'Thomas Linley, 1756–78, and his Vocal Music', *MT* 119 (1978), 669–71, has attributed all six to the younger Linley, two of them positively.

more a Lenten substitute for an opera or a play than a displacement of something better heard in a concert-room. But any public performance in a venue other than a theatre would certainly count as a concert, and the potential repertory ranged from elaborate works for voices and instruments to solo items. Most concerts were mixed in character: it was rare for an evening to consist solely of orchestral music, though this became at this period the *raison d'être* of several series of concerts. Almost all musical forms, therefore, could be heard in the context of a public concert: the distinction between a 'concert' and a 'recital' was yet to emerge.

It will be useful to note here the various types of venue available to promoters in the later eighteenth and early nineteenth century. Taverns, pleasure gardens, assembly rooms, churches, and chapels (these last mostly for charitable concerts) were all inherited from the previous period; so to a certain extent was the dedicated concert-room ('hall' is a later usage), but several important such rooms came into being (through new building or the adaptation of an existing building) during the period under discussion. The most important of these in London was the Hanover Square Rooms, built in 1774 to house the concerts of J. C. Bach and C. F. Abel from 1775 onwards, and subsequently the principal venue of the Professional Concert and of J. P. Salomon's famous series from 1786. Its great rival was the Pantheon in Oxford Street, built in 1772 and the home of a concert series run by its own management from 1774 until it was adapted as a theatre in 1789.[47]

The principal focus of concert promotion was the subscription series, though the clientele was often artificially limited by high prices and by aristocratic control of the subscription lists. The concerts given by Mrs Cornelys in the 1760s at New Carlisle House in Soho Square, mostly under the superintendence of Bach and Abel, were more like private soirées, with refreshments, cards, and dancing. Bach and Abel operated independently at another venue, Almack's Rooms in King Street, from early in 1768 to 1774, after which they moved to Hanover Square Rooms.[48] The heyday of the subscription series was the 1780s and early 1790s, when the Pantheon (until 1789), the Professional Concert, and Salomon (whose great draw was the presence of Haydn in 1791–2 and 1794–5) were all in rivalry. After that there was a decline—though not to the extent once believed—until the establishment of the Royal Philharmonic Society in 1813.[49]

But there were many other types of concert promotion, in addition to 'oratorio' concerts and the summer entertainments of the pleasure gardens

[47] See above, p. 95. It was burnt in 1792, and reopened in 1795.
[48] McVeigh, *Concert Life*, 14–15. Almack's Rooms were later known as Willis's Rooms.
[49] See ibid. 234–7 for lists of series in each year from 1750 to 1800. In addition to those mentioned above were Harrison and Knyvett's 'Vocal Concert' and the 'Opera Concert' in the King's Theatre Room, a large room adjacent to the theatre itself.

already mentioned. Amongst the most important was the Concert of Ancient Music, founded in 1776 by the Earl of Sandwich; to begin with, at least, this shared some of the features of the now moribund Academy of Ancient Music.[50] One of these was the amateur control of repertory and personnel, and a degree of amateur participation, though in due course the performances became fully professional. 'Ancient' in this context, as already noted, meant music more than twenty years old, though there was (again at first) a presumption in favour of 'learned' contrapuntal music in any medium.[51]

The combination of amateur and professional forces, with amateur control, was also characteristic of many provincial series, such as those of Oxford and (to glance briefly outside England) Edinburgh.[52] Small-scale concerts in London and elsewhere were likewise not necessarily aristocratic in tone: those of the Wesley family, designed to show off the talents of the young Charles and Samuel, made a respectable profit but were not conditioned by a desire for social exclusivity;[53] and the same must have been true of many a gathering in the provinces.

Turning to the repertory itself, we shall be disappointed if we are looking for a flourishing tradition of orchestral music by English-born composers. Developments in taste were led by foreigners, whether they came to reside more or less permanently, like J. C. Bach, Abel, and later Clementi, or visited for a longer or shorter period, like Haydn, Viotti, and Dussek, or whether their music was merely imported. The idiom made fashionable by J. C. Bach was an Italianate proto-Classicism of the kind often referred to as *galant*, a derivative of opera both by virtue of the origin of the concert symphony in the three-movement operatic overture or *sinfonia* and because of the relation between the concerto and the operatic aria and ensemble. Abel's style was essentially similar, though he lacked a theatrical background and apparently resented the 'Italian' label.[54] Any influence there may have been from early Viennese or Parisian symphonism tended to merge with this, but a more sharply distinctive idiom, though itself based on Italian models, was that associated with the electoral court orchestra at Mannheim.[55] The best-known British exponent of this style is the Scotsman Thomas Alexander Erskine, sixth Earl of Kelly, but it also had its English imitators.

J. C. Bach also championed the use of the piano for both solo and concertante work, and while he himself achieved no great renown as a

---

[50] See Ch. 1: the Academy did, however, limp on until 1797 (cf. McVeigh, 34).

[51] The Concert of Ancient Music continued until 1848.

[52] J. Burchell, *Polite or Commercial Concerts?*, passim.

[53] McVeigh, 48–9.

[54] Ibid. 122 and 262 n. 10, citing *Boswell in Holland*, ed. A. F. Pottle (London, 1952), 52. McVeigh describes this idiom as a 'lingua franca' of the early Classical style (ibid. 122).

[55] Cf. E. K. Wolf, 'Mannheim Style', in *NGD*, xi. 629–30.

virtuoso, he paved the way for what has been dubbed the 'London pianoforte school' of the period 1780–1840. This again was dominated by
composers of foreign birth: Clementi, J. B. Cramer, Dussek, and Clementi's
gifted Irish apprentice John Field. This development of keyboard virtuosity
was paralleled by the achievements of several violinists, beginning with the
Italian Felice Giardini (1716–96), who arrived in 1750 and remained until
1784.[56] Although Giardini was a versatile composer, his main contribution
was to enhance the standard of orchestral playing in London. Amongst a
large number of foreign violinists resident in London during the later
eighteenth century, G. B. Viotti stands out as a composer, mainly of
concertos in which virtuosity is always subordinate to the claims of melodic
interest and structural development.[57]

The earliest phase of English symphonic writing in this period is represented by Boyce and Arne, whose published symphonies and 'overtures' are
drawn largely from their vocal works.[58] Whatever their stylistic merits (and
both composers, but Arne in particular, were capable of moving away from
the restrictions of a Baroque-based idiom), they are invariably small in scale,
with finales often designed to lead into an opening vocal number rather than
to round off the work effectively. Arne's *Four New Overtures or Symphonies*,
published in 1767, are independent of any vocal work and are in that sense
more ambitious, with elements of the Mannheim fire in their 'repeated–
note' passages; but a purely symphonic idiom is constantly being kept at bay
by elements of pretty melodiousness, and the finales (except perhaps that of
no. 1) are tame affairs.

Many of the symphonic works by English composers that reached publication and/or concert performance were originally theatrical overtures.
English convention made no distinction between 'symphony' and 'overture' (except that works in the French overture style, now almost defunct,
were rarely if ever called symphonies); the largest concert works (such as
Haydn's symphonies) were frequently called overtures, and theatrical overtures, which still usually had three movements, were as often called symphony or *sinfonia*. Only in the early nineteenth century, when concert
works had grown enormously in size and significance, did the modern
distinction between a multi-movement symphony and a single-movement
overture, theatrical or otherwise, take root.

---

[56] He returned briefly in 1790. See S. McVeigh, 'Felice Giardini: A Violinist in Late Eighteenth-
Century London', *ML* 64 (1983), 162–72; and, more generally, id., *The Violinist in London's Concert Life
1750–1784* (New York and London, 1989).

[57] Other visiting foreign violinists included Wilhelm Cramer, G. M. Giornovichi (Jarnowick), and
Maddalena Sirmen. Sirmen (née Lombardini) appeared with great success in London in 1771 and 1772
(her concertos Op. 3 were published in London and Paris, c.1770), but later chose to appear as a singer, in
which capacity she was markedly less successful.

[58] For a useful list of published parts of theatre overtures, 1740–1800, see Fiske, *English Theatre Music*,
594–6. Interestingly, there is nothing by Arnold in the list.

Published collections (in parts) of overtures or symphonies often contained one or more works of theatrical origin; such pieces were also published separately or as part of a series such as Robert Bremner's *Periodical Overture* (begun in 1763 with a symphony in D by J. C. Bach). Much of the most admired music, however, remained in manuscript, by which a composer or entrepreneur hoped to preserve its value as a rarity: published music was not protected by a workable copyright law, and the few published full scores (mostly of operas and oratorios) could also be used to generate parts. Published music was intended primarily for semi-professional and private or provincial use, though some sets of printed parts must have been used at the major concert-series. Conversely, some music that remained in manuscript did so because its appeal was limited: such, perhaps, was the fate of William Herschel's twenty-four symphonies and those of Samuel Wesley.[59]

A Mannheim-inspired style was adopted in the symphonic music of such minor composers as John Collett (c.1735–75) and J. A. Fisher (1744–1806), and in George Rush's popular overture to *The Royal Shepherd*, while that of William Smethergell is somewhat more Italianate. All these works, like those of Bach and Abel, include a figured bass; the most usual scoring is for two oboes, two horns, and strings (the standard 'eight parts'), though additional woodwind, and even trumpets and drums, are occasionally found. 'Orchestra quartets', also with figured bass, were composed by George Rush (*Three Quartets*, c.1775) and F.-H. Barthélemon (one of his *Six Quartets*, c.1790). In this latter case the composer himself makes a clear distinction between the orchestral and the chamber quartet; there are also a few examples of the orchestrally conceived trio for two violins and bass on the lines of Johann Stamitz's Op. 1 no. 1.[60]

Many English works of the period display some originality, though this often manifests itself as a kind of quirkiness that is not compensated for by the underlying depth that characterizes Haydn's mature symphonism. The symphonies of Thomas Norris, a hard-drinking Oxford organist who also pursued a London singing career, are formally original but in a rather undeveloped way.[61] As with so much other published work, it is difficult to estimate the level of their reception, but it is likely to have been short-lived and restricted to minor gatherings in London or the provinces. The same is true of the published symphonies of such later enthusiasts as John Marsh and Thomas Haigh.[62] Even the playhouse overture declined in popularity as a concert item: according to McVeigh, 'only a few facile overtures of the 1780s by Hook and Arnold maintained a place at Vauxhall;

[59] Herschel's symphonies are in Brit. Lib., Add. 49624–32; three are in *The Symphony*, E III (nos. 1–3).

[60] See *BHMB*, iv. 329. Symphonies and 'overtures' by Collett, Fisher, Rush (including *The Royal Shepherd* and three orchestra-quartets), Smethergell, and Barthélemon (not the orchestra-quartet) are in *The Symphony*, E I.

[61] *BHMB*, iv. 223–4; publication was in London, c.1774.

[62] *The Symphony*, E I, nos. 19, 20.

no instrumental music by Shield, Storace or Attwood passed into the concert repertoire'.[63]

Four of Samuel Wesley's five symphonies were evidently written for the subscription series at his parents' home. As such they will have made little stir in the wider musical world, but the teenaged composer shows in them an enviable skill and imagination, all the more noteworthy for being exercised with such a small instrumental palette. The earliest (1781) is a 'sinfonia obligato' [sic] for solo organ, violin, cello, and strings; the other three are for two horns and strings—two, in D and E flat, dated 1784 and the third, in A, undated.[64] Fundamentally they are in the galant idiom of J. C. Bach and Abel, but there are touches of Haydn, too, particularly in the exquisite slow movement of the A major work, a miniature that deserves quotation (Ex. 2.8). It is a tragedy that such promise was not given the single-minded encouragement that Mozart, who drew from the same fountain, received from his father. But Charles senior, himself a clergyman, was doubtless also swayed by the opposition of his brother John, the evangelist and founder of Methodism, to a musical career for either of them. Wesley's other symphony, dated 1802, is for larger forces and may never have been performed.[65]

By 1800, in any case, London's concert life was less robust, with the Ancient Concert the principal agent of continuity. Very few concert symphonies by English composers were written between 1800 and 1810: the emphasis in this decade was on theatrical entertainment at all levels.[66] The founding of the Philharmonic Society in 1813 may have contributed to a revival: a couple of manuscript symphonies by the indefatigable James Hook survive from that year, and in 1814 Crotch completed a four-movement symphony in F, performed by the Society in 1815.[67] Another, begun in 1808, was apparently never completed orchestrally, though it was published as a piano duet.[68] Composing symphonies was now a much more laborious business: they were expected to be considerably longer and more fully scored than formerly. Even Clementi had stopped composing symphonies by 1800; but the Philharmonic Society performed one in 1815, and he resumed their composition on a larger scale after that.

[63] McVeigh, Concert Life, 126; but Burchell (Polite or Commercial Concerts, 223–4, 332) reports the performance of a 'Grand Overture' by Attwood at Oxford in 1799.

[64] The Sinfonia obligato is in The Symphony, E III, no. 8; those in D and A are ed. R. Platt (London, 1974 = MC 12, 13).

[65] The Symphony, E III, no. 9.

[66] Concert life was by no means extinguished during this period—see e.g. P. Young in BHMB, v. 358—but it rarely fostered new English orchestral music. Even so, the young Henry Bishop composed a 'Grand Sinfonia' (1805). On the Philharmonic Society, a venture of cardinal importance, see C. Erlich, First Philharmonic (Oxford, 1995).

[67] Hook in Cambridge, University Library, Add. 6639; Crotch ed. in facs. in The Symphony, E IV.

[68] Brit. Lib., Add. 30394 ('revised 1817'). Other symphonists in this transitional period include such minor composer as J. F. Burrowes.

Ex. 2.8

(1) MS: each time

continued

Ex. 2.8, continued

S. Wesley, Symphony in A, 2nd mvt.: London, Brit. Lib., Add. 35011, fos. 147ᵛ–148ʳ (the tempo indication and some slurs are taken from the parts, fos. 153ʳ–158ʳ)

In many ways the English concerto was a more viable form than the English symphony. Here too the beacon for change was lit by J. C. Bach and Abel, who between them published several sets of six keyboard concertos, mostly 'for the harpsichord or piano forte'. The accompaniment was usually just for two violins and cellos, making them suitable for chamber music in the home, and several English composers—Rush, Hook, and Smethergell, for example—followed this pattern in the 1770s. Sometimes the writing makes it clear that the piano was the instrument actually intended. More surprising is the survival of the organ as a concerto-instrument in the post-Baroque era. The English organ of the period was usually a small affair, even in the theatres, where it was customary to erect one on the stage on oratorio nights in Lent (though experience suggests that it must normally have been got ready for the season and simply moved out of sight when not needed). The pleasure gardens and some concert rooms had an organ, and it was not uncommon in the home—the Wesley family had two. Charles Wesley wrote fourteen organ concertos—not merely Handelian, as has been suggested, but with their own individuality of melody and orchestration.[69] Three of Philip Hayes's *Six Concertos* (1769) are for organ. John Stanley published a set of six, with the regulation two violins and cello accompaniment, in 1770 (Op. 10), in a mixture of conventional and more up-to-date style (no. 3 is borrowed entirely from Op. 2 no. 6, a string concerto published in 1740). Arne's six keyboard concertos may have been composed for the most part in the 1750s, but they seem to have been revised subsequently, and were published only in 1793, long after his death: they are agreeably light and *galant* in idiom.[70] James Hook wrote numerous concertos for the Vauxhall

[69] Cf. *BHMB*, iv. 235. It is also an exaggeration to say that Charles wrote nothing of interest after 1785 (p. 236), though it is true that his later work was highly conservative.

[70] Ed. R. Langley (London, 1981 = MC 81–6).

Gardens: about twenty have survived, but only seven with their 'orchestral' accompaniment. Samuel Wesley's early *Sinfonia obligato* (see above) is very largely an organ concerto, and he wrote another three in later life, with much fuller orchestration; and there are three striking examples by Crotch.[71]

Beside this very parochial phenomenon the true piano concerto was able to draw on a vigorous European tradition. After Bach and Abel, the main protagonists were such figures as Clementi, Cramer, Steibelt, and Dussek. Muzio Clementi (1752–1832) had been 'adopted' by a wealthy Englishman, Peter Beckford, in 1766 at the age of 14, and he spent most of his working life in England. But although he frequently appeared as a concerto soloist up to about 1790, only one of his concertos survives complete.[72] John Baptist Cramer (1771–1858) published piano concertos in London, as did Daniel Gottlieb Steibelt (1765–1823), who lived in London from 1796 to 1799, and Jan Ladislav Dussek (1760–1812), who was in London from 1789 to 1799, when his financial affairs dictated the prudence of withdrawal. In the later 1790s the young John Field (1782–1849) began to create a stir as a piano soloist, and in 1799 he played his own first piano concerto at a concert in the King's Theatre Room (the work was later published, like his six others, in St Petersburg and Leipzig). Of these composers only Clementi and Cramer could be regarded as 'English' in any real sense, but there were also some native-born practitioners, such as George Rush (three concertos, published separately in the 1770s), William Smethergell (six concertos, *c.*1775, and a further one in 1784), Thomas Haigh (six concertos, *c.*1785), and Joseph Mazzinghi (1800).[73]

Concertos for instruments other than the keyboard continued to be produced by English composers, though they were often overshadowed by the offerings of visiting foreign virtuosi. As we have seen (Ch. 1), conventional sets of concertos 'in seven parts' sometimes included solo concertos (e.g. for trumpet or oboe) or for unusual combinations of instruments. Concerti grossi for strings were rarely published after 1760, except for reprints of the most admired works of Corelli, Handel, and Geminiani.[74] Concertos for two or more different instruments had come to be designated *sinfonia concertante* on the Continent: this *galant* form was introduced to England by J. C. Bach and Abel, and it was cultivated mostly by visiting or temporarily resident foreigners such as Gyrowetz, F. H. Graf, Pleyel, and

---

[71] Langley has reconstructed Hook's Op. 20 no. 2 (MC 59); others forthcoming in MB. Wesley's later concertos are in Brit. Lib., Add. 35009; those of Crotch (one published in London, *c.*1805) are in Norwich, Norfolk Record Office, 11250, 11274).

[72] MS in Vienna, Gesellschaft der Musikfreunde; published as a piano sonata, Op. 33 no. 3.

[73] Mazzinghi (1765–1844) was an English composer of Corsican stock, a composer of many dramatic works and ballets. His concerto is a 'concertante' for piano, flute, and strings (see n. 75 below).

[74] Somewhat exceptionally, Capel Bond's set of six concertos, published in 1766, included four concerti grossi (for the other two see below). Charles Avison's *Twelve Concertos in Four Parts*, Op. 9, and *Six Concertos in Seven Parts*, Op. 10, all primarily for strings, were issued in 1766 and 1769 respectively. Charles Wesley published a concerto grosso, *c.*1782.

(not least) Haydn.[75] More parochial were such things as the trumpet and bassoon concertos by Capel Bond, the oboe concertos of J. C. Fischer (who settled in London in 1768 or thereabouts), and the solitary surviving clarinet concerto of John Mahon (1775). J. A. Fisher wrote and published violin concertos, as did F.-H. Barthélemon (1775), Thomas Shaw (c.1780) and James Brooks (c.1790).[76] Quite a number of violin concertos by Samuel Wesley are preserved in manuscript, but again the native genius was overshadowed by the more powerfully influential figures of Continental virtuosi such as G. B. Viotti, who was a familiar figure on the London concert platform in the 1790s.

Chamber Music

As with orchestral music, the *galant* and Classical types of chamber music only gradually overtook the Baroque in England. The trio sonata and the solo sonata with (keyboard) bass were amenable in any case to stylistic modification, and if publication figures are any guide their cultivation by native composers if anything increased during the last forty years of the century.[77] While some published trio sonatas are resolutely Baroque in idiom, others (such as those of F. E. Fisher's Op. 2, c.1760) are mixed, and yet others (like those of the Oxford composer James Lates's Op. 4, c.1768) more consistently *galant* or Mannheim-influenced and in three or even two movements. Most are for two violins and bass; some were devised so as to be played either as trio sonatas or as concerti grossi (John Cushin, John Alcock jun.). A few sets, or examples within sets, were for two flutes (James Hook published a set for flutes or violins in 1776), and one also encounters the medium of violin, cello, and bass (Lates, Op. 5, c.1775), a sort of half-way house between solo and trio sonata.[78]

As for the solo sonata with bass—potentially a vehicle for expression and virtuosity in the manner of Giardini, Nardini, or Pugnani, all of whom had sets of violin sonatas published in London in the 1760s and 1770s[79]—few English composers at this period met the challenge with distinction. James Lates (Op. 3, c.1765) and J. A. Fisher (*Six Solos*, c.1774) are two of the more ambitious, the former still in a largely Baroque idiom, the latter in a more up-to-date manner.[80] The flute solo with bass was in decline (there is a set

---

[75] The genre was originally a Parisian one, usually known simply as concertante (McVeigh, *Concert Life*, 106).

[76] For some comments on the works of Fisher, Shaw, and Brooks, see O. Edwards, 'English String Concertos Before 1800', *PRMA* 95 (1968–9), 1–13 at 10–11.   [77] *BHMB*, iv. 324, 328.

[78] Abel's Op. 9 is of this kind. The two-movement form common in works of this type consisted usually of an extended binary ('sonata') movement and a minuet.

[79] Giardini, Opp. [10] (1765), 16 (19 (1777); Nardini, Opp. [1] (c.1760), 5 (c.1769) Pugnani, Opp. 7 (1770 or later), [8] (n.d.) (London publications only cited here).

[80] For a discussion of the violin solo in England from c.1750 onwards see McVeigh, *The Violinist in London's Concert Life*, 213–43; to which should be added a reference to Abel's Op. 6 (1765).

by Hook, 1774, and little else thereafter), but there is more interest in the cello sonatas of Stephen Paxton (1735–87: Op. 1, 1772, and Op. 3, c. 1778), James Cervetto (c.1748–1837: three sets of solos and three sets of duets), Hook (Op. 24, 1782), and William Flackton, who included four viola sonatas along with two for cello (Op. 2, 1770, enlarged by two further cello sonatas in 1775). Most of Abel's sonatas for viola da gamba and bass remained unpublished.

The decline of the continuo sonata coincided with the rise of the accompanied keyboard sonata, the precursor of the duo sonata, piano trio, piano quartet, and piano quintet. While the development of the accompanied sonata was closely paralleled by that of the sonata for solo piano, it would be wrong to think of the latter as the predecessor of the accompanied sonata, at least as far as England is concerned. Stylistic advances occurred at least as early in the accompanied varieties, while the expression 'with accompaniments' by no means always indicates that these parts are inessential, particularly as regards the (first) violin. The earliest examples to be published in England seem to have been those of Giardini's Op. 3 (1751, for keyboard and violin), in which the keyboard sometimes acts as a continuo accompaniment to the violin, sometimes as the predominant partner, and sometimes as an equal partner.[81] These two-movement works were an important harbinger of the *galant* style in English chamber music: few contemporary compositions in other media, even the early violin solos of Giardini himself, were so advanced.

Not all the accompanied sonatas of the 1750s and 1760s are so consistently *galant* or so adventurous in their textural variety. Those of F.-X. Richter, much of whose music was published in London, include cello parts (two sets of six sonatas, 1759 and c.1763, and a further two sets with two violins and cello) but are more conservative in idiom. In the 1760s and 1770s numerous such publications by Abel and Bach appeared in all three instrumental forms, usually with the alternative of a flute for the (first) violin. While violin parts were often given essential melodic material, cello parts were much more subservient, usually following the bass line quite slavishly and often being entirely dispensable.[82] During these decades, moreover, the pianoforte came to be mentioned on title-pages (as it did in the unaccompanied sonata), either in first or in second place relative to the harpsichord. The proto-Classical orchestral style, with its sudden dynamic contrasts and occasional crescendos, was much more readily transferred to the piano

---

[81] McVeigh, *The Violinist*, 243. The title is in Italian: *Sei sonate di cembalo con violino o' flauto traverso* (ibid. 357). On the accompanied sonata see R. R. Kidd, 'The Sonata for Keyboard with Violin Accompaniment in England', Ph.D. diss. (Yale University, 1967); id., 'The Emergence of Chamber Music with Obligato Keyboard in England', *AcM* 44 (1972), 122–44; F. Moroni, 'Keyboard Ensembles in Britain: Piano Trios, Quartets, Quintets and their Antecedents', D.Phil. thesis (University of Oxford, 1996).

[82] *BHMB*, iv. 337, citing in addition Johann Schobert and Mattia Vento as composers whose music was well known in London.

than to the harpsichord and was increasingly adopted in the accompanied sonata.

The earliest examples of the genre by an English composer seem to be the works for two violins, cello, and keyboard by Avison (Op. 5, 1756, followed by Op. 7, 1760, and Op. 8, 1764);[83] these, however, are somewhat Baroque in idiom and were thought of by the composer rather as keyboard concertos without 'symphonies' (i.e. ritornelli). Much more advanced were the violin-accompanied sonatas by William Jackson 'of Exeter' (Op. 2, c.1760): here the textures are admirably varied. In the following decades numerous sets of sonatas for keyboard with violin or with violin and cello appeared, many of them simple works with optional string parts, others more elaborate and technically demanding. Amongst the more imaginative are some of those of James Hook for piano and violin (or flute) and those of Stephen Storace for piano, violin, and cello.[84] A great deal of the immense quantity of music published for these forces in the 1780s and 1790s is somewhat bland in character and sometimes barely competent, but the best of it merits revival. Still later the tragically short-lived George Frederick Pinto (1785–1806) produced four fine sonatas for violin and piano, and the accompanied forms were assiduously cultivated by Clementi and Cramer.

The vogue for works for keyboard with two violins and cello—whether of the type represented by those of Avison or of the rather different kind published by Richter or Giardini in his Op. 21, c.1778—came to an end by about 1790. Giardini's Op. 21 also included three works for violin, viola, cello, and harpsichord, all six being called quartettos, though this early use of what was to become the standard 'piano quartet' medium was not, apparently, taken up by English composers. Giardini also composed a set of 'quintetti', Op. 11 (1767, now lost) for harpsichord, two violins, cello, and 'bass', while a set for the later standard combination of keyboard and string quartet was published in London and Frankfurt by Tommaso Giordani in 1771. English examples of piano quintets of various kinds include those of William Jackson (Op. 10, 1773: the 'tenor' part is not extant), William Tindall (c.1785), and the two by Stephen Storace (1784), who also included a sextet (with additional flute) in the same publication.

---

[83] Note also those of James Nares (one work in his Op. 2, 1759), John Garth 'of Durham', a friend of Avison (Opp. 4–7 c.1772–82), Thomas Ebdon, also of Durham (*Six Sonata's*, c.1780), and Matthias Hawdon (d. Newcastle upon Tyne, 1787: *Six Conversation Sonatas*, Op. 2, c.1776).

[84] *NGD* lists twenty publications of accompanied works by Hook; of these his Opp. 16, 17 (both c.1775), and 30 (*Six Grand Lessons*, 1784), all for harpsichord or piano with flute or violin, are especially noteworthy. Storace's three *Sonatas* (or trios) for piano, violin, and cello were published in *Storace's Collection of Original Harpsichord Music* (1788–9) and in a reprint by Preston & Son (c.1790, with a set of variations added). Attwood may have been the first in England to use the word 'trio' of this combination: see his Op. 1 (? 1787), and a further work in *Storace's Collection* (1789); in his *Sonatas* Op. 2, by contrast, the stringed instruments are *ad libitum*.

The variety of instrumental textures available for use with harpsichord or piano—not to mention the guitar and harp—was considerable, though some possibilities, such as that of wind instruments with piano, remained largely unexplored in England. The same variety is evident in chamber music without keyboard. In fact, however, the distinction between these two genres is not as clear-cut as one might imagine. Works scored for one or two melodic instruments and a bass might seem inevitably to call for a keyboard accompaniment (with or without cello or viola da gamba), but title-pages often leave open the possibility of an unharmonized bass, one that could be justified where, for example, a violin (or viola da gamba) part has a good deal of multiple stopping, or where the bass part is itself melodious and demands to be treated as an equal partner.[85] In larger ensembles, such as the quintets of J. C. Bach, Op. 11 (1774, for flute, oboe, violin, viola, and 'bass'), the word may imply no more than a cello. Even the presence of figuring does not settle the matter: figuring was sometimes added to a 'bass' part when not intended by the composer (as in the case of some London editions of Haydn's quartets). Even when supplied by the composers themselves, figuring may often have been a purely conventional element designed to aid ensemble in amateur performances.[86]

The simplest type of ensemble music without keyboard is represented by the numerous sets of works—mostly short sonatas under whatever title—for a pair of identical instruments: two violins, flutes, cellos, or even horns. Many such works (not to mention numerous arrangements, especially for flutes) were written as teaching pieces or for the amateur market, though a few, such as those of J. A. Fisher (c.1773) and Shield's Op. 1 (1777), both for violins, are more ambitious. There are trios for like instruments, too, at any rate for flutes: a solitary one of James Hook's (not at all a bad work) has bizarrely achieved 'canonic' status through publication as a Boosey & Hawkes miniature score.[87] For unlike instruments there are duets for violin and cello by Robert Wainwright (1748–82) and Stephen Paxton, and some for violin and viola by Benjamin Blake (three sets) and by C. H. Wilton (Op. 1, 1780). String trios (for violin, viola, and cello) are rare—there is a set of six by Shield, published in 1796—and string quartets little less so, though London publishers put out quite a lot of Continental music in this form.

It is in the context of the quartet, as well as of the quintet and even larger ensembles, that one encounters a greater variety of instrumentation than might be expected, even within the confines of a single publication. The usual variant was the substitution of the flute for the (first) violin, but the oboe is also found, for example in one of Shield's quartets Op. 3 (1782). The earliest English quartet publications were those of Abel

[85] McVeigh, The Violinist in London's Concert Life, 241–3.
[86] Figuring is not, therefore, necessarily a sign of the orchestra-quartet or trio (see above, p. 127).
[87] From a set of six, Op. 83 (c.1797), alternatively for three violins or for flute, violin, and viola.

(Op. 8, 1769) and J. C. Bach; Joseph Gibbs issued a set with figured bass (c.1778), and there were published collections by the young Charles Wesley (c.1778), Barthélemon, and others as well as the set by Shield. This last is certainly the best of its time—the work of an assured string-player and a master of the Viennese Classical idiom who was not ashamed to resort to a native tunefulness in his slow movements and finales. English composers do not seem to have attempted to write for larger ensembles without keyboard, even with a lowest part designated as 'bass': the set by Bach mentioned above was not emulated.

Serious chamber music for strings, the preserve of professionals and a matter for the public concert-platform, suffered the same fate as symphonic music in the 1790s, namely the challenge from Haydn and even from Haydn's pupil Pleyel, some of whose quartets are far from negligible. It all but vanished from sight, and there are no signs of a revival until well on in the nineteenth century.

Harpsichord and Piano Music

English solo keyboard music (other than organ music, which developed on rather different lines) probably underwent a greater stylistic transformation in the half-century covered in this chapter than did any other kind. Even allowing for the very different natures of the harpsichord and the piano, the extent of the change is remarkable. The professional keyboardist was expected to be doing something very different in 1815 compared with 1760, and even the amateur (usually a lady) had rather different aspirations, that is when the piano was chosen in preference to the equally popular harp.

A considerable amount of the solo keyboard music published in the 1760s and 1770s was still essentially Baroque in idiom and conceived for the harpsichord. The sonatas of Joseph Kelway (d. 1782), for example, published in 1764, are still much influenced by Scarlatti; Burney had a low opinion of them, though he had a tendency to set unreasonably high standards of euphony. The published sets of lessons by John Jones, organist of St Paul's Cathedral (1754, 1761), James Nares, Master of the Choristers at the Chapel Royal (Op. 2, 1759, and in Il principio, 1760), and John Burton (1766) are transitional in style and (in the case of Jones and Nares at any rate) of considerable merit.[88] Burton used the designation 'sonata' for his set, though he was not the first English composer to adopt it for solo keyboard music,[89] and it was published as 'for the harpsichord, organ, or piano forte'. Not too much attention need be paid to the details of such nomenclature at this period: Burton's accompanied sonatas, Op. 2 (c.1770) placed the options

---

[88] Cf. BHMB, iv. 198–9, 336–7. There is a sonata by Burton (Op. 1, no. 1) in LPS 7/1–6 (facs.); for Nares's Il principio see n. 103 below.

[89] Cf. T. A. Arne, VIII Sonatas or Lessons ([1756]); C. Avison, Six Sonatas . . . with accompanyments, Op. 5 (1756).

in the order 'piano forte, harpsichord or organ', but the expression 'harpsichord or pianoforte' continued to be used long after that, even in so advanced a work as J. C. Bach's sonatas Op. 17 (c.1779).

As for innovations in style, they owed much, as we have seen, to Giardini, though he published no original works for keyboard alone. Nor did Abel publish any such works in London,[90] so that the main catalyst for change in this medium seems to have come from J. C. Bach, whose sonatas 'for the piano forte or harpsichord', Op. 5, were published c.1768.[91] These are unquestionably pianistic in idiom, with contrasts of loud and soft that would sound ridiculous if obtained by manual-change on the harpsichord, and incorporating at least one crescendo. Some of the writing in fact, both in this set and in Op. 17, is distinctly 'orchestral' in quality, the piano being as effective a deliverer of the early Classical orchestral style as the harpsichord had been (in numerous published arrangements) of the Baroque.

Bach's sonatas display well-developed binary structures in their first movements and sometimes in their finales; if there are three movements rather than merely two the slow movements are songlike; other forms of finale are the variation-set and a rondo or ternary design.[92] Dishearteningly few English composers seemed to be able to capitalize effectively on these opportunities, though innumerable rondos and sets of variations on popular tunes were published separately in the 1780s and 1790s. Among those who published sonatas at this period were Samuel Arnold, whose latest set was the *Three Grand Sonatas*, Op. 23 (1783), Thomas Haigh, Thomas Busby (1755–1838), Samuel Wesley, and William Crotch.[93] English composers were by no means averse to the flashier aspects of keyboard style as the century neared its end, their principal mentors in this respect being Dussek and the young Field, whose Op. 1 sonatas were published in 1801.[94] Mozartian Classicism was largely eschewed, though one cannot discount the influence of Haydn, whose last three piano sonatas were written for London.[95]

A more durable strand was represented by Clementi and J. B. Cramer (1771–1858), who settled in England and formed the backbone of the 'London pianoforte school'. Clementi published a considerable number of piano sonatas up to 1804:[96] many are rather mechanically brilliant, but the

[90] His only known publication for solo keyboard is *Six Easy Sonattas* (Amsterdam, c.1771, alternatively for a melody-instrument and bass).

[91] So Hogwood in his facs. edn. of Opp. 5 and 17 ([London, 1973]); *NGD* (Warburton) gives 1766.

[92] Op. 5 no. 6 is an introduction, fugue, and gavotte.

[93] For these and several others, see LPS 7.

[94] LPS 6 (Dussek and others), 12 (Field). A certain amount of Field's later music (LPS 12, 13) was also published in London.

[95] Only two—Hob. XVI/52 in E flat (as Op. 78, in 1799) and XVI/50 in C (as Op. 79, in 1801)— were published in London (facs. in LPS 6, pp. 13, 35). C. I. Latrobe's three sonatas Op. 3 (? 1793) were dedicated to Haydn (facs. in LPS 7).

[96] LPS 1–3 (facs.).

best of the later ones have a pianistic gravitas that is already reminiscent of Beethoven. The sonatas of J. B. Cramer (about sixty published in London by 1815, excluding accompanied works), not to mention the outstanding *Studio per il pianoforte*, are in general more thoughtful and reflective, however technically demanding. After 1800 the piano music of Mozart and Beethoven, together with that of J. N. Hummel and other more 'brilliant' composers, was becoming more widely available through publication in London and through performances. English-born composers who wrote and published piano sonatas in the early nineteenth century include Haigh, Pinto (*Two Grand Sonatas*, Op. 3, and two others), and Samuel Wesley (a *Sonata*, 1808, in addition to earlier works); those of Pinto are fine, imaginative pieces in a genuinely Romantic vein.[97]

A final strand in the piano repertory is that of the duet, usually for four hands on one instrument. J. C. Bach initiated the form in England; it was pursued to a greater or lesser degree by Theodore Smith (or rather Schmidt, a German resident for a time in London), Clementi, Cramer, Samuel Wesley (who also wrote duets for the organ), and numerous minor composers. The roll of light-hearted trivia continued apace—for piano solo or duet, for harp, and for piano accompanied by percussion, including cymbals, triangle, and even the tambourine in various combinations. Only Wesley, perhaps, managed to raise the status of the variations or rondo on a popular tune to that of a minor art-form.[98]

Organ Music

Organ music is in one sense a branch of church music, but we should not overlook the widespread use of the organ at concert venues and in the home, and it is convenient here to survey the repertory as a whole. It is a strikingly impressive achievement by a body of composers who were in general more independent of Continental influence than in other instrumental genres, and who were largely unaffected by competition with music from abroad. Its development is the continuation of a tradition that was unbroken since the Restoration in 1660 and which could be said to have lasted until the 1870s, when the death of S. S. Wesley removed from the scene one of the last defenders of the native organ-building tradition. However, it is still possible to consider as a group the successors of Stanley, Walond, Travers, and Bennett (to name the four most significant of those whose voluntaries were composed and/or published before 1760) and to review here the work of (amongst others) John Alcock sen. (1715–1806), T. S. Dupuis (1733–96), James Nares (1715–82), John Keeble (1711–86), Starling Goodwin (1775), Jacob Kirkman (1746–1812), the Wesley brothers,

[97] LPS 7 (Haigh, Wesley), 14 (Pinto), all facs.
[98] The duet repertory is in LPS 19 (four hands at one piano), 20 (duets for two pianos).

and William Russell (1777–1813), leaving that of such figures as Thomas Adams and Samuel Webbe jun. to the following chapter.[99]

Even John Keeble, who was an almost exact contemporary of Stanley, displays considerably more adventurousness than the latter in his four sets of *Select pieces*. These were published 'for the author' in the late 1770s, and almost immediately reissued by Longman & Broderip (and again by Broderip & Wilkinson around 1800). They may of course be recent products of those years, while Stanley had stopped composing voluntaries in the 1750s; but one cannot help being struck by the free handling of the form in what are in effect multipartite voluntaries, and by the vigour and resourcefulness of the fugues. The slow movements are particularly imaginative, starting usually quite simply but going on to develop in unexpected ways. A work like the fourth of the *Third Set* is really a minor masterpiece, with its ruminative introduction, a 'duo' that becomes a trio and dissolves into almost Bachian fantasy to introduce the concluding fugue.[100]

Fugal writing is often handled imaginatively by the composers of this generation. The fugues of Nares, for example (*Six Fuges with Introductory Voluntary's*, [1772]), are exceptionally good.[101] Three are provided with massive introductions; two of the others are marked 'alla capella', but all are lively, with ingenious subjects and vigorous working out. In the case of composers of relatively modest attainment (Alcock sen., Dupuis, Charles Wesley, and many others), their fugal writing is often their strongest point; in some others, particularly Samuel Wesley and William Russell, not to speak of the later Thomas Adams, it can be of outstanding quality. In an era when Continental fugues are often either a purely conventional device (Cherubini) or a struggle against superhuman odds (Beethoven), it is quite refreshing to encounter numerous examples that are inventive without unduly straining the musical language.

The ten voluntaries of Alcock, who became organist of Lichfield cathedral in 1750 but left under a cloud in the early 1760s, are of no great originality, but the pieces and voluntaries of Dupuis, who became a Chapel Royal organist in 1779, show a degree of imagination and flair in a variety of styles.[102] Starling Goodwin and Jacob Kirkman were composers of relatively modest attainment: Kirkman was the English-born son of the famous

---

[99] Of the many others who might be mentioned, Jonathan Battishill (1738–1801) was a London organist, singer, and composer noted for his powers of extemporization; but the haul of his posthumously published organ pieces (ed. J. Page, c.1805) is very meagre. Altogether about fifty composers had organ voluntaries published during the period covered by this chapter (including the posthumous publications and reprints of music by earlier composers).

[100] *English Organ Music*, ed. R. Langley (London, 1987–8), vi, no. 1.

[101] Facs. ed. R. Langley ([London, 1974]).

[102] *Nine Voluntaries* (c.1800, posth.); also a later set 'for the use of juveniles' (c.1808), with which it has sometimes been confused. For the difficulties associated with Alcock's tenure of the Lichfield post see W. Shaw, *The Succession of Organists of the Chapel Royal and the Cathedrals of England and Wales from c.1538* (Oxford, 1991), 149–51.

Alsatian immigrant instrument-maker, and in addition he collaborated with Keeble in the production of a set of psalm-interludes (*c.*1787). Goodwin produced his own set, *The Organists's Pocket Companion*, around 1775, and several similar collections are known.

Three or four composers at least included instructions for playing and interpretation with their publications. Nares's *Il principio* (1760) was intended for organists as well as harpsichordists.[103] More interesting from the organist's point of view are Jonas Blewitt's *Complete Treatise on the Organ, to which is added a Set of Explanatory Voluntaries*, Op. 4 (*c.*1795), and John Marsh's *Eighteen Voluntaries . . . to which is prefix'd an Explanation of the . . . Stops . . . with a few Thoughts on Style, Extempore Playing* (1791). Both writers describe the use of the different registers in appropriate combinations, though their approach remains conservative. The English organ of this period did not display much advance over that of the earlier eighteenth century. A 'great organ' of seven or eight stops, and a 'choir organ' of four or five, were usual except on small chamber instruments; a swell or echo organ, descending only to *g*, was sometimes added, and composers often assume its availability, though few emulated Walond in indicating crescendo and diminuendo. The long compass (usually G_1-e''' at this period) was a traditional feature and provided some of the depth missing through the lack of a pedal division on nearly all English organs; not all the stops, however, descended so low, and some were solo right-hand stops descending only to c♯' sharp. An example of this was the multi-rank cornet so often utilized in the fast movements of these voluntaries; others of limited compass were some reed stops (such as the cremona) and of course all the stops on the short-compass swell.

The early years of the nineteenth century witnessed a considerable amount of stylistic experiment in response, perhaps, to advances in the design of larger organs. More of them were now provided with pedals, though these added little or nothing to the tonal repertory of the instrument and were merely an adjunct to the lower part of the manual compass, now sometimes extended down to F_1. Sometimes the pedals merely operated on the manual stops: if they had one or two of their own, these would be of 'eight-foot' (i.e. unison), not 'sixteen-foot' pitch. Only subsequently was sixteen-foot tone adopted, and then not for the entire downward compass.[104]

The first composer to write expressly for organ with pedals seems to have been William Russell, though Samuel Wesley may have written some of his similarly scored pieces at around the same time. The pedal parts, however,

---

[103] Facs. ed. R. Langley (Oxford, 1981). Hook's *Guida di Musica*, Op. 37 (*c.*1785), with its *Second Part*, Op. 75 (1794) and *New Guida di Musica*, Op. 81 (1796) were addressed primarily to harpsichordists and pianists.

[104] For some details of English organs, 1800–10, see C. W. Pearce, *Notes on English Organs . . . from the MS of Henry Leffler* (London, 1911); id., *The Evolution of the Pedal Organ* (London, 1927).

do no more than merely 'help out' the manual parts here and there. More significant is the stylistic advance apparent in each composer. Russell's voluntaries are mostly two-movement works consisting of either an introduction and fugue or a pair of movements in a freer, more graceful style: despite some longueurs, he brings a high level of inventiveness even to the more conventional forms. Wesley exhibits a similar range in the twelve voluntaries issued separately from 1802 to 1808 and in his other mature works, such as the *Full Voluntary* attached to the *Twelve* (really thirteen) *Short Pieces* published in 1815 or 1816. Such works as the C minor voluntary no. 3, with its extraordinary chromatic fugue, and the almost Regerish introduction to the D-minor *Full Voluntary*, betray the workings of a searching mind, while the short pieces themselves (with others printed later or remaining in manuscript) show the more genial side of his personality, with their attractive tunefulness and impeccable craftsmanship.[105]

Much organ music of the early to mid-nineteenth century was published with the suggested alternative of performance on the piano, and curiously enough it often sounds well on that instrument despite the use of pedals and the instructions given for registration. This applies even to those who relied largely on older idioms, like Charles Wesley, who was inclined to pad out a perfectly respectable introduction and fugue with a couple of weaker movements or even an arrangement from Handel.[106] Matthew Camidge (1764–1844), organist of York Minster from 1803 until his death, even made a virtue of imitating the style of Handel and Corelli in his *Six Concertos for the Organ or Grand Piano Forte* (c.1815), though the imitation is not a particularly close one.[107] There is no indication that these concertos were ever given an orchestral accompaniment; keyboard concertos were so often played as solos that Camidge may not have thought it worth his while to provide one. Amongst numerous other composers of voluntaries in the early nineteenth century was James Hook (*Ten Voluntaries*, with fifty psalm-preludes and interludes, Op. 146, c.1812, and a single *Voluntary*, c.1815 or possibly earlier);[108] he too writes a very capable fugue.

Song

As we have seen, the distinction between an orchestrally accompanied song or cantata and a chamber work with instrumental obbligati can be a rather

[105] Five of Russell's voluntaries in *English Organ Music*, vi, no. 4, and ix, nos. 2–5. S. Wesley, Op. 6 nos. 3, 6, ibid. vi, nos. 8, 9; the *Short Pieces* and *Full Voluntary*, ed. G. Phillips (London, 1957); Op. 6, nos. 9–10, with the *Full Voluntary* and three other works, ed. R. Langley as *Six Voluntaries and Fugues* (London, 1981); the same editor has given us *Fourteen Short Pieces*, from various printed and MS sources (London, 1981).

[106] *Voluntary... No. 1* [–6] (c.1815); partial edns. of nos. 5 and 3 in *The Wesleys*, Sets 1 and 2, ed. G. Phillips and P. F. Williams respectively (London, 1960, 1961).

[107] The second concerto, in G minor, ed. F. Jackson (London, 1966).

[108] *English Organ Music*, vi, no. 3 (with the date c.1810).

fine one. The formal distinction between a cantata and a multipartite song is also not always easy to draw, although in this period the growing importance of the song as a small-scale genre independent of the theatre and the decline of the chamber cantata itself combine to make this less of a problem than before. This development can be illustrated by the later songs of William Jackson 'of Exeter', whose first set of songs was discussed in the previous chapter. His later sets, such as his Opp. 4, 7, and 16, preserve the instrumental variety of his Op. 1 but are on the whole less ambitious formally. In Op. 16 (c.1785) the instrumentation varies considerably: three are accompanied by four-part strings, one has strings and two flutes, another strings, two flutes, and two horns; one has a viola da gamba obbligato with 'Violoncello o Piano Forte' (a figured bass), while the remaining six have only the pianoforte, written out in full on two staves.[109] These are in some ways more 'advanced' than the other songs in the collection, though they betray the limitations of a composer whose instincts were fundamentally Baroque; the keyboard parts, though not unidiomatic, double the vocal line almost throughout. The songs are almost entirely in the major key, but the opening of no. 9, 'While Delia with averted eye', is in the minor, and (unusually) without an initial ritornello: it may serve to illustrate a very tentative step in the direction of Romantic sentiment (Ex. 2.9).

The simplest kind of piano-accompanied song could be written out on two staves, just like a continuo-song; the one genre merged imperceptibly into the other, even while more elaborate types of piano accompaniment were being tried out. The number of songs published in this period is enormous. Many—perhaps the majority—were taken from stage works by such composers as Arnold, Hook, Shield, and Dibdin; and indeed there is no difference between these songs in their individual state and their collective publication in the vocal score of a theatre piece. Many were published on two staves, with instrumental cues for the ritornelli and sometimes for minor interjections (printed usually in small notes) during the course of a vocal section. Others were printed on three (occasionally more) staves, with the voice-part directly above the bass. Either way, the song as published could easily be accompanied by the harpsichord or piano alone. Finally, the genuine keyboard reduction, on two staves below the voice, made its appearance.[110]

There was also a continuing and gradually increasing cultivation of songs originating outside the theatre. These vary enormously in style and weight, from the elaborate orchestrally accompanied *scena* (the successor to the

---

[109] There are two songs with 'cembalo solo' accompaniment in his Op. 7 (c.1770).

[110] It is not easy to give a precise date for this innovation, but it became inevitable with developments in orchestration on 'Classical' lines. It appears in Attwood's first opera, *The Prisoner* (1792), and was usual with him thereafter; but this had been preceded by a general tendency not to indicate orchestration in detail, either in two-stave reductions of overtures or in vocal numbers laid out in the old style.

Ex. 2.9

William Jackson, 'While Delia with averted eye': *Twelve Songs*, Op. 16 (London, *c.*1785),
no. 9, p. 30

dramatic cantata) to the simplest of popular ditties. English composers seem
not to have cultivated the fully orchestral concert-*scena* or concert-aria in
the late eighteenth and early nineteenth centuries, though examples by
Haydn were performed in London in the 1790s.[111] With the decline of
the Baroque type of song, which was often accompanied by an instrumental

[111] The principal one was the *Scena di Berenice* ('Berenice, che fai'), from Metastasio's *Antigone*; his
cantata *Arianna a Naxos* ('Teseo mio ben'), which was popular in London, has piano accompaniment.

ensemble, the emphasis came to be very much on piano-accompanied song in the concert-hall as against orchestrally accompanied song in the theatre. Even so, there was a considerable body of hybrid material in the form of popular songs originally introduced into a variety of entertainments of all kinds (such as for instance Dibdin's 'one-man' entertainments) and originally accompanied by a lightweight (sometimes very lightweight) theatre band.

Although most published songs were introduced as having been sung 'to great applause' by Mr or Miss So-and-so, either on the stage or in the concert-hall, some sets and individual numbers were published on a speculative basis, sometimes (if rarely) to fine poetry as a serious artistic endeavour. From the late eighteenth century come such things as Ambrose Pitman's 'Laura', a setting of a Petrarch translation published in short score (on three staves) with violin and 'hautboy' obbligati, and the *Ten Songs* [1796] by the Wells cathedral organist Dodd Perkins (*c*.1750–1820). All but two of these are printed on two staves (one of the exceptions is a three-part unaccompanied song), including the most ambitious, an 'accompanied' recitative and a reflective air entitled 'The Storm'. The recitative has figures as well as written-out chords, small notes being used both for chordal filling and for melody-writing to be distinguished from the vocal part (Ex. 2.10).

The influence of Haydn's *Creation* seems fairly obvious here, but it was Haydn's *Six Original Canzonettas* (1796, and a second set subsequently) that were the most fruitful model for more serious and ambitious composers:[112] indeed 'canzonet' or 'canzonetta' became the favoured term for an accomplished and pleasing, often picturesque setting with a fully developed piano accompaniment. The little-known James B. Adams (fl. 1770–1820) adopted such a style, which represented a considerable advance both on Perkins and on the piano-accompanied songs of Jackson; he published seventeen (or more) *Select Songs* of this kind (as well as a series of *Airs* 'for the Voice and Harpsichord with other Accompanyments'), the best of which are of considerable sophistication. In 'Come Peace repose with me' the rather straightforward vocal melody is doubled almost throughout, but there is a genuine vein of expression in the quasi-orchestral dynamics of the accompaniment (Ex. 2.11). 'The Nightingale' is a largely successful attempt at Haydnesque tone-painting in which the roulades of the introduction invade the subsequent accompaniment as well (Ex. 2.12).

The most promising composer in this style was undoubtedly the young George Pinto, who published *Six Canzonets* (Birmingham, [1804]), *Four Canzonets and a Sonata* (London, [1808, posth.]) as well as four individual

---

[112] There were also a number of spurious compositions and adaptations, for example by Samuel Arnold.

Ex. 2.10

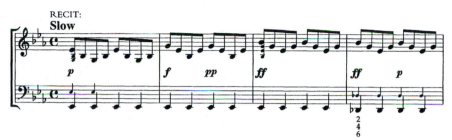

Dodd Perkins, *The Storm: Ten Songs* (London, 1796), no. 8, p. 16

Ex. 2.11

Ex. 2.11, continued

seats   of   bliss,   And   come, con - verse   with __ me:

J. B. Adams, *Come Peace Repose with Me*: *Select Songs*, no. 15 (London, [1798]), pp. 2–3

canzonets. Of these last 'Sapho to Phaon', which sets the first eight lines of Pope's well-known Ovidian paraphrase, exhibits a sense of harmonic colour that seems almost to anticipate Schubert, a quality that is of course also found in late Haydn (Ex. 2.13).[113] 'The Wish' is even more Haydnesque at the outset, but goes on to develop a Beethovenish sonority in the sequel (Ex. 2.14).

Many of Thomas Attwood's separately published songs are early theatre pieces, and while he subsequently developed an individual vein, the best of his later songs (with the exception, perhaps, of his highly individual setting of Walter Scott's *Coronach*, written and published in 1810) postdate the limits of this chapter. He was a pioneer of early Romantic song in England, and will be considered in that light, together with John Clarke(-Whitfeld) and other transitional figures, in the next chapter.[114]

The period also saw a large output of piano-accompanied duets, mostly of a rather slender kind, and of unaccompanied vocal music in the form of the madrigal and glee. The madrigal was a revival that owed its cultivation to the 'ancient music' movement and appealed to the amateur societies that sprang up in the later eighteenth century.[115] Unlike earlier Italian examples (for example by Steffani), which represented the dying embers of a long

[113] In the first setting of the final line in Ex. 2.13, the source reads 'this Love'; Pope, however, wrote 'thy Love', and it is quite likely that the printer of the song simply misread Pinto's handwriting at that point. There is a modern edn. of 'Eloisa to Abelard' (Pope) from *Four Canzonets* and of 'Little Warbler cheerful be' from *Six Canzonets* by N. Temperley (London, 1965); the former also in *English Songs 1800–1860*, ed. Temperley (London, 1979 = MB 43), no. 11, with two more from *Six Canzonets* (ibid. nos. 9, 10).

[114] Attwood's *Coronach* (also set by Clarke) is in *English Songs*, no. 1; the same volume contains two of a large number of sacred and secular solo songs by S. Wesley, very few of which have ever been published (see lists in *NGD*).

[115] See Ch. 9 for details of some of these.

Ex. 2.12

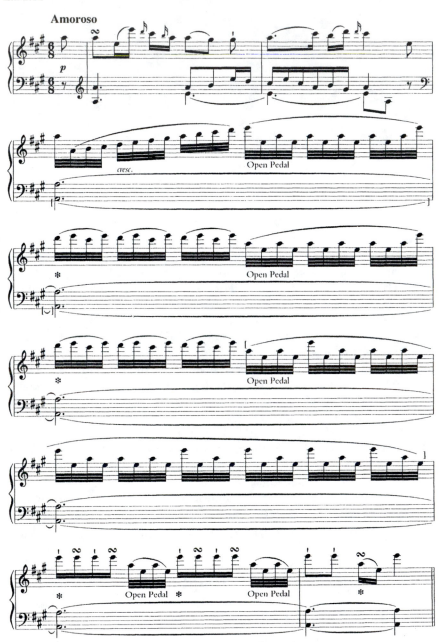

Ex. 2.12, continued

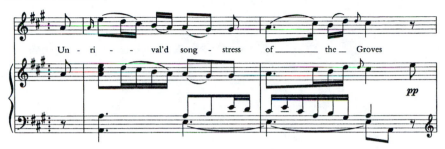

Un - ri - - - val'd song - stress of _____ the _ Groves

Sweet Night - in - gale,   sweet

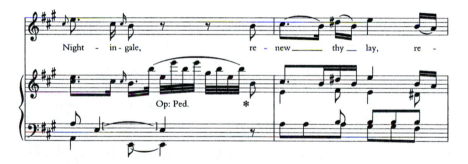

Night - in - gale,   re - new_____ thy _ lay,   re -

-new_____ thy lay, Sweet Night - in - gale re - new - thy _ lay.

continued

Ex. 2.12, continued

J. B. Adams, *The Nightingale: Select Songs*, no. 13 (London, [1798]), pp. 1–2

tradition and had incorporated the convention of the basso continuo, English examples were a revival of the medium, if not always of the form and spirit, of the unaccompanied Renaissance madrigal. Madrigal societies usually employed boys, recruited from the local cathedral or other ecclesiastical foundation, to sing the treble parts. The madrigals of Thomas Linley the younger are miniature da capo or sonata movements with a decorative melodic idiom and a strong sense of tonal direction;[116] they are amongst the most attractive pieces in the posthumously collected vocal music of the father and son, precursors of the later Victorian part-song but devoid of sentimentality (let alone heartiness) and enduringly fresh in their appeal.

The glee, like the madrigal, was intended in the first instance for amateurs but flourished also in concerts, particularly those of Harrison and Knyvett's 'Vocal Concert', a popular late eighteenth-century London series.[117] Glees were usually more purely chordal than madrigals and scored for adult male voices only in three or four parts (though some adopt a full vocal range). It has been estimated that some 10,000 glees were composed between 1760 and 1830; though often of minimal interest, the best examples—by such

[116] Two ed. G. Beechey (London, 1978); Beechey believes, however, that they were composed for domestic use.
[117] McVeigh, *Concert Life*, 236–7: there were four seasons, 1791–5.

Ex. 2.13

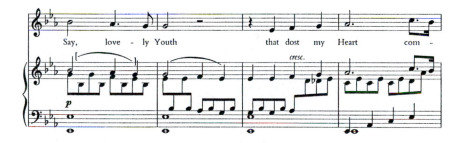

Say, love - ly Youth that dost my Heart com -

-mand, Can Pha-on's Eyes for - get his Sa - - pho's

(1) *g' e'* for *a' f'*

continued

Ex. 2.13, continued

G. F. Pinto, *Sapho to Phaon* (London, *c.*1805), pp. 1–3

Ex. 2.14

Poco adagio con espressione

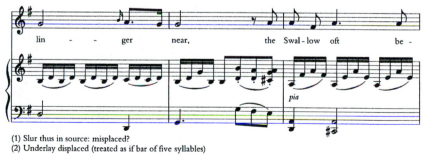

(1) Slur thus in source: misplaced?
(2) Underlay displaced (treated as if bar of five syllables)

continued

Ex. 2.14, continued

neath my thatch,   shall twit - - ter from her   clay built nest,

Oft   shall   the   Pil - grim lift the   latch,   and share my

meal,   a wel - come guest.

G. F. Pinto, *The Wish* (London, *c.*1805), pp. 1–3

composers as Samuel Webbe, jun. and sen., J. S. Smith, R. J. S. Stevens, Thomas Attwood, and John Wall Callcott (1766–1821)—show individuality and taste.[118]

At a still lower level were the numerous catches and rounds for equal voices that continued to be written, perhaps for the last time in appreciable numbers at this period. These were entirely convivial and usually male-orientated, a striking testimony to the continued popularity of gentlemen's clubs as a resort for purely mirthful as well as for more intellectually stimulating activities. Even so, they too frequently figure in professional concert programmes.

Church Music

The cathedral music of the late eighteenth and early nineteenth centuries has been almost universally condemned as the least worthy of the entire Anglican tradition. It is true that there is a good deal of evidence for poor standards of performance in this period and indeed up to the middle of the nineteenth century. We read of widespread absenteeism amongst the poorly paid gentlemen of the choir, indiscipline amongst the boys, lack of adequate rehearsal (or indeed of any rehearsal at all), lack of support from the clergy, insufficient finance for the maintenance of the music and the organ, and a seeming casualness from all concerned except for those few cathedral organists who actually voiced a protest. One might add that the entire structure of the Anglican Church was showing signs of decay, not least in the fabric of the buildings themselves. An extraordinarily lax attitude to the fulfilment of ministerial duty was matched by the poor physical state of the great medieval cathedrals and other churches up and down the land, the patchwork nature of their essential repairs, and the installation of inappropriate furnishings.

Yet there is another side to the picture. The image of a lazy, well-fed clergy is countered by many signs of faithful, unobtrusive service, and above all by its humane response to genuine need, 'the continual fount of charity' as it has been described in relation to one country priest.[119] The clergy were

[118] The upper parts in madrigals, and in glees for the full vocal range, could be taken by either boys or women; glees, moreover, were often accompanied on the piano, whether published with an accompaniment or not. Glees were included in operas (for example by Hook, as seen above, and Bishop); non-theatrical glees could also be quite elaborate in form and style. There is an obvious overlap with the madrigal and other types of secular part-song, but the prevailing ethos of the glee was of gentlemanly solidarity. The Recollections of R. J. S. Stevens, ed. M. Argent (London, 1992), together with his upublished papers, give an amusing picture of the composition and performance of glees and associated genres in the late 18th and early 19th cc. There are extensive MS collections for the use of (e.g.) a 'Harmonic Society' est. in Oxford, 1796 (Bod. Lib., Ten. 598–600) and of the Vicars Choral at Hereford; there is an anthology by P. Young, The English Glee (Oxford, 1990).

[119] The Diary of a Country Parson [James Woodforde], ed. J. Beresford, 5 vols. (Oxford, 1924–31), iii, p. xi. Parson Woodforde was, however, no friend of music in his churches: his altercations with the singers at Castle Cary are detailed in vol. i, 92–3, 95. He registers disappointment at the standard of

well educated—to a standard virtually unattainable today—and their influence was apparent in the schooling for which they were largely responsible in cathedral closes and elsewhere. If we could visit our cathedrals as they were before the Victorian restorers and reformers got their hands on them we should be astonished by what they retained of their collegiate or monastic origins: architecturally in the great stone screens that in nearly every case divided the choir from the nave, ecclesiastically in the maintenance of colleges of vicars and other institutions in their fullness, and in the quiet if humdrum maintenance of the daily office year in and year out.

It is in this context of a daily routine faithfully maintained that we must appreciate the legacy of cathedral music from the period. Even the abuses of the system bear witness to an enviable professionalism. Gentlemen and boys sang from manuscript partbooks, mostly of music with which they had long been familiar but which occasionally at least they must have had to learn at very short notice.[120] Very little full rehearsal of new music, and none of old, can have taken place; sometimes the choice of a service-setting was left to the canon in residence and conveyed to the choir and organist during the reading of the first lesson.[121] There was no conductor: decani and cantoris maintained eye-contact when necessary for ensemble. The organist accompanied everything, including chanted psalms, from a figured bass, though this (like the use of C-clefs in the boys' parts) was changing: Arnold provided a volume of fully written-out organ parts in his *Cathedral Music* (1790) 'the reason for which will appear too obvious to point out', and Page included them in his edition of Battishill's anthems (1804), though without removing the bass figuring. After that the practice became usual in printed editions, though a dependence on figured bass (except, of course, where a solo verse called for an obbligato instrumental line) continued for some time in cathedral organ lofts.

The sumptuous folio editions in which some of this repertory is preserved were not intended for use in choir or on the whole in the organ loft either, but were a repository for study and from which parts could be copied. Boyce's *Cathedral Music* (in three volumes, 1760–73), contains mainly an older repertory, but Arnold's similarly entitled three volumes (1790, with its fourth, organ part) included some music of the previous thirty years, while John Page's *Harmonia Sacra* (1800, also in three volumes) was still more up to

singing at his new church at Weston in Norfolk (ibid. 152: 'only the Clerk and one man, and both intolerably bad'); yet after his death in 1803 the news is: 'We are to have singing at Church' (ibid. v. 413).

[120] Only C-clefs and the bass clef were used in these partbooks as a rule until near the end of the 18th c. Arnold substituted the treble clef for the soprano in his *Cathedral Music*, and the practice became usual thereafter. The treble clef was first adopted for the alto and (with octave transposition) for the tenor in publications for parish use.

[121] D. H. Robertson, *Sarum Close* (Bath, 1969), 279–80, quoting an account of conditions in the late 1820s. This delightful book includes a wealth of information on life in Salisbury cathedral and its schools in the 18th and 19th cc.

date. Page intended his collection 'for Cathedral and Parochial Churches', an interesting anticipation of what was to become a widespread aim amongst Victorian popularizers of the cathedral repertory. He was a vicar choral of St Paul's and also edited posthumous collections of Jonathan Battishill's anthems and keyboard works.

Several composers, following the lead given by Croft, Greene, and others, published collections of their own cathedral music: they include James Kent (1700–76: *Twelve Anthems*, 1773), John Alcock sen. (*Six and twenty Anthems in Score*, 1771), James Nares (*Twenty Anthems in Score*, 1778), William Jackson, John Stafford Smith (1750–1836), and John Clarke (-Whitfeld) (four volumes of services and anthems, 1800–c.1822). Others, like Battishill, had collections published posthumously: they include Boyce (1780, 1790, both edited by Philip Hayes), William Hayes (1795, also edited by his son Philip), Jackson again (1819), and Attwood (ed. T. A. Walmisley, 1852). Even so, the amount of music copied in manuscript, often by local composers who never achieved wider fame, by far exceeds that which found its way into print.

Cathedral-like establishments were maintained by the Chapel Royal and the Royal Peculiars of Westminster Abbey and St George's, Windsor; these, together with St Paul's, represented the summit of the late Georgian achievement, unsatisfactory though that was in certain respects. (The standards of the provincial cathedrals varied widely, but they seem at their worst to have been considerably lower.) In addition there were several other 'professional' choral establishments, for example at certain colleges at Oxford and Cambridge (including Oxford's cathedral, Christ Church), and those collegiate churches that had withstood the hands of the reformers: the northern minsters of Beverley, Ripon, and Southwell, St Anne's in Manchester (the last three of these later to become cathedrals), and Wimborne Minster in Dorset, for example. Lower down the scale were those urban parish churches that aspired to cathedral-like music, usually on a purely voluntary basis;[122] below that again, the much larger number of local churches, town and country, that provided harmonized music through gallery choirs and instrumentalists. Theirs was a diet of metrical psalms and hymns, with simple 'anthems', either composed and arranged locally or drawn from the commercially inspired collections of metropolitan publishers. Dissenting congregations made use of similar materials, while Roman Catholics were beginning to recreate their own traditions on the basis of the practice of the London embassy chapels.

[122] At this period and for long after, Trinity College, Cambridge, had a professional choir of boys and men in addition to King's and St John's Colleges; so also St John's, Oxford, in addition to Magdalen, New College, and Christ Church. Eton and Winchester Colleges also maintained similar choirs until fairly recently. Some urban parishes (and some colleges) were able to maintain cathedral-like music by taking their boy singers not from their own choir-school but from another local school.

The reputation of the cathedral music of this period has suffered from a tradition of criticism that goes back (implicitly or explicitly) to the Victorian reformers. That standards of performance needed to be improved can hardly be questioned, but the idea that the repertory itself is predominantly dull or meretricious is a myth created by the rather different ideals of the Victorians themselves.

The charge of dullness is most easily laid at the door of numerous 'services' in *stile antico*—settings, that is, of Te Deum and Jubilate (or other canticles) for Morning Prayer, Kyrie eleeson [*sic*] and Nicene Creed, sometimes with introductory Sanctus, for Communion, and Magnificat and Nunc Dimittis for Evening Prayer.[123] Convention and practicality favoured a simple idiom for such settings, but the worst that can be said of the majority of them is that their rhythms are predictable, their phrases four-square, and their harmonies plain. But their contrapuntal craftsmanship, in the hands of such as Benjamin Cooke, Samuel Arnold, Kent, and Jackson, is usually impeccable, and in their straightforward alternation between 'full', 'decani', 'cantoris', and 'verse' scoring they offer innumerable variations on the theme of quiet functionalism.[124]

The 'full' style (with its legitimate contrasts of scoring) was also adopted in anthems, sometimes in a masterly fashion. Two of the finest examples are by Jonathan Battishill (1738–1801), a former chorister of St Paul's who aspired to, but never attained, the post of organist there: these are the seven-part 'O Lord look down from heav'n' and 'Call to remembrance'. The first of these has long been admired, not only for its command of contrapuntal structure but for its imaginative use of dramatic pauses suggested, perhaps, by the reverberant acoustic of St Paul's.[125] 'Call to remembrance', composed in the 1760s but revised in 1797, is described in Page's collection as a 'full anthem with verses'; the opening section in E minor (which already displays contrasts in scoring) in fact gives way to a comfortable 'verse' (marked 'pathetic') in E major, which is then followed by a concluding chorus on the same material (Ex. 2.15).

Music of this calibre makes one wonder why so little is heard of Battishill outside these two works. He has been represented as a lazy man overfond of the bottle; but he was in his youth an admired tenor singer and collaborated

---

[123] The 1662 *Book of Common Prayer* has alternative canticles for Morning and Evening Prayer (Benedicite and Jubilate for Morning Prayer, Cantate Domino and Deus Misereatur for Evening Prayer: the Jubilate was often preferred to the Benedictus in musical settings). The Venite at Morning Prayer was normally sung to a composed chant, like the other psalms, at this period. The responses to the Ten Commandments were often dignified by the term 'Kyrie eleeson'; the Communion Service was sung, if at all, only to the end of the Creed, the Sanctus (if set) being used as an introit. (The offence at Castle Cary (see n. 119) was the singing of the first response to the Commandments.)

[124] Two characteristic examples, by Benjamin Cooke (1734–93, organist of Westminster Abbey from 1762: a Magnificat in G) and Samuel Arnold (Cooke's successor: Nunc Dimittis in A) are in *TECM*, iv, nos. 1, 3.

[125] *TECM*, iv. 9–17 (from an edn. by G. C. Martin, London, 1916).

Ex. 2.15

continued

Ex. 2.15, continued

Ex. 2.15, continued

Jonathan Battishill, 'Call to Remembrance': J. Page, *Harmonia Sacra* (London, 1800), i: (*a*) pp. 92–3; (*b*) p. 96

in an operatic venture (*Almena*) whose failure is generally attributed to the libretto. He composed numerous glees as well as anthems and organ music; but he seems to have been not much concerned about preserving his music for posterity, and the manuscripts from which Page made his selections have apparently disappeared.

Few if any composers quite matched Battishill's ability to harness fine counterpoint to expressive purposes, but there is a wealth of able music in the 'verse' style of the period, either as part of an otherwise full anthem or in a verse anthem properly so called (in which the choral element was essentially responsive). One of the difficulties for our present purposes is the absence for the most part of precise chronology, so that the retrospective or posthumously published collections of (for example) Boyce, Nares, King, and Jackson cannot always be used to defend the quality of their productions in this period. In any case, their later work was essentially a continuation of the flourishing tradition previously described. Two composers junior to Battishill whose work has been justly admired are John 'Christmas' Beckwith (c.1750–1809) and John Stafford Smith (1750–1836).[126] Samuel and Charles Wesley both wrote anthems for Anglican use; Samuel is in most respects the better composer, but it is Charles who comes out more strongly in *Harmonia Sacra* with the fine, if conventional, verse anthem 'My soul hath patiently waited for the Lord'.

It was Attwood who became organist of St Paul's in 1796, and he was at that stage already writing church music of a far more serious and reflective nature than can be found in his stage music and other early songs. 'Teach me O Lord', his earliest surviving anthem, is already a fully mature piece, in which the opening chorus (familiar as a separate item) and the succeeding bass verse demonstrate his command of fairly conventional idioms (Ex. 2.16).[127]

Attwood eventually went beyond the exploitation of long-established conventions, as well as beyond the confines of his Mozartian training (not that its beneficial effects were ever lost), and it will be necessary to return to his church music in the next chapter. John Clarke of Cambridge (1770–1836), who became John Clarke-Whitfeld from about 1814, was another transitional figure, though one more firmly rooted in tradition. Some of his earlier anthems—such as 'Behold God is my salvation' and 'O praise God in his holiness', both from his first miscellaneous collection (1800)—include picturesquely accompanied solo airs (see Ex. 2.17). But he can also be dull and short-winded, as so often in his services and in the subsequently very popular 'Behold how good and joyful a thing it is', the simplicity of which made it appropriate for parochial use.[128]

Parochial music varied widely at this period, from quite elaborate music in some urban parishes to unaccompanied monophonic metrical psalmody

---

[126] Beckwith (whose date of birth is disputed) published *Six Anthems in Score* (c.1785); he was organist at St Peter Mancroft in Norwich and, towards the end of his life, at the cathedral; like Battishill he was a noted extempore player. Stafford Smith, also a musical antiquarian, published a collection of twenty *Anthems* (c.1793); they are in the same rather richly extravagant style as his few published organ voluntaries.

[127] Page, *Harmonia Sacra*, i. 111. The obbligato in the first air may originally have been intended for a cello, although it has evidently been adapted for organ performance in the published version.

[128] *A Morning and Evening Service, with Six Full Anthems* . . . (London, c.1822), 43–7. All the music in this later collection (whenever it was composed) is simple in style and long remained popular.

Ex. 2.16

(a)

continued

Ex. 2.16, continued

(1) See n.127 above

Thomas Attwood, 'Teach me O Lord' (J. Page, *Harmonia Sacra* (London, 1800), i: (*a*) p. 111; (*b*) p. 114

(if that) in others, town or country.[129] Increasing numbers of town parishes came to possess an organ, which could be used (with givings-out and interludes) to support the unison singing of metrical psalms and, where vocal resources permitted, the accompaniment of harmonized psalms and hymns or even short anthems. On the whole the style of this harmonized music was based on Baroque practice, for one, two, or three voices with

[129] N. Temperley, *Music of the English Parish Church*, chs. 5–7. See also R. M. Wilson, *Anglican Chant and Chanting in England, Scotland, and America* (Oxford, 1996).

Ex. 2.17

(a)

Allegro moderato

Full Org.

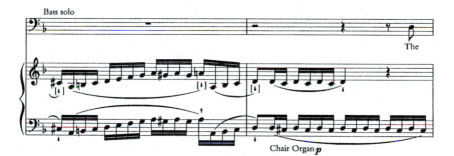

Bass solo

The

Chair Organ *p*

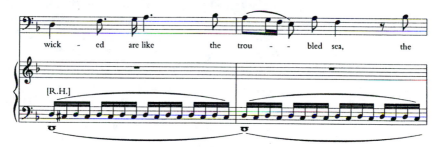

wick - ed are like the trou - - bled sea, the

[R.H.]

continued

Ex. 2.17, continued

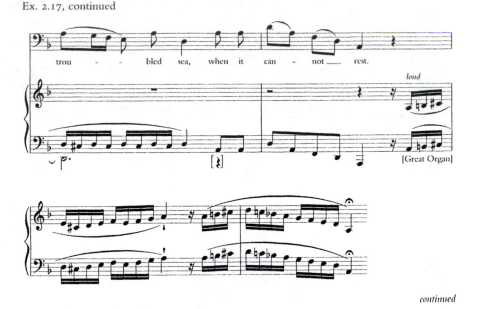

trou - - bled sea, when it can - not rest.

continued

organ continuo. Early collections such as that of John Chetham (*A Book of Psalmody*, 1718, with ten further editions up to 1787) long remained popular and were widely emulated. In due course the simpler cathedral repertory became accessible, as we have seen, to well-equipped parish churches.[130]

Beside this relatively conventional repertory, composed and arranged by professional musicians, there grew up a less formal but equally vigorous repertory in the country parishes. This seems to have arisen essentially as a local effort to enhance the tradition of monophonic congregational psalms, 'given out' line by line and repeated by the people. They were at first strengthened by a few gallery singers, and in due course the tunes were supplemented, or even supplanted, by harmonized settings and short anthems. Such churches rarely if ever possessed an organ (except in some cases a barrel organ): the singing came to be supported by a gallery 'orchestra', usually a motley collection of stringed and wind instruments.[131]

[130] The singers were usually charity children (boys and girls), supplemented sometimes by adult volunteers. In some cases an arrangement with a local boys' school facilitated the performance of more elaborate music, but there was no attempt as yet to emulate the ceremonial function of a cathedral choir: the music was performed usually, though not invariably, from a west-end gallery.

[131] For the barrel organ see L. G. Langwill and N. Boston, *Church and Chamber Barrel Organs* (2nd edn., Edinburgh, 1970); this includes a list of nearly 500 churches which are thought to have or in some cases still have a barrel organ. A further seven pages are devoted to records of other musical instruments

Ex. 2.17, continued

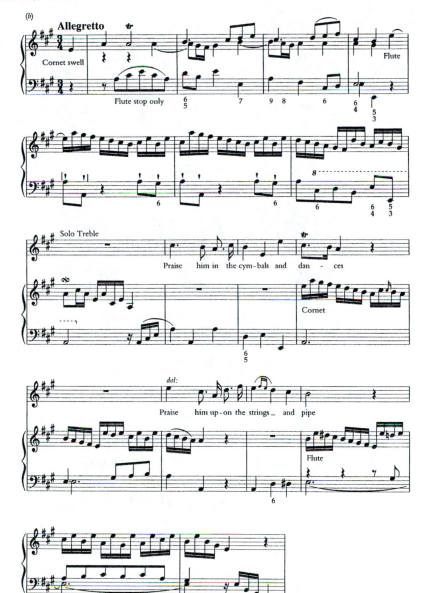

John Clarke-Whitfeld: (*a*) aria 'The wicked are like the troubled sea' from 'Behold, God is my salvation': *A Morning and Evening Service, with Six Anthems in Score* (London, 1800), i. 39; (*b*) aria 'Praise him in the cymbals and dances' from 'Praise God in his Holiness': *A Morning and Evening Service*, i. 55

The musical idiom of these locally composed settings is sometimes very curious, but it cannot be dismissed as incompetent. Such features as parallel fifths and octaves, bare harmony, and swift transitions between short sections of music are widespread and cannot have been an object of local dissatisfaction. Many of these features arose in the preceding period, both in the context of simple harmonizations of tunes new and old (with the tune in the tenor) and in the new 'fuging tunes' that enjoyed a sudden wave of popularity in the 1740s and 1750s.[132] In these freely composed strophic settings of metrical psalms one or more lines would be treated in imitative fashion, a method originally introduced by relatively sophisticated composers. The practice quickly became a cliché exploited by country musicians with little or no grounding in conventional counterpoint. The term is generally extended to any tune with an element of textual overlap, whether fugal or not in the usual sense.

The parochial anthem often exhibits many of the same features, accentuated by a division of the piece into short contrasting sections and by strange discrepancies between verbal and musical rhythm.[133] The vocal parts of such pieces could be, and presumably often were, doubled by gallery instrumentalists; but later ones are sometimes given independent instrumental parts, as are some anthem-like settings of metrical psalms and hymns.

Repertories of sophisticated and unsophisticated parochial music were cultivated in parallel throughout the eighteenth and early nineteenth centuries, while a similar development took place in the non-conformist chapels. Eventually the less sophisticated elements disappeared, partly through the recovery and reharmonization of some of the best new tunes of the eighteenth century.[134] Indeed the enduring legacy of the parochial and dissenting repertories was a wealth of fine tunes, enshrined not only in 'country' collections but in more outwardly conventional publications such as Martin Madan's *Collection of Psalm and Hymn Tunes* (1769) for the use of the Lock Hospital.[135] These too, being often (as with Madan) for solo or duet singing with figured bass, required adaptation subsequently to fit nineteenth-century conventions: most of them are still too little known, let alone performed, in their original form.[136]

---

in churches, in some cases into the present century. See also K. H. MacDermott, *The Old Church Gallery Minstrels* (London, 1948) and, for some further observations, Ch. 8 below.

[132] N. Temperley, 'The Origins of the Fuging Tune', *RMARC* 17 (1981), 1–32.

[133] There is a characteristic example of such music, George FFitch's anthem 'Hallelujah, now is Christ risen', in Temperley, *Music of the English Parish Church*, ii, no. 35.

[134] A good example of this is Thomas Greatorex's reharmonization (with the tune in the soprano) of William Knapp's tune 'Wareham' (ibid., nos. 44, 55).

[135] For this repertory see Temperley, 'The Lock Hospital Chapel'; his *Music of the English Parish Church* gives two of Madan's tune-settings (ii, nos. 45, 46), the second being of the well-known tune 'Helmsley' in its earliest known form.

[136] See also Ch. 1, p. 85 and Ex. 1.16.

An indigenous Roman Catholic tradition, finally, re-emerged in this period with the gradual relaxation of repressive legislation. The plainchant repertory was recovered, largely through the printing and copying activities of John Francis Wade,[137] and simple polyphony was composed by (e.g.) T. A. Arne, S. Webbe sen., S. Wesley, Vincent Novello (1781–1861), all of whom composed short Masses, and Charles Barbandt. Webbe was organist of the Sardinian embassy (as Novello was, from 1798, of the Portuguese): his *Motetts or Antiphons* (1792) provide very simple, sometimes rather jejune settings of canticles, hymns, antiphons, and other liturgical items, sometimes based on chant, with a number of motets of no specific function. The tunes in this book for the 'O salutaris' and 'Tantum ergo' for Benediction of the Blessed Sacrament have since become widely known.

Wesley, who subsequently lapsed from the faith to which he had seemingly been converted, is reckoned to have composed altogether fifty or so works to Latin texts, ranging from simple solos to the huge setting of Psalm 110 (111), 'Confitebor tibi', for soloists, choir, and orchestra. This was a purely speculative effort, written in 1799 but not performed until 1826 (and infrequently thereafter).[138] More characteristic of his normal level are the finely wrought polyphonic motets in from four to eight voices, amongst them the once well-known 'In exitu Israel' and 'Dixit Dominus', both for double chorus (eight voices) and organ.[139] Though Wesley was in some respects an oddity whose undoubted genius never reached complete fulfilment, his Latin music is just one part of his output that deserves to be far better known than it is.

Writings on Music

The period we are discussing saw the emergence of musical historiography and a burgeoning of aesthetic theory and criticism. Charles Burney (1726–1814) and Sir John Hawkins (1719–89) were pioneers in the narration of musical history. One places Burney first for more than alphabetical reasons, but in some ways the achievement of Hawkins was the more remarkable. Without professional training as a musician (he was a lawyer with a well-stocked literary mind, a friend of Samuel Johnson and his first biographer), he produced all his four volumes in 1776, the year of Burney's first. He brought to his task a love of 'ancient' music (by which is meant in his case

---

[137] B. Zon, 'Plainchant in the Roman Catholic Church in England, 1737–1834', D.Phil. thesis (University of Oxford, 1993); id., *The English Plainchant Revival* (Oxford, 1999).

[138] Ed. J. Marsh (MB 41).

[139] These, with 'Exsultate Deo' (for 5 voices and orchestra) and 'Tu es sacerdos' (for 6 voices) became well known initially through adaptations to English texts (for the former see *TECM*, iv. 29–51). Another setting of 'Tu es sacerdos' (for 4 voices) with 'Constitues eos principes' (5 voices) have been ed. by J. Marsh (London, 1974); also 'Deus majestatis intonuit', for double choir, organ, and strings, ed. J. I. Schwarz (Borough Green, 1984).

serious, contrapuntally conceived music from the early sixteenth century to Geminiani) and a willingness to explore difficult texts in Greek and Latin, not to mention Middle English and other European languages. His work is *A General History of the Science and Practice of Music*, and it is not for nothing that the 'science' comes first. A lengthy treatment of the music of the ancients (that is, of ancient Greek musical theory, not 'ancient music' as just defined) is followed by a leisurely stroll, with much backtracking, through the garden of medieval theory: the scalar and other innovations attributed to Guido of Arezzo, the mensural system attributed to Franco of Cologne (then believed to have lived in the eleventh century), and the refinements of later writers, not least the anonymous works that he had discovered in the Cotton and Lansdowne collections in the British Museum. His earlier musical examples are nearly all drawn from treatises: Josquin and his contemporaries from Glareanus, and so on. He was unsympathetic to the innovations of his own day, but his range of interests is astonishingly wide. The greatest weakness of his *History* is its lack of a sense of period-division governed by stylistic change; two of its many strengths are its prose style and its positive view of monastic intellectual achievements. It was reprinted, with annotations based on the manuscript comments in his own copy in the British Museum, in 1853, and again in 1875 (a reprint of the 1853 edition).

Burney lacked, or did not aspire to, the sonorous majesty of Hawkins's prose, but he was in his own way a witty and cutting writer, and he had two immeasurable advantages: a willingness to go out and search Europe for examples of music in a practical format, and a profound sympathy for the musical developments of his own day. He agreed with Hawkins that no value could be placed on assertions of the superiority of the music of 'the ancients', though he also devoted a quantity of space—the whole of his first book, in fact—to the subject. Like Hawkins, he treated the subsequent development of the art very much as a series of technical 'improvements' which composers had at their disposal. He too is largely innocent of 'periodization', though he writes of the 'middle ages' and implies a transition to the modern world with the invention of printing and the religious Reformation of the sixteenth century. He freely scatters remarks about 'monkish darkness' and 'Gothic trammels', but this is countered by his quotations of (for example) trouvère songs from original sources. His final volume is concerned entirely with eighteenth-century music, for the most part that of the Italian opera in London.

There were precedents, some English, some Continental, for the writing of musical history, but none exhibited the genuinely historical sense of Burney or Hawkins. They were not much influenced, if at all, by the annotations to Tudway's collection of church music, to Talbot, to North, or to Boyce's published collection of cathedral music, important though this last was as a work of scholarship in its own right.[140] They had read Mersenne, Kircher, Doni, Bontempi, Printz, and Gerbert, and the first two volumes of the *Storia della musica* by their own most significant precursor, G. B. Martini.[141] Perhaps they were as much influenced by such endeavours as Hume's *History of Great Britain* (1754–61), Warton's *History of English Poetry* (1774–81), and the monumental *Histoire littéraire de la France*, of which the first twelve volumes had appeared between 1733 and 1763. Certainly this last was an important source of information and misinformation, an example of the latter being the misdating of Franco of Cologne by two centuries. But in the last resort they created their own genre, at least for English-speaking readers, and in the opinion of many set standards that overshadowed even the reputation of Martini.

Burney and Hawkins assumed aesthetic principles that in many points agreed but differed in emphasis. Hawkins's standards were primarily intellectual: what he admired above all was 'the artful contexture of the parts'. For Burney, music was an innocent recreation, devoted to 'the gratification of the sense of hearing': he detested 'crudities' that compromised this pleasure. Burney's aesthetic is disappointingly bland in view of his frequent references to music as a 'language', but it probably corresponded to the intuitions of the majority of his readers. Hawkins, on the other hand, gave the impression of an intellectual penetration which, while partly illusory, may have ensured the posthumous reputation of his *History*.

Amongst other historians and critics of repute in the period one may mention Thomas Busby (1755–1838), though his own *History* appeared only in 1819, John Stafford Smith (*A Collection of English Songs*, 1779; *Musica antiqua*, 1812), and Joseph Ritson (*Ancient Songs and Ballads*, 1790, and other works). The two latter were influenced by the efforts of Bishop Percy in English poetry, though Percy's views on minstrelsy were strongly attacked by the ungracious Ritson. Scholarship in more up-to-date fields included Arnold's editing of Handel, and Samuel Wesley's pioneering advocacy of J. S. Bach. Finally, mention should be made of the astonishing achievement

---

[140] For Tudway, Talbot, and North, see above, Ch. 1, p. 88 and n. 154; also Vol. I, p. 612 n. 122 Boyce's *Cathedral Music* (3 vols., 1760–73) included biographical notes on the composers represented.
[141] M. Mersenne, *Harmonie universelle*, 3 vols. (Paris, 1636–7); A. Kircher, *Musurgia universalis* (Rome, 1650); G. B. Doni, *De praestantia musicae veteris libri tres* (Florence, 1647); G. A. Bontempi, *Historia musica* (Perugia, 1695); W. C. Printz, *Historische Beschreibung der edelen Sing-und Kling-Kunst* (Dresden, 1690); M. Gerbert, *De cantu et musica sacra*, 3 vols. (St. Blasien, 1774; vol. i printed before 1768); G. B. Martini, *Storia della musica*, 3 vols. (Bologna, 1761 [dated 1757], 1770, 1781). They also used Marpurg's *Kritische Einleitung* (Berlin, 1759), Mattheson's *Grundlage einer Ehren-Pforte* (Hamburg, 1740), and the dictionaries of Brossard (1701, 1703; also transl. J. Grassineau, 1740) and Walther (1732). They were well read in ancient and modern theory, using such editions as those of Meibom (*Antiquae musicae auctores septem*, Amsterdam, 1652), J. Wallis (his edn. of Ptolemy, 1683, reprinted with the commentary of Porphyry in his *Opera mathematica*, iii, Oxford, 1699) and the works of Renaissance theorists such as Glareanus (*Dodecachordon*, 1547), S. Calvisius, Zarlino, and Salinas (whom Hawkins discusses at inordinate length).

of Sir William Jones in his article 'On the Musical Modes of the Hindus', published in *Asiatic Researches*, vol. iii (1792).

Most musical criticism of the period was of an ephemeral nature, consisting of reports of concerts and discussions of new music in newspapers and journals not devoted specifically to music. But there were serious discussions of aesthetic issues, mostly in the context of other arts, for example by James Beattie, Sir William Jones, Daniel Webb, Adam Smith, and Thomas Twining. A frequent topic was the Aristotelian doctrine of imitation as it applied to music; since all were agreed that music did not, as a rule, imitate the actual sounds of the material world, it was necessary either to explain away the doctrine somehow or to discard it altogether.[142]

A good deal of scientific research in those days was devoted to acoustical matters, and the Royal Society continued to provide a forum for discussion.[143] Public music lectures were promoted by the Royal Institution and by Gresham College in the City of London; one of the most distinguished, though conservative, lecturers of his day was William Crotch, who drew Burney's fire after reports of his lukewarm reaction to Haydn's *Creation*. Nevertheless Crotch, who illustrated his talks at the harpsichord, must have been an entertaining lecturer, and possibly the most versatile Professor of Music Oxford has ever had.[144]

The late eighteenth-century 'rage for music' was matched by a voracious curiosity about its history and the nature of its appeal. Of course not all who enjoyed music were in the least interested in such things, but in the discussion of aesthetic issues (as we should call them) a wide range of philosophical concerns was brought together. Music was considered in the light of poetry or painting, for example, and few philosophers would have considered it unworthy of their enquiry. The incipient philistinism of the succeeding era did not yet cast a shadow over the legitimacy of music as an object of study; the objections to music, if any, were social and moral rather than intellectual. In the pleasure-loving ambience of the early nineteenth century, however, before the onset of a new wave of moral earnestness, its detractors were unable to mount a concerted attack. While the overwhelming bulk of musical entertainment was of an essentially trivial

---

[142] Beattie (*Essays on Poetry and Music*, 1776) and Jones (in an essay included with his *Poems*, 1772, pp. 201–17) were inclined to reject the doctrine of imitation in music altogether; Twining, in translating Aristotle's *Poetics*, argued that it referred to the power of music over the 'affections'. Adam Smith was unusual in addressing the aesthetics of purely instrumental music (in an essay published posthumously in 1795); Beattie and Smith were of course Scots. See T. McGeary in *BHMB*, iv. 417–21, for a more extended discussion of the contributions of these and others to aesthetic theory; and for the early 19th cent., ibid. v. 455–7. For Twining as a practical musician, see p. 547, n. 8.

[143] Kassler, *The Science of Music in Britain, 1714–1830*.

[144] Kassler, 'The Royal Institution Music Lectures, 1800–1831: A Preliminary Study', *RMARC* 19 (1983–5), 1–30; V. Duckles in *BHMB*, v. 488–9 (for Crotch and for the Gresham Professorship, held by R. S. J. Stevens from 1801 until his death in 1837). Crotch's *Specimens of Various Styles of Music*, the illustrations to his lectures, were published in 3 vols. in 1801; see also above, n. 38.

nature, there was not yet a great gulf fixed between the light-hearted and the serious: the same people, on the whole, enjoyed both, and indeed composed both. The widening of that gulf in later periods was due, at least in part, to developments in aesthetic theory and towards a view of art that enabled it in some sense to offer an alternative to religious experience.

3

FROM THE LATER
GEORGIAN TO THE
MID-VICTORIAN AGE

WHEREAS the previous period could be said to have witnessed a drastic lowering of the average composer's aspirations, the present age (1815–70) saw the rise of a new seriousness—a development paralleled by changes in the general political and ecclesiastical outlook of the nation. Whether the artistic results of this phase of consciousness bore any qualitative relation to it would be a matter of opinion; a firm moral purpose is no guarantee of musical or any other form of artistic inspiration. But it was inevitable that English composers should respond somehow or other to the Romantic movement, with its political and moral overtones—both to the impact of English (and indeed German) Romantic literature and to that of early musical Romanticism on the Continent. The widening of access to European opera—by Weber, Spontini, Bellini, Meyerbeer, to name no others—to the instrumental music and songs of Beethoven, Schumann, Mendelssohn, and Chopin, and to the new Continental oratorio tradition of Spohr and Mendelssohn, was bound to have its effect, beneficial or not.

The fact has to be faced, however, that the English reaction to most of this was at first patchy and in the end doomed to failure through lack of artistic resolution in the face of a fickle public taste. This failure of response—the recognition of which is not at all to condemn a repertory which may well deserve plaudits from other critical points of view—is due to a number of factors. In the field of opera, for example, there was a deep-seated antipathy to the idea of an all-sung opera in English, certainly on the part of audiences and managers. It is hardly too much to say that between *Dido* and *Peter Grimes* virtually every all-sung English opera (with the exception of small-scale pastorals and masques) has an experimental character: even the best and most successful examples (these being by no means the same thing) have never become regular repertory pieces in this country or anywhere else. The English, on the other hand, had adopted dialogue-opera with enthusiasm as the national form *par excellence*; but this was easily diluted by the subordination of songs to the spoken text, and corrupted by the practice of pasticcio. A visit to the opera in English was essentially a form of play-going, and audiences were by and large content with that.

There is nothing wrong, of course, with dialogue-opera, but neither the German nor the French repertories rested so heavily on it and in the Italian it was largely excluded. The English challenge to Romantic opera therefore ran the risk of being either shallow or pretentious: shallow when spoken dialogue assumed too preponderant a role, and pretentious if, with continuous music, the form was being raised above its natural level.[1]

In the sphere of instrumental music there are a number of reasons for the rather insular turn that these forms were liable to take. The first (in no particular order) is the continuing failure of the English to make their own contribution to virtuoso display. Since most virtuosi were also composers and mostly performed their own music, there was no indigenous tradition of providing excitement through its creative use. This was not a new situation, but it made for increasing insularity in the face of the challenge from Chopin, Paganini, Moscheles, and Liszt. A rather different factor was the liking of English audiences for variety in their concerts. After about 1820 the European practice developed of distinguishing between orchestral concerts on the one hand and solo or chamber recitals on the other; the English continued to prefer a mixture of items and were slow to build concert-halls of a type specially suited to music requiring a relatively large orchestra. This was a factor inhibiting the growth of connoisseurship of instrumental forms in specific media and the appreciation of differences between them. Finally the English were slow to adopt novelties in techniques of orchestral composition and performance (including conducting), although some composers (amongst them Crotch, Bishop, and Sterndale Bennett) developed an acute ear for orchestral sonority.

It was in the realm of oratorio that a combination of indifferent models and ethical high-mindedness had the most disastrous consequences. Oratorio finally lost both its stylistic and its social affinity with opera, becoming instead a vehicle for worthy sentiment (couched usually in Old Testament language) of a kind suited to the growing army of amateur choralists and their largely provincial audiences. The fully-fledged choral society was indeed a powerful new performing medium, one that eventually inspired the creation of a number of masterpieces entirely worthy of it, and worthy

---

[1] G. Biddlecombe, *English Opera from 1834 to 1864 with Particular Reference to the Works of Michael Balfe* (New York and London, 1994), can name only three all-sung operas produced during the period covered by this chapter: Horn's *Dirce* (1821), and Balfe's *Catherine Grey* (1837) and *The Daughter of St Mark* (1884) (p. 58). Balfe himself was Irish by birth, but like that of Wallace (Irish) and Benedict (German-born) his work for the London stage is too important to be disregarded here.

in its turn of a Continental repertory conceived under rather different conditions; but these triumphs were yet to come.

In some other forms English composers were able to make a valuable contribution. Solo song is one. Only a tiny fraction of the repertory has become readily available in recent years, and while that fraction may well represent it at its best, there is a great deal of exploration still to be done. Victorian song as a whole has suffered from the twentieth-century prejudice against what is thought of as sentimentality as well as from comparisons with the most exalted strata of German Lieder. In fact sentimentality is an essential component in all Romantic song, and it can easily be detected in the songs of Schubert, Schumann, and Brahms, not to mention those of their countless lesser contemporaries. Much of the enormous repertory of German song descends to the level of commonplace vulgarity, and while that is no excuse for its appearance elsewhere, the fact should teach us not to cavil at qualities that are inseparable from the genre and which would be more generally recognized if the words of German songs were always fully attended to by their listeners.

The other main area for healthy growth was that of church music (or more specifically cathedral music and its imitations). There are admittedly limits to the degree of enthusiasm that can be mustered for the genre in all its manifestations, and it was intrinsically a non-exportable one; but it had its roots in a firm tradition, and blossomed in ways that both depended on that tradition and yet outshone it at times.

As in the two previous chapters we shall consider each class of musical production in turn, beginning with that of the lyric theatre.

Opera and Theatre Music

The earlier part of this period saw no change in the nature of theatre-music compared with what had gone before. Indeed the upheavals of the previous quarter of a century—the burning and rebuilding of the major London theatres, and the rise and eclipse of the Pantheon as an opera-house—were followed by a return to normality. Drury Lane and Covent Garden remained the only fully licensed theatres in the metropolis, empowered to present stage plays (though almost always with music) as well as other forms of entertainment. The King's Theatre continued as the bastion of Italian opera, though with a repertory based more and more on acknowledged masterpieces and with an occasional foray into German opera.[2] Other theatres cultivated pantomime, burletta, melodrama, and the like: the ban on spoken dialogue, arising from their unlicensed status, became progres-

---

[2] *Der Freischütz* and *Fidelio* were both performed in German in 1832 during Monk Mason's short tenure as manager of the King's Theatre. H. F. Chorley, *Thirty Years' Musical Recollections* (London, 1862), i. 44; 50–9 (discussion of *Fidelio*).

sively less observed as the distinction between the 'legitimate' theatre and these other forms became more generally recognized in any case.

Three events of importance dictated the changed circumstances of the early and middle Victorian periods. The first was the opening of the 'New Theatre Royal, Lyceum, and English Opera House' in 1834 with a production of E. J. Loder's *Nourjahad*. The second was the passing of the Theatre Regulation Act in 1843, which laid down conditions for the licensing of all theatres and extended the censorship of play-texts to all forms of dramatic entertainment under the direction of the Lord Chamberlain. Although these laws might seem more draconian than those they replaced, they were actually fairer and more logical. The licensing of all theatres now depended primarily on the consideration of public health and safety, while the reading of operatic libretti and the texts of other musical theatre-pieces became very largely a formality.[3]

The third event was the establishment of the 'Royal Italian Opera' at Covent Garden in 1847, formed by Michael Costa and a number of singers at Her Majesty's Theatre (as the King's Theatre was renamed in 1837) after their disillusionment with its management. It was an interesting moment to choose: Her Majesty's had just premiered its first and only Verdi commission, *I Masnadieri*, conducted by the composer himself. But in retrospect this step turned out to be crucial. Covent Garden—burned again in 1856 and rebuilt in 1858 (the present theatre)—slowly became England's main opera-house as the operatic fortunes of Drury Lane, the Lyceum, and Her Majesty's declined. While opera was normally given in Italian both at Covent Garden and at Her Majesty's throughout this period, Covent Garden was leased to Louisa Pyne and William Harrison's 'Royal English Opera Company' for six winter seasons from 1858 to 1864 and by a successor company for two seasons after that. The end of 1864, in fact, marked a significant break in the production of new opera in England.

At the beginning of our period Henry Rowley Bishop (1786–1855) was firmly established as the capital's main theatrical entrepreneur and composer. After two early successes, as we have seen, he became from the 1810–11 season musical director and composer at Covent Garden. In 1824 he moved back to Drury Lane, where his *Aladdin* (1826), intended as a counterblast to Weber's *Oberon* at Covent Garden, proved a disastrous failure. He subsequently continued to alternate between the two theatres before bowing out of the theatrical world for good in 1840.[4] From then until its demise in 1848 he directed the Concert of Ancient Music; in 1842 he was knighted, and from 1848 until his death was Professor of Music at Oxford in succession to

---

[3] The Lord Chamberlain's powers of censorship were abolished in 1968. Cf. Biddlecombe, *English Opera*, 48–9.

[4] He was at Covent Garden again in 1829, back at Drury Lane in 1831, and finally at Covent Garden in 1839–40.

Crotch. Unlike (say) Arnold before him, therefore, his careers as a theatrical composer and adaptor and as an establishment figure were successive rather than concurrent; yet the former was a natural precursor to the latter, the medium in which he gained the experience in the field and the guarantor of his solidly based musicianship. No other English composer of the nineteenth century, however distinguished, served so long and demanding an apprenticeship.

Bishop the composer has been much maligned, above all for his readiness to adapt the work of others, to mingle theirs with his own, and for his failure to espouse an all-sung form of opera. But these objections are anachronistic: we should accept the English musical theatre of its day for what it was, not reject it for not fitting our own preconceptions. Within certain limitations, Bishop was a gifted composer with a flair for quickly establishing a mood. Most successful, perhaps, are the simple songs or ballads that were a feature of almost every theatrical production of the day. The form was an indigenous one, traceable to such composers as Carey and Leveridge; but in the early nineteenth century it acquired a tinge of Continental Romanticism, drawing on the simpler elements in (for example) Rossini and Weber in their cavatinas and similar pieces. A fuller and more idiomatic orchestration contributed to the setting of mood. The melodic line had to be at once simple and a challenge to the singer's control of legato and dynamics.

Not all Bishop's efforts in this line hit the nail on the head; indeed the form was almost 'hit or miss' by definition, though fine singing could (and apparently often did) redeem an earthbound melody. One of the best of Bishop's songs, 'By the Simplicity of Venus' Loves', was composed for *A Midsummer Night's Dream*, one of a series of Shakespearean adaptations by Frederick Reynolds.[5] Such entertainments are virtually unstageable nowadays: the songs were normally made available with piano accompaniments for domestic and concert use and can be so sung today, but they are at their best in their original orchestral garb. Alternatively, 'theatrical ballads' sometimes originated outside the theatre: 'Home, sweet home' in *Clari* (1823) was originally published in 1821 as an anonymous 'Sicilian' air.[6]

It is hard to define the limits of a ballad, but it is clearly distinguishable from the comic song on the one hand and the bravura aria on the other: Bishop's 'Lo hear the gentle lark', for soprano with obbligato flute in F, from the *Comedy of Errors*, is a good example of the latter. Indeed a satisfactory variety of genres was essential for the success of an entertainment. Apart from the solo genres one might encounter duets, trios, accompanied glees, the concerted finale, and a multi-movement overture. The Mozartian type of concerted ensemble was as far beyond Bishop (and, no doubt, his

---

[5] *English Songs 1800–1860*, no. 12; extract from orchestral version on p. 130.

[6] In a collection entitled *Melodies of Various Nations*; Bishop was later accused of having stolen his own melody.

librettists) as it had been beyond his predecessors, Hook, Arnold, and Dibdin; and his finales in particular suffer from an inability to combine musical and dramatic incident.

An elaborate typology of musical theatre at this period is difficult to maintain, but we can distinguish between what are essentially plays, in which the music is purely incidental, and operas, in which the action is partly carried on in the musical numbers. Even so, there is a certain amount of overlap, and opera never abjured the convention of the song that really is a song in its dramatic context. One writer has distinguished in addition the Shakespearean adaptations, 'musical dramas' (less ambitious than operas, and lacking a principal male singing role), and a number of subgenres (ballets, pageants) which had continuous music. Melodramas, on the other hand, were spoken plays (normally afterpieces) with a certain amount of 'action music' and an occasional chorus or ballad. 'An operatic work could be performed as a mélodrame, simply by removing most of its music, as in the case of Rodwell's *The Sexton of Cologne* in 1837.'[7] Nevertheless, the precise definition of a melodrama and its French cognate remained rather vague.

Charles Edward Horn (1786–1849), son of the German immigrant musician Karl Friedrich Horn, embarked on a theatrical career—initially as a singer—at more or less the same time as Bishop. His stage works included *The Devil's Bridge* (Lyceum, 1812) and *Dirce*, an all-sung Metastasian opera in English (Drury Lane, 1821: lost); however, his enduring legacy is his setting of Herrick's 'Cherry ripe', a 'cavatina' inserted in the play *Paul Pry* (Haymarket, 1825). Unlike the strophic ballad, this appealing melody adopts the rounded form of the German *Cavatine* as well as capturing something of its simple melodic idiom.[8] But in 1827 Horn emigrated permanently to the United States and disappears from our story.

Bishop's *Aladdin* (1826) is interesting for its use of recurrent melodic material, a technique stimulated no doubt by Weber's *Der Freischütz*, performed in 1824 in no fewer than seven English adaptations, 'of which the last and most faithful was by Bishop'.[9] Weber's *Oberon* (Covent Garden, 1826) was one of the most spectacular operas ever written for the London stage, and a fine example of what could be made of the English conventions by a real master. *Aladdin* was hardly a serious competitor, but it deserves more attention than its failure has allowed it to receive. Bishop was more successful with his music for Byron's *Manfred* (Covent Garden, 1834, in an adaptation of which the poet would never have approved): this was a highly

---

[7] Biddlecombe, 19; cf. B. Carr in *BHMB*, v. 292–3.

[8] The form may have been suggested by Agathe's *Cavatine* 'Und ob die Wolke sich verhülle' from *Der Freischütz* (see below), though Horn's song is a rondo with two episodes rather than a simple ternary. Both have the abbreviated final statement that is also characteristic.

[9] *BHMB*, v. 302.

Weberish score (the overture is even by Weber), in which the techniques of recurrence are taken much further than in *Aladdin*.

A number of other composers may be mentioned beside Bishop and Horn as active in the 1820s and early 1830s. John Barnett (1802–90), George Rodwell (1800–52), and George Alexander Lee (1802–51) were amongst those who continued to write new operas after the 1834 watershed. The main operatic venue apart from Covent Garden and Drury Lane had been the Lyceum Theatre in Wellington Street (Strand). Originally a concert-hall, this had been bought by Samuel Arnold in 1792 and converted to a theatre; but he had been unable to obtain a licence. From 1809 until 1812 it was used by the homeless Drury Lane Company, and when they left, Arnold's son S. J. Arnold (1774–1852) was able to retain a licence for the summer months, which he used for plays and for opera, calling the theatre for that purpose 'The English Opera House'. It was rebuilt in 1815–16 and was used for opera in English as well as for plays, melodramas, and the like until 1830, when it was burnt down.

Other venues for opera at the time included the Adelphi in the Strand, originally the Sans Pareil (built in 1806). It was renamed in 1819, enlarged in 1827, and replaced in 1858 by the 'Royal Adelphi'. In 1810 a concert-room in Tottenham Court Road, at one time the home of the Concert of Ancient Music, was rebuilt as a theatre, known variously during its history as 'The New Theatre in Tottenham Road', the Regency, the West London, Queen's, Fitzroy, Prince of Wales (1865), and finally (in 1905) the Scala.[10] In 1831 it saw an unsuccessful attempt by the Macfarrens, father and son, to establish English opera. The Olympic Theatre had a chequered career from its first opening in 1805 until its final closure in 1899. The Surrey Theatre, originally a riding-school and later (1782) the Royal Circus, was converted to theatrical use in 1809.[11]

The annals of these and other theatres of the time, engaged as they were in a constant struggle with the licensed theatres to present 'plays', show to what an extent operas, plays with music, melodramas, ballets, and panto-mimes were all part and parcel of a multifarious entertainment industry that was not much concerned with boundaries between genres. At the same time a number of individuals—amongst them George Rodwell, who pro-posed an ambitious scheme for a national opera in 1833—were concerned about the difficulties faced by English composers of serious opera and the need to educate the taste of the public. Essentially these were calls for subsidy of a kind that was not to materialize for another century.

The reopening of the 'English Opera House' in 1834 undoubtedly raised the profile of 'serious' opera in English for a time, though it could not

[10] It was closed in 1969 and subsequently demolished.
[11] It was finally pulled down in 1937.

guarantee artistic worth. S. J. Arnold at first continued as manager, but after two years he went bankrupt. John Braham then took over (1835–8), followed by John Barnett (in 1840), and finally Michael Balfe (1841). Although the theatre was used intermittently for opera thereafter until the outbreak of World War II, it never fulfilled the hopes initially placed in it. Those who promoted opera at the other London theatres fared equally badly. Alfred Bunn, impresario and librettist, managed Drury Lane from 1833 to 1839; he was bankrupted in 1840, but returned there for two further periods, 1843–7 and 1851–2. His trite professionalism pervaded the English operatic scene during those years. Covent Garden played only a minor part in the cause of English opera until the days of the Pyne–Harrison English Opera Company, which promoted seasons there every autumn and winter from 1858/9 to 1864/5. The Theatre Royal and Her Majesty's (both in the Haymarket) were amongst the other London theatres that occasionally mounted English opera in this period, while Brighton, Bristol, Liverpool, Manchester, Newcastle, and Sheffield also saw such productions from time to time.

The opening production at the new English Opera House was E. J. Loder's *Nourjahad* (21 July 1834), a successful but rather slight work and its composer's first opera. More substantial was Barnett's *The Mountain Sylph*, produced on 25 August in the same year. These, together with the earlier works of Balfe, nearly all of which were produced at Drury Lane, were the most significant new English operas of the decade 1834–43.

John Barnett, though he lived to a great age, did not ultimately fulfil his early promise—the product of a natural facility and a thorough training under S. J. Arnold, C. E. Horn, and Beethoven's friend Ferdinand Ries, who lived in London from 1813 to 1824. (Ries himself had an English opera, *The Sorceress*, produced in London at the Adelphi in 1831.) Barnett had written music for numerous stage works prior to 1834; *The Mountain Sylph*, however, he regarded as 'my first attempt at legitimate opera', a remark that is more significant as an indication of contemporary aspirations than as marking a clear-cut technical distinction. Evidently the succession of songs and ensembles with which he had previously had to be content as the musical substance even of works called operas did not satisfy him, and it is unlikely that he looked to his English predecessors for models worthy of his emulation. In fact it was Weber's *Der Freischütz* that offered the main inspiration to composers of English romantic opera: it showed how even with extensive dialogue it was possible to achieve characterization by musical means and to incorporate lengthy set pieces, both solos and ensemble, that allowed for emotional development during their course.[12] It also

---

[12] These include in *Der Freischütz* Agathe's *Szene und Arie* 'Wie nahte mir der Schlummer', the *Terzett* 'Wie?, Was?, Entsetzen', and the Finales of Acts II and III.

strengthened (like *Don Giovanni*, produced at the King's Theatre in 1817) the legitimacy of the supernatural as a source of motivation in 'serious' opera, a point that has some bearing on our reception of its English imitations.

Barnett's German-oriented training (and he was himself of German descent) ensured the technical competence of his work, and apart from Weber his style in *The Mountain Sylph* shows affinities with that of Schubert and Mendelssohn as well as an occasional glance back to Mozart. (It is much less dependent on the Italian and French idioms that attracted Balfe, for example.) The overture introduces, even in its slow introduction, two of the main musical ideas of the work: a syncopated idea associated with the villain, Hela, and a gentler theme associated with the rural community to which the hero and his intended bride belong. The main section of the overture is strikingly ambivalent in tonality, at least to begin with, but the piece is far too long and is fatally weakened by the plodding treatment of the 'rural' theme as a 'second subject' (Ex. 3.1).[13]

The plot of *The Mountain Sylph* is based on that of *La Sylphide*, the first of the great Romantic ballets (Paris, 1832: the music by J.-M. Schneitzhoeffer). Donald (the names in the opera are changed, though the action remains in Scotland) is betrothed to Jessie but falls in love with a sylph, Aeolia. The conflicts which this engenders are resolved only when the Queen of the Sylphs transforms Aeolia into a human being. The progress of Donald's seduction is effectively handled, for example with a *scena* beginning as in Ex. 3.2 (the accompaniment in the aria incorporates a popular Scottish melody, 'Roy's wife of Aldivalloch')[14] and then in a duet that recalls Schubert's modulatory skill (Ex. 3.3).

Two of Barnett's later operas—*Fair Rosamund* and *Farinelli*—were performed at Drury Lane, but in 1841 he moved to Cheltenham and his two last operas (a third, *Marie*, was left incomplete) remained unperformed. *Fair Rosamund* (produced on 28 February 1837) was longer, and stylistically more diffuse (or adventurous) than *The Mountain Sylph*, with its echoes of Rossini, Auber, and even of the canonic quartet in *Fidelio*.[15] But Barnett was beginning to run out of steam, both as a composer and as a theatre manager, and he could no longer compete in the world that revolved around Michael William Balfe. Even so, *The Mountain Sylph* enjoyed several revivals and foreign productions.

Although Loder had two more operas produced at the English Opera House before Balfe's *Siege of Rochelle* appeared at Drury Lane in 1835, it was Balfe who dominated the rest of this first decade. Of Irish birth, and a baritone who had sung in Italian opera in Paris, Milan, and Palermo

---

[13] Musical examples of stage works are drawn from the 1st edn. of the vocal score unless otherwise noted.

[14] Biddlecombe, 78; this aria leads straight into the Sylph's aria 'Deep in a forest dell'.

[15] Biddlecombe, 83, and his Ex. 5.19.

Ex. 3.1

(a)

continued

Ex. 3.1, continued

Allegretto scherzando

Ex. 3.1, continued

(b)

John Barnett, Overture, *The Mountain Sylph*: vocal score (London, [1834]): (a) pp. 1–2; (b) p. 5

(where his own first opera was produced), Balfe was more fully acquainted with the latest Italianate idioms than either Barnett or Loder and adapted them more skilfully to the needs of opera in English. It would be more difficult to identify a personal voice in his music, and he could be tiresomely eclectic, but he worked hard at the English ballad idiom and produced a handful of immensely popular songs of that type. He was less fortunate in his librettists than Barnett or Loder, and was himself notoriously insensitive to verbal accentuation. Yet he offered the English operatic stage a professionalism and consistency that it had previously lacked—a professionalism sharpened by his continuing to write operas in Italian (*Falstaff*, 1838, for Her Majesty's, and *Pittore e Duca*, 1854, for Trieste) as well as in French (*Les Puits d'Amour*, 1843, and *Les quatre fils Aymon*, 1844, both for the Opéra Comique, and *L'Étoile de Séville*, 1845, for the Opéra itself: he had in fact assimilated the French operatic manner long before then).

The Siege of Rochelle (Drury Lane, 29 October 1835) was immensely successful, as its librettist Edward Fitzball later recalled.[16] While its idiom is predominantly Italianate, it is not unaffected by that of *Der Freischütz*. The overture inhabits the world where Weber and Rossini meet, though its 'second subject' is pure Rossini—a welcome change from the bland 'contrasting' themes of less fluent composers. The opening of the first-act finale is also Rossinian, with its repeated semiquavers and its element of mock

---

[16] E. Fitzball, *Thirty-five Years of a Dramatic Author's Life*, 2 vols. (London, 1859), ii. 25; cited Biddlecombe, 103.

Ex. 3.2

Ex. 3.2, continued

When en-chant-ing fair   shall I be-hold a - gain that form be-witch-ing

which must e-ver reign   Fix'd firm   in Do-nald's all be-wil-der'd brain.

Andantino

Art   thou   a   form   of

continued

Ex. 3.2, continued

mor - tal birth   With charms___ so wond'-rous fair   so wond'-rous

fair.

John Barnett, 'Poor Jessie', *The Mountain Sylph*: vocal score (London, [1834]), pp. 61–2

horror (see Ex. 3.4); but Clara's ballad-like air 'Mid the scenes of early youth' has echoes, faint but detectable, of Agathe's *Cavatine* 'Und ob die Wolke' from *Der Freischütz* (see Ex. 3.5). The ensembles are convincingly handled within the limitations imposed by the technique and experience of the singers, and even the scenario is free of the inconsequentialities and improbabilities so often associated with the libretti of Fitzball himself and Alfred Bunn.

Balfe did not always repeat this success, though he persisted with English opera throughout the course of his life: there are twenty-one in all, not including the English versions of his French operas. He worked quickly, sometimes revising material from his foreign works, and this fluency undoubtedly led him into carelessness and to an overemphasis on the potential market for the resale of single numbers. Nevertheless he was responsible for the only two surviving all-sung operas in English from the period covered by this chapter, which argues for his underlying seriousness of intent.[17] The problem with these was the need to compose a substantial

---

[17] See n. 1 above. The vocal score of *Catherine Grey* does not include the recitatives: they are in the autograph score, Brit. Lib., Add. 29329–30.

Ex. 3.3

Fare-well for e — ver Since doom'd to sev — er To o-ther

climes _____ I _ fly To na - tive bowers _____ To once lov'd

flow — ers With them, with them to fade and die Too fa - tal

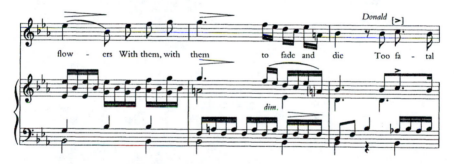

beau — ty What faith or du — ty Can e'er op - pose, op - pose thy _

continued

Ex. 3.3, continued

John Barnett, 'Farewell for ever', *The Mountain Sylph*: vocal score (London, [1834]), pp. 72–3

Ex. 3.4

continued

Ex. 3.4, continued

Ex. 3.4, continued

William Balfe, 'Father Azino' (Finale Act I), *The Siege of Rochelle*: vocal score (London, [1836]), pp. 112–13

amount of recitative. The difficulties were not all due to Balfe himself: he had written recitatives for his own earlier Italian operas (including *Falstaff*), and subsequently supplied them for *Fidelio* at Her Majesty's and for *La*

Ex. 3.5

Ex. 3.5, continued

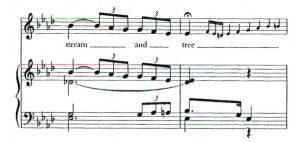

stream _____ and ____ tree

William Balfe, 'Mid the scenes of early youth', *The Siege of Rochelle*: vocal score (London, [1836]), pp. 59–60

Zingara, his own adaptation of *The Bohemian Girl*.[18] But his earlier Italian recitatives were essentially of the traditional Rossinian type; the newer manner, cultivated both in Italy and in French *grand opéra*, involved continuously 'accompanied' declamation in a less predictable, often more *arioso* style. Even Donizetti and Bellini did not always succeed in managing this stylistic transition. Balfe was further hindered by his librettists' lack of expertise, and in particular their inability to create a suitably flexible verse-form for recitative. In response to criticisms of his word-setting, finally, it could be said that he probably expected considerable freedom of delivery.

Catherine Grey and *The Daughter of St Mark*, however, also suffered from faults of construction and improbabilities of scenario, and neither found their composer in his best form. *The Maid of Artois* (1836), written for the popular soprano Marie Malibran, scored him a second success, while in *The Bohemian Girl* (1843) he reached the peak of his fame. The enthusiastic reception given to this opera was due above all to its ballads, in particular 'When other lips' and 'I dreamt that I dwelt in marble halls', written for William Harrison and Elizabeth Rainforth respectively. But it is in general a colourful and lively score. The overture, in A major/minor, is formally intriguing. After an introduction based on the theme of 'I dreamt that I dwelt', the first subject, in A minor, is based on a supposedly Hussite song.[19]

[18] As previously noted, *Fidelio* had been given in German in 1832. Recitatives were required for its revival in Italian in 1851 (Her Majesty's and Covent Garden) and in 1854 and 1855 (Covent Garden: Chorley, ii. 132, 144, 210, 217). A copy of the first edition of the full score (Paris, 1826, German and French texts) with recitatives to Italian texts added by hand, mostly by Balfe, is in the Brit. Lib., Add. MS 34226. (*Der Freischütz* was also given in Italian, as *Il franco arciero*, at Covent Garden in 1851, presumably with recitatives.) There were two versions of *La Zingara* (Trieste, 1854, and Paris, 1869): the autograph full score of the latter, entitled *La bohémienne*, is in the Brit. Lib., Add. 29336. Cf. Biddlecombe, 129.

[19] But actually by Joseph Knoff and popularized by Liszt in 1840. Biddlecombe, 110, and his Ex. 7.16, p. 243.

But because it begins with a chord of C major there is an air of tonal ambiguity: the second subject is in G, and the preparation for the recapitulation is a very emphatic dominant seventh of C. A most unusual feature is the lengthy solo for 'corno bassetto', in F, as an introduction to another ballad, 'The heart bow'd down' for bass, which is in G flat (see Ex. 3.6).[20]

After *The Daughter of St Mark* in 1844 and a number of other not particularly successful efforts, Balfe's fortunes revived with *The Rose of Castille* in 1857. The French element is stronger than before, though without displacing the Italian altogether; in fact, given the strong reliance on Italian idioms in French opera, it might be truer to say that Balfe had fully absorbed the (non-Teutonic) international style of his day. Like all his remaining operas (except for the operetta *The Sleeping Queen*) it was written for the Pyne–Harrison English Opera Company, which in the 1857–8 season occupied the Lyceum Theatre; Louisa Pyne was a far more accomplished singer than most of the sopranos previously available to Balfe, and this is celebrated in the virtuoso writing for the part of Elvira (some of it borrowed from his own Parisian opera *L'Étoile de Séville*).[21]

Balfe's last six completed operas in fact represent an Indian summer for the ageing composer, one in which his style and approach developed little but in which his fluent musicianship never deserted him. It is often hard to pinpoint a precise model for a particular episode, even when the writing points unequivocally to an inherited tradition, as in this trio from the Act II finale from *The Puritan's Daughter* (1861) (Ex. 3.7). If his facility and his desire to entertain led to the sacrifice of dramatic intensity, it can nevertheless be said that he, more than any other, established English Romantic opera in its 'classical' form.

We should return briefly to the younger Loder, whose career was cut short by a tragic illness. After *Nourjahad* he enjoyed little success until *The Night Dancers*, produced at The Princess's Theatre in 1846. In his Germanic training Loder had more in common with Barnett than with Balfe, and he lacked the acumen which enabled Balfe to found his reputation in opera. He was obliged to earn his living by composing popular ballads in large numbers (though some of them are actually rather good), and some of his operas—*Francis I* (1838) in particular—are nothing but a string of separate numbers around which a plot was subsequently hung. The same could be said of many of his contemporaries, but the promise of *Nourjahad* could not be entirely suppressed. Loder became manager of the Princess's in 1846 and immediately took the opportunity to display his real strengths. *The Night Dancers* is far from perfect, but it shows real dramatic imagination. George

---

[20] Sung by Borrani, for whose convenience the awkward modulation from F to G flat was presumably designed. A later popular version of this song bowdlerized the Neapolitan progression in the final phrase.

[21] This is the case with the celebrated *Rondo mauresque*: Biddlecombe, 119.

Ex. 3.6

continued

Soane's libretto was based on the German myth of *Giselle*, but its real impetus came from the ballet of that name with music by Adolphe Adam, first heard in London in 1842.

It would be difficult to interest a modern opera audience in this tale of dreams and supernatural spirits (the Wilis), even though Puccini used it in his first opera (*Le Villi*, 1884), and tolerable though it may still be in ballet; but Loder's music has real dramatic force, particularly in the ambitious finale to Act I, in which Giselle meets her death. Giselle's 'Grand Scena', 'I dreamt

Ex. 3.6, continued

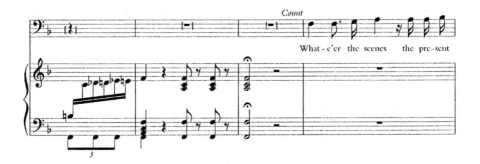

(1) Misprinted as ♭

Ex. 3.6, continued

scenes of past ___ de - light. The

heart, bow'd down by weight of woe, To weak - est hopes will cling;

William Balfe, 'Whate'er the scenes', *The Bohemian Girl*: vocal score (London, [1843]):
(*a*) p. 183; (*b*) pp. 184–6

we stood before the altar', had both Continental and English precedents (the
form of the *scena* was normally recitative, slow air, interlude, and faster air);
its opening idea is reproduced in the 'intrada' to Act II, where the scene is
that of Giselle's tomb. Here the arrangement of harmonies in a sequence of
rising thirds is perhaps somewhat mechanical, but it embodies the spirit of
early German Romantic opera, the source of inspiration for Wagner himself
(Ex. 3.8).

In 1851 Loder moved to the Theatre Royal in Manchester, where his
Raymond and Agnes was given in 1855. He returned to London, by now
seriously ill, but managed to revise the opera for production at St James's
Theatre in 1859. It is an ambitious and musically effective work, at least in
part, though its elaborate scenario is not altogether convincing (the libretto
is lost).[22] The main section of the overture is a powerful allegro in 12/8 time

Ex. 3.7

Ex. 3.7, continued

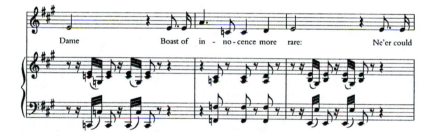

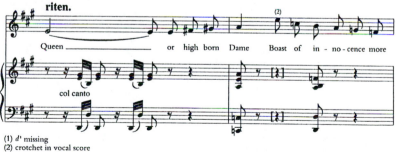

(1) *d'* missing
(2) crotchet in vocal score

continued

Ex. 3.7, continued

Ex. 3.7, continued

William Balfe, 'What man worthy of the name', *The Puritan's Daughter*: vocal score (London, c.1862), pp. 219–21

(D minor). The finale of Act II is in three sections and incorporates an effective quintet as a middle section in the flat submediant key (B major in relation to E flat).[23] Not only is this reminiscent of Italian practice; it also prefigures the telling quintet from the Act I finale of Wallace's *The Amber Witch*.

Apart from an operetta, *Never Judge by Appearances*, composed in Manchester and performed in the same London season as *Raymond and Agnes*, Loder produced no more operas. His last four years were spent in a coma. His life was a tragedy of lost opportunities as well as in a personal sense; yet in his two best operas he demonstrated a genuine gift for a dramatic idiom in an amalgam of the German and Italian styles.

Sir Julius Benedict, a native of Germany, was even more solidly teutonic in outlook, though this did not prevent him from adopting a thoroughly Italian style in his early Italian operas (he produced three while in Naples, where he worked from 1825 to 1834). His earlier English operas are not of any great interest, but *The Lily of Killarney* (1862), based on Boucicault's play *The Colleen Bawn*, has been highly praised. One interesting feature is the use

[23] Biddlecombe, 95; quoted ibid. 225–6; also, from MS full score, in *BHMB*, v. 324–7 (Ex. 14.3).

Ex. 3.8

(a) **Allegro agitato**

I dreamt we stood be-fore ___ the Al – tar, With joy - ous

hearts and lips that fal – ter,

Ex. 3.8, continued

E. J. Loder: (*a*) 'I dreamt we stood before the altar'; (*b*) *Intrada*, Act II, *The Night-Dancers*: vocal score (London, *c*.1847): (*a*) p. 62; (*b*) p. 163

of an Irish folk-like idiom for the peasants and a more sophisticated, predominantly Germanic one for the gentry, who are in dramatic conflict in the plot. The convention is suspended for the elaborate *scena* in which the hero's faithful servant resolves to murder the peasant girl to whom the hero is secretly married: here the idiom is broadly Italianate though this is discarded for the cantabile 'The Colleen Bawn', where local colour again prevails (Ex. 3.9). But there is a certain stiffness in the musical phrasing and harmony that prevents the work, thoughtfully constructed though it is, from making the most of its potential.

Much the same may be said of the operas of George Macfarren (1813–87). His German-based training (with Cipriani Potter at the newly founded Royal Academy of Music) is evident in his earlier works and gave him the technical assurance that led ultimately to his principalship of the Academy and to his knighthood as a pillar of the musical establishment. His later

Ex. 3.9

Jules Benedict, 'The Colleen Bawn', *The Lily of Killarney*: vocal score (London, *c.*1862), pp. 164–5

operas, not to mention his cantatas and oratorios, often embody a self-consciously national style that makes him an important precursor of the founding figures of the 'English musical renaissance'. His main success amongst several later works for the stage (including two so-called *opere di camera, Jessy Lea* and *The Soldier's Legacy*) was *Robin Hood* (1860), but here again the rather four-square style and the self-conscious nationalism (of a politically liberal type) are something of a hindrance. One instance of musical humour may be noted in the course of a lengthy two-section 'song' for the Sompnour, as it must be one of the first to use falsetto to denote the ironic imitation of a woman's voice (Ex. 3.10); the lurch back to the natural voice is amusingly handled. The nationalist element is maintained in his two last operas, *She Stoops to Conquer*, based closely on Goldsmith's play, and *Hellvelyn*, both produced in 1864.

Ex. 3.10

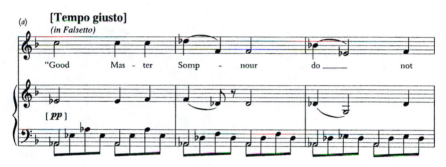

continued

Ex. 3.10, continued

G. F. Macfarren, *The Sompnour's Song* from *Robin Hood*: vocal score (London, *c.*1860): (*a*) p. 46; (*b*) pp. 47–8

We may finally consider William Vincent Wallace, an Irishman who travelled extensively before settling in London in 1845, when his opera *Maritana* was produced at Drury Lane. Though somewhat eclectic, the idiom is predominantly Italianate, above all in the characteristic *cantabile-cabaletta* aria 'This heart by woe o'ertaken' from the third act. *Lurline* (1860) is a far finer work, and perhaps the most inventive of all the operas of the 1860s. Based on the *Lorelei* legend that had attracted Mendelssohn shortly before his death, it contains some imaginative musical scene-painting. The overture, one of the best of its type, certainly carries overtones of Weber (for example in the opening for four horns), but it is almost reminiscent of Berlioz's early style in its boldness and vigour. There is a fine orchestral introduction to Act III, in F sharp minor, a key which returns later in the act to describe the rushing waters of the Rhine, and a long *scena*, 'Sad as my soul' (composed, like much of Act I, as early as 1847 but an effective vehicle in 1860 for Louisa Pyne). *The Amber Witch*, though less successful at the time, is almost as good; the libretto, however, despite being the work of the censorious Chorley, is as feeble in diction as anything by Fitzball, the librettist of *Lurline*. The overture is imaginative and ambitious, and the opera is noteworthy for having more extended musical scenes than was usually the case: the overture and the first four vocal numbers, for example, together make up a single unit in E flat. The Act I finale is long and elaborate, incorporating the quintet already referred to. The opera ends with a brilliant rondo for the heroine, though this was surpassed by that of Balfe's *The Puritan's Daughter* later that year.

Wallace's other late operas are rather facile, shorter works (though a number of others remained unperformed). Yet despite a tendency to court easy popularity, both his works and Balfe's show a surer instinct for theatrical effectiveness than those of Benedict or Macfarren. Unfortunately the absurdities of plot and the almost complete failure of the librettists to forge a viable operatic mode of discourse make the staged revival of any of these works, except on an experimental basis, more or less unthinkable. Despite this, the Pyne–Harrison company achieved in the late 1850s and early 1860s something that had eluded all previous idealistic ventures in English opera, namely the establishment of a genuine, if short-lived, tradition of commercially viable works. One priceless advantage was a guarantee of fine singing, mainly from Pyne herself, something previously only intermittently available to English opera. With the demise of this company, the production of serious opera in English came virtually to a halt for the time being.

Of course the musical theatre of the day did not depend entirely on the most ambitious forms. As we have already seen, the musical theatre of the nineteenth century up to 1834 was largely of a trivial kind, notwithstanding the use of the term opera and the production in English adaptations of some influential masterpieces, in particular *Der Freischütz* and *Fidelio*.

An important figure of this period was Lucia Elizabeth Vestris (1797–1856), the deserted wife of a French dancer of Italian extraction. She was primarily a gifted contralto singer, but she was also a 'straight' actress, and theatrical manager at the Olympic Theatre (1831–8), Covent Garden (1839–42), and Lyceum Theatre (1847–55), the last two together with her second husband Charles Matthews (1776–1835). In addition to singing in a number of demanding Italian roles and in Weber's *Oberon*, she cultivated the 'lower' forms of musical theatre with considerable success.

The usual catch-all term for these forms was 'burletta'; other names for them were 'burlesque' (more strictly parodic) and 'extravaganza'.[24] Their principal purveyor was James Robinson Planché (1796–1880, of Huguenot descent), a versatile man of letters who amongst other things wrote the

---

[24] 'Burletta' was a term employed for productions with at least five songs in each act, thereby qualifying them for performance at the minor theatres. As a result it was used for a wide variety of genres, even Shakespearean adaptations. See *Oxford Companion to the Theatre*, s.v. 'Burlesque'.

libretto for *Oberon* and a number of English adaptations of foreign operas. He specialized in the extravaganza, which proved to be an ideal vehicle for 'Madame Vestris', though he also wrote burlesques for her and others. The scores were rarely if ever the work of a single composer. At an early stage the composers included such figures as Barnett, Bishop, and Horn. The purloining of the music of popular composers (such as Balfe) was frequent, and when later on new music was written it was rarely by composers of distinction. The burlesque survived as a dramatic form into the 1880s, by which time completely new scores had become the norm; by then, however, it was under increasing pressure from operetta on the one hand and music-hall entertainment on the other. Music-hall itself developed in the 1850s and 1860s as a form of entertainment in rooms (the 'music halls') attached to taverns, but its real expansion came only in the following period.

The operetta as a distinctive genre also came into being during the 1850s and 1860s, though the term was rarely used and the form is not easy to define. In the eighteenth and early nineteenth centuries light comic operas were generally played as interludes (between the acts of a more serious piece) or as afterpieces. The term may be applied to light operas in which there is a higher proportion of spoken dialogue to music and an undemanding plot: there are clear examples by Loder (*Never Judge by Appearances*, 1859), Macfarren (*Jessy Lea*, 1863, and *The Soldier's Legacy*, 1864), and Benedict (*The Bride of Song*, 1864). But operetta in its English form did not really come into its own until Sullivan began to produce his little masterpieces in the 1870s.

Oratorio and Cantata

It can at least be said of the 'English' contribution to this nation's musical theatre that it fulfilled a valuable public function. The texture of theatrical life was such that despite its variety and range, managing, writing, composing, and performing were closely interwoven. Opera from abroad, whether adapted and sung in English or not, was enjoyed by an increasing proportion of society, but it did not displace the native product. One cannot say the same of concert life, except at the level of the music-hall. Where English music prevailed, as it did in oratorio and cantata, the forms themselves had become parochial; in the instrumental genres the homegrown element was an increasingly alien and specialized one, and even the inclusion in otherwise serious concerts of popular English songs bespoke a provincial attitude to programming.

It has been suggested in a penetrating essay[25] that a great many of the oratorios, cantatas, and part-songs of the mid-Victorian era were the

---

[25] S. Banfield in *BHMB*, v. 14–15; cf. also W. J. Gatens, *Victorian Cathedral Music in Theory and Practice* (Cambridge, 1986), ch. 2, 'Morality, singing, and church music'.

product of a crusade to improve the moral outlook of the middle and working classes. It was certainly the popularity of communal singing at all levels that encouraged their composition, while the pious form so many of them took confirms the increasing influence of a Calvinist intellectual élite. The combination of a morally uplifting social activity with the desire to give concert-going the aura of virtue resulted in the Victorian oratorio, performed by amateur choral societies (usually with a professional or semi-professional orchestra) and attended by a self-satisfied bourgeoisie. Their primary focus was the provincial music festival, though in due course the major centres could count on the permanent availability of a choral society capable of a high level of music-making. (Such societies are of course a continuing valuable feature of our musical life, having survived the complete collapse of the conditions that brought them into being.)

We have seen already how the abandonment of dramatic form and even much narrative interest, combined with the deadly sententiousness and feeble diction of the librettists, had brought the oratorio to a low point irrespective of its composers' talents. Social changes, too, had resulted in the decline of the secular ode; only in a few specialized contexts, such as the ceremonies for the installation of university chancellors, did it live on for a while. Its successor was the secular choral cantata, a concert genre without serious social function.

The older composers of this period—Crotch, Clarke-Whitfeld, Bishop, and Barnett—adopted an oratorio style modelled on that of Handel, lightened by reminiscences of Haydn and sometimes also of Mozart, Beethoven, and Schubert. Clarke-Whitfeld's *Crucifixion* and *Resurrection*, published as a single work but produced in instalments in 1822 and 1825 at Hereford, where he was organist, exemplify the limitations of the genre. Some of the arias, like those in his anthems (see above, Ch. 2), are agreeably picturesque, though this can be taken a bit too far, as with the clucking noises at the words 'even as a hen' in the aria 'O Jerusalem, Jerusalem'. The story is carried on through words selected and 'adapted' from the four gospels, with solo recitatives and arias and 'dramatic' choruses, though there is no equation between the characters and the choice of solo voice. One senses that Clarke-Whitfeld may somehow have become acquainted with Bach's Passions and possibly others in the German tradition, but the comparison is rendered odious through the C-major jollity of the 'crowd' choruses and a general air of the inappropriate: the final chorus of *The Crucifixion* even ends with allelujahs.

Clarke-Whitfeld was really out of his depth in oratorio, as William Russell had been before him. Barnett had a much better sense of the musically appropriate, but his *Omnipresence of the Deity* is saddled with a dreary libretto by Robert Montgomery, who specialized in verse of this kind.[26] The work is really an extended cantata (though described as an oratorio on the title-page of the vocal score); it seems in any case not to have been performed.

Bishop's *The Seventh Day* (1834), on the other hand, a work that has been praised for its 'enjoyable vulgarity', really was called a cantata: the words are taken from Book VII of *Paradise Lost*. Its picturesqueness is of a more controlled kind than Clarke-Whitfeld's, and if it is unashamedly Haydn-esque in places, there are worse models. There is some imaginative scoring (such as the use of four cellos to accompany a section of recitative) and harmony (augmented sixths at 'temper'd soft tunings', powerful unisons at 'Thee that day thy thunders magnified' (Ex. 3.11).[27] Bishop must have been

Ex. 3.11

[26] Even so, it hardly warrants inclusion within the scope of Temperley's remark, 'His sacred music is grotesque' (*NGD*). The MS full score appears not to be extant: the MS vocal score is in the Boston Public Library.

[27] The printed full score advertised on the vocal score seems not to have been published, and I cannot locate the MS: observations on scoring are based on MS indications in the vocal score (copy in Bod. Lib.). There are some comparable felicities in Barnett's *Abraham on the Altar of his Son* (1823).

Ex. 3.11, continued

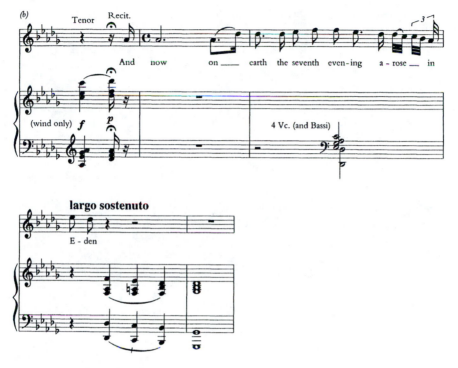

continued

pleased with its reception, since he followed it up with *The Departure from Paradise* (based on Milton's Book XI), for solo voice and orchestra, two years later; and his oratorio *The Fallen Angel* was given in Oxford in 1839.[28]

Crotch's second oratorio to be called *The Captivity of Judah*[29] was composed between 1812 and 1815, though it was finalized only in 1828 and not heard until 1834, when it was put on at Oxford during the celebrations for the installation of the duke of Wellington as chancellor. It is no more advanced than *Palestine*, but the biblical words are a help, and there are some imaginative touches of scoring and harmony. Such qualities are also evident in the ode 'When these are days of old', written for the same occasion to words by John Keble. The task was evidently a struggle for poor Keble, who as Professor of Poetry was obliged to carry it out, but Crotch was in his element, writing a short sharp dominant seventh to represent the shot that brought down the 'vulture' (Ex. 3.12), and directing

---

[28] Not published; MS in Stanford University Library, California.
[29] For the first, a juvenile work, see Ch. 2, p. 110.

Ex. 3.11, continued

Ex. 3.11, continued

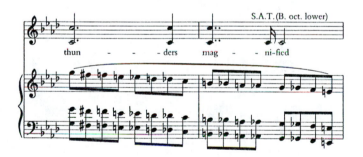

H. R. Bishop, *The Seventh Day*: vocal score (London, *c*.1835): (*a*) p. 10; (*b*) p. 10; (*c*) pp. 11–12; (*d*) pp. 14–15; instrumental indications from MS annotations to copy in Oxford, Bod. Lib., Tenbury Mus.c.232 (16)

the timpanist at one point 'no note—let down to imitate Cañon' [*sic*]: this in a score in which the bass is figured throughout.[30]

---

[30] There is even some recitative accompanied by figured bass alone, a tradition also still current at the Italian opera in London.

Ex. 3.12

William Crotch, Ode, 'When these are days of old' (Keble) (London, 1834), p. 40

The professors of music and poetry were similarly employed in 1853, when the earl of Derby was installed. This time Bishop and the Revd T. L. Claughton were responsible. Bishop managed a charming introduction, complete with horn calls, harp arpeggios, and a sustained melody for the cellos, but even he was defeated by having to set the first sixty or so lines of Claughton's execrable verse as accompanied recitative. The odes by composers such as W. S. Bennett and S. S. Wesley for openings of the North London Working Men's Industrial Exhibition represent a change of style: Wesley's work of 1864 has a somewhat Beethovenian character, though it descends in places to the level of the glee; in any case it is paralysed by W. H. Bellamy's insufferably didactic text.[31]

There are two or three odes by Frederick Arthur Gore Ouseley (1825–99), who also contributed to a late flowering of the traditional oratorio style in his *Martyrdom of St Polycarp* (1854). This was his 'exercise' for the Oxford doctorate of Music; by the time he had it published (in 1855 in full score, possibly at his own expense) he had become Professor in succession to Bishop.

Ouseley was a remarkable man: a child prodigy who had composed a Metastasian opera at the age of eight, even before he had learnt to read music;[32] an idealist who did much to rescue the Anglican cathedral tradition from complete extinction; and a baronet who became an Anglican priest as well as an Oxford MA and D.Mus., Professor of Music, and writer on musical subjects. We shall have occasion to return to him more than once.

The Martyrdom of St Polycarp is indeed in many ways as traditional as its composer's gentlemanly temperament would lead one to expect. Its idiom is the usual blend of Handel, Haydn, and Mozart, but with a strong admixture of Mendelssohn. At the bottom of the score is a part for 'cembalo ad lib.', though it is really just a fairly serviceable reduction of the full score. In addition some of the choral movements call for organ support for the voices (as in, for example, Brahms's *Requiem*), aided in this case by a little bass figuring. But the real significance of this score lies in its extraordinarily passionate character. The subject may have been suggested by the prominence given to the study of the Fathers by the Tractarians:[33] the eyewitness account of St Polycarp's death in the second century is an important early patristic text. The libretto is, most unusually at this period, dramatic in form, and the double chorus for the most part represents Christians and pagans in opposition. It is not at all a distinguished libretto, but it did offer the composer the essentials of a dramatic conflict.

The work is above all a masterpiece of naïve art. The problem with the naïve treatment of a serious subject is that it will give the sophisticated cause for unseemly mirth, even where the musical idiom as such is unexceptionable. For example, it is disconcerting to be reminded of the Commendatore's appeal to Don Giovanni to repent in the scene in which the Proconsul of Smyrna tries to persuade Polycarp to renounce Christ (see Ex. 3.13).

---

[31] Bennett also wrote, in the same year as his Industrial Exhibition ode (1862), another for the installation of the duke of Devonshire as chancellor; the very last such example of which I am aware was Stanford's in 1892 (Cambridge). Bennett's work is lost, except for a minuet reused in his 5th symphony and preserved in its original form in an organ arrangement by Charles Steggall.

[32] So Gatens, *Victorian Cathedral Music*, 149; though the inference, from the fact that he was said to have been able to improvise whole scenes and that the (piano-accompaniment) score is not in his hand, may not be entirely correct. The MS is in the Bodleian Library, Tenbury 1087a: apart from anything else, it displays an ear for Italian word-setting that can have arisen only from prolonged immersion in the style.

[33] For the Anglo-Catholic Tractarian movement see below, p. 241.

Ex. 3.13

F. A. G. Ouseley, *The Martyrdom of St Polycarp* (London, 1855), pp. 70–1

Here it is the reversal of roles that makes the resemblance unintentionally amusing;[34] at other times we may be struck by the undercharacterization of

[34] There is also a hint of Caspar's aria in Act I of *Der Freischütz*: the martyrdom was itself considered a triumph, this time of good over evil.

pagan malice or by a superfluity of surface energy in an essentially bland idiom. In these ways it is a successor to Clarke-Whitfeld's diptych; but it succeeds, where the latter does not, by virtue of its dramatic integrity and an inner conviction that cannot but command respect.

No mid-century composer of oratorio could have escaped the influence of Mendelssohn, whose *St Paul* was given its first English performance at the Birmingham Festival in September 1837, and whose *Elijah* was first performed there, in August 1846. These works are narratives based on a selection of scriptural texts, a form which with a greater or lesser admixture of non-scriptural additions was to remain standard until Elgar reverted (temporarily) to the setting of a dramatic poem. The stylistic influence varied from composer to composer: it is less marked, perhaps, in Michael Costa (*Eli*, Birmingham Festival, 1855) and Hugo Pierson (*Jerusalem*, Norwich Festival, 1852), but it is pronounced in Bennett. Costa, of Italian birth, was an impresario and opera conductor whose *Eli* is a solitary masterpiece much overlaid with Italian operatic idioms;[35] Pierson, like Benedict (*St Peter*, Birmingham Festival, 1870) was more in tune with the older German tradition of Beethoven, Weber, and Spohr, whose *Last Judgement* had also been influential in England over a long period. (Pierson had actually emigrated to Germany in 1844, though without relinquishing his links with England.)

William Sterndale Bennett (1816–75) apparently regarded Mendelssohn as the only legitimate post-classical model, though some of his earlier piano music is markedly Schumannesque. In the sphere of sacred concert music, however, the Mendelssohnian manner predominates, and that in its least appealing form. *The Woman of Samaria* (Birmingham Festival, 1867), described as a 'sacred cantata', is a narrative based on John 4: 5–42, with choruses and airs to other biblical words added. There is also an introductory chorale, and a free setting of the hymn 'Abide with me'.[36] The narrative is given to a contralto and the words of the woman to a soprano; the words of Jesus, however, are introduced by the bass voice of the soloist himself. One would probably tolerate the narrative recitative more readily if the inserted movements showed any spark of life, but their tone is predominantly reverent and elegiac, even in defiance of the sense of the words.

One could hardly describe *The Woman of Samaria* as worthless, since Bennett was a good craftsman whose only fault was a dread of the operatic. This shows even in *The May Queen* (Birmingham Festival, 1858), a 'pastoral' for which the libretto, by Henry Chorley, is at least nominally dramatic in form. One could forgive Chorley's inadequacies more readily if he had not previously been so critical of Alfred Bunn, but the genre was one in which

---

[35] His *Naaman* (Birmingham, 1864) is much less successful.

[36] Whose author, H. F. Lyte (d. 1847), is not acknowledged in the vocal score. (Lyte also wrote a little-known tune for this hymn.)

sentimental gadzookery was virtually inevitable. Bennett prefaced it with the excellent Mendelssohnian overture *Marie du Bois* (1843–4), but the rest of the work is tame stuff. Both it and *The Woman of Samaria* achieved immense longstanding popularity, however, and may be considered as the narrative prototypes for the later Victorian secular and sacred forms respectively. Their success was surely due to Bennett's skill in writing straightforwardly but effectively for solo and choral voices, and in conforming to the current standards of taste and respectability.

Orchestral Music

While many of these choral works were first heard at a provincial music festival (that of Birmingham being the most significant), others were written for performance in a regular concert season, a context to which the more successful festival works were also transferred. London's concert life was revitalized by the formation of the Philharmonic (later the Royal Philharmonic) Society in 1813.[37] The society was responsible for a renewed interest in the orchestral music of German composers (notably Beethoven, whose Ninth Symphony it commissioned), and its programmes included chamber music, cantatas, and songs; but it also encouraged the composition of orchestral music by English composers. Clementi, Cramer, and Crotch were amongst these to begin with, later Cipriani Potter (1792–1871), George Macfarren, and W. S. Bennett. (These three, like Crotch, all became principals of the Royal Academy of Music, though in every case their best work preceded their appointment. Even the little-known Charles Lucas (1808–69, president 1859–66) wrote several symphonies in the years before his presidency.) Most of them (including Cramer) also wrote piano concertos, and there are descriptive concert-overtures, often on Shakespearean subjects, by Potter, Macfarren, and Bennett.[38]

Of these composers Potter was essentially a late classicist—his G minor symphony 'no. 12' is forcefully reminiscent of early Schubert, although his *Tempest* overture (1837) is more maturely Romantic.[39] In Macfarren and Bennett a Mendelssohnian influence is readily apparent, both in 'abstract' and in descriptive music. Bennett is rightly admired for his early piano concertos and for a few concert-overtures such as *The Naiads* (1836); his later music is less successful, though the G minor Symphony no. 5 (1864/7)

---

[37] See C. Ehrlich, *First Philharmonic*.

[38] A few works by T. A. Walmisley survive in MS, including a 'Second Organ Concerto' (RSCM), a late survivor of a dying breed.

[39] His *Antony and Cleopatra* overture was intended to precede the play, but may never have been so used. In this era of elaborate incidental music (Sullivan's music for *The Tempest*, originally written in 1861 on a speculative basis, is a good example), it is sometimes difficult to establish the composer's intention. Macfarren's overture to *Romeo and Juliet* was eventually used with the play for a time, as was the whole of Sullivan's *Tempest* score on at least one occasion.

is interesting for its Schumannesque attempt at continuity between the movements.[40] Macfarren was also an instinctively conservative composer: he produced in all nine symphonies, seven concert-overtures, and four concertos for various instruments.

In general, English orchestral music fared less well after the middle of the century. Standards of performance improved dramatically with the appointment of Costa as permanent conductor of the Royal Philharmonic Society's orchestra (1846–54), and there were innovations such as the promenade concerts (1841–59) organized by the flamboyant Louis Jullien (1812–60), the formation of the New Philharmonic Society (1852–79), and the still more durable series of concerts at the Crystal Palace in Sydenham (south London), conducted by August Manns (1825–1907) from 1855 to 1901. A series of popular concerts was started at St James's Hall in 1858, and in the same year Charles Hallé founded his own orchestra in Manchester. Much of this activity was entrusted to foreign-born musicians, and while not unsympathetic to the claims of English composers, they were (with the exception of Jullien, whose programmes included a good deal of light entertainment) primarily interested in establishing and developing a sound tradition of performing the teutonic classics.

The only younger composer in this period who showed real promise— alas unfulfilled—of becoming an orchestral composer of distinction was Arthur Sullivan (1842–1900). A symphony, a cello concerto, and two overtures came out in the years 1866–7, and in 1870 he produced his sparkling *Overture di ballo* for the Birmingham Festival.[41] After that, however, he wrote no purely orchestral music, and the native tradition had to await revival by younger and less precocious figures.

Chamber Music

Much the same is true of the chamber music of the period. There is, however, an important difference in that composers were more likely to write speculatively, as it were, for small ensembles in the hope of public or private performance. Chamber music had long been a feature of public concerts, and this continued to be the case for some time. Public concerts devoted solely to chamber music are reported to have begun only in 1835, though this by no means spelt the end of miscellaneous concerts.[42] Even so,

---

[40] This continuity was established in the revision of 1867, represented in the published score (Leipzig, [1872]: facs. in The Symphony, E VII, pp. 105–273); a third, slow, movement was also added at this stage, the work having originally been performed as 'Allegro, Menuetto, and Rondo Finale'. For the minuet see above, n. 31.

[41] The score of the cello concerto is lost, but a reconstruction has been made on the basis of the surviving solo part (which includes orchestral 'cues').

[42] BHMB, v. 382, citing N. Temperley, 'Instrumental Music in England, 1800–1850' Ph.D. diss. (University of Cambridge, 1959), 92–103.

the opportunities offered for the public performance of indigenous chamber music were not very considerable, partly because of the competition from foreign works and partly because of a strong preference among audiences for music involving instrumental display, whether solo or ensemble. Many of the best efforts of English composers at this time, therefore, are likely to have been heard privately if at all—for example at the concerts of the Society of British Musicians, founded in 1834.

For the reasons given, chamber music with piano was more likely to win a wider audience than music without. In any case, a firm foundation had been laid in the works of this kind by Storace, Attwood, and Pinto, together with the foreign-born leaders of the 'London pianoforte school', Cramer, Clementi, and others. Samuel Wesley's very charming Trio in F, for two flutes and piano (1826), represents a somewhat old-fashioned debt to Mozart,[43] while Potter's three *Grand Trios*, Op. 12 (1835), one of which is for clarinet, bassoon, and piano, owe more to Beethoven. Bennett in turn exhibits the technical developments associated primarily with Mendelssohn, namely an increased brilliance and a greater flexibility in the handling of the relationships between the instruments. His sextet in F sharp minor for the unusual combination of piano, string quartet, and double bass, Op. 8 (1835) is an ambitious work on a large scale, while the splendid Trio in A (Op. 26, 1844) owes much to Schumann; indeed the headlong triplets of its finale carry a distinct echo of the finale to Schumann's *Concert sans orchestre*, though the medium permitted a technically simpler piano part. The *Sonata Duo* for cello and piano, Op. 32 (1854), is again on a large scale; its passionate lyricism is a gift to cellists, and it is hard to understand why a such work once again made readily available should not take its place in the standard repertory.[44] If Bennett has a fault it is in the tendency towards a *moto perpetuo* treatment of figuration in the fast movements—a rather Schumannesque failing, perhaps, but also one in which he anticipates Fauré to some extent. A liking for retaining the same key-note in each movement of a multipartite work, as in the present sonata, may also be traced back to Schumann.

Apart from the inevitable offerings of entirely minor composers, we may note the interesting quintet in G minor by George Macfarren (1843), written for the same instruments as Schubert's 'Trout' Quintet (piano, violin, viola, cello, and double bass), a couple of smoothly written works by Balfe—a cello sonata and a piano trio—and, less expectedly, a flute sonata by Loder.[45] Bennett's real potential successor was again Sullivan, whose *Duo*

[43] Ed. H. Cobbe (MC 12; London, 1973), from Brit. Lib. Add. 48302; first published *c*.1830.

[44] This work and the Trio are in Sterndale Bennett, *Piano and Chamber Music*, ed. G. Bush (MB 27; London, 1972). Schumann's *Concert*, in F minor, was published as a three-movement work in 1836; in 1853 it became his third sonata, somewhat revised but with one of its original five movements restored.

[45] Royal College of Music, MS 2272: the MS lacks the final page (*BHMB*, v. 389).

concertante for cello (1868) is in a single large movement. But here too the early promise remained unfulfilled.

The string quartet was cultivated throughout this period, largely one must assume through personal enthusiasm, since the opportunities for public performance and widespread appreciation were rare. Henry Bishop wrote a good Mozartian specimen early on in his career (1816); there are three by T. A. Walmisley, one by Potter, five by Macfarren (the last dating from 1878), and two rather conventional ones by Ouseley, published in 1868 (and another that remained unpublished).

Solo Piano Music

Apart from the later works of Clementi and Cramer (which include Clementi's *Gradus ad Parnassum* and a number of sonatas by both composers), the main contributions to the solo piano repertory in this period are those by Potter and Bennett.[46] Quite a number of minor figures wrote interesting pieces, as did others better known for other achievements (such as Loder, Balfe, Wallace, and S. S. Wesley); but only Potter and Bennett can stand comparison with the best of the foreign composers whose music was published in London and who resided there for longer or shorter periods of time. The most important of these was Ignaz Moscheles (1794–1870), who lived in London from 1825 to 1846. His main significance was as a pianist of formidable virtuosity, but his compositions also show a strong sense of classical form and harmony. Frédéric Kalkbrenner (1785–1849), who lived in England from 1814 to 1824, also helped to enhance the technical horizons of English-born composers, while Mendelssohn through his several visits and a number of influential publications in London achieved an ideal balance of brilliance and sentiment that was widely admired and imitated.

Potter built on the technical foundations of Clementi and Cramer, while his musical thought was also influenced by the Viennese classics. He composed three piano sonatas early on in life (the best of which, Op. 4 in E minor, was published in Leipzig but not in England) and a certain amount of salon music; but his finest achievement is undoubtedly the two books of *Studies . . . in all the Major and Minor Keys* (Op. 19, 1826), 'composed for the use of the Royal Academy of Music'. Though their classicism recalls that of Cramer (*Eighty-four Studies*) and Clementi (*Gradus ad Parnassum*, published in London, Leipzig, and Paris in three parts, 1817–26), it exceeds even the latter in its technical demands. What is evident throughout is the unity of technical idea and musical substance. Like the studies of Chopin, which in some respects the set seems to prefigure, there is poetry even in the most

---

[46] Much of the material mentioned in this section is published in annotated facsimile in The London Pianoforte School (LPS). For the references, see under individual composers in the Bibliography.

fleet-footed, while some of the slower ones (those, for example in A minor and B flat minor) have a truly captivating lyricism. Potter also shows an attentiveness to technical problems in Beethoven's music (the E flat major study, for example, recalls the figuration of the second movement of Op. 78), either directly or through the medium of Beethoven's pupils, Czerny and Ries.[47]

Bennett was a student of Potter at the Academy, and his earliest works (such as the *Six Studies*, 1835, later reissued as Op. 11) were composed while he was still a student there. His burgeoning Romanticism is apparent in the *Three Musical Sketches*, Op. 10, and *Three Impromptus*, Op. 12, both of 1836: here the influence of Mendelssohn is mainly apparent. By the time of his first major work, the sonata in F minor, Op. 13 (first published in Leipzig, 1837), despite its dedication to Mendelssohn, an indebtedness to Schumann cannot be mistaken: as with the Trio in A, the model seems to be Schumann's *Concert sans orchestre* in F minor, published the previous year.[48] Bennett never again equalled this passionate, extended composition in a solo piano work, though the *Suite de pièces*, Op. 24 (Leipzig and London, 1842) comes close to it in the creative use of bravura. He continued to write attractive music in an 'international' Romantic idiom during the 1840s and 1850s, after which the flow virtually ceased. The late sonata *Die Jungfrau von Orleans*, Op. 46 (1873), based on Schiller's drama, is an interesting curiosity, but hardly more than that. The second movement, 'In the Field', is an eccentric reflection of the Schumannesque march idiom as seen, for example, in the middle movement of the *Phantasie*, Op. 17, while the first movement carries an occasional echo of Chopin (Ex. 3.14).

A number of other composers, such as Loder, Benedict, Balfe, and Macfarren, contributed to the Romantic piano repertory in a small way, while the short-lived Francis Edward Bache (1833–58) showed promise of finer things to come. Minor figures like Samuel Wesley, William Horsley (1822–76) and Walter Macfarren (1826–1905) wrote respectable salon music, and there are a few works by composers better known as organists: S. S. Wesley and the redoubtable W. T. Best (1826–97), for example, not to mention the virtually unknown Edmund Thomas Chipp (1823–86), organist of Ely cathedral from 1866 until his death.

Solo Organ Music

The solo organ repertory should itself be considered here, as it was by no means an exclusively ecclesiastical genre. A number of publications in the 1810s and 1820s, in any case, were advertised as 'for organ or pianoforte';

---

[47] Ferdinand Ries (1784–1838)—pupil, assistant, and biographer of Beethoven—lived in London from 1813 to 1824, where he made a considerable impact as a composer and pianist.

[48] Cf. above at n. 44.

Ex. 3.14

W. S. Bennett, Sonata, *Die Jungfrau von Orleans* (London, 1873), 1st mvt., p. 4

one recalls the *Concertos* (*c*.1815) of Camidge, the *Three Voluntaries* (*c*. 1815) of Samuel Webbe jun. (*c*.1770–1843), and the *Six Fugues* (*c*.1820) of Thomas Adams (1785–1858). Adams was an enterprising and is still too little-known a composer, very much in the tradition of William Russell and Samuel Wesley, particularly as a writer of fugue. Indeed the six fugues mentioned— his earliest published work—are just that, each one being prefaced with the words 'Introduction ad libitum'. The twelve organ voluntaries of 1824 (four books of three each) make a virtue of their (somewhat Mozartian) intro- ductions, while the *Six Organ Pieces* (*c*.1830, dedicated to Attwood) and the *Grand Organ Piece* (also *c*.1830, dedicated to the 'Minister of St. George, Camberwell', where he was organist) show a greater flexibility of design. Adams was undoubtedly influenced by the fugues of J. S. Bach, by the complex chromatic harmony to be found in the later Mozart (not least in the slow sections of his pieces for mechanical organ), and by the ornamental Classicism that we find not only in late Mozart but also in some of the nocturnes of Field, in the voluntaries of Webbe just mentioned, and in Beethoven and Schubert.[49]

The first of the *Six Pieces*, for example, offers a fine Bachian fugue in C minor, a C major *andante* in 3/4 of the Mozartian type, and a second fugue with a livelier subject that eventually combines with that of the first fugue in close stretto. *The Grand Organ Piece* consists of a C minor Mozartian introduction in 3/4, a 'rococo' sonata *allegretto* in C major, 4/4, and a double fugue based on the subject of the *allegretto*.[50] The only weakness in this and some other works of Adams is in the grandiose conclusion, which relies on weight of organ tone rather than on musical working out for its effect.

This fine native tradition, based on a love of complex part-writing and full manual textures, reached its culmination in the organ music of Samuel Sebastian Wesley. Like his father, Samuel Sebastian was a true original. Knowledgeable of Bach, of Mozart, and of his English heritage, he blended all three into a highly personal mixture that revealed itself in many different forms and genres. His organ music is small in quantity but of considerable merit. It centres around the two sets of *Three Pieces* (1848, 1868) for a chamber organ—though in fact they are not at all unsuited to the traditional smaller church organ with limited range and power in the pedals.

The first set includes the famous *Choral Song*, a splendidly crafted piece of pageantry, with its somewhat less convincing fugue, and the expansive Andante in F, which carries the 'rococo sonata' style to extremes. In the *Second Set*, the Larghetto in F sharp minor and the Andante in E flat are both fine pieces, the former with its wistful melody and the latter with its

---

[49] Cf. e.g. Field, Nocturne no. 14 in C, itself related to Beethoven, Op. 31, no. 1 (2nd movement); Mozart, Quartet in D, K. 499 (3rd movement); Schubert, Sonata in G, D. 894, Finale.
[50] *English Organ Music*, ed. R. Langley, vi. 27–42 (no. 5).

ingenious spinning out of Mozartian material. A brief extract from each of the three statements of the opening theme of this piece will serve to illustrate Wesley's compositional ingenuity: the strange third chord of the second statement arises from a plan to have the bass descending in thirds, while in the third statement the same chord (with seventh added) arises out of a descending semitonal scale in the bass (Ex. 3.15). Amongst the

Ex. 3.15

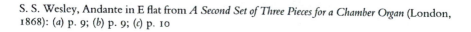

S. S. Wesley, Andante in E flat from *A Second Set of Three Pieces for a Chamber Organ* (London, 1868): (*a*) p. 9; (*b*) p. 9; (*c*) p. 10

Ex. 3.16

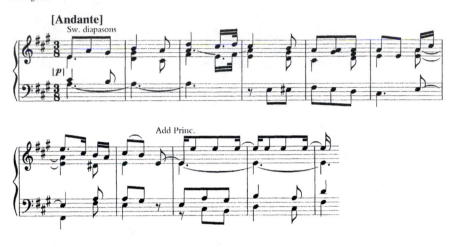

S. S. Wesley, *Andante (in A) for the Organ* (London, *c*.1880), p. 2

posthumously published pieces, an Andante in A owes more perhaps than is healthy to the slow movement of Beethoven's Second Symphony, but disarms criticism through the originality of its large-scale structure and a recurrent wistfulness in its harmony (Ex. 3.16).[51]

Nothing by Adams or either Wesley quite parallels the extraordinary Op. 1 of the short-lived Egerton Webbe (1810–40), a *Prelude and Fugue in A major... With a Part for the Pedal Obligato*, published in 1837.[52] From the very first arpeggio in C sharp minor, any concept of tonal stability seems irrelevant to the composer's thought. Otherwise there is little to be said for the increasing amount of humdrum material being published. The replacement of church gallery orchestras with harmoniums and even small pipe organs in parish churches called for the publication of a great quantity of simple music with and without pedals. Meanwhile ever larger instruments were being installed in the cathedrals and in the town halls; a standard Continental compass was adopted in manuals and pedals, but instead of a return to classic principles of design, more and more effort was put into the imitation of orchestral and other 'effects', for the accomplishment of which ever more ingenious devices were needed: additional manual divisions, couplers, combination pistons, and a novel 'pneumatic action'. The repertory of solo music, apart from the ubiquitous improvisation, came to consist very largely of orchestral transcriptions, which were especially favoured in

[51] Ibid., x. 59–73 (no. 9: the last of an anthology of pieces by S. S. Wesley).
[52] Ibid., ix. 55–68 (no. 9).

the town halls as a substitute for the expense of maintaining an orchestra. A revival of serious organ music had to await the arrival of Parry, Stanford, and Elgar, for the last of whom the organ was indeed a quasi-orchestral medium.

Song

'English song 1815–70' is above all the story of the ballad, although some songs cannot sensibly be so described. 'Ballad' is a term of very wide application, but in general it remained, as it always had been, the favoured word to describe a strophic poem whose stanzas are sung to the same music. Not all so-called ballads fit that description precisely, and there are strophic songs that are not so called. There are a number of 'subtexts' for the definition of a ballad: one of them refers to a simple homely style (in both words and music), another to the telling of a tale in verse. These are sometimes applicable over and above the general definition, but the term did not yet carry a pejorative connotation. If some ballads fall below our own perception of good taste, that is not because they are ballads but because no form of art operates at a constant level or is immune to a lowering of standards for the sake of popular appeal.

Critical judgement is in any case a highly subjective affair, and many a song that would at one time have fallen foul of prevailing opinion might now easily pass the test of a more catholic aesthetic. Some of the most popular songs of their day—Balfe's 'When other lips', for example—are among the best of their kind. This song raises the important question of the relationship of the ballad to the theatre, to the role of the singer associated with it, and to the commercial exploitation of its qualities, above all its potential for sentimentality. These factors eventually brought the ballad low and gave it a bad name—but not for the time being. There had long been a fruitful interaction between the theatre and the detachable song—particularly in England where spoken dialogue 'spaced out' the musical numbers in most forms of theatre. By far the majority of published songs from 1660 to (say) 1860 either originated in the theatre or acquired a connection with it. The vocal scores of theatrical works (and full scores were hardly ever published) were basically collections of vocal pieces that could be run off separately if they offered the chance of independent sales.

The role of the singer was vital. In the days before recordings and broadcasts, the name of the singer on the title-page was the key to the song's worth and the indispensable encouragement for amateur singers to buy it. An origin in the theatre offered the necessary initial publicity, and even the most serious operas depended on the inclusion of a few simple songs, both to enhance their own success and as a detachable product that would justify the expense of engraving a complete vocal score. Singers then came to be paid a fee—a 'royalty'—whenever they sang a particular song on the stage or in a concert, a system that enhanced its popularity and generated further sales. So was born the publisher's 'ballad concert'—those of John Boosey began in 1867—and the ultimate degeneration of the form into a vehicle for tawdry sentimentality. Once that had happened, serious composers had to abandon the term.

A good deal of ballad verse was new or recent, but this was not always so. Shakespearean adaptations, such as those by Reynolds with music by Bishop, called for Shakespearean or quasi-Shakespearean songs; the Caroline lyrists (notably Herrick, author of 'Cherry ripe') and other seventeenth- and eighteenth-century poets were called into service for non-theatrical songs; and more recent poetry, for example by Shelley and Tennyson, was set both in ballad style (whether or not the term was used) and in more complex forms. These were sometimes designated by such terms as 'cavatina' (generally for a song in ternary or rondo form) and 'canzonetta', which usually implied a formally well-developed song in the Classical mould and with important material in the accompaniment. On the whole, however, the use of specialist terminology diminished as time went on.

The Irish poet Thomas Moore (1779–1852) exerted a strong influence on English song-making and on the musical preferences of the non-expert. He was a composer of tunes (though he needed help with the accompaniments) and exercised the profession of poet in some of the usual ways, but his real métier was the writing of new verses to existing tunes. His three collections were *A Selection of Irish Melodies* (ten numbers and a supplement, or five vols., Dublin and London, 1808–34, and numerous later issues and editions), *A Selection of National Airs* (six numbers, 1818–28), and *A Selection of Sacred Songs* (two numbers, 1816–24). Of these the *Irish Melodies* were by far the most significant. Moore's collaborators were the Irishman Sir John Stevenson (1761–1833), himself a composer of songs and glees, and later Henry Bishop. His melodies were drawn from good sources (notably Bunting),[53] and though they finally emerged with the civilizing gloss of introductory symphonies and polite harmonies, the resulting combination of exoticism and homely sentiment offered a distinct *frisson* within an unexceptionable framework.

To some extent Burns and Scott had done something similar for Scots song, though they had mingled adaptations of the anonymous originals with their entirely new creations. But although many Scots melodies became favourites in England, the genre did not transplant well, partly at least because of the primitive accompaniments given in Johnson's *Scots Musical Museum*,[54] partly because of Scott's own lack of interest in the melodies, and

---

[53] E. Bunting, *A General Collection of the Ancient Music of Ireland*, vol. i (London, [1796]); a second volume, misleadingly labelled 'Vol. 1st', appeared in 1809, and a third, *The Ancient Music of Ireland*, in Dublin in 1840.

[54] 6 vols., Edinburgh, 1787–1803.

partly because of the lack of a commercial link with London. The efforts of George Thomson (1757–1851) to popularize the tunes in settings by Classical composers also failed in the end, this time because the settings did too much violence to the character of the tunes.

Moore was also enormously influential though his *Lalla Rookh*, a sequence of four verse tales linked by a prose narrative. Both the tales individually and their linking narrative became the subjects of operas (in England and elsewhere), while short passages of the poems were used as song-texts. The book itself was published in May 1817 and had passed through at least six editions by the end of the year; and songs based on it began to be published almost immediately.

Moore encapsulated in his work that affinity with the exotic that had already led to the collection (and publication in London) of many Scots and Irish songs, to the publication of 'ancient ballads' and the like, and to the eighteenth-century Celtic fraud, the poems of 'Ossian'.[55] If he did not inaugurate popular orientalism, he certainly gave it an impetus that later produced two further outstandingly influential works: E. W. Lane's (slightly bowdlerized) translation of *The Thousand and One Nights* (3 volumes, 1839–41), and Edward Fitzgerald's *Rubáiyát* [i.e. quatrains] *of Omar Khayyám* (1859, anonymously).

Thomas Attwood was amongst those captivated by *Lalla Rookh* when it first appeared: there are four songs of his to words from it, all of them showing an individuality that takes him well beyond his apprentice manner as well as his experience of writing the theatrically commonplace. *The Fire-Worshippers* (its title is that of the third poem, from which the lines it sets are taken) deals in a tender and solemn manner with the perennial theme of lovers mismatched in religion and culture (Ex. 3.17). In this and a few other songs there is a hint of a talent never fully exploited, though it found some outlet in his later church music.

John Clarke-Whitfeld is another whose track record would not predispose one to anticipate great things in song; yet his underlying Classicism is put to good expressive use in such things as the canzonet 'One struggle more' (Byron) and the songs in his *Twelve Vocal Pieces* (c.1817).[56] John Barnett's *Lyric Illustrations of the Modern Poets* (1834) aims a good deal higher: these are lengthy through-composed pieces in a well-assimilated early Romantic style. They were not, however, a great commercial success; the

---

[55] J. Macpherson, *Fragments of Ancient Poetry* (1760), *Fingal* (1762), and other works, purportedly translated from the Gaelic of 'Ossian son of Finn'. At best these can have been only marginally related to Gaelic originals and were vigorously denounced by Samuel Johnson; but they were enormously influential on Romantic poetry in England and Europe. More poetically respectable were Byron's *Hebrew Melodies* (1815), to melodies arranged by J. Braham.

[56] *English Songs 1800–1860* (MB 43), no. 7. Other songs by Attwood, Clarke-Whitfeld, and two of Barnett's, are included in this volume.

Ex. 3.17

Ex. 3.17, continued

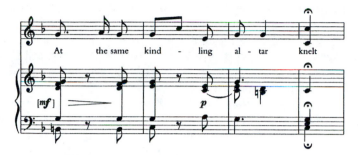

Thomas Attwood, *The Fireworshipper* (London, *c*.1817), pp. 3–4

composer rather naïvely expected the original plates to be intact when preparing a second edition in 1877, but they had already been reused.

John Liptrot Hatton (1809–86) also set out to do justice to fine poetry, in this case of the seventeenth century, in his *Songs . . . by Herrick, Ben Jonson, and Sedley* (1850). 'To Anthea', from this collection, was long one of the most popular songs in the language, notwithstanding its noisy accompaniment of repeated chords. Another popular song of the period was Balfe's 'Come into the garden, Maud'—a setting of one of Tennyson's less happy efforts, and whose appreciation has suffered since. In fact it is a well-made piece with an imaginative vocal line (the use of the 7th degree in an accentuated position in the first bar is an example of a technical novelty that later became associated with weak sentimentality).[57]

Another famous Tennyson setting was Wallace's 'Sweet and low'[58] (though not as famous as Joseph Barnby's part-song was to become). But the most prolific songwriter of the opera composers was Loder, partly because he was bound by a notorious contract to write one song every week for his publisher. It has been widely assumed that anything written under such conditions must be *ipso facto* beneath consideration; but while Loder's very best songs (such as the haunting *Lamentation*[59] from his series of separately published *Sacred Songs*) are indeed exceptional, his craftsmanship and his feeling for an effective vocal phrase rarely deserted him. If when taken *en masse* they are not a wholly persuasive monument, that is due at least in part to the inferiority of many of their texts.

It would be a great mistake, in any case, to overlook the frankly popular songs, by composers virtually unknown today, that were published in

[57] Ibid., nos. 19 (Hatton), 17 (Balfe), with another by each composer.
[58] Ibid., no. 23.
[59] Ibid., no. 26.

enormous quantities during the middle years of the century. A trifle like Thomas Pettman's 'Good Bye' is charming light music of a kind about which even the most partisan enthusiast has not had a great deal to say (Ex. 3.18). J. M. Jolly, described on the title-page of *A Set of Six Songs of the Wild Flowers of Spring* as 'Composer, Leader, & Musical Director, at the Surrey Theatre', was another composer of the same kind, but there were scores of other similarly employed professionals.

The successors of Clarke-Whitfeld, Barnett, and Hatton were such figures as Bennett, Macfarren, and Pierson (or Pearson, as he was originally known). Essentially they continued in the German Romantic tradition first exploited by Barnett, adopting in turn the idioms of Mendelssohn and

Ex. 3.18

Thomas Pettman, 'Good Bye' (London, *c.*1840), p. 2

Schumann. As usual, Macfarren cuts a relatively prim figure in this company, though he conveys a fine sense of desolation in his setting of Shelley's *The Widow Bird*, with its haunting clarinet obbligato (the idea of which, but hardly its application, may have come from Schubert's *Der Hirt auf dem Felsen*).[60]

Henry Hugo Pierson (1815–73) lived more or less permanently in Germany from 1843, apart from a brief and unsatisfactory period as Reid Professor in Edinburgh (1844). In a sense he became an adoptive writer of lieder, publishing them in the Continental fashion as small collections of up to six songs (as opposed to the English fashion of publishing single songs or, occasionally, sets of twelve). Yet he almost invariably set English texts in the first instance and published them with the English and German words. It is perhaps in his imaginative and fully integrated accompaniments that he most consistently avoids the triviality of much contemporary song, in this respect following the tradition of Barnett, though it has to be said that Loder, and even Balfe and Wallace, occasionally achieved equally artistic results.

Bennett's songs were originally published in similar fashion (mostly in Leipzig like those of Pierson), though he never settled in Germany. His earlier songs (and he published very few after 1855) are exquisitely judged, essentially Mendelssohnian affairs; again the integration and coherence of their accompaniments is a strong feature.

One striking failure by English composers was that they did not emulate the song-cycle, either of the loosely linked Schubertian type or the more fully integrated kind cultivated by Beethoven and Schumann. Collections of songs like Barnett's *Lyric Illustrations* pursued a literary aspiration rather than an emotional theme; in this they are closer to Hugo Wolf's collections, but their songs lack the epigrammatic qualities that would have enabled them to count as 'cycles' in that sense. And one can hardly put Jolly's *Wild Flowers* into the category of serious artistic endeavour.

Music for Vocal Ensemble

There was a large repertory of piano-accompanied vocal duets, almost always for female voices, and even trios and quartets; and a still larger repertory of glees, madrigals, and part-songs for unaccompanied voices. Glees were now often (and to a certain extent had previously been) written for mixed voices, but the genre was, to a much greater degree than the other forms, a multi-sectional one in which the successive strophes of a poem were usually given contrasting treatment.[61] Madrigals, on the other hand,

---

[60] Ibid., no. 25; this volume also includes several other songs by Loder, and by G. A. Macfarren, Pierson, and Bennett.

[61] Cf. Ch. 2 n. 117: written piano accompaniments became more usual in this period. Cf. also Gatens, *Victorian Cathedral Music*, 94, citing W. A. Barrett, *English Glee and Madrigal Writers* (London, 1877) and *English Glees and Part-Songs* (London, 1886).

were generally single movements in a contrapuntal idiom supposedly based on that of the Elizabethans. One of the best practitioners of this form was Robert Lucas Pearsall (1795–1856), whose imitations of the style are sufficiently distinctive (or insufficiently exact, depending on the point of view) for them to count as individual creations rather than as pure pastiche (in the modern sense of that word).

As for the part-song, it is really a catch-all term that only emerged as a separate genre after the distinctive features of the glee and the madrigal had gone out of fashion (though there was to be a revival of pseudo-madrigalianism in the twentieth century). The unaccompanied part-song (the term is also applicable, however, to songs for chorus and orchestra) flourished on the back of the sight-singing movement of the 1840s and beyond; it was from the outset a choral genre (the glee and the madrigal having become so by fashion rather than by musical necessity); its musical simplicity and its generally high moral tone were adapted to the needs of singing classes rather than of the more upper-class glee clubs and madrigal societies. Eventually the admission by madrigal societies of women (as opposed to boy treble and male alto) singers and the custom of duplicating the parts made the musical distinction a rather pointless one, but the Victorian part-song was in origin a more democratic genre.

Although the unaccompanied choral part-song reached artistic maturity only in the following period, it exerted an enormous influence on other forms. The choral idiom of the middle and late Victorian oratorio and cantata depended on it (the sequence of orchestrally accompanied part-songs is a near relative of the cantata); it infiltrated the choral element in opera (where the prevailing idiom had been Italianate); and it affected the style of the church anthem and even the congregational hymn. All this was a result of the enormous popularity of the adult singing-class movement, which enabled amateurs in due course to supplant professionals entirely in innumerable choral societies up and down the country and to form mixed parochial choirs (though the Tractarian movement also introduced surpliced choirs of boys and men into some parish churches). Even in opera the idiom had the advantage of facilitating amateur performances, an activity that began to appear during the following period. In all this, music and a kind of puritanical moral earnestness went hand in hand: it was by no means confined to apologists for the established church (of whatever theological persuasion), but also embraced the dissenting tradition and even scientific rationalism, for which a non-ecclesiastical outlet for the maintenance of public morality had its attractions. Beside the established forms of prayer and praise, therefore, emerged a sanitized admiration for nature, a carefully controlled access to springtime revelry, and the deification of productive work. We have already encountered these in the larger forms: it was in the choral part-song and some other simple vocal types (including 'national' songs) that their assiduous cultivation began.[62]

Church Music

The tradition of cathedral music was at first immune from these developments, since its texts were drawn almost exclusively from the Bible and the *Book of Common Prayer* and since its contrapuntal and freer forms were developed rather than replaced. The music that was published in the earlier nineteenth century as fit for parochial use was often a simplified form of cathedral music: the technical freedoms characteristic of some eighteenth-century parochial anthems and metrical psalm-settings were gradually eliminated as incorrect and hence unworthy, so that both the anthems and services of the more ambitious parishes and the metrical psalmody that they all shared came once more to depend on approved cathedral models and on long-standing professional practice respectively. Only towards the end of the period can one begin to speak of a distinctly parochial repertory once more, this time technically unexceptionable and the work of centrally trained composers, allied to the new hymnody of which we have spoken. Here the dissenting tradition played an important part, as did Roman Catholicism both in its own right and as an influence on an appreciable segment of Anglican opinion.

Of the older cathedral composers who continued to compose after 1815, only Attwood developed his style further. Two major works were his coronation anthems for George IV ('I was glad', 1821) and William IV ('O Lord grant thy king a long life', 1831), both with orchestral accompaniment (a similar anthem for Queen Victoria was left incomplete at his death). In general his later works, both anthems and service-music, have a greater degree of continuity than he had previously espoused. He was one of the first to exploit a form of choral unison recitation,[63] later a standby of S. S. Wesley, and to write out an idiomatic organ accompaniment in choral and ensemble sections. But he never entirely abjured the Mozartian idiom of his younger days, though he developed it in ways that can be paralleled elsewhere in Catholic liturgical music both foreign and English (which he could have encountered at embassy chapels and through contacts with Vincent Novello). Whatever its exact origin, the idiom is seen at its simplest in the famous 'Come Holy Ghost', a treble solo written, it is said, in the carriage on the way to an ordination at St Paul's on Trinity Sunday, 1831. Quite apart from its melodic charm, it is an ingenious treatment of the hymn-text, the four quatrains and two-line conclusion of which are rearranged to make

[62] For the sight-singing movement and its intellectual foundations see B. Rainbow, *The Land Without Music* (London, 1967), and the first two chapters of Gatens, *Victorian Cathedral Music*.

[63] e.g. in his anthem 'Enter not into judgement' (1834).

three six-line stanzas. This does less violence to the words than might be supposed, and eliminates musical monotony while preserving a hymnic form.

Attwood's cathedral music was published collectively in 1851 by his godson Thomas Attwood Walmisley (1814–56), himself a composer of cathedral music and Clarke-Whitfeld's successor as Professor at Cambridge. Walmisley was undoubtedly conventional by temperament, though he broke new ground in his ambitious anthem 'The Lord shall comfort Zion' (1840), where the influence of Mendelssohn's *St Paul* has been convincingly asserted.[64] The Evening Service in B flat, for double choir and organ (published in 1845), is a fine work of a more traditional kind, though it was for long surpassed in popularity by the (still familiar) Evening Service in D minor (1855). So very traditional is this in style that it has been held to be a deliberate archaism, a suggestion that is encouraged by the composer's use of material by Henri Dumont in the two Glorias but contradicted by the triple-time verse 'He rememb'ring his mercy', reminiscent of the era of Battishill and Attwood. On the whole it seems preferable to take the piece as an expression of its composer's natural language, and its final 'Phrygian-mode' cadence as the last word in a *prima pratica* that had never been entirely discontinued.[65]

John Goss (1800–80), though considerably older than Walmisley, was a far more adventurous composer, particularly in the composition of large-scale single-movement anthems in an extended sonata or comparable form. His best and most characteristic works belong to the 1850s and 1860s, though as a younger man he had been a versatile composer in many genres. It is, however, in style rather than in form that his work makes the transition to a properly Victorian idiom—an essentially diatonic style but divorced from the *prima pratica* through its free use of discord and a more declamatory approach to word-setting, even in a nominally contrapuntal context. It is here that one can point to the influence of the part-song, though the idiomatic range of a lengthy anthem is naturally much wider. But Goss also wrote some telling miniatures that are in all essential respects neither more nor less than sacred part-songs.[66]

Some of these characteristics held good also for S. S. Welsey, the most considerable of all the nineteenth-century composers of cathedral music (some would place him at the apex of the entire musical pyramid). But Wesley's musical character was a complex one and included traditional as

---

[64] Gatens, 110.

[65] Given complete in TECM, iv. 109–22. According to J. Bumpus, *A History of English Cathedral Music* (1908 edn., p. 471, cited Gatens, 115), the practice had arisen of reversing the two Glorias so as to end in the tonic! Despite the prevailing archaism, however, the organ part essentially is independent.

[66] Two such works—'If we believe that Jesus died' and 'O saviour of the world'—are in TECM, iv. 62, 69.

well as advanced traits. His approach to counterpoint, for example, was more rigorous than that of Goss, and insofar as it diverged from the cathedral model it depended on his knowledge of J. S. Bach and on the Fuxian tradition. His longer anthems are all multi-sectional, though often with a symphonic breadth and continuity that distinguishes them from their predecessors. He also preferred the old-fashioned F-compass organ and the unison singing of hymns and metrical psalms, for which he wrote some characteristically ebullient introductions and interludes.

Wesley's first two anthems[67] (and his first major compositions of any kind), 'The Wilderness' and 'Blessed be the God and Father', were written during his first appointment, at Hereford cathedral (1832–5), in 1832 and 1834 respectively. 'The Wilderness' was a memorable achievement for a young man of 22 who had been plunged into the decrepit world of a provincial cathedral of those days. It is rich in choral declamation, a style he can only have picked up from its more cautious use in Attwood, and while it is not free of naïvety it is a forceful and original piece. 'Blessed be the God and Father'[68] received what must have been an inauspicious first performance from an incomplete choir on Easter Day, 1834: stylistically it is very close to 'The Wilderness'. Wesley then moved to Exeter cathedral, where he spent seven unhappy years, and in 1842 to Leeds parish church, where he stayed until 1849. Conditions at Leeds did not materially differ from those at a well-ordered cathedral, following the acceptance by the vicar, Walter Hook, of the arguments promoted by the Revd John Jebb in favour of introducing the choral service in selected parishes. Indeed it could be said that the 'cathedral ideal' was more enthusiastically pursued there than in most cathedrals, the attitude of which was to induce Ouseley to found St Michael's College, Tenbury, in 1856. But Wesley moved to Winchester cathedral in 1849 and to Gloucester in 1865, where his death at the age of 66 finally concluded a turbulent career. He had been a tireless campaigner for reform 'from within', and had ruffled not a few feathers through his volatile and irascible temperament.

Unfortunately, Wesley was not by any reasonable yardstick a 'great' composer. He tried his hand at many forms outside those of the Anglican liturgy, but they all have a somewhat experimental character. So too do many of his anthems, but these are also characterized by an inherent conservatism that sits oddly with their superficial novelties. How far removed they are from the mainstream of musical development can be seen from the orchestral versions of 'The Wilderness' and one of his largest later anthems, 'Ascribe unto the Lord'. While the orchestration as such is

[67] Wesley's anthems are edited by Peter Horton in MB 57 (1990), 63 (1993), and in a third volume yet to appear. The second of these includes 'The Wilderness' and 'Ascribe unto the Lord' with their orchestral accompaniments as well as in their original form.

[68] Complete also in TECM, iv. 73–80, with three shorter anthems, 81–99.

irreproachable, their inventive shortcomings are more obvious in their orchestrally accompanied dress. While Wesley's reputation will always be sustained by miniatures such as 'Wash me throughly' and 'Thou wilt keep him in perfect peace', his career tellingly illustrates the final parting of the cathedral tradition from its European roots.

Conservatism and provincialism sat much more happily on the shoulders of Frederick Ouseley. His early brilliance and his freedom from financial care might have set him on a very different path, but his piety and his antiquarianism directed him towards the priesthood and the preservation of tradition in cathedral worship. Like Jebb's, his campaign for reform took a more practical turn than that of Wesley: his foundation at Tenbury was intended to preserve and develop what the cathedrals were in danger of losing. To it he devoted all the care and energy not demanded by his Oxford chair, building up a fine library to buttress his practical endeavours.

Ouseley's church music differs sometimes in technical detail but scarcely in underlying aim from composers as remote from him in generation as Crotch and Attwood. As with Goss, there are traces of Mendelssohn here and there, but even in the orchestrally accompanied anthems (of which several survive, apparently for use at Tenbury) there is little that at least conceptually would not have felt out of place at the beginning of the century.[69]

Although cathedral music had further to go before the century was out, it is fair to say that it had assumed a 'high Victorian' character by 1870, above all in the hands of John Goss. Unfortunately that transition was fated to lead into a cul-de-sac.

In a rather similar way, the many fine hymn-tunes that are one of the Victorian period's most significant legacies occupy a very small corner in the English musical garden. That is to say, their significance is primarily cultural rather than as a pervasive element in contemporary art-music as a whole, as the Lutheran chorale-melody had been for hundreds of years. The flavour of the Victorian hymn-tune requires a performance with choir, congregation, and organ, perhaps with an occasional unaccompanied verse. There can be a wide range of expression, because dynamic levels are indicated against the words of the hymns; the congregation can read and can be expected to 'pick up' a new tune quickly; some members of the congregation may have their own music books and may indeed sing a part other than the tune.

The Victorian hymn-tune reached its apogee in the last quarter of the century and can be looked at more closely in the next chapter. However, it

---

[69] Some of his later anthems, such as 'It is a good thing to give thanks' (Salisbury, 1889, with orchestra), are indeed more adventurous, though hardly innovative for their period (quoted in Gatens, 167).

had set into its pattern by 1870,[70] a pattern that was also imposed (against the views of Wesley, for example) on the large existing repertory of metrical psalm-tunes and others borrowed from the dissenting and Continental traditions. (The revivalist part-song, however, had a life of its own and may also have influenced, as it certainly infiltrated, Anglican hymnody.) A similar pattern was imposed on the cathedral chant repertory, where an approximation to speech-rhythm began to be attempted and to which parochial congregations were gradually introduced.

While both the introduction of cathedral-style worship into many parishes, and the development of Anglican hymnody, stemmed alike from the common ground eventually worked out between Tractarians and Evangelicals, there were also churches where a distinctly Anglo-Catholic ethos prevailed. The Tractarian movement, which took its name from a series of *Tracts for the Times* promoted and partly written by John Henry Newman in Oxford in the 1830s and early 1840s, emphasized what it saw as the 'Catholic' nature of the Church of England: a Catholicism often ignored in the past and threatened by recent and proposed political reforms, but which they held not only to be inherent in the Church of England but preserved there in a purer form than in the Church of Rome.

While the validity of this thesis at the deepest level is hardly a matter for this book, it may be said that its contradictions at the level on which it was then argued soon became apparent both to its opponents and to many of its proponents, some of whom did indeed convert to Roman Catholicism. The most spectacular, though not the earliest, of these conversions was that of Newman himself, and it encouraged the view that Tractarianism was but a back door to 'Romanism' in the Church of England. In the circumstances the development and survival of a strong Anglo-Catholic movement that drew much of its inspiration from the contemporary Roman Church is surprising: it was bitterly opposed by many, and its warmest supporters were always in danger of falling off (or 'going over'). Yet it survived, not only in an 'extreme' form but in ways that enabled it permanently to alter the centre of gravity, so to speak, in the Church of England.

One of the consequences was an 'ecclesiological' movement that insisted on (among other things) the exclusive use of Gregorian chant in worship, which in practice meant the adaptation of the responses, psalms, and canticles of Matins and Evensong, together with the Ordinary of the Mass, to English texts. The chief musical exponent of this view was the Revd Thomas Helmore (1811–90). In its extreme form such a movement

---

[70] Especially in *Hymns Ancient and Modern* (1861, with Appendix, 1868). Wesley's *The European Psalmist* (1872) contains over 600 tunes and first stanzas from a wide variety of sources, all harmonized in four parts, together with some service-music, chants, and short anthems; but it did not catch on, except as a source for other compilations. Wesley had earlier resisted a four-part format for hymns and metrical psalms.

was doomed to failure, but its influence was incalculable. Though opposed by many, the use of plainsong actually provided a link with the deepest layer of Anglican Cathedral usage as currently employed, that is in its chanted responses and prayers. Even Anglican chant (i.e. for the psalms) was ultimately grounded on plainsong, while on a different level Marbeck's newly revived music for the Communion service was itself a form of chant. In due course the idiom of chant became available for use in composed music, as it had never ceased to be in that of the Roman Catholic Church. Finally, it decisively enlarged the repertory of Anglican hymn-tunes through its adoption of numerous hymns translated from the medieval breviary.

At another extreme the Anglo-Catholic movement fostered the intro-duction of more elaborate forms of Continental church music, such as the Masses of Haydn, Mozart, and Schubert currently in favour in the Roman Catholic Church. The re-establishment of a Catholic hierarchy in England in 1850 decisively altered that Church's public profile, and a tradition of elaborate music was established at Brompton Oratory, as also, much later, at Westminster Cathedral. Anglican ecclesiologists also drew inspiration from Rome itself and (reflecting a different emphasis) from the medieval English liturgies. Altogether a not entirely digestible mixture of influences was being brought to bear on English parochial worship by the last quarter of the century.

Musical Thought and Scholarship

The main feature of advanced musical thought in the early and middle years of Victoria's reign was a move away from eighteenth-century utilitarianism, according to which music was essentially a recreation whose moral force, if any, was a reflection of the words set.[71] It is true that a moral usefulness continued to be claimed for music of the 'right' kind. Outside the Church itself, where its value continued to be a subject of lively debate, musical activity was, as we have seen, often thought of as a means of inspiring urban populations towards virtuous and productive lives. Here an almost Marxist praise of nature and of physical labour could supplant Christian ethics in certain cases, though this did not necessarily affect musical style. But in any case music could hardly be immune from the new agnosticism.

What this new era contributed above all, however, was an understanding of music as a form of communication in its own right, subject to its own laws and independent of accompanying verbal text. It cannot be said that

[71] I have adopted the word 'utilitarianism' in a non-technical sense here, although there is a link with the philosophical principle of utility—that which results in the greatest good of the greatest number—as expounded by J. Bentham and refined by J. S. Mill. Music could serve either innocent pleasure or the moral betterment of the individual, according to the 18th-c. view, and its success in doing so would be judged by the breadth of its appeal.

English writers were at the forefront of this intellectual development; they were, however, receptive to its European propagation, above all by the 'Leipzig' school headed by Mendelssohn and Schumann. Earlier English writers, such as Burney, had thought of music as a language whose purpose was to stimulate the 'affections', but they were unable to explain how it could do this. Crotch, whose lectures were not published until 1831, could still refer only to music's 'magic influence'.[72]

The most influential European thinker of the mid-century was Eduard Hanslick, whose book *Vom Musikalisch-Schönen* (*Beauty in Music*) was published in 1854 (though not translated into English until 1891). His most devoted English follower was Edmund Gurney, whose book *The Power of Sound* appeared in 1880. But Hanslick's denial of the necessity for expressive content in music—its significance being invested solely in its own actuality—was no doubt widely circulated before then and offered a philosophical basis for the cultivation of 'pure' music.

The Darwinist explanation of biological evolution (the idea of evolution as such was not new) stimulated the search for 'origins' in other spheres. In 1857—before the publication of *The Origin of Species*—Herbert Spencer produced an article on 'The Origin and Function of Music', deriving music from the 'natural' propensities of the human voice in the expression of emotion and seeing it as initially a heightening of speech. Interestingly, Darwin himself did not accept this theory; but the subsequent controversies in which Spencer continued to engage took place in the later years of the century.

On the whole, therefore, the mid-century was more significant for the birth and reception of new ideas and enlarged perceptions than for their systematic working out in full-scale monographs. It saw an enormous expansion of musical journalism and its growth in the columns of the daily press, which now began to claim a seriousness of purpose previously reserved for monthly and quarterly journals. The specialist musical journal, too, was invented: amongst the more significant to be started in this period were *The Harmonicon* (1832–3), edited by William Ayrton, *The Musical World* (1836–91), and *The Musical Times and Singing-Class Circular*, founded in 1844 and still running as *The Musical Times*. These were a vehicle for more penetrating criticism than could be accommodated elsewhere, though the two latter in particular also offered a lively commentary on the passing musical fashions of their day—whether they took them seriously or not.

The Musical Times was, as its full title indicated, the primary organ of the adult singing-class movement. A whole range of educational primers, the fruits of the teaching methods pioneered by Sarah Glover (1786–1867), the Revd John Curwen (1816–80), and John Hullah (1812–84),

---

[72] *Substance of Several Courses of Lectures on Music* (London, 1831), 64.

came into existence, aimed initially at children only but having the long-term effect of fostering the movement as a whole.[73] Large quantities of music were printed in tonic-sol-fa notation, with or without staff-notation in addition. Meanwhile the supplements of simple part-songs and anthems issued with *The Musical Times* came to occupy a major position in the operations of Novello, its publisher.

The theory of composition and its associated discipline of harmony developed markedly during the period. The decline in the practice of playing from a figured bass encouraged this, for books like Crotch's *Elements* (1812) had assumed its necessity as part of a comprehensive training in practical music. The primacy of counterpoint also gave way to that of harmonic theory as a basis for the technique of composition, as it already had done in Continental treatises such as those of Reicha. The basis of all such theory in the nineteenth century was a modified version of Rameau's theory of roots and inversions. *A Treatise on Harmony* by Alfred Day (1810–49), published in 1845, proved to be a controversial contribution, mainly because of its restriction of possible roots to three (tonic, supertonic, and dominant) in any key. Counter-intuitive though this seemed to be, it had the effect of emancipating the higher discords and could be said to have revealed harmonic potential more fully than conventional theory. Macfarren's warm support for it led to his resignation as Professor of Composition at the Academy, though when he later returned as Principal he was in a strong enough position to issue a second, revised edition (1885). His own books included *Rudiments of Harmony* (1860) and *Six Lectures on Harmony* (1867), which like Ouseley's *Treatise on Harmony* (1868) adopted many of Day's ideas.

It could be argued that the emphasis on the teaching of harmony had a markedly deleterious effect on musical composition, in England even more than in Europe. Contrapuntal writing had been one of English composers' great strengths up to about 1820, after which it survived mainly as an archaism for academic and church use. A rigorous training in Fuxian counterpoint, supplemented by the practical use of figured bass, had not only fostered skill in the contrapuntal forms themselves but had informed the conduct of the parts in all styles. Many composers—S. S. Wesley, Ouseley, Bennett, Sullivan, and others—continued to value counterpoint and to absorb it into their personal style; but the enfeebled idiom of so much church and other choral music from the 1840s onwards can surely be traced to a reliance on harmony for harmony's sake.

Musical history and scholarship, finally, made considerable progress during the period. It was difficult to challenge the massive achievements of Burney and Hawkins in the previous century—Hawkins's *History* was in

---

[73] The progress of the movement is chronicled in detail by Rainbow, *The Land Without Music*.

fact reissued in 1853 with annotations drawn from his own manuscript notes—and the contributions of Busby and Hogarth are largely based on them. But John Hullah took a notable step forward in his publications of 1862 and 1865, in which he adopted a 'periodization' of musical history that anticipates current usage.[74] Not only do his first three divisions correspond to our medieval, Renaissance, and Baroque (the fourth, or modern, period extended from 1750 to his own day); the whole concept of a periodization based on style was then still something of a novelty in England, though drawn in all probability from the burgeoning German school of historiography represented by Kiesewetter's *Geschichte der... Musik* (published in English in 1848).

Musical research—or musicology as we should now call it—was still in its infancy in the nineteenth century, notwithstanding the pioneering work of earlier writers, including Burney and Hawkins. Research into musical practice, ancient or modern, rubbed shoulders with acoustical investigations in a way that suggests a confusion of aims, if not on the part of the authors themselves then on that of the editors of journals, organizers of lecture-series, and other such enablers. Nevertheless, the investigation and interpretation of historical source-material bore fruit both in journals such as *The Harmonicon* and in the printing of older music in new editions. These latter drew away from their eighteenth-century prototypes, the cathedral collections of Boyce and Arnold, towards a more secular-orientated repertory, and from the antiquarian bias of Joseph Ritson and J. S. Smith (or of Crotch's *Specimens*)[75] towards the concept of the practical performing edition. E. F. Rimbault (1816–76), though a somewhat eccentric (not to mention acquisitive) personality, was a key figure in this development, with editions to his credit such as those of *Parthenia* (1847) and of the works of the English madrigalists in the publications of the Musical Antiquarian Society. His co-founder in this latter enterprise was William Chappell, whose historical interest was centred on the popular and national music 'of the olden time'.[76] Although much of their work has now been superseded and more exacting standards of scholarship introduced, the middle years of the nineteenth century saw a flowering of intellectual curiosity in matters musical that was surpassed only with the development of a stronger organizational infrastructure in the later nineteenth and early twentieth centuries.

[74] T. Busby, *A General History of Music* (London, 1819); G. Hogarth, *Musical History, Biography and Criticism* (London, 1835); J. P. Hullah, *The History of Modern Music* (London, 1862); *The Third or Transition Period of Musical History* [i.e. 1601–1750] (London, 1865).

[75] For Smith and Ritson, see Ch. 2, p. 171; Crotch, *Specimens of Various Styles of Music*, 3 vols. (London, 1808).

[76] See Ch. 8 below.

4

LATER VICTORIAN MUSIC AND THE 'ENGLISH RENAISSANCE', 1870–1914

Opera and Theatre Music

THE collapse of the Pyne–Harrison English Opera Company in 1866 was undoubtedly a setback, but it coincided with the passing of a tradition that had outlived its usefulness. Balfe and Wallace in particular had perfected a style of opera with dialogue that placed a high value on sheer entertainment: their pieces had supposedly serious but in any case romantic plots, and music that was sparkling or sentimental as occasion required. But the often threadbare dramaturgy and the sometimes comically stilted dialogue were beginning to pall, while the mid-century Franco-Italian musical idiom could not be milked for ever. The genre offered little opportunity for further development other than through Verdian pastiche; even in France, the vastly more gifted Bizet was initially unsuccessful in his bid to raise the level of *opéra comique* with *Carmen* (1875).[1] Similarly, the more Germanic idiom espoused by Barnett, Loder, and Benedict was incapable of further development except through the adoption of thoroughgoing Wagnerism. Middle and late Victorian audiences increasingly had the opportunity of hearing the latest masterpieces at Her Majesty's and at Covent Garden, admittedly in Italian for the most part even when the originals were not, but later on, especially under the management of Augustus Harris, 1888–96, in the original languages too.

One result of this greater accessibility of foreign opera to the music-loving public was an increasing polarization between it and the traditional English genre. There had always been comic dialogue-opera in England, including some reasonably successful examples by Loder, Benedict, and Macfarren; quite suddenly, however, dialogue-opera became comic almost

---

[1] *Carmen* was given at Her Majesty's Theatre on 22 June 1878, presumably in Italian and with Guiraud's recitatives, however.

by definition, and serious works by English composers had to compete for the attention of a sceptical public with the greatest foreign works. In the circumstances it is not surprising that comic opera flourished where they did not. Partly for reasons of chronology, but also because of their inheritance of a living English tradition, it makes sense to look first at comic opera with dialogue.

Even so, there would be little of interest to discuss had not Arthur Sullivan and W. S. Gilbert discovered in each other a very nearly perfect foil for their respective talents. Gilbert was a successful playwright with a flair for the carefully plotted paradox and for elaborate word-play. His plays are farce rather than comedy, though without the impropriety of the French genre, which would by this date have scandalized the broad public. Sullivan's musical gifts were considerably greater than Gilbert's literary talent, but by 1870 he was developing an alarming tendency to rest on his laurels. He had already realized in himself a penchant for light music. *Cox and Box*, an adaptation of a farce by J. M. Morton with a libretto by F. C. Burnand, had been given privately, with piano accompaniment, in 1866; but it was so successful that it soon reached the public stage, was orchestrated and given an overture, and was published in vocal score.[2] A second work by Burnand and Sullivan, *The Contrabandista* (1867) was less successful; it was, however, the composer's first two-act opera.

Sullivan's first operatic collaboration with Gilbert was *Thespis, or The Gods Grown Old*, first performed as a two-act afterpiece on 26 December 1871 at the Gaiety Theatre. Most of the music is lost, but like *Cox and Box* it was probably much influenced by Offenbach. In many ways the genre came to fulfil a social role comparable to that of Offenbach's *opérettes*, though its humour was more restrained and its music on the whole more sophisticated. London audiences could in any case enjoy both, but 'Gilbert and Sullivan' could be safely relied upon for family entertainment in an increasingly prudish age. Much of their work's extraordinary success must have been due to this factor.

Thespis was not initially successful, as it happened, and it was apparently too slight to bear revival. *Trial by Jury* (Royalty, 25 March 1875) was also an afterpiece, but in one act and with continuous music. It has always been considered one of Sullivan's most enchanting scores—while *The Zoo*, another one-acter with continuous music and a libretto by B. C. Stephenson ('Bolton Row': produced 5 June 1875 at St James's) was almost immediately forgotten until the present century. But even *Trial by Jury* was not the stuff of which genres are made.

The regular series, as it might be called, began with *The Sorcerer* (1877) and continued until *The Grand Duke* (1896). The first four operas—*The*

[2] A. Jacobs, *Arthur Sullivan* (2nd edn., Aldershot, 1992), 51–3.

Sorcerer, *HMS Pinafore*, *The Pirates of Penzance*, and *Patience*—were staged at the Opera Comique; the remainder, from *Iolanthe* on, at Richard D'Oyly Carte's new Savoy Theatre. Even the less successful of these twelve works have their warm admirers, but there would be widespread agreement in seeing *Iolanthe* (1882) and *The Yeomen of the Guard* (1888) as the musical peaks. In these scores the composer's profound instinct for parody becomes something more like the sincerest form of flattery—of Donizetti, of Schubert, of many others. But *The Yeomen* is marred by a vein of cloying sentimentality in the libretto, leaving *Iolanthe* to survive as the perfect embodiment of light comedy in music.

The vein of parody ran deep, and is sometimes thought to be overdone in, for example, *The Pirates of Penzance*. But parody is an essential point in the continuum running from subconscious emulation to burlesque, and it served as a subtle method of underlining the kid-gloved ironies of Gilbert's libretti. All comic opera depends on parody to a certain extent, but in Sullivan it is so many-layered that the point of reference is not always easy to discover. The well-drilled choruses may in some cases hark back to nowadays unfamiliar examples in Barnett and Balfe, in others to models in Weber and Donizetti. The essence of parody is the adoption of a serious manner in a comic context. The patter-songs adopt a manner made familiar by Rossini, but they cannot be said to parody him. The best of them all, the Lord Chancellor's Song in Act II of *Iolanthe*, is a highly creative application of the genre, a worthy response to the challenge of Gilbert's twenty-two-(or twenty-three-)syllabled lines.

The orchestration, still largely inaccessible for study,[3] is a natural consequence of superb craftsmanship applied to small forces. It rarely draws attention to itself, but is unfailingly colourful and supportive.

Some techniques are drawn without parody from the reserves of traditional English operatic idioms. An occasional ballad—such as the heroine's 'Love is a plaintive song' from Act II of *Patience*—is free not only of musical parody but of the verbal trickery that Gilbert could rarely resist (except when being mawkish). The occasional 'madrigal', whether so-called (*Mikado*, Act II) or not (*Patience*, Act I sestette, 'I hear the soft note of the echoing voice'), harks back to the operatic glees of Hook or Bishop, though occasionally a 'madrigal' or even a 'glee' (*Mikado*, Act II) is essentially a solo with chorus. A full study of genre in Sullivan's light operas would no doubt reveal a considerable variety, all of which helped to ensure the popularity and longevity of his works.

After *The Gondoliers* had been launched with immense success (7 December 1889), a row about the expenses (initially between Carte and Gilbert)

---

[3] There is an Eulenberg score of *The Gondoliers* and a facsimile of *Mikado*. A collected edition is in progress.

led to a rupture between the two collaborators, and Sullivan's next Savoy opera, *Haddon Hall* (1892), had a libretto by Sidney Grundy; in the same year Alfred Cellier set Gilbert's *The Mountebanks*, which was produced at the Lyric Theatre. The partnership was resumed for *Utopia Limited* (1893) and *The Grand Duke*, but neither of these was a great success, and Sullivan's last three Savoy operas had other librettists. The last of them all, *The Emerald Isle*, was left unfinished at his death and was completed by Edward German.

In truth the genre had played itself out. A century after the collaboration finally ended it is difficult to account for the phenomenal success of its half-dozen best-known representatives. The two men must have struck a chord that responded to that curious desire of a puritanical society to be entertained without being forced to ponder. Doubtless there are hints in the libretti that went unnoticed or could be ignored, but the sheer safety of the entertainment, not to mention its pandering to innate prejudices, must have had a good deal to do with its popularity both then and later. The operas remained the property of the D'Oyly Carte Company and until the expiry of the Gilbert copyright in 1961 were continuously produced in a manner that (supposedly) retained every feature of the original stagings. They proved immensely popular too with amateur societies and their audiences, but the full scores were not made available. With the expiry of the copyright it became possible to mount alternative productions of those operas of which the manuscript full scores had reached public libraries, but the free exercise of scholarship and performance has remained inhibited and a full assessment is still awaited.

A few of Sullivan's contemporaries and successors strove to maintain his standards of stylish entertainment: the most successful of them were Cellier (1844–91), whose *Mountebanks* we have just encountered, and Edward German (1862–1936), who after completing *The Emerald Isle* went on to produce two masterpieces of their kind, *Merrie England* (Savoy, 1902) and *Tom Jones* (Prince's Theatre, Manchester, 1907). Sir Alexander Mackenzie (1847–1935) had *His Majesty* produced at the Savoy in 1897. But a parting of the ways between a 'high' artistic tradition in comic opera and mass entertainment was inevitable, and these works of German fell firmly in the latter sphere.

Even so, *Merrie England* and *Tom Jones* do not quite come into the category of 'musical comedy' that was burgeoning at the time. A closer approximation would have been Cellier's *Dorothy* (Gaiety, 1886), itself one of the more respectable products of that theatre at the time. The Gaiety was famous for its burlesques, the music of which was generally a pasticcio cobbled together by its 'house' composer W. M. Lutz (1829–1903), and drawing on the songs of composers such as Edward Solomon (1855–95) and Sidney Jones (1861–1946). These two also composed more conventional operettas, like Solomon's *The Nautch Girl* (Savoy, 1891), which nevertheless betrays its 'musical comedy' tendencies in the division of the libretto into 'book' (by G. Dance) and 'lyrics' (by Dance and F. Desprez).[4] Eventually the burlesque was superseded by musical comedy at the Gaiety and its place in London entertainment taken by a form of 'music hall', played no longer in tavern annexes but in luxuriously appointed theatres: in fact 'variety' and 'music hall' now came to mean very much the same sort of thing.[5]

Sidney Jones was the main composer of musical comedy: *The Gaiety Girl* (Prince of Wales, 1893), was followed by others at the Gaiety itself and at his impresario George Edwardes's other main theatre, Daly's, where *The Geisha* (1896) was the outstanding success. In musical comedy the music was generally of the frothiest, however workmanlike, but the scenario and dialogue were free of the buffoonery and punning that had characterized the burlesque. A certain opulence of décor and costume doubtless contributed to the 'feel-good' factor that was of the essence of the genre. Apart from Jones, Leslie Stuart (1864–1928), Ivan Caryll (1861–1921, of Belgian birth), Lionel Monckton (1861–1924), Paul Rubens (1875–1914), and Howard Talbot (1865–1928, of American birth) were the most prolific composers of the period 1890–1914. One can at least say of this form of light music that its workmanship (sometimes with the help of specialist orchestrators) was usually impeccable and its tone above reproach. Most of these composers, of course, also supplied the variety theatres and drawing rooms with the fodder which they required; some of their theatre pieces, moreover, remained popular for decades afterwards.

The seriously intended comic operas of the 'high' tradition were needless to say far less of a commercial proposition. Their roots lay deep in the comedies, full-length or otherwise, of the 1860s, like Macfarren's *Jessy Lea* (Royal Gallery of Illustration, 1863) and *She Stoops to Conquer* (Covent Garden, 1864), in which the effort to forge a recognizably English idiom is sometimes painfully apparent. The number of successful later comic operas of this type, with or without spoken dialogue, can be counted on the fingers of one hand. Stanford's *Shamus O'Brien* (Opera Comique, 1896), despite its weaknesses, is certainly one of them, and it is mercifully free of the bogus Irish folkiness with which it could so easily have been afflicted.[6] His *Much Ado about Nothing* (Covent Garden, 1901), which has continuous music, is well written but failed to establish itself; it is, however, a significant prototype for British Shakespearean opera in the inter-war years. Ethel

⁴ Jacobs, 335–6.
⁵ Other semi-dramatic genres were pantomime, ballet, and revue. See A. Lamb in *BHMB*, v. 104–8; the following paragraph is indebted to pp. 97–104 of that volume.
⁶ It does of course have an Irish flavour, but Stanford claimed in the vocal score to have used only one Irish folk song and one Cornish ('The Glory of the West').

Smyth (1858–1944) had considerable operatic experience by the time she wrote *The Boatswain's Mate* in 1913–14; it was produced by Beecham at the Shaftesbury Theatre in 1916 and was frequently revived between the wars. Its first part uses spoken dialogue, while its second has continuous music. Another pre-war comedy that had to wait for a production, this time until after the war, was Vaughan Williams's *Hugh the Drover*, a strongly nationalist work that uses a good deal of folk song.

Serious opera in the period was equally subject to problems of artistic and commercial viability, its competitor being the wide repertory of Continental masterpieces by then available to London audiences. The earlier tradition of English opera had not failed, but had simply come to the end of its natural span. It had tolerated, indeed thrived on, spoken dialogue; now the effort had to be made to establish a tradition based on continuous music. It was unsuccessful—and remained so until 1945—partly because of the foreign competition but primarily because the idioms natural to English composers were not inherently musico-dramatic. Certainly fine and revivable operas were written—those of Delius spring to mind—but they are isolated instances.

The most conspicuous of all the operatic failures of the late Victorian period was Sullivan's *Ivanhoe*. Not that its music is especially weak; indeed its general level is as high as that of any of Sullivan's serious works. But it failed commercially despite its extraordinary initial run of 160 performances in 1891 (with revivals in Liverpool and in Berlin in 1895). *Ivanhoe* had been commissioned for the opening of Carte's ambitious new Royal English Opera House at Cambridge Circus, and as there were no other works with which it could alternate it was staged on successive evenings with variable casting. But it had to be discontinued before it had paid its way, though it was revived in alternation with Messager's *La Basoche* (given in English) in November 1891. But even Messager's lively score failed to catch on, and the theatre was sold early in 1892. (It reopened at the end of that year as The Palace Theatre of Varieties, now simply The Palace.)

Probably the finest opera of its day, produced in such circumstances without subsidy (supposing there to have been an English composer able to write it) would have succumbed to commercial forces. But *Ivanhoe* suffers also from weaknesses of design and (for want of a better word) 'tone'—essentially there is a mismatch between ambition and content. Gilbert had sensibly declined to be involved, and Julian Sturgis's libretto is both a travesty of Scott's novel and feeble in itself. Previous operatic adaptations (including Rossini's, which Scott saw in Paris in 1826 and enjoyed) had of course dismembered the novel and were perhaps no literary masterpieces; nor was Sturgis's verse noticeably inferior to that of (say) Bunn or Fitzball. But the context here was that of an endeavour to raise the level of English opera by superhuman effort to a great height; and it would have been hard for any composer to respond effectively to such lines as 'Ah, would that thou and I might lead our sheep Among the folded hills! The winter is past, the rain is over and gone; The singing birds *are come beside the rills*. Arise, beloved one!' (my italics).

A long-standing difficulty in English opera had been that of coping adequately with recitative. Sullivan's design of writing continuous but detached scenes (nine in all) does not conceal this inherited weakness (which is also evident, incidentally, in the comic operas), since clearly some variation in lyrical mode, as in an old-fashioned 'number-opera', was essential. Neither this variety nor the lack of continuity between scenes was abnormal at the time: it is perhaps the sense of hiatus *within* scenes, the prevalent impression of earthbound melody, and the futility of the composer's efforts to conceal this through harmony and orchestration, that are ultimately wearying. Yet there are whole scenes that can be enjoyed: the third scene of Act II, in which Rebecca encounters first the soothsaying Ulrica and then the lustful Templar, has real dramatic power, even though it could almost be a finale from an Italianate opera of the 1840s. Perhaps that is the solution to the problem of *Ivanhoe*: it works best when the composer could relax in the security of an idiom he knew well, and when the conventions of Romantic drama can be accepted at face value. As a whole, however, it is simply tedious.

Ivanhoe was probably the most eagerly awaited serious opera of its day, and the one on which the greatest hopes were pinned; yet it was far from unique either in its ambition or in its inability to find its own voice. Frederic Cowen (1852–1935) began well enough with *Pauline* (Lyceum, 1876), an old-fashioned opera in the idiom of Balfe and Wallace; but *Thorgrim* (Drury Lane, 1890), an attempt to claim Nordic myth for the English musical theatre, suffers even more than *Ivanhoe* from poorly digested Wagnerism. Arthur Goring Thomas (1850–92) was more indebted to French models in his operas, *Esmerelda* (1883) and *Nadeshda* (1885), but the problems of stylistic misalliance recur in those of Alexander Mackenzie (*Columba*, 1883; *The Troubadour*, 1886; *The Cricket on the Hearth*, published 1901).[7] Perhaps the most consistent toiler in the operatic vineyard in the 1880s and subsequently was Charles Villiers Stanford (1852–1924). Like Cowen he studied in Leipzig and Berlin. Unlike Cowen, however, he forged a personal style based on an amalgamation of the German school now led by Brahms, his Irish roots, and his adoptive English heritage; and he did not desert this even for opera. *The Veiled Prophet of Khorassan* (after Moore's *Lalla Rookh*), composed in 1877, was first staged in Hanover in 1881; several

[7] *The Cricket on the Hearth* was not performed until 1914, and then not professionally but by students at the Royal Academy of Music. Mackenzie (1847–1935), a Scot who finally came to live in London in 1885, became Principal of the Academy in 1888 and thereafter settled into the mould of a respected establishment figure.

others followed (some unpublished and a few not even performed), but only *Shamus O'Brien* was at all successful.

Whatever claim Cowen, Thomas, Mackenzie, and Stanford may have to belong to the vanguard of what came to be called the English musical renaissance, it would not be based on their operas. Those of Frederic Delius (1862–1934) are far more significant in this respect, notwithstanding their own tangential relationship with Wagnerian music-drama. He was indeed a decade younger than Stanford and Cowen; he spent almost his entire adult life abroad, and during his lifetime nearly all productions of his operas took place in Germany (*Koanga*, Elberfeld, 1904; *A Village Romeo and Juliet*, Berlin, 1907; *Fennimore and Gerda*, Frankfurt-am-Main, 1919, all composed long before their first performances). *A Village Romeo and Juliet* came to Covent Garden under Beecham in 1910. His first opera, *Irmelin*, was not heard until 1953 (in Oxford, again under Beecham).

Delius's operas therefore can have had very little impact on English audiences or on other English composers. Yet they cannot be wholly detached from English musical history: their musical language, notwithstanding its responsiveness to much of what was new in pre-war Germany and elsewhere, is that of an Englishman in exile, at least if its pastoral waywardness is any indication. Its frequent shifts from the blandly diatonic to the richly chromatic can be disconcerting, and its rhythms are often monotonous. At times we seem to have invaded the hot-house world of pre-war Vienna (Ex. 4.1). The famous interlude that follows this scene in *A Village Romeo and Juliet* ('The Walk to the Paradise Garden') reverts to a plainer style, characterized by slow-moving harmonies and the use of one-bar rhythmic cells in 4/4 time. Yet in its dramatic context it is extremely poignant. Delius's musical dramaturgy was far more advanced than that of (say) Richard Strauss at this period; it has more in common with that of Debussy's *Pelléas* in being based on a juxtaposition of images each lit by a single musical affect.

Two or three other composers deserve at least passing mention. Joseph Holbrooke (1878–1958), an ambitious young man, was commissioned by Lord Howard de Walden to write a trilogy of operas based on his version of the *Mabinogion* legend. The first two, *The Children of Don* and *Dylan*, were given in 1912 and 1914; the third, *Bronwen*, had to wait until 1929 for a performance, by which time the first two had fallen from favour. Rutland Boughton (1878–1960) together with the poet Reginald Buckley contrived a cycle of Arthurian operas and a festival at Glastonbury at which to present them (an obviously Wagnerian idea); the first two, *The Birth of Arthur* (1908–9) and *The Round Table* (1915–16), received their first complete performances in 1920. The festival came to an end in 1927 and of the remaining three operas of the cycle the last two were never performed.

Ex. 4.1

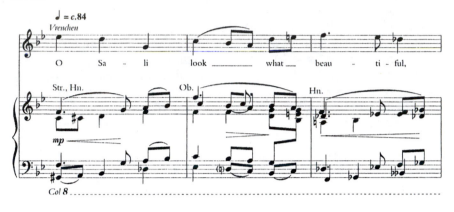

Ex. 4.1, continued

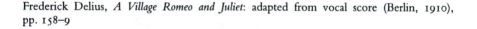

Frederick Delius, *A Village Romeo and Juliet*: adapted from vocal score (Berlin, 1910), pp. 158–9.

Of Boughton's other operas, the most successful was *The Immortal Hour* (Glastonbury, 1914), in which he abandoned Wagnerian complexity in favour of a smaller scale and a simpler harmonic idiom.[8]

The only other English opera-composer of note at this period was Ethel Smyth, whose *Boatswain's Mate* was mentioned above.[9] A woman of extra-ordinary tenacity and courage, Smyth studied in Leipzig and achieved a thorough grounding in the German instrumental style; like those of Delius

---

[8] For a sympathetic study see M. Hurd, *Rutland Boughton and the Glastonbury Festivals* (Oxford, 1993).

[9] Holst's opera *Sita*, finished in 1906, was never performed. *Savitri*, though composed in 1908, was first performed only in 1916 by the London School of Opera, and publicly for the first time in 1921. It will be discussed in the following chapter. Parry's *Guenever* (1885) never reached performance and only a MS vocal score, not quite complete, survives. It is discussed in J. Dibble, *C. Hubert H. Parry: His Life and Music* (Oxford, 1992), 236–43.

(who also studied there), her earliest operatic productions were in Germany: *Fantasio*, later rejected by her, in Weimar, 1898 (and in 1901 in Karlsruhe), and *Der Wald* (Berlin, 1902, later at Covent Garden and New York). Her next opera, *The Wreckers*, was originally composed to a French text, *Les naufrageurs*, but it was eventually produced in Leipzig as *Strandrecht*, and in London in 1909. (All Smyth's operatic libretti were her own, though the English version of *The Wreckers* is attributed to Henry Brewster.) Although her music is in many ways so different from that of Delius—furiously energetic where his is predominantly languid—it shares the same preoccupation with illuminating the lives of ordinary people in their occupations, their vices, their sufferings, and their merrymaking.

But whereas Delius absorbed his influences to create a unique sound-world, Smyth's music remained predominantly eclectic, though based ultimately on a Brahmsian foundation. One must not deny her a considerable measure of originality, but her melodic invention was not always strong, and the frequent changes of mood can become wearisome. The remarkable prelude to Act II of *The Wreckers*, entitled 'On the Cliffs of Cornwall', shows these qualities in their most favourable light; its swift juxtaposition and alternation of ideas in some ways resembles Janáček, while the use of instrumental music to denote the forces of nature, like the subject-matter of the whole opera, looks forward to *Peter Grimes* (Ex. 4.2).[10]

Elaborate incidental music continued to be cultivated in the late nineteenth century: Sullivan followed *The Tempest* with *The Merchant of Venice* (1871), *The Merry Wives of Windsor* (1874), and *Henry VIII* (1877), all produced in Manchester, and finally *Macbeth* (1888, at the Lyceum in London). Mackenzie wrote music for half a dozen plays, including Shakespeare's *Coriolanus* (1901). Apart from the then fashionably opulent productions of the professional companies there was a vogue in Oxford and Cambridge for enhancing Greek plays in the same way. Macfarren, Stanford, and Wood at Cambridge, and Parry and Parratt at Oxford, were the chief contributors; to them should be added Vaughan Williams, whose music for *The Wasps* was used at Cambridge in 1909. (Vaughan Williams wrote music for three more such plays before 1914, but it seems not to have been used; he also provided several scores for Shakespeare plays—and for one by Shaw—at Stratford-upon-Avon in 1913.)

Such music stands little chance of revival in its original context. The same may be said of a number of ballet scores from the period. Most of them were ephemeral concoctions devoid of dramatic interest. It is not entirely clear why a genre of Romantic ballet on the French model did not spring up; Sullivan's *L'isle enchantée*, given at Covent Garden in 1864 as an afterpiece to

---

[10] The MS full score is Brit. Lib., Add. 45939–41; the Preludes to Acts I and II were also printed separately in full score.

Ex. 4.2

Ethel Smyth, *The Wreckers*, Introduction to Act II: adapted from vocal score (London, 1916), pp. 129–30

Bellini's *La somnambula*, might have inaugurated one, but it did not. (Sullivan reused some of its music in *Victoria and Merrie England*, written for the diamond jubilee in 1897.) Ballet was a frequent adornment of other kinds of entertainment, dramatic and otherwise, but the time was not yet ripe for a serious approach to ballet by English composers.

Cantata and Oratorio

While opera necessarily remained a doubtful path for composers trying to escape from the shackles of mid-Victorian convention, it was quite otherwise in the case of cantata and oratorio, where the financial and practical obstacles to the production of ambitious new work were far less severe. It is true that the first performance of Elgar's *Gerontius*, the climactic endeavour in this development, was a disaster, because of under-rehearsal; but this was exceptional, and the work quickly established itself thereafter. It is in the context of these forms, together with orchestral music, that the idea of an 'English renaissance' is best explored. First, however, we should ask whether the use of the expression is still justified, and if so what exactly it ought to mean.

The term 'renaissance' has been applied since at least 1900 to the movement of musical growth and emancipation that began in the later nineteenth century and continued for long into the twentieth.[11] It had indeed two distinct aspects, for which growth and emancipation respectively are appropriate designations. The first was an expansion of English musical life and its penetration into a wider spectrum of society than hitherto. The second was a growing freedom from Continental models in composition. These were closely related, but not so much so that they cannot be considered separately.

The expansion of musical life can be illustrated by several factors, of which the development of amateur singing, the folk-song movement, the rediscovery of Tudor music, and the Bach revival are the most important. Frank Howes has also cited the gradual acceptance of music as a subject of scholarship akin to other 'arts' subjects in the universities, and as a focus of connoisseurship of the standing long held by literature and the fine arts. These are significant matters, but some of them are more important to compositional development than others. The sight-singing movement and its effect on amateur choralism up and down the country, for example, was a necessary but not a sufficient precondition for the stylistic advances possible in choral works by Parry, Stanford, Elgar, and Vaughan Williams. On the other hand the folk-song, Tudor, and Bach revivals could be translated directly into musical style, although in isolation their effects would be

[11] F. Howes, *The English Musical Renaissance* (London, 1966), 228, citing Ernest Newman. Cf. also pp. 20–1 and 38–9 for similar usages by J. A. Fuller-Maitland, Ernest Walker (1907), and Charles Stanford.

limited. The last factor, the growth of an intellectual interest in music *per se*, is the least tangible but in some ways the most complex and interesting. It took many forms: an advance in musical scholarship, illustrated by such things as the foundation of the Musical Association and other bodies, the editing of older music, and the publication of Sir George Grove's famous *Dictionary*; the growth of musical study and practice at Oxford and Cambridge, more particularly under the guidance of Parry and Stanford respectively; the establishment of genuine conservatory training in London, at first in the newly founded Royal College of Music, then with the reconstitution of the Royal Academy; and the subsequent involvement of both Parry and Stanford at the College, Parry as Director in succession to Grove and Stanford as Professor of Composition. The cumulative effect of all this activity prior to World War I was incalculable.[12]

It is harder to pin down the specific characteristics of a renaissance in composition. A healthy independence from Continental models is certainly a factor, but it is not the only one. Parry and Stanford, who are by far the most significant figures in the earliest manifestations of a renewed vigour, made it their business to master the expanded techniques of the modern German music of their day—especially that of Brahms, though without prejudice against the Wagnerian element. In terms of attitude this scarcely differs from the earlier cult of Mendelssohn, which Parry at any rate was slow to shake off. Nor was either composer at all nationalist in any obvious sense (discounting for present purposes the Irish element in Stanford).

Part of the answer seems to lie in the nature of the preferred model. Like that of Mendelssohn, Brahms's idiom proved to be highly adaptable; but it was far 'stronger' to begin with, owing nothing to Mendelssohn and not a great deal to Schumann but going past them to the common inheritance of the Viennese classics, and beyond those to Bach and even further to Schütz and the classics of the Renaissance itself. Brahms's grasp of contrapuntal idiom, and his ability to integrate it with classical form and tonality and with the expanded harmonic horizons of the later nineteenth century, far outshone Mendelssohn's superficial amalgam of similar elements; and his followers found in his music an intellectual coherence that could be translated as it were into the English vernacular without doing violence either to the thought or to the new linguistic context. The adaptation of Mendelssohn had proved all too easy; that of Brahms took more trouble but was more rewarding in the end.

It is difficult to assert a special case for Parry and Stanford without seeming to disregard the very real advances made by some of their predecessors and contemporaries. Stanford himself cited Wesley and Bennett as 'the first fruits of the Renaissance of English Music';[13] but Wesley's

---

[12] See further below, pp. 317–20.   [13] Howes, 39.

achievement was a very individual one, leading to no 'school', while as a composer Bennett deteriorated so markedly in later life, without doing more than hold the fort as an administrator and enabler, that he cannot be compared with those who held important positions in English musical life subsequently. Macfarren, despite a certain honest independence and a resourceful technique, was at heart a Mendelssohnian conservative. Cowen and Mackenzie, notwithstanding their early promise, lapsed into mediocrity, while Arthur Goring Thomas (1850–92) died too young to contribute anything decisively to the movement.

Sullivan, Macfarren, and J. F. Barnett (1837–1916, nephew of John Barnett) were the chief composers of choral music in the high Victorian tradition. Their work, particularly that of Sullivan, has plenty of zest and colour, but its idiom is unadventurous and the subject matter (when not biblical) is at best conventionally Romantic, at worst jejune. Secular cantatas were either dramatic in form, like Bennett's *The May Queen* (1858; Sullivan's *Kenilworth*, 1864, described as a masque, with words by the same ineffable Chorley, and his *On Shore and Sea*, 1871, a 'dramatic cantata' to words by Thomas Taylor, were of this type), or narrative, like Barnett's *The Ancient Mariner* (1867). The reliance on an established verse classic did not, unfortunately, betoken a comparable stature in its musical treatment, though it foreshadowed a more fruitful symbiosis of poets and composers in the years to come. Mackenzie's 'dramatic oratorio' *The Rose of Sharon* was produced in 1884; the most interesting oratorio in dramatic form before *Gerontius* was Sullivan's *The Martyr of Antioch* (1880), which was actually performed as an opera by the Carl Rosa company in 1898.

Hubert Parry (1848–1918) was, amongst his other merits, acutely sensitive to literary quality; he was wholly averse to the least suggestion of the banal (which saved him from the cult of Longfellow that seduced Barnett, Sullivan, the young Stanford, and Elgar)[14] while not being immune from the lure of the merely worthy, to which category his own versified efforts might be said to belong. His first work for voices and orchestra (apart from his youthful exercise for the degree of Bachelor of Music) was his *Scenes from Prometheus Unbound* (1880), based on Shelley's verse drama.

Although *Prometheus* is flawed both dramatically and musically, it is justifiably regarded as a landmark in English musical history.[15] Parry brought to it a wealth of experience in the handling of pure instrumental form and of word-setting in the smaller genres of anthem, part-song, and solo song. His idiom, though rooted ultimately on a traditional Anglo-Mendelssohnianism, had absorbed a great deal of Brahmsian and even Wagnerian technique. His choice of material was determined by his innate seriousness and his

---

[14] *The Golden Legend* was used by both Stanford (1875) and Sullivan (1886); for Elgar's use of Longfellow see below.
[15] E. Walker, *A History of Music in England* (Oxford, 1907), 300.

hatred of organized religion: in few of his subsequent choral works (except for some settings of liturgical or ceremonial texts) would he endorse a wholly orthodox stance, and in some of the later ones he would attempt a purely philosophical discourse in oratorio form. *Prometheus*, while nominally secular, has as its theme the destruction of the old gods and human self-sufficiency.

Too little of Shelley's poem was retained for dramatic cohesion; even so, the quantity of decasyllabic blank verse remaining posed a challenge that would have daunted even a finer composer than Parry. The wooden declamation of Prometheus' opening monologue is a disappointment after the atmospheric orchestral prelude; even some of the choral writing remains earthbound, and the predominantly slow or moderate speeds are wearisome in the long run. All Parry's longer works suffer in the same way to some degree. Yet his underlying integrity saves his cantatas and oratorios from the shallow appeal of so many of his contemporaries. He was an inspired melodist, but he made a virtue of restraint; there is a line to be drawn between restraint and dullness, and he did not always judge it accurately.

Parry pursued his aims in the oratorios *Judith* (1888), *Job* (1892), and *King Saul* (1894), all of which combine biblical matter with additions of his own. His *Invocation to Music* (1895) and *A Song of Darkness and Light* (1898), both to texts by Robert Bridges, foreshadow his later attempts at purely philosophical works to texts of his own devising. But he struck a far happier note in some of his shorter, less pretentious choral works. Supreme amongst these is his setting for eight-part choir and orchestra of Milton's ode 'Blest pair of sirens' (1887), in which the convoluted sentence structure of the poem, no less than its imagery, is matched with uncanny precision in the music. Every nuance of the words is caught somehow or other in a style that draws on the richest vein of Anglican anthem-writing, yet is welded into a powerfully convincing symphonic whole.

After 1900 neither Parry nor Stanford (who by then had composed several successful choral works)[16] could reasonably claim musical leadership, though Parry scored a sensational success with his coronation anthem 'I was glad' (1902, recast in the now familiar form for the coronation of George V in 1911), and could be said to have embodied the 'dignified part' of the English musical constitution in his later years. Moreover *The Pied Piper of Hamelin*, produced in 1905 but written earlier, is a genuine comic creation, a straight setting of Browning's poem in which the choir acts as narrator, sometimes in amusing juxtaposition with the direct speech of the two soloists. Finally, in his setting of William Dunbar's *Ode on the Nativity* (1912), for soprano solo, chorus, and orchestra, Parry achieved a perfect

---

[16] The most notable are *The Revenge* (Tennyson, 1886), *Eden* (Bridges, 1891), and *Phaudrig Crohoore* (J. S. Le Fanu, 1896).

fusion of strophic form and continuous musical development in a work that must surely rank as one of the finest of its kind in the years immediately before the First World War.

The case is rather different with Edward Elgar (1857–1934), who was without question the outstanding English composer in the years 1900–14; at the same time, his choral music, except for *Gerontius*, has weathered less well than the symphonic. Elgar's musical and social background differed markedly from Parry's. While Parry had had the educational advantages of Eton and Oxford, and had made excellent use of the opportunities of the relaxed system of those days to further his interest in composition—indeed he had satisfied the requirements for a B.Mus. even before going up to Oxford—he nevertheless found himself without a foothold in the profession on going down; and having contracted a socially difficult marriage he initially entered a partnership in Lloyd's of London. His determination to succeed as a composer, in which he was helped by the admirable Edward Dannreuther (1844–1905), a pianist and scholar of German origin, was rewarded in due course, and it is an inspiring story of courage on the part of a diffident young man. Elgar's story is no less inspiring, but his beginnings were quite different. The son of a Worcester music-seller, he enjoyed a decent Catholic education until the age of 15, after which he was initially destined for the Law. Disappointed of his ambition to study in Germany,[17] he earned his living for years as a violinist and teacher before making his name generally known as a composer. An important early influence was the Catholic liturgical repertory—to which he himself occasionally contributed—at the church of St George, Worcester, where he played the organ; but he also studied and listened to the Anglican music at the cathedral and was kept on his toes by the need to arrange and compose all sorts of things, vocal and instrumental, for local amateurs. Like Parry, he married above his station; unlike him, he enjoyed his wife's wholehearted support throughout his years of frustration and subsequent success. When she died, his muse left him.

In the 1890s the primary objective of an English composer was still recognition through the commissioning and performance of major choral works, whether in London or in the provinces. Elgar's Worcester origins were a help here (as his Gloucester connections had been for Parry), and *The Black Knight* was duly given there on 18 April 1893 (but not at the Festival in September of that year). *The Black Knight* suffers from a text, or rather a translation, by Longfellow; but unlike, say, Sullivan's *The Golden Legend*, or indeed Parry's *Prometheus*, it is not a botched reduction of a verse drama. It is in effect a symphonic poem for chorus and orchestra, without soloists, and while its style ranges from the simply diatonic to the highly chromatic, it

---

[17] J. N. Moore, *Edward Elgar: A Creative Life* (Oxford, 1984), 55.

Ex. 4.3

Edward Elgar, *The Black Knight*: adapted from vocal score (London, 1893), p. 22

compares favourably (again) with Sullivan in the homogeneity of its idiom and the sureness of its harmonic touch. One passage (quoted by W. H. Reed) will illustrate not merely an early instance of a favourite chromatic idea but an intriguing reminiscence of *Die Walküre* (Ex. 4.3).[18]

For *King Olaf* (1896), H. A. Acworth supplemented Longfellow's narrative with dramatic scenes; according to a note by Elgar, 'the performers should be looked upon as a gathering of skalds (bards); all, in turn, take part in the narration of the saga and occasionally, at the more dramatic points, personify some important character.' The text of *Caractacus* (1898) is entirely by Acworth, and is dramatic throughout. The inadequacies of its verse diction are less evident in Elgar's setting than one might expect, since they are cleverly disguised by irregularities of phrasing, repetition of words, and unexpected modulations (Ex. 4.4).[19] These are indeed increasingly evident in all three cantatas, but it is in *Caractacus* that they finally evolve into a musical medium that is not merely dramatic in an abstract sense but positively operatic. *Caractacus* cries out for staging, and would make a splendid opera were it not for the jingoistic final chorus.

[18] *Elgar* (London, 1939), 38. Reed also cites two passages from *The Apostles*, in which the addition of a pedal-point strengthens the allusion; and N. Burton in *BHMB*, v. 239 quotes (even more appropriately perhaps) from Walford Davies's *Everyman*.

[19] For its composition see Moore, *Edward Elgar*, 236–40.

Ex. 4.4

Edward Elgar, *Caractacus*: adapted from vocal score (London, 1898), pp. 95–7

All three of these works—together with the less ambitious *Scenes from the Bavarian Highlands* (first heard in 1896) and *The Banner of St George* (1897)— have a ringing confidence and a security of technique that would well repay more performances, notwithstanding the receding tide of fashion that has left their subject matter high and dry. One can hardly say the same of *The Light of Life* (also known as *Lux Christi*), a 'short oratorio' given at the Worcester (Three Choirs') Festival in September, 1896. The familiar mixture of narrative and drama, a compilation by the Revd E. Capel-Cure based on the gospel narrative of the healing of a blind man, was uninspiring stuff, and Elgar responded with cautious ideas and wooden word-setting.[20] But as his largest religious work before *Gerontius* it has the interest of a dry run for that masterpiece, even though *Gerontius* in some ways has more in common with its secular predecessors.

The Dream of Gerontius itself, when it came in 1900, far outshone even those predecessors as well as all other English oratorios since those of Handel. There are a number of reasons for this, not least of which is the rapid development of the composer's style and technique, and another the style and circumstances that once again permitted the conjunction of a boldly innovative idiom and the exigencies of English festival oratorio. But it would be wrong to overlook the solid excellence of its libretto. In Handel's day the marriage of fine music and indifferent verse could result in oratorios that neither offended contemporary susceptibilities nor resist revival in our own day. But a sentimental or feebly versified text usually brought out the worst in a Victorian composer and can still set modern nerves jangling. Newman was not perhaps a great poet, but he was a master of the English language, and a simple reading of the abridged text at the beginning of the vocal score is sufficient to reveal a skill in versification and an absence of mawkishness that made his poem a highly suitable vehicle for musical setting.

The text of *Gerontius* is dramatic in form but not operatic in spirit: it is a drama of the mind, to be experienced in the imagination alone. For this reason it is ideal for oratorio. It was much criticized, apropos Elgar's setting, for its overt Catholicism, and the oratorio suffered accordingly in reputation in certain quarters. Nevertheless, it is a 'far from conventional' expression of Catholic doctrine,[21] and it can in any case be interpreted not as a drama of actuality but as a vision of a possibility or even as an allegory of the progress of a soul irrespective of intervening death.

However Elgar himself may have interpreted the poem, he set it *con amore*, inscribing the score at the end with the famous words 'this is the best of me'. Its disastrous first performance, which no amount of enthusiasm from his friends could mitigate, is said to have lost him his faith, and there is

---

[20] For a more generous estimate see *BHMB*, v. 230.   [21] I. Ker, *Newman* (Oxford, 1988), 575.

a profound irony in the very different circumstances of his own departure from life thirty-three years later.[22]

But while *Gerontius* is not operatic in the theatrical sense it draws on operatic techniques: a system of leading motives analogous to Wagner's though less detailed and thorough and—a Verdian rather than a Wagnerian idea—the introduction of a new melody at the end (the Angel's 'Softly and gently'), though not in such a way as to exclude a final reminiscence of the angelicals' 'Praise to the Holiest'. Amongst other purely musical influences that go to make up the mature composer's very individual style, that of Schumann may be singled out; it is overt in the Andantino section of the prelude (fig. 12 of the score),[23] and even when it is not overt it seems to lie behind the composer's fondness for harmonically complex sequential structures and the various forms of thematic imitation to which they give rise (cf. Ex. 4.4 above)—not to mention those elements of wistfulness, nobility, and playfulness that both composers share.

After *Gerontius* Elgar projected a trilogy of works on the foundations and ultimate destiny of Christianity, reverting to a selection of biblical texts. Only the first two, *The Apostles* (1903) and *The Kingdom* (1906), were finished and performed, and while they contain much absorbing music they seem to lack the overall grandeur of conception that their theme demands. The lack of the third member, *The Last Judgement*, is obviously a contributory factor, but it is perhaps a want of engagement at the deepest level that accounts for their relative colourlessness. His cantata *The Music Makers* (1912) is interesting chiefly for its Straussian use of self-quotation.

By 1900 the conventions of the choral cantata and oratorio had broadened to admit a wide variety of approaches and a loosening of the boundaries between genres. Works like *The Golden Legend* and *King Olaf* were essentially secular, notwithstanding their Christian overtones, and in a mixture of dramatic and narrative modes. Longfellow was again the basis of the most popular of all secular choral works of its time, Samuel Coleridge-Taylor's *Scenes from the Song of Hiawatha*, whose three parts were premièred in 1898, 1899, and 1900 respectively.[24] This tradition continued into the twentieth century, as we have seen, alongside the pioneering work of Stanford and Parry, to which Elgar's later works seem more fittingly to belong. Composers younger than Elgar (including Coleridge-Taylor) offered both tradition and innovation; two of the most innovative were Delius and Vaughan Williams.

[22] Moore, *Edward Elgar*, 818–23.

[23] Cf. *Kreisleriana*, no. 2.

[24] Coleridge-Taylor (1875–1912), of West African origin though born in London, was a prolific composer in many genres. After *Hiawatha*, eight major choral works appeared in London and the provinces.

Delius's major choral works, like his operas, were first heard in Germany: *Appalachia* at Elberfeld in 1904, *Sea Drift* (Whitman) at Essen in 1906, and Part II of *A Mass of Life* (Nietzsche) at Munich in 1908, though they were later given in England by Fritz Cassirer (*Appalachia*, London, 1907), Henry Wood (*Sea Drift*, Sheffield, 1908), and Beecham (*A Mass of Life*, complete, London, 1909).[25] *A Mass of Life*, with its pronouncedly atheistic philosophy, was hardly matter for an English choral festival; its (admittedly limited) acceptance in England rather signifies the transference of the genre of major choral works from the festival to the subscription series, in which orchestral music formed the staple fare. The choice of Whitman's poetry in *Sea Drift* corresponds more closely to the sense of nostalgia and yearning that can be detected in the more thoughtful English composers at the time, even though the poet was as purely American as it is possible to be.

Ralph Vaughan Williams, a decade younger than Delius, also chose Whitman in his *Toward the Unknown Region* (Leeds, 1907), its composer's first major success. He followed this with a far larger choral work based on Whitman—*A Sea Symphony*, composed between 1903 and 1909 and first heard in Leeds in October 1910. It is one of the few examples of a true 'choral symphony', fully vocal throughout and cast in a large four-movement form.[26] The lengthy final movement, with its intensely meditative close, seems prophetic of future uncertainties in an era of confidence scarcely justified by events. Its idiom, too, while anchored in the national tradition, is highly innovative, though in ways as far removed from the contemporary explorations of Schoenberg and other Europeans as can well be imagined. A simple juxtaposition of unrelated concords, as at the very beginning of this symphony, cuts the Gordian knot that the increasing chromaticism of Wagner, Strauss, and their English imitators seemed capable only of tying more tightly. With this work, together with half a dozen others prior to the First World War, Vaughan Williams set the agenda both for his own subsequent development and for that of numerous others whose idioms differed widely from his.

Henry Walford Davies (1869–1941) was at this period another innovator whose composing career was subsequently abandoned in favour of popular education: his book *The Pursuit of Music* (1934) and his broadcast talks later fostered the enthusiasm of many. His cantata *Everyman* (1904) adopts an advanced chromaticism in places and is a more successful adaptation of a literary drama (in this case a Tudor morality play) than most. Granville Bantock (1868–1946) was another who wrote little of consequence after the First World War; he too could be regarded as innovatory in the English

---

[25] *Appalachia* was written originally as an orchestral work (1896), but never performed in that form. Delius himself conducted it at Hanley in 1908.

[26] There are also Holst's *First Choral Symphony* and Britten's *Spring Symphony* from a later period; and several choral suites, from *The Black Knight* onwards, are analogous.

context, though in a purely post–Wagnerian direction that proved to be an artistic dead end. His largest choral work was his setting of *Omar Kháyyám* (a characteristically Romantic choice), first heard complete at Birmingham in 1909 and hardly ever since (it was revived at the Festival of Britain in 1951).[27] He also wrote three *unaccompanied* choral symphonies: *Atalanta in Calydon* (Manchester, 1912), *Vanity of Vanities* (Liverpool, 1914), and *A Pageant of Human Life* (1913, unperformed).

Other vocal genres with orchestra included settings of Latin liturgical texts, accompanied part-songs, and accompanied solo songs, the two latter usually also available for performance with piano accompaniment (as distinct from being provided with a piano reduction purely for rehearsal purposes). Parry wrote a fine Te Deum (later revised with English text) in addition to the splendid English coronation Te Deum (1911), and a less successful Magnificat, whose use of a plainsong intonation gives it a somewhat unfortunate thematic resemblance to the opening of Mendelssohn's *Lobgesang*. Stanford wrote a Verdian Requiem (1897), a Te Deum (1898), and a Stabat Mater (1907) as well as a liturgical Mass with orchestra (1893), and provided orchestrations for some of his Anglican service-music.

The line between a choral cantata and a set of accompanied part-songs is a fine one, and in any case the part-song idiom permeated a great deal of English choral writing, whatever the genre. However, Elgar's *Scenes from the Bavarian Highlands* (1896) is a clear example, and Stanford's *Songs of the Sea* (1904) and *Songs of the Fleet* (1910) should also be mentioned, though these also use a solo voice. Elgar again provides the best example of an orchestrally accompanied song-cycle in his *Sea Pictures* (1899). Its harmonic idiom is less advanced than that of (say) *Caractacus*, and its sentiments nowadays seem faded; yet it is still an effective vehicle for fine contralto singing and it is picturesquely scored. His subsequent set of three orchestral songs (out of a projected set of six) to poems by Gilbert Parker (Op. 59, first given at the Jaeger memorial concert in January 1910) is less well known but deserves revival as a maturer specimen of his highly individual, almost instrumental, approach to song. But the most striking work of the period for solo voice and orchestra is Gustav Holst's *The Mystic Trumpeter* (1904, revised 1912; performed in 1905, and in 1913 as revised), to words from Walt Whitman's poem 'From Noon to Starry Night'. The use of soft trumpet calls in diatonic triads was hardly a novelty, but their underpinning by fourths-based harmony in unrelated keys was decidedly so, even for Holst himself, who had previously made free use of diatonic dissonance but had hitherto scarcely ventured into such quasi-atonal territory (Ex. 4.5).[28]

---

[27] Howes, *The English Musical Renaissance*, 200. There are also some valuable recent recordings.

[28] Ed. C. Matthews (London, 1989); Brit. Lib., Add. MS 47817. One should also mention here Bantock's orchestral song-cycles *Ferishta's Fancies* (1905, after Browning), for tenor, and the extraordinary *Sappho* (1906, first performed 1908), for contralto.

Ex. 4.5

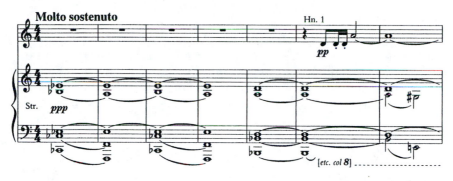

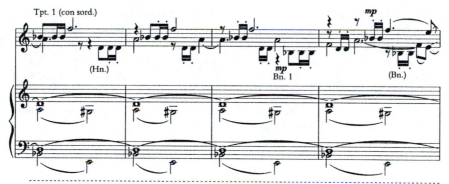

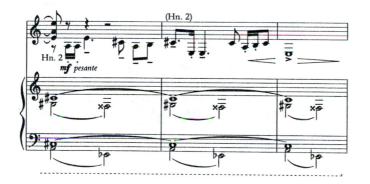

Gustav Holst, *The Mystic Trumpeter* (London, 1989), pp. 1–2

Of Holst's other works for voices and orchestra from this period the *Choral Hymns from the Rig Veda*, Op. 26, are the most prophetic of his later, elliptical style: here are the irregular metres, the ostinati, the pedal-points, the strange scales, and the clashes of tonality that recur in varying degrees and combinations in the *Hymn of Jesus*, the *First Choral Symphony*, and the *Choral Fantasia*. Only the first of the four *Rig Veda* sets is for full choir and orchestra: the second is for female voices and orchestra, the third for female voices and harp, and the fourth for male voices and strings with optional brass.

Part-Songs and Other Unaccompanied Vocal Forms

The part-song was such a prominent feature of later Victorian musical life, and its idiom so all-pervading in other choral forms, that it must necessarily receive more attention here than the intrinsic worth of the great majority of its representatives would warrant. In general it subsumed the existing traditions of glee and madrigal, though the persistence of the madrigal as a genre in its own right, even after 1900, somewhat complicates the issue and raises problems of definition.

From one point of view the distinction is social. Madrigal societies—certainly those of London (founded in 1741) and Bristol (founded 1837)—were all-male clubs, using boys for the upper line or lines, even up to the Second World War in these cases at least.[29] (In this they resembled glee clubs, which makes it difficult to distinguish between the madrigal and glee on social grounds.) Part-songs, on the other hand, emanated as we have seen form the amateur singing-class movement, in which women participated from the outset. In neither context was one voice to a part the norm. On the other hand, both madrigals and part-songs (and even glees, up to a point) were amenable to transfer to the domestic context, in which case a smaller number of singers (but including women) could be expected. Then again, some unaccompanied works designated as anthems or motets could as well (or even better) be sung by mixed choirs outside the church; and in time the conventions of the mixed choir (in which the alto line would be taken wholly or partly by women) came to affect the tessitura of the upper parts and the textural character of the whole, even in specifically liturgical music. Nor were any of these forms immune from the possibility of accompaniment.

The madrigal, then, and *a fortiori* the glee, are not easily distinguished from the part-song on the grounds of the vocal forces required. If there is a distinction at all (other than the fact of performance by, or submission for a prize offered by, a madrigal society or glee club), it must be on grounds of idiom. The glee had effectively come to an end as a distinct form by 1870; the madrigal, so called, survived for longer, though with less and less to

[29] H. Byard, *The Bristol Madrigal Society* (Bristol, 1966), 3, 5.

distinguish it in idiom from the more ambitious type of part-song.[30] It inherited from the days of Pearsall and Walmisley a tendency towards the archaic, but the element of pastiche, never absolute in any case, became less and less important as time went on.

The part-song itself, on the other hand, quickly became emancipated from the idiom of simply harmonized melody, four-square in rhythm and phrase structure, with which it began. Its main weakness in the later Victorian period was sentimentality, a quality much derided in the early twentieth century. But even sentimentality has its uses, and a work like Sullivan's 'The long day closes' (to Chorley's words) is a perfectly turned miniature of its kind. Stanford and Parry strove for a more elevated musical language and generally chose good poetry, old or new, for their settings. Stanford's 'The blue bird' is surprisingly adventurous harmonically, especially in its inconclusive ending (see Ex. 4.6).[31] Elgar wrote unaccompanied part-songs in the Victorian tradition throughout his composing career, as well as the *Scenes from the Bavarian Highlands*, in which the piano accompaniment is a genuine performing alternative, not just a substitute for the purposes of rehearsal. Parry's masterpiece in the idiom, and one which represents the form at its apogee, is the set of six *Songs of Farewell*, composed during the First World War. These are described as motets, but in reality they are extraordinarily dignified settings of religious and quasi-religious English poetry, with nothing of an ecclesiastical idiom about them.

That is not quite true of Stanford's set of three Latin motets (Op. 38, 1905), the first of which, the four-part 'Justorum animae', is one of his finest inspirations. Perhaps it is that the choice of Latin biblical texts fostered a more musically extended, less 'wordy' idiom.[32] There is a later set of 'motets' for unaccompanied voices, Op. 135 (1913), to English poetry, which have more of the part-song about them. While church music as such will be dealt with later, it is significant that some of the best of it at this period was written for unaccompanied choir.

There are a few early part-songs with and without accompaniment by Vaughan Williams, and a great many more by Holst, to whom the medium in its many guises came naturally. He seems to have enjoyed disciplining himself to write for amateurs without sacrificing his individuality. His teaching duties (and in particular his lifelong post at St Paul's Girls' School, which he took up in 1905) were an essential part of his creative life. During the War he was to carry this further by establishing annual Whitsuntide

[30] Sir John Goss (1800–80) was the last effective practitioner of the glee. Cyril Rootham, who was the son of Daniel Rootham, Musical Director of the Bristol Madrigal Society, 1865–1915, wrote a couple of madrigals so named, one of which, 'Sweet echo', won the (London) Madrigal Society's prize in 1906.

[31] Op. 119, no. 3, publ. in 1910; the words are by Mary Coleridge.

[32] In this context, perhaps, 'motet' signals an element of archaism analogous to that implied by 'madrigal'. This is still more evident in the other two motets of this set, 'Coelos ascendit' (*a 8*) and 'Beati quorum via' (*a 6*).

Ex. 4.6

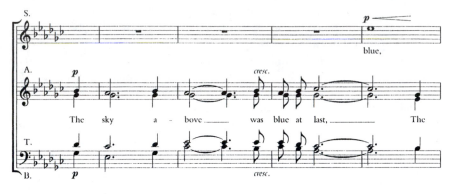

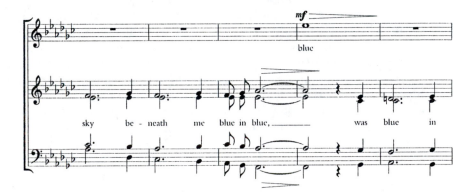

Ex. 4.6, continued

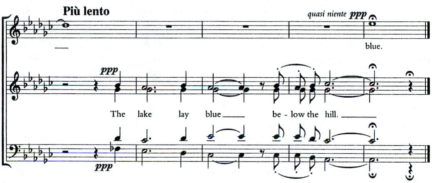

C. V. Stanford, *The Blue Bird* (London, 1910), pp. 3–4

festivals at Thaxted: it was to these singers that Vaughan Williams dedicated
his G minor Mass in 1922.

Solo Song

Solo song, in this as in all periods, is an extraordinarily diverse phenomenon.
It may be extended to include works for as many as four (only very rarely
more) solo voices with accompaniment; and the accompaniment itself,
though normally since the late eighteenth century for piano alone, may be
for a chamber ensemble small or large. (Orchestrally accompanied songs in
this period are discussed above, as belonging rather to the cantata tradition as
far as England is concerned; though the distinction is weakened by the fact
that a piano accompaniment is almost invariably sanctioned, at least by the

publisher with the presumed connivance of the composer, as a legitimate alternative.)

As regards the years 1870–1914, classification is complicated by issues of taste and reception. One may be able to single out instances of high artistic endeavour, but it is hardly possible to create a category for them in purely objective terms. It is certainly not possible to do so on commercial grounds, for the great majority of the songs of the later Victorian and Edwardian periods that we know of were sold by their composers to a publisher for some small consideration; they were accepted in the hope of a profit, small or large, by the publisher. This could be boosted by an adroit dedication, the name of a well-known singer on the title-page, or the choice of a fashionable poet in the setting; the identity of the composer was generally a song's least enticing feature. If anyone was paid a royalty, it was the nominal singer on the basis of copies sold;[33] the composer was rarely so rewarded, and never until he (or she) had become firmly established.

Even the name of a famous singer could not turn every song so labelled into a goldmine; royalties were only paid (and were only worth having) on songs designed to appeal broadly. These were customarily known as ballads, a term as we have seen with a long and honourable history but which now became discredited (except when used historically) by the low status of most of its representatives. But there is no easy distinction to be made between an 'art-song' and a commercial ballad. Some composers, like Frederick Cowen, aimed high but rarely reached their target; sometimes a publisher's ballad, or at any rate a song so called, achieved a sort of artistry. Some composers, like the young John Ireland (1879–1962), were so conscious of the distinction that they had their ballads marketed under a pseudonym.[34] Others, like Sullivan and Elgar, swooped high and low without apparent consciousness of any anomaly.

The higher type of song can be distinguished not only from its sentimental offshoot the 'drawing-room ballad' but from the popular (comic or sentimental) songs of the music hall and similar outlets, and from urban and rural folk music. Here too there are difficulties of definition, and a considerable degree of overlap existed both within these categories and between them and more genteel types of song. Rural folk music, the least

---

[33] Cf. E. D. Mackerness, *A Social History of English Music* (London, 1966), 231–2. But there was more to it than '[paying] singers to include them in ballad-concert programmes'. Percy Scholes (*Oxford Companion to Music*, e.g. 3rd edn. 1941, s.v. 'Ballad', p. 67) is worth quoting: 'Some of the principal publishers pushed the lucrative sale amongst tasteless amateurs by paying a fixed sum (or 'royalty') to professional vocalists for every inclusion of a particular ballad in a public programme, or by paying very eminent vocalists a royalty for a term of years on the complete sales of ballads which they undertook to introduce to the public. . . . [Royalty ballads] tended to die out during the period of the Great War (1914–18) and probably received their *coup de grâce* from the radio, which placed the domestic warbler at a discount and so reduced sales to a very low point.'

[34] 'Turlay Royce': noted by G. Bush (ed.) in *Songs 1860–1900* (MB 56; London, 1989), a useful selection on which the following observations are to some extent based.

understood of these types to begin with, was avidly collected by connois-
seurs in the Edwardian period; but their published collections, with piano
accompaniments for general use, like those of John and Lucy Broadwood
earlier on, brought them into the realm of 'serious' song. Urban folk song
(including the street ballad) was not always easy to distinguish from the rural
type—indeed some of their tunes were shared[35]—though the distinction
became sharper as time went on, and urban folk song merged instead with
the popular music of the urban proletariat.

These phenomena are not our immediate concern. The quantity of
'serious' song produced in the period is in any case enormous. At least
fifty composers of worthwhile achievement could be named, from the older
Victorians to the generation of George Butterworth (1885–1916) and Ivor
Gurney (1890–1937), with thousands of songs to their credit.[36] They set
mainly English words, of course, but there was a striking vogue for Ger-
man-language song and a lesser one for French. Some composers—Ethel
Smyth (1858–1944) and Maude Valérie White (1855–1937), for example—
cultivated both; Delius wrote songs in five languages, including English.
The effect was often to induce a passable imitation of the host national style,
as is very clear in the French songs of White, who even achieved echoes of
Fauré, and of Arthur Goring Thomas (1850–92), who was closer to Bizet
and Ambroise Thomas. The German tradition went back to Pierson, who
had emigrated, and Bennett; it was continued in the work of Liza Lehmann
(1862–1918) and Delius, both of German extraction, Stanford, and Parry,
who even chose to set four Shakespeare sonnets in a German translation.
These last sound exactly like indigenous lieder, though they do not precisely
imitate any one composer: in harmony they seem closest to Brahms, but
their accompaniments are often more assertive and melodically significant.
But in due course Parry turned exclusively to the English language.

Arthur Sullivan was the archetypal Victorian song-composer (though not
the oldest of those still active), both in his merits and in his weaknesses. His
idiom was built on a Mendelssohnian foundation, though his fondness for
Schubert is often betrayed. Some of his best songs—the Shakespeare settings
and those of the Tennyson cycle, for example—are products of the 1860s.
The Tennyson cycle, *The Window, or The Song of the Wrens*, was a conscious
effort to introduce the German form to England. Tennyson seems to have
regarded the invitation to write the words as an opportunity for triviality,
and he subsequently tried to prevent the completed work from being
published; Sullivan, however, insisted, and the set appeared in 1871. It is
not particularly successful as a cycle, but the songs individually are attractive,

---

[35] Cf. R. Middleton in *BHMB*, v. 68–9, comparing two versions of 'The Miller of Dee'. See further in Ch. 8 below.

[36] Cf. S. Banfield, *Sensibility and English Song* (Cambridge, 1985). This important book lists in full the song-output (up to 1945) of fifty-four composers active in the 20th c.

as is for example *The Window* (the second song of the set, 'Vine, vine and eglantine'), where the style is that of a sentimentalized Beethoven. Tennyson's verse, like Longfellow's in the case of cantata-writers, was overestimated by composers of songs, who often chose to set his weakest efforts: one of the most popular was the appalling 'What does little birdie say?',[37] while *Maud* was frequently evoked, most spectacularly by Arthur Somervell (1863–1937) in his own Tennyson cycle of 1898.

An insecurity in the choice of modern verse was a significant element in the overall weakness of much late Victorian song. It is hard to say what drew Macfarren (in 1866) and Sullivan to Adelaide Proctor's *The Lost Chord*, even if its opening lines do hint at a possible classical prototype.[38] Sullivan eventually set the poem in 1877—at his brother's death-bed, so it is said—and his song exemplifies the awful potential of maudlin verse combined with apposite music. Clara Butt's famous observation—'What we need now is more songs like *The Lost Chord*: there is something of the grandeur of Beethoven in it'—is as much a curiosity of criticism as the song itself is of song-writing. Its hymnic harmonies and its static melodic line are undoubtedly suited to the words, but the relentlessness with which they are pursued serves only to emphasize the underlying shallowness. One thing is certain: there never *could* be another song like it.[39]

It would be unfair to judge Sullivan by *The Lost Chord*, and few Victorian or Edwardian composers maintained a consistently high level. Alexander Mackenzie wrote at least one little masterpiece in his 'Dormi, Jesu' for voice, violin or cello, and piano,[40] but many of his songs are disfigured by a striving for effect and an overelaborate 'splashy' accompaniment. In this he was far from unique; it is a valid criticism of Elgar, for example, and not only in his songs. The 'renaissance' was characterized by access to a much wider range of expression than had been available hitherto, and it was tempting to misuse it. The most successful songs were often technically restrained, whether in a harmonically conventional idiom or in the expanded language that became possible in the early twentieth century.

Of the composers already referred to, Liza Lehmann deserves further brief mention for the sake of her song-cycles, which include *In a Persian Garden* (1896, Fitzgerald, for four voices and piano), and *In memoriam*

---

[37] Composers were only echoing contemporary taste: 'What does little birdie say?' is the second poem in the Second Series of Palgrave's *Golden Treasury* (1897).

[38] Proctor's poem was published in 1858. It is tempting to conjecture that she had been idly turning the pages of E. J. Hopkins and E. F. Rimbault, *The Organ* (London, 1855), where on pp. 14–15 she would have found a quatrain by Claudian with the phrase 'Et qui magna levi detrudens murmura tactu . . . Intonet erranti digito', and a Greek epigram (attributed to Julian the Apostate) to much the same effect; though she would have had to dismiss Rimbault's (mistaken) denial that its words imply the existence of a keyboard.

[39] Temperley's encomium (*BHMB*, v. 129–30) seems wanton; but it occurs within a valuable treatment of the ballad tradition.

[40] *Songs 1860–1900*, no. 7.

(Tennyson, 1899). The medium of the former was unusual but not unique: there are examples by Somervell and Stanford, amongst others, with possible prototypes in Schubert, Schumann, and Brahms. *In memoriam* suffered in comparison with Somervell's *Maud*,[41] which had appeared in the previous year. Neither is particularly successful as a cycle, though both contain individually satisfying songs. The same is true of Somervell's later cycles, which include one from Housman's *A Shropshire Lad* (1904—the first Housman settings of any note) and Browning's *James Lee's Wife* (1907).

On the whole English composers fared best with collections of between three and six or seven songs, often linked by their choice of poet but otherwise making no great pretensions to unity. Stanford published twenty-two such collections (nineteen up to 1914); these include two sets of *Six Songs* to words of Heine (Op. 4 and Op. 7, 1893), and two 'Irish' cycles, so called (Op. 118, 1910, and Op. 139, 1913). These latter have but seven songs apiece; the first of them has an optional orchestral accompaniment. In all these sets and in numerous separate songs a certain level of craftsmanship and good taste is maintained; but inspiration did not always materialize, and the idiom is surprisingly unadventurous. Even the Irish element (there are three sets of 'Irish' songs in addition to the two cycles) is underplayed in musical terms, and in a song like 'Since thou, O fondest and truest', the first of three Bridge settings (Op. 43, 1897), Stanford came very close to an English 'folk' melody (Ex. 4.7).[42] But neither this song nor its

Ex. 4.7

C. V. Stanford, 'Since thou O fondest and truest' (Bridges): (*Album of 12 English Songs* (London and Leipzig, 1893–7)

---

[41] Ibid., nos. 29–40 (complete). For a more positive assessment of Somervell's cycles, see Banfield, *Sensibility and English Song*, 42–53.

[42] C. Villiers Stanford, *Songs*, ed. G. Bush (MB 52; London, 1986), no. 13; and an earlier version, ibid., no. 45.

two companions make the best of their undeniable melodic charm; the harmony is at times as near to being careless as Stanford ever gets, and the possibility of continuity between the stanzas is altogether ignored in the first of them. Stanford wrote too quickly and freely to achieve absolute perfection, though his idiomatic restraint was a potential merit and puts him at an advantage even over Elgar at this time.

Elgar himself advanced beyond the extroversion of *Sea Pictures* in some of his later songs, in which the public image often gives way to the wistful intimacy that is at the heart of his musical language. A song such as *Pleading* (Op. 48, no. 1, also with orchestral accompaniment)[43] is quintessentially Elgarian both in its unabashed sentimentality and in its poignant questioning (Ex. 4.8). As with the Parker cycle mentioned earlier, however, the vocal line could almost be a solo violin part.

Elgar's choice of, and response to, lyric poetry was at best uncertain. Quite the reverse is true of Parry, whose twelve sets of *English Lyrics*—the format in which much of his mature output was deployed—are a uniquely satisfying and consistent monument of their kind. Most of their contents— even of the last three books, published in 1918 (Book X) and 1920 (Books XI and XII)—were composed before the outbreak of war. Critical reception has not always been enthusiastic, and indeed the fondness for moderate 4/4 time and the restricted choice of keys can seem wearisome to the student of the songs as a whole. The weaker ones sometimes adopt conventional gestures reminiscent of a high Victorian idiom. Yet the preponderance of purely musical qualities, as opposed to flashy 'effect', is their greatest advantage: the melodies respond in a shapely fashion to the words, and the accompaniments have the Brahmsian merit of contrapuntal viability within a wholly pianistic idiom. Such virtues are in abundance throughout (say) the *Fourth Set*, an astonishing achievement for an English composer in 1896, and one that firmly places English song on the level of the later Romantic lied. The opening of the first song will illustrate these qualities (Ex. 4.9), though it is not the finest of the set (the anticipation here of Elgar's cello concerto, incidentally, is curious).[44]

In the early years of the twentieth century the idiomatic boundaries widened in the work of composers younger than those so far mentioned—except that is for Delius, who was the same age as Lehmann and a year older than Somervell. Delius is a special case, writing songs in German, French, Norwegian, and Danish as well as in English; but though his influence in England was at first limited he was chronologically at least the standard-bearer of an idiom based on an enhanced chromaticism that was to a certain extent independent of contrapuntal logic. In this, and in his

---

[43] Novello & Co., 1908. There were no further nos. in this opus.
[44] The last three of the set are in Hubert Parry, *Songs*, ed. G. Bush (MB 49; London, 1982), nos. 16–18.

Ex. 4.8

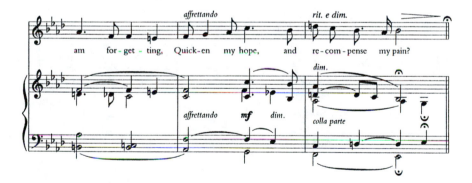

Edward Elgar, *Pleading* (Salmon), Op. 48 no. 1 (London, 1908), p. 1

Ex. 4.9

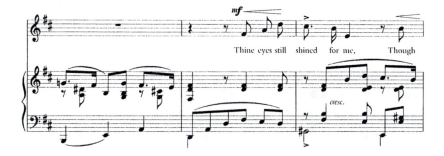

C. H. H. Parry, 'Thine eyes still shined for me' (Emerson) (*English Lyrics (Fourth Set)* (London, 1896), no. 1, pp. 1–2

preference for short repeated melodic units, he resembles Debussy (we have mentioned his Debussyan dramaturgy above); but his very personal style also embraced straightforward diatonicism and a more contrapuntally-based chromaticism (cf. Ex. 4.1 above, p. 254).

The expanded tonality of the early twentieth century, therefore, could be derived either from non-structural chromaticism or from the contrapuntal treatment of chromatic melody. Few composers adopted one or the other procedure exclusively, but in the context of song the most 'Delian' figure was probably Cyril Scott (1879–1970), who had written nearly ninety songs by 1914, and the most Wagnerian Granville Bantock (1868–1946), with about 120 songs up to the same date. Scott is assigned to a 'Frankfurt' school with Norman O'Neill (1875–1934), Balfour Gardiner (1877–1950),[45] and Roger Quilter (1877–1953); but their shared training there had little bearing on their later idiomatic preferences, which vary considerably both in their attachment to chromaticism and in the form which it took. All continued song-writing after the war (Quilter to a very substantial extent), as did Bantock, Arnold Bax (1883–1953), and several others of their generation. Two more individuals who made a significant contribution up to 1914 were Frank Bridge (1879–1941) and Joseph Holbrooke; Bridge later developed modernist tendencies (there is a fascinating parallel with Albert Roussel, ten years his senior), but his natural language was that of thirds-based chromaticism.

Much of this outpouring of song is worth detailed exploration, but it is less significant in historical terms than the more sober but at the same time more emancipated repertory associated with Vaughan Williams, Gustav Holst (1874–1934), William Hurlstone (1876–1906), John Ireland (1879–1962), and the younger group led by George Butterworth (1885–1916) and Ivor Gurney (1890–1937). Butterworth was the most gifted of those killed in action (though strong claims have been made for Denis Browne, 1888–1915); Ivor Gurney was shattered by the war, though his large output of songs mostly post-dates it. Of the older group Hurlstone is hard to evaluate because of his early death: like Vaughan Williams, he built on foundations laid by Stanford but had little time to achieve real individuality.[46] Ireland destroyed all his songs prior to *Songs of a Wayfarer*, published in 1912.

---

[45] Cf. S. Lloyd, *H. Balfour Gardiner* (Cambridge, 1984). Gardiner composed little in all; many of his earlier works are now untraceable, but his few surviving songs are of value, and he was an enthusiastic collector and arranger of folk songs.

[46] Charles Wood, another pupil of Stanford, wrote numerous songs up to the First World War (many published later or not at all). Only one, a setting of Walt Whitman's 'Ethiopia saluting the colours' (*Songs 1860–1900*, no. 41) is at all remarkable (first published 1898). This odd poem, which hardly satisfies modern standards of 'political correctness', also attracted Vaughan Williams, both in middle and in later life (sketches, 1908, 1957–8: M. Kennedy, *A Catalogue of the Works of Ralph Vaughan Williams* (2nd. edn., Oxford, 1996), 45, 258).

Vaughan Williams was in any case the leader of the movement. His strength lay in his solid though hard-won technique—he had studied with and admired both Stanford and Parry, sharing with them a broadly based university education and an appreciation of fine poetry, both old and new— and in his sturdy independence of fashion. His earliest songs were conventional enough, but he soon established a personal voice in such songs as *Linden Lea*, composed in 1901, and *Silent Noon* (1903), which became the second song in a D. G. Rosetti cycle, *The House of Life* (1904). The opening of this still popular setting is sufficient to indicate his individuality in a distonic context (Ex. 4.10). Some of the other, more experimental, songs in the set lack cohesion, but the *Songs of Travel* (Stevenson), also from 1904, are more completely assured. (Curiously the ninth and last song, which gives the cycle its unity, was never performed in the composer's lifetime and remained unpublished, its existence unsuspected, until after his death.)[47] The masterpiece of these early years, however, is *On Wenlock Edge* (1909), a cycle drawn from poems by Housman and scored for tenor, piano, and string quartet. (The quartet can be dispensed with, though its omission deprives the work of an important coloristic element; the accompaniment was later orchestrated.) Here the composer's unique combination of chromaticism and modal diatonicism is fully developed. It is interesting to compare the fifth song, *Bredon Hill*, with Butterworth's more austere setting in his second set of Housman songs, published in 1912. Quite apart from Vaughan Williams's far more atmospheric treatment of the church bells, his melodic line has an irregularity that evokes the freedom of the folk singer, whereas Butterworth's phrases (justified by his accompaniment) are far more mechanical (Ex. 4.11).

By this time, in fact, Vaughan Williams had become an experienced collector of folk songs and had published the first of several collections with piano accompaniment. His work on the *English Hymnal* (published in 1906) had similarly acquainted him with the wellsprings of English melody, both in plainsong and in the old metrical psalm-tunes and their Renaissance settings. The personal voice that he acquired before the war as a result of these influences, combined with that of a great deal of more recent European music (including Wagner's), never deserted him throughout his long career.

Holst too was much influenced by folk song, but he was less prone than his great friend to romanticize it, and it had to take its place beside his other great enthusiasm, which was for Sanskrit literature and lore.[48] Apart from the four groups of *Choral Hymns from the Rig Veda* (1908–12) he published a set of nine solo *Vedic Hymns* with piano accompaniment, in which his

---

[47] Kennedy, ibid., 28.
[48] This he shared with John Foulds (1880–1939), a minor but fairly prolific composer whose book *Music Today* (London, 1934) reveals a degree of saturation in the occult.

Ex. 4.10

Ralph Vaughan Williams, *Silent Noon* (D. G. Rossetti) (London, 1903), version in E flat, pp. 1–2 = *House of Life* (London, 1903), pp. 9–10

Ex. 4.11

'In summertime on Bredon' (Housman): (*a*) Ralph Vaughan Williams, *On Wenlock Edge* (London, 1911), pp. 29–30; (*b*) George Butterworth, *Bredon Hill* (London, 1912), no. 1, pp. 1–2

characteristically spare textures and fourths-based harmony are effectively deployed. Although Holst had earlier written a substantial number of songs, his characteristic voice emerged only in this set and was not often heard subsequently in the medium.[49]

As for Butterworth himself, also a collector of folk songs, it is hard to say how he would have fared given a longer span of life. The second Housman cycle is a remarkable achievement by any standards. It is not in the least self-indulgent: indeed the songs have a strong flavour of sobriety. If the occasional splash of harmonic colour in *Bredon Hill* or the ghostly marching of 'On the idle hill of summer' are reminiscent of Debussy, the motivic persistence of the latter song also offers a foretaste of Britten (Ex. 4.12).

[49] *Four Songs*, Op. 35, for voice and violin (composed 1916–17), and *Twelve Songs*, Op. 48 (Humbert Wolfe, composed 1929), are his main later contributions.

Ex. 4.12

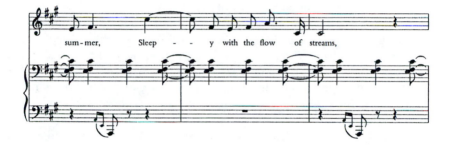

George Butterworth, 'On the idle hill of summer' (Housman): *Bredon Hill* (London, 1912), no. 4, p. 14

The undertone of intense sadness and its expansion in simple folk-like melody is only one facet of a complex musical personality.

Orchestral Music

It is perhaps in orchestral music that the greatest changes can be seen over the course of this period. In 1870 the English contribution was a distinctly parochial affair, even in the country of its origin. Sullivan's early efforts had come to a premature halt, and the later ones of Macfarren belonged to a vanishing age. Mackenzie seemed less and less able to fulfil his early promise, except perhaps in his violin concerto (1885), *Britannia* overture (1894), and *Scottish Concerto* for piano (1897). The time was ripe for a renaissance, but the prospects were poor. Hans Richter and August Manns, who were with Hallé the most prominent conductors of the later Victorian years, while not unsympathetic to the promotion of British music, had a not unnatural predilection for the German classics. Manns could be extraordinarily obstinate in the face of what he considered to be modernist or experimental. It is disheartening to read of the rebuffs faced by Parry when trying to get his early orchestral music even rehearsed and so to gain vital experience. Stanford, with his more aggressive manner, fared better; as a result his orchestral music is, on the whole, better scored in a straightforward fashion.

It is a great credit to the Cambridge University Musical Society, and none at all to London's professional musical life, that it was able to mount first performances of several demanding and sometimes (with hindsight) important orchestral works, including the second symphonies of both Stanford (1882) and Parry (under Stanford, 1883). The provincial festivals were another major outlet. Three of Stanford's symphonies and over half of his other orchestral works remained unpublished; the same is true of the less prolific Parry's first symphony, his piano concerto, and several other works. In Parry's case, publication often occurred only long after their first performances and even long after their subsequent revision. (Parry was an inveterate reviser, and such delays did him less harm than precipitate publication might have done.) Elgar moved heaven and earth to get his *Froissart* overture published by Novello, which they did in time for its first performance in Worcester in 1890.[50] The only other English composer of important orchestral music before 1900 was Delius, whose German connections enabled him to get his demanding music performed and published in Germany.

Stanford's orchestral music is perhaps more significant for the flag it flew than for its lasting qualities. The overall impression created by his

---

[50] Only the full score and the string parts were engraved; the other parts were copied by hand for hire. But the engraving of the score was itself an achievement: publishers often did no more than make the composer's autograph, or a MS copy, available to conductors.

symphonies is that we should be glad of them if it were not for those of Brahms or Dvořák; which prompts the further reflection that if it were not for those of Brahms and Dvořák we probably should not have Stanford's either. Casual impressions, however, can be misleading: the second symphony, which sounds suspiciously like Dvořák's seventh, predates it by three years. Could Dvořák have become acquainted with it when he visited England in 1884? Viewed as a prototype, Stanford's ambitious work is worthier of our respect. Its first movement is an energetic 6/8 in D minor, though its main modulation is to the relative major, not to Dvořák's submediant major. The second movement is in 4/4, F major, though less ornamented than Dvořák's; the scherzo is again in 6/8, D minor, with a D major trio, 'Tranquillo ma l'istesso tempo' (Dvořák notates in 6/4 but the two movements have much in common). Only the two finales differ greatly: Stanford begins with a portentous introduction which accelerates into a D major Allegro based on a cheeky 'Irish' folk melody (Ex. 4.13).[51] Stanford did not quite have it in him to become an Irish Dvořák, though he came close to being so in his third ('Irish') symphony (arguably his best) and in the five Irish rhapsodies (four for orchestra and one for solo cello and orchestra).

In 1883 came the charming serenade in G, a Brahmsian score that keeps its secret until the very end: a concluding *Lullaby* of exquisite tenderness (Ex. 4.14).[52] In the next two decades he wrote a wealth of orchestral music: several concertos, the remaining symphonies, and other pieces of various kinds. The second piano concerto, composed in 1911 but first performed in America in 1915 (and published only in 1916), is a fine work with hints of Rakhmaninov's second. The clarinet concerto, composed in 1902 for Richard Mühlfeld, is a striking piece, but never performed and subsequently withdrawn (it has since been published as a facsimile of a manuscript copy owned by Boosey and Hawkes).[53] Mühlfeld did not like it: its challenging virtuosity goes well beyond anything in the late works that Brahms had written for him, and its aggressiveness is not very like anything else in Stanford either.

But most of Stanford's later orchestral music is less rewarding than the earlier. The seventh symphony, also in D minor (composed in 1911) is still very much in the Brahmsian mould, like so much of Parry's. Parry had written some ambitious chamber music, mostly unpublished, before he had an orchestral work of comparable stature performed. This was the overture *Guillem de Castabanh*, which received a disastrous hearing under Manns in 1879. Manns was out of sympathy with its 'modernism', and the musical establishment generally gave Parry the least possible encouragement.[54] His

---

[51] Cambridge, Univ. Lib., Add. 9042 (copy).
[52] Ibid., Add. 9041 (copy: also publ. Boosey and Hawkes, n.d.).
[53] Published by Cramer, 1977.
[54] Dibble, *C. Hubert H. Parry*, 171–5.

Ex. 4.13

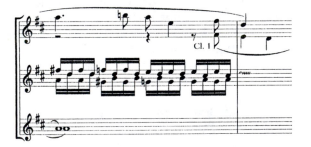

C. V. Stanford, Second Symphony, Finale: Cambridge, University Library, Add. 9042

Ex. 4.14

C. V. Stanford, Serenade in G, *Lullaby*: four-hand arrangement (London, 1882), pp. 52–3

one and only piano concerto (1880) was better received (with Dannreuther as soloist), and was repeated a couple of times. Thereafter the composition of orchestral music had to be fitted in with an increasing demand for his choral music following the (relative) success of *Prometheus Unbound*.

Parry was not a naturally fluent orchestrator, but it can at least be said that his orchestration matches his somewhat monochrome style; from that point of view it has a certain aptness. His first symphony occupied him for two years and was finally given at Birmingham under Richter in 1882 (like Stanford's *Serenade*). It was repeated under Manns in 1883, but neither conductor was at ease with it; it has never been published.[55] A second symphony was written for Cambridge in 1883 at Stanford's invitation. It was twice revised, for performance in 1887 and 1895, and published in 1906. The third and fourth symphonies had similarly lengthy periods of gestation and revision; the fourth (revised 1910) and a Symphonic Fantasia (1912) were published only after Parry's death. The title of the fourth symphony as revised, 'Finding the Way', and that of his symphonic poem 'From

---

[55] For Manns's patronizing attitude, see Dibble, 201.

Ex. 4.15

C. H. H. Parry, Symphony in E minor [no. 4], 2nd mvt. (London, [1921]), pp. 66–7

death to life' (1914, unpublished), reveal his later preoccupation with abstract philosophical ideas and his compulsion to express them in musical terms.

All these larger orchestral works contain much finely wrought music, soberly presented. But Parry's sense of a fitting restraint, particularly in his melodic lines, often strikes the listener as a failure to realise the implications of his finest ideas (except perhaps in the lighter and more 'accessible' third symphony). A good example is in the 'Molto adagio' slow movement of the fourth symphony, where, however, the overall effect (in its revised version) is of an overpowering introspection (it is subtitled 'Thinking on it') (Ex. 4.15).[56] The whole work is characteristic of Parry's intensely serious approach to symphonic composition.

Two of his shorter orchestral works, the *Overture to an Unwritten Tragedy* and the *Symphonic Variations*, enjoyed greater esteem in his lifetime. The former, first given in 1893 and twice revised before publication in 1906, is as weighty as any of his symphonic first movements. Quite unlike Brahms's

[56] For the revisions see Dibble, 434–41. The subtitles do not appear in the published full score (Novello, 1921).

Tragic Overture, it has on the contrary a certain Schumannesque character: the opening is suggestive of that of Schumann's Second Symphony, and there are further echoes of him in the taut, animated semiquaver figures of the main Allegro. The *Symphonic Variations* (1897), which won much critical acclaim, adopt Dvořák's plan of a short theme, its metrical structure being retained for some time before greater freedom is introduced. But Parry's theme is undistinguished (whereas Dvořák's could be called quirky), and the scoring is somewhat drab and occasionally ineffective. After six variations a flute solo, in a manner too reminiscent of Brahms, leads from E minor to the tonic major, and while the galumphing gait of the theme is temporarily abandoned we are not allowed to forget it for long.

In an ideal world the best of Stanford's and Parry's orchestral music would receive repeated hearings and be accorded the respect due to (mostly) sound craftsmanship and its historical importance. But their contribution was overshadowed in their lifetime by that of Elgar and Vaughan Williams in particular, and to a lesser extent by that of Delius (whose major works were only occasionally to be heard in England), Holst (who had not quite found his voice in the orchestral medium prior to *The Planets*), and several minor but enterprising figures.

Elgar rightly claims supremacy in that the years 1899–1913 coincided with his orchestral maturity and his international recognition. Although Stanford and Delius (in their very different ways and for different reasons) enjoyed considerable foreign esteem, it is only of Elgar that it could be said that his music quickly achieved (and retained) 'canonic' status in England and abroad. The reasons are not far to seek. His highly personal, recognizably English yet German-based style and his phenomenal command of orchestral colour endeared him to conductors and audiences alike. After his death his music suffered an eclipse as being perhaps too harmonically and tonally straightforward for a 'modern' composer; but it has always had its warm admirers and is now enjoyed both for its own sake and with a better understanding of its musico-historical context.

Before the *Enigma* variations there had come (apart from some quite minor pot-boilers) the *Froissart* overture (1890) and the E minor *Serenade* for strings (1892). *Froissart* seems indebted to Parry in some of its ideas, such as the dotted rhythms in moderate 4/4 that we also find in 'Blest Pair of Sirens'. Whether or not this particular work was a subconscious source, Elgar was certainly influenced by Parry and greatly admired him—a touching instance of regard from a by no means deferential genius. But even at this early stage Elgar's command of orchestral resources, based on his insider's knowledge as an orchestral violinist and an intensive study of scores, far exceeded Parry's. The *Serenade* illustrates his ability to write simply but effectively for strings, just as the later *Introduction and Allegro* was to display his flair for virtuoso string-ensemble writing.

The *Enigma* variations (1899), so very different from those of Brahms and Dvořák in their approach to the form, catapulted him into fame. The model here is less the Classical idea of a variation set than a Schumannesque succession of character-studies, though the freer concept of variation embodied in Strauss's *Don Quixote* (1897–8) may have played a part. In any case the relationship of each variation to the theme becomes ever looser as the set proceeds. Though the style in this work shows little dependence on either Schumann or Strauss, the general air of fantasy and mystery, helped by the use of initials, asterisks, and nicknames, is a markedly Schumannesque trait. So is the idea of a 'hidden theme' going along with the overt one; it occurs in the *Humoreske* and (less clandestinely) in the last movement of *Kreisleriana*.[57] The 'Enigma' (properly the title of the theme itself) has never been satisfactorily explained, unless it is simply that it indicates Elgar's own 'Eusebian' nature (his 'Florestanian' side being represented in the Finale).[58]

Bold orchestral characterization of external scenes, action, and moods is maintained in the overtures *Cockaigne* (produced in 1901) and *In the South* (1904), and in the 'Symphonic Study' *Falstaff* (1913). *Cockaigne*, like the *Introduction and Allegro* (1905), adopts a straightforward diatonic brilliance (notwithstanding moments of wistful introspection in both) that seems old-fashioned for its time. *In the South* is perhaps the most Straussian of all Elgar's orchestral works—the specific indebtedness is to *Ein Heldenleben*—and it is weakened, as Strauss's own tone-poems often are, by passages so bizarre that they seem to fall right out of the conventional symphonic frame in which they are set. *Falstaff* is Straussian in conception but not in execution (except insofar as the ending has affinities with those of *Don Juan* and *Don Quixote*). The composer thought it his finest achievement, and it is with hesitation that one dissents. But if the acid test of good programme music is that it is comprehensible independently of its programme, then *Falstaff* satisfies it only with difficulty. The themes themselves, though apt in terms of characterization, are not on the whole amongst Elgar's most compelling, and their formal treatment is highly discursive.

It is in the two symphonies, together with the violin concerto (and finally the cello concerto) that Elgar's grasp of large-scale form is most apparent. The symphonies were at first thought too diffuse to be genuinely symphonic, but that was before the huge structures of Mahler and Bruckner were generally known and appreciated in this country. In fact they are surprisingly compact, given the scale, and in that sense closer to Bruckner than to Mahler. As for the style, the usual foundation of Schumann and Brahms overlaid with Strauss is readily apparent; but Elgar also achieved a

---

[57] *Kreisleriana* often crops up, no doubt unconsciously, at this period: for example, in Parry's *Blest Pair* (3/4 section) and in his song 'No longer mourn for me' (*English Lyrics*, Set 2, no. 3), and in *The Dream of Gerontius*, as noted above.

[58] Cf. Reed, *Elgar*, 55: 'He was himself the Enigma, and remained so to the end of his life.'

highly personal form of harmonic chromaticism that owes little to any Continental example and which, when allied to his more conventional use of diatonic dissonance, gives his finest music much of its unique flavour.

The First Symphony (1908) seems to begin where the *Enigma* variations left off (Ex. 4.16). As for its own conclusion, this adopts not the same upward sixth but the upward fourth that had originally occurred with the repetition of a thematic segment at the end of the first statement of the complete theme (Ex. 4.17). It is not an entirely convincing strategy, and the orchestral pyrotechnics that accompany the final motif suggest that the composer himself was not convinced by it either. It is a slight but detectable flaw in a work that in most respects exhibits consummate

Ex. 4.16

Edward Elgar: (a) *Variations on an Original Theme* (*Enigma*) (London, 1899), pp. 126–7; (b) First Symphony (London, 1908), p. 3

Ex. 4.17

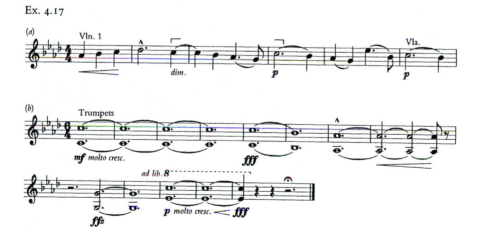

Edward Elgar, First Symphony (London, 1908): (a) motto theme, p. 6; (b) conclusion, pp. 169–70

mastery. The interweaving of the noble motto with the frenzied utterances of the main section of the first movement is handled with great skill; the middle movements are sharply characterized, their common thematic basis noticeable only to someone previously primed; and the finale has a thrilling momentum that in a fine performance can enable us to suspend disbelief until the final chord is over.

The end of the violin concerto (1910) adopts a similar but more effective strategy. Here the opening motif is given out triumphantly, in horns and cellos, in the major key, ending on the fifth of the scale. The accompanying virtuosity is confined to the soloist, from whom it is expected. Elgar's achievement in this work can be equated with that of Sibelius in its application of the grand Romantic manner to the purposes of the new century. The first movement, though it has a substantial orchestral 'exposition', and a melting 'second subject' which in true Elgarian fashion can never bring itself to come to an end, is formally unique. If it is really true that Elgar composed the work in bits and decided how to fit them together only at a later stage, the outcome is remarkably successful.[59] The slow movement exudes the calm serenity and the florid ornament that we associate with Beethoven's comparable movement or for that matter the slow movement of Brahms's second piano concerto, with which it shares its key and its first few notes. The finale is distinguished by the magic of an accompanied reminiscing cadenza prior to the energetic conclusion.

But it is the Second Symphony (1911) that crowns Elgar's orchestral achievement, and England's too, in these years. 'Rarely, rarely comest thou, Spirit of Delight', Elgar inscribed on the score; and rarely has a motto been so patently apt. For the spirit of delight, which often deserted Elgar, is present here in that rarified form that comes of the experience of despair. The slow movement is a threnody under a clouded sky, but a sky which the sun cannot help breaking through. If this movement and the Finale look back to past glory, the first movement revels in the actuality of delight and the scherzo in a terrifying agility. The formal control in the enormous first movement is absolute, and there are few more gripping returns to the opening material than here: the prancing steed is reined in for the biggest hurdle, as it were, and with a rush we are over and away. The end of the whole work is a glorious sunset which seems to have puzzled its first audiences but which can now be seen as the inevitable consequence of all that has gone before. 'Most most beautiful', commented the composer's wife after the second rehearsal.[60]

If Elgar's music invites a relaxation from objective criticism it is because of its exuberant Romanticism. But it also has an inner toughness that has secured its permanent appeal compared with that of (say) Granville Bantock,

---

[59] Cf. Reed, *Elgar*, 101; Moore, *Edward Elgar*, 462, 552, 562–87.   [60] Ibid. 615.

who was far more prolific, and equally skilful in the handling of large-scale form and the orchestral medium. His music does not deserve its present neglect in the concert-hall (*Fifine at the Fair*, based on Browning's poem and the third of six tone-poems produced between 1900 and 1902, has received an occasional well-merited revival).[61] His musical personality and his technical assurance are comparable to those of (say) Saint-Saëns and Rimsky-Korsakov, and these seems no good reason why his music should not have entered the repertory on a comparable footing.

Delius is sometimes regarded as a marginal figure in the national context. He was indeed a cosmopolitan, drawing his inspiration from many sources and preferring to live in Germany and, later, in France. But his music was to be heard in England before the Great War; he chose English as well as European subjects as the inspiration of his works, and (a small but telling point) he preferred to write his indications of speed and expression in the English vernacular.[62]

Delius, like Elgar, was largely self-taught and a late developer. The orchestral tone-poem *Paris* was composed in 1899 and first heard at Elberfeld in 1901; it was preceded by a number of smaller works and an unsatisfactory piano concerto (first heard in 1904), but only in *Paris* did Delius's command of orchestral resources become fully evident. By 1907, when *Brigg Fair* was composed and performed (in Basle), he had become well known. *Brigg Fair* is no aimless rhapsody, despite its subtitle, but a tautly constructed set of variations with interludes well placed to secure structural variety and an element of repose. *In a Summer Garden* and the first *Dance Rhapsody* (both 1908) are also less indulgent formally than their titles might suggest. Delius cultivated a small orchestra in *Summer Night on the River* and *On Hearing the First Cuckoo in Spring* (given in Leipzig in 1913);[63] his last orchestral work before the war was *North Country Sketches* (given by Beecham in 1913). The two former are exquisite miniatures; the latter is a major work in four movements, somewhat Debussyan in places but a masterly score that deserves to be far better known than it is.

In the reactionary atmosphere of pre-war London Delius's large-scale works were often thought to be impracticable until Beecham took some of them in hand, reducing their orchestration (the six horns of *Brigg Fair*, for example, are easily reduced to four) and annotating the scores with supplementary dynamics and articulation. Thus there arose the myth of Delius the

---

[61] It was revised in 1912, as was *Dante and Beatrice* (originally *Dante*, no. 2 of the set) in 1910. His *Helena Variations* appeared in 1899, the year of Elgar's *Enigma*. Some recent recordings have begun to redress the balance.

[62] See also Ch. 5, p. 330–1.

[63] Published in reverse order as *Zwei Stücke für kleines Orchester* (Cologne: Tischer and Jagenberg, 1914; reissued as *Two Pieces for Small Orchestra* by Oxford University Press, 1930). R. Threlfall, *A Catalogue of the Compositions of Frederick Delius* (London, 1977), and *Frederick Delius: A Supplementary Catalogue*, (London, 1986), no. VI/19.

scarcely competent. He himself admired Beecham's performances, but it is essential for the student to consult the scores as Delius wrote them, if possible from corrected versions of the often inaccurate original impressions.[64] He was an imaginative orchestrator and skilful in large-scale design. His scores do indeed need sensitive interpretation, but (to cite just one instance of his supposed carelessness) he often seems to have intended the particular effect of separate bow-strokes in quiet music: the absence of slurs is not necessarily due to inattention.

The use of folk tunes as a basis of orchestral works enjoyed a considerable vogue in the early years of the twentieth century. Stanford, as we have seen, wrote five Irish rhapsodies; Vaughan Williams three Norfolk rhapsodies (two unpublished and later suppressed); Delius used folk melodies in *Brigg Fair*, in the *North Country Sketches*, and in *Appalachia* (for chorus and orchestra); Holst wrote *Songs of the West* and *A Somerset Rhapsody* (Op. 21), both being revisions of more amorphous 'selections'; and Butterworth used folk songs in his *Two English Idylls* (1911), *A Shropshire Lad* (1912), and *The Banks of Green Willow* (1913).[65] Such works demonstrate musical nationalism in its most obvious form, but the genre had its limitations, however ingeniously the tunes might be forced into a musically coherent structure. Holst's *Rhapsody* (written in 1906–7 but first performed in 1910), for example, combines its four tunes in various ways; his use of bitonality and fourths-based harmony gives it an astringency not often encountered in works of this kind.

Holst's *Cotswolds Symphony*, completed in 1900 and first performed in 1902, has little in it of the composer's mature style.[66] There is more individuality in Vaughan Williams's *In the Fen Country*, composed in 1904 but not heard until 1909, when Beecham gave a performance. Neither work is based explicitly on folk song, though there is the flavour of it in both. Apart from the Norfolk rhapsodies and the instrumental music to *The Wasps*,[67] Vaughan Williams's main pre-war contributions were the *Fantasia on a Theme by Thomas Tallis*, for double string orchestra, composed and first heard (in Gloucester cathedral) in 1910, and *A London Symphony*, completed in 1913 and first given on 27 March 1914. Both were subsequently revised: the *Fantasia* in 1913 for a London performance, and again in 1919 (and

---

[64] The complete works are now in course of publication: the Delius Trust has issued a series of facsimiles, and several works have been issued in corrected reprints or new editions. See Threlfall, *Catalogue* and *Supplementary Catalogue*, for details.

[65] In this nomenclature, an idyll is based on a single tune, a rhapsody on two or more (*Brigg Fair* is an exception). *A Shropshire Lad* is a rhapsody, *The Banks of Green Willow* an idyll.

[66] Though unpublished, it was given the opus no. 8 (originally 10). I. Holst, *A Thematic Catalogue of Gustav Holst's Music* (London, 1974), no. 47. A more ambitious early work was the symphonic poem *Indra* (Op. 13, 1903: Holst no. 66): this was his first Sanskrit-inspired orchestral work.

[67] This was arranged for a larger orchestra and published as a five-movement suite in 1914 (first heard in this form in 1912). Details of all works in Kennedy, *Catalogue of the Works of Ralph Vaughan Williams*.

published in 1921); and the *London Symphony* in 1918, 1920 (when it was published), and finally in 1933 (and republished in 1936).

This pattern of extensive revision was not unusual at this time, when English composers had little opportunity of hearing their orchestral music performed and often found that they had miscalculated their effects. Delays in publication at least made it less embarrassing to make adjustments. In Vaughan Williams's case there was also a tendency to prolixity that he later felt he had to curb. The Scherzo of the *London Symphony*, for example, originally had two trios, with a corresponding further repetition of the main section. The excision of the second trio is a pity in some ways, for a certain gigantism is part of the aesthetic of the work. But there is still enough of it left, even after these revisions. Michael Kennedy rightly places it beside Elgar's two symphonies for its opulence and its copiousness of invention;[68] and we may discern in its touching epilogue not only the mysterious sadness at the heart of life (and not least of the teeming life of a huge city) but a farewell to a world which for all its wickedness one could hardly bear to see slipping away for ever.

The Tallis *Fantasia* had also ended on a quiet G major chord, but its message is of timeless permanence, not of an imperfect but much loved temporality. Its inspiration was a discovery by Vaughan Williams for *The English Hymnal*, the third of Tallis's eight tunes for Archbishop Parker's Psalter. In the original version the tune is in the tenor part of four. *The English Hymnal* gives it both in that form and with the tune transferred to the treble. Vaughan Williams was able to make play both with the tune *per se* and with Tallis's original upper part. But his piece is no archaizing or 'period' fantasia, even if the renewed interest in Tudor music then taking place provided the impulse for a string piece so titled. It takes a highly romanticized view of the form, retaining only the convention of a sectionalized structure of loosely related parts. The new idea first introduced on the viola is indeed treated contrapuntally, but the counterpoint is soon abandoned. The episode also offers a tonal contrast by emphasizing the E Phrygian modality of the original tune, the outer sections having transposed it to G. The piece successfully evokes a golden age of the remote past and projects it, idealized as it is, into the present. It is a work to gladden the heart, but it was received at Gloucester with patronizing indifference.

Other composers of orchestral music in the early twentieth century include Cyril Rootham (1875–1938), Frank Bridge (1879–1941), Donald Tovey (1875–1940), Benjamin Dale (1885–1943), and George Butterworth. Rootham was a Bristolian who became organist of St John's College, Cambridge; his talent was really a very minor one, though he attained a certain celebrity with his setting of Laurence Binyon's *For the Fallen* (1915).

[68] *The Works of Ralph Vaughan Williams* (2nd edn., London, 1980), 140.

His overture *To the Spirit of Comedy* and his short tone-poem *A Passer By* (based on a poem by Bridges)[69] are afflicted by a penchant for sliding chromaticisms that achieve a valid comic effect in the overture but are a distraction in the other work. Bridge was anything but a minor talent, and his pre-war music for orchestra such as his tone-poem *The Sea* has a panache that would have justified its greater popularity had it not had to compete with that of Elgar and Vaughan Williams. After the war Bridge's style changed quite radically, as we have already noted, and the complexity of his musical *persona* has proved a continued barrier to a fuller appreciation.

Donald Tovey is nowadays thought of mainly as a scholar and educator, but as a young man he was a pianist of distinction and a composer of promise. His early orchestral works were a piano concerto (1903) and a symphony (1913). Unfortunately, his immense enthusiasm for the German classical tradition led him into pedantry, though there is something to be said for some of his chamber music. He became Reid Professor at Edinburgh University in 1914 and remained there for the rest of his life.

Dale was a precocious musician whose early orchestral music showed great promise; his wartime experiences may have been responsible for a marked falling-off in his later years. Butterworth achieved, in the small number of works mentioned above, a personal voice of great distinction, although it was destined not to be expressed in a work of symphonic dimensions.

Chamber Music

A good deal of English chamber music in this period seems to have been written simply in order to exploit established forms and to demonstrate a kind of parity with Continental models. It did not have to be commissioned or even composed with particular performers in mind (though it often was), so that it satisfied a less obvious external need than choral and orchestral music. Like songs, chamber works were offered speculatively to publishers, who in most cases could hope to make little money from them. Much of it therefore remained, and still remains, in manuscript.

Except for a few examples by younger composers in the early years of the twentieth century, the chamber music of the period is much less interesting than the orchestral. If it is good, it is usually because it is derived from a good model. The medium excluded (or was generally considered to exclude) wholesale formal innovation, the use of short single movements (apart from trifles), or programmatic content; and it very largely excluded instrumental novelty even within its self-imposed confines. In return for the possibility of

---

[69] MSS in Cambridge, Univ. Lib., Add. 9100 (1907), 9102 (1910?). Other MSS of Rootham are to be found there and at St John's College.

wider dissemination, composers settled on the whole for the safety of routine.

Macfarren's later chamber works include his last string quartet (in G, 1878), a flute sonata (B flat, 1883), a violin sonata (E minor, 1887) and, it is true, some lighter works for one or two solo instruments and piano. Of the younger generation, Mackenzie wrote little of importance, and nothing at all after settling in London in 1885 (he was, of course, concentrating on larger forms). During the 1880s the cult of Brahms, led by Stanford, became the main influence on serious English chamber music. Parry too was affected by it, since although he was far from being an exclusively Brahmsian composer this seemed the only viable model for the medium. At first the influence was a beneficial one, since it superseded the all-pervading Mendelssohnianism of the preceding era and offered a dialectical toughness that had previously been lacking.

Parry's chamber music, apart from a couple of suites for violin and piano, was all written by 1900, though some of it was later revised. Much of it remained unpublished. After a good deal of experimental work he wrote an ambitious Nonet for wind instruments, also experimental and not in the event performed in his lifetime, but at the same time tightly organized and worthy of his maturity. The piano trio in E minor, published in 1879, is more obviously Brahmsian, like the piano quartet in A flat (1879, published in 1884) and the cello sonata in A (1879–80, published in 1883). The string quintet in E flat is his major (and only published) chamber work without piano; certainly it is Brahmsian, but its energy and spirit, especially in the scherzo and finale, make it an admirable concert piece, well worth revival. It was composed in 1883–4, revised in 1896 and 1902, and finally published (in score only) in 1909. It bears comparison with the equally Brahmsian piano trio in B minor (composed and published in 1884), his last major chamber work and a fine piece despite its unevenness.

Stanford's output of chamber music was larger than Parry's and extended almost to the end of his life (the last two quartets, which are also his last major chamber works, are datable c.1919). There are eight string quartets in all (only the first three and the fifth published), of which the earlier ones are generally considered the best. The fifth (1908), composed in memory of Joachim, may be taken as representative. It is Brahmsian, but never oppressively so, and its passionate slow movement, with a triple fugato worthy of Bach, lifts the whole work a long way above the ordinary, as does the lyricism of the second idea, quoted here from its reappearance in the tonic major (Ex. 4.18).[70] Not all Stanford's work, however, is on this level. The outer movements of the clarinet sonata (Op. 133, composed c.1912) are

---

[70] Cf. *Kreisleriana*, again, for the dotted figure with demisemiquavers; and perhaps Schumann's Second Symphony (slow movement) for the lyricism in (b).

Ex. 4.18

Ex. 4.18, continued

C. V. Stanford, Fifth String Quartet, Op. 104, 3rd mvt. (London, 1908): (*a*) pp. 30–1; (*b*) p. 33

mere Brahms-and-water, little more than students' pastiche; the middle movement is the well-known *Caoine* (Lament), though even this lacks the intensity of the movement just quoted. Unfortunately, Stanford's failure, in his later years, to develop beyond his inherited tradition was more a symptom of stagnation than of golden serenity.

Stanford had a pupil, Charles Wood (1866–1926), whose string quartets should not be forgotten. He was, like Stanford, an Irishman, and he eventually succeeded his master as Professor of Music at Cambridge. After his death his eight quartets (one of which is a set of variations on an Irish folk tune) were edited by E. J. Dent and published by Oxford University Press at the expense of the Master and Fellows of Gonville and Caius, Wood's Cambridge college. The quartets range from 1885 to 1916, though some are undated. The eighth work is a single undated movement, probably early. Wood obtained a mastery of the medium at an early age; his work is free of pedantry, and in fact the gentle counterpoint of his later quartets has much in it of the freedom usually associated with younger composers. After the war this was transmuted into a rather self-conscious archaism that found its outlet in simple church music, but at this period there was nothing self-conscious about his quiet Romanticism. Incidentally the orchestral prelude to his music for *Ion* (produced in Cambridge in 1890) is a short tone-poem of quite remarkable beauty.[71]

Donald Tovey was another composer whose main contribution lay in the field of chamber music. Some of the chamber music with piano, dating from 1899 to 1910, is attractive in a neo-Brahmsian fashion. The two string quartets, both dating from 1909, are strange works. The first, in G major (Op. 23), starts like a French overture, 'Andante pomposo e galante', though the real inspiration for this 2/4 piece is the first movement of Beethoven's last quartet. The influence of Beethoven predominates throughout the work, though its instrumental complexity exceeds Beethoven's at his most elaborate. Unfortunately, the composer was heading rapidly down a cul-de-sac.

More innovative voices than Tovey's, however, were making themselves heard in the 1900s. The Tudor revival sparked off a vogue for 'phantasy' quartets and quintets, originally as a result of a competition for a prize offered for the first time in 1905 by Walter Cobbett, an amateur enthusiast for and subsequently encyclopaedist of chamber music. The prize was won by William Hurlstone, who died the following year at a young age but who had already begun to make a reputation for a less academic approach to composition.[72] Cobbett later commissioned one of the best of such works, Vaughan Williams's *Phantasy Quintet* (1911), though it is only fair to add as a measure of his eclecticism that he also commissioned Tovey's piano quintet in 1912.[73]

Vaughan Williams was undoubtedly the most promising of the composers then in their thirties, in chamber music as in so much else, though even he had achieved little in terms of quantity by 1914. Both the first string quartet and the *Phantasy Quintet* are attractive as well as innovative pieces. The quartet was received with incomprehension when it was first heard in 1908; it was revised and published after the war. One can only guess what would have been the reaction of its critics to the quartets of Debussy and Ravel; that of Vaughan Williams may have been indebted to Debussy's in its choice of key and certain technical details, and it was certainly indebted in a general sense to Ravel, from whom he had recently been taking lessons. (Vaughan Williams even seems to anticipate the minuet of *Le tombeau de Couperin* in his use of quiet consecutive triads in G Dorian; possibly he encountered the idiom in some earlier work of Ravel. Whatever the truth may be, this feature was destined to become one of his most characteristic

[71] Cambridge, Gonville and Caius Coll., Wood archive, envelope 4.
[72] He was a pupil of Stanford, who treated him very roughly.
[73] *BHMB*, v. 399.

devices.) The use of the Dorian scale in G minor (i.e. with E natural) pervades the opening of this work and is even more characteristic of the composer than the Phrygian scale used (very freely of course) in the 'Tallis' *Fantasia*. It is frequently found in folk song, which for Vaughan Williams was as valid a key to our musical origins as the newly revived Tudor repertory.

The quartet also makes great play with proportional rhythms (such as four crotchets in the time of three), possibly also deduced from Tudor practice and another fruitful device in later years. The Minuet (which comes second) is almost an Austrian Ländler, particularly in the Trio, which is about as close to Mahler as any English composer got in that decade. A charming Romance, starting and ending in 5/4, follows, and then a wild Finale. The *Phantasy Quintet*, which justifies its title by linking its four movements together without a break, is no less inventive and playful. Its opening pentatonic theme deserves to be quoted as a perfectly shaped example of its kind and to illustrate the irreducible kernel from which Vaughan Williams's chromatically enhanced modality springs (Ex. 4.19). The rest of the movement explores further chromaticisms and tonalities before repeating

Ex. 4.19

Ralph Vaughan Williams, *Phantasy Quintet*, 1st mvt. (London, 1921), pp. 1–2.

the opening phrase. The second movement is a spiky Scherzo in 7/4, D minor; the third a tender Sarabanda for the four upper parts, starting in A flat but ending on F; the last movement, a Burlesca, begins in F but ends in D (major). The whole thing could be described as a dialogue about keys a minor third apart and about the scales to be adopted and the possibilities of their chromatic extension; as such it is a paradigm for much of the later Vaughan Williams.

The only composer to equal Vaughan Williams in this field before the war was Frank Bridge, who wrote a *Phantasie Quartet* in F minor in 1905 and the first of three string quartets, in E minor, in the following year.[74] The E minor quartet is a passionate work on a generous scale, in essence highly Romantic but with elements of the astringency that was later to become his hallmark: it should surely be given an occasional hearing. There are also a number of pre-war chamber works with piano, including a *Phantasie Trio* (*c.*1907) and a *Phantasie Quartet* (1910).

Piano Music

Music for piano alone (including duets and duos) occupies only a small corner of the English musical garden at this period. Even the best of it, such as the shorter characteristic pieces of Parry (*Shulbrede Tunes*, 1914) and the *Capriccios* of Stanford (Op. 136, 1913) seems pale in comparison with its Brahmsian or Schumannesque model; and the worst of it is decidedly inferior. Stanford's early *Rhapsodies* (published in 1904 as Op. 92) are more interesting, Lisztian rather than Brahmsian in derivation, but they are not wholly convincing.

There is one exception to these gloomy generalizations, and that is the remarkable early *Sonata in D minor* by Benjamin Dale, completed in 1905 and published in the following year. It is an enormous work of great technical difficulty, but for anyone accustomed to the demands of Schumann's hardest pieces or of Liszt's sonata it is surmountable. In style, too, it occupies a similar area; if the first movement has a strongly Lisztian flavour, the variations which follow recall the Schumann of the *Études symphoniques*. This movement, which combines the elements of slow movement, scherzo, and finale, is the chief formal point of interest in the work. The Scherzo begins at Variation V; Variation VI is a Mazurka, and Variation VII a furious Prestissimo, after which a lengthy lyrical episode, rising once more to the heights of Lisztian passion, breaks into the energetic finale. The key-scheme of this second part of the work proceeds from G sharp minor to D major, with a short quiet coda in the minor. The sudden appearance of so precocious a work is best explained by the development of piano studies at the Royal Academy of Music, where Dale was a pupil of York Bowen

---

[74] A fourth string quartet dates from 1937.

(1884–1961), himself only a year older and one of the most gifted English pianists of his generation. Bowen himself wrote three piano concertos in the early 1900s (not to mention a symphony in 1912), though he concentrated mainly on shorter piano pieces then and later. Dale also wrote a pioneering large-scale Suite for viola and piano (1906); after the war, however, he turned to educational projects and in particular the work of the Associated Board of the Royal Schools of Music, which had been founded as an examining body in 1889.

Organ Music

The organ music of the period is also of relatively small interest, except to enthusiasts. The advantages of adopting the standard Continental compass in both manuals and pedals were dissipated by the increasing size and complexity of most instruments, which in general sought to achieve the greatest possible range of orchestral effects. (On village organs, needless to say, resources were usually minimal.) Organ music, whether written by cathedral or concert organists, tended to exploit these opportunities and in doing so created a demand for ever more such effects.

The organ music of Samuel Sebastian Wesley was republished with the newer type of instrument in mind, and it offered a suitable model for the more sober-minded composers of the day, such as Henry Smart (1813–79) in his later years, and afterwards Stanford and Parry. The influence of Bach popularized the chorale prelude, usually based on an older tune of English origin. Eventually a series of really distinguished works of this type appeared in Parry's two sets of *Chorale Preludes* (1912, 1916) and three *Chorale Fantasies* (1915). Those of Stanford are less interesting, though he occasionally produced a short freely composed piece of real individuality, like the last of the *Six Preludes and Postludes*, Op. 105 (Ex. 4.20). Stanford, like numerous other composers, wrote organ sonatas (though they belong to his later life), as did such figures as Alan Gray (1855–1935) and Basil Harwood (1859–1949). Gray and Harwood were primarily organists—Gray at Trinity College, Cambridge (1893–1930, in succession to Stanford), Harwood at Ely cathedral and later at Christ Church, Oxford—though both also attempted work outside the routine of church and organ music. The best-known, and indeed the best, of all late Victorian organ sonatas is Elgar's (Op. 28, 1895), which is quite devoid of any ecclesiastical overtones; indeed it is a medium-length symphony scored for organ.

Harwood's two sonatas and other pieces illustrate the extravagance of the rhetorical gestures that were often adopted at this period. His *Dithyramb* (Op. 7, 1892) is essentially a large sonata-movement with exaggerated contrasts of mood (there is perhaps an analogy with the first movement of Brahms's piano sonata, Op. 5). Ex. 4.21 shows its first and second subjects

Ex. 4.20

C. V. Stanford, *Six Short Preludes and Postludes*, Op. 105 no. 6 (London, 1908), p. 18

Ex. 4.21

Ex. 4.21, continued

Basil Harwood, *Dithyramb*, Op. 7 (London, 1893): (*a*) p. 1; (*b*) p. 3

(to use the by then well-established terminology of what had come to be known in England as 'sonata form').[75] William Wolstenholme (1865–1931), a blind Lancashire organist, wrote in a similar vein. Not until Herbert Howells wrote and published his *Three Rhapsodies* (1917) did a new and distinctive voice emerge.

Church Music

As usual this category covers a wide range, from celebratory anthems and services for special occasions to the hymnody of parochial and dissenting congregations. Some of the former have already been referred to, but the best of them often passed into more general use, with accompaniment arranged for organ. A good example of this is Parry's Coronation anthem 'I was glad' (1902, revised 1911), which actually benefits from the removal of its 'Vivat' calls. The reverse could also happen, as when Stanford orchestrated the Te Deum from his B flat service (1879) for the coronation of 1902. (This was replaced in 1911 by Parry's new setting, but on that occasion Stanford provided a splendid orchestrally accompanied

[75] Ouseley, *A Treatise on Musical Form and General Composition* (London, 1875), still called it 'modern binary form'. The modern conventional English terminology is well established in E. Prout, *Applied Forms* (London, 1895).

Communion.) There are also orchestral versions of the B flat, A, G, and C major services.[76]

Stanford's five services[77] are a bright spot in a genre that often drew only routine work. All included the Communion items,[78] and their straightforwardness made them popular with parochial surpliced choirs, which in this period became a common sight in urban churches. All have distinctive features: the use of Gregorian intonations and the 'Dresden Amen' in the B flat service, for example, and the pastoral soprano solo that opens the G major Magnificat. Charles Wood wrote restrained services early in his career, as well as several anthems long popular. Of innumerable other sets, Alan Gray's splendid evening canticles in A flat for double choir unaccompanied can be singled out for their almost orchestral use of the medium.

It would be tedious to survey the enormous output of Victorian anthems in detail. Composers increasingly turned to the shorter forms, which could be used more easily in parish churches. Many of the anthems of John Stainer (1840–1900) and Joseph Barnby (1838–96) are of this type, though both men also wrote lengthier anthems and, indeed, services.[79] Unfortunately, they are often weakened by an enervating chromaticism and a static movement of the vocal parts. One of the sadder aspects of the repertory is the element of 'writing down' for less well equipped choirs; they were often given music that was not just technically straightforward but feeble in melody and harmony. Not all such music is sentimental, of course, nor is sentimentality necessarily associated with musical weakness; the shallow triumphalism of some parochial music is equally depressing. The output of J. H. Maunder (1858–1920) and Caleb Simper (b. 1856) represents the genre at its lowest.

The Victorians earnestly revived the harmonized singing of chants and responses, creating many new settings and plugging gaps where they thought that tradition was wanting. The Tractarian movement had created a demand for settings of the Communion service, not only (or even primarily) in cathedrals but in many parish churches. Harwood's *Office for the Holy Communion* in A flat (1892), which was part of a trilogy that included the morning and evening canticles in the same key, set the responses to the commandments, the Gloria tibi before the gospel, the Credo, the Sursum corda, the Sanctus, Benedictus, Agnus Dei, Gloria in

---

[76] These are complete except for the C major service, for which only the Te Deum, Magnificat, and Nunc dimittis were orchestrated. See Hudson, 'A Revised and Extended Catalogue of the Works of Charles Villiers Stanford (1852–1924)', *MR* 37 (1976), 106–29.

[77] i.e. those in B flat, F, A, G, and C; there are also two early sets of evening canticles, a unison service (Morning, Communion, and Evening), and some further canticles (Opp. 98, 164), and an organ version of the *Festal Communion Service* (1911). Hudson, ibid.

[78] Benedictus and Agnus Dei were added separately to the B flat and F major services; they were advertised for the G major service but were apparently not written.

[79] For selective lists of their work from this period see Gatens, *Victorian Cathedral Music*, 184–5, 195.

excelsis, and final Amen. Plainsong melodies were used in the Sursum corda and Amen (two settings), with the alternative of a plain harmonization in the case of the Sursum corda. This amounted to a complete 'ordinary' for Anglo-Catholic use; the inclusion of the Benedictus and Agnus Dei was, however, controversial, and many settings left them out.[80] The style of Harwood's setting is generally simple and dignified, but it attempts too concentrated and specific a response to the text for a small-scale work. An episode from the Credo will illustrate his concern for word-painting (Ex. 4.22).

A word is due on Stainer's *Crucifixion* (1887), the English parochial equivalent of a Bach Passion. Whatever its usefulness (and few sacred works on its theme have been so widely performed), it can hardly be called an artistic success. Its recitatives and other solos are wooden, its choruses ruined by inapposite word-repetition. Its redeeming feature is a wealth of fine hymn-tunes, which in accordance with the prevailing view regarding the chorales in Bach's Passions were given to the congregation. But for all its faults it is a better effort than Maunder's *From Olivet to Calvary* (1904).

A more sturdy approach to the anthem came from Stanford and some of his pupils, who included Charles Wood and John Ireland. Ireland wrote very little church music, but his anthem (or motet) *Greater love hath no man* (1912, beginning 'Many waters cannot quench love'), for treble and baritone solo, chorus, and organ, is a masterpiece, a miniature tone-poem of great beauty and emotional strength that has never lost its appeal.[81] Unfortunately, the major figures of the early twentieth century wrote little or no Anglican church music, a sad symptom of the national Church's slow disengagement from the musical currents of its own day. Elgar wrote some simple, rather sentimental Latin church music, some of it still in use, and Stanford an elaborate Mass for soloists, choir, and orchestra in G major for Brompton Oratory (1893), as well as the three Latin motets already mentioned. (His Requiem, Te Deum, and Stabat Mater, on the other hand, were concert works intended in the first instance for festival performance.)

But if not all the repertory of this epoch can be welcomed with open arms, it can at least be said that the late Victorian period witnessed a rise in standards of performance and lifted the dignity of music in cathedrals and larger churches. It was an age of antiquarianism and restoration, and just as it is nowadays difficult to find a medieval church that has not received the sometimes unnecessary and impertinent attentions of the Victorian restorer, so also does our conception of what is fitting in cathedral worship owe a great deal to the ideals of the Victorians. If they were sometimes misled, we can still enjoy the best of their contribution in the spirit in which it was made while discarding what has lost its lustre.

---

[80] See n. 78 for Stanford's additional movements.
[81] It achieved an unwelcome topicality on the outbreak of war in 1914.

Ex. 4.22

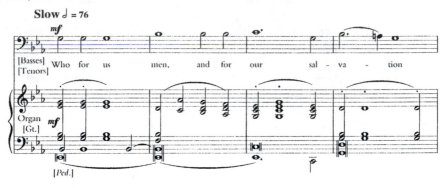

Ex. 4.22, continued

Basil Harwood, *Communion Service in A flat*, Creed (London, 1892), pp. 8–10

In no area is that more true than in hymnody. The Victorian Church witnessed a great revival of newly written verse for hymn-singing, following a longer Dissenting tradition and drawing on much of that for its own use. It retained the best of its older metrical psalmody and began to translate the great riches of medieval and oriental hymnody for liturgical purposes together with that of the German Evangelical Church.[82] For this purpose a wealth of older musical material was investigated: Sarum plainchant, Genevan psalm-tunes, Lutheran chorales, folk tunes, and the older English sources. Except for the plainchant melodies, this material was usually harmonized, or reharmonized, for four voices in part-song or simple anthem style, and the tunes themselves were often adapted (cf. Ch. 3). Finally, a great body of new harmonized tunes found its way into the standard hymnals.

The first edition of *Hymns Ancient and Modern* appeared in 1861, the second in 1868 and, with a supplement, in 1889. A completely new edition came out in 1904, and a second supplement in 1916. In 1922 the 1889 edition was reset with the second supplement added.[83] The 1889 edition may be taken as a representative, though not a complete, collection of the hymns in general use in the late Victorian era. There are also collected editions of the tunes of Sullivan and of John Bacchus Dykes (1823–76). Many of the hundreds of newer tunes in these collections have fallen out of use, and deservedly so, but many more have kept their place or are worthy of revival. One cannot but admire the ingenuity with which the challenge of setting a fixed number of syllables in notes of equal value has been met in the best tunes of S. S. Wesley, Smart, and Stainer. In such a situation harmony becomes important, as it can often supply the tonal direction that the melodic sequence alone would not.[84] Triple-time tunes for iambic hymns are still found, but they are less common than before. In another type of tune, especially for long-lined stanzas, an element of rhythmic variety is introduced: tunes of this kind include *Strength and Stay* (Dykes), *Eventide* (W. H. Monk, for 'Abide with me'), *Ellers* (E. J. Hopkins, to J. Ellerton's 'Saviour, again to thy dear name'), and Monk's *Unde et memores* ('And now, O Father, mindful of the Love', a fine eucharistic hymn by W. Bright), all specimens of the more sentimental type and relying much on repeated chords. A still more elaborate type is represented by Dykes's *Lux benigna* for Newman's 'Lead kindly light', a complex stanza with variable caesura and enjambment, all of which is catered for in Dykes's ingenious setting (Ex. 4.23). The more elaborate the tune, of course, the greater the danger of

---

[82] The standard work of reference is J. Julian, *A Dictionary of Hymnology*, 2 vols. (2nd edn., London, 1907; repr. New York, 1957).

[83] The musical edition of 1922 restored the original harmonies of tunes bowdlerized in 1904, but added alternative (and generally better) plainchant harmonizations.

[84] e.g. Smart, *Rex gloriae* (no. 148) and *Everton* (no. 362); Stainer, *Iona* (no. 359).

Ex. 4.23

1. Lead kind - ly Light, a - mid the en - circ - ling gloom,___
2. I was not e - ver thus, nor pray'd that Thou___
3. So long Thy power hath blest me, sure it still___

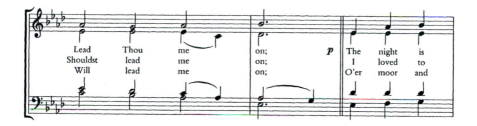

Lead Thou me on; The night is
Shouldst lead me on; I loved to
Will lead me on; O'er moor and

dark, and I am far from home,___ Lead Thou me on.___
choose and see my path;(p)but now___ Lead Thou me on.___
fen, o'er crag and tor - rent,(p) till___ The night is gone;___

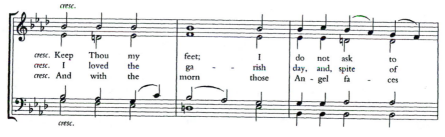

cresc. Keep Thou my feet; I do not ask to
cresc. I loved the ga - - rish day, and, spite of
cresc. And with the morn those An - gel fa - ces

continued

Ex. 4.23, continued

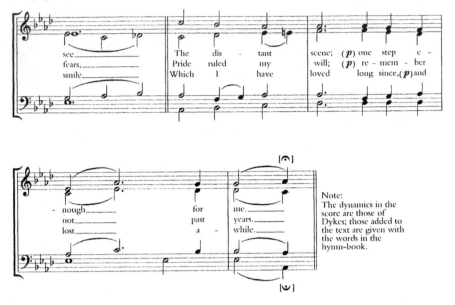

J. B. Dykes, *Lux benigna* ('Lead, kindly light', Newman): *Hymns Ancient and Modern*, no. 266;
Dykes, *Hymn Tunes* (London, *c*.1900), p. 164

lapsing into the style of a short anthem: several of Dykes's tunes are of this
kind. A final category used chanted chords in free rhythm, one of the best
examples being Stainer's setting of 'Hail, gladdening light', a translation
from the Greek by John Keble.

By the end of the century taste was changing. The 1904 edition of *Hymns
Ancient and Modern* bowdlerized some of the harmonizations of the Victorian tunes and introduced many new ones. But its reforms were overtaken in
1906 by the fresh approach and (in most respects) superior scholarship of *The
English Hymnal*, edited as to the music by Vaughan Williams. It too bowdlerized the Victorian hymns and added some preposterously slow tempo
markings, but it gave plainchant melodies in a well-designed square notation and with new harmonizations; it restored the original rhythms of the
metrical psalm-tunes and gave several of them in authentic polyphonic
settings with the tune in the tenor; and it drew on other national traditions
and on folk song to a far greater extent than its rival. Finally, and despite a
proclaimed emphasis on the familiar, it contains many fine new tunes by

such composers as Walford Davies, Gustav Holst, Walter Parratt, and (not least) Vaughan Williams himself under the cloak of anonymity. One of the best of these last is *Salve festa dies*, written for M. F. Bell's ingenious English equivalent of Fortunatus's elegiac couplets. Vaughan Williams was by no means wholly bound by these metrical constraints, however (see Ex. 4.24).

Ex. 4.24

continued

Ex. 4.24, continued

Ev - ery good gift of the year___ now with its Mas - ter re -

Repeat *'Hail thee'* in chorus

Verse 3,5,7,9 and 11
Clerks only

turns.___ 3. He who was nailed to the Cross is God and the

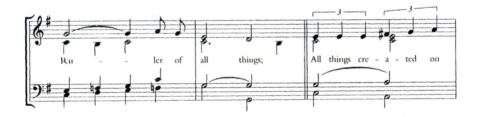

Ru - - ler of all things; All things cre - a - ted on

earth wor - ship the Ma - ster of all.___

Note:
Rhythmic details as for
verses quoted. The
refrain is sung once only,
in chorus, after each
verse, using the 2nd time
bar.

[D.C. *chorus*]

Ralph Vaughan Williams, 'Hail thee festival day': *The English Hymnal* (London, [1906]),
no. 624

The English Hymnal reflected a view of congregational hymnody that was intended to place it in a wider focus than hitherto. It was conspicuously more Anglo-Catholic than its rival (though the latter too had represented this sector of ecclesiastical opinion very fairly), and it rapidly became standard in churches of that type. This is not the place to discuss hymnody in greater detail, but it should be mentioned that the scholarship found in *The English Hymnal* was pioneered in G. R. Woodward's *Songs of Syon* (1904 and subsequent revisions) and *The Yattendon Hymnal*, edited by Robert Bridges (1899).[85]

There was also a class of hymnody current that fell well below the standards attempted in any of the books so far mentioned. It would be unfair to charge the Dissenting traditions with inherently lower expectations of congregational music—the Methodists, for instance, had inherited a fine tradition, and Roman Catholics a far longer and more diverse one—but they proved to be easy prey to essentially revivalist elements. Much the most powerful influence was that of the Americans D. Moody and I. D. Sankey, who first came to Britain in 1873: indeed 'Moody and Sankey' came to be a catch-phrase for a particular kind of 'gospel song'. Catholicism never descended to these depths, but it resorted to a sentimental appeal in verses by F. W. Faber and others, and often found tunes comparable to them in saccharine effect. Some but by no means all of these were eliminated in R. R. Terry's *Westminster Hymnal* (1912, subsequently revised several times), and Terry himself wrote several good, if old-fashioned, tunes.[86]

Musical Literature and Education

Late Victorian and Edwardian England experienced a revolution in attitudes to music. It became a subject of scholarship: the Musical Association was founded in 1874, the Plainsong and Mediæval Music Society in 1888, and the Folk-Song Society in 1898; Sir George Grove published his *Dictionary* in four volumes in 1879–89; the Purcell Society edition and *Tudor Church Music* were initiated, and E. H. Fellowes embarked on his editions of Byrd and of the English madrigalists and lutenists. G. P. Arkwright, W. H. Cummings, A. H. Mann, J. Fuller-Maitland, W. Barclay Squire, and R. R. Terry all made important contributions in the fields of editing and/ or bibliography. Augustus Hughes-Hughes produced his catalogue of musical manuscripts in the British Museum, Squire his catalogues of printed music there and in the King's Library; similar services were performed for

---

[85] The first three editions of *Songs of Syon* were of tunes only. Amongst the contributors of tunes to *The Yattendon Hymnal* was T. B. Strong, bishop of Oxford: his fine modal tune *Poplar*, to the words 'God be in my head', was given wider currency in the Second Supplement to *Hymns Ancient and Modern* (no. 695).

[86] Terry (1865–1938) was organist and director of music at Westminster Cathedral, 1901–24. He was a scholar of distinction, and his uncompromising attitude to values in church music led to his resignation.

Christ Church by Arkwright (1915) and by Mann and Fuller-Maitland for the Fitzwilliam Museum. Fuller-Maitland and Squire edited *The Fitzwilliam Virginal Book* (1899), Arkwright produced his series *The Old English Edition*, and W. H. Frere, bishop of Truro, edited the Sarum Gradual and Antiphonal in facsimile, with extensive introductions, for the Plainsong and Mediæval Music Society (PMMS).

In the popularization of musical culture, in addition to Grove, the preeminent figures were Ernest Walker, also a composer, W. H. Hadow, and Tovey, all educated at Oxford in Classics as the foundation of their intellectual life. The degrees in Music at Oxford and Cambridge were taken seriously in those days by aspiring composers. Oxford also initiated a *History of Music* to which P. C. Buck, Parry, and H. E. Wooldridge (Slade Professor of Fine Art and a notable scholar of medieval music) contributed. Stainer, an earlier Professor of Music at Oxford, together with his children, J. F. R. and C. Stainer, edited *Early Bodleian Music*, a volume of facsimiles and one of transcriptions (1901); he also wrote an analytical introduction to the latter's remarkable *Dufay and his Contemporaries* (1898), a selection from the Italian fifteenth-century Bodleian manuscript Canonici Misc. 213. Bodley's Librarian, W. B. Nicholson, contributed to this a masterly palaeographical study, and later produced a volume of early medieval facsimiles on his own account (*Early Bodleian Music*, vol. iii, 1913). Wooldridge edited *Early English Harmony* in facsimile for the PMMS (1897), and the young H. V. Hughes (later Dom Anselm Hughes) contributed a flawed volume of transcriptions.

It is worth emphasizing here the extraordinary concentration of new ventures in the period 1870–1914 and the versatility of many of the people responsible for them. Scholarship, composition, performance, and teaching were not isolated activities but interrelated. Parry and Stanford not only taught and managed the music at their respective universities but were in differing degrees composers and performers; in addition they occupied the key posts at the Royal College of Music and as such were the two most influential people of their day, above all on composers of the next generation.

The Royal College came into being in 1883 as a continuation of the National Training School for Music, founded in 1876 with Sullivan as Principal. Grove became the Royal College's first director, followed later by Parry. It was at the time the leading professional institution, for the Royal Academy was in some disarray, though the latter soon recovered sufficiently, under Mackenzie's principalship, to mount the competitive challenge that has ensured the health of both institutions ever since. They became, and have remained, England's leading conservatories, although there were already by 1900 numerous other professional schools in London and the provinces, in particular those of Birmingham (1886) and Manchester (1893).

It should not be imagined that all of this activity attracted wide public notice, though the royal patronage of the College and the Academy ensured a certain cachet. The future Edward VII, as Prince of Wales, was a vigorous patron of the arts and a supporter of musical good causes, but the aristocratic interest in music, to the extent that it existed at all, was usually limited to fashionable novelty (which essentially meant foreign composers and per-formers) and to light music.[87] A large body of political and intellectual opinion was either indifferent or even hostile to the pursuit of music, at least as a career or as a consuming interest. But the public recognition of the most eminent members of the profession through knighthoods, and by the even more illustrious award of the OM to Elgar (1911),[88] gave it a dignity that had been slow in coming as the nineteenth century progressed. Many cathedral and college organists, too, almost all of whom were in some measure composers and teachers, were similarly honoured.

Popular interest in serious music was fostered not only by the writings of Walker, Hadow, and others (amongst which must be counted the London programme notes and the *Encyclopaedia Britannica* articles of the young Tovey)[89] but by newspaper criticism and by journals such as *The Musical Times* and *The Monthly Musical Record*. Newspaper criticism was often marred by pomposity and by a patronizing attitude to new music by writers who could not themselves have strung together two notes; but its coverage of London and provincial musical life was impressive. Bernard Shaw was something of a maverick; he was guilty of much exaggeration, but even at his most opinionated he usually hit upon some essential truth.[90]

In addition to the professionally orientated activity that we have been discussing (but without excluding the contributions of the leisured, the clergy, and the community of polymaths of whom Grove and Wooldridge were eminent examples), there were two other important movements. One was the advance of music in general education and amongst adults. As we have seen, this was very largely concerned with the promotion of singing in schools and in the formation of bodies for adult recreational singing, and it had an appreciable effect on the growth of amateur choralism, especially that of the large provincial festivals. The notion that instrumental perform-ance and a knowledgeable appreciation of music might properly form part of a school's curriculum was slower in coming, but it began to take root in the public schools (including girls' schools) in the 1860s and 1870s and from

[87] The two individuals most responsible for the encouragement of serious English music in the Edwardian era were Sir Thomas Beecham, who was knighted 'for services to music' in 1916 as well as succeeding to his baronetcy in that year, and Balfour Gardiner, who organized a memorable series of concerts at the Queen's Hall in 1912–13.

[88] Elgar had been knighted in 1904, and was to be made a baronet in 1931.

[89] *The Encyclopaedia Britannica* articles were written for the 11th edn. (1910) and they were published in book form in 1944.

[90] His collected criticism is published as *Shaw's Music*, ed. D. H. Laurence, 3 vols. (London, 1981).

that vantage point helped to foster a fuller musical life in the universities, not only in Oxford and Cambridge but also London (King's College), Durham, Birmingham (where Elgar became first Peyton Professor in 1904), Bristol, Liverpool, and other new foundations.

The other strand was that of philosophical or theological enquiry into the nature and purpose of music. Books like the Revd Hugh Haweis's *Music and Morals* (1871) and Edmund Gurney's *The Power of Sound* (1880) explored issues previously in currency, but they achieved something like a classic statement of well-defended positions. Both considered music as essentially the arouser of emotional feeling in the listener. For Haweis this inevitably meant that music had a moral content, since different emotions affect the personality in morally worthy or reprehensible ways, and the composer had a choice in the arousal of good or bad emotions. (An important predecessor in this line of thought was A. B. Marx, whose *General Music Instruction* (1854), a translation of his *Allgemeine Musiklehre* (1839), contains several chapters on the subject.) Gurney, on the other hand, claimed, like Hanslick, that the emotional content of music resided in its formal content. His emphases were in some ways different from Hanslick's, but he rejected a simplistic correlation between musical processes and emotional states, and hence a direct link between the intentions of the composer and a moral outcome in the listener.[91]

In arguing for the self-sufficiency of music, Haweis and Gurney were at one with a long-standing tradition of European thought. Stainer, in his inaugural lecture at Oxford (*Music in its Relation to the Intellect and the Emotions*, 1892), characterized musical effect as 'an appeal to the Emotions by means of the Intellect'.[92] The essential optimism of late Victorian musical thought was reflected in Parry's *Art of Music* (1893), later republished as *The Evolution of the Art of Music* (1896). Essentially a historical survey, it treated music as evolving to a point at which it had become fully equipped as an expressive medium in its own right. Parry the agnostic was a convinced Darwinian, and more than any of his musical contemporaries sought to understand his art in an evolutionary sense. Evolutionary concepts were also introduced into the study of harmony by C. H. Kitson (1874–1944) at the end of this period. As the Preface to his *Evolution of Harmony* (1914) explains:

Now it must be obvious to anyone who has studied the history of music that the growth of harmonic resource is a natural evolution. And it is of the utmost importance that the student should grasp the basis of harmony, that is, the conditions that obtained at the close of the Polyphonic Period (1600). Any one who has studied strict counterpoint historically will have a very firm grasp of essential principles. Later procedure is but a logical extension of them.

[91] For Haweis and Gurney see Gatens, *Victorian Cathedral Music*, 34–9.
[92] Cited *BHMB*, v. 464.

Although the evolutionary stance is really evident only in the opening and closing chapters of this book (and the latter is well worth reading as the considered view of a thoughtful pedagogue), Kitson was right to challenge current theories of functional harmony, based as they were on dubious acoustic foundations. Acoustical knowledge had made a quantum leap in the work of Helmholtz, translated by the great English physicist A. J. Ellis (1814–90) as *On the Sensations of Tone as a Physiological Basis for the Theory of Music* (1875). Ellis also wrote some interesting (and still in many ways authoritative) original works on musical pitch, tuning systems, and scales. Writers such as Ouseley, Macfarren, and Stainer grappled with the problems of reconciling harmonic practice with acoustic theory.[93] But the doyen of all musical theorists (by which is meant here writers on the elements of musical composition) was Ebenezer Prout (1835–1909), who was also a composer and became well known for his edition with additional accompaniments of Handel's *Messiah* (1902). In 1901, in the sixteenth edition of *Harmony: Its Theory and Practice*,[94] he had the courage to abandon acoustical theory as the basis of harmony. But harmony as such remained the foundation of compositional teaching, both by Prout and others. In Prout's magisterial scheme the treatise on harmony was followed by those on counterpoint, fugue, form, and orchestration, each occupying two volumes. Kitson wrote books on counterpoint (1907) and fugue (1909) prior to *The Evolution of Harmony*, but harmony obstinately maintained its pedagogical primacy both then and later.

It will now be obvious that England's musical life underwent in later Victorian and in Edwardian times a revitalization that had no real earlier parallel. It was not so much a reaction to stagnation, however, as a discovery of possibilities, essentially of an educational character in the broadest sense. But the term 'renaissance' can be fully justified only if musical composition itself can be shown to have been reborn. On a certain level it is difficult to assent to such a proposition. In purely quantitative terms, there is no truth in it at all; but it is necessary also to contend with a re-evaluation of eighteenth- and, especially, nineteenth-century music as a whole in order to address the issue. In the same way, however, medieval art, literature, and music have been re-evaluated, but without ever quite displacing the proclamation of a new era by its proponents in the fourteenth and fifteenth centuries. It may not seem quite right to regard English music of the eighteenth and earlier nineteenth centuries as 'medieval', but there is an

---

[93] F. A. G. Ouseley, *A Treatise on Harmony* (London, 1868), followed by works on counterpoint (1869) and form (1875); G. A. Macfarren, *The Rudiments of Harmony* (London, 1860) and other works, notably his revised edition of Day's *Treatise on Harmony* (London, 1885); J. Stainer, *A Theory of Harmony* (London, 1871).

[94] This was really a 2nd edn., following fifteen earlier impressions. The publishers continued to make the 15th impression available.

analogy in its largely unquestioning acceptance of established forms and procedures. It evolved, but slowly and without any sudden upsurge of new thought.[95]

In the late nineteenth century, however, traditional procedures came to be challenged in ways that went beyond a mere preference for Brahms and Wagner over Mendelssohn or Schumann as models for imitation. It amounted to a wholesale discarding of accumulated rubbish and the forging of a new bond between music and her intellectual sisters. In due course there was achieved a liberation of music, not so much from specific constraints as from constraint in principle.

There can be no question but that Parry and Stanford were at the forefront of this process. They may be compared, only half facetiously, with Vasari's Cimabue and Giotto, the first of whom in Vasari's words '[gave] the first lights [i primi lumi] to the art of painting'. It would certainly be facetious to pursue such an analogy further, but it can all the same be argued that Elgar occupied an anomalous position similar to that often encountered in the history of Renaissance art. On the one hand he was a typical late Victorian—there is much truth in the view that sees him as in some sense the heir of Sullivan—while on the other hand he branched out to an unprecedented extent in his later choral and orchestral works. But for a complete change in the essential quality of musical experience we must look to the generation and attitudes represented by Delius, Holst, and Vaughan Williams. It was Vaughan Williams above all who by virtue of his versatility and his artistic stamina proved to be best equipped to carry the torch of musical freedom into the post-war era.

[95] A comprehensive discussion of the issues is now available in R. Stradling and M. Hughes, *The English Musical Renaissance 1860–1940: Construction and Deconstruction* (London, 1993).

5

POST-ROMANTICISM, 1914–1945

THIS chapter begins and ends with a period of war, not just to pad out an inconveniently short inter-war period of little more than twenty years but because 1914 and 1945 were more of an end and a beginning respectively than 1918 and 1939 were a beginning and an end. There had been 'ends of an era' before 1914—at the death of Victoria in 1901 and at the death of Edward VII in 1910—but the outbreak of war in August 1914, even though its full consequences could not then be foreseen, was accompanied by the instinctive feeling that whatever the outcome, certain qualities of life would have disappeared for ever by the time it ended. Perhaps there were similar emotions during the autumn of 1939; but this came after two decades of political and diplomatic turbulence, and there was less left by then to bemoan. 1945, in contrast, was marked by a determination not to repeat the mistakes of the 1920s and 1930s; and with hindsight we can see that, whatever mistakes there may have been, they were not the same ones. 1945 did genuinely mark a fresh start.

Here we are concerned only with the tangible consequences for music and the arts of great events whose causes and effects are still debated. But the two World Wars did affect cultural life to a far greater extent than any previous conflict since the Civil War. Though conscription was not introduced until 1916,[1] the national crisis provoked an immediate outburst of patriotism and a surge of voluntary enlistment. As the war dragged on and its horrendous implications became clear, the early optimism was succeeded by a grim determination. The second war was like a rerun whose likely consequences were all too predictable—except that they were in many respects worse. But the nature of the enemy persuaded the nation to grit its teeth and, together with its allies, to win through in the end. At least

---

[1] A. J. P. Taylor, *English History 1914–1945* (2nd edn., London, 1970, repr. with revised bibliography, 1975), 86–9.

the failure of enemy invasion kept the country's integrity intact on both occasions.[2]

It is not possible to identify a 'war music', comparable to 'war poetry', as a direct product of the First World War (that of the Second World War had far less impact). The genre of war poetry, of course, is not solely generated by the participants in a particular conflict, either during its course or subsequently; but equally obviously there was no musical legacy from the first war comparable to that of (say) Wilfred Owen or Siegfried Sassoon. Apart from anything else it is much harder, for various practical reasons, for a composer to compose than for a poet to write in the theatre of war. Even songs, the most likely genre to emerge from the front, seem to have been composed there in very small numbers, mostly (if not entirely) by Gurney, though more will have been written, or finalized, during periods of leave. Larger forms were, for fighting soldiers, unthinkable.

There was, however, a larger-scale reaction to war and its consequences in a good deal of English music written between the wars and afterwards. It seems likely, for example, that Vaughan Williams's third, fourth, fifth, and sixth symphonies were all in some ways inspired or affected by the experience of war, even though in none of them is it overtly alluded to.[3] It accounts for much in the work of Britten and Tippett, both pacifists, and there have been many settings of war poems since their effective prototype, Butterworth's prophetic setting of Housman's 'On the idle hill of summer', published in 1912 (see Ch. 4). Although the more extreme forms of Continental iconoclasm were avoided by English composers, the satirical and ironical element in much of their music in the 1920s and 1930s and later can be seen as a form of reaction to war and a reflection of its coarsening effect on the human psyche. At the same time, and usually within the context of a liberal agnosticism, there has been a disposition to use music as a vehicle for the promotion of greater tolerance in the aftermath of the social upheavals generated by war and the economic depression.

All this is to look further ahead than is our present concern; and in any case the English experience needs to be seen in its European context. The tally of significant musical works from 1914 to 1918 is a small one.[4] Butterworth was killed early in the war, and several others of promise—Denis Browne, the Australian Frederick Kelly, and Ernest Farrar amongst them—also fell. Ivor Gurney, generally more adventurous as a poet than as a composer, wrote a number of attractive songs, many of which are deeply

[2] With the significant exception of the Channel Islands in the Second World War, where John Ireland had taken refuge and from where he escaped only at the last minute. M. V. Searle, *John Ireland: The Man and his Music* (Tunbridge Wells, 1979), 97–8.

[3] For the *Pastoral Symphony* see below. The fifth symphony is a proclamation of peace in time of war; the fourth and the sixth give voice to its effects, material and spiritual. Taylor's remarks (*English History*, 489) are uncharitable and inaccurate.

[4] There is a useful survey in Banfield, *Sensibility and English Song*, 133–9.

moving. So also did John Ireland and, for example, the young Peter Warlock (1894–1930). Vaughan Williams served throughout the war, and had little time for composition. Holst, being thought medically unsuitable, was not called up until late in the war, by which time he had composed *The Planets*. Older composers contributed patriotic music: Elgar, whose 'Land of hope and glory' was revived with enthusiasm, wrote accompaniments to the recitation of poems by the Belgian Émile Cammaerts; a setting of *The Fringes of the Fleet* by Kipling, who objected and caused the work to be withdrawn; and most notably the trilogy *The Spirit of England* (Laurence Binyon, 1916–17) for soprano or tenor solo, chorus, and orchestra—these in addition to three masterly chamber works in 1918–19. Parry in a fit of inspiration produced *Jerusalem*, and he and Stanford wrote several other patriotic pieces.

After the war, English musical life had to be reconstructed, a process assisted by growth in the recording industry and by the development of broadcasting in the 1920s. Performers had to be trained to meet more exacting international standards. For composers, there was the opportunity to strike out on new paths or to retrieve the pre-war threads. For some, the war effectively spelt an end to their activities. Such eminent Victorians as Cowen and Mackenzie never again wrote a substantial work that could be taken seriously. Parry had died in 1918, and Stanford, though he refused to give in, wrote nothing further of significance and died in 1924. Elgar produced his final masterpiece, the cello concerto, in 1919. On the other hand the inter-war years were enormously productive for Holst (until he died after an operation in 1934) and Vaughan Williams, and they were also the arena for the new generation of Bliss, Rubbra, Walton, Rawsthorne, and, towards the end of the 1930s, Tippett and the more precocious Britten. It will be useful first to offer a vignette of the work of these and some others, to the extent that it falls within the limits of this chapter, before considering that of lesser figures in the context of the genres which they mainly cultivated.

Elgar

Elgar would have been entitled to relax after his war effort, which had exhausted him physically; yet the summer of 1918 and the better part of 1919 were occupied—in the by no means tranquil circumstances of his wife's deteriorating health—with the composition of four major works: the violin sonata, string quartet, piano quintet, and cello concerto. Elgar was a fast worker, but he had never before tackled in quick succession such a series of works in Classical instrumental forms. They should be seen as the group of late masterpieces that they certainly are, even though the concerto alone has kept a regular place in the repertory.

Yet it is hard to do them adequate justice. In a rather obvious sense it can be maintained that they are, for their period, conventional, even reactionary, in harmony and form. It was certainly an achievement to breathe such fresh life into long-standing models—and these works are in no sense 'neo'-Classical. No—they are in and of the great tradition; and yet, quintessentially Elgarian though they are, they develop his style anew, along a path suggested by *Falstaff* but within a more disciplined formality. There is a concision that is manifest not so much in overall length as in character: an economy of material and its treatment that issues not in the miniaturesque but in the decently proportioned. There is also an oddity of constructional method that is hard to pin down but can perhaps be traced back to the violin concerto: there is hardly anywhere an element of repose or closure in a contrasting key such as characterizes both the sonata principle and the 'rounded' forms (ternary or rondo) as handled by the German Classicists.[5] In particular the dominant is largely avoided for such a purpose: if anything, the subdominant is stressed (perhaps a Schumannesque feature), as in the finale of the quartet, or the relative, or the tonic major or minor; but even here repose is avoided.[6] One result is to create an effect of concentrated tonal unity within each movement; another, paradoxically enough, is a constant shifting of tonal ground that can make even the conclusion of a movement sound surprising. Elgar's range of chromatic resource was always wide—we have commented on his use of semitonal sequence in comparatively early works—and the chord of the flat supertonic, sometimes treated temporarily as a tonic, remained a favourite device.[7]

The quintet is the most obviously grandiose and Brahmsian of these works, notwithstanding the ghostly opening material, seemingly devoid of any tonal base, that recurs in various guises in an almost nightmarish fashion (Ex. 5.1).[8] It has a beautifully serene slow movement, but that of the quartet is a still greater achievement, perhaps the finest of its kind in Elgar or even in the post-Beethovenian tradition as a whole—a large claim, though certainly sustainable if one is sufficiently precise as to 'its kind'. Marked 'Piacevole (poco andante)', it exhales the modest spirit of the slow movement of Beethoven's Op. 59, no. 3. All grows from its quiet opening idea (Ex. 5.2), the rhythmic and tonal constraints of which are scarcely exceeded; yet the emotional range, the feeling of ground covered, is immense. When a

---

[5] The middle section of the Romance of the violin sonata is an exception to this generalization.

[6] It is striking that three of the four works are in E minor.

[7] See e.g. the ends of the quartet and of the concerto. The slow movement of the concerto is particularly imaginative in its use of sequence.

[8] Cf. Moore, *Edward Elgar*, 725–6, and the introduction by Michael Pope to the Eulenberg miniature score. There is no evidence, however, that Elgar intended an allusion (in the first four notes) to the ancient *Salve Regina* chant: he is more likely, in any case, to have associated that text with the 'simple tone' in mode 5.

Ex. 5.1

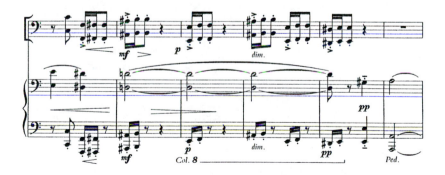

Edward Elgar, Piano Quintet, 1st mvt. (London, 1919), pp. 1–2

Ex. 5.2

(a)

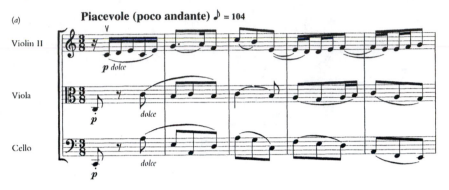

(b)

Edward Elgar, String Quartet, 2nd mvt. (London, 1919): (a) p. 18; (b) p. 25

(a)   (b)

(c)

PLATE I. (a) John Christopher Pepusch (1667–1752). Portrait by an unknown artist. Faculty of Music, Oxford; (b) Carl Friedrich Abel (1723–1787). Portrait by an unknown artist. Faculty of Music, Oxford; (c) Ticket for a Bach–Abel concert season. Royal College of Music

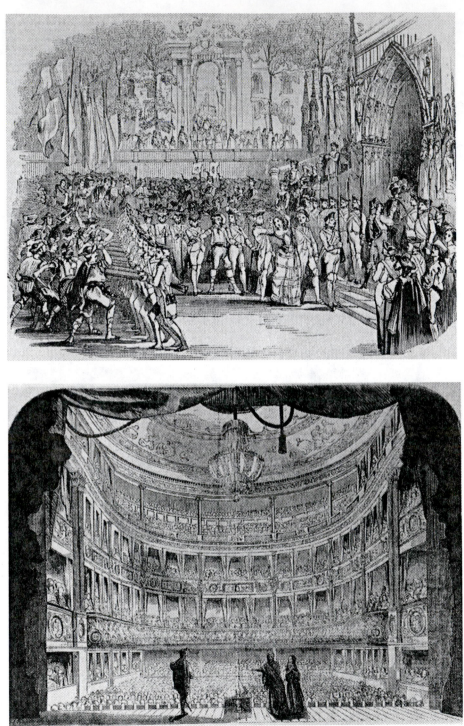

(a)

(b)

PLATE II. (a) *The Bohemian Girl* at Drury Lane. *Illustrated London News*, 23 December 1843. Royal College of Music; (b) Lyceum Theatre, interior, 1856. *Illustrated London News*. Royal College of Music

(*a*)

(*b*)

(*c*)

PLATE III. (*a*) Charles Dibdin
(1745–1814). Watercolour by Robert
Dighton. Royal College of Music;
(*b*) Thomas Attwood (1765–1838).
Portrait by an unknown artist, *c*.1815.
Royal College of Music; (*c*) Samuel
Sebastian Wesley (1810–76). Portrait
by William Keighley Briggs, 1849.
Royal College of Music

(a)

(b)

PLATE IV. (a) Louis Jullien conducting at Covent Garden. *Illustrated London News*,
7 November 1846. Royal College of Music; (b) The former Colston Hall, Bristol (from
a postcard, c.1940). Royal College of Music

PLATE V. (a) Granville Bantock, Barry Jackson, Edward Elgar, H. K. Ayliff, Cedric Hard-
wicke, Edith Evans, and G. B. Shaw, Malvern, c. 1930. Royal College of Music; (b) Ethyl
Smyth (1858–1944). Portrait by Neville Lytton, 1936; (c) Herbert Howells (1892–1983).
Drawing by William Rothenstein, 1919

PLATE VI (*a*). Arthur Sullivan (1842–1900). Marble bust by W. G. John, 1902. Royal College of Music

PLATE VI (*b*). George Grove (1820–1900). Bronze bust by Alfred Gilbert, 1895. Royal College of Music

PLATE VII. A rehearsal for *The Rape of Lucretia* at Glyndebourne: Ernest Ansermet (directing Nancy Evans and Flora Nielsen, out of sight), Benjamin Britten (at the piano), and Reginald Goodall, who conducted some of the performances. *Picture Post*, 13 July 1946. Hulton–Getty

PLATE VIII. Peter Maxwell Davies (b. 1934). Portrait by Fred Schley, 1997.
Royal College of Music, reproduced by permission of the artist

friend and admirer said to Elgar: 'Surely that is as fine as a movement by Beethoven' the composer could only answer 'Yes it is...'.[9]

The cello concerto transforms the cyclic principle into a *raison d'être*; there is an inevitability about the return of the cello's opening gesture that transcends its use as a stock Romantic device. The four-movement scheme emphasizes the effect of concision: none of the movements is lengthy, and even those with a recognizably 'sonata' design (the second and the fourth) handle it as economically as possible. The slow movement, timeless as it seems to be, occupies a mere four pages (eight systems) of score. The first movement is based on one of those malleable themes that can survive numerous transformations without losing their identity; the material of the scherzo vies with a return to the work's opening material before finally breaking out into independent life. After that there is no explicit *attacca* from one movement to another, but the remaining breaks need to be kept to a minimum. The slow movement ends with a dominant-key cadence that neither 'leads in' to the finale, despite the latter's opening in B flat minor, nor concludes the movement definitely: in effect we have both the cake—a melancholy aposiopesis—and its eating in a tonal resolution. The last movement then quickly leads to the reassertion of the tonic of the work. Its long drawn-out conclusion (reminiscent in its strategy of Dvořák's concerto) draws attention, as in Beethoven's late quartets, to an underlying unity of thematic material in these works (Ex. 5.3; cf. also Exx. 5.1 and 5.2 above), a gesture that here reinforces the sadness at the heart of all four of them.

Ex. 5.3

Edward Elgar, Cello Concerto, 4th mvt. (London, 1921), pp. 95–6

---

[9] The friend was Troyte Griffith, the 'Troyte' of the *Enigma* variations. Elgar continued: 'and there is something in it that has never been done before'. When asked what that was, he refused to say (Moore,

Elgar composed no great music thereafter, though the *Severn Suite* for brass band and—especially—the *Nursery Suite* are attractive light music. (The latter was written by Elgar as Master of the King's Musick with the young children of the then duke and duchess of York—the present monarch and her sister in mind.)[10] But we can hardly complain that the sketches for major works in his later years—for *The Last Judgement*, a third symphony, an opera, and others—came to nothing. The sketches for the symphony[11] demonstrate no significant development of his musical language, and emotionally he can have had little to add to the cello concerto. He had given of his best, and had seen his finest music join the canon of classical masterpieces.

Delius

While Elgar languished after 1920, Delius, five years his junior, unleashed a final burst of creative energy both during and after the war. He had lived with his wife at Grez-sur-Loing, south of Paris, since 1897 (the house was eventually bought for him by Balfour Gardiner), but he came to England for part of the war and, while returning to Grez thereafter, maintained his links with his native country. The political climate did not impede the production of *Fennimore and Gerda* (composed in 1908–10) at Frankfurt in 1919; his *Requiem* (composed in 1913–16) was dedicated 'to the memory of all young artists fallen in the war' and performed in London in 1922, where its profoundly pantheist content caused great offence.[12] The first signs of his subsequent paralysis (of syphilitic origin) appeared in that year; four years later he became blind and totally helpless. In 1928 Eric Fenby, a young Yorkshireman and a devout Catholic, learnt of his inability to finalize his latest music and offered to help. The extraordinary story of their collaboration, a product of personalities so opposed in temperament and philosophy, was movingly told by Fenby after Delius's death in 1934.[13] Although Delius's music was still not widely heard by then, it had not been neglected in England (and less so there than abroad, where it had become unfashion-

731). For a recent discussion and a possible solution see B. Newbould, '"Never done before": Elgar's Other Enigma', *ML* 77 (1996), 228–41.

[10] Moore, 787, 791.

[11] These, or a substantial selection of them, were published in line-facsimile in *The Listener*, 14 (1935), in a supplement to the issue of 28 Aug., with an extensive commentary by W. H. Reed. Anthony Payne's recent reconstruction has nevertheless proved remarkably successful.

[12] According to Delius's contract with Universal Edition the text is by Heinrich Simon; it is evidently based on *Ecclesiastes* and Nietzsche and was translated into English by Ernest Newman for the first performance, and for inclusion in the published vocal and full scores. The reissue of the study score by Boosey & Hawkes in 1986 includes important corrections. Threlfall, *A Catalogue of the Compositions of Frederick Delius*, 70 (no. II/8); *A Supplementary Catalogue*, 41.

[13] *Delius as I Knew Him* (London, 1936). Delius was reburied (after temporary interment at Grez) at Limpsfield, Surrey, in May 1935: it made a nice day out for Vaughan Williams and his (first) wife. U. Vaughan Williams, *R.V.W.: A Biography of Ralph Vaughan Williams* (London, 1964), 206.

able). Beecham was a tireless advocate: there were recordings, and a festival of six concerts in 1929, which Delius was able to attend and was at that time made a Companion of Honour. In 1932 he also became a Freeman of the City of Bradford.

Apart from the *Requiem* Delius's wartime works, all of which had to wait until after the war for a hearing, included a double concerto for violin, cello, and orchestra, a violin concerto, the second *Dance Rhapsody*, the tone-poem *Eventyr*, *A Song Before Sunrise* (for small orchestra), a string quartet, and a cello sonata—a remarkable tally and a demonstration of a growing interest in 'abstract' forms. The monolithic *Requiem*, in four short movements, is not a very satisfactory piece—its controversial nature aside—lacking as it does the colour and spirit of *A Mass of Life*. *Eventyr* is an expansive work with a strong Nordic flavour (it is subtitled 'Once upon a time: after Asbjørnsen's Folklore'), its discursive form compensated for by its motivic economy.[14] As for the abstract works, neither they nor their successors—two violin sonatas, the second and third, were to follow—can be regarded as entirely successful. Delius's musical thought was expressed in short, cell-like motifs, and his structural principle was paratactic rather than syntactic. In this way he could build up a satisfying mosaic from the juxtaposition or repetition of brief fragments, each often dependent on a single chord; but such methods are ill-suited to organic development, and the sonatas and concertos are an odd mixture of rhapsodic meandering and periodic phrase-structure. There is more to be said for the quartet, despite its poor reputation,[15] since it has a Debussyan fluidity. But there is plenty to admire in Delius's later work, even though his style developed little after the war: *A Song of Summer* (1929–30), for orchestra, was resurrected from the earlier *Poem of Life and Love*, which Fenby thought was below Delius's best and told him so; and most of all the *Songs of Farewell* (Whitman), for chorus and orchestra (1930), which draw into one final statement his message of languorous beauty and ultimate pessimism.

Holst

Holst was the third major composer to die in the fatal year 1934;[16] and of the three he was the most adventurous in his post-war quest. Much younger than Delius and Elgar, he had not really found his feet as a composer by 1914, notwithstanding the emergence of the real Holst in works like *The*

---

[14] But not by any economy of resources: a chorus of 'about 20 men' is required for two pitched shouts off-stage. Programme-planners beware: this requirement is not shown in the preliminary list of instruments.

[15] Fenby, 65. The third movement, 'Late Swallows', is a survivor from an earlier, unpublished quartet.

[16] But chronologically the second, on 25 May (Elgar died on 23 Feb. and Delius on 10 June). In addition, Norman O'Neill died on 3 Mar.

Mystic Trumpeter, Savitri (as yet unperformed), and some of the *Rig Veda* settings. He found them with a vengeance in *The Planets*, composed in 1914–16, in which he showed how his personal penchant for ostinati, fourths-based harmony, and slowly shifting chordal progressions could be coupled with brilliant scoring and sharp characterization to create a large-scale work with broad appeal. In 1917 he wrote *The Hymn of Jesus*, to his own translation from the Greek; after the war it was taken up by choral societies with enthusiasm. Nothing he wrote thereafter enjoyed the same success, though his prominence as a composer and teacher was assured. He remains an enigmatic figure, with his unrestrained enthusiasms and his relentless pursuit of originality; it cannot be claimed that he possessed the universality of Vaughan Williams, his great friend and lifelong associate.[17]

Savitri, though composed in 1908–9, was not heard until 1916, and then privately;[18] the first public performance, conducted by Arthur Bliss, was at the Lyric Theatre, Hammersmith, on 23 June 1921. Holst's style in this short one-act piece is not as advanced as it later became, but the work is nevertheless distinguished by its economy of means: it is in fact the first 'modern' chamber opera of any consequence. Holst himself wrote the libretto on the basis of a story from the *Mahabharata*, translating from the Sanskrit a simple tale of wifely devotion and ingenuity in the face of Death. There are but three characters, and the scoring is for two string quartets, double bass, two flutes, cor anglais, and a hidden wordless chorus. Few English operas first heard between 1918 and 1940 are as cogent, but it has suffered from the difficulty of devising a satisfactory double or triple bill to include it. Vaughan Williams's *Riders to the Sea* is almost the only English work of comparable stature from the inter-war years; but it requires larger forces, and in any case lasts only 37 minutes.[19]

Holst's next opera, *The Perfect Fool* (produced at Covent Garden on 14 May 1923), was also a one-acter but requires a full orchestra and is a not entirely convincing parody of operatic conventions. (Its opening ballet music is well-written light music and was long popular as a separate item.) Holst's two last operas, again in one act each, were *At the Boar's Head* (1924, produced in 1925) and *The Wandering Scholar* (1929–30, produced early in 1934), the first making use (like Vaughan Williams's *Hugh the Drover*) of folk tunes and the second adopting a folk-like idiom. All these operatic ventures exhibit something like a failure of musical nerve in their use of parody or a 'folk' style. Holst wanted in each case to write a genuinely comic opera and

---

[17] The record of their friendship, or much of it, is preserved in U. Vaughan Williams and I. Holst (eds.), *Heirs and Rebels: Letters to Each Other and Occasional Writings on Music by Ralph Vaughan Williams and Gustav Holst* (London, 1959).

[18] By the London School of Opera on 5 Dec.

[19] It also, like *Savitri*, requires an off-stage chorus for women (Holst had rewritten his off-stage choral music for women's voices in time for the first performance: M. Short, *Gustav Holst: The Man and his Music* (Oxford and New York, 1990), 77).

had some good ideas for them; but—his weakness as a librettist aside—he did not bring to them the seriousness of compositional approach that was within his grasp.

It was far otherwise in the case of his large-scale orchestral and choral works, and in that of many of his smaller pieces as well. There is, however, little pattern of achievement in Holst: practically everything he wrote was *sui generis*. *The Planets* was a gigantic orchestral 'suite' like no other, but by no means a symphony. *The Hymn of Jesus* is unique, though there is an extended parallel in Vaughan Williams's later *Sancta Civitas*. Holst here created his own language of semi-Christian spirituality out of elements previously used in his Vedic works, to which he added two plainchant melodies from *The English Hymnal*, those of 'Pange lingua gloriosae prelium certaminis' and 'Vexilla regis prodeunt', both initially stated by the trombone. Its essentially triparte form of slow—fast—slow anticipates by over a decade that of the third movement of Stravinsky's *Symphony of Psalms*. (Holst was clearly influenced in certain respects by the Stravinsky of the great ballets, though his rhythmic ostinati are regular and monolithic where Stravinsky's are highly irregular; there is also the element of 'mysticism' that we find in Skryabin.)[20]

Holst's choral masterpiece is the *First Choral Symphony*, composed in 1923–4 and first heard in October 1925 at the Leeds Festival. (There are only a few sketches extant for a second choral symphony, and the late *Choral Fantasia* is an occasional work of much less interest.)[21] The predominant tone is of the cool paganism of Keats's poetry. The work was much criticized after its first performance, largely because of what was seen as Holst's cavalier selection of verse. Such criticism is entirely misplaced: a composer has every right to deal with a poetic resource in the way that suits his purposes, a point which numerous poets, as well as critics, have failed to understand, sometimes to the extent of forbidding the setting of their verse. Nowadays this point of view is less common and can be ignored, at any rate as part of a critique of this fine work. It is of truly symphonic stature, despite its cantata-like scoring for soprano solo, chorus, and orchestra and its dependence on a verbal matrix. It is precisely in the creative selectivity of text that its symphonic dimension is attained: Holst has fashioned a scheme embracing a lively first movement ('Song and Bacchanal', with a 'Prelude: Invocation to Pan'), a slow movement setting the *Ode on a Grecian Urn* complete, a scherzo ('Ever let the Fancy roam', with *Folly's Song* as a pendant), and a finale, 'Spirit here that reignest', predominantly slow and solemn. The work is completely free of the turgidity that a reliance on ostinato and the slow pace of much of it might have induced; the scoring is

---

[20] Holst apparently found the text of the *Hymn* in the work of a theosophist, G. R. S. Mead (Short, *Gustav Holst*, 147).

[21] According to I. Holst, the *Fantasia* elicited his worst ever press notice when first performed at Gloucester Cathedral on 8 Sept. 1931 (*Catalogue*, 180 [no. 177]).

comparatively light and the choral textures are luminous. But it is the formal economy that is most striking; the texts are expeditiously delivered, and there is no superfluous padding. Perhaps it is this aspect of Holst's post-Romantic style that most disconcerted his first audiences.

The sense of economy is paramount in all Holst's later music, even such of it as was written for large forces. He made use of older compositional procedures in works like *A Fugal Overture* (1922), its companion *A Fugal Concerto* for flute, oboe, and strings (1923), and the *Double Concerto* for two violins and orchestra (1929)—though in unusual ways. Far more compelling than these is *Egdon Heath (Homage to Thomas Hardy)*, composed in 1927 and first heard in New York in February 1928. Like a good deal of Holst's later music, it was uncomprehendingly received: the composer of *The Planets* had been duly type-cast and was failing to deliver the goods. *Egdon Heath* was inspired by Hardy's *Return of the Native*, a quotation from which is prefixed to the score:

A place perfectly accordant with man's nature—neither ghastly, nor ugly; neither commonplace, unmeaning, nor tame; but, like man, slighted and enduring; and withal singularly colossal and mysterious in its swarthy monotony!

Something of the paradox of this description is preserved in Holst's music, which is pared down to its expressive essentials yet has in it both the colossal and the mysterious. The form is original, discursive without seeming rhapsodic. We may envisage a wanderer standing at the very edge of the heath before walking across it; as he walks, he encounters images that act powerfully on the imagination, yielding in turn a maelstrom of devilry, a solemn procession, a ghostly dance; eventually the far side is reached, fervid imaginings reduced to dim recollections. Such a picture, however fanciful, is truer to the work than a formal motivic, or tonal analysis:[22] certainly it has form (a free rondo), certainly there are melodic cells that help to bind the work together, and certainly one can think in terms of an ultimate G minor; yet even at the end, where some of the earlier mystery is resolved, it is only to emphasize the disparity of the main ideas and, perhaps, the irresolution at the heart of the human condition (Ex. 5.4).

In his chamber music and songs, too, Holst came to whittle down his expressive means to a minimum. The *Four Songs for Voice and Violin* (1916–17, published in 1920), using medieval poems, are concise in the extreme, but their tonal language, despite the medium, is still fairly conventional. The *Twelve Songs* to poems by Humbert Wolfe, published singly in 1930,[23] are

---

[22] There is, however, a fine analysis by R. Greene, *Gustav Holst and a Rhetoric of Musical Character* (New York and London, 1994), 135–51, and in his article 'A Musico-Historical Outline of Holst's "Egdon Heath"', *ML* 73 (1992), 244–67, in which both technical and metaphysical aspects of the work are fully explored.

[23] Newly ed. and ordered as a set by I. Holst (London, 1970).

less spare in texture but exhibit a maturer sense of harmonic idiom. There is in some of the accompaniments (to *Persephone*, *The Floral Bandit*, and *Rhyme* in particular) an ornamental quality that anticipates Britten and, especially, Tippett, though others, like the famous *Betelgeuse*, are stark. The composer did not consider them a cycle (an *Epilogue* was subsequently abandoned), but their contrasts make a collective performance an attractive proposition.

Holst explored the possibilities of polytonality in several later works, most thoroughly in the *Terzetto* for flute, oboe, and viola (1925). The results are curious, since in striving for compatibility the composer achieved non-functional triadic harmony rather than his by then normal astringent idiom.

An estimate of Holst would be very one-sided if it did not refer to the numerous works in a more straightforward idiom that he wrote or arranged for amateur choirs and orchestras. He was passionately devoted to the amateur cultivation of music and found pleasure in the uphill task of preparing untrained singers and players for great challenges. Some of these works, like the *St Paul's Suite* (1913) and *Brook Green Suite* (1933) for strings, or the part-song *This have I done for my true love* ('To morrow shall be my dancing day') for mixed choir (1916, published in 1919) are small masterpieces in a comfortably approachable idiom. On the other hand, the late and very characteristic prelude and scherzo *Hammersmith* (1930) was written for

Ex. 5.4

continued

Ex. 5.4, continued

Gustav Holst, *Egdon Heath* (London, 1928): (*a*) p. 1; (*b*) p. 3; (*c*) pp. 5–6; (*d*) pp. 24–5

a professional body, the BBC Wireless Military Band.[24] His last orchestral compositions were a *Lyric Movement* for viola and small orchestra, and a *Scherzo* (1933–4) for a symphony that was never completed.

Holst, despite his wide sympathies and his questing nature, did not quite achieve the breadth of musical insight that marks the truly great composer. His teaching, to which he devoted so much energy, distracted him too readily from his creative purposes, and his physique—despite his enthusiasm for walking and cycling—played him sad tricks. His eyesight was poor, he suffered increasingly from 'neuritis' in his right hand, and at the end he lacked the resilience to recover from an operation to remove an ulcer. He was much respected by his colleagues and pupils, but he suffered from the patronizing indifference, faint praise, or even downright hostility of some critics, especially in later life. All this affected Holst, notwithstanding his moral stature, to the extent that his handful of real masterpieces is set beside a large body of work that is for the most part entirely characteristic but either too obviously experimental or too down-to-earth to be of lasting value.

Vaughan Williams

Vaughan Williams attained the breadth of appeal that eluded Holst in his later years. Like Holst, whom he invariably admired and encouraged, he wrote a good deal for amateurs, singers in particular. Much of his smaller-scale output—music for unaccompanied choirs, folk song arrangements, music for military and brass bands, church music, minor cantatas, and so on—is of only ephemeral interest. But beside this must be placed a substantial body of music in the major forms: three of his symphonies, *Job*, at least one of his operas, two major and several lesser choral works, instrumental concertos, chamber music, and songs. Even a summary of this sort excludes masterpieces that resist categorization, like *Flos campi*, and risks linking splendid works such as the G minor Mass or *Dona nobis pacem* with the 'ephemera', which they certainly are not. Some of his tiniest works, moreover, are pearls of great price. Like Holst again, he will have seen all his activity (including arranging, editing, teaching, writing, and performing) as of a piece; the difference is that he was able to project a more consistent image of his musical personality throughout the range of his endeavours.

At the forefront of those endeavours stand the third, fourth, and fifth symphonies, to which we may add here the sixth, composed in 1945–7 and first performed in 1948.[25] The third, *A Pastoral Symphony*, was written

---

[24] It was soon arranged for a normal orchestra; the original version was not publicly performed, despite the commission, until 1954 (I. Holst, *A Catalogue*, 181 [no. 178]). Like *Egdon Heath* it is a scenescape, this time animated by real people.

[25] Kennedy, *A Catalogue of the Works of Ralph Vaughan Williams*, 285–6, 290.

mainly in 1921 and first heard in 1922. Its title points to an obvious contrast with *A London Symphony* (no. 2), though mental images of an idyllic landscape are misleading: the passages for natural trumpet and natural horn in the slow movement really evoke the practising of an army bugler amid the desolation of wartime France.[26] Even that desolation, however, had a certain beauty—or rather it could not wholly displace the beauty of nature—and the third symphony, like so much of Vaughan Williams's music, conveys the paradoxical liaison of pleasure and melancholy rather than any pictorial qualities. It would certainly be a mistake to dismiss it as limited in emotional range or as deficient in variety, notwithstanding its preponderance of moderate and slow tempi.[27] The first movement (Molto moderato) is in an abbreviated sonata form, to which the continuous flow of the composer's modally structured melody is readily suited. The slow movement, with its horn and trumpet calls, resists a conventional formal or tonal analysis, but the bitonal opening (a pentatonic tune in C major against the chords of F minor) and the E flat tonality of the trumpet call find a piquant resolution in the coda (Ex. 5.5).[28] The third movement is a heavy dance in 3/4 (another Ländler, in fact, like that of the G minor quartet) with a faster 'trio' and (a surprise) a creepy Presto coda. The last movement, again tripartite in form, begins and ends with the celebrated wordless soprano melisma.[29] Tonal ambiguity persists to the last, for the singer's final E is left unresolved against the high A in the violins—a note that in theory returns to the opening of the movement but in its context sounds alien and disorientating.

The fourth symphony, 'in F minor' (all Vaughan Williams's subsequent symphonies, except for the *Antartica*, no. 7, are in a named key) is by contrast straightforward in its tonal toughness and in its clear-cut use of short motifs. His contemporaries were surprised by its level of dissonance, although there is nothing in the work that does not emerge naturally as a consequence of the composer's well-established idiom. The Fifth, in D, is on the other hand warm and euphonious: composed and first performed during the Second World War, it shares some of its music with his 'morality' *The Pilgrim's Progress*, on which he had been working since 1909 (and also with the 1938 pageant *England's Pleasant Land*). The sixth symphony, in E minor, effectively rounds off this phase of symphonic composition. The first three movements mark a return to the toughness—and the jokey parody of

---

[26] U. Vaughan Williams, *R.V.W.*, 121. The use of the natural trumpet in E flat and a natural horn in F, or their equivalent effect on valved instruments, results in a pitch for the seventh note of the harmonic series that is decidedly flatter than its counterpart in equal temperament.

[27] Kennedy's commentary (*The Works of Ralph Vaughan Williams*, 168–72) is exemplary.

[28] The violin phrases are reminiscent of the *Tom Thumb* movement in Ravel's *Ma mère l'oye* (orchestrated in 1911).

[29] Alternatively for clarinet or (incredibly) tenor. As in most of Vaughan Williams's orchestral works, certain instruments are optional, their material being 'cued' into other parts.

popular idioms—of the fourth symphony, but the last is a study in despairing nihilism. It is impossible not to see in this work a comment on war and its aftermath, though the terrifying theme of the slow movement, with its

Ex. 5.5

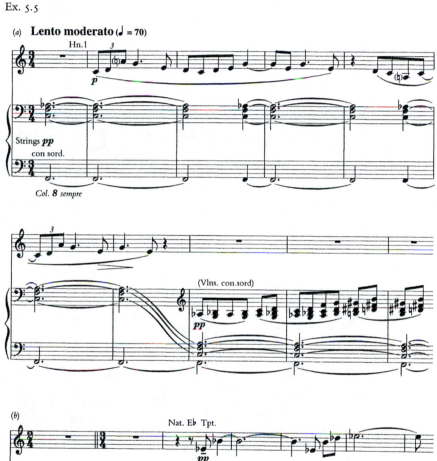

continued

Ex. 5.5, continued

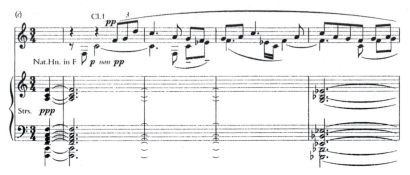

Ralph Vaughan Williams, *A Pastoral Symphony*, 2nd mvt. (London, 1924): (*a*) p. 33; (*b*) p. 41;
(*c*) pp. 48–9

inexorable repetition of the ⸪ rhythm, originated, improbably enough, in the score to a wartime film, 'Flemish Farm'. The composer seems to have become increasingly anxious to deflect attention from any external message in his music by the facetiousness of his programme notes: those for the sixth symphony[30] are painfully at odds with its searing challenge to the psyche.

With the symphonies we may consider *Job*, described in the score as 'A Masque for Dancing Founded on Blake's "Illustrations for the Book of Job"'. The scenario is credited to Geoffrey Keynes and Gwendolen Raverat. The fruitful idea of animating Blake's illustrations, as it were, to music resulted in by far the most enduring of twentieth-century ballets with music by an English composer. It works best in the theatre, as indeed it should: the music is not quite a self-standing symphonic work, with its optional repetitions and cuts and its moments of lesser substance. Nevertheless the complete score is a masterly achievement, realizing a hieratic quality that fits perfectly with the schematic and pictorial elements of the scenario.

The concertante principle is surprisingly prominent in the output of a composer for whom instrumental display was far from being a priority. Yet the relationship of an instrumental soloist to the larger body is clearly a problem that fascinated Vaughan Williams throughout his composing life, at any rate from the early *Fantasia* for piano and orchestra (1896–1902, revised 1904: unpublished) to the tuba concerto of 1954. Nor was it confined to avowedly concertante works: the *Pastoral Symphony*, in addition to its use of the solo voice and some striking wind solos, has in the first movement a prominent part for solo violin, mostly in dialogue with various woodwind instruments, once with a solo viola. During the years 1914–45 he composed three concertos and four other works for a solo instrument and orchestra.

The violin and viola were perhaps those with which he had the greatest instinctive sympathy. *The Lark Ascending*, a 'Romance' for violin and small orchestra[31] (1914, revised and performed 1920), is a kind of extended accompanied cadenza: a purely atmospheric evocation of the soaring bird. The *Concerto Accademico* (1924–5: the epithet was removed on revision in 1951) for violin and strings is very different, a piece of creative pastiche in an idiom distantly related to the Baroque but as much a reflection of Vaughan Williams's personality as any of his works. *Flos campi*, composed around the same time, is different again: a six-movement suite for viola, wordless chorus, and small orchestra. The title alludes to the Song of Songs, quotations from which in Latin head each movement. The composer seems to have been motivated simply by the sensuous and pictorial qualities of these texts, but they gave rise to querulous comments, prompting the composer

---

[30] Cited in full, as always, by Kennedy, *A Catalogue*, 191–4.
[31] The orchestra, small as it is, can be further reduced if desired.

to explain them in a later programme note and to disclaim any 'ecclesiastical basis' for the music.

There was also a *Fantasia on Sussex Folk Tunes* for cello and orchestra (1930, unpublished and later withdrawn) and, more importantly, the piano concerto in C (1926–31). This massive (though not overlong) work was later revised (in 1946, with the aid of Joseph Cooper) for two solo pianos and orchestra, although any doubts about the viability of the one-piano version are misplaced.[32] Its introductory toccata in 7/8 time and the chromatic fugal section of the finale are evidence of the composer's exploratory mind at this period; the use of fugue in a finale recurs, of course, in the fourth symphony, where it rather more convincingly functions as an 'epilogue': here it is followed by a cadenza and a 'finale alla tedesca'.[33] Perhaps the most striking feature of the work is its very free use of a percussion section that includes a tam-tam as well as side-drum, cymbals, and bass drum. Lastly (before 1945) is the exquisite concerto for oboe and strings, first performed in September 1944. It would be hard to match this record of creativity in the concertante forms—even more so if the later *Romance* for harmonica and strings and the tuba concerto are taken into account.[34]

Instrumental chamber music and solo song were less important in this period than previously, although there is a second string quartet (1942–4), 'For Jean on her birthday', and, amongst his songs, sets devoted to poems by Fredegond Shove (1925), Whitman (1925), Shakespeare (1925), and Housman (1927, revised 1954). Far more significant was a galaxy of choral works, most of which have remained in the repertory of ambitious choral societies. The Mass in G minor, for unaccompanied voices (1922), is a strictly liturgical setting, though it was dedicated 'to Gustav Holst and his Whitsuntide Singers' and was first performed by the City of Birmingham Choir. Reflective and vigorous by turns, it is a remarkable piece of vocal 'orchestration', unsurpassed as such in the period and challenged in this respect only by Britten's *Hymn to St Cecilia*.

More characteristic is a batch of medium-length works for one or more soloists, chorus, and orchestra. The *Benedicite*, a setting of *The Hundredth Psalm*, and *Three Choral Hymns* were all composed (together with *Three Children's Songs*) in 1929 for the Leith Hill Music Festival at Dorking and first given there in 1930: this was a festival of which Vaughan Williams had been the guiding spirit since its foundation in 1904 and with which he remained associated to the end of his days.[35] *Dona nobis pacem*, a response to rumours of war (1936), is similar to the *Benedicite* in character. In 1937 he

---

[32] There are, however, other minor changes in the two-piano version, possibly improvements.
[33] Despite the terminology, the fugue, cadenza, and *alla tedesca* are all part of the same movement.
[34] There are also extensive sketches for a cello concerto dating from 1942–3.
[35] The 1958 festival was 'the first he had ever missed'. U. Vaughan Williams, *R.V.W.*, 395.

wrote a *Festival Te Deum* for the coronation of George VI as well as a *Flourish for a Coronation* for concert use. In 1938 came the euphonious *Serenade to Music*, a setting of Lorenzo's speech from *The Merchant of Venice* (Act V, Sc. 1) for sixteen solo voices and orchestra, a tribute to Sir Henry Wood and unofficially to a galaxy of British vocal talent.

Two major choral works stand out. *Sancta Civitas* (1925, first given in Oxford in 1926)[36] is his finest religious piece, described as an oratorio though it lasts for little more than half an hour. Whatever Vaughan Williams's reservations about the Christian faith, it would be hard to match this work for intensity of feeling conveyed through a biblical text.[37] A small but telling detail—more informative, perhaps, than the quotation from *Phaedo* at the beginning of the score—is the omission of the holy name from the closing words of the text: 'Amen, even so come Lord [Jesus]'. But even this could have been done for musical reasons as much as from philosophical doubt. Otherwise the selection and rearrangement of the words seems to serve purely artistic purposes: the lament for the fall of Babylon (ch. 18) is placed between the account of the heavenly army and its war against the 'kings of the earth' (ch. 19) and the description of a 'new heaven and a new earth' (ch. 21). This satisfying tripartite scheme is enhanced by an outer layer of material devoted to the praise of God in heaven, and around that an opening and a closing passage depicting the beginning of the vision and the final prophecy of and prayer for the Second Coming. Tonal relationships are employed for rhetorical purposes: a distant trumpet and chorus of sopranos and altos introduce the 'heavenly' area of A flat major, while the 'new earth', linked to it by the enharmonic equivalence A flat/G sharp, is represented by E major. On the other hand, the heavenly army is tonally mobile, its war pursued with extreme dissonance, and the central lament is 'closed' within a refrain-element ('Babylon is fallen') in G minor. The beginning and end are virtually keyless, and the work fades away into tonal nothingness (Ex. 5.6).

The *Five Tudor Portraits* (1935, first performed 1936) are, of course, secular, and far less radical in musical language. Certainly the societies that in the 1860s had rejoiced in *The May Queen* had come a long way by their acceptance of this rumbustious and irreverent setting of portions of Skelton's verse; even so, the composer has omitted 'certain lines that look well

---

[36] In the Sheldonian Theatre on 7 May, during the general strike. The conductor was Hugh Allen. The acoustics of this building, though somewhat clinical, will have enabled every detail of this complex score to be heard.

[37] This is described as being taken 'from the "Authorized Version" [i.e. of The Revelation of St John the Divine] with additions from "Taverner's Bible" and other sources'. The only passage not to be found in Revelation is a completion, towards the end, of the liturgical Sanctus from the *Book of Common Prayer*. The very few departures from the wording of the Authorized Version, except for the omission noted below and when dictated by the composer's selection and arrangement of verses, are to be attributed to the use of Taverner's translation.

Ex. 5.6

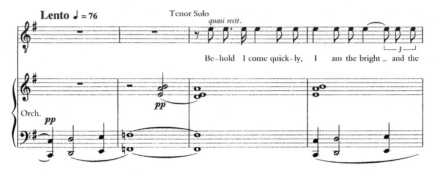

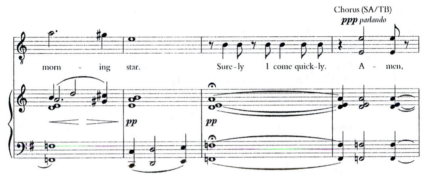

Ralph Vaughan Williams, *Sancta Civitas*: vocal score (London, 1925), pp. 55–6

when read [but] cannot conveniently be sung'—a euphemism in itself.[38] The two most substantial pieces (both in quality and in length) are the first, *The Tunning of Elinor Rumming*, and the fourth, *Jane Scroop*, a haunting lament for her pet sparrow for the women's voices. But the impression of a fading period-piece is hard to resist.

Of Vaughan Williams's operas, *Hugh the Drover* was composed between 1910 and 1914, but first performed only in 1924 and much revised thereafter, most recently in 1956 (and republished as such in 1959). Despite the claims that have been made for it,[39] this attempt at a 'romantic ballad opera' is not entirely convincing; the comic element (undermined in any case by the poverty of Harold Child's libretto) is tinged with earnestness, and the use of folk tunes (eight in all) and folk-like material impedes the development of a natural musico-dramatic language—a difficulty that would be less serious if the music were not continuous. The same objection can be raised against *Sir John in Love* (1928, first performed at the Royal College of Music in 1929), although the immeasurably greater strength of the 'libretto' (an adaptation of *The Merry Wives of Windsor*), and a greater fluency in adapting folk-like material (and actual folk tunes) to dramatic purposes, make it a far more satisfying proposition than *Hugh the Drover*. *The Poisoned Kiss*, a dialogue-opera which originated at the same time but did not reach the stage until 1936—and then only in a student production at Cambridge— suffers from the facetiousness that had been the bane of *The Perfect Fool* and to which neither Holst nor Vaughan Williams were able to respond (or could disguise) with genuinely witty and acerbic music. *Sir John in Love*, therefore, is much the best of Vaughan Williams's comic operas and would merit professional revival.

But all three are thrown into the shade by *Riders to the Sea*, composed between 1925 and 1932 but not published until 1936,[40] and first performed (again at the Royal College of Music) in 1937. Here for once a literary masterpiece, J. M. Synge's play about poverty-stricken life on the west coast of Ireland, made a perfect libretto with hardly any shortening. Despite the work's long gestation, it shows none of the hesitations and uncertainties that marked most of Vaughan Williams's operatic ventures. The preponderance of free declamatory writing throws the more lyrical moments into sharp relief; there is a subtle use of motif (for example the descending semitone associated with Maurya, the old woman), and the harmonic idiom is as

---

[38] The missing line in no. 3, *John Jayberd of Diss*, following '*per asinum et mulum*' ('the devil kiss his *culum*') is represented by an orchestral phrase, though a long-standing tradition has the men whistle it at this point.

[39] e.g. by Kennedy, *The Works of Ralph Vaughan Williams*, 179–84. Appendix I of Mrs Vaughan Williams's book is devoted to the genesis of this work.

[40] This was a vocal score, elegantly printed but by no means fault-free. The full score was published only in 1972.

uncompromising as anywhere in Vaughan Williams. One can truly say of such a work that it adds a dimension of experience unobtainable from speech alone; Maurya's reconciliation with the death of all her sons gives expression to a catharsis that is deeply moving yet at the very end is not allowed to eliminate the keening of those still uncomforted (Ex. 5.7).

The other major operatic work of this period was *The Pilgrim's Progress*, begun perhaps as early as 1909 though not performed until 1951 and revised even after that for performance in 1952, in which year the vocal score was published. It is best considered as in substance a work of the inter-war years; the shepherd's episode (Act IV, Sc. 2), which started life as an independent work, *The Shepherds of the Delectable Mountains*, was composed in 1921 and first heard in 1922; substantial parts of the whole work were broadcast in 1942, and it was effectively complete in 1949. No other composition occupied Vaughan Williams over such an extended length of time.

The Pilgrim's Progress, described as 'a morality in a prologue, four acts and an epilogue founded on Bunyan's allegory of the same name', was regarded as difficult to stage in the 1950s,[41] and it has often been thought of as intrinsically untheatrical. This is unjust. Didactic works have succeeded on the stage—Hindemith's *Mathis der Maler* is similar in scope and dramatic method, though not of course in stylistic detail—and this opera is far more cogent than any of Vaughan Williams's other full-length stage works (all of them comedies). There are indeed weak moments, particularly in the more animated scenes, whereas the passages of rapt contemplation, and indeed of spiritual doubt, as usual brought out the composer's best. His readiness to adapt the length of the interludes between the scenes by means of optional cuts and repetitions is taken to greater lengths than in (say) *Job* and is suggestive of a composer unable or unwilling to impose his operatic vision as a whole. In this respect the opera is *too* theatrical, exhibiting as it does a kind of professionalism that is almost amateurish in its lack of musical self-confidence.[42] But, these weaknesses once discounted, we can readily admit that the whole is greater than the sum of its parts. It has a grand and universal theme, and its clean, picture-book morality is encapsulated in the clear G major of its opening and closing as well as in the more complex processes of its several episodes. As Kennedy says, its day may yet come.

---

[41] Like *Hugh the Drover* and *Sir John in Love* it calls for a large cast; although some parts can be doubled, this has perhaps limited the opportunities for professional production in all three cases.

[42] Similarly, the optional omission of certain instruments, the arrangement of operas as cantatas, and the numerous examples of rescoring, while originating in a genuine desire by Vaughan Williams, Holst, and others to make their work widely available, became in the end a form of artistic appeasement that casts a sad light on the opportunities for professional performance in Britain in the 1920s and 1930s and indeed up to about 1960.

Ex. 5.7

Ex. 5.7, continued

Ralph Vaughan Williams, *Riders to the Sea*: vocal score (London, 1936): (*a*) p. 53; (*b*) p. 60

Bridge, Ireland

Bridge and Ireland, both born in 1879, were very different in musical personality, united only (perhaps) by having taught Benjamin Britten.[43] Bridge continued in his markedly novel path after the First World War, one that led at times to extremes of dissonance bordering on atonality (we have already noted an analogy with Roussel). He became incomprehensible to most of his contemporaries, and his death in 1941 contributed to an obscurity that has never wholly been lifted. His post-war chamber music—a piano sonata (1921–4), two string quartets (nos. 3, 1926, and 4, 1937), a string trio (*Rhapsody*, 1928), and a violin sonata (1934)—best exemplifies his new 'tough' approach.[44] The orchestral music preserves something of his pre-war opulence, with which the new tonal language does not always make a good 'fit'; it includes *Enter Spring* (1927), *Phantasm* for piano and orchestra (1931), and a one-movement cello concerto, *Oration* (1930). There are also some imaginative songs, some with orchestral (or optional orchestral) accompaniment.

If Bridge strove to realize European ideals, Ireland remained resolutely English. His impeccable craftsmanship never deserted him, but neither did his style develop much after the First World War, being based above all on a comprehensive grasp of late Romantic pianism such as we find in Rakhmaninov or Metner. His most characteristic work was in piano music and song, but there is enough of value outside these fields to justify his status as more than a merely minor, though interesting, figure.

It was during the first war, in fact, that Ireland's credentials became firmly established. His second violin sonata (1915–17) matched the times with a grittiness rare in his work; his orchestral Prelude *The Forgotten Rite* (1913) was premiered in 1917; there was a second piano trio (in F, in one movement, 1917); a piano *Rhapsody* (1915), four Preludes (1913–15), one of them the much arranged and all too popular *The Holy Boy*, and the three *London Pieces* (1917); and a number of war-inspired songs.[45] His immediate post-war output included a piano sonata (1918–20), the symphonic rhapsody *Mai-Dun* (1920–1), and a cello sonata (1923). Otherwise the 1920s were occupied mainly with songs (including the Housman cycle *The Land of Lost Content*, 1920–1) and shorter piano works. Ireland had not, however, stopped thinking in terms of the larger forms. In 1930 came his piano concerto, long popular, in 1933 his *Legend* for piano and orchestra, and in 1936 'These things shall be' (Symonds), for baritone (or tenor) solo, chorus, and orchestra. In the same year came the slight but effective *London*

---

[43] Both had studied with Stanford, like so many others.

[44] He enjoyed at this period the patronage of Mrs Elizabeth Sprague Coolidge, a wealthy American who (like Paul Sacher in Basle) encouraged modernist tendencies with enthusiasm.

[45] Ireland neither enlisted nor was called up for war service.

Overture, and in 1939 a *Concertino pastorale* for strings. *Sarnia: an Island Sequence*, inspired by his beloved Channel Islands, was his last important piano work (1940–1), but the *Fantasy-Sonata* (1943), for clarinet and piano, is still full of vitality. After the war he wrote nothing of real importance, though the overture *Satyricon* (1946) was a final well-written gesture in the direction of the standard orchestral forms.

If we ask why a conservative composer of relatively modest output should be singled out, it is because his achievement is practically unique in its cultivation of an extended chromaticism that nevertheless keeps its feet firmly on tonal ground. Light music used a limited repertory of higher chromatic discords in this way, and improvised jazz a considerably larger one, but Ireland usually avoided the perils of a relapse into the commonplace through his melodic originality and metrical sophistication. That he could retain inventiveness as well as his stylistic integrity into his sixties is shown by the *Fantasy-Sonata*, in which an endemic tendency to rhapsodize is held in check by a strong grasp of formal rhetoric. Perhaps the melodic descent of a perfect fifth, the common feature of several Lisztian transformations, is a little obvious; but in tracing its occurrences we can also take measure of the tonal language in which they are cast, and observe a little of the almost Oriental improvisatory quality that is again restrained by a rigorously controlled structure of harmony and metre (Ex. 5.8).[46]

Bax

Arnold Bax (1883–1953), a little junior to Ireland, was in many ways a musician of the same cast, though altogether more prolific and enterprising. Like so many of his generation he emerged but slowly from studentship, in this case under Frederick Corder at the Royal Academy. His pre-war music is enviably fluent, but shows little of his later individuality. His lifelong fascination with Irish mystery and romance began as early as 1902, but it was not at first easy to imbue his idiom with the 'Celtic' spirit, particularly as he sought more subtle methods than the mere quotation of folk tunes. The orchestral tone-poem became his most characteristic means of expression, and he had written several examples before his first real success, *In the Faery Hills* (1909, performed under Wood, 1910).[47] Several more followed before *The Garden of Fand* (1913–16, first performed in Chicago, 1920). 'The Garden of Fand is the sea', as the composer tells us; thus it anticipates the better-known *Tintagel*, not only in its ostensible subject but in its rich

---

[46] As the harmonic reduction of the third extract shows, the bass pedal, which occupies bars 220–44, functions enharmonically both as the diatonic 7th in D and the flat 7th in E flat (the key of the work).

[47] This was the second part of the trilogy *Eire*; the first part, *Into the Twilight*, had been given by Beecham in 1908, less successfully; the third, *Roscatha* (1910), was not heard until 1970. L. Foreman, *Bax: A Composer and his Times* (2nd edn., Aldershot, 1988), 56–7, 74–5, 408: the present section is much indebted to Foreman's work.

Ex. 5.8

continued

Ex. 5.8, continued

Ex. 5.8, continued

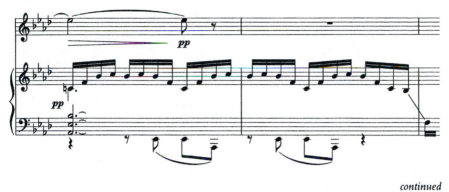

continued

orchestration and free use of higher chromatic discord. Indeed Bax had already arrived at the point at which any semitonal combination could be justified in the context of any key-centre, the orchestration serving either to soften the dissonance or, for pictorial effect, to exacerbate it. We are not far from the world of the big Stravinsky ballets, except that Bax, unlike Stravinsky, was still devoted to older norms of rhythmic continuity. The Strauss of *Salome* and *Elektra* also had a hand in the forging of his idiom, but Bax never succumbed to Strauss's penchant (even in *Elektra*) for lapsing into comfortable diatonic repose. As an orchestral colourist he came to rival Bantock, but his altogether more sinewy idiom made his music a considerably greater force to be reckoned with between the wars.

After *The Garden of Fand* came *November Woods* (1917) and *Tintagel* (1917–19), as well as other works, all produced during the emotional upheaval of his affair with Harriet Cohen and consequent separation from his wife and children. Bax was still able to postpone the instrumentation of a work as orchestrally conceived as *Tintagel* for two years, so that *November Woods*, formally and conceptually the more adventurous, was actually ready first.

These two works are the high point in Bax's production of Romantic tone-poems. It could hardly have been predicted that he would go on to write seven symphonies between 1922 and 1939. The cultivation of concertante works, on the other hand, had effectively been initiated with the *Symphonic Variations* for piano and orchestra (1917), an enormous and demanding work written for Harriet Cohen and subsequently shortened and simplified for her. These changes, while making the work more practicable, are generally thought nowadays to have weakened the piece, but the original version is once more available and is surely to be

Ex. 5.8, continued

John Ireland, Fantasy-Sonata for clarinet and piano (London, 1945): (a) p. 1; (b) pp. 8–9; (c) p. 18, with harmonic reduction added

preferred.[48] In 1920 came the *Phantasy* for viola and orchestra, in 1930 the *Winter Legends* for piano and orchestra, in 1936 a cello concerto, and in 1938 a violin concerto; after the war, in 1949, there were completed a *Concertante* for three wind instruments and orchestra (for cor anglais, clarinet, and horn, each with a movement of its own, and for all three together in the finale), and the not very successful *Concertante* for piano (left hand) and orchestra, written for the now disabled Harriet Cohen.[49] In addition to all these there were a number of lesser orchestral works, several unpublished and unperformed at the time.

The seven symphonies are, collectively, a remarkable achievement, virtually unparalleled for the short period in which they were written and hard to match for the ambitious pursuit of the symphonic ideal. It is fair to ask, however, whether that ideal, insofar as it can be technically evaluated, was truly symphonic. Bax's flow of opulently harmonized and scored ideas never ceased, but they lack, on the whole, the capacity to generate a closely argued dialectic, without which twentieth-century symphonism is of little use. Nor is there the colour, variety, and sheer cussedness that permits acceptance of Vaughan Williams as a wholly original symphonic thinker. Bax did not possess this kind of originality, though he did command formidable technical resource and an enviable grammatical fluency. Nor was he unoriginal: he pursued progressive tonality (in his second symphony) and was formally inventive to the last; it is rather that the scope of his originality was circumscribed by his innate preconceptions as to the way music behaves. One could make a similar observation of Edmund Rubbra's symphonic work, in spite of its very different idiomatic framework.

As for the concertante works, these, together with much of the mature chamber music, may ultimately prove more durable than the tone-poems and symphonies themselves: despite their general opulence of style, there is an incisiveness in the solo instrumental writing and a clarity of texture in the chamber music that one often seeks in vain elsewhere. The four published piano sonatas, together with the sonata for two pianos (1929), are another monument of persistence: the second in particular (1919) is an arresting work of Lisztian proportions. The songs on the other hand, including those with orchestra, do not represent him at his best; well over half, in any case, pre-date the First World War and lack the disciplined cohesion that a properly lyrical expression demands. The few choral works are of small importance.

[48] Foreman, 144–5. Cohen's difficulties were excusable: her small hands could stretch no more than an octave.

[49] It says much for her professional detachment that she could continue to be associated with Bax's music, as she had learnt of his long-standing relationship with Mary Gleaves only the previous year. Foreman, 240.

Bliss, Howells

At first sight the pairing of these two composers may seem odd, but they were among Stanford's last pupils of any consequence (Ivor Gurney, a third, will be considered further on), and their musical personalities, or at any rate their historical positions, are not as different as may at first appear. Both, moreover, enjoyed long lives and continued to write in their characteristic and assured manners well after 1945; of the composers already singled out that is true only of Vaughan Williams, since neither Ireland nor Bax had much of importance to offer in their later years.

Arthur Bliss (1891–1975) was one of the few composers (and the only one of any distinction) both to have served in the first war and to have survived it. His early post-war works—including *Madame Noy* (1918), *Rhapsody* (1919), *Rout* (1920), and *Conversations* (1919)—the first three for ensemble with voice or voices, the last for five instruments—demonstrate a vein of iconoclasm that is closer to Milhaud than to Stravinsky, though the most characteristic expression of this in Milhaud, his *Machines agricoles*, appeared only in 1920, too late to be influential. Still, Bliss must have been acquainted with the earlier experimental work of Milhaud and his French (and Swiss) compatriots who—again in 1920—under the influence of Cocteau and Satie briefly united as 'Les Six'. While the Stravinskian precedent was also no doubt significant, Bliss's rather less radical type of anamorphosis soon merged into a less distorting neo-Romanticism such as we find as early as the *Colour Symphony* (1922, revised 1932) and in another symphony, this time for orator, chorus, and orchestra, *Morning Heroes* (1930), his most deeply considered large-scale work of the period and an effective personal catharsis from the emotional legacy of the war. Neo-Romanticism is carried to excess in the piano concerto (1938), a big and bold but musically slighter work; the ballet *Checkmate* (1937) similarly exhibits a disturbing facility for which the tiresome scenario offers scant compensation. But there were always two sides to Bliss's nature, and the musician who conducted the first public performance of *Savitri*, once he had thrown off the merely modish elements in his post-war adventurism, went on to write well-crafted, fine-textured chamber music—an oboe quintet (1927), a clarinet quintet (1931), and a viola sonata (1933)—and the equally sophisticated *Music for Strings* (1935), perhaps the most rewarding of all his instrumental works. The *Pastoral: Lie Strewn the White Flocks*, for mezzo-soprano, chorus, and strings with solo flute and timpani (1928), suffers from a rather four-square quality in the choral writing;[50] as a setting of secular Elizabethan and Jacobean poetry with prominent instrumental sections it anticipates and

---

[50] It was apparently intended specifically for amateur choirs (*NGD* s.v. 'Bliss'). The dedication to Elgar does not seem to reflect any musical indebtedness: Bliss's admiration found expression only in his ceremonial works.

may have influenced Constant Lambert's *Summer's Last Will and Testament*, but is far less challenging both technically and stylistically.

Herbert Howells (1892–1983) is probably best known nowadays for his Anglican church music and in particular for his series of services for a number of different choral establishments. But these, like the *Missa Sabrinensis* and the *Stabat mater*, date mostly from after the second war (the first, *Collegium Regale*, was written in 1944), while the *Hymnus Paradisi*, though composed in 1938, was not performed until 1950. On the other hand, the best of his organ music, in which he forged a distinctive personal idiom, was written by 1945, when five of the *Six Pieces* had been completed. From the period of the first war and into the 1920s, moreover, emerged a striking series of chamber works. The orchestral music is of little moment, except for the beautiful *Concerto for String Orchestra*, but *Lambert's Clavichord* (1927), a charming set of keyboard pieces in a vein of semi-pastiche, lives on as the prototype of many such things.[51]

The early chamber music is of a distinction that makes one regret that Howells did not pursue his quest further. Perhaps he sensed that his idiom had little further potential in that context, characterized as it was by richly chromatic harmony, tonal vacillation, and extended linear development—a kind of Romantic *Fortspinnung* in which the line may be passed from one instrument to another but in which cadences are avoided as far as possible—as in the ecstatic passage from the *Rhapsodic Quintet* for clarinet and strings shown in Ex. 5.9. By 1923, when the second string quartet ('In Gloucestershire') and the third violin sonata appeared,[52] this manner had had its day, though it experienced a late flowering in the oboe and clarinet sonatas (1943, 1949). With the organ, Howells persisted longer. The (first) three Rhapsodies (1915–18) and the first set of *Three Psalm Preludes* (1915–16) are bold, striking works for a large, orchestrally coloured instrument. By the time of the sonata of 1933[53] his idiom had become terser, but he still demanded the resources of a Romantic monster, perhaps a concert-organ in this case, and the outcome is a dichotomy between style and resource, especially in the lengthy first movement, where the music is bespattered with accents that cannot be literally represented on an organ at all. The second set of *Three Psalm Preludes* (1938) and the *Six Pieces*[54] are less amenable to this criticism, though the more vigorous movements still perpetuate a gap between expectation and a feasible result. The more

---

[51] Including his own *Howells' Clavichord*, published in 1961. Peter Warlock's *Capriol Suite* for strings or piano duet appeared in 1926, but this consists essentially (like Stravinsky's *Pulcinella*) of developed transcriptions.

[52] The first two violin sonatas, and the *Phantasy String Quartet* [no. 1] were all composed in 1918.

[53] There was also an earlier sonata, *c*.1911, in C minor.

[54] Of these, four (nos. 1, 3, 4, and 6 of the set as eventually published in 1953) are dated 1940; no. 5 is dated 1945, and no. 2, the *Sarabande for the Morning of Easter*, is undated but was first published in 1949.

Ex. 5.9

(1) actual sounds

Ex. 5.9, continued

Herbert Howells, *Rhapsodic Quintet* (London, 1921), pp. 3–4

reflective pieces, however, even though they may (as in *Master Tallis's Testament*) entail a spurious archaism, are among the most satisfying English organ works of the mid-century.

The *Concerto for String Orchestra* fulfils many of the expectations only partially realized in the organ sonata. It had a complicated genesis. The slow movement (1934–5) was written as a memorial to Elgar and to Howells's young son, who had died of meningitis in 1935. The first movement, however, was a reworking of the first movement of an early *Suite for Strings* (1917), while the finale was completed in 1938 and the whole first performed in 1940.[55] The stylistic homogeneity is remarkable in the circumstances, the command of the medium impressive, and the whole a worthy rival to Bliss's better-known *Music for Strings*.

Hymnus Paradisi too is a memorial, this time on an extended scale, to the son whose loss he felt so deeply: its opening notes recall those of the slow movement of the *Concerto*, though they evolve into a different, chant-like phrase which recurs frequently and reappears at the end of the work. *Hymnus Paradisi* is certainly Howells's pre-war masterpiece, perhaps his finest work altogether. The text is an imaginative re-creation of the idea of a Requiem: the opening words of the Latin introit, in its universalized version with plural pronouns, gives way to a setting of Ps. 23; the Latin Sanctus is integrated with Ps. 121, and after two more liturgical texts in English the opening Latin words recur (as in a liturgical Requiem) to make a framework for the whole. The soaring lines, the predominantly meditative tone, and the passionate climaxes are all welded into a unified work that breathes sincerity from first to last and never loses its structural grasp.

It would be easy to dismiss Howells as a mannered individualist with a restricted appeal, and indeed the public perception of him in the 1930s must have been in decline, certainly as compared with that of Bax, Bliss, and Vaughan Williams. But his resurgence after 1945 testifies to an enviable resilience on his part—a resilience due largely to the reliability of his idiom as an expression of his personal testament and as a convincing vindication of traditional values in the later twentieth century.

Warlock, Moeran

Peter Warlock—the pseudonym of Philip Heseltine (1894–1930)—and E. J. Moeran (1894–1950) were for a time companions in conviviality as well as exact contemporaries. Unfortunately, a serious war wound had rendered Moeran unusually susceptible to the effects of alcohol, though few in any case could have kept up with Heseltine in his cups.[56] Heseltine himself was possessed of a volatile temperament and eventually took his own life, much lamented by the many who had been charmed by his personality and were appreciative of his multi-faceted talent.

Peter Warlock, as we should call him, was a musical scholar as well as a composer, using his pseudonym for both purposes.[57] As a very young man he became obsessed with Delius and his music; later he came into contact with the Dutch-born exile Bernard van Dieren (1887–1936), from whom he informally learnt a good deal. Warlock's output consists very largely of

[55] The score was published posthumously in 1985 (Novello) with a note by Giles Easterbrook.

[56] G. Self, *The Music of E. J. Moeran* (n.p., 1986), 19–20; cf. L. Foreman, *Bax*, 224.

[57] The pseudonym was first adopted in 1919 as a subterfuge involving Heseltine's dealings with his publishers. There is no truth in the suggestion that 'Heseltine' and 'Warlock' represented two sides of his personality, as maintained by Cecil Gray, *Peter Warlock* (London, 1934).

songs, and they leave a decidedly mixed impression. Many of them—too many, for a composer of serious pretensions—resort to archaism or are straightforwardly popular: a song like *Captain Stratton's Fancy* (Masefield) is pure modernized Dibdin—and none the worse for that, but hardly the stuff of which reputations are made. At his straightforward best, as in 'Bright is the ring of words' (Stevenson), a deceptively simple opening disguises an idiom susceptible to much chromatic manipulation, while a comparison of the music for the two successive stanzas reveals a highly sophisticated application of age-old strophic variation.[58] But even this (and much else like it) is the art of a miniaturist and linguistic conservative.

But there was a more searching side to Warlock's nature, and it found early expression in two of the songs later published as *Saudades*: these are written entirely without metrical restraint, somewhat Satie-like in appearance but owing most to the influence of van Dieren.[59] They in turn led to *The Curlew*, a continuous setting for tenor, flute, cor anglais, and string quartet of four poems by Yeats (1920–2), generally, and surely rightly, accounted Warlock's masterpiece.[60] Here the metres are necessarily specified, though the effect in performance is of considerable freedom. Even so, the harmonic language is fairly limited, exploiting mainly the sharp seventh and higher discords over a minor triad. The bass is often static, though the underlying simplicity is well disguised by instrumentation and a fluid tempo. A powerful sense of desolation is conveyed by the arching melodic lines, with their frequent falling minor thirds, and is accentuated by the doleful tones of the cor anglais. Warlock's friend and later biographer Cecil Gray found the piece unbearably sad, and it is indeed unique in the quality of its pessimism. The problem for Warlock was that neither technically nor emotionally could this work form the basis of future development. The remaining years of the 1920s saw the best of his scholarship, a great deal of song, much of it rather lightweight, the *Capriol Suite*,[61] and some very effective part-songs and carols. Warlock's powers of entertainment (both in music and in other ways) were considerable, but it is not unlikely that in the end he saw himself as having failed in his deepest ambitions.

[58] These comments are based on the version published in 1922. Both this and an earlier version (1918) are given in the *Peter Warlock Collected Edition*, ed. F. Tomlinson, 8 vols., n.p., 1982–93), vol. ii, nos. 1A, 1B transposed to G flat. The song was included in its original key of A flat as the first of a selection of *Thirteen Songs*, ed. P. Pears (Great Yarmouth, 1970). The *Collected Edition* is a useful, indeed, essential, resource: the songs are printed chronologically, but it is a pity that the decision was made to transpose some songs against Warlock's known wishes. No volumes beyond the eight devoted to songs with piano accompaniment have appeared.

[59] *Heraclitus* (1917), *Along the Stream* (1917); published in 1923, with 'Take, o take those lips away' (1916), as *Saudades* (1923). Collected Edition, ii, nos. 9, 10, 7, and as a set, pp. 34–9 (in the order 10, 7, 9).

[60] Score (Stainer and Bell, 1924) reissued with an introductory note by F. Tomlinson (1973).

[61] An earlier work for strings was the *Serenade* written for Delius's 60th birthday (1922). There are accounts of Warlock's music by I. A. Copley: *The Music of Peter Warlock: A Critical Survey* (London, 1979), and B. Collins, *Peter Warlock: The Composer* (Aldershot, 1996).

Moeran's origins and temperament were quite different from Warlock's. The son of a Norfolk clergyman, he profited from his education, musical and otherwise, at Uppingham (unlike Warlock at Eton), and entered the Royal College of Music in 1913. From 1920 to 1923 he continued his studies with John Ireland, who became the major formative influence on his style. He was a serious, ambitious, and personable young man: by 1925 he had written a respectable body of piano pieces, songs, chamber music, and orchestral music, much of it already published by then. He had also collected a large number of folk songs, mainly from Norfolk.[62]

From 1925 to 1928 he lived with Warlock in Eynsford in Kent, a regime devoted to convivial weekends and (in theory) working weeks. It nearly destroyed Moeran, and the rest of his life, once he had broken away (though he maintained his friendship with Warlock), was devoted to regaining his lost creativity. It says much for his resilience that he very largely succeeded, sustained by the discovery of his affinity with south-west Ireland and ultimately by his relationship with the cellist Peers Coetmore, whom he married in 1945. After 1947, however, he deteriorated both physically and mentally, and his death in 1950 cut short no realistic prospects of further achievement.[63]

It is in his music of 1929 and subsequently that interest in Moeran mainly centres. It includes some excellent songs, beginning with a set of seven to poems by James Joyce,[64] two sets of part-songs (*Songs of Springtime*, and the choral suite *Phyllida and Corydon*), several chamber and orchestral works, and the *Nocturne* for baritone, chorus, and orchestra (1934). Amongst the chamber music is the splendid string trio (1931, published in 1936), which seems to anticipate the earlier Tippett in its flexible rhythms, its contrapuntal freedom of line, and the adoption of diatonic consonance as a framework for wide-ranging harmonic and modulatory processes. All these are easily identified in the opening of the first movement (Ex. 5.10), which is just the first part of a masterly transition to the folk-like second theme in the dominant. The later chamber music (principally the *Fantasy Quartet* for oboe and strings, 1946, and the cello sonata, 1947) marks no real advance on this work, but the orchestral music, and especially the symphony on which he had worked for so long (1924–37) exhibits a satisfying grasp of a more powerful and public idiom. The symphony does admittedly show signs of its protracted genesis: parts of the first movement are very

[62] Self, *The Music of E. J. Moeran*, 48–9. Self carefully sifts the main influences on Moeran's early work, including that of Ireland, Delius, Vaughan Williams, and Ravel.

[63] He had attempted, and discarded, a second symphony. 'Such manuscript sketches as are available do not suggest a further advance of style, nor a maintenance of quality' (Self, 227, with supporting quotations).

[64] These are from *Chamber Music*; Moeran also contributed the song *Tilly* to the collective study of Joyce's *Pomes Pennyeach* and published as *The Joyce Book* in 1933. (Banfield has published a memorable verse account by C. W. Orr of the genesis of this collection: *Sensibility and English Song*, 397–8.)

Ex. 5.10

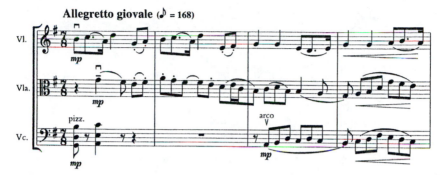

continued

Ex. 5.10, continued

J. E. Moeran, String Trio, 1st mvt. (London, 1936), pp. 1–2

Tchaikovskian, in ethos if not in idiomatic detail, while later on, particularly in the fleet scherzo and the peroration of the finale, Sibelian images predominate. Sibelius was widely admired and much imitated at this time,[65] so Moeran's susceptibility, even if it is at times rather obvious, is quite understandable. Much of the apparently derivative matter in this work is subsumed, in any case, within a re-creation of folk-like idioms of both English and Irish origin.

The violin concerto (1937–41) is also derivative in the same creative fashion: in its amalgam of familiar elements, at least, it is an original and effective work. Much the same is true of the cello concerto (1945), though not of the rather monotonous *Rhapsody* for piano and orchestra (1942–3).

---

[65] Sibelius's works were vaunted by Constant Lambert in his *Music Ho!* (London, 1934) as the 'music of the future' (in contradistinction, for example, to that of Schoenberg, Stravinsky, and Bartók); Sibelian music of the 1930s and 1940s includes Walton's first and Vaughan Williams's fifth symphonies. Moeran's symphony, like Walton's first, concludes with a gesture too evidently derived from the end of Sibelius's fifth; numerous references to his and other composers' music in this work are noted by Self in his extended discussion, op. cit., 102–33.

The *Sinfonietta* (1944) introduces an attractive, though very belated, neo-classicism into Moeran's language, while the *Serenade* (1948) is skilfully scored light music, some of it salvaged from earlier work.

No one could reasonably claim major stature for Moeran, but his musical personality, like Ireland's, is too vivid to be ignored. Unlike the more prolific Bax he cultivated a fastidiousness and clarity of texture that in itself compels admiration.

Rubbra, Finzi

Edmund Rubbra (1901–86) and Gerald Finzi (1901–56), the first of our selection to have been born in the twentieth century and the first to have been too young to serve in the Great War, were very different in their origins, circumstances, and artistic predilections. Rubbra's life's work is a monument of patient endeavour, built on early pianistic promise in unpro-pitious personal circumstances, an insatiable curiosity about music and its spiritual hinterland, and the opportunity in due course for study at the Royal College (1921–4) under Cyril Scott, Holst, and R. O. Morris. From about 1925 he began to get his music published and performed, and by the mid-1930s it was widely known and respected.

Rubbra's early mastery of large-scale form and an indication of his life-long preferences are shown in such works as the *Sinfonia concertante* for piano and orchestra, Op. 38 (1934), and the second violin sonata, Op. 31 (1931). The sonata is energetically neo-Romantic. So too is the *Sinfonia concertante*, but the harmonic vocabulary is bolder and the formal plan more adventur-ous. The last movement, in memory of Holst, is a prelude and slow fugue, the latter on a tortuous subject announced by the cor anglais. The first four symphonies are the most ambitious of his pre-war works.[66] The early infatuation with Cyril Scott's music may be discounted as a lasting influ-ence, but that of Holst is apparent in the harmonic bleakness, an occasional element of bitonality, and in the use of ostinato and fugue. R. O. Morris[67] will have given him a more strongly traditional grasp of counterpoint and a penchant for an academic style of fugue that we find (for example) in the C sharp minor subject and countersubject of the third symphony. His study of Bartók may have influenced his pianistic style and certainly encouraged him to think motivically. It is possible, indeed probable, that Milhaud exercised

---

[66] The dates conventionally given are: no. 1, Op. 44 (1935–7); no. 2, Op. 45 (1938, rev. 1951); no. 3, Op. 49 (1939); no. 4, Op. 53 (1942). Those of nos. 2–4 are essentially dates of publication and, perhaps, final revision: Rubbra served in the army, 1941–5, and abandoned composition for the duration of the war (information given to the author, *c.*1960).

[67] (1886–1948). He was an influential teacher at the Royal College and elsewhere, author of *Contra-puntal Technique in the Sixteenth Century* (1922), and a minor composer on his own account. His other pupils included Finzi and Lambert. In 1915 he married the sister of Vaughan Williams's first wife Adeline.

an early influence. Milhaud's schematic approach to orchestration, in which different ideas or ornamental figures are often assigned to various instrumental groups sounding simultaneously, is very evident in the first symphony, and the use of an eighteenth-century tune of southern origin in its second movement (*Perigourdienne*) supports this hypothesis.[68]

Rubbra's symphonic achievement is undeniably an impressive one, despite a tendency to textural heaviness and a contrapuntal idiom that does not always lend itself naturally to the orchestral medium. His song accompaniments are often dense, too, but a meticulous weighing of keyboard textures and a matching care for word-setting create an intensity of expression, even in the more light-hearted songs, far removed from the casual lyricism then generally prevalent. His unaccompanied choral music, such as the five motets, Op. 37, is equally resourceful in its exploitation of vocal colour and expressive potential.

It is as a composer of vocal music that Finzi is nowadays chiefly remembered, though there is some orchestral music, including the post-war clarinet concerto (1949), and some chamber music, including the still popular set of *Five Bagatelles* for clarinet and piano. His extreme stylistic conservatism embraced a fastidious archaism, a kind of neo-Bachianism that probably owed more to the example of Parry than to the teaching of Morris. This is particularly evident in the cantata-like *Dies natalis* (Traherne), for tenor and strings, commissioned for the Hereford Festival in 1939 but based mostly on material composed earlier.[69] There are some other early songs with accompaniment for strings or small orchestra, but the spiritual descendant of *Dies natalis*, and his most successful post-war work, was *In terra pax* (1954, with chorus, to a poem of Robert Bridges), produced at a time when its idiom seemed even more at odds with the spirit of the age.

It is in his substantial body of Hardy settings[70] that Finzi is at his best. Even here, the idiom is better suited to the light and shade of Hardy's poetry than to its harsher side. But the word-setting is immaculate in its response to the inflections of the verse—it is almost exclusively syllabic, in fact—and the songs are capable of conveying a desolation as profound as those of (say) Ireland or, later, Britten, though usually by very simple harmonic means. Finzi was a far less searching composer than Rubbra or even Howells (whose artistic credo was in many respects comparable), but within his limitations he achieved a kind of perfection. Much is owed to him, too, for his

---

[68] Less seriously, Rubbra shared Milhaud's obsession with opus-numbers, assigning them to the most trivial works, though he came nowhere near the Frenchman's astonishing total.

[69] The outbreak of war put paid to the Hereford performance; the work was first given in London in 1940. Banfield, *Sensibility and English Song*, 444.

[70] *By Footpath and Stile*, Op. 2, for baritone and string quartet, later withdrawn; *A Young Man's Exhortation*, Op. 14; *Earth and Air and Rain*, Op. 15; and *Before and After Summer*, Op. 16, published in 1949, are the main collections composed wholly or substantially between the wars. The entire corpus is discussed by Banfield, 275–300.

championship of eighteenth-century English music and for his persistence
(with his wife Joy) in the recovery of Gurney's songs for posterity.

Walton, Lambert

William Walton (1902–83) and Constant Lambert (1905–51) shared similar
aims and experiences in early manhood, though Walton's considerably
greater resilience, both physical and temperamental, ensured his position
in the English mainstream both before and after the war, while Lambert,
more genuinely original, failed to keep a hold on the popular acclaim
secured by his *Rio Grande* (1927). Both passed through the refining fire of
Sitwellian patronage and influence in the 1920s: Lambert was the narrator in
some performances of Walton's *Façade*, and *The Rio Grande* sets a poem by
Sacheverell Sitwell.

For Walton, the friendship of the Sitwells was decisive in broadening his
musical and cultural horizons. He had already shown astonishing precocity,
first as a chorister at Christ Church, Oxford, subsequently as an undergraduate, where, however, his inability (or unwillingness) to satisfy minimal
academic requirements meant that he never took a degree.[71] His ability was
recognized, nevertheless, above all by the musical dean of Christ Church
(later bishop of Oxford), T. B. Strong. Walton's *Litany* ('Drop, drop, slow
tears') for unaccompanied choir was composed at the age of 14 and is still
sung; his piano quartet, composed at Oxford in 1918–19 though later
revised (definitively for publication in 1976), has kept its place in the
'canon'.[72] *Façade*, an 'entertainment' consisting of poems by Edith Sitwell
recited to the accompaniment of a small ensemble, was also much revised
over the years: so much so that the version heard in 1922 seems to have been
scarcely the same work as the one eventually popularized and published. A
'definitive version' appeared only in 1951 (though a *Façade 2*, a reworking of
numbers previously discarded, was given at Aldeburgh in 1979).[73]

The parodic element in *Façade* was soon jettisoned (except insofar as the
various revisions and derived works—orchestral suites, ballets, and so on—
occupied him throughout his life), but a sardonic bitterness and irony
remained as a permanent residue, colouring (or perhaps discolouring) a

---

[71] For the details of Walton's Oxford career see M. Kennedy, *Portrait of Walton* (Oxford, 1989), the
most trustworthy biography that has appeared.

[72] The string quartet started at Oxford and disastrously given at the first festival of the International
Contemporary Music Society at Salzburg in 1923 was later withdrawn. See S. R. Craggs, *William
Walton: A Thematic Catalogue of his Musical Works* (London, 1977) for details of this and other works
discussed below.

[73] The bibliography can be agreeably complicated by the publication history of Sitwell's poems: for
example, *Façade* was first published privately, but more poems were included under that heading in her
Bucolic Comedies (1923), together with some that formed part of the entertainment but which she chose to
place elsewhere in the book. She should in any case be considered part-composer of the music, for her
poems are metrical exercises, and their rhythms were carefully worked out in collaboration with Walton.

fundamentally Romantic idiom. The rawness of *Façade* is rendered down into harmless diatonic discord in the overture *Portsmouth Point* (1925), but the characteristically Waltonian pathos, partly a product of major–minor antithesis in melody and harmony, reappears in the exquisite short *Siesta* for small orchestra (1926) and in the viola concerto (1929).[74] Also in the viola concerto is the earliest full-scale representative of a typical Walton scherzo (though here in 2/4 time), such as recurs in the first symphony and in the violin concerto. The viola concerto is his first masterpiece, formally and emotionally on a tight rein yet unashamedly direct in expression.

Belshazzar's Feast (1931), the very next work in the catalogue, is of an extraordinary self-confidence and ebullience. Compared with, say, Vaughan Williams's *Sancta Civitas*, which it oddly resembles in size, shape, and literary basis,[75] it would seem to be quite devoid of spiritual content. Yet its very directness of response to vivid textural imagery is immensely compelling. It has become fashionable to regard the more robust sections with faint disdain, but it would hardly be *Belshazzar's Feast* without them. Essentially the composer succeeded in broadening his idiom to embrace the expression of starkly opposed human emotions without any sacrifice of accessibility: the idiom of ceremonial rejoicing was to serve him well in many a *pièce d'occasion*, but in *Belshazzar* it takes its place alongside the more searching elements to create a work of great dramatic power.

Walton's next major commission, from Sir Hamilton Harty for a symphony, presented him with the problem of reconciling an idiom perfected for its dramatic appositeness with the expectations of large-scale instrumental composition. He could not, at least in a symphony, retreat to the point he had reached in the viola concerto. A monumental affirmation was called for, but the new public persona, while suited to large-scale rhetoric, carried with it the risk of lapsing into mere gesture. That Walton was triumphantly successful in maintaining boldness of utterance without any loss of integrity would now be generally conceded, although the difficulties he faced may be judged by the length of time it took him to complete the finale, performed only in November 1935, nearly a year after the first three movements had been given as they stood.

That finale has itself been criticized as a retreat to a less challenging language, but with hindsight we can see that the whole symphony is markedly traditional in conception, reaching back beyond Elgar and Sibelius to the aesthetic values and even the processes of Beethoven's Ninth. The mysterious opening, with its bare fifths (quickly supplemented but not

[74] The rather heavily written *Sinfonia concertante* for piano and orchestra (1928) is less representative; it was revised in 1943. The viola concerto was revised, with reduced orchestra, in 1961, but the original version is on balance preferable.

[75] Both last about 35 minutes, are scored for large forces, and draw almost exclusively on the Authorized Version of the Bible, the Fall of Babylon being a central event in each. Walton does not, however, use the term oratorio: in fact his work carries no genre-designation.

negated by Walton), is transformed into a terrifying outburst at the reprise, where the shock in this instance comes from the inclusion of the flat seventh in a resolution prepared for by no fewer than fifty bars of dominant harmony (Ex. 5.11). The placing of the scherzo second and the 'different'

Ex. 5.11

continued

Ex. 5.11, continued

William Walton, Symphony [no. 1], 1st mvt. (London, 1936): (*a*) p. 1; (*b*) pp. 52–3

(though not of course choral) nature of the finale, with its opening challenge as it were to 'leave off these sounds', are implicitly Beethovenian. On the other hand, the strategy for avoiding the perils of a 'contrasting second subject' in the first movement—its reduction to a fragmentary motif—is Sibelian, while the fugal section of the finale is analogous to that in Elgar's *Introduction and Allegro* in its stringy vigour.

These remarks do not detract from the evidence of Walton's individuality on every page of the score. But the very success of his solution to the problem of the symphony in this case only postponed the question for him of an idiomatically coherent symphonism in general—a challenge currently being met in varying ways by Vaughan Williams, Bax, and Rubbra. The eventual answer lay in his acceptance after the war of a return to lyricism. His last substantial pre-war work, the violin concerto of 1939,[76] clearly prefigures this trend. Formally it resembles the viola concerto, while tonally a more subtle use of variable scale-forms coexists with a greater refinement of dissonance. The lyricism is made still more piquant by the high tessitura of the solo instrument and by a constant vigilance against harmonic repose, the latter a guarantee against the sentimental weakness always dangerously close to the surface of his later idiom.

Constant Lambert's aesthetic, initially so close to Walton's, retreated into a world constrained at first by an obsession with jazz and subsequently by elements of quasi-Warlockian archaism. *The Rio Grande*, for chorus, piano solo, strings, brass, and percussion, suffers from the usual weakness of symphonic jazz, namely the artificiality of its notated rhythms when interpreted outside the context of collective improvisation. The simplicity of the choral writing seems at odds with the frenetic nature of the instrumental parts, though it has ensured the work's popularity until comparatively recent times. The other jazz-inspired works—the concerto for piano and nine players, the *Music for Orchestra*, and the piano sonata—all suffer from a lack of formal cohesion, though the *Music for Orchestra* is based on a potentially attractive scheme of three fugues, each faster than the last. The sonata is in any event far too long. Lambert had better luck with ballet, particularly *Horoscope* (1937), by which time he had started to explore older dance measures. But his masterpiece in the re-creation of an earlier aesthetic is *Summer's Last Will and Testament* (1933–5), a 'masque' for orchestra, chorus, and baritone solo in seven movements. A profoundly pessimistic response to the scourge of plague has been fashioned from Nashe's 'pleasant comedy' of 1600, though not to the exclusion of more light-hearted elements. Lambert here prefigures *Horoscope* in the use of older forms, both vocal and instru-

---

[76] It was followed in 1940 by the overture *Scapino*, but by no further major work until the post-war string quartet. Walton was not a conscientious objector, but was excused military service to allow him to write music for patriotic films. Two of his film scores—*The First of the Few* and *Henry V*—are superlative examples of their genre. For these and his other wartime music, see Kennedy, *Portrait of Walton*, 119–26.

mental—there is an opening instrumental *Intrata*, two madrigals 'con ritornelli', a vocal coranto, 'Brawles', and final saraband, while the penultimate
movement, 'King Pest', is a *Rondo Burlesca* for orchestra alone. But the
idiom is anything but archaic: a kind of harmonic sourness pervades the
whole, and in the livelier sections Waltonian cross-rhythms and displaced
accents have replaced the old jazziness. It is a less immediately appealing
work than Vaughan Williams's *Five Tudor Portraits*, with which it is in some
ways comparable, but it is infinitely more searching and indeed responsive
to the temper of its time.

Lambert was not to repeat even the limited success of either this work or
Horoscope (the post-war ballet *Tirésias*, however, would merit reconsidera-
tion).[77] Had he lived, the problem of idiom would have remained, as it did
for Walton, but its solution would have had to rest on a narrower stylistic
base.

Berkeley, Rawsthorne, Lutyens, Maconchy

The bulk of these composers' work falls into the post-war period, but a
preliminary glance at their pre-war achievement will help to establish the
circumstances behind what was in each case a clear and consistent pattern of
development.

Compared with (say) Rubbra or Walton, Lennox Berkeley (1903–89)
was a late starter. He studied in Paris from 1927 to 1932 with Stravinsky's
admirer Nadia Boulanger, and his early music exhibits the textural clarity
and diatonic astringency that one might expect from her teaching, together
with the more direct influence of Stravinsky himself. By 1940 he had
produced several songs, keyboard and chamber works, a ballet, *The Judgement of Paris* (1938), a couple of choral works (*Jonah*, later withdrawn, and
Domini est terra, 1937), and some orchestral music, including his first
symphony (1940). Two significant wartime works were the *Divertimento*,
Op. 18, and the string trio, Op. 19, both of 1943. One of the least pompous
of composers, he had a high regard for the entertainment value of 'serious'
music—an attitude shared with, for example, Hindemith and Prokofiev at
this date—but there are signs of a growing austerity in the choral works. His
finest music, however, was yet to come.

Alan Rawsthorne (1905–71) had written still less by 1940, but had nevertheless—with very little formal teaching—forged a highly distinctive style
based on the use of atonal elements within a tonal, or potentially tonal,
framework. These atonal elements were not particularly dissonant: the
augmented triad is used a good deal, both melodically and harmonically,

---

[77] It is sympathetically discussed in R. McGrady, 'The Music of Constant Lambert', *ML* 51 (1970),
242–58. On the sources of Lambert's jazz idiom see C. Palmer, 'Constant Lambert—A Postscript', *ML*
52 (1971), 173–6. The standard biography is R. Shead, *Constant Lambert* (London, 1973).

and has for him the useful property of being both atonal in itself and capable of being reinterpreted within a tonal framework in order to provide large-scale coherence. The tonal references in the very promising clarinet concerto (1936) and piano *Bagatelles* (1938) are purely local, while the first string quartet (theme and variations, 1939) is more clearly in A minor, a key scarcely perceptible at the opening but confirmed by the end of the theme and (in a transformation to major) at the end of the whole work (Ex. 5.12). The tonal orientation of the *Symphonic Studies* (1938), his first major success, is even stronger, though it relates to a note (B) rather than a triad. In his later music, however, the magnetism of the triad was to prevail, though often ambiguously as to mode and always subject to the influence of neighbouring chromaticism. During the war he found time, despite the pressures of military service, to compose another substantial orchestral work, *Cortèges* (1945, dedicated to Lambert), and the slighter overture *Street Corner* (1944); he also rescored his first piano concerto (1939, with strings and percussion) for a full orchestral accompaniment (1942). This is a superbly entertaining piece in an idiom that owes nothing either to neo-classicism or to neo-Romanticism but is wholly and uniquely the composer's own.

Elisabeth Lutyens (1906–83) and Elizabeth Maconchy (1907–94) were destined to achieve a great deal in post-war Britain. Lutyens developed slowly, partly because her studies (with Harold Darke at the Royal College,

Ex. 5.12

(a) **Tempo giusto, espressivo e poco agitato**

(b) [ending of theme]

continued

Ex. 5.12, continued

Alan Rawsthorne, String Quartet [no. 1] (London, 1946): (*a*) p. 1; (*b*) p. 2; (*c*) p. 20

1926–30) encouraged insularity (her year in Paris at the École Normale, 1922–3, had done little to focus her aspirations). It was not until the late 1930s that she began to find her true voice, at first in some chamber music for strings; with the *Chamber Concerto* no. 1 for string trio and six wind instruments (1939) she embraced a personal blend of serialism. She and her husband Edward Clark (1888–1962) were tireless in their promotion of challenging new music by British composers, and her dedication was eventually to reap rich rewards.

Elizabeth Maconchy, of Irish descent, studied at first with Wood and Vaughan Williams, and later in Prague. In the 1930s she developed a concentrated, dissonant style and pursued it in a remarkable series of string quartets, the first four of which were composed in the decade 1933–43. Her reliance on taut motivic structures, somewhat in the manner of Bartók but on a smaller scale, might have led her into an impasse; but her post-war style was to become more broadly based with the extension of her interests to opera, choral music, and the larger orchestral forms.

Tippett, Britten

Michael Tippett (1905–98), has often been considered a 'late developer'; yet his achievement by the end of the war was at least comparable with that of

Berkeley and Rawsthorne in terms of quantity, and arguably more promising than theirs as regards stylistic potential. His first string quartet (1934–5)
and his first piano sonata (1938, then called 'Fantasy Sonata') were revised
and published in 1943 and 1942 respectively;[78] his concerto for double
string orchestra was composed in 1938–9, a second string quartet in 1942,
the oratorio *A Child of Our Time* in 1939–41 (it was first heard in 1944), and
the 'cantata' *Boyhood's End*, for tenor and piano, in 1943. All these are works
of full, if early, maturity: Tippett had also before the late thirties written a
number of interesting works that were destined to remain unpublished but
show incipient signs of his individuality. His first symphony (apart from an
apprentice work, unnumbered) was begun towards the end of the war.[79]

Tippett's formal training in composition—under Wood, Kitson, and R.
O. Morris—was insular and somewhat conservative, but it was supplemented by a receptive attitude to all kinds of stimuli, musical and otherwise. The
study and performance of English madrigals—together with the reading of
Morris's *Contrapuntal Technique*—made him aware of the possibilities of
rhythmically irregular counterpoint, which he developed in such works as
the *Concerto* and the two quartets. The danger in this was that the rhythmic
complexity might be too much for the less highly developed melodic and
harmonic elements of his style. The *Concerto* is for this reason—and also
because of its general uniformity of texture—a rather arid work, its relentless
rhythmic drive somewhat at odds with its featureless melodic topography
and diatonic blandness. This is far less evident in (say) the second quartet,
where the textures are lighter and other compositional elements are also
prominent, and the slow movement of the first quartet already reveals a
capacity for sustained lyricism. The piano sonata is, like the concerto,
relentlessly rhythmical in its fast movements, but here the arabesque-like
treatment of the piano in certain sections (chiefly in the 'Meno mosso'
variation in the first movement, the middle section of the second movement, and much of the fourth) provides a welcome change and prefigures
an important element in Tippett's later style.

A Child of Our Time and *Boyhood's End*, though very different from each
other, enabled Tippett to address the emotions through the verbal as well as
the musical element for the first time in his mature work; and as regards the
former to do so in a conspicuously public fashion. This fine oratorio, as it is
specifically called, is noteworthy for its simplification of musical language
(though it might be truer to say that it draws on a strand of Tippett's thought
less evident in the instrumental works that we have discussed) and directness

---

[78] The term 'fantasy' was dropped when the sonata was republished (without significant further
change) in 1954. I. Kemp, *Tippett: The Composer and his Music* (London, 1984), 489 n. 16: this is the most
comprehensive account of Tippett's music to date, but see also A. Whittall, *The Music of Britten and
Tippett: Studies in Themes and Techniques* (2nd edn., Cambridge, 1990).

[79] Minor wartime works are discussed in Kemp, 179–84.

of utterance. The composer's libretto, while lacking independent literary distinction, successfully universalizes the specific and topical horror of the Nazi pogrom that followed the shooting of the German ambassador to Paris by a 17-year-old Jewish boy.[80] Musically, and in line with the plan of its libretto, it achieves a persuasive symbiosis of modern and older elements within the oratorio tradition. The tripartite scheme is derived from that of Handel's *Messiah*, while the use of Negro spirituals is analogous to that of chorales in a Lutheran Passion. Archaic harmonies in the recitatives reinforce a generalized impression of the Baroque, but one can go still further. The severity of the opening introduction and chorus, with its use of strings, bass, and lower woodwind, recalls Schütz, and the mixture of narrative and drama both Schütz and Carissimi. On the other hand, the swiftness of the action and of musical change are suggestive of Honegger's *Le Roi David* (1921), itself a 'dramatic psalm' with archaic features. If these parallels are real (though not necessarily conscious), they testify to the composer's depth of musical reference, just as his scenario and libretto testify to his philosophical maturity and the warmth of his response to the human predicament.

The spirituals, so much discussed then and later, typify the composer's approach to his task. To the audience, they represent points of musical repose and relative familiarity, and a sufficiently universal (because supra-denominational) expression of a religious (and indeed Christian) dimension within a fundamentally agnostic framework. For the composer, they offered not only these advantages but also a point of contact, in their rhythmic fluidity, with his own style. Melodically and tonally, too, they were compatible with the roots of his inspiration and with one end of his wide technical spectrum. The brilliance of their re-creation within the parameters of his score as a whole is perhaps the crucial factor in this work's enduring relevance.

Boyhood's End similarly extends the appeal of Tippett's writing by the eloquence of its vocal line and by the homogeneity of that line and its instrumental complement.[81] The exhilarating counterpoint of the two—in *melos*, in rhythm, and in texture—may be sampled from the opening of the third and last section of this tripartite work (Ex. 5.13). Indeed this is far from being a nostalgic piece: rather is it a celebration of innocent youth before both youth and innocence are inevitably lost, their idealization its central purpose.

Benjamin Britten (1913–76), eight years Tippett's junior, was producing work of comparable maturity in the later thirties and early forties. Though hardly a prodigy in the Mozartian sense, he was composing large amounts of music in a fairly conventional style from an early age. In the autumn of

---

[80] Kemp, 150–1, gives the full background: his discussion of the work in all its aspects occupies pp. 149–79. Tippett originally asked T. S. Eliot to write the libretto: ibid. 152–3.

[81] The text is taken from W. H. Hudson's autobiography *Far Away and Long Ago*; the title is that of the chapter in question.

Ex. 5.13

continued

Ex. 5.13, continued

Michael Tippett, *Boyhood's End* (London, 1945), pp. 15–16

1927,[82] when he was nearly 14, he began to take lessons intermittently with
Frank Bridge; at 16 (i.e. in the summer of 1930) he left school and
that autumn entered the Royal College of Music, where his composition
teacher was John Ireland. All the same it was Bridge, with his own relentlessly questioning nature, not Ireland, who was by far the greater influence,
both technically and inspirationally. Britten quickly began to absorb 'modernist' influences, even before his RCM days (the *Quartettino*, written early
in 1930, is highly chromatic, almost expressionist), and while there he wrote
what were (almost) the earliest of his works to be published: a *Sinfonietta* for
chamber orchestra (1932, published in 1935 as Op. 1), a *Phantasy Quartet* for
oboe and strings (1932, published in 1935 as Op. 2), and the variations for
unaccompanied choir *A Boy Was Born* (1933, published in 1934 as Op. 3).[83]

[82] C. Mark, *Early Benjamin Britten: A Study of Stylistic and Technical Evolution* (New York and London,
1995), 7; this book, which covers the period to 1943, has a useful chapter on the juvenilia.
[83] Still earlier were a song, *The Birds* (1929), and *A Hymn to the Virgin* for unaccompanied choir
(1930), both later revised for publication in 1935. The *Simple Symphony*, Op. 4 (1934, published in 1935),

The *Sinfonietta* is by far the most original of these early works, and experiment continued to sit alongside more conventional writing for some time. In a sense the antithesis never vanished in Britten: some of his most imaginative works juxtapose the simplest ideas, often triadically harmonized, with adventurous chromaticisms and rhythmically complex structures. It was his ability to revitalize older elements in the musical language and to synthesize them with newer ones that gave his music its universality; and this ability was fully in evidence by the end of the 1930s.[84]

The years from 1935 to May 1939, when Britten sailed for the USA with Peter Pears, were productive ones: in addition to his major works— *Our Hunting Fathers* for high voice and orchestra (1936, a song-cycle with words by Auden), *Variations on a Theme of Frank Bridge* for string orchestra (1937), *On This Island* (song-cycle, Auden, 1937), and a piano concerto (1938, later revised)—he collaborated with Auden in films and theatre music and wrote several lesser scores: he was also active as a pianist and conductor. His American years were marred by illness and depression, yet the flow of major works continued: a violin concerto, later revised; *Les Illuminations* for high voice and strings (Rimbaud, 1939); the *Sinfonia da Requiem* (1940, in memory of his parents); the *Seven Sonnets of Michelangelo* (1940); and the first string quartet (1941). He also wrote with Auden an operetta, *Paul Bunyan*, performed once and then abandoned for many years, and several minor works.[85] During his return to England in 1942 he completed the *Hymn to St Cecilia* (Auden), for unaccompanied choir; there followed the *Ceremony of Carols*, for treble voices and harp, the *Prelude and Fugue* for string orchestra, *Rejoice in the Lamb* for choir and organ, and the *Serenade* for tenor, horn, and string orchestra, all completed by the end of 1943. Then, in 1944–5, he tackled *Peter Grimes*, which was produced a month after VE day on 7 June 1945. It is an astonishing achievement, even for a conscientious objector excused military service, since he was obliged to fulfil a demanding schedule of musical activities in 1942–5.[86]

---

was arranged from much earlier material, while the recently discovered and edited double concerto for violin and voila is another work of 1932. Britten's first publisher was Oxford University Press, who published *Three Two-Part Songs* (1932), *A Boy Was Born*, the *Simple Symphony*, and the Te Deum in C for voices and organ (1935); but a rare misjudgement by the enterprising founder and head of OUP's Music Department, Hubert Foss, led to Britten's subsequent long-standing arrangement with Boosey & Hawkes: see D. Hinnells, *An Extraordinary Performance: Hubert Foss, Music Publishing, and the Oxford University Press* (Oxford, 1998), 43–6.

[84] Tippett had similar aims, and undoubtedly achieved them at a technical level, but his music, both then and later, often seems more contrived than Britten's.

[85] Of these *Young Apollo*, Op. 16, and *AMDG* (Hopkins, Op. 17) were soon withdrawn. Cf. Mark, 163–6. *Paul Bunyan* was revised and revived in 1976, and has proved to be strikingly successful in its assimilation of popular musical styles.

[86] *Peter Grimes* will be discussed in the following chapter. Tippett was, like Britten, a conscientious objector; unlike him, he declined alternative work and was imprisoned for three months.

A full account of Britten's extraordinary development in the decade 1935–45 would be impossible here.[87] In general it is the story of his approach to the synthesis mentioned above—at least in some form or another, for Britten's solutions varied from one work to the next. In many ways his intellectual development parallels that of W. H. Auden, with whom he collaborated so often. Auden retreated from self-regarding modernism in 1933,[88] aiming with variable success at a more public persona: Britten must have been conscious of a similar obligation. On the other hand, the return to England marked a parting of the ways: Auden remained, and even returned to his Anglican roots (which Britten did not, though like Vaughan Williams he frequently adopted religious forms as a medium for communication with a society still outwardly Anglican in observance). That parting is symbolized by the *Hymn to St Cecilia*, a final acknowledgement of an intellectual apprenticeship.

Two fundamental elements in Britten's musicality were an extreme sensitivity to verbal nuance (both rhythmic and tonal) and a very positive attitude to instrumental fluency (both as a composer and as performer). The reconciliation of these elements was one aspect of his development. In many of his purely instrumental works—the two concertos, the first quartet, and the *Sinfonia da Requiem*, for example—the fluency, or the attachment to aurally extreme devices, has a tendency to run riot. The early solo vocal works—*Our Hunting Fathers* and to a lesser extent *Les Illuminations*—are strongly affected by an instrumental quality in the vocal line as well as by the brilliance of the accompaniment itself. In the *Michelangelo Sonnets* this tendency gives way to a more idiomatic treatment of the voice and a compensating adjustment in the piano writing that proclaim this as the first of the great song-cycles.[89] The *Hymn to St Cecilia* moves in the opposite direction: the bland conventions of unaccompanied choral music (not that Britten's earlier work for this medium was bland) are invigorated by a quasi-instrumental three-movement design and a manner of vocal orchestration that extends even to the imitation of specific instruments.

The *Serenade* is the great masterpiece of the wartime years, not merely as a summation of his achievement to date but also in many ways as a prophecy of what was to come. At the same time it is oddly resistant to analysis beyond simple factual observations about the form of each song individually. Its

[87] A number of detailed studies, in addition to that of Mark, exist. The most useful for general purposes are: D. Mitchell and H. Keller (eds.), *Benjamin Britten: A Commentary on His Works from a Group of Specialists* (London, 1952); P. Evans, *The Music of Benjamin Britten* (2nd edn., London, 1989; reissued with additions, Oxford, 1996); and Whittall, *The Music of Britten and Tippett*. For the biography see esp. M. Kennedy, *Britten* (London, 1981: also with musical comment), and H. Carpenter, *Benjamin Britten: A Biography* (London, 1992).

[88] See e.g. *Selected Poems*, ed. E. Mendelson (London, 1979), p. xii.

[89] The use of Italian, rather than Auden's English or Rimbaud's French, was no doubt a factor in this development.

unity, if it has any other than is supplied by the opening and concluding horn-call, is simply one of musico-poetic appositeness at every turn; its poetic theme is that of sundown, night, and sleep. The horn-call itself—using only the natural harmonics in F—transports us into a magic world (possibly that of Windsor Forest: cf. the opening of Act III, Sc. ii in Verdi's *Falstaff*); its last note becomes the bass of the opening progression in the first song, a simple strophic setting of Charles Cotton's 'The Day's grown old'. Horn-calls recur for the refrain ('Blow, bugle, blow') in Tennyson's 'The splendour falls on castle walls', also strophic, but with modal transformation in the middle stanza. 'O Rose, thou art sick' (Blake) is treated as a mono-strophic recitative with a long instrumental prelude and postlude. The anonymous dirge 'This ae night' treats its stanza as an unchanging six-bar ostinato, unrelieved by any rest, in the high-lying tenor part; it is accompanied by a fugue on a four-bar subject, polytonal both internally and against the voice.[90] Ben Jonson's 'Queen and huntress', apostrophizing the moon, is a brisk ternary-form scherzo; again the horn fulfils a descriptive role. Finally Keats's sonnet 'O soft embalmer of the still midnight' brings sleep; at its close the horn, off-stage, sounds its call once more, this time perhaps to exert Oberon's magic.

We shall encounter more strictly controlled parameters in some of Britten's later music, and the bugles will resound more tragically in the *War Requiem*, but the poetry of repose will not again be so hauntingly evoked.

Song

Of all the genres that engage minor as well as major composers, song is most often found to be the one in which they excel. Among those already discussed in this chapter, Warlock and Finzi might well be said to exemplify the point, while for Ireland, Howells, and Moeran, song was more than usually significant in their output. Of those not so far mentioned Ivor Gurney, (1890–1937) was at his best a master, while in such composers as Norman O'Neill (1875–1934), Roger Quilter (1877–1953), Cyril Scott (1879–1970), Armstrong Gibbs (1889–1960), Benjamin Burrows (1891–1966), C. W. Orr (1893–1976), Patrick Hadley (1899–1973), and Michael Head (1900–76), it offers their best title to consideration. Even for such versatile but tangential figures as Lord Berners (1883–1950), Havergal Brian (1876–1972), Alan Bush (1900–95), Bernard van Dieren (1887–1936), John

---

[90] Attempts to discover an internal rationale for the key-sequence of the fugal entries (cf. Mark, 262–3) are unconvincing; it is more likely to have been dictated by the need for a continuing relationship with the independent progress of the voice. The G A flat G of the vocal opening coincides with bass E in the accompaniment at the centre of the song to reverse the major–minor opposition of the previous number; at its end, the vocal G F♯ G follows the final E flat in the bass (the 'instrumental' tonic) to recreate it a semitone lower.

Foulds (1880–1939), Eugene Goossens (1893–1962), and Joseph Holbrooke (1878–1958) it was of more than passing significance. Yet others (Bantock, Walford Davies, Rutland Boughton, and many more), much of whose best work preceded the Great War, were still active beyond its end.

It is manifestly impossible to cover this enormous field here, even in a cursory fashion.[91] An essential preliminary is the study of English verse (and not only English, although the height of the vogue for setting foreign-language verse had passed, only to be revived by Britten from 1939 onwards). Even 'English' includes American and Irish (less often Scottish and Welsh) and must take account of an increasingly catholic taste. In the inter-war years the range of possibilities extended beyond the Elizabethans to medieval lyric, partly through anthologies such as Quiller-Couch's *Oxford Book of English Verse*. A wider range of translated verse, such as Helen Waddell's of medieval Latin lyrics, was also becoming available (D. G. Rossetti had earlier been a celebrated translator from the Italian). Shakespeare remained popular, but a larger number of Elizabethan, Jacobean, and Caroline poets was coming to be appreciated, particularly, for example, Donne and Jonson; the lyric verse of the later seventeenth and eighteenth centuries was newly explored while from the nineteenth century a wider choice of minor poets, helped again by the use of anthologies, was cultivated at the expense of (for example) Byron and Tennyson. D. G. Rossetti, who together with Holman Hunt and John Everett Millais had founded the Pre-Raphaelite Brotherhood in 1848, was well liked in the early decades of the century but less so thereafter. The American Walt Whitman (1819–92), whose use of free verse made him a harbinger of modernism, was set from time to time in twentieth-century solo song as well as in several celebrated choral works.

English poetry itself underwent a 'renaissance' comparable to that in music, and it is interesting to observe its course in relation to music and to fashions in musical settings.[92] Pre-Raphaelitism was a forerunner of what was to come, though it was primarily a movement of the visual arts, D. G. Rossetti himself being a painter as well as (like his sister Christina) a poet of exceptional sensitivity. The new spirit emerged, somewhat earlier than in music, in a group of poets born in the 1840s, in particular Thomas Hardy (1840–1928), Robert Bridges (1844–1930), and Gerard Manley Hopkins (1844–89). Hardy and Bridges were often set, Hopkins scarcely at all (his

---

[91] It is the subject of Banfield's *Sensibility and English Song*, a masterly study whose main weight falls on the inter-war years and also deals with the songs of the major composers already discussed above, together with such figures as Percy Grainger (1882–1961, Australian-born and later an American citizen but active in England in the early years of the century) and the enormously prolific Fritz Hart (1874–1949), who emigrated to Australia in 1908.

[92] Banfield's index offers a complete list of poets set during the first half of the 20th c. A comprehensive index with a different remit is B. N. S. Gooch and D. S. Thatcher, *Musical Settings of Late Victorian and Modern British Literature: A Catalogue* (New York and London, 1976).

poetry remained little known until it was edited by Bridges in 1918). A later wave of pre-modern lyricists included A. E. Housman (1859–1936) and the Irish poet W. B. Yeats (1865–1939), who became two of the most favoured writers for musical setting. Housman claimed to be unmusical and could not understand why composers should want to set his verse (although he did not actively prevent it); but the concentrated, jewel-like quality of his thought and versification made it ideal for the purpose, and its understated nostalgia a temptation to 'spell out' in music what he had chosen to conceal.

A modernist movement in verse was well under way before 1914, fuelled by the Americans Eliot and Pound among others. 'Imagism' survived into the 1930s, though its poets (apart from Joyce) were rarely set. A more modest, somewhat reactionary movement was that of 'Georgian' poetry, the label of a series of anthologies published between 1911 and 1922 and featuring such names as Rupert Brooke, W. H. Davies, Walter De la Mare, D. H. Lawrence (also an Imagist), John Masefield, Siegfried Sassoon, Robert Graves, and Edmund Blunden. It excluded (at least as far as the anthologies were concerned) Edward Thomas (1878–1917), Wilfred Owen (1893–1918), and Ivor Gurney, of whom Thomas and Owen were killed in action and had collections published in 1920. Owen was set scarcely at all before 1945,[93] and Gurney, who had published small collections in 1917 and 1919, only by himself and by Finzi. Edith Sitwell and W. H. Auden, finally, flew the modernist flag in the 1920s and early 1930s respectively: T. S. Eliot, who settled in England, was never set.[94]

The poetic movements of the immediate pre-war and inter-war years are therefore only partly related to movements in English song—partly for the negative reason that composers were either unaware of or indifferent to contemporary developments in verse (or even more mundanely because of copyright difficulties), and partly for the positive reason that they were newly open to the stimulus of an enormously wider range of verse in English than hitherto. Nevertheless the predominant 'sensibility' of poets and composers in the inter-war years was essentially comparable, as can be seen above all in the work of Ivor Gurney and in his choice of poetry, for the most part not his own.

It is not easy to get a good idea of Gurney's song-writing as a whole: he published only a small fraction of his output—chiefly four song-cycles or sets of songs—while a selection of fifty was published posthumously in five volumes (1938–79), in all about a quarter of the total. The *Five Elizabethan*

[93] Banfield refers to a setting in Bliss's choral symphony *Morning Heroes*; he also points out that war-inspired music has tended to be on a larger scale and that: 'Until Britten began to reconstitute the elements of expression in song composition in the 1930s there was a manifest assumption that technical advance was out of place in song and a tacit agreement to leave war verse, like the new poetry of Eliot and Pound, untouched.' *Sensibility and English Song*, 134–5.

[94] Apart from the 'tacit agreement' mentioned in n. 93, Eliot was notoriously hostile to the setting of his verse.

Songs (1920) were originally scored for woodwind instruments and harp but published only with piano accompaniment. Two other sets, both of poems by Housman—*Ludlow and Teme* (1923) and *The Western Playland (and of Sorrow)* (1926)—were scored for piano and string quartet (the parallel with Vaughan Williams's *On Wenlock Edge* is inescapable) and published both in that form and with the accompaniment arranged for piano alone. These Housman songs, all composed or revised in the years 1920–1, do not really show him at his best: there is little interest of a cyclic kind, and a tendency to over-elaboration. But they belong to an extremely fertile post-war period (1918–22, with an extension to 1926) during which he composed about five-sixths of his output of over 300 songs.[95] It was a heroic endeavour for a man who entered a mental hospital in 1922, and who in addition wrote 1,700 poems. It seems certain that his control over his materials deteriorated well before his final attempts at composition, but even so it is possible that something of value remains unpublished.[96]

In what seem to be Gurney's most characteristic songs there is an intensity of expression in both melody and accompaniment that strikes one as Germanic (in the Schumann–Brahms–Wolf tradition), but more complex and improvisatory in melody and harmonic tonality. Banfield analyses in detail one of Gurney's finest songs, 'Most holy night' (Belloc) and prints it in full, so it will not be discussed here;[97] but a complete short song, 'Brown is my love' from the fourth posthumous collection, can be given to illustrate the potential for what might be called 'strophic paraphrase' in the treatment of (in this case) a second stanza (Ex. 5.14). The poem is taken from the second book of *Musica transalpina* (1597), an interestingly adventurous choice. We can agree that the harmony is often 'weak' in functional terms (as for example in the repetition of the chord in bars 1–2), but so often is Wolf's. Sometimes Gurney did not get the balance quite right, as when an ordinary melody is simply harmonized inefficiently; but in the published selections at least he is more often convincing than not.

Roger Quilter was the most consistent songwriter of the 'Frankfurt group' that also included O'Neill, Scott, and Balfour Gardiner. All had

---

[95] There was a good deal of instrumental music, too, from the years 1919–21, when he returned to the Royal College as a rather mature student. See M. Hurd, *The Ordeal of Ivor Gurney* (Oxford, 1978), 135–40. In 1926 a fourth cycle, *Lights Out* (Edward Thomas) for voice and piano, was published.

[96] This conflicts with Hurd's view, who in preparing the 1979 volume of ten songs wrote: 'A further volume of ten *new* songs would not have been easy, or even advisable, to put together. But a volume which brought under one cover the five songs that the Oxford University Press already publish as separate items, plus *five* new songs, is another matter, and this is what the fifth volume comprises.' The view expressed above is based on statistical probability and the fact (reported by Banfield, 182) that Gerald Finzi, who originally sorted out the songs with Howard Ferguson, 'gave a double or a single tick [meaning 'good' and 'good or adequate' respectively] to about 100 songs'.

[97] Banfield, 201–6. His analysis of the third stanza (a 'strophic paraphrase' in the terminology adopted below) is well founded; but the four-semiquaver units in the postlude should be scanned as 4123, not 1234, and their direction, as much as their exact intervals, given significance.

Ex. 5.14

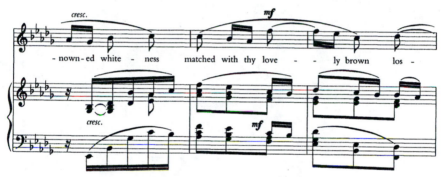

continued

Ex. 5.14, continued

Fair is my Love, but scorn — ful:

Yet have I seen ____ de - spis — ed

Dain - ty white li - — lies, and sad

Ex. 5.14, continued

Ivor Gurney, 'Brown is my love' (Nash): *A Fourth Volume of Ten Songs* (London, 1959), pp. 4–5

achieved characteristic work before the Great War, and Gardiner virtually abandoned composition thereafter. All were periodically subject to over-elaborate accompaniment, mainly in order to support harmonic complexity, in a way that could easily detract from the vocal line. It was an inheritance from Mackenzie and Somervell (who continued writing until near his death in 1937), not easily shaken off. In Gurney's best songs the accompaniment can have a concentrated intensity that mitigates the elaboration. The Frank-furt composers did not aspire to this, and their harmonic language was generally more superficially chromatic; but Quilter at least contrived a balance that exhibits considerable artistry. His style—marked by modest chromaticism and a free use of the higher discords—hardly changed throughout his long composing life (he was still being published even after the second war), and his choice of verse remained catholic: sixteenth- and seventeenth-century lyrics, including of course Shakespeare; Blake, Byron, Stevenson, and a large clutch of lesser moderns.

Many composers of Gurney's generation aspired no higher than cultivated artistry within an established idiom. Gibbs and Burrows set De la Mare and his 'Georgian' contemporaries effectively; C. W. Orr concentrated on Housman. There is little sense of exploration in their song-writing, nor in that of the singer Michael Head. Ireland, Bax, and Howells had stronger musical personalities, but even here it was Ireland, the least radical of them, who took most easily to song in his settings of Housman (*The Land of Lost Content*, 1921), Hardy, D. G. Rossetti, and Georgians such as Alice Meynell. Again the idiom was essentially ready-made. Finzi was even more conservative, as we have seen, despite his penchant for Hardy. Moeran in his settings of Irish poets (Joyce and, at the end of the war, Seamas O'Sullivan—he also set his share of the Elizabethans, Housman, and the Georgians) achieved the concentration that eluded Bax and which made him much the more successful songwriter of the two. Warlock has been sufficiently considered above.

Of the others mentioned, Holbrooke was too much wrapped up in his own ego—like his exact contemporary Rutland Boughton he had a propensity for grandiose but doomed operatic schemes—to be a successful songwriter. In the end Holbrooke's poverty of invention and innate conventionality broke through the façade of self-promotion. Hadley's small output of song was almost exclusively for accompaniment by chamber ensemble or orchestra; his idiom was traditional. Some of those who, like Brian and Foulds, were more adventurous tended to be technically insecure; Lord Berners,[98] van Dieren, and Goossens, together with Lambert and Bridge, were much more successful in bringing song into the orbit of modernism.

But in the end it was Rubbra, Berkeley, Rawsthorne, Tippett, and Britten who as it were reinvented song, revitalizing it for the purposes of the later twentieth century and building to a certain extent on the example of Holst and Vaughan Williams (whose inter-war songs are of considerable distinction). Their growth in lyrical sensibility went *pari passu* with their technical development, so that there was no risk of a divorce between 'song' and the rest of their output. (The same was to be true, after the war, of Walton and several younger composers: Walton's pre-war output, except for *Façade*, was negligible.) Above all it was Britten who achieved the stylistic freedom to bend the lyrical impulse to his own will. The wartime sets of folk song arrangements illustrate this brilliantly, departing as they do so radically from the traditional approach without losing the identity of the

---

[98] Gerald Tyrwhitt-Wilson (1883–1950), who succeeded to the barony in 1918. His gift for vocal comedy was as strong as Walton's in *Façade*, and moreover expressed in song proper.

songs themselves. With these, and the *Michelangelo Sonnets*, the way was open for the exploration of Donne, Hardy, and much else.

Piano and Chamber Music

As with song, instrumental music for small forces often brought out the best in minor composers. A common factor is the idiomatic use of the piano, so that song, piano music, and chamber music with piano embody stylistic preferences that overlap but are not coterminous with those presupposed by the cultivation of chamber music without piano. Of course such a distinction is equally apposite in (say) Brahms, which may serve to remind us of the Brahmsian bedrock on which so much English piano-writing depends in composers as different as Elgar and Howard Ferguson. The Brahmsian textural language proved capable of sustaining harmonic innovations, as it had in Germany, but there were other potential influences available: those of Liszt, Skryabin, Debussy, and Ravel, for example. The Lisztian manner, after Benjamin Dale, was more often applied to concertos, though even here Rakhmaninov was generally the preferred model. Skryabin and Debussy supplied precedents for more specific developments in harmonic language while also encouraging a more impressionistic approach to melodic continuity; they were for obvious reasons less influential in chamber music.

The solo medium was also preferable for short (not necessarily miniaturesque) pieces, and for the suite of loosely associated movements. Here the parallel with songs and song-sets is particularly close. Apart from Ireland, Bridge, and Bax, lesser figures such as Cyril Scott and York Bowen (1884–1961) wrote a good deal of this sort of thing, much of it indeed before the Great War but a certain amount during it or subsequently. Scott wrote in all the major forms, but he was probably most successful as a miniaturist: even so, his chromatic excesses are apt to conceal poverty of substance. A piece like *Rainbow Trout*, published in 1916, is quite atonal, though not so very dissonant in effect because of the high pitch of the semitonal clashes: an extract will illustrate the incantatory but purely decorative quality of much of his writing (Ex. 5.15). One of his three piano sonatas and several chamber works (out of about twenty dating from 1900 to 1968) belong to the interwar years: the reassessment called for in 1980[99] is clearly desirable but has not yet taken place.

Bowen likewise produced major works over an extended period, and his music on the whole has more backbone (but perhaps less genuine originality) than Scott's. The fourth suite (*Suite Mignonne*, published in 1915 and a better work than its formidably difficult predecessor) has outer movements reminiscent of Debussy's *Pour le piano*, though the middle movement is a

[99] By Hurd in *NGD*.

Ex. 5.15

Ex. 5.15, continued

Cyril Scott, *Rainbow Trout* (London, 1916), pp. 8–9

Ravellian waltz. The third movement of his *Curiosity Suite*, Op. 42 (1916, a work with facetious titles throughout), called 'The "Futurist" Piece. To those with a sense of humour—not to admirers of this particular cult', is an amusing parody of what was no doubt thought of as the Schoenbergian manner. But for genuine musical humour at this period one could profitably turn to Lord Berners;[100] his *Le poisson d'or* (1915), preceded by a poem of his own in French, is a true forerunner of minimalism.

The inter-war years are better represented, for solo piano music, by Ireland and Bax, whose four piano sonatas (1910; revised 1917–21, 1919, 1926, 1932) are comparable in structural invention to his symphonies. The sonata by Bridge (1921–4), written in memory of Ernest Farrar, is still more intense in musical language, while Ireland's equally weighty work (1918–20) is, as one would expect, more traditional. All three composers wrote smaller pieces, but their sonatas, with those of Scott, demonstrated a more serious potential, a challenge grasped above all by Tippett and continued by him and others after the second war. Howard Ferguson (b. 1908) wrote a cogent sonata (1938–40) as well as an attractive set of *Bagatelles* (1944).

Bridge, Ireland, and Bax were also the leading composers between the wars of chamber music with piano, and again a neo-Brahmsian approach to texture, and sometimes also to form, tends to overshadow their considerable originality at a local level. Of minor composers Rebecca Clarke (1886–1979)[101] wrote an admirable viola sonata (1919) and a piano trio (1921), both of which won prizes in the United States. The duo-sonata became something of a speciality amongst English composers at this period: apart from those previously mentioned, there is a vigorous, well-crafted violin sonata by Howard Ferguson (1931), while one of Rawsthorne's earliest mature works was a viola sonata (1935, later revised).[102] The Hindemithian influence detectable in this work was far more pronounced in the music of Franz Reizenstein (1911–68), who, though of German birth, came to live permanently in England in 1934. The sonatina for oboe and piano (1937) is typical of his texturally clear style, which he continued to pursue in a variety of media (including orchestral) until his death.[103]

The 'phantasy' mania—sparked off by the enthusiasm of W. W. Cobbett and the competition he inaugurated in 1906—showed no signs of abating. In fact it rested on two different, though related, sources of inspiration: the older English contrapuntal, often multi-sectional, form, newly strengthened by Warlock's championship of Locke and Purcell as well as of older

---

[100] *The Collected Music for Solo Piano*, ed. P. Dickinson (London, 1982), a volume of forty-eight pages.
[101] She married the Scottish composer James Friskin (1886–1967) and settled with him in the USA.
[102] Another worthwhile violin sonata is that of Arthur Bliss (1933).
[103] Another minor composer who studied with Hindemith and was much influenced by him is Arnold Cooke (b. 1906), who produced a solid output of chamber and orchestral music both before and after 1945.

composers,[104] and the aesthetic of the sonata 'quasi una fantasia' as practised (for example) by Beethoven, in which each movement (which might well be formally complete) follows its predecessor without a break. Schumann and Liszt offer additional parallels, particularly the latter, whose piano *Sonata*, like so many English 'fantasy' works, compresses four 'movements' into a single one, making the last a recapitulation. On the whole 'phantasy' (or 'fantasy') works without piano had a closer relationship with the older forms, though here too elements of later sonata procedures are normally found.

Not all composers were wholly at ease with all-string textures; a single clarinet or oboe is the commonest addition to the string ensemble. Ferguson's *Octet*, for the same instruments as Schubert's, is an agreeable and very well scored companion to it and deserves to be better known. Moeran's *Fantasy Quartet* for oboe and strings (1946) is perhaps the last successful expression of an idiom that had already outlived its usefulness.

Bridge's violin sonata and Ireland's for clarinet, not to mention several other works by Bridge and Bax, displayed a far tougher approach to the 'fantasy' aesthetic; but the string quartet, untrammelled by preconceived formal objectives, offered the best opportunity for ambitious writing. Bridge's third and fourth quartets (1926, 1937) are practically atonal, resembling in this Bartók's second, third, and fourth (1917, 1927, 1928) rather than anything by Schoenberg, since although they possess expressionistic features they are not serial. A certain hankering after pentatonic shapes reveals Bridge's national predilections behind the façade and in the last resort might seem to threaten stylistic coherence. Even so, these fine works deserve more attention than they generally receive.

Amongst lesser composers may be mentioned van Dieren, in whose six quartets (nos. 2–5 dating from 1917 to 1928: nos. 4 and 5 use a double bass) technical novelty disguises an innately conventional temperament; Eugene Goossens (1893–1962), whose large output includes two string quartets;[105] and Alan Bush, whose strange *Dialectic* (1929) seems unsuited to the medium. An earlier quartet by Bush in A minor (1924) betrays 'folk'-inspired modality. *Dialectic*, in a single movement of scarcely varying tempo, substitutes more abstract shapes and introduces more dissonant harmony, but it remains essentially rooted in the aesthetic of (say) John Ireland, two decades his senior, in its reliance on a large-scale tonal argument subservient to triadic harmony. Lacking even the musical radicalism of Bridge, still less could Bush anticipate the innovations of Rawsthorne, Maconchy, Lutyens, Tippett, or Britten.[106]

---

[104] The four-part consorts of Locke and the fantasias of Purcell were edited, in versions for modern stringed instruments, by Warlock and André Mangeot (Chester, 1932, and Curwen, n.d., respectively).

[105] Amongst his other works is a *Phantasy Sextet*, Op. 37, for the unusual combination of three violins, viola, and two cellos.

[106] Lutyens's first string quartet (1937) was withdrawn, but the second (1938), together with a sonata for solo viola (1938) and a string trio (1939), are representative of her earliest maturity.

Orchestral and Choral Music

The orchestral medium presented the greatest challenge to composers between the wars. In some ways the circumstances were propitious. Orchestral standards were gradually improving; the Promenade Concerts, the BBC, and the provincial festivals, as well as the regular series in London, Liverpool, Manchester, Birmingham, and Bournemouth, offered a variety of opportunities; and a new generation of conductors, led by Adrian Boult (1889–1983) and John Barbirolli (1899–1970) became actively interested in promoting English music. The provincial choral societies were at their zenith, and while a great deal of new choral music was second-rate or worse, the festivals allowed for a wide choice of music, old and new, purely orchestral as well as choral. On the other hand, there was little or no state subsidy available;[107] what the open market could not achieve had to be sponsored by private patronage (including, for example, that of Beecham and his friends on a massive scale). Orchestral standards were maintained by formidable skills in sight-reading; even complex new works might be done on a single rehearsal (or part of one), since the finances allowed of no more, while freelancing and the deputy system eroded useful preparation even further.[108]

The symphony—which was sometimes wholly or partly choral—was the form to which the highest aspirations were directed. The British inter-war symphony was a neo-Romantic form par excellence—hardly ever was it neoclassical, like Prokofiev's first or Stravinsky's two. It was an aspiration paralleled in Soviet Russia and the United States, but influence from these quarters was minimal. The model was provided by the heroic German tradition of Beethoven and Brahms, supplemented by Sibelius (but not Nielsen, whose music was then little known) and the pre-war English innovators, Elgar and Vaughan Williams. Tchaikovsky was ignored except as an orchestrator, and so seemingly was Mahler, except by Havergal Brian. Contemporary models from Western Europe were by and large lacking: the symphony was not cultivated by Hindemith (except for the operatic derivative *Mathis der Mahler*) before he emigrated to America, nor by Stravinsky before he too emigrated, nor by Bartók at all; the pre-war symphonies of Prokofiev (except for the *Classical*, his first) were hardly known; Milhaud's series (little regarded in England in any case), like that of K. A. Hartmann, began only in 1940; Honegger's first (1929–30) was probably little known and less liked, and his second, for strings and trumpet (1941), a maverick.

---

[107] Local authorities supported the orchestras in Bournemouth (from 1897) and Birmingham (from 1920). The BBC on its foundation in 1927 was able to use the licence fee (initially 10s. [50p] p.a.: there were 2¼ million licence-holders early in that year, and 8¼ million by 1937) for artistic patronage. CEMA (Council for the Encouragement of Music and the Arts) was set up in 1940 to allocate government grants for musical activity in the provinces.

[108] C. Ehrlich, *The Music Profession in Britain Since the Eighteenth Century* (Oxford, 1985), 207–8; cf. 215–16.

English composers had by and large to invent their criteria, and the sheer originality of Vaughan Williams, Bax, and Rubbra, the three most important symphonists of the era—whatever one may think of their solutions—was the outcome.

Of minor composers in this field the long-lived Havergal Brian (1876–1972) occupies a special place—indeed that he is minor at all would be disputed by some. But irrespective of his calibre in absolute terms, the very fact that none of his thirty-two symphonies was performed until 1954 (no. 8) must make him a marginal figure in inter-war music; indeed very little of his music had ever been performed, except for some early orchestral music before 1914. Brian's *Gothic Symphony* (1919–27), his first, is on a gigantic scale:[109] he alone of English symphonists seems to have emulated Mahlerian proportions and methods. Three instrumental movements are followed by a massive Te Deum. The second symphony (1930–1) is equally massive, though purely instrumental. By the end of the second war he had completed five, one more of them (no. 4) with chorus, one (no. 5) with baritone solo. The style remained essentially post-Wagnerian, until after the war he began to cultivate more concise structures and a lighter idiom.

Concertante music was surprisingly often written, considering the English tradition of aversion to writing for virtuoso playing, though few such works entered the canon. Walton's concertos for viola and violin quickly eclipsed all English rivals for strings, and Ireland's for piano was practically unique in securing a regular place, at least in English programmes, not granted to those of Vaughan Williams, Bax, Bliss, or Walton.

Ballet and film occupied a good deal of attention. English ballets to new scores (not counting unfortunate escapades like Walton's *The Wise Virgins*, arranged from Bach) appeared at regular intervals from 1931,[110] their music readily susceptible to recycling in the form of suites, or even to concert performances as they stood. Film music was less amenable to such treatment: much of it was necessarily subsidiary to the action, and it is normally irrecoverable except in the form of the soundtrack itself. Bliss's music for *Things to Come* (1935), a film based on H. G. Wells, is both a fine score and one of the earliest of any merit by an English composer (or indeed by any composer).[111] Vaughan Williams, Walton, and Britten all wrote excellent film scores, as did comparatively minor composers like Benjamin Frankel (1906–73), whose serious music post-dates the war but who contributed to several pre-war films. Walton extracted the *Spitfire Prelude and*

---

[109] It was first performed in 1961, and again (for the composer's ninetieth birthday) in 1966.

[110] The Camargo Society gave Vaughan Williams's *Job* in the Cambridge Theatre, London, in 1931; the company was absorbed into the newly founded Vic–Wells Ballet later that year, and *Job* was repeated at the Old Vic Theatre in September. Lambert and Berners, who had previously written ballets for Diaghilev's Ballets Russes, both wrote for the Sadler's Wells company in the 1930s.

[111] Walton's music for *Escape Me Never* was written in 1934; the film was released in 1935.

Fugue from *The First of the Few* (1942) and two pieces from *Henry V* (1943–4); Bliss made a suite of *Things to Come*; and (to anticipate) Vaughan Williams made a symphony of *Scott of the Antarctic* (1948); but these were the exceptions.[112]

George Dyson (1883–1964) came into prominence as a composer of choral music in the inter-war years.[113] The festival tradition was still capable of supporting a new repertory of wide appeal, though only the Three Choirs' was to continue effectively after the war. *Belshazzar's Feast* was commissioned for Leeds (1931), and *Five Tudor Portraits* for Norwich (1936). Dyson's *The Canterbury Pilgrims* (1931) was commissioned for Winchester Cathedral and shows the limitations of the secular choral cantata in hands less resourceful than those of Vaughan Williams. Its craftsmanship cannot be faulted, but the sheer tameness of the musical language and the obviousness of the design (after a succession of movements describing each pilgrim more or less in Chaucer's words we are to imagine the procession moving off to a return of the opening music) are exacerbated by the feeble archaisms of the modernized text. Such works had the amateur market in mind, but this one is at any rate a cut above Thomas Dunhill's *John Gilpin*.[114] Dyson's *Quo vadis* (written for Hereford, 1939, but not heard complete until 1950) aims higher, but is still no match for Howells or Finzi.

Opera and Other Theatre Music

New opera by English composers needs to be considered, as always, in the light of two factors: the general cultivation of opera in England at the time, and the undercurrent of less demanding musical theatre.

Operetta, musical comedy, revue, and music hall were the main forms of popular musical theatre, the two latter of course not based on a connected scenario. Christmas pantomime, and the children's play with music, might be added to the list. (Almost all theatres employed a pianist or a small group of players to provide music before and after the show and between the acts of spoken plays: fairly elaborate incidental music was still provided in Shakespearean and other non-contemporary drama.) The styles in musical comedy and revue were interchangeable; popular songs from dramatic works found their way into revues and music-hall entertainments, and in due course into broadcast programmes. Overtures were a medley of tunes,

---

[112] For further details see *BHMB*, vi. 131–4.

[113] Dyson taught music at several schools and became Director of the Royal College in 1937. He wrote a number of orchestral works (including a symphony, 1937), and in addition to those mentioned below the oratorios *St Paul's Voyage to Melita* (Hereford, 1933) and *Nebuchadnezzar* (Worcester, 1935). He also wrote books, including the influential *The New Music* (Oxford, 1924).

[114] Dunhill (1877–1946), a pupil of Stanford, himself taught at the Royal College. Before the Great War he organized performances of chamber music by himself and others; between the wars he mainly wrote light operas and ballets. His educational piano music was once familiar to many.

and any form more complex than the strophic song (even for the chorus) was virtually unknown. The musically illiterate 'composer' emerged in the person of Noel Coward:[115] his tunes had to be harmonized and scored by others, and owed much of their popularity to their efforts. Dance-band scoring came to be preferred over small-orchestra and piano-trio combinations for the frothier types of musical comedy as well as for revue. In this, as in the musical idiom itself, the influence of America became paramount, with its emphasis on jazz-influenced dance rhythms.

The only established repertoire pieces from an earlier period were those constituting the attenuated canon of 'Gilbert and Sullivan' operettas, regularly staged and toured by the D'Oyly Carte company, which owned the material and reserved exclusive rights of professional performance. Amateurs, of course, continued to play them as well as the most enduring works by other composers: *Merrie England* and *Tom Jones*, by Edward German, and Alfred Cellier's *Dorothy*, for example. These, with such foreign importations as Franz Lehár's *Frederica* and Rudolf Friml's *The Three Musketeers*, were the staple of local 'operatic societies'.[116]

Some element of artistry in musical comedy and operetta was preserved by Ivor Novello (1893–1951), one of whose librettists was Christopher Hassall, later to write the words of Walton's *Troilus and Cressida*. A series of shows put on in the 1930s reacted against American influence and reverted to the standards of pre-1914 operetta, offering a mixture of comedy and sentimentality in a sub-Puccinian idiom.[117]

Opera itself was in the doldrums during the 1920s and 1930s, with Covent Garden reverting for lengthy periods to its historic function of providing a mixture of entertainment. The British National Opera Company (BNOC), formed in 1922 by orphans of the Beecham Opera Company (which had collapsed in 1920), performed in Covent Garden and in the provinces until 1924; it was then excluded from Covent Garden, which was wanted primarily for German opera, but taken over by Covent Garden itself from 1929 to 1932. From 1932 to 1939 Beecham was in charge at Covent Garden and promoted a wider choice of works than had obtained since 1924. In 1939 the theatre became a dance hall for the duration of the war.

From 1931 an operatic repertory, together with ballet, could also be heard at the new Sadler's Wells theatre in Rosebery Avenue in North London, at first in alternation with Shakespeare, but from 1934 exclusively, in

---

[115] Cf., however, Thomas Moore previously (Ch. 3 above): he composed tunes as well as using existing ones.

[116] These examples are drawn from a Chappell advertisement of c.1935: numerous examples by Sigmund Romberg (1887–1951), Lionel Monckton (1861–1924), and Friml himself (1879–1972) could be added. (Friml and Romberg were Americans of east European origin.) *The Beggar's Opera* was very successfully (and very inauthentically) revived in 1920, and Offenbach's operettas, in particular *La Vie parisienne*, continued to be popular in English adaptations.

[117] *BHMB*, vi. 111 (and for more information generally, 107–18).

performances by the resident opera and ballet companies. The enterprising operatic repertory included many English premières of foreign operas as well as operas, new and old, by English composers. In 1940 the companies took to touring. Opera was sung in English from the outset.

In the circumstances of the time, with no public subsidy and a declining confidence, both political and financial, in the 1930s, the enterprise of the BNOC and the Sadler's Wells companies (in ballet as well as opera) is surprising. What was still lacking was an established tradition of serious English opera, the result of decades of hand-to-mouth enterprise since the 1860s. Beecham did sterling work at Covent Garden, both before and after the Great War, but even he could not finance an enduring tradition single-handed. But the BNOC performed Holst's *The Perfect Fool* (1923) and *At the Boar's Head* (1925), Boughton's *Alkestis* (1924) and Vaughan Williams's *Hugh the Drover* (1924), while the Sadler's Wells company revived works by Smyth and Stanford.

Important scores by Vaughan Williams, however, had to be produced by amateurs or students: *Sir John in Love* and *Riders to the Sea* at the Royal College (1929, 1937), *The Poisoned Kiss* at Cambridge (1936, conducted by Cyril Rootham) and, the year after, at the Juilliard School in New York. Discouragement doubtless played a part in the long-delayed completion of *A Pilgrim's Progress*.

Smyth's comic opera *The Boatswain's Mate*, curiously designed with spoken dialogue in the first act and continuous music in the second, was produced in 1916 and enjoyed considerable success thereafter. Rutland Boughton's later operas included, in addition to *Alkestis* (Glastonbury, 1922), *The Queen of Cornwall* (Glastonbury, 1926) and *The Lily Maid* (Stroud, 1934); but none of these achieved the astonishing success of *The Immortal Hour* (1914), which had a run of 216 performances in London in 1922–3 and a further 160 in the following season. The final opera, *Bronwen*, in Holbrooke's *Maginobion* trilogy *The Cauldron of Anwen*, was given in London in 1929, heavily subsidized, no doubt, by its eccentric librettist Lord Howard de Walden.

A few minor composers may be added. Amongst university musicians Charles Wood produced two Dickensian comedies in the 1920s, Cyril Rootham *The Two Sisters* (1920), and Tovey *The Bride of Dionysus* (Edinburgh, 1929). Lord Berners wrote a satirical work, *La Carosse du Saint-Sacrement* (Paris, 1923). The operas of the critic Cecil Gray (1895–1951) have sunk without trace, but the first of four by Arthur Benjamin (1893–1960, Australian-born), *The Devil Take Her* (1931), showed a promise that bore fruit in the later operas, all produced after the second war.[118]

---

[118] See further *BHMB*, vi. 343–58. Two operas by the young George Lloyd (1913–98)—*Iernin* (1934) and *The Serf* (1938)—were well received and added to the impression given by his first three symphonies of a precocious if conventional talent.

All in all, however, the predominant impression is of isolated efforts dogged by indifferent performances in unpropitious circumstances. In Italy, Germany, and France, new work, even if of doubtful value, could take its chance alongside established national classics (even though the rise of Nazism in Germany compromised the healthy growth of the new). In England there was no such living tradition to provide a context: its re-establishment would have to await the end of the Second World War.

Writing and Scholarship

The inter-war years saw the continuation of several endeavours initiated before 1914. The activities of the Plainsong and Mediæval Music Society proceeded with the completion of the facsimile of the *Antiphonale Sarisburiense* (1901–24) and with the publication of *Worcester Mediæval Harmony* (1928), *Anglo-French Sequelæ* (1934), and *The Old Hall Manuscript* (1933–8).[119] The Purcell Society continued its slow progress. The *Oxford History of Music* was revised and extended under the editorship of P. C. Buck. E. H. Fellowes initiated *The English Madrigal School* in 1914; it was followed by *The English School of Lutenist Song-Writers* (1920–32) and *The Collected Works of William Byrd* (1937–50). *Tudor Church Music*, one of the projects financed by the Carnegie Trust, appeared in ten massive volumes (1922–9) under an editorial committee comprising R. R. Terry, Buck, Fellowes, Ramsbotham, and Sylvia Townsend Warner.[120] Subsequently an octavo series of leaflets appeared, edited by Fellowes.

Much of this editorial activity was the work of amateurs, several of them ordained Anglicans. Terry and H. B. Collins, both performing musicians, were, or became, Roman Catholics. Collins was organist at the Birmingham Oratory from 1915 until his death: like Terry and Fellowes, he issued a large amount of sixteenth-century music—Continental as well as English—in octavo format. Although some of the editorial work at this period was intended primarily as a contribution to scholarship, the bulk of it was directed to practical use. Even the heavy folios of the Purcell Society edition included realized continuo parts, sometimes unashamedly pianistic in idiom. (But this venture too spawned a 'popular edition'.) Editorial methods reveal much about performing style, especially amongst choral groups. Fellowes evidently thought of the madrigal principally as a vehicle for

---

[119] The *Antiphonale* was edited by W. H. Frere, bishop of Truro; *Worcester Mediæval Harmony* and *Anglo-French Sequelæ* by Dom Anselm Hughes (H. V. Hughes, by now a monk of the Anglican abbey of Nashdom); and *The Old Hall Manuscript* by Bishop A. Ramsbotham (1870–1932), Hughes, and H. B. Collins (1870–1941). Collins had also produced a fine edition of the Mass 'O quam suavis' for the PMMS in 1927.

[120] For Terry's sad role in his decline, and for much other information, see R. Turbet, 'An Affair of Honour: "Tudor Church Music", the Ousting of Richard Terry, and a Trust Vindicated', *ML* 76 (1995), 593–600.

amateur choirs—which indeed it already was and long had been in England. But by now the performers were not solely the long-established madrigal societies but less experienced groups with women sopranos and altos.[121] For them Fellowes introduced variable barring (as also in *Tudor Church Music*), accent-signs (sometimes over rests), dynamics, and keyboard reductions 'for practice only'. In such ways his editions came to resemble the part-songs and folk song arrangements that were already part of the repertory, and we can be fairly sure that the performing style was unchanged, too. Conversely, however, the newly available madrigalian material[122] came to influence contemporary English writing for choir.

Much the same applies, *mutatis mutandis*, to sacred vocal music, though women had not yet penetrated the chancel stalls of Anglican churches. It was brave of Fellowes, in the lute-song repertory, to include the tablature (in the 'first series' only), but he eliminated the original bass parts (vocal or instrumental as the case may be) and the alternative part-song versions where these existed. Warlock also published selections from this repertory, including an edition of the manuscript 'Willow Song', and his book *The English Ayre* was long an attractive introduction. Fellowes issued *English Madrigal Verse* (including lute-song verse) in 1920, and published books on Byrd and Gibbons, on the English madrigal (1925), and on English cathedral music (1941). They are now superseded, but they were valuable in their day and for long afterwards.

There was no long-standing tradition of academic musicology at this period, though the majority of scholars had taken a university degree, often in Classics. Others had taken a B.Mus. as part of a general degree course, and might proceed also to a doctorate: these were still essentially composers' degrees and fitted their holders at best for an organist's or a pedagogical position, or for the two in combination. Typical was Sir Hugh Allen (1869–1946), who became organist of New College in 1901 and Professor of Music at Oxford, as well as director of the Royal College of Music, in 1918.[123] His scholarship, which was considerable, was directed entirely to the performance of music, old and new, at these institutions and elsewhere.

Meanwhile E. J. Dent (1876–1957), the most considerable English scholar of the inter-war years, was carving out a new pattern at Cambridge, where he was appointed Professor in 1926. He began by widening the B.Mus. curriculum to embrace history and performance, though as there was still no music 'tripos' candidates had also to take a BA. As a brilliant linguist he not

---

[121] For the introduction of women into madrigal societies see above, p. 270.

[122] Much of it had, indeed, been republished in the 19th c.; but those editions were regarded as impracticable and were in any case no longer obtainable. Arkwright's *Old English Edition* (1889–1902), though in a more practical format, was also out of print.

[123] Though organ scholar of Christ's College, Cambridge from 1892 (BA 1895, MA 1899), he took the Oxford degrees of B.Mus. (1893) and D.Mus. (1898). The rules were later tightened up: see n. 129 below.

only translated several operatic libretti with great flair but was a natural leader of English musicology abroad: he became the first president of the International Society for Contemporary Music, 1923–38, and was president of the International Musicological Society, 1931–46 (and of the Royal Musical Association from 1928 to 1935). He was an opinionated and at times exasperating writer: his brief remarks on Elgar in Guido Adler's *Handbuch der Musikgeschichte* (Frankfurt am Main, 1924, p. 938) caused outrage, as much perhaps for their dismissive brevity as for any specific criticism.[124] But he contributed notably to the study of opera in his books *Alessandro Scarlatti* (1905), *Mozart's Operas* (1913), and *Foundations of English Opera* (1928); and he was generous with practical advice to composers and producers.

P. C. Buck (1871–1947), though far from being a scholar of Dent's standing, published some interesting lectures (*The Scope of Music*, 1924), *A History of Music* (1929), and supervised, as we have seen, the second edition of the *Oxford History*. Nor, despite his commitment to pedagogy, did he achieve as much as Dent at Cambridge. He was King Edward VII Professor at London University from 1925 to 1937, and participated much in the administrative and educational spheres in London and the provinces. He was also, in a small way, a composer, and his *Unfigured Harmony* (1911, 2nd edn. 1920) was widely used.

Dent had been a journalist before taking up the Cambridge chair, and one of the younger contributors to the *Oxford History*, J. A. Westrup (1904–75), was also a journalist in the 1930s. His main contribution to pedagogy was to come after the war, but he had already made his mark as a scholar and conductor, notably of Monteverdi's *Orfeo*, which he edited and performed as an Oxford undergraduate—reading Classics—in 1925. In 1937 came his outstanding short book on Purcell. This was an era, in fact, in which many of the most important works of scholarship were written by journalists. Ernest Newman (1868–1959) produced his four-volume *Life of Richard Wagner* between 1933 and 1947, the most substantial of his many books. Cecil Gray (1895–1951) wrote *inter alia* on *Sibelius* (1931) and *Peter Warlock* (1934), and H. C. Colles (1879–1943) the influential *Voice and Verse* (1928).[125]

More general works of criticism and aesthetics are on the whole less distinguished. George Dyson's *The New Music* (1924) and Constant Lambert's *Music Ho!* (1934) offer trenchant criticism—particularly in Lambert's case—as well as evocative description. Holbrooke's *Contemporary British*

---

[124] They are put into perspective by B. Trowell, 'Elgar's Use of Literature', in R. Monk (ed.), *Edward Elgar: Music and Literature* (Aldershot, 1993), 182–326, esp. pp. 182–5.

[125] Newman was on *The Sunday Times*, 1920–58; Gray wrote for *The Daily Telegraph* and *The Manchester Guardian*. Colles, who also edited the 3rd and 4th edns. of *Grove's Dictionary* (1927, 1940) and wrote Vol. VII of the *Oxford History* (1934), was chief critic of *The Times*, 1911–43.

Composers (1925), by contrast, is unbalanced. Lambert faltered only in his failure to spot the potential of Bartók and by exaggerating the position of Sibelius as 'the music of the future'—curiously, for a composer so little influenced by him. Otherwise his thrusts are well directed and expressed with consummate wit. 1934, the year of so many composers' deaths, saw a plethora of books on music. Apart from those just mentioned, there were popularizing works like *The Musical Companion*, edited by A. L. Bacharach,[126] and Walford Davies's *The Pursuit of Music*. One could hardly so describe John Foulds's *Music To-day*, though it too professes to be written for the 'musical public'. Foulds (1880–1939) was a composer of some temporary repute, notably for *A World Requiem*, written in memory of those fallen in the Great War and performed annually thereafter for some years. He was too preoccupied with psychical research and novel techniques to be a good composer, but the same preoccupations, taken with a pinch of salt, make for entertaining reading. He discusses an extended modal system, microtones, atonal music, and a host of issues relating to the psychology of music. The book's most distinctive, and slightly sinister, feature is an obsession with the occult. Despite this, and a propensity to sincerely believed but ill-founded generalizations (such as: 'Exceptions do nothing to shake the conclusion long held by many specialists that women are comparatively impotent as creative artists'), it is a remarkably open-minded piece of writing.

Another lone figure of the period, though a more prolific composer, was Kaikhosru Sorabji (1892–88), of Parsi/Spanish-Sicilian descent. His tendency to Oriental prolixity and complexity is evident in his *Opus clavicembalisticum* for solo piano (1929–30), three hours in duration and formidably difficult to play. His strongly expressed views can be sampled in *Around Music* (1932) and the later *Mi contra fa* (1947). In 1940 he banned further performances of his music, a sure way to sustain interest in it (the ban was partially lifted in 1976).

Minor Genres and Summary

The picture presented by the years 1914–45, and above all of the inter-war years, is of a restless search for identity. Futurism, the father of a more generalized modernism, had appeared before 1914, but it had had little effect on English musical development at the time and was arrested by the outbreak of war. After the war, there was no shortage of English composers of an experimental bent. A Sitwellian iconoclasm, related to that of Satie, Cocteau, and *Les Six*, was at first embraced by Lambert, Walton, and Bliss, and more deep-seatedly by Berners, on whom Stravinsky and his exact

---

[126] The contributors were W. R. Anderson, Eric Blom, F. Bonavia, Dent, Edwin Evans, Julius Harrison, Dyneley Hussey, and Francis Toye.

contemporary Alfredo Casella (1883–1947), a pre-war apostle of extreme modernism, were also influential. Composers like John Foulds dabbled with atonality, extremes of tonal chromaticism, and quarter-tones, the last under the influence of the Czech composer Alois Hába (1893–1973), who established a department of microtonal music at Prague Conservatory in 1924. A more serious response to Continental atonality and chromaticism was offered by Cyril Scott and (especially) Frank Bridge. But although Bridge occasionally invented twelve-note themes, there was little use of the serial principle by English composers. One of the earliest English serial works, and certainly the earliest of any substance, was Lutyens's *Concerto* for nine instruments (1939), by which time the preferred model was Webern rather than Schoenberg. A younger composer, Humphrey Searle (1915–82), was to become an ardent advocate of the method, but he had achieved little by 1945. The Webernesque element is indeed already strong in his *Night Music*, Op. 2 (1943), for chamber orchestra, but this is not yet a truly serial composition.

It is surprising that Berg, with his free use of and partial abandonment of serialism, sometimes in favour of tonal direction, was not more influential. The same is true of Bartók (notwithstanding some traces in Bridge's quartets). Hindemith's very personal idiom impressed minor figures like his pupils Reizenstein and Cooke. Walton was an admirer of Hindemith, who premièred his viola concerto after Lionel Tertis had withdrawn, and one of his best later works is based on a theme of his. But stylistically the gulf was considerable. Sibelius was highly regarded (and the supposedly finished eighth symphony eagerly awaited during the 1930s), but his influence, bolstered by the plaudits of Gray and Lambert, was more in the sphere of a generalized symphonic idealism, dedicated to tonal integrity and 'organic' development, than in stylistic detail. At the same time the bright, perky neoclassicism of the 1920s, enlivened by the importation of jazz, was gradually discarded, as indeed it had been to a certain extent by its own protagonists such as Stravinsky, Milhaud, Poulenc, Honegger, and Prokofiev.

It would be foolish to judge England's musical achievements in this period by the standards of Continental innovators. At the same time it would be pointless to deny the undercurrents of a deeply rooted conservatism, fostered indeed by the 'conservatory' training of the Royal College and the Royal Academy, where the teaching of composition passed more and more into the hands of traditionalists and where performance was increasingly geared to the interpretation of standard classics. The 'English renaissance' might well have run into the ground had it not been for the sturdy individualism of Holst and Vaughan Williams and the sophisticated responses to tradition by composers as diverse as Bax, Bridge, Bliss, and Walton. The use of folk music by Holst and Vaughan Williams (and by 'lesser' contemporaries such as Butterworth and Moeran) as an expression of

musical nationhood had many Continental parallels, especially from eastern
Europe (Stravinsky, Bartók, Kodály, Martinů, Janáček, to name no others),
but the effect of these parallels on their music was negligible, largely because
their material was so different. In any case, the English adoption of folk
songs and the impact of their modality on style proceeded very largely,
before 1914, without the benefit of Continental precedent; it was a truly
'original' movement, and it continued for long under its own steam.

Tudorism and the Bach revival also affected English composers in ways
not readily paralleled elsewhere. Doubtless there were foreigners, such as
Gian Francesco Malipiero and Hans Pfitzner, whose development owed
something to Renaissance influence, but they were little known in England.
The direct effects of the new understanding of Tudor music and of a portion
of the Continental repertory (in particular Palestrina) are evident above all
in the adoption of rhythmic flexibility and linear independence in works
that in other ways might seem quite conventional. The Bach revival, or
rather the particular wave of enthusiasm for Bach that was initiated in the
later nineteenth century, continued unabated,[127] encapsulated for this
period in the annual performances of the St Matthew Passion at Dorking
under Vaughan Williams and by the provision of a new edition (with a
much improved English text) by Elgar and Ivor Atkins, organist of Worcester cathedral, in 1911. Vaughan Williams was himself deeply influenced by
Bach, and a reverence for him is even more apparent in the music of Gerald
Finzi. For both, the precedent was no doubt Parry.

The underlying conservatism was strongest (leaving aside the increasing
caution of recitalists, conductors, and concert promoters)[128] amongst
church musicians. They had inherited and continued to maintain a highly
traditional pattern of training in composition and organ-playing, the former
leading to the baccalaureate and doctorate in Music at Oxford or Cambridge (or, it might be, Durham or Trinity College, Dublin, where no other
qualifications, residential or otherwise, were needed in support).[129] These,
with the FRCO for organ-playing and 'paperwork', were the normal
qualifications for a career in the organ-loft of a cathedral or collegiate
foundation. Many of them proved in the event of no account at all as
composers, whatever might be their talents for performance and administration. Others, such as Edward Bairstow (1874–1946: organist of York

---

[127] The London Bach Choir, for example, was founded in 1927.

[128] This was a European phenomenon, hardly affected by such ventures as Schoenberg's Society for
Private Musical Performances (Vienna, 1919–21), Paul Sacher's activities in Basle, or in England the
Macnaghten–Lemare concerts (from 1931); nor yet by the partial adventurousness of (say) Fürtwängler
or Boult, Walther or Beecham.

[129] At Oxford and Cambridge the examination for B.Mus. could be taken, but the degree not
awarded, without prior completion of the requirements for at least a 'pass' degree of BA. The doctorate
required as a preliminary either the B.Mus. or an MA (automatically available to a BA seven years from
matriculation).

minster from 1913) and W. H. Harris (1883–1973: organist of New College, 1919–29, of Christ Church cathedral, 1929–33, and of St George's chapel, Windsor, 1933–61), contributed modestly to the repertory in such admirable, if highly conservative, pieces as 'Let all mortal flesh keep silence' (Bairstow)[130] and 'Faire is the heaven' (Harris, a double-choir setting of Spenser's sonnet), both of 1925. Bairstow's masterpiece is probably 'Blessed City, Heavenly Salem', an extended anthem based on the plainchant hymn 'Urbs beata Jerusalem' (quoted in Vol. I, p. 65, with different words). Edgar Bainton (1880–1960) was not a church musician, and he left England for Australia in 1933. Before then, however, he had published a good deal of music in all forms (his choral symphony 'Before Sunrise', composed in 1907, won a Carnegie award in 1917), including his still popular anthem 'I saw a new Heaven'. Much of Charles Wood's church music, some of it in a deliberately archaic idiom, dates from after the war.[131]

In the 1920s and 1930s one could still walk into virtually any English cathedral or collegiate church on a weekday morning and hear choral Mattins, as well as Evensong in the afternoon or early evening, professionally sung and with a repertory drawn largely from the later nineteenth and early twentieth centuries but now with a slight admixture of Tudor and Jacobean polyphony, at least in the more enlightened centres. Several large urban churches (notably at Leeds) maintained a choir of boys and men and a cathedral-like pattern of worship. Westminster Cathedral supported a similar choir, and high standards were maintained at the Brompton and Birmingham oratories. Smaller churches, Anglican and otherwise, were generally less successful or less interested, and neither Roman Catholicism nor the Anglo-Catholic movement in the Church of England gave rise to genuine creativity. Even the best days of hymn-tune composition were now over.[132]

'Serious' music between the wars existed in an uneasy relationship with popular music of all kinds. There was widespread condemnation in high places of the shallowness and sentimentality of popular song, on and off the stage, and of dance-band music, much of it now fully Americanized in idiom if not actually of American origin. Sometimes it was satirized in scores such as *Façade*, and in the ballets of Berners and Lambert. Jazz in its many forms was harder to assimilate, but it was taken seriously, if not always successfully integrated, in works by Lambert and others. A pianist-composer

---

[130] *TECM*, v. 39–44; this volume contains a representative selection of shorter 20th-c. works.

[131] Ibid. 67–77 (Bainton), 15–17 (from Wood's *Short Communion Service in the Phrygian Mode*, 1919).

[132] The encouragement of parochial music was put into the care of the School of English Church Music, founded in 1927 by Sydney Nicholson (1875–1947); it became the Royal School of Church Music in 1945. Unfortunately, Nicholson, who had been organist successively at Carlisle, Manchester, and Westminster Abbey, personifies the malaise of church music in the period. Having presided over the bowdlerization of Victorian hymn-tunes in 1904, he proceeded to devise a simplified but badly pointed *Parish Psalter*, published in 1932. His own church music is nondescript at best.

like Billy Mayerl (1902–59) reached out in both directions, but his appeal was essentially to the dance-band temperament. Eric Coates (1886–1957) similarly specialized in light orchestral music.[133] The restricted appeal of serious music was not new; what was changing was the rapid development of light music on quite different lines, leaving its origins in Sullivan and German far behind. It is true that Walton could provide for the 1937 coronation a *Crown Imperial* march that had wide appeal, but in general the separation of light and serious music was now an established fact, the gap bridgeable only by satire or in comparatively restricted areas such as film-music and patriotic music (the two sometimes coinciding). In that connection, the lighter concert-organ music of a Percy Whitlock (1903–46, municipal organist at Bournemouth) counted for more than the sonatas of a Bairstow or the plainsong fantasias of a Bainton.

Innovative serious music was thus becoming increasingly distanced from hitherto complementary forms of musical life. It was becoming detached from the performing tradition of classical masterpieces, a tendency for which Adrian Boult's championship of Elgar, Holst, and Vaughan Williams offered only partial compensation; it was becoming less and less involved with the 'establishment' circuit of church and organ music, the universities, and the Three Choirs' Festival; and it was becoming remote indeed from the musical entertainment of the urban or suburban masses. Its isolation began to place a strain on its financial viability, for which the patronage of the BBC and of private persons offered only limited respite. Programmes were designed to sugar the pill by an admixture of the familiar and the spectacular, but it now became clear that serious modern music could not, and never would, pay its way. When after the Second World War the principle of state subsidy was at last conceded, new music found itself in competition with a host of other contenders. Its resilience in very different circumstances will be examined in the next chapter.

[133] See further in Ch. 8 below.

6

TRADITION AND AVANT-GARDE, 1945–1975

Opera and Music Theatre

IF ever a musical event had symbolic importance it was the first performance of Britten's opera *Peter Grimes* at the Sadler's Wells Theatre on 7 June 1945, almost one month after Victory in Europe. The opera was, however, the fruit of a long gestation of fully four years, and initial reactions were decidedly mixed; with hindsight one is in a better position to judge of its significance than at the time, yet the coincidence of material and artistic recovery was rapidly confirmed by the international success of the work in the immediately following years. Indeed a striking feature of the post-war period was the place of music in the regeneration of cultural life, commensurately almost with architecture, which for obvious reasons had primacy at the time. Opera at Sadler's Wells, Covent Garden, and Glyndebourne (and ballet at Sadler's Wells) were all revived in forms that proved durable; other festivals were those at Cheltenham (from 1945, devoted to contemporary British Music), Aldeburgh (from 1948,) and, to glance briefly across the border, Edinburgh (from 1947). Britten's English Opera Group catered for operatic adventures that the established companies could not then be expected to entertain. The Arts Council of Great Britain was set up in 1945 as a successor to the wartime Council for the Encouragement of Music and the Arts and to administer the state subsidy of the arts that now for the first time in Britain became an established feature of peacetime life. The climax to this phase came with the Festival of Britain in 1951; the Royal Festival Hall on the South Bank, opened in that year and later provided with an imposing new organ (1954) to the design of Ralph Downes, its dry acoustic since softened, has always seemed both an attractive and a useful symbol of confidence in Britain's musical future.

It is indeed from this period that a conscious projection of 'British' music as such came to predominate over earlier perceptions of 'English'. A. L. Bacharach, a noted popularizer, edited a collection of essays entitled *British Music of Our Time*, first published in 1946 and then, in an expanded edition, in 1951. But after 1951 the freshness of the enterprise faded. The coronation in June 1953 of Elizabeth II, who had come to the throne in 1952, provided an occasion for festive musical activity, but the real work of the 1950s and 1960s was to consolidate, often in the context of financial uncertainty, the position established in the late 1940s.[1]

It was its unexpected and lasting success as an opera that made and still makes *Peter Grimes* such a potent symbol. It was a decided breakthrough in a form which to many people seemed to have only Purcell's *Dido* as a serious English precursor. Britten's own first opera, the lightweight *Paul Bunyan* (1941), had been a failure with the American critics, though 'the public seemed to find something enjoyable in the performances'.[2] Britten wanted to do more in that line. In the same year he came across an article by E. M. Forster on George Crabbe, the Suffolk poet (1754–1832); subsequently he and Peter Pears settled on the story of Peter Grimes, from Crabbe's *The Borough*, as the basis of the opera. By the time the librettist, Montagu Slater, had been found, Britten and Pears had worked out a scenario and had agreed to make Grimes a far more sympathetic figure than in Crabbe's poem, a tortured visionary driven to extremes by his desire for recognition rather than the psychopath who 'wanted some obedient boy to stand / And bear the blow of his outrageous hand'. The villain of the opera is not Grimes, despite his tendency to violence, but the unfeeling chorus of townsfolk.

Slater was in many ways the ideal librettist, though he had to accept the criticisms of Britten, Pears, and their sympathetic colleague from the Sadler's Wells company, Eric Crozier. He took the scenario as given, and supplied the details of motivation and characterization which make this one of the most convincingly structured of operas, all in a flexible verse that owes something, but not much, to Crabbe's prototype.[3]

[1] To the Labour Government of 1945–50 must go the credit for establishing the principle of peace-time subsidy, but the arts have neither then nor since been lavishly supported in Britain by government funds. New music, in particular, has depended a great deal on private funding both by individuals (or their trusts) and by corporations, not necessarily English. *Peter Grimes* was commissioned by the Koussevitsky Foundation. The continuing role of the BBC, whose Third Programme was founded in 1946, and of some local authorities, should not be overlooked.

[2] B. Britten, 'Introduction', in E. Crozier (ed.), *Benjamin Britten: Peter Grimes* (London, 1946: Sadler's Wells Opera Books, No. 3), an important source-book reprinted in P. Brett (ed.), *Benjamin Britten: 'Peter Grimes'* (Cambridge, 1983). See also B. Banks (ed.), *The Making of 'Peter Grimes'*, 2 vols. (Woodbridge, 1996). For the revival of *Paul Bunyan* see Ch. 5 n. 85.

[3] Only the opening and closing choruses quote Crabbe directly at length. Crabbe's phrase ' "Grimes is at his exercise" ', the villagers' ironic comment on hearing one of his apprentice's cries, is less apposite in the opera, from which the element of pure sadism has been eliminated: we do not know exactly how the first boy died, it is true, but the second died at worst of culpable negligence. Nor, *a fortiori*, does the opera contain a homoerotic element in plot or characterization; its overriding emotion is of sympathy for the lonely and the outcast. Britten and Pears, as pacifists and homosexuals, were themselves potential outcasts, but their rejection of physical and moral oppression was a deep-seated conviction expressed here in terms quite independent of their own circumstances. (For a different and powerfully argued view, see Brett, *Peter Grimes*.)

As for Britten's music, it achieves a deeper and more consistent resonance than any previous large-scale work of his. The disparate elements of his style are here resolved into a convincing whole. It is one of the most vivid of operatic scores: the grinding of surf against shingle as the gulls cry overhead in the first interlude, the jangle of rigging against masts in the storm, the play of light in the morning sunshine as the church-bells sound, and the dense fog of the final interlude—all these are evoked. Its structure as a series of 'numbers' linked by more flexible declamation is handled so as not to disrupt continuity—in this it has the virtues of (say) Verdi's *Otello*—and its word-setting benefits from the composer's long apprenticeship in song. Among many other operatic influences, that of *Wozzeck* has perhaps been understressed; there are parallels in a concern for formal symmetries, small and large, in the realism with which the suffocating atmosphere of the pub and the abandon of the barndance are delineated, and in the importance given to the orchestral interludes and to self-contained forms elsewhere in the opera, not to mention many a telling detail. But its style is far more conservative than Berg's; even so, one of the oddities of its reception was the complaint of E. J. Dent, a former president of the International Society for Contemporary Music, that its music sounded like 'the noise of a motor bike starting up'.[4] This is a salutary reminder that musical England in 1945 had not the least idea what a modern opera, as represented by (say) *Wozzeck*, *The Lady Macbeth of Mtsensk*, or *Mathis der Maler* might be.[5] There were, however, some intelligent and perceptive reactions to *Peter Grimes*, despite the indifference of the Sadler's Wells company to its fate. It was taken up by Covent Garden in 1947 and toured in the provinces with enormous success. In this way *Grimes* became a great educative force, inspiring many young musicians with their own ambitions for the future.

A survey of notable new operatic productions in the period 1945–76 shows Britten in a commanding lead, with Tippett, Walton, and Berkeley far behind in terms of quantity. But even Britten's output demonstrates a variety of approach and a penchant for experiment far removed from the comparative uniformity to be found in Verdi, Puccini, or Strauss. It is not even agreed whether the 'parables for church performance' should count as operas at all (the view taken here is that they should). There are works with and for children, chamber operas, and religious works, not of course mutually exclusive categories, and 'realizations', as well as full-length, fully scored operas. *Owen Wingrave*, produced on television in 1971, was revived in a stage version in 1973. *Paul Bunyan*, discarded in 1941, was produced in a revised version in 1976, the year of Britten's death. There is a full-length

[4] Reported by Kennedy, *Britten*, 46. But in *Penguin Music Magazine*, 1 (1946), 18, Dent described *Grimes* as 'a work of outstanding originality, quite unlike any other modern opera'.

[5] The first British productions of these were respectively in 1952 (Covent Garden), 1987 (Covent Garden), and 1952 (Edinburgh). Britten knew and admired all three.

ballet, *The Prince of the Pagodas* (produced on 1 January 1957), and a certain amount of incidental music from the decade 1945–55.

Britten's third opera, *The Rape of Lucretia*, to a libretto by Ronald Duncan based on a play by André Obey, was written in 1946 for the reopening of the Glyndebourne opera-house after the war. Its production was attributed to the 'Glyndebourne English Opera Company', formed to complement the more usual activities of the festival company. After it had been performed there and widely toured, Glyndebourne's founder and owner John Christie withdrew from the venture and the company was refounded as the English Opera Group (and re-formed in 1976 as English Music Theatre). *The Rape*, which like many other 'difficult' works has been triumphantly revived on numerous occasions, was not well received at first. A chamber opera, though ideal for Glyndebourne's (then) small theatre, did not provide the kind of musical experience that most opera-goers expected; the subject was thought dangerous, to put it mildly; and, as a final piece of captiousness, some critics objected to its framework of Christian morality. (They had probably forgotten that Greek temples were sometimes transformed into Christian churches, and that Virgil had been Dante's guide. Duncan, though he found the Christianizing element in his source, was evidently sympathetic, as was Britten himself, to such continuities.)

The Rape is one of Britten's finest scores, fastidious to the last degree and coolly elevated in tone, though not without dramatic effect in its own terms. A lack of engagement with the heroine's dilemma has been complained of, but Britten and his librettist deliberately cultivated a certain detachment. It is a didactic, courtly work, like a Carissimi oratorio—a dramatic poem, to be turned this way and that in the memory long after the last sounds have died away.

Britten's next three works for the stage were lighter in character. *Albert Herring* (1947) is a comedy such as Stanford, Smyth, Vaughan Williams, and Holst never remotely approached—a comedy with roots not in the folky antiquarianism of the 1920s and 1930s, nor even in the light-entertainment tradition of Sullivan and German, but in the broader and franker humour of eighteenth-century comic opera and of the spoken drama that paralleled it—though this is an 'all sung' piece, with piano-accompanied recitatives and an accompanying ensemble similar to that of *The Rape*. Here Britten displays a gift for the musical characterization of comic—even embarrassing—episodes (such as Albert's attack of hiccups) that surfaces again in *Noye's Fludde* and *A Midsummer Night's Dream*. It is a gift not to be despised, that of making an audience laugh through music that enhances rather than trivializes the comedy.

Albert Herring, though first given at Glyndebourne, was written for the newly formed English Opera Group, a company independent of any existing theatre. Its real home was to be Aldeburgh, where it became the mainstay of the annual festival in addition to its touring, training, and broader educational functions. Britten's lively re-creation of *The Beggar's Opera* was given by the company in Cambridge in 1948, and *Let's Make an Opera*, incorporating *The Little Sweep*, at Aldeburgh in 1949. *Let's Make an Opera*, like Britten's other music for children, should not be disregarded. Its introductory section, in which adults and children together plan the opera, is an integral part of the work.[6] Here Britten displays in their simplest form his principles of musical characterization, linking his most sophisticated procedures to a literally childish level of invention. A phrase like the descending chromatic scale used for 'Oh my poor feet' will linger in a child's mind for a lifetime, so apt is it and yet so little of a cliché. The opera itself focuses on the miseries of child labour, offering a sympathy for the victims that in *Peter Grimes* had been diverted to Grimes himself.

Britten's principal contribution to the Festival of Britain was *Billy Budd*, first given at Covent Garden on 1 December 1951.[7] It is arguably his finest full-length opera, on a large scale (in four acts, later reduced to two), with a large orchestra once more and with a prose libretto by Forster and Crozier based on Melville's short story; but its all-male cast, as demanded by the plot, tended to diminish its appeal to the wider opera-going public. The framework of an opera within a narration is also somewhat distancing, creating an artificiality that is entirely appropriate in more intimate examples such as *The Rape*, but which again erects a psychological barrier that is absent from *Grimes*. It is perhaps for these reasons that *Billy Budd* long failed to achieve the recognition that its musico-dramatic qualities deserved. Yet again an opera by Britten focuses on a victim of unjust oppression: a young man is impressed into naval service, incurs the resentment of his immediate superior, is taunted into unintentional homicide, and is executed by hanging from the yardarm. It is a brutal tale, and perhaps it would be unbearable if told otherwise than as the recollection of a retired mariner.

Gloriana was composed to celebrate the coronation of Elizabeth II and performed in her presence on 8 June 1953, six days after the coronation itself. The complaint that its story of Elizabeth I's relationship with Essex was inappropriate for the occasion has a measure of justification, and the opera long suffered under this cloud. It now seems a workmanlike, but not an outstanding opera. It was quickly overshadowed by *The Turn of the Screw*, a major masterpiece in chamber-opera form first heard at La Fenice, Venice, on 14 September 1954. As a set of fifteen variations on a twelve-note theme, the whole corresponding to a dramatic action in two acts of eight scenes

[6] There is an obvious parallel in the prologue to Strauss's *Ariadne auf Naxos*, though the ambience—and indeed the compositional prehistory—of this opera are wholly different.

[7] A month after completion on 2 Nov. An equally timely offering was his 'realization', with Imogen Holst, of Purcell's *Dido*, produced at the Lyric Theatre, Hammersmith, on 1 May. But the flowering of the early music movement has made Britten's version of Purcell seem dated.

each (with a short prologue preceding the first scene), the opera has long been recognized as possessing a musical cohesion rarely achieved in dramatic forms. Henry James's ghost story offered an opportunity for the suggestion of evil too deep to be specified; of the two children, Flora is saved and Miles is lost in the context of a dualism that contributes powerfully to the opera's sinister effect.

Britten's next opera was a setting of a Chester mystery play, *Noye's Fludde*, first given in Orford parish church on 18 June 1958. It is both Britten's most ambitious work to include amateur performers and a foretaste of his later conception of the 'church parable'. The amateur contribution, from both adults and children, is integral to the conception, which involves a wholesale adoption of the deliberately naïve, represented by music for solo children's voices, amateur bugle-players and percussionists, and by the inclusion of congregational hymns. While the community spirit of a medieval mystery play is thus brilliantly recreated, the opera is thereby restricted to productions in comparable circumstances.

Then in 1960 came *A Midsummer Night's Dream* (Aldeburgh, 11 June), a shortened version of Shakespeare's play made by the composer and Peter Pears. It is a magically evocative score, capped by some wonderfully knock-about musical humour for the 'rude mechanicals' and their play of 'Pyramus and Thisbe'. It is a less artfully constructed but at the same time a more spontaneous and appealing work than *The Turn of the Screw*; it was also to be Britten's last full-length opera of more or less conventional design. It marks a watershed in his composing career, and it is a convenient point at which to take stock of other operatic endeavours in the fifteen years since *Grimes*.

Britten's hope then that 'the willingness of the [Sadler's Wells] Company to undertake the presentation of new operas will encourage other composers to write works in what is, in my opinion, the most exciting of musical forms'[8] was not immediately fulfilled. The Sadler's Wells company retreated from its initiative, for one thing, and it was the English Opera Group that was to provide the principal framework for operatic innovation both by Britten himself and, with his friendly encouragement, one or two others. The chief of these was Lennox Berkeley, whose *Nelson* was one of Sadler's Wells's few enterprises in those years but alas a not very successful one (22 September 1954); earlier that year his mildly amusing one-act opera *A Dinner Engagement* had been given at Aldeburgh. Berkeley's *Ruth*, a short biblical opera in three scenes with a libretto by Crozier, was produced at the Scala Theatre in London in 1956.

Surprisingly enough it was Covent Garden, under vigorous and realistic management, and with adequate if hardly generous funding, that offered the

---

[8] Britten, 'Introduction', 8.

greatest scope for new English operas in the conventional format; the Royal Opera had in any case taken over *Peter Grimes* and subsequently produced *Billy Budd* and *Gloriana*. After *Grimes* its first new opera of note was Bliss's *The Olympians* (1949), with a potentially attractive scenario based on a legend according to which the gods, after belief in them had lapsed, descended to earth disguised as a troupe of strolling players. From time to time (at least in the opera) they resume their divine powers. But J. B. Priestley made ponderous work of the libretto and the music nowhere achieves the dramatic aptitude for which Britten had demonstrated such flair in *Albert Herring*, surely the best of models for a story of intrigue in a small French town in 1836. Christopher Hassall, whose uneasy collaboration with Walton had been a feat of heroic endurance, provided the libretto for Bliss's *Tobias and the Angel*, devised for television (1960) and given a stage production in 1961. But it too has left no lasting mark.

Vaughan Williams's *The Pilgrim's Progress* (1951) has been discussed already,[9] and the next new English opera at Covent Garden, after *Billy Budd* and *Gloriana*, was Walton's *Troilus and Cressida*, produced after a prolonged gestation in 1954. Hassall was an experienced man of the theatre, a long-standing collaborator with Ivor Novello, but hardly an obvious choice as librettist for an opera meant to challenge and emulate Britten on his own ground. In the event, *Troilus* offered a viable stylistic alternative within the conventions broadly assumed in *Grimes* and *Budd*. Walton's lyrical gift, when it can be discerned beneath the surface activity, was of a more conventional cast than Britten's, not only in purely melodic terms but also as regards its underlying harmonic processes; even so, it offers enough in the way of aural challenge to offset the ever-present threat of sentimentality. Walton was acutely conscious of this and always tried to prevent conductors of his music from dawdling (the choice of Malcolm Sargent for *Troilus* led inevitably to friction, for he seems not to have bothered even to master the score).[10] When *Troilus* was revived in 1976 Walton cut the score mercilessly, with some benefits to its dramatic cohesion; nevertheless, a body of critical opinion still prefers the earlier version. At that stage the part of Cressida was remodelled to fit the mezzo-soprano range of Janet Baker. One cannot help feeling that so much agonizing over the work—the subject had been proposed as far back as 1947—stemmed from a fundamental insecurity: so tragic a tale of deception and treachery needed a directness of response that was in neither the composer's nor the librettist's nature.[11]

---

[9] See Ch. 5, p. 346.

[10] Kennedy, *Portrait of Walton*, 179–80, citing R. T. Savage, *A Voice from the Pit: Reminiscences of an Orchestral Musician* (Newton Abbott, 1988), 151–2.

[11] Walton had been direct enough in *Belshazzar's Feast*, it is true, but he had since developed a fastidiousness that may have been the result of a subconscious recognition of his limitations.

Walton's second opera, *The Bear*, based on a short play by Chekhov, is much more successful in its very different way, using parody to point up the absurdities of the plot and character. Its gifted librettist was Paul Dehn, who also wrote the book for Berkeley's one-act opera *Castaway*. Both were given at the Aldeburgh Festival in 1967.

The year after *Troilus*, Covent Garden staged Tippett's *Midsummer Marriage*, the first opera by a composer whose dramatic potential was proved in the event to be the equal of Britten's. As in *A Child of our Time* he wrote the libretto himself, as he was to do in all his subsequent operas. Except for *King Priam*, moreover, he was his own myth-maker. At a local level the diction of his operas is often forced and the incidents scarcely believable; but the words are clothed in wonderfully apposite music and the underlying imagery is often powerful and coherent. *The Midsummer Marriage* has as its subject the reconciliation not of opposites but of two characters whose natures have to be refined before they are capable of harmonized union. The parallel with *The Magic Flute* is obvious. The entire action is encompassed within twenty-four hours of midsummer, and is set in a no-man's land between the worlds of reality and of magic. It is a land where ordinary passions and the events to which they give rise are mingled with a culture of worship in dance and song, a realm of heightened imagination in which the participants are free to address their own natures. The music has that springy vitality so characteristic of the earlier Tippett, where contact is kept with the roots of his style in Renaissance counterpoint and Baroque formalism. There is an infectious optimism about the whole score, even during the trials that precede the final reunion, that marks this as one of Tippett's sunniest creations.

King Priam, which followed in 1962, has a good claim to be considered Tippett's finest opera, partly because his inexhaustible thirst for complex imagery and cultural cross-reference are here subordinated to the demands of a universal myth. Although it differs sharply from *The Midsummer Marriage* in mood and consequently in style, *King Priam* now seems to represent less of a distinct change of direction than a striking development of certain aspects of Tippett's long-established idiom. Rhythmic drive is enhanced by means of more subtle durational schemes and by a flexible technique of 'tempo modulation'; vocal declamation has become freer, and a propensity for ornamental accompaniment (cf. Ex. 5.13 above) is carried to a greater extreme. The harmonic idiom has become more complex, but a tonal basis has not been discarded. The score is at once a work of superabundant originality and a disciplined, even ascetic, response to the pity of war and the inescapability of its evil.

Commissioned (like Britten's *War Requiem*) for the Coventry Festival and given there on 29 May 1962, *King Priam* won critical respect from the outset, though its idiom was still regarded as strange. The wildly rushing violin passages associated with Hecuba had to be transferred to the piano, being thought unplayable as they stood.[12] It had a much less rapturous welcome than the *War Requiem*, which was also bedevilled by imperfections in its first performance, but time has softened its harder edges and the composer's entire approach now seems fully justified.

We may look ahead briefly to *The Knot Garden*, Tippett's third opera, which was given at Covent Garden on 2 December 1970. Conceptually this reverts to the world of *The Midsummer Marriage*, but the scenario now involves a more complex play of sexual relationships, including homosexual relationships, while at the same time the treatment is tauter and the interplay (musical as well as dramatic) more ornately patterned. On the other hand, the idiom is anything but restrained. Its violence, however, is related exclusively to the inner world of the characters and their sharply circumscribed external world, bounded as it is by the enclosed garden of their society. It is this sense of musical and social delimitation that makes *The Knot Garden* so disturbing an experience.

In three widely spaced masterpieces Tippett had redefined the parameters of opera without questioning the relevance of the traditional theatrical form. In his three 'parables for church performance', Britten did precisely that. It must be admitted that in the 1960s the temptation to achieve significance through the interpretation of widely divergent cultural referents—a practice traceable to Pound and Eliot in English poetry and avidly seized on by Tippett in the 1940s and 1950s—was still as strong as ever. In his *War Requiem* Britten juxtaposed the timeless liturgy of the Catholic Church with the indignant poetry of Wilfred Owen. In *Curlew River* (1964), a Japanese Noh play about a woman's search for the soul of her son is transposed to a medieval East Anglian setting, a monastic evening service in which the abbot and his monks act out the story as it unfolds. Costumed singers and instrumentalists walk in procession down the aisle of the church while singing the Compline plainsong hymn 'Te lucis ante terminum'; at the end they resume it as they return. That the details of the medieval setting are quite unhistorical is beside the point. An atmosphere is created, not just by the setting in (ideally) a medieval church but above all by the spare, metrically free, tonally evocative music of chanting, recitative, and ornamental accompaniment by a small instrumental group.

In the two subsequent parables Britten and William Plomer, his librettist, drew on biblical material, so making a trilogy of works of respectively Oriental, Hebrew, and Christian inspiration, all subsumed within the same orbit of a medieval Christian meditation. Perhaps 'meditative' is the

---

[12] E. W. White, *Tippett and his Operas* (London, 1979), 92. The writing, despite the optimistic view expressed there, has continued to give trouble, but a more recent and far more convincing device has been to divide these unison torrents of sound between the 1st and 2nd violins (personal communication from Mr Barry Griffiths, leader of the ENO orchestra). Quite why no one thought of that in 1962 is hard to understand.

best adjective with which to describe the group as a whole; this need not exclude the colourful barbarities of the Babylonian court in *The Burning Fiery Furnace* (1966) or the emotional drama of *The Prodigal Son* (1968), but it makes clear the reflective response invited by all these works. In this they resemble Britten's five canticles, but within a more generous framework.

The parables occupied all Britten's operatic energies during the 1960s, but after that he reverted to a more theatrical mode. *Owen Wingrave*, written for television and broadcast in 1971, is inevitably compared with *The Turn of the Screw*, being another adaptation from Henry James by Myfanwy Piper. Skilful though it is, and more complex in its imaginative use of twelve-note material, the opera suffers in the comparison, mainly because of its less subtle characterization. It was staged in 1973, and should be considered as definitive in that form: television, despite many experiments, is not usually an effective medium for opera.

In that same year Britten produced his final operatic masterpiece and (at last, one might think) allowed himself the overt expression of homoeroticism in a stage work.[13] *Death in Venice*, based on Thomas Mann's novella, portrays the obsession of the writer Aschenbach for Tadzio, the Polish boy whom he watches but never meets. This is the psychological drama of Aschenbach himself; Tadzio and his family only dance, not sing, and the other vocal elements remain in the background. The preponderance of recitative, accompanied, as so often before in Britten's operas, by the piano, gives a dry touch that aptly characterizes Aschenbach's personality while throwing into bright relief the contrast of the surrounding sunlit holiday-making. In the end the vision of beauty fades: the holiday-makers go home and the old man dies without achieving either a physical or a spiritual union, too fastidious for the former and morally unfit for the latter.

Death in Venice, like the novella itself, is a depressing work, since its protagonist so plainly falls short of his ideals. Perhaps its message is that the worship of human beauty—male or female—will never succeed in exalting the human spirit above the ephemeral.[14] At the heart of this opera is an ambiguity that manifests itself in the breaking down of formal and tonal norms. As in the church parables, the audience is invited to reflect, this time on the imperfection of purely terrestrial ideals. It is difficult not to identify a biographical element in Britten's choice of subject.

---

[13] It is implicit in previous operas, especially *Billy Budd* and *The Turn of the Screw*. Britten's greater daring in *Death in Venice* cannot be unconnected with the partial decriminalization of homosexual acts in 1967; yet that would not have legalized a sexual encounter between Aschenbach and Tadzio. More significant, perhaps, is the growing tolerance by a broad public of a pervading element throughout European literature and of its exploration on the stage as well as in other art-forms. As Britten's opera shows, that is not incompatible with a moral theme independent of sexual orientation.

[14] For an appraisal of the work's philosophical basis see C. Hindley, 'Platonic Elements in "Death in Venice"', *ML* 73 (1992), 407–29; his reading is somewhat more optimistic than mine.

Britten's operatic œuvre was enormously influential from the outset. At first it stimulated the writing of full-length operas for large forces, and it offered encouragement in that respect to the one other major force of the period, Michael Tippett. Then the adoption of chamber-operatic forms enabled further experiment to take place on a manageable scale, and a less self-conscious approach to comedy in music widened the scope of operatic experience. Finally the church-parable form sparked off (or at the very least was an integral part of) a movement towards a mixed genre of 'music theatre', principally amongst the younger generation led by Peter Maxwell Davies and Harrison Birtwistle. But the basis of Britten's achievement was ultimately his profound understanding of the human voice and of its potential for expressing in song the most delicate inflections of the English language. If in the last resort the finest fruits of that understanding are to be found in his settings of great European literature, its application to the necessarily more mundane products of his librettists (Shakespeare alone excepted) is what gives his operas their special quality of an intimate engagement with the developing emotions of his characters. To this was added an instinctive grasp of musico-dramatic pace, something acquired from a deep knowledge of the Italian tradition at its best and remote in its aesthetic from the Wagnerian, but with an important contribution from the French and Russian approach to word-setting.[15]

Of a large number of composers who tried their hand at opera between 1945 and 1975, few succeeded in having their works brought to the professional stage, and fewer still in writing work of lasting appeal. Elizabeth Maconchy created interest in 1957 with a one-act comic opera, *The Sofa*, later joined by two others to make a trilogy first performed in 1977. Phyllis Tate's *The Lodger*, given at the Royal Academy in 1960, was warmly received but has not entered the repertory. A more populist approach was espoused by Antony Hopkins (b. 1921) and Joseph Horowitz (b. 1926) in their short pieces for The Intimate Opera Company, founded in 1952 to bring piano-accompanied opera to small provincial towns. Unfortunately, their derivative idiom has not worn well. A word should be spared for Alan Bush (1900–95), a Communist whose socialist-inspired operas were all first heard in East Germany. *Wat Tyler* was awarded a Festival of Britain prize in 1951 but was first given in Leipzig in 1953 (and in England only in 1974); the best of the others, *Men of Blackmoor*, was produced in Weimar (1956), and by the Oxford University Opera Club in 1961. But the idiom of these is sadly unoriginal. One of the more prolific and successful opera composers of the period was Malcolm Williamson (b. 1931), an Australian who came to England in 1953 and who in 1975 became Master of the Queen's Music on

---

[15] *Pelléas et Mélisande* is an obvious instance of this, but it is tempting also to postulate the influence of Dargomïzhsky's all-recitative Pushkin opera *The Stone Guest* amongst numerous better-known Russian works.

the death of Bliss. Richard Rodney Bennett had several operas (two of them substantial) produced in the decade 1961–70, while Nicholas Maw (b. 1935) had his second opera, *The Rising of the Moon*, produced at Glyndebourne in 1970. Gordon Crosse (b. 1937) set Yeats's *Purgatory* for the Cheltenham Festival in 1966 and followed this success with *The Grace of Todd* (1967) and *The Story of Vasco* (1974). Each of these last three composers has ventured a relatively exploratory idiom, with variable success, in a genre that depends above all on communicability.

The earlier dramatic works of Peter Maxwell Davies (b. 1934) and Harrison Birtwistle (b. 1934) injected new life into a medium that in the hands of more conservative composers normally offered neither the challenge of the wholly original nor the prospect of wide and lasting appeal. Like Alexander Goehr (b. 1932), son of the German composer, conductor, and musicologist Walter Goehr, they studied composition in the early 1950s at the Royal Manchester College of Music under Richard Hall (1903–82), himself a composer of distinction.[16] Goehr's own *Arden muss sterben* was produced at Hamburg in 1967, and in London, as *Arden must die*, in 1974; like his two colleagues, he contributed, at first more effectively than in opera, to what came to be known as 'music theatre', notably in the 'triptych' consisting of *Naboth's Vineyard* (1968), *Shadowplay* (1970), and *Sonata about Jerusalem* (1970).

Music theatre, if taken to exclude opera, is hard to define: it tends to involve such features as small instrumental and vocal forces, an element of ballet, and a mixture of narrative and drama, separately or in any combination. Britten's church parables, though expressly not conceived for the theatre, are valid representatives of it, and indeed it is characteristic that secular examples are also readily transferable to the concert or recital hall.

Maxwell Davies, whose dramatic œuvre is conspicuous for its overall variety, was an early and radical innovator in this genre, which became linked indissolubly with the activities of his performing group The Pierrot Players and its successor The Fires of London. Neither group was expressly or exclusively theatrical in aim; it was rather that a growing desire, especially by Davies and Birtwistle, to exploit various levels of expression—movement, sound (words and notes), and scenery—led inexorably to quasi-dramatic forms. Birtwistle's *Punch and Judy*, first performed at Aldeburgh in 1968, is classed as a one-act opera, but its ritualized form and brutal sound-world ally it to music theatre.[17] Davies's *Revelation and Fall*

---

[16] Hall became Director of Music at Dartington Hall in 1956 and exercised a beneficial influence on numerous aspiring composers who attended its regular courses and its summer schools. His own idiom was founded on Schoenbergian serialism.

[17] The gifted librettist of this and several similar works was Stephen Pruslin, a pianist and an ardent advocate of both composers. The concept of music theatre, though not the name, can be traced back to Stravinsky's *Reynard* and *The Soldier's Tale*; The Pierrot Players was formed expressly to perform

(translated from a prose-poem by Georg Trakl; later revised) was first given in London (Conway Hall) in 1968; there followed *L'homme armé* (1968), *Eight Songs for a Mad King* (1969), *Vesalii Icones* (1969), and a ballet, *Nocturnal Dances* (1970).

Meanwhile Birtwistle had written (in addition to *Monodrama, Linoi II,* and *Medusa*, all withdrawn) *Down by the Greenwood Side* (1969), perhaps the most enduring of all such works first heard in the late 1960s. The strange juxtaposition of the folk play of St George with the traditional ballad 'The Cruel Mother' has no obvious justification, but they are brought into relationship towards the end, when Father Christmas (from the play) becomes the narrator of the ballad; the whole, despite its contrasts of black humour and genuine tragedy, is curiously evocative. The range of instrumental sonorities drawn from the ensemble of nine players is extraordinary: Birtwistle in this and other works of the period created a personal soundscape that at times achieves a ferocity matched by few other composers.

While Birtwistle pursued other experimental genres in the early 1970s, Davies built on his dramatic instincts to create the 'masque' *Blind Man's Buff* (1972) and *Miss Donnithorne's Maggot* (1974); he also revised *L'homme armé* as *Missa L'homme armé* (1971), and above all finalized his opera *Taverner*, written in 1962–8 and eventually performed at Covent Garden in July 1972. *Taverner* was the largest of a series of works deriving from a preoccupation with both the technology and the historical context of Renaissance music, from the early orchestral *Prolation* (1958) onwards. In particular he had explored some aspects of Renaissance Mass composition in the ironical and sacrilegious *Missa L'homme armé*, and English instrumental writing in two orchestral fantasias 'on an In nomine of John Taverner' (1962, 1964), and in a series of seven 'In nomines' (partly arrangements) for wind quintet, harp, and string quartet (1963). The opera, which is comparatively straightforward in idiom, at least on the rhythmic level, deals with the dilemma of a composer caught up in religious controversy to the detriment of his work.[18] The atonal sound-world of nearly all this music, however, is as remote from that of the sixteenth century as it is possible to imagine: the raw material has been transmuted into something quite alien. This alienation from a norm that is assumed but not necessarily perceived is essential to Davies's art; it sometimes takes on a blasphemous character, reflecting perhaps a personal

Schoenberg's *Pierrot Lunaire*, not a dramatic work but an expressionist one that has certainly been influential. In many ways the English avant-garde of the 1960s and 1970s has simply continued that of the second and third decades of the century, emulating both its musical techniques and its propensity for genre-crossing.

[18] Davies reflected a common misunderstanding in his belief that Taverner wrote more than one In nomine, and in his assumption that Taverner stopped composing Latin church music after becoming an agent of Cromwell in Boston (see Vol. I, pp. 226–7). The Sept. 1972 issue of *Tempo* is devoted to *Taverner*.

antipathy or ambivalence but in any case distorting the religious images that are often present in his work.

Other Genres: The Older Composers

Naturally there were many composers born before 1900 who were still active in 1945; but the disturbing effect of two world wars and the concomitant radical changes in society and its predilections made them (or now make them) seem more old-fashioned than they really were. Figures like Cyril Scott (d. 1970) and Roger Quilter (d. 1953), though they continued to compose and to publish, were now quite out of touch with contemporary developments. Bax (d. 1953) and Moeran (d. 1950) had run out of new ideas, the former kept in the public eye through being Master of the King's (and finally the Queen's) Musick, the latter inspired by his wife to write a series of works for cello as well as composing the charming but insubstantial oboe quartet. Ireland (d. 1962) had virtually stopped composing. Bliss (d. 1975), who succeeded Bax as Master of the Queen's Musick, was not at all inactive during these years, but his style developed little. His later choral works, *The Beatitudes* (for the Coventry Festival in 1962) and *Mary of Magdala* (1963), are perhaps the most effective, traditional without being entirely predictable, but he also wrote the orchestral *Meditations on a Theme of John Blow* and a violin concerto, both in 1955, and the more adventurous *Knot of Riddles* for baritone and eleven instruments (1963). There is more to be said for the later choral and organ music of Howells, whose *Hymnus Paradisi* was first heard in 1950 and who followed this with the equally striking but less personal *Missa Sabrinensis* (1954) and *Stabat mater* (1963).

Havergal Brian (1876–1972) stands out in this period as a lone survivor who never relinquished his quest for originality. Between the wars he wrote a good deal of ambitious choral and orchestral music, very little of it published or even performed. After the second war signs of interest began to appear in a composer whose enormous *Gothic Symphony* had become a legend; at the same time he himself was paring down the scale of his music, adopting an almost Haydnesque approach to symphonic form. His symphonies nos. 6–32 belong to this late period: none of them is long, and none of them calls for the vocal forces required by three of their predecessors, though a large orchestra is still used. It is harder to define the idiom. The Straussian approach to harmony and tonality, which had long fortified Brian as it had Bantock, Bax, and Bridge, has been replaced by a dour soundscape in which strong tonal referents are articulated by seemingly casual progressions. The eighth symphony—composed in 1949, first performed in 1954, published in facsimile in 1973—in B flat minor, in one movement, exemplifies these characteristics. The large orchestra includes triple woodwind, standard brass with the addition of a euphonium, and up to ten percussionists, together with piano, harp, and organ pedals. If there is a parallel, it is with Sibelius's seventh symphony or for that matter *Tapiola*, with which it shares a brooding intensity; yet it lacks their variety and at times is even more clotted in texture. Nor does it succeed in achieving, out of perhaps equally unpromising materials, the melodic organicism that distinguishes Sibelius's method of progressive development. Indeed its pedestrian melodic content, yoked as it is to an unadventurous rhythmic idiom, is this symphony's weakest feature. Yet that is not quite the whole story, for the work is formally ingenious, embracing two passacaglias of which the first at least is an imaginatively austere invention, the whole conception having the cohesion as well as the solidity of a marmoreal tragedy.[19]

The strange figure of Kaikhosru Sorabji (1892–1988) made little impact at this period, for he banned performances of his music in 1940 and permitted them once more (apart from a few recordings made by himself in the 1960s) only in 1976. He continued to compose in what one assumes to have been a development of his earlier, impossibly complex, idiom, but he kept himself in the public eye as essayist (*Mi contra fa*, 1947) and in a series of pungent contributions to *The Musical Times*. He may have been misunderstood, but if so he had only himself to blame.

Quite different from that of Brian (let alone of Sorabji) was the achievement of and recognition accorded to Vaughan Williams in his old age. Of the major works first heard after the war, *The Pilgrim's Progress* had been several decades in the writing, and the sixth symphony (completed in 1947 and premiered in 1948) belongs with the fourth and fifth as a trilogy of essentially abstract works.[20] He wrote several film scores between 1946 and 1950, one of which, for *Scott of the Antarctic*, provided some of the material for the *Sinfonia Antartica* (1952, first performed in January 1953). The composition of this sombre large-scale work, for soprano solo, women's chorus (both wordless), and orchestra, seemed to have a liberating effect on Vaughan Williams, for he went on to compose two more symphonies (no. 8 in D minor, finalized in 1956, and no. 9 in E minor, finalized in 1958), not to mention the cantata *Hodie*, the tuba concerto (both 1954), and numerous smaller vocal and instrumental works. In all of these there is a tendency towards stylistic simplification, countered in the larger compositions by an uninhibited approach to orchestral colour. In 'O taste and see', a tiny unaccompanied anthem (with organ introduction) composed for the

[19] The published score has a sympathetic introduction by Robert Simpson. The standard work is M. MacDonald, *The Symphonies of Havergal Brian*, 3 vols. (London, 1974–83).

[20] See above, pp. 346, 338–41. One listener at least, a critic of the older generation, was profoundly moved by *The Pilgrim's Progress*: 'I think I shall never forget Vaughan Williams's music, so utterly, transcendently sincere, speaking in a universal language to every man in the audience, conveying so devoutly and faithfully the transcendent message of another great Englishman three centuries removed' (Stephen Williams in *Music 1952*, ed. A. Robertson (Harmondsworth, 1952), 198–9; this volume also contains some interesting comment on provincial music in the festival year of 1951).

coronation of Elizabeth II, or in the Lullaby 'Sweet was the song' from *Hodie*, we seem to be transported to the primary roots of Vaughan Williams's inspiration, so straightforward are they in their diatonic simplicity, and yet so completely characteristic of the composer.[21]

Rather different is the style represented by the *Prayer to the Father of Heaven* (Skelton's 'O radiant Luminary of light interminable'), a short motet for unaccompanied chorus (1948) which shares the harmonic language of the sixth symphony but counters its supposed pessimism with an orthodox prayer of transparent sincerity. Sincerity, too, is the hallmark of *Hodie*, a large-scale celebration of the joys of Christmas based on texts from a variety of sources. Its joyous simplicity is sustained in the tuba concerto and in the last two symphonies, the latter marked also by their bold instrumentation and their shafts of wit. And while the eighth descends at times to the absurd, the ninth recaptures at its end the nobility that was at the centre of its composer's character. Few composers have bidden farewell to their public on a note of such striking affirmation.[22]

The Middle Generation: Walton, Rubbra, Rawsthorne, Berkeley

Originality, or the lack of it, is not entirely age-related, and some composers born in the 1890s, like Gordon Jacob (1895–1984) and Eugene Goossens (1893–1962), maintained an idiomatic freshness in their later years that was denied to most of their exact contemporaries. Jacob was noted for skilful orchestration and for a witty Classicism (it hardly deserves to be called 'neo-') in his chamber music, Goossens for a more complex and ornate idiom (though his post-war works are few in number). Even George Dyson's two concertos for strings (1949) have a certain pleasant asperity. But collectively their music counts for little compared with that of (say) Bliss or Howells.

William Walton, who died in 1983, epitomizes the plight of the seeming radical whose underlying musicality is of an essentially conservative cast. No other composer entered the post-war period to such high expectations, and the disappointment—except amongst loyal enthusiasts—was general. His film and occasional music was widely appreciated—he was much more adept at providing for royal ceremonial than Bax or Bliss—but his more

---

[21] The downward opening—soh me ray doh—of 'O taste and see' is a Vaughan Williams 'fingerprint': see Kennedy, *The Works of Ralph Vaughan Williams*, 79.

[22] Not all critics welcomed Vaughan Williams's later music. Kennedy (ibid. 330–1) cites Donald Mitchell's acerbic reaction to *Hodie*: Mitchell was entirely representative of the movement then current for the modernizing and Europeanizing of English music, a powerful advocate of Britten and much preoccupied, in reviewing new music for *The Musical Times*, with defining the limits of a 'valid' style. With the perspective of forty or more years' distance we can begin to evaluate this at times strange music without style-directed inhibitions. Amongst the late works not mentioned in the text a word must be found for the *Ten Blake Songs* for voice and oboe (1957, composed for a film about Blake but extended from eight to ten songs and first performed in Oct. 1958); they reveal an astonishing capacity for the expressive exploitation of minimal resources.

ambitious works seemed to lack the pre-war fire. Both the string quartet (1947) and the violin sonata (1949) are conventionally tonal, and while there is plenty of rhythmic vitality and localized harmonic diversion, the Romantic, almost Brahmsian, bedrock keeps showing through. Walton's rather un-English penchant for instrumental virtuosity sits somewhat uneasily on the sonata, but it is given a more appropriate setting in the unashamedly Romantic concerto for cello (1956–7), a work that attracted little praise when first heard but which has gained in esteem as the polemics of the 1950s have faded. The best of his later orchestral works are the second symphony (1960) and the *Variations on a Theme of Hindemith* (1963). The symphony displays the composer's sardonic wit and his melancholy in the first two movements, concluding with a more powerful passacaglia (on a twelve-note theme) that finally returns the work to its tonal and motivic roots. It is characteristically Waltonian in its instrumental brilliance; less weighty and shorter than the first symphony, it nevertheless possesses a substance not to be expected of the composer's light orchestral works. The 'Hindemith' variations were a labour of love, a long-delayed requital for Hindemith's short-notice first performance of the viola concerto in 1929. The haunting theme[23] infuses the whole work with a Hindemithian flavour which blends well with Walton's snappier idiom, until at the close it is recalled and the work ends peacefully as it had begun.

Some of Walton's smaller orchestral works are enjoyable enough, but he was less happy with his choral *pièces d'occasion*—the coronation Te Deum is a noteworthy exception—and he seemed to find liturgical texts generally uninspiring. The short setting for unaccompanied mixed voices of St Francis of Assisi's *Cantico del Sole* (1974) is on the other hand notable for its expressive intensity. But in the main Walton's later work is characterized by an emotional reticence that may have been born of his extreme sensitivity, not least to criticism of his music—a sensitivity to which the pages of Kennedy's biography bear ample witness. The schoolboy humour was a protective mask paralleled in the gloss of brilliance that is rarely absent from his scores; he too often concealed his inner self for fear of being, like Belshazzar, found wanting, and as a result his music still arouses ambivalent reactions.

Edmund Rubbra pursued an increasingly isolated path after the war. In 1945 his stock stood high: with four symphonies and several other major works to his credit, he was considered the prophet of a new era of counterpoint, a translator of Renaissance polyphony into the modern orchestral medium. In the sixth symphony (1955) he managed to write a comparatively extrovert and effectively scored work; but few of his other post-war orchestral compositions, which include four more symphonies (one choral)

---

[23] From the second movement of the cello concerto (1940).

and three concertos, lived up to this promise of a more aerated style. Peter Evans's lapidary summary of the prospects of a re-evaluation—'The indisputable originality of his methods may never overcome the sobriety of his materials'—is singularly apt.[24] Rubbra will probably be found to have achieved more in his varied output of chamber music, songs, and religious works, many of these last to Latin words. A note of spiritual anguish seems to penetrate his settings even of more joyful texts: the 'Lauda Sion' (1960) for double chorus (with a few phrases for soprano and baritone solo), cruelly difficult to sing, is characteristic, if not without a debt to Britten's *Hymn to St Cecilia*.

The dangers for this generation of composers are aptly illustrated by the later career of Alan Rawsthorne. His technical mastery allowed him to develop an idiom both chromatic and tonal without any loss of individuality. The distinctiveness of the idiom made the pre-war works seem uncommonly promising; its limitations became apparent in a series of post-war works in conventional forms: three symphonies, a second piano concerto, two violin concertos, and yet others for oboe and cello. A wide range of miscellaneous orchestral, chamber, piano, and vocal music testifies to his industry and to the residual attractiveness of his style, but he lacked the sheer panache that often enabled Walton to make an arresting statement out of material fundamentally no more distinguished.

Lennox Berkeley fared better: though equally fastidious, he had a wider palette at his disposal and did not attempt the harsher rigours of tonal argument. At its least persuasive, his music can seem inconsequential (as can Stravinsky's). In the lightweight violin concerto (1961), scored with classical 'chamber orchestra' of strings, two oboes, and two horns, for example, we should be hard put to it to find a clear hint before the end of the first movement of its C major goal, which is demonstrated in the finale to be a genuine focus. In between comes a set of variations on a twelve-note theme, treated almost haphazardly. Yet there is motivic cohesion throughout; the music is neither atonal nor potentially dissonant, but crisp and clear. The openings of the first two movements, and the theme of the finale, will give an idea of the flavour and some of the motivic ingredients (Ex. 6.1). The short third symphony (described as being 'in one movement', though really in three connected movements) has similar virtues but suffers from a lack of incident: the material is really rather insignificant, and the casualness of the tonal argument (if it can be called that) is merely irritating.

Berkeley, like Rubbra, wrote a fair amount of sacred music to Latin texts, both for concert and for liturgical use. The *Stabat mater* (1947) is a fine, austere work. There is also a large output in the smaller forms: part-songs, solo songs, chamber music, and compositions for piano. His music stands for

---

[24] *BHMB*, vi. 229, following a sympathetic review of the orchestral music.

Ex. 6.1

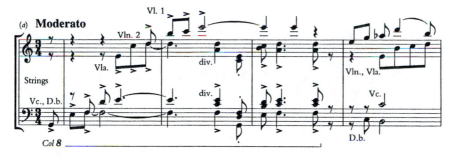

continued

Ex. 6.1, continued

Lennox Berkeley, Violin Concerto (London, 1962): (*a*) pp. 1–2 (1st mvt.); (*b*) p. 24 (theme of 2nd mvt.); (*c*) p. 37 (main theme of finale)

taste, style, and approachability; but while he evaded the shadows of the past that haunted Walton, his invention lacks the distinction that marks Tippett and Britten as the masters of their generation in this period.

Tippett, Britten: Non-operatic Work

It was *A Child of our Time* that brought Tippett to wider public notice in the 1940s, but he did not court easy popularity, and he was thought to be a difficult, even a maverick, composer, during most of the period under discussion. In addition to his operas he wrote amongst other works a third string quartet (1945–6), a second and a third symphony (1956–7, 1970–2), the fine song-cycle *The Heart's Assurance* (1950–1), a second and a third piano sonata (1962, 1972), a piano concerto (1953), the *Concerto for Orchestra* (1962–3), and his oratorio *The Vision of St Augustine* (1962–3). Indeed one could single out the 1950s and 1960s as a particularly fruitful and rewarding period for Tippett, despite public hesitation. In the early 1970s, just as his acceptance was becoming assured, he discovered new ways to shock: stylistic discongruity exacerbated by undigested quotation (for example from Beethoven's ninth symphony in his own third symphony), and the exploration of unconventional modern life-styles in *The Knot Garden* and subsequently.

A certain dryness in the harmony makes Tippett's music for piano alone and for strings alone somewhat forbidding; he is much more approachable when these are combined with the voice or with other instruments. His sensitivity to literary texts is shown in *The Heart's Assurance* (to poems by Sidney Keyes and Alun Lewis), which takes the ecstatic vocal writing and ornamental pianism of *Boyhood's End* to new heights in the context of a genuine cycle of songs. His mastery of orchestral writing is shown above all in the second symphony and in the *Concerto for Orchestra*, in both of which the chamber-like treatment of groups of instruments is shown to be quite compatible with a genuinely orchestral conception. The symphony is surely the outstanding example of its kind from the 1950s—excluding only the scarcely comparable ones by Vaughan Williams but bearing in mind everything that Brian, Rubbra, Rawsthorne, Berkeley, Searle, Fricker, Simpson, Arnold, Alwyn, and others were able to produce during that ten-year span. It possesses the solid brilliance of a carefully executed chalk drawing: every tonal area, including the rock-like C around which the whole work revolves, attracts a series of fifth-related tonalities that shade off, as it were, into the tonal distance; so that everything seems related to everything else, and marked changes of tonal direction, when they occur, are all the more arresting. The 'second subject' of the first movement, for example, has an iridescence produced by this tonal glow: melodically it cadences in A flat, but the subordinate parts occupy the areas of E flat, B flat, F, and even beyond (Ex. 6.2). The scherzo is a rhythmic invention of extraordinary ebullience (Ex. 6.3), while the finale is an energetic passacaglia. The work was found difficult to play, and actually broke down at its first performance; yet it is one of those pieces in which every note is in place and which, once mastered, speaks with a luminous voice from first to last.

The same can be said of the *Concerto for Orchestra*, which opposes groups of instruments characterized by their own material as well as combining them (and their constituents) in novel ways. The result is a more chamber-like quality than in the symphonies and a dynamic restraint that belies the implications of its title. It is rhetorically novel, too, in abandoning symphonic dialectic for the sake of simple juxtaposition; and it ends as it began, without the usual gestures of inchoation or finality.

The Vision of St Augustine (1963–5) is a kind of meditation on time and eternity, based on a passage from the *Confessions* with additions from the Bible and the liturgy, and scored for baritone solo, chorus, and orchestra. It exhibits many of the stylistic features of his other works of the 1960s, not least *King Priam*; but the commanding role given to the baritone solo (representing St Augustine), and the low accompanying registers that it generates, make this a rather drab work, notwithstanding some exultant

Ex. 6.2

Michael Tippett, Symphony no. 2, 1st mvt. (London, 1958), pp. 7–8 (some performance
indications omitted)

Ex. 6.3

Michael Tippett, Symphony no. 2, 3rd mvt. (London, 1958), p. 70 (some performance indications omitted)

choral writing at the visionary climax. It stands rather uncomfortably between *A Child of our Time* and *The Mask of Time*, which reflect Tippett's humanitarian concerns and his philosophy of life respectively. One might infer that Tippett was moved by St Augustine's vision of eternity mainly on the intellectual level; his essentially agnostic outlook precluded a complete identification with Christian mysticism, and the artificiality of his Latin compilation seems to bear this out. All the same, it is a work of substance that does not yield its secrets to the casual listener, and it has few parallels (Messiaen's *Chronochromie* springs to mind) as an exercise in the musical expression of the idea of time.[25]

[25] Tippett must have been well aware of Messiaen's temporal language, and his work presents many analogies in this and other respects. There is a sympathetic account of *The Vision* in Kemp, *Tippett*, 386–401.

Tippett's third symphony (1970–2) seems in retrospect to stand at the beginning of a prolonged 'third period', anticipated in *The Knot Garden* and its offshoot *Songs for Dov* (1969–70), in which the formal classicism of his middle works is discarded in favour of a freer use of his rhythmic and colouristic discoveries and a questioning, if not a total abandonment, of musical and social convention. This development in Tippett's work will be considered in the following chapter.

Benjamin Britten was a much more prolific composer than Tippett, perhaps because he was always more at ease with what might be called the 'common practice' of the years 1918–45, a sort of neoclassicism based on long-standing tonal principles but allowing a large measure of harmonic freedom. We may see this at work in Britten's second string quartet (1945), where the core C major of the opening soon gives way first to G, then to D, and after that to a less stable tonal environment. Rhythmically it is a straightforward work, with a wild 6/8 tarantella in second place and a 'Chacony' (in obvious homage to Purcell, for the 250th anniversary of whose death it was written) in slow 3/2 to conclude. It was one of Britten's technical achievements in his later years to evade the shackles of conventional rhythmic organization while resisting abstract structuralism and excessive complexity; similarly he developed the possibilities of motivic organization from being a mere gloss on tonally focused melody to a principle of construction, but without recourse to wholesale serialism.

Britten in fact wrote very little music in the conventional abstract forms: not a single symphony of a standard type (though the wartime *Sinfonia da Requiem* is close to being one), and of the later chamber works only the third string quartet (1975) and a cello sonata (1961) are at all significant. The most enduring orchestral work of this period is the *Symphony for Cello and Orchestra* (1962–3), a concerto, or at least a *sinfonia concertante*, in all but name.

These works of the 1960s and early 1970s are all important, and to them one should add their predecessor the *Six Metamorphoses after Ovid*, for oboe solo (1951), and their contemporaries the three suites for solo cello (1964, 1967, and 1971), which like the symphony and the sonata were written for his great friend Rostropovich. But it was in vocal music of all kinds, including the operas, that Britten made his most distinctive contribution. The cantata *St Nicolas* (1948) and the *Spring Symphony* (1949) are joyous celebrations: the former devised to exploit the resources of a boys' public school,[26] the latter a cantata in all but name, an anthology of poems from the sixteenth century to Auden, arranged in four movements and set for three soloists, mixed chorus, boys' choir, and orchestra. The *War Requiem*,

---

[26] Lancing College, for its centenary; but the first performance took place at Aldeburgh (Kennedy, *Britten*, 188).

composed for the Coventry Festival of 1962 and in a spirit of reconciliation between two countries that had wrought so much destruction on each other, is one of the very few large-scale English choral works of the present century to have won universal acceptance—*Gerontius* is certainly one and *Belshazzar's Feast* (though much shorter and devoid of spirituality) perhaps another. It is rewarding to sing, ingenious in structure, and varied in mood while maintaining a level of high seriousness throughout. The poems of Wilfred Owen are like a modern trope to the liturgical text, to which they often act as an ironical comment: this is nowhere more so than when Owen's savage poem about the sacrifice of Isaac, in which 'Abram' slays not only his son but 'half the seed of Europe one by one', follows the 'Quam olim Abrahae' of the Offertorium, the promise of holy light to Abraham and his seed for ever. At the very end, when the blood and thunder of the 'Libera me' have died away, and the ethereal notes of the 'In paradisum' have run their course, the clanging bells introduce the solemn chords that we have heard twice before to recall us to the task of prayer for the dead.

It seems that Britten—whatever his actual beliefs—possessed, like Handel, Elgar, and Vaughan Williams, the capacity to evoke a genuinely religious response within a framework of established Christianity, be it Catholic or Protestant. His at times childlike (but never childish) use of religious imagery is reminiscent of Haydn but can more readily be traced back to the late-medieval use of popular drama and the static visual images that once adorned our churches in great profusion. Britten's identification with these roots was one of his great strengths, and together with his profound knowledge of English—and of a great part of European—literature enabled him to address his generation with a unique poetic authority.

It is difficult not to accept that the majority of Britten's finest vocal works have a religious content; and—given that a complete survey would be impracticable here—a few words will be said about the religious songs. *The Holy Sonnets of John Donne* were composed in the *annus mirabilis* of 1945 and achieve an even greater intensity than the *Michelangelo Sonnets*, as well as being his only sonnet sequence in English. He subsequently channelled his small-scale religious settings into the form of the 'canticle', a nomenclature stumbled on as a description for his setting of a strange poem by Francis Quarles, 'My beloved is mine', for high voice (preferably tenor) and piano (1947). This is hardly more than an extended song, but Britten afterwards employed the concept to cover a variety of approaches. The second canticle, *Abraham and Isaac* (1952), is a setting of a Chester miracle play for alto (originally female),[27] tenor, and piano, the voice of God being represented by the two voices in unearthly proximity. The shocking directness of the medieval telling of this story is handled with no trace of irony; that was to

[27] The first singers were Kathleen Ferrier and Peter Pears.

come, with an appropriate musical reminiscence, in the quite different context of the *War Requiem*. Canticle III, 'Still falls the rain' (Edith Sitwell, 1956) is for tenor, horn, and piano and takes the form of a theme and variations for horn and piano interspersed with vocal verses in recitative. At the end all three join together. This is perhaps the most impressive of all the canticles. The fourth, a setting of T. S. Eliot's *Journey of the Magi*, for three male voices (countertenor, tenor, and baritone) and piano, was written early in 1971. In this and the fifth canticle, a setting of T. S. Eliot's early poem *The Death of Saint Narcissus* for tenor and harp (1974), the religious imagery is strained and the mannerisms—amongst them an over-fondness for verbal repetition—become irritating.

One other late vocal work deserves mention here and is sufficient to efface an impression of tiredness left by the last two canticles. This is *Phaedra*, a genuine dramatic cantata for mezzo-soprano (originally Janet Baker) accompanied by orchestral strings, percussion, and harpsichord (1975). The idiom is pared down to the essentials in this scene from Racine's play (in the translation by Robert Lowell), and the composer bids farewell to his dramatic muse with an economy that only emphasizes the tragedy of a heroine ruined by her obsession. Just one major work, the serene third quartet (its last movement, a Recitative and Passacaglia, is indeed called *La Serenissima* in reference to the Venice he loved), intervened before his own death.

One cannot do adequate justice to so universal a figure in a few short paragraphs: several major works, among them the Hardy, Hölderlin, Blake, and Pushkin song-cycles, have been left out of account altogether, and little enough has been said about Britten's educational, liturgical, and occasional works—such as the immensely popular *Young Person's Guide to the Orchestra*, the much-performed *Missa brevis* for boys' voices and organ, and a long list of other choral works, sacred and secular, accompanied and unaccompanied. His reputation has had its peaks and its troughs, but it is difficult to imagine a cultural future in which his music does not play an essential part.

Older Modernists: Lutyens, Frankel, Searle

Amongst the numerous composers striving for attention and struggling to make a living in the post-war years were several contemporaries of Tippett and Britten whose outlook was considerably more 'advanced', in purely technical respects, than theirs. They included Elisabeth Lutyens (1906–83) and Benjamin Frankel (1906–73), the oldest English-born composers to espouse serial composition—essentially the twelve-note system—in a thorough-going way. The acceptance of this method was helped by a number of factors; two of them were an awakening curiosity about the music of Schoenberg, Berg, and Webern, whose music at that time was virtually unknown in England, and the arrival of several immigrant composers, driven here by war or by intolerable political conditions at home. These included the Austrian-born Egon Wellesz (1885–1974), the Spanish-born Roberto Gerhard (1896–1970, of Swiss parentage), Berthold Goldschmidt (1903–96), and the Hungarian Mátyás Seiber (1905–60), both of whom had left Germany for England in 1935. Wellesz, who was also a distinguished scholar in the field of Byzantine music, had been a pupil of Schoenberg in 1905–6, long before the twelve-note method had been devised; but he remained keenly in touch with its development throughout his Viennese years and adopted it in many of his major works, including the nine symphonies that he wrote in England between 1945 and 1971. Gerhard, more experimentally minded than either Wellesz or Seiber, attracted a considerable following in the 1950s and 1960s, becoming a kind of father-figure to the new avant-garde in England; the colour and vitality of his music would repay a renewed interest in it now that the obligatory post-mortem eclipse has run its course.

Lutyens and Frankel had much in common, besides their age. Both were highly professional figures, determined to make a living from composition, writing music for numerous films and for other ephemeral purposes. All their more significant music post-dates the war, though Lutyens was begin-ning to forge a characteristic idiom by the late 1930s (see Ch. 5). Frankel was primarily an instrumental composer, achieving, for example, eight sym-phonies between 1952 and 1972, a violin concerto (1951), and five string quartets (1944–65). He often devised note-rows that would permit quasi-tonal argument: Berg's violin concerto was a seminal influence on com-posers who, like Frankel, were searching for a point of contact with common musical experience while adopting a rigorous method. His symphonies have not held a place in the repertoire, but Frankel was a master of orchestral texture and they deserve to be heard.

Lutyens was made of sterner stuff, an apostle of her cause and a leader of her profession. Apart from her six string quartets (1937–52), she wrote little instrumental music in conventional forms; but there are five operas of a very varied nature, and numerous vocal, orchestral, and chamber works tailored to suit a verbal text or a poetic idea. She was an imaginative colourist, especially when working with a small ensemble, and the clarity and preci-sion of her music are noteworthy. She attracted attention in 1946 with the short Webernesque cantata 'O saisons, ô châteaux' (Rimbaud) for soprano and string orchestra with mandoline, guitar, harp, and solo violin. The twelve-note row is easily traced and leaves an indelible mark on the expressive voice part: the effect is haunting, although a more extended work would require greater sophistication if monotony were to be avoided (Ex. 6.4). The *Wind Quintet* (1960) shows this greater sophistication, and the marked influence of Webern's *Concerto* both in its more advanced rhythmic

Ex. 6.4

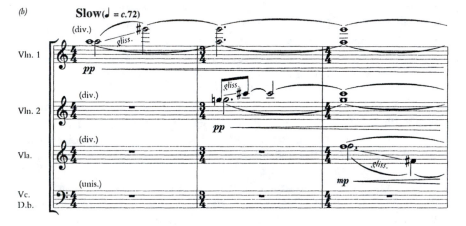

continued

language and in the use of a row comprised of four (though not here identical) three-note units. In the same year she produced her most celebrated work, *Quincunx*, scored for a large orchestra with baritone and soprano solos. This elaborately organized work falls into five 'tutti' sections interspersed with 'soli' sections for woodwind, strings, percussion, and brass respectively. The third tutti is introduced by the baritone, unaccompanied, singing an extract from Sir Thomas Browne: 'But the Quincunx of Heaven runs low...'; the tutti itself incorporates a wordless soprano line. The violence and unpredictability of this work are disturbing, but it well illustrates the formidable expressive range of a still underrated composer.

Humphrey Searle (1915–82) was another serialist who initially seemed to be a disciple of Webern, though he also pursued a Lisztian rhetoric wholly at variance with that model, and eventually followed his own lights. In a large and varied output the predominant impression is of density and weight,

Ex. 6.4, continued

continued

Ex. 6.4, continued

Elisabeth Lutyens, 'O saisons, ô châteaux' (Rimbaud) (London, 1960): (*a*) note-row; (*b*) pp. 1–2 (doubling in mandolin, guitar, and harp, and some performance indications, omitted); (*c*) p. 6

even when, as in the comparatively late *Labyrinth* (1971) for orchestra, use is made of a 'pointilliste' technique by which the notes of a melodic line are passed from one instrument to another. It has been noted that his serial technique grew stricter in his later music,[28] but this process was not always matched by a commensurate lucidity. Perhaps his most successful works are those in which he still exercised a certain freedom, as in the first symphony (1953), where the B A C H motive predominates, and in the imaginative *Poem* for twenty-two solo strings (1950). He also wrote a number of works for speaker (or speakers): there is the immense trilogy consisting of *Gold Coast Customs* (Sitwell, 1949), *The Riverrun* (Joyce, 1951), and *The Shadow of Cain* (Sitwell, 1951), each with orchestra, and the first and third with male

---

[28] *NGD*, s.v. 'Searle, Humphrey'.

chorus in addition; at the other end of the scale is the amusing *Owl and the Pussy-cat* (Lear, 1951) for speaker, flute, cello, and guitar. There are three operas to his own texts, one an Ionescan comedy for radio (*The Photo of the Colonel*, 1964), but none of them at all successful. Searle was a man of superabundant energy, working in turn for the BBC and for Sadler's Wells Ballet (he wrote three ballet scores), and active in various organizations for new music; he was also a scholar, writing a book on Liszt and contributing chapters to books on Liszt, Chopin, and twentieth-century composers. Few have achieved so much in a diversity of fields, yet the creative personality remains obscure.

Reginald Smith Brindle, born in 1917, deserves brief mention amongst the composers of this generation, though he trained as an architect and only began to study music seriously in 1946. He is best thought of as an explorer of novel techniques and as a teacher sufficiently eclectic to be of use to a wide range of pupils: he was Professor of Music at Surrey University from 1970 until 1985. He has written books on serial technique and on writing for percussion instruments, and has translated Bruno Bartolozzi's *New Sounds for Woodwind*; he has also used serial, electronic, and aleatory techniques in his own music. All this displayed in the 1960s and 1970s the innovatory instincts of a much younger man, and no discussion of the avant-garde in England can ignore his influence.

Younger Traditionalists: Simpson, Fricker, Arnold

'Traditional' is an unsatisfactory label for three such diverse figures as these, none of whom would presumably have wished to cast himself as a conservative. But except for Fricker, who occasionally adopted it in a very personal form, none of them espoused serialism, preferring instead the exploitation of tonal relationships as the basis of their musical dialectic.

Like such older composers as Berkeley, Rawsthorne, Maconchy, and Alwyn,[29] only more singlemindedly than any of them, Robert Simpson (1921–97) has seen the symphony and the string quartet as central to a concept of organic development on tonal lines (though one discarded early symphony was apparently a serial composition). In all there are eleven symphonies and fifteen quartets, together with a good deal of other music of various kinds. They vary considerably in length, weight, and style, but they have in common a concern for both 'visible' and 'audible' coherence. That is, their argument is both amenable to analysis in the strict sense and

---

[29] For Berkeley and Rawsthorne, see above. Maconchy (see Ch. 5) wrote only one symphony, for double string orchestra, but eleven quartets from 1933 to 1977. Alwyn (1905–85) discarded all his work prior to the Divertimento for solo flute (1939, an impressive *tour de force*); his subsequent works include song-cycles and an opera, *The Libertine* (1965–71) and, amongst a substantial body of instrumental music, five symphonies and two string quartets. The third and fourth symphonies employ a personal brand of tonal serialism. Alwyn also composed about sixty film scores.

apprehensible by the listener as a rhetorical unit, sometimes with the aid of one-movement form. In some ways the quartet medium has suited Simpson's purposes better, since a wide range of colour is not central to his language. The first quartet illustrates one kind of tonal argument, starting very simply in E flat and ending, equally simply, in its antithesis, A. The seventh quartet, in one movement, begins and ends 'on' D, with a wide range of tonal reference in between. The first and second symphonies are much weaker than the first quartet, mainly because of a certain orchestral thinness and no very great distinction of ideas. The third symphony is based on a tonal opposition (B flat as against C) that is not resolved but is itself the focus of the argument.[30]

Simpson's general indebtedness is to Beethoven, followed by Sibelius, on each of whom (together with Nielsen and Bruckner) he has written persuasively. But to invest such a substantial proportion of the emulative effort in symphonic form has risked a limitation on creative freedom (allowing indeed for a very considerable variety of method within the framework) and greatly restricted the range of his appeal. It is tempting to assert that the self-imposed task became an anachronism, but a final judgement (if such a thing is ever possible) must await a further revolution in taste.

Peter Racine Fricker (1920–90) was considered one of the most promising composers of his generation immediately after the war. His wind quintet Op. 5 (1947) won the Clements Memorial Prize, his first symphony won the Koussevitzky Prize in 1949, and a second was commissioned for the Liverpool Festival in 1951. His strong technique, the product of study with Seiber and founded on a post-Bartókian handling of dissonance and tonality, gave his music both the requisite toughness and the potential of a wider appeal. The wind quintet is an enchanting work, exceptionally well written for this difficult medium and formally and rhythmically ingenious. A number of vocal and instrumental works followed, including a third symphony and an exuberant orchestral *Dance Scene* that was popular for a while. But the major achievement of the 1950s was the oratorio *The Vision of Judgement* (1957–9, based on the Old English poetry of Cynewulf), even though it has not retained a place in the repertory. His music withstands examination by the strictest criteria, and it seems almost perverse to argue that (like so much music by central Europeans such as Blacher, Fortner, Seiber himself, and Petrovićs) it steers an uneasy path between drabness and popularism. In 1964, Fricker emigrated permanently to the United States, teaching in California and refining his style to include elements of serialism within an essentially tonal framework. He may therefore be allowed to pass from our story, though not without a plea for the rounded assessment that is now overdue.

---

[30] Samson concludes rather (*BHMB*, vi. 282) that 'the overall conflict between C and B flat is resolved by the final bars in such a way that derivations from a cycle of 5ths become clear'.

There could never be any suggestion of drabness about Malcolm Arnold (b. 1921), whose sense of musical fun perhaps stems from his early life as an orchestral trumpeter. The danger, rather, has always been that colourfulness might degenerate into vulgarity, a reasonable indulgence in a 'Hoffnung' concert but otherwise an intrusion. (Gerard Hoffnung, 1925–59, was an illustrator and cartoonist, a refugee from Nazi Germany who from 1956 organized an annual 'Hoffnung Music Festival' in London. Arnold contributed a 'Grand Grand Overture for Hoovers, Rifles, Cannon, Organ, and Full Orchestra' for the first festival concert, which took place at the Royal Festival Hall.) It is perhaps surprising that symphonies should loom so large in the work of a professed jester—he had written seven by 1973—but there is a serious side to Arnold, expressed most characteristically in a sustained lyricism that often distinguishes his slow movements. Orchestrally he is never less than highly effective, though his uncanny instinct for maximization of sonority can result in the deafening outbursts encountered in (for example) the overture *Tam O' Shanter* (1955) or the conclusion of the third symphony (1957). He has often written jokey melodies characterized by absurd appoggiaturas of a type used by second-rate dance-band players, as for example in the Divertimento for flute, oboe, and clarinet (1952) and the finale of the second symphony (1953): see Ex. 6.5 The finale of the

Ex. 6.5

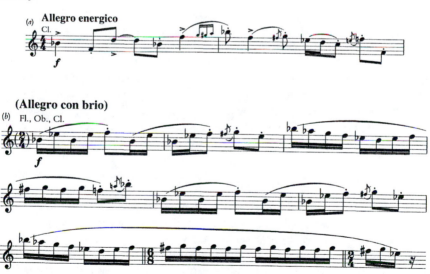

Malcolm Arnold: (*a*) Divertimento for flute, oboe, and clarinet, 1st mvt. (London, 1952), p. 1; (*b*) Symphony no. 2, 4th mvt. (London, 1953), pp. 91–2

Divertimento incorporates a preposterous parody of a ceremonial fanfare, reminiscent of Ibert in its boisterous mockery. There are numerous concertos and solo instrumental works, for which Arnold's talents have been eminently suited, two short operas, ballets, and innumerable film-scores, most conspicuously for *The Bridge on the River Kwai*.

Younger Modernists (1): Goehr, Wood, Maw, Bennett

Alexander Goehr was, as already mentioned, a fellow-student of Davies and Birtwistle in the early 1950s, but he is slightly older than they, as well as being of German parentage, and his radicalism has been of a less extreme kind. Initially the foundation of his technique was Schoenbergian serialism, but during a long career that has enabled him to develop at his own pace, he has evolved an atonal harmonic language derived from serial procedures without being dependent on them; this has given his writing a flexibility often lacking in the work of strict serialists. He has written in most of the standard instrumental forms, but there are a good number of works that are *sui generis*, and in general there is a high level of formal, if not always of melodic, invention in his work. His characteristically gritty idiom is evident at this period in such works as the *Little Symphony* (1963), the *Little Music for Strings* (1963), the Concerto for eleven instruments (1970), the cantatas *The Deluge* (1957–8) and *Sutter's Gold* (1959–60), and in a respectable body of chamber music and song.

Hugh Wood (b. 1932), an exact contemporary of Goehr, and a long-standing Cambridge colleague, is also a Schoenbergian who later broadened his idiom through other influences such as that of Messiaen. His early works, including a string quartet in B flat, were discarded, and the nominal first quartet (1962) is one of the first to show a mastery of serial technique. Although Wood has written a fair amount of vocal music, including several song-cycles, his most characteristic achievements have been in the 'standard' instrumental forms of the quartet, concerto, and symphony. The cello concerto (1969), in one movement, is by common consent a masterpiece, both in the formal control achieved by subordinating the elements of slow movement and cadenza to the main material, and as an effectively written piece in a difficult medium. His other major instrumental works in this period were a *Chamber Concerto* (1971, later revised), a violin concerto (1972), a second string quartet (1970), and some further chamber music.

A comparison between these two composers and Nicholas Maw (b. 1935) is instructive, since Maw evolved and persisted with a non-serialist form of post-Romantic modernism. Some commentators would deny him the modernist label altogether, but he explored all the stages of the European avant-garde from early Schoenberg to Boulez, building on them for his own purposes rather than adopting their techniques. It is interesting to consider his approach by looking at one of his more 'Romantic' works, the *Scenes and Arias* for soprano, mezzo-soprano, contralto, and orchestra (1962, revised 1966). Such a work is 'modernist' (as well as original) in several respects, despite its freedom from structuralism and its relatively warm harmonic content. For one thing its text is treated as little more than a peg on which to hang the piece that Maw wanted to write. This text is a love-poem, written in alternating lines of French, English, and Latin, as from a man to a woman, followed by a 'Responcio' in the same verse-form as from the woman to the man. Of its content and dramatic form only the division into two parts remains. The words are allocated irrespective of meaning to one, two, or all three soloists, with no distinction at all between the two halves of the piece. Neither the vocal lines themselves nor the orchestral accompaniment bear any relation to the semantic content, and indeed the words as declaimed, quite apart from the obscurity of the medieval language, could scarcely be grasped by even the most attentive listener.[31]

These are not necessarily criticisms, but observations intended simply to indicate that the piece is 'modernist' in its treatment of verbal text. As for its general style, selective quotation cannot do it justice, but a passage in which the words of the second stanza are set a second time (for no apparent reason), taking up some previously used ideas in a new context, may be given: note the three-octave descending octatonic scale that binds the whole together while never suggesting a conventionally tonal focus (Ex. 6.6). Chord collocations do in fact have a quasi-tonal function, as may be shown quite clearly by the opening and close of this work, where the same chord is used; but their significance depends on the listener's aural memory (as does actual key in a lengthy tonal work), rather than on an instinctive appreciation of standard procedures at the microchronic level.

Maw, in contrast to Wood, has written very little in standard genres, unless one counts his only partially successful comic opera *The Rising of the Moon*, where the complexity of the idiom tends to undermine the dramatic impact. He continues to pursue a rich and ornamental idiom. Richard Rodney Bennett (b. 1936), on the other hand, has cultivated a lighter style while retaining a serial basis in his major works. In the tradition of Lutyens and Frankel, both also serialists, he has been the complete professional, writing the music for numerous films and for other forms of commercial entertainment; he is also a fine jazz pianist. His operas, already mentioned, have a sure touch. His output is so large and varied that it is difficult both to generalize about his music and to be sure of doing him justice. The first piano concerto (1968), in four movements, may be taken as representative of his middle-period music in the standard forms. It is freely serial, attractively decorative in the piano part, and effectively scored. There

---

[31] This is partly because of the cruelly high *tessitura* of the soprano part.

Ex. 6.6

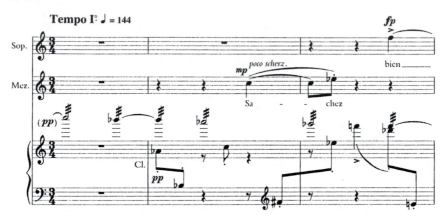

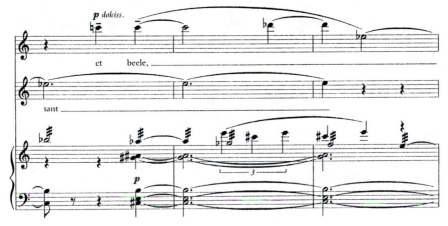

Ex. 6.6, continued

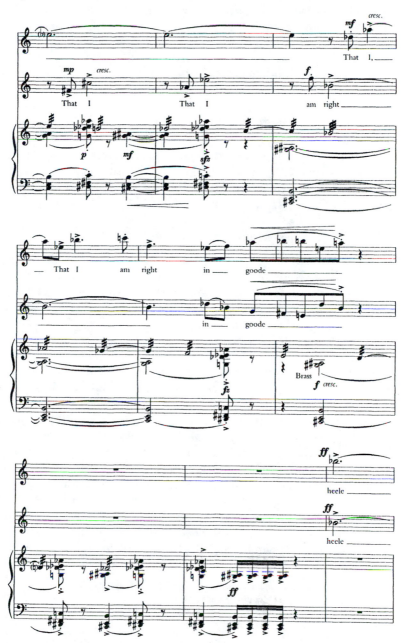

Nicholas Maw, *Scenes and Arias*: vocal score (London, 1968), pp. 11–12

is a clear model for its relaxed manner in Schoenberg's piano concerto, and there is something of Schoenberg's melodic expansiveness in the impassioned slow movement. Elsewhere, however, there is more concentration on motif and pattern: indeed the scherzo is almost Webernesque, except in its rhythmic straightforwardness.

Accessibility, on various levels, is a feature of Bennett's music as a whole, and it should not be regarded as a failing in a high culture then dominated by the challenges of the most acerbic modernism. Indeed it is clearly an important and fully intentional part of his aesthetic, and he might legitimately be thought of as a prophet of a greater readiness to blend popular and serious elements within a unified but broadly based idiom. It is true that his activities have remained to a certain extent compartmentalized, but he is one of the few in his generation to have achieved aural attractiveness in a modern 'serious' context, and that in itself is no small achievement.

Younger Modernists (2): Davies, Birtwistle

Davies and Birtwistle were born within two months of each other, in Manchester or near by, and they clearly have much in common. They were the first English-born composers to become fully immersed in the new European avant-garde as promoted at the post-war festivals at Darmstadt and Donaueschingen and associated with the names of Pierre Boulez, Karlheinz Stockhausen, Luigi Nono, and Bruno Maderna.[32] One of their early objectives was the serialization or predetermination of all 'parameters', that is to say of pitch, duration, dynamics, colour, articulation, and so on, either independently or as a single composite 'series'. Oliver Messaien was an important precursor, since he was the first to achieve the linking of parameters, though without serial predetermination, in the impossibly difficult piano piece *Mode de valeurs at d'intensités* (1949).[33] The use of a series of twelve durations based on aggregates of a small unit such as the demisemiquaver, semiquaver, or quaver (Messiaen uses all three of these units in combination, yielding not 36 but 24 different durations) led to very complex rhythms, which were generally notated in measures of 2/4 for orientation. (Tippett, perhaps influenced by Messiaen, has used 2/4 time for purposes of orientation when writing irregular rhythmic units in combination, e.g. in the second symphony.) Boulez's *Structures*, for two pianos (in

---

[32] The Darmstadt concerts were part of an International Summer Course each year, starting in 1946; this venture had a sort of foster-child in the Dartington Summer School, begun at Bryanston School in 1948 and transferred to Dartington, Devon, in 1953. The Donaueschingen Festival was revived on a permanent footing, after a long gap, in 1950.

[33] This was not Messiaen's first composition to link parameters, but it was the most thoroughgoing and the first to make the device the sole basis of a composition. He also pioneered the 'interversion', or mathematically predetermined variability, of a durational series, which when applied to pitches would yield a lengthy note row (as in change-ringing).

two books, 1952 and 1956–61 respectively), represents the *ne plus ultra* in the serial organization of several linked parameters, at least with human performers. Sensing a dead end, composers, including Boulez, began to loosen their techniques: multiple-choice progressions from one section of a piece to another, a freer use of the complexities induced by the serialization of duration, strict and free rhythms in combination, yet other types of 'aleatory' or 'stochastic' (chance) organization, and the use of electronic tape, were all tried. Henri Pousseur pioneered *musique concrète* (the capturing, distortion, and utilization of alien sounds on tape for artistic purposes), while the American John Cage introduced 'live' chance elements (such as the sound of radio sets randomly tuned and even the adventitious sonorities associated with pre-planned silence).[34] Some of this was little more than licensed buffoonery, but many of the new discoveries, and especially the aleatory control of rhythm and form, together with the electro-acoustic generation of sound, have proved astonishingly fruitful and indeed a scarcely noticed part of daily life in the context of films, radio, and television.

Davies and Birtwistle, fresh from their College in Manchester, reacted to all this with enthusiasm in their own different ways. Davies's orchestral *Prolation* (1958: the word is derived from a medieval concept of rhythmic organization) serializes pitch and duration but does not link them. In subsequent works, many also based on medieval or Renaissance concepts and/or materials, he introduced systems of schematic distortion intended both to disguise what might seem naively inappropriate material and for the purpose of symbolic or actual shock. It is sometimes difficult to discern the motive behind such distortions. The large-scale orchestral 'motet' *Worldes Blis* (1966–9) adopts as its basis a simple thirteenth-century song (cf. Vol. I, p. 68); if the resultant mass of sound is intended to imply the worthlessness of present joy it is an entirely successful exercise in aversion-therapy, but in any event all trace of the original song, let alone any suggestion of actual pleasure, is lacking. The apparently sacrilegious nature of some of Davies's music has been referred to already, but it is only right to add that his output includes some perfectly straightforward sacred music, music for children without dubious overtones, the unconventional use of various mythologies, and a parodic element intended purely to entertain. It must be confessed that Davies's music is not always as entertaining as it professes to be. *St Thomas Wake: Foxtrot for Orchestra on a Pavan by John Bull* (1969: one notes the counter-intuitive combination of materials) takes a good long time to get going, while *Vesalii Icones*, its questionable use of a naked dancer apart, is in places undercomposed to the point of tedium.

---

[34] In the notorious 'piano' piece 4′ 33″ (1952). John Cage also discovered the potentially ruinous device of the 'prepared' piano. There is a useful study of Cage by P. Griffiths (Oxford, 1981).

In the early 1970s Davies settled in Orkney and a new phase of work began, much of it directed towards his new home and towards Scotland in general (the St Magnus Festival, the series of Strathclyde concertos), but without his losing touch with London and international audiences. That, and the later work of Birtwistle, are matter for the next chapter. As for Birtwistle's earlier non-dramatic music, a few words must suffice. It is if anything even harsher and more dense than Davies's, and bleaker even in its quieter moments. It too has its longueurs, a common problem with composers who have rejected conventional methods of rhythmic organization. Characteristic of his work is the formal principle of episode and refrain, deriving perhaps from Stravinsky (*Symphonies of Wind Instruments*, Mass) and Messiaen (*Cinq Rechants, Oiseaux exotiques, Chronochromie*), both of whom have clearly been influential in matters of rhythm and instrumentation as well as in form. The cyclic or recurrent element has been a persistent feature of Birtwistle's work from the outset, adding a ritual quality even to works that do not otherwise suggest it. *Refrains and Choruses* for wind quartet (1957), *Tragoedia* for wind quintet, harp, and string quartet (1965), and *Verses for Ensembles* (nine wind instruments and percussion, 1969) are examples from various phases of his career, while his orchestral masterpiece *The Triumph of Time* (1972), based on a painting by Breughel, rivals Davies's *Worldes Blis* in its massive bulk, adding to this a sense of progression as Time's unwieldy chariot is made to move across the frame of the aural imagination. His vocal works (for example, *Ring a Dumb Carillon, Nenia on the Death of Orpheus, Meridian*, all with non-standard instrumental accompaniments) are akin to his music-theatre works in style and ideology. Finally, Birtwistle had achieved by 1975 some notable works using electronic tape, notably *Medusa* (later revised) and *Chronometer* for eight-track tape alone (1971).

Younger Modernists (3): Sherlaw Johnson, Crosse, Harvey

These three composers have little in common save that they were born in the 1930s and belong to the moderate avant-garde. They are representative of a larger group whose reputation was established during the 1960s and in most cases still continues. Two more extreme figures may be briefly mentioned. David Lumsdaine, born in Sydney in 1931, has consistently worked at the outer reaches of modernist expressionism, absorbing a variety of influences but faithful on the whole to contemporary European radicalism (Berio, Ligeti, etc.) and making use (since 1970) of electronic and computer-generated techniques. Cornelius Cardew (1936–81), after immersion in the post-war developments in Europe, became influenced by Cage and started to pursue indeterminate methods. He also worked as a graphic artist and introduced 'graphic' forms of notation, often giving performers only a vague idea (if that) of what to play or sing; he fostered collective improvisation and worked extensively with amateurs—the Scratch Orchestra was started in 1969 and was devoted to experimental performance. In the nature of things Cardew did not leave behind a significant body of permanently accessible work, but his influence as a teacher was considerable and—more than that—he conveyed a sense of enjoyment in experimental and improvisatory music-making. In later life, however, he repudiated much of this achievement and came to see music as an instrument of socialist propaganda.

Robert Sherlaw Johnson (b. 1932) was, like most of his generation, influenced by post-Webernian tendencies, serial and otherwise, but his style evolved in a personal and convincing way. A second important influence was that of Messiaen, with whom he studied in Paris and on whom he published a book in 1974; he also studied plainchant in depth and, while this had little direct effect on his style, it has been a factor in the melodically directed and temporally flexible character of his music, which often sounds free even when it is, in fact, carefully controlled. There are few techniques that he has not at some time addressed: his writing for voices is effective, he has adopted indeterminacy (in a series of six *Improvisations* for various instrumental forces, 1966–9), and he has used electro-acoustic methods from time to time. He has written short works for the Catholic liturgy, instrumental works in standard forms (two string quartets and two piano sonatas), and a variety of other vocal and instrumental pieces of diverse inspiration. Of the works of the 1960s the two piano sonatas (1963, 1967) are outstanding, not least for their imaginative use of the instrument's potential.[35] In the early 1970s he expanded his expressive horizons in two works in particular, *Carmina vernalia* (1972) for soprano and ten instruments (those of Webern's *Concerto* with the addition of a cello) and *Asterogenesis* for piano solo (1973), a short but intricate and telling piece. This move towards a more expansive and accessible manner has continued with an opera (*The Lambton Worm*) and a slowly increasing body of orchestral music. His influence as a university teacher has been considerable.

Gordon Crosse (b. 1937) moved in a similar direction, from a somewhat rebarbative modernism to a greater accessibility exemplified in his operas and in a number of works for children. He has been more prolific than Sherlaw Johnson, having written by 1975 several orchestral works of which the most ambitious and effective is the second symphony, written and performed in that year.[36] As a man of wide-ranging interests, musical and otherwise (he studied fifteenth-century music at Oxford), he has drawn on medieval and Renaissance sources more intuitively and sympathetically than, say, Davies or Maw, while his choices of extra-musical subject-matter are invariably dictated by a sensitive appreciation of literary quality.

[35] In the second sonata and some other works the player has to operate the strings internally in various ways.
[36] The first symphony, dated 1976, is a revision of his *Sinfonia Concertante*.

Amongst other modern writers he has set (for example) verse by Robert Graves, Ted Hughes, Geoffrey Hill, and Stevie Smith, finding in their agnostic humanism as potent a source of inspiration as the medieval Christian verse to which he has responded without irony or affectation.

Jonathan Harvey (b. 1939) has been a more thoroughgoing modernist than either Sherlaw Johnson or Crosse, though he has been equally concerned with communicability. Early influences were very diverse, and his music of the 1960s—though some of it, like *Ludus amoris* (1969, the fourth in a series of seven cantatas for various forces), is very impressive—did not yet exhibit complete consistency of style. In 1969–70 a period of study with Milton Babbitt at Princeton enabled him to consolidate his technique, and while the idiom remained eclectic, a new control of aims and methods seemed to be in evidence. A proportionately greater part of his achievement, therefore (compared with Crosse, only two years his senior) belongs to the period discussed in the following chapter.

New Voices

Composers still younger than Harvey[37] began to make an impact in the later 1960s and early 1970s, either with methods ardently modernist or else by essaying a new rapprochement with tradition and popular culture. Chance, collage, minimalism, and electro-acoustic devices were some of the novelties, or relative novelties, that were brought to bear on the task of redefining the scope of the art and the range of its appeal. Amongst the modernists may be accounted Bill Hopkins (1943–81), a disciple of Boulez and Barraqué, Brian Ferneyhough (b. 1943), and Roger Smalley (b. 1943)—though from the perspective of the end of the century such a grouping might seem less appropriate. More flexible and pragmatic in their aims were Robin Holloway (b. 1943), Tim Souster (1943–94), and John Tavener (b. 1944). Tavener at this time might have seemed a more extravagant version of Jonathan Harvey, seeking a profound spirituality in his large-scale choral works *The Whale* (1966) and *Celtic Requiem* (1969), both of which make conspicuous use of collage. Another arresting composition of the same general type was the *African Requiem* (1972) by David Fanshawe (b. 1942). All of these continued (though for a tragically short time in the case of the talented Hopkins) to pursue their aims in the subsequent years.

Song and Church Music

The rather artificial preservation of the part-song in Novello's monthly supplements to *The Musical Times* in these decades reveals an ever-widening

---

[37] And some older ones not so far mentioned, including Peter Dickinson (b. 1934), David Blake (b. 1936), David Bedford (b. 1937), and Edwin Roxburgh (b. 1937).

range of style in a genre that one would have thought impervious to modernism. A large majority of these songs (and of the sacred works published in equal numbers), both unaccompanied and accompanied, were indeed very old-fashioned, sometimes positively reactionary, in manner, especially in the 1940s and 1950s, though occasionally a real gem like Howells's *Walking in the snow* (John Buxton, 1951) or John Joubert's 'O Lorde, the maker of al thing' (1953) penetrated the defences.[38] Maxwell Davies's 'Ave Maria...Hail, blessed flower' (1961) was something of a landmark (not that it is anything but straightforward in rhythm and tonality, with only a few oddly spaced dissonances to ripple the placid surface), but in general the most that could be aspired to was a sub-Waltonian bite in a number of carols and anthems. An attractive archaism sometimes marks the work of Howells's pupil Richard Drakeford (b. 1936: see for example his 'Now the fields are laughing', 1957, a translation by Helen Waddell from the medieval Latin) and Brian Brockless (1926–95: 'Christ is now rysen agayne', 1958). By 1975 a thoroughgoing modernism had been permitted to intrude within the hallowed precincts, and in that year a whole series of 'advanced' works was published, in particular by Anthony Payne (b. 1936), Jonathan Harvey, Nicola LeFanu (b. 1947), and Naresh Sohal (b. 1939).[39] By this time, however, the unaccompanied part-song (though not the carol and the anthem) was nearing extinction, and the series was discontinued in 1979.

As for piano-accompanied solo song, this certainly flourished in the hands of Britten and Tippett. Elsewhere, however, it languished, uneasily seeking a compromise between nostalgic reminiscence (Quilter, Finzi, Geoffrey Bush, C. W. Orr) and the newer tendency to combine the voice with ad hoc instrumental ensembles. Even so, composers as diverse as Walton, Lennox Berkeley, and Hugh Wood contributed thoughtfully to the genre, most often and most successfully in song-cycle form.

It is tempting to relegate the composition of new church music at this period to the status of a sociological phenomenon, but this would be misleading. Herbert Howells, for one, played a vital part in the rejuvenation of Anglican cathedral music after the war. It was never to be revived, it is true, on the pre-war scale. The principal casualty was daily choral Mattins, now thought to be an unwarrantable intrusion into the school day for the boys of the choir and an unrealistic expectation of men who of necessity held other jobs. Mattins was still sung on Sundays at most cathedrals and comparable establishments, before or after or instead of choral

[38] Joubert (b. 1927) is of South African origin; he settled in England after the war, at first to study and subsequently to enjoy a career as a university teacher and respected composer, a middle-of-the-road modernist with an impressive list of works in the public domain.

[39] Payne is a respected critic and scholar, and a composer of Schoenbergian leanings. Sohal, of Indian birth, settled in England in 1962; he has employed microtones in some of his music, while this particular work, *Poets to Come* (Whitman), employs both speech and song and a specially devised notation.

Communion, so a use for new morning canticles did not disappear; but the emphasis was bound to be on the evening canticles, Magnificat and Nunc dimittis, from then on.

In 1944 Howells inaugurated a series of canticles for different choral establishments, beginning with a set of four for King's College, Cambridge. It is strange that he had not tried this genre before, but whatever the reason, he now applied his peculiar vein of warm lyricism to the medium of organ and voices with singularly happy effect. True, they are the work of a middle-aged man of no very radical temperament, and in aggregate they may seem limited in invention and excessively mannered. There were to be six such sets in all, with a Communion Service, the *Missa Aedis Christi* for Christ Church, Oxford (as well as two other Mass-settings), but Howells never surpassed the outpouring of melody that distinguishes the set composed for Gloucester, the cathedral in which he had been trained as a boy (1946).

Like many others, Howells also wrote motets and anthems. A good deal of published church music was intended for parochial use, while established composers (Britten, Tippett, Walton) wrote works for special occasions or as the result of a commission for some other reason.[40] Music for the Catholic liturgy was being composed more regularly than before, especially by Catholic composers like Rubbra, Berkeley, Anthony Milner (b. 1927), and Sherlaw Johnson, but also by Britten, whose *Missa brevis* was written for Westminster Cathedral. Anglican churches, too, began to use settings of the Latin Mass Ordinary untranslated, both from earlier periods and by con-temporary composers. The Second Vatican Council (1962–5) and the resulting introduction of a simplified vernacular liturgy struck deeply at this repertory, though the number of Catholic centres for good liturgical music had always been limited in England (and by then were few and far between even in Catholic Europe). It became clear, however, once the dust had settled, that the use of the Latin Ordinary was by no means ruled out in places where it had been the tradition. The Anglican liturgy was also being subjected to scrutiny and new texts introduced for optional use, but this again, while encouraging new settings in a more accessible style, did not make the older tradition obsolete.

Below the level of the major musical centres, however, a strong move towards congregational participation encouraged the growth of idioms based on secular popular music. While the results of this were in some respects utterly deplorable, they need not be considered in a wholly neg-ative light. Geoffrey Beaumont's Anglican *Folk Mass* (1956), which has achieved something like classic status, was much criticized at the time but can now be seen as an interesting, if pallid, reflection of 'Rock 'n' Roll' in its

---

[40] There was a striking contribution in the nine motets (1952) by Bernard Naylor (1907–86), who spent most of his adult life in Canada, but who taught in England from 1950 to 1959.

earliest phrase. The organ (unless electronic) being generally unsuited to such a style, the piano, guitars, and other instruments began to invade gallery and chancel, much to the distress of conservative musicians and congregations. In the Catholic world, Dom Gregory Murray (1905–92) adapted the psalmodic formulae of Joseph Gélineau for English use and composed several fine hymn-tunes.[41]

Style and Criticism

The post-war period is one in which English musical criticism may truly be said to have come of age. There had long been a tradition of intelligent journalism, and serious contributions to scholarship had been made by newspaper critics and other journalists as well as by freelance writers and university teachers. But this was the first time in which one can observe a genuinely constructive engagement with contemporary composers' aspirations and achievements and an attempt to mediate between composers and the public. It was assisted by the BBC, which with the founding of the Third Programme in 1946 was able to offer more consistently than before a platform for new music of all kinds and a forum for critical discussion, much of which then found its way into the pages of its weekly publication *The Listener*.

In 1959 William Glock (b. 1908) became Controller of Music of the BBC, and as such in charge of the Promenade Concerts, but he had been an influential figure long before that. It was he who founded the Summer School at Bryanston, later transferred to Dartington, as already mentioned (see n. 32). In 1949 he founded and became editor of *The Score*, of which twenty-eight numbers appeared, somewhat irregularly, over a period of thirteen years. *The Score* provided an opportunity for the discussion of new music, but it was nevertheless quite wide in its scope, with articles on subjects ranging from the Middle Ages to its own day. Each issue contained the score of one or more new works, usually in a facsimile of the composer's manuscript. Lest it should be thought that Glock's interests were at all partisan, it might be noted that his editorial for the eighth number (September 1953) singled out Anthony Milner and Bernard Naylor as two composers of 'remarkable gifts'; Naylor himself provided an article on Milner, and his Advent motet 'Come ye, and let us go up to the mountain of the Lord' was one of the two scores printed (a monodic setting of a poem from Donne's *Devotions* by Priaulx Rainier being the other).[42]

---

[41] Most popular hymnody is beneath consideration, but there are some good modern tunes amongst the dross in collections such as *100 Hymns for Today* (1969) and *More Hymns for Today* (1980), both supplements to *Hymns Ancient and Modern*, and in several other publications of the 1960s and subsequently.

[42] Rainier (1903–86) was of South African (English-Huguenot) origin, passing most of her professional life in England. Her idiom combines native African influences with an individual response to

Glock, while willing to promote the avant-garde, was a force for sane modernity in British music. The same is true of Donald Mitchell (b. 1925) and Hans Keller (1919–85), the latter an Austrian refugee from the *Anschluss* of 1938. Mitchell founded *Music Survey* (1947–52), an incisive journal that occasionally ventured into the near-libellous; Keller joined him as co-editor in 1949. Both men, though steeped in the progressive tradition of the second Viennese school, became enthusiasts for Britten, and in 1952 collaborated on a symposium[43] that provoked a backlash of hostility. Martin Cooper, commenting critically enough on *Gloriana* in *The Score* (September 1953), noted that it had been 'very generally over-blamed . . . with an almost sadistic relish or glee that has little to do with musical merit or demerit . . . [Britten] has been ill served, with the best of intentions, by a fanatical clique of admirers, whose exaggerated claims on his behalf have combined with an hysterical resentment of all critical comment to alienate large sections of the musical world'.

If this was a swipe at Mitchell and Keller it will have missed the mark, for the *Commentary* exaggerates, if at all, only in the fact of its existence, there being no such books, for example, on the older (but less prolific) Walton, Berkeley, Tippett, or Rawsthorne. Mitchell continued to promote Britten's music, but both he and Keller had many other interests. Mitchell became a powerful advocate for Mahler; his lively comments on new British music in *The Musical Times* (mainly from 1954 to 1956 under the heading 'London Concerts') have already been mentioned. Keller was an eccentric: his 'functional analyses', dispensing with words and demonstrating motivic relationships by means of newly juxtaposed fragments of the score under review, provoked derision, though they were based on a deep knowledge of, and sympathy with, the central European understanding of musical processes as formulated (for example) by Rudolf Reti and as enshrined in twelve-note serial composition.

Other critics notable for their sympathetic understanding of new musical trends at this period included Peter Heyworth (*Observer* from 1955); Peter Stadlen (an Austrian pianist who joined *The Daily Telegraph* in 1959); Anthony Payne (*Daily Telegraph*); Colin Mason (*Manchester Guardian*, 1950–64, *Daily Telegraph*, 1964–71; also chairman of the Macnaghten concerts in the 1960s and editor of *Tempo*, 1964–71); Michael Kennedy (northern music critic of the *Daily Telegraph*, 1950, and northern editor, 1960); and Robert Henderson (*Daily Telegraph*). For a time, indeed, *The Observer* and the *Telegraph* were essential reading for intelligent amateurs of new music, English and otherwise. *The Sunday Times* (under Ernest Newman until

European canons of harmony and tonality. Another important forum for the discussion of new music was (and is) *Tempo*, started before the war as a Boosey and Hawkes house newsletter but refounded in 1946 on a less exclusive basis.

[43] *Benjamin Britten: A Commentary on His Works from a Group of Specialists* (London, 1952).

1958) and *The Times* (anonymous, but under Frank Howes from 1943 to 1960) were, at any rate to begin with, less sympathetic, though Desmond Shawe-Taylor in the former was to welcome *The War Requiem* with the greatest warmth. The important thing about this generation of critics (and one could add such figures as Ernest Bradbury, of *The Yorkshire Post*, A. K. Holland, of *The Liverpool Daily Post*, and John Waterhouse, of *The Birmingham Post*) was not their individual likes and dislikes but the positive way in which they sought to engage their readers in the issues of style and technique that were at the forefront of the composers' minds as they grappled with the problem of addressing their audiences in a meaningful fashion.

There is no doubt that style was the great preoccupation at this period. Progressive composers and critics were concerned at the historic 'backwardness' of English music. As we have seen, the English were slow to adopt atonal serialism between the wars, though the same was true of France, Italy, and the musical establishment in Germany and Austria. Nor was Schoenberg's inter-war music performed here in any quantity, let alone that of Berg or Webern.[44] After the Second World War it seemed that there was a great deal of catching up to do, with Webern's intricately patterned dodecaphony superseding Schoenberg's, and the new 'post-Webernian' techniques of total serialism and aggressively disjointed *pointillisme* superseding Webern's comparatively straightforward methods. English composers could attach themselves to these developments at any point, and subsequently to electro-acoustic composition and indeterminacy, though it was not until the later 1950s that the discoveries of the new avant-garde began to sink in, partly as a result of the greater accessibility of works like Boulez's *Le marteau sans maître* (1953–5) and Stockhausen's *Zeitmasse* (1955–6).

The common ground in all these techniques was atonality, which need not be serial and eventually was often not so, once strict serialism had ceased to be thought of as an essential guarantee of rational organization. In general English serialists were either eclectics, like Lutyens, Frankel, and Bennett, willing to write in other styles to suit the occasion, or committed Schoenbergians like Searle, Goehr, Payne, and Wood, abandoning or relaxing the method only when they felt they had exhausted its possibilities. But the majority of composers did not want to write atonally at all, and their style-problem was far more acute. Neither conventional harmonic processes, even if saturated with advanced chromaticism, nor pentatonically inclined modalism as espoused by Vaughan Williams, seemed appropriate to

---

[44] There were no works by Schoenberg newly introduced at the Proms between 1918 and 1938, except for a couple of Bach chorale-prelude arrangements; though Webern's non-serial *Passacaglia*, Op. 1 (1908) was given its first English performance in 1931 and the BBC had broadcast some of his music before his death in 1945.

forward-looking composers as vehicles of musical expression. Three European inter-war composers in particular—Stravinsky, Hindemith, and Bartók (all, incidentally, of impeccable political credentials)—seemed to offer a model for a modern tonally directed idiom. Stravinsky and Bartók found virtually no direct imitators, though there are echoes of Stravinsky to be found here and there, for example in Tippett, while Fricker came temporarily close to Bartók through the influence of Seiber. Hindemith, as already noted, found at least two close followers in Franz Reizenstein (1911–68) and Arnold Cooke (b. 1906), both of whom continued active in their established idiom after the war.

Rawsthorne was one of the few post-war composers to achieve a really 'clean' tonally directed style, though he came to rely more and more on older norms of tonal attraction. Otherwise the choice was between a certain capriciousness (Berkeley) or latent Romanticism (Walton). Britten, without being beholden to either (though he was to demonstrate a personal and professional regard for both), exhibits a mixture of the two tendencies, while capriciousness was elevated into a positive system by Tippett.

Despite the fuss occasionally made by progressive critics, the breadth of the recognition accorded to Britten reflected a genuine and generally welcomed rapprochement of various tendencies. *The Turn of the Screw*, given its flirtation with serial methods, was a highly appropriate and much appreciated contribution to the Biennale Festival of Contemporary Music at Venice in 1954. With the 1960s, some of the sting was withdrawn from conflicts of style. Berio and Xenakis, with their freer (though still radical) modernism, came to the fore, while Boulez, Stockhausen, Nono, and Maderna continued to experiment. Political protest was voiced in musically radical terms, for example in Nono's works on Hiroshima and Auschwitz, and less brutally in the socialist-inspired works of Hans Werner Henze. Britten's apolitical humanism, often expressed in the context of Christian convention, was able to make use of Henze's less dogmatic technical armoury, however different their outlook, and the same is true of Tippett, who benefited from as well as contributing to the newer freedom of expression.[45]

Davies and Birtwistle lost none of their power to shock, but their abandonment of traditional genres and their boldly experimental dramatic work marked a further expansion of expressive range. Their freedom from formal, harmonic, and rhythmic restraint was matched at the other end of the spectrum by Britten's church parables, and later by his *Death in Venice*.

---

[45] It should be added that the highly organized, toughly dissonant music of the American Elliott Carter (b. 1908) provided a countervailing influence on Tippett and several others. The influence of Messiaen (1908–92) has been pervasive, but generally so well assimilated as to be little evident, even on his pupil Sherlaw Johnson. Shostakovich has had a somewhat marginal influence, mainly on Britten, who became a warm friend in the 1960s.

The 1960s were, in any case, a decade that saw new liberties of expression. The law on obscenity was tested to destruction when the full text of *Lady Chatterley's Lover* was published and those involved in its publication and distribution acquitted (1962); homosexual acts between consenting adults were legalized in 1967. The office of Lord Chamberlain, with his powers of censorship, was abolished in 1968. Popular as well as serious music and theatre took advantage of the new freedoms, and the growing radicalism of 'pop' music and culture began to approximate, at least philosophically if not quite technically, to that of 'serious' music. A show like *Oh! Calcutta!* or its American predecessor *Hair*, with their exaggerated permissiveness, evoked responses not entirely dissimilar to those prompted by *Vesalii Icones*, even though there may have been little or no overlap between the audiences for the two kinds of spectacle.

The critical reaction to all this was muted. The older generation of progressive critics was puzzled, while conservative critics dismissed new musical modes and the growing influence of pop culture altogether. But extreme radicalism aside, the conflict of the 1950s gave way to a new tolerance of a great diversity. The 'Arts' sections of national newspapers began to be more wide-ranging, devoting less space to the canonical repertory and its performance but more to revivals of 'early music' (as it was coming to be known), to new music of all kinds, and to the recognition of popular music as worthy of sophisticated comment. If William Mann's enthusiasm for The Beatles in *The Times* now seems exaggerated, his articles and those of others were nevertheless the harbingers of a scholarly literature and even a collected edition.[46] In short, the 1960s and early 1970s set the scene for the variegated musical culture to be considered in the next chapter.

[46] See e.g. W. Mellers, *Twilight of the Gods: The Beatles in Retrospect* (London, 1973); *Beatles Complete* (London, 1972: for a later issue see Bibliography).

7

MODERNISM AND POSTMODERNISM, 1976–1997

'MODERNISM' and 'postmodernism'—terms used here in their primary sense as defining a culture or a style—do not fully account for the variety of musical language heard in this twenty-year period. There are also the older traditional forms of expression and the more innovative styles of 'rock' or 'pop', with which serious composers have sometimes attempted a rapprochement. Modernism itself, if it is a valid concept, is essentially a continuation of the old avant-garde—as practised, that is, by English (or British) composers in the 1950s and 1960s. As for postmodernism, it is inherently a cultural phenomenon rather than a technically exact expression: it articulates a sense that the cup of modernism, usually perceived as brutal, artificial, or nihilistic, has been drained to the full, and that the whole experience needs to be put behind one. It implies that truly modernist work—in music, architecture, fine art, or literature—is of limited absolute value, but that the experience of it, in an artist's own work or in that of others, has had a purifying and liberating effect. Naturally no composer would wish to be associated solely with modernism so construed, and I have preferred the term avant-garde, where it seems appropriate, though more for its historical associations than in any literal sense. Nor do I single out a generation of postmodernists as such. Almost all, a few traditionalists excepted (and they too might contest the label), have been through the refining fire. The outcome is not a return to older norms but a redeployment of all available techniques and materials, often with disturbing effect but always with a sense of liberation.

One composer, Michael Tippett, stood in a commanding position in relation to these developments. Never himself truly avant-garde or modernist, his pioneering spirit pervaded all his work throughout his composing life, and never more so than in his youthful old age. He alone, perhaps, reached postmodernism through the natural route of a long-lasting personal creative curve. Strongly susceptible to external influences, literary and musical, he nevertheless preserved his individuality, never subordinating it to the tide of fashion. His late music, supremely original and totally in control, offers a standard by which other achievements can be measured.

Tippett

Tippett had from the outset been absorbing the current cultural climate, so to speak; from early manhood a friend of T. S. Eliot, he found the mitigated modernism of Eliot's later poetry and drama, with its combination of spiritual striving and social irony, a fruitful stimulus in *A Midsummer Marriage* and its satellite works. With Eliot came also much of the apparatus of classical and medieval scholarship, mythological symbolism, and psychology that has so exercised Tippett's imagination. *King Priam* (1962) is his finest achievement in classically inspired symbolism, a work that shocks us, as the Greek tragedians often do, with its strange matter-of-factness and the triviality (no accidental word) of the mechanisms by which the necessities of fate are carried through. In the later 1960s the composer identified himself with the cultural revolution of a younger generation, a liberation not merely from conventional moral assumptions but from many hitherto restraining disciplines of social life and of art. This, the true source of Tippett's and indeed of all postmodernism, found expression in *The Knot-Garden*, the *Songs for Dov*, and the third symphony (first performed in 1972). The symphony, for orchestra and solo voice, is a brilliantly inventive work, but it is fatally weakened by a direct quotation from the finale of Beethoven's ninth symphony[1]—fittingly enough, as a way of introducing the vocal conclusion of a hitherto instrumental work, but creating so profound an aesthetic shock that the listener's intuitive sympathy is dislocated beyond recovery and any valid symbolism neutralized.

The third symphony is also one of Tippett's less successful attempts at providing his own text. Deprived of dramatic context, the poem seems merely didactic, although in musical terms its setting is of a characteristically exalted beauty. No such doubts need assail one's appreciation of the fourth symphony (1977), a formidably difficult one-movement work for orchestra alone. As in most of the later non-dramatic works, a vestige of cyclic tonality is retained,[2] though the harmonic freedom of this music would make it next to impossible for any listener without absolute pitch to follow a tonal argument from beginning to end. Whether there *is* a tonal argument, other than truistically, is open to question. The sense of progress and recall is

---

[1] The quotation is closest to the version at the beginning of Beethoven's finale, i.e. without supporting strings. An odd pendant is succeeded without pause by a Lento introducing the 'Blues' of the first solo-voice section. In subsequent works quotations and allusions are more circumspect. For a positive appraisal of this particular instance see Kemp, *Tippett*, 449.

[2] As in (say) the *Triple Concerto* and *Byzantium* (1991). Dramatic works are not tonally unified by historic necessity, and so the charting of tonal argument in the later operas (or even in *King Priam*) and in *The Mask of Time* is fraught with difficulty.

achieved by sequences of easily recognizable ideas in statement, development, and recapitulation within a framework of three distinct tempi: there is
an analogy with that seminal work of 1960, Messiaen's *Chronochromie*, and
also perhaps with Stravinsky's *Concerto in D* for strings, and other works too,
in which carefully regulated tempo-relations are formally significant.
Orchestrally the work is a showpiece of the most demanding kind: brass,
strings, woodwind, and percussion, together with harp and piano, are
treated as separate but interlocking families. A wind-machine ('gently
breathing' at the beginning and end) helps to create the impression that
the work is one huge disturbing dream.[3]

The *Triple Concerto* (for violin, viola, cello, and orchestra, first performed
in 1980) has similar virtues, though it is more exotic (the percussion sections
of the two, which are similar, each have vibraphone, glockenspiel, and
marimba as well as a variety of untuned instruments, but the concerto has in
addition five tuned gongs and a set of tubular bells), not only in the
deployment of the instruments in numerous inventive combinations but
in the element of quasi-improvisatory ornamental melody and exhilarating
cross-rhythm. The latter almost disintegrates in the final swift 5/4, but a
generalized impression of complex drumming remains as the twentieth
semiquaver of the last bar is knocked into place. The work is again in a
single large movement, with 'interludes' and other episodes; the tonal
framework consists of an E in the bass with a strong fourth (A) in the
harmony above; but for most of the work this is lost sight of.

Tippett's later operas resemble *The Knot Garden* (and *The Midsummer
Marriage*) in their disturbing combination of humdrum reality and strange
apparitions. Like *The Knot Garden*, they exploit the tragedies of modern life
made so familiar by the mass media—prison camps, separations, riots, deaths
and injuries, drug-induced fantasy. The music is violent and unpredictable,
but it helps to bind the disparate elements together by means of its stylistic
coherence. In *The Ice Break* (1977), the scene is modern America; in *New Year*
(1989) it is alternately 'Somewhere and Today' and 'Nowhere and Tomor-
row', but it is not hard to recognize the land of the dispossessed and their
illusions. *The Ice Break* adds an electronic organ to Tippett's already comprehensive instrumental palette; the part of Astron, the 'psychedelic mes-
senger', is sung by two voices, soprano and counter-tenor, in approximate
unison, through a loudspeaker, the sound being manipulated ad lib by an
engineer. *New Year* incorporates 'specially prepared electronic ingredients'
to represent the arrival and departure of a space-ship and other products of
the imagination. The space-ship, however, is really a time-machine whose
inhabitants are able to make contact with the world of today, even to the

---

[3] According to Tippett himself, as reported by Kemp, *Tippett*, 477, the symphony is a 'birth to death'
piece. Kemp also mentions (p. 497) the desirability of substituting 'actual or synthesized human breathing' for the wind machine, which 'cannot avoid sounding like real wind'.

extent of a declaration of love; when they depart once more into the future, the protagonist of the present is mysteriously released from her entrapment and finds that she can, after all, face the outside world of 'Terror Town'.

The 'myth' of *New Year* is less convincing than that of *The Ice Break*, in which the image of spring correlates with the meeting of a son with the father he has not previously encountered. In *New Year* the liberating image is that of a rose, which nevertheless disintegrates, leaving only the memory of love as a source of strength. The composer's preoccupations are more fruitfully recalled in his last, and most beautiful, orchestral work *The Rose Lake* (1993), in which a spiritual contentment is achieved in purely musical terms—a contentment analogous to that reached at the end of Eliot's *Four Quartets*, 'When the tongues of flame are in-folded / Into the crowned knot of fire / And the fire and the rose are one'.

It is not easy to come to terms with the later Tippett.[4] The violent and abrupt musical language, while consistent with the violence and disorientation of his operatic myths, might be suspected of concealing a lack of substance. As for the myths themselves, it is possible to accept the sincerity of the message while questioning (as one might with *Lulu*) the practicality of an assimilation to operatic cultural norms. In *The Mask of Time* (first heard in 1984) a personal creation-myth is presented through music of such complexity that shafts of light are rare (it is scored for a large orchestra with four solo singers and a predominantly six-part chorus). The most striking of its ten sections is the seventh, 'Mirror of Whitening Light', a set of variations on the plainsong hymn 'Veni creator spiritus' that recalls Berg conceptually if not in technical detail. The analogy here is with the end of Berg's violin concerto, but it is possible to see a wider parallel with works such as *Lulu* and the *Chamber Concerto* in Tippett's near-fatal temptation to excesses of complexity. But a more serious problem is that Tippett's myths may themselves encounter either principled objections or, more prosaically, a simple lack of enthusiasm for their private world. In much the same way the most passionate admirer of Blake's lyricism might well jib at *The Four Zoas*. Tippett's gift was an essentially lyrical one, though of a musical rather than a literary kind, and it is perhaps sufficient to be grateful for the generosity of its outpouring over a mature creative life of some sixty years.

Older Traditionalists

Tippett was unique in his perpetually creative longevity. Few other composers born before the Great War remained active for long after 1975, and

---

[4] Kemp's book is an excellent commentary as far as it goes: *The Ice Break* is discussed in detail, and the fourth symphony, fourth quartet, and *Triple Concerto* are described more briefly in a Postscript. There is an illuminating account of *The Mask of Time* by P. Driver, ' "The Mask of Time" ', *Tempo*, 149 (June 1984), 39–44.

none achieved a comparable renewal of style. Rubbra, Walton, and Berkeley all lived and continued to compose in the 1980s, and Maconchy indeed into the 1990s, but they had by and large fulfilled their potential before then.[5]

Traditionalism, for these composers, implies a strong sense of tonal orientation, however it might be achieved. Contrapuntal movement towards a tonal centre was more important than a harmonically directed technique, although elements of this are still apparent, especially in Rubbra and Walton. Of a slightly younger generation Robert Simpson and Malcolm Arnold, both born in 1921, stand out, though for different reasons. Simpson continued to plough his lonely furrow, pursuing older ideas of symphonic cohesion while retaining a sturdy individuality. Arnold has remained accessible in continuing to cultivate the more Romantic traditions of the symphony and the concerto. Of several others who might be mentioned, Kenneth Leighton (1929–88) adopted a somewhat acerbic form of Hindemithian counterpoint. To a certain extent public perception of his achievement has suffered, not because he was unproductive in his later years but because of an inevitable distancing from concert life; he ended his career as Reid Professor at Edinburgh. The much younger John McCabe (b. 1939), while not immune from modernist influence, has remained at heart a traditionalist.

Older Eclectics

To this category belongs a group of composers most of whom have explored serialism, but who have increasingly wished to develop it in a personal manner or discard it altogether. Goehr, Wood, and Maw are perhaps the chief of these, though one could add several others: Robert Sherlaw Johnson, Richard Rodney Bennett, David Blake, Anthony Payne, and Gordon Crosse, for example, while Peter Dickinson, David Bedford, and Jonathan Harvey, to make a selective list of those born in the 1930s, have cultivated a still wider eclecticism.

Alexander Goehr has always maintained a strong link with his Schoenbergian roots. Even in his most elaborate compositions, and in those least committed to strict serialism, there is an austerity and an underlying simplicity that is capable of great eloquence. He has even been able to introduce tonal elements without any apparent incongruity. Something of this strange austerity can be seen in the opening of his song-cycle *Das Gesetz der Quadrille*, a setting of some posthumous prose fragments by Franz Kafka

---

[5] The same could be said of the 'older serialists', Lutyens and Searle. It should be borne in mind in the following, inevitably selective, discussion, that several Welsh and Scottish composers, important in a 'British' context, are excluded (they are referred to in Ch. 9), as is the Polish-born Andrzej Panufnik (1914–91: emigrated 1954, naturalized 1961, knighted 1991), who despite a complete assimilation into English musical life remained, as a composer, a continuator of his inherited tradition.

(1979). It is hard to make sense of these fragments individually or collectively, but Goehr manages to encapsulate in musical terms that uneasy
waywardness. Much of the cycle is purely atonal, but the opening (recap-
itulated at the beginning of the eighth and penultimate song) adopts a fitful
tonality in laying out some basic ideas that will recur, without a tonal gloss,
in the final desolate song (Ex. 7.1). This capacity to utilize a diatonic idea
recurs in ... *a musical offering (J.S.B. 1985)* ..., for fourteen players, in which a
range of Bachian devices and idioms are allusively presented (the dots in the
title perhaps signify an incompleteness of homage rather than any lack of a
persuasive beginning and end). Here the material is drawn from the plainsong Alleluia 'Veni Domine', stated at the outset by the horn and echoed by
the trombone in augmentation; this becomes the main idea of the third and
last movement, a 'Ricercar', and finally emerges as the bass of the chorale-
like conclusion (Ex. 7.2). The *Sinfonia*, Op. 42 (1980), in which the
character and sequence of movements owes something to Beethoven's
late quartets (Opp. 131 and 132 in particular), ends with a short 'Dankgesang' that quotes the elder Milton's psalm-tune 'Pray that Jerusalem may
have peace and felicity'—a re-creation of the stylistic incongruity in
Beethoven's own 'Heiliger Dankgesang'.

Each of these middle-period works is of a pronounced Germanic inspiration while exhibiting a readiness to flout the expectations that such an idiom
raises. Much of Goehr's later music has a similar ambivalence. Even his
strange opera *Arianna* (1994), which combines Monteverdi's surviving
lament with an exotic sound-world of its own, has its Germanic side:
Goehr's father, Walter, himself a composer, edited Monteverdi's *Vespers*
and *Poppea*; Hans Redlich (1903–68) was another composer-scholar, Austrian-born, who had published work on Monteverdi before settling in
England. But this Germanicism is not a nostalgic element; it is, rather, an
inherited feature that sits well with a complete identification with English
musical culture and a strong sympathy for its traditions of scholarship.[6]
Hugh Wood has also broadened his stylistic range in recent years, but
without introducing disconcerting dichotomies of style. Nicholas Maw
has perhaps been more successful than either in forging an idiom that is
neither beholden to the serialism he once espoused nor in the least retro-
gressive. His abundant œuvre is, however, somewhat uneven. At its least
approachable it can seem both clotted and prolix. The density of the *Life
Studies* for fifteen solo strings,[7] and the longueurs of the enormous orchestral
Odyssey, first heard complete in 1989, are still apparent in the orchestral

---

[6] One would hope for no less in a Cambridge professor, but Goehr has been outstandingly successful
in bridging the gap between academic life and contemporary musical culture.

[7] The *Life Studies* were first performed in 1973, but the eighth and last Study was added only in 1974,
and the second (the first two having been compressed into one) in 1976. Part of the work can be played
by a string orchestra, and in both versions the number and order of the movements can be varied.

Ex. 7.1

Ex. 7.1, continued

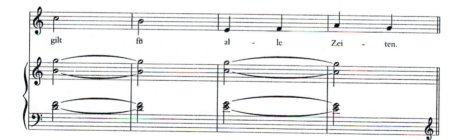

Alexander Goehr, *Das Gesetz der Quadrille* (Kafka) (London, 1983): (*a*) pp. 2–3 (first song); (*b*) ninth song (p. 35)

Ex. 7.2

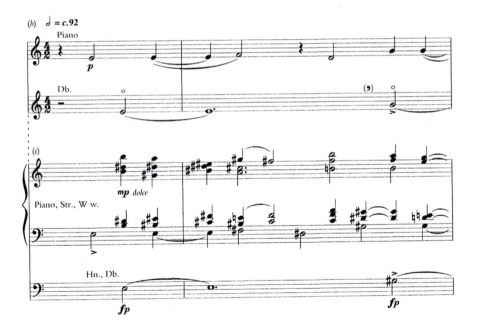

Ex. 7.2, continued

Alexander Goehr, ... *a musical offering* ...: (*a*) p. 1 (1st mvt.); (*b*) p. 56 and (*c*) pp. 76–7 (3rd mut)

Variations that appeared in 1995. Maw's work for smaller forces is often more immediately likeable: the flute quartet (1981) is enjoyable light music, in a definite key moreover, if still a little longer than it need be;[8] while *La Vita Nuova*, a setting of five Italian poems from Cavalcanti to the sixteenth century, achieves a still more satisfying lyricism. Maw's Italianism is akin to Walton's and Britten's: it casts a warm glow without compromising stylistic integrity.[9] *La Vita Nuova* is scored for soprano accompanied by wind quartet, harp, and string quartet; its idiomatic range extends from a diatonic opening to seeming atonality without inconsistency. On the other hand, the series of six piano pieces collectively known as *Personae* (I–III 1973, IV–VI 1985) is uniformly dissonant, and terrifyingly complex and savage at its climactic moments.

While Maw's musical personality is at the very least a strongly compelling one, some equally gifted contemporaries for one reason or another have made less of an impression on the public at large. Robert Sherlaw Johnson has been most successful in smaller forms, particularly those involving the voice. Clear textures in a highly organized atonality, elements of pointillisme, and the occasional use of electro-acoustic material might seem to ally him with the older avant-garde, and indeed his willingness to write for amateurs and to modify his style accordingly has its parallels in Maxwell Davies. Time has, however, softened the impact of his modernism; his larger works (primarily the concertos for piano and for clarinet, and *The Lambton Worm*), have been less exploratory and less genuinely arresting than some of those for small groups, and the predominant impression left by his work as a whole is of fastidious craftmanship. One might say the same of Gordon Crosse, though he has written a good deal more for larger forces. Again a willingness to write for children and for amateurs, and a responsibility towards regional musical cultures, together with a softening of idiom, has converted a potential challenger of Davies into an equally—indeed more—likeable but less powerful contemporary voice.

David Blake and Anthony Payne have both moved outwards during the last two decades from a starting-point of Schoenbergian serialism, cultivating a genuine eclecticism that in Blake's case can embrace simple juxtaposition (*Capriccio* for septet, 1980) as well as synthesis. His capacity for assimilating a diversity of idioms has resulted in two outstanding operas: *Toussaint* (1977), on the subject of the eighteenth-century Haitian revolutionary, and *The Plumber's Gift* (1989), a fantasy with elements of comedy. Payne's eclecticism has been fuelled by his interest in, and scholarly work on, earlier twentieth-century British music. Whether his attempt to incor-

---

[8] The finale is somewhat reminiscent of that of Strauss's oboe concerto.

[9] The word-setting is, however, not always idiomatic; it rarely observes the elisions demanded by metre, even where the sense runs on.

porate this instinctive sympathy into his own style has been entirely successful it is perhaps too early to say, but it certainly marks an advance on the
unyielding serialism that he was inclined to pursue (even in unaccompanied
vocal music) in the 1960s and earlier 1970s. Bennett, on the other hand, has
continued to alternate light-textured, but strictly serial, works with a large
quantity of more directly assimilable music for a variety of forces including
unaccompanied chorus (e.g. the choral suite *Sea Change*, 1984). He has
continued to be enormously prolific, for example in a series of concertos
and chamber works; but in retrospect he seems more and more a minor,
though at his best a highly entertaining, figure.

Peter Dickinson (b. 1934) has combined a scholarly interest in modern
American music with an essentially traditional style of his own much
influenced by popular elements. Satie, another preoccupation, provided
the inspiration for the orchestral *Transformations* (1969–70, based on the
Trois Gymnopédies), and a series of concertos since then is testimony to an
increasing interest in the larger forms. David Bedford (b. 1937), whose
techniques have sometimes verged on the minimalist, has continued to
write a large number of works in a wide variety of styles and for all sorts
of media.

Jonathan Harvey (b. 1939) has written his most impressive work since
1975, and has indeed disclaimed much of what he had written earlier.
However, he had been composing prolifically since at least 1962, when he
won the Clements prize with a string quartet. His year of study at Princeton
in 1969–70 markedly increased his grasp of the whole range of twentieth-
century techniques. More recently a spell at IRCAM in Paris has resulted
not only in pieces for electronic tape alone but in some striking uses of
synthesized sound within conventionally scored works.

It is difficult to characterize briefly the work of so diverse a composer,
but underlying all of it is a deep concern with the spiritual potential of
musical expression. Initially this was expressed in a quasi-minimalist form
that could seem monotonous, but in the mature work there is a much
greater sense of purpose. Even so, an ability to harness the simplest of
materials to his own ends is apparent in the exquisite short anthem for
unaccompanied voices 'I love the Lord',[10] basically a fantasia on a G major
triad. A willingness to explore both orthodox Christian and secular themes
suggests a comparison with Messiaen, though the musical language remains
quite independent; more significant, perhaps, is the sheer energy that has
produced a series of masterpieces culminating in the cello concerto (1990)
and the opera *Inquest of Love*, produced at the Coliseum in 1993. The opera,
like the earlier *Madonna of Winter and Spring* (1986), combines 'live' synthe-
sizers with conventional forces (on the whole a more satisfactory device

[10] Published as a *Musical Times* supplement in Nov. 1977.

than the use of pre-recorded tape, such as is used in some of the earlier works)[11] to strikingly beautiful effect. As so often in the later twentieth century, the dramatic context justifies a breadth of idiomatic range that might seem questionable in the concert-hall; yet Harvey's own concert works exercise precisely the discipline that prevents them from being amorphous or indulgent.

The Older Avant-Garde

Davies and Birtwistle are the main representatives of this movement, which has continued to occupy a central place in the last twenty years and has been the strongest single influence on younger composers generally. It is by no means a restrictive or exclusive movement, however; it has strong affinities both with the older eclecticism and the newer pragmatism, and Davies in particular has cultivated a number of stylistic gradations to suit various performing contexts, including those involving children and amateurs. Birtwistle has been less flexible, but he has developed an idiom that transcends mere modernism in its challenging public persona.

Older than either of them is the enigmatic figure of John Buller (b. 1927), who despite an earlier leaning towards composition practised architecture before deciding to pursue musical study with Anthony Milner during the years 1959–64. Even after that he continued his former career and only took to composing full time in the early 1970s. He leapt into prominence with *Proença* (1977), a large-scale work for mezzo-soprano and orchestra, securing a growing reputation with the orchestral *Theatre of Memory* (1981) and, more recently, with his opera *The Bacchae* (*BAKXAI*, 1992). Some of his chamber music has used electronic tape. Much of his work is of unmitigated complexity, but he has simplified and diversified the idiom in his choral works *Finnegan's Floras* (1972) and *The Mime of Mick, Nick, and The Maggies* (first heard in full in 1978), both based on James Joyce's *Finnegans Wake*.

Buller's choice of subjects and his treatment of them bear the mark of a high intellect. *The Bacchae* uses the original Greek text, like the earlier *Kommos* ('lament') from the *Agamemnon* of Aeschylus, set for four solo singers and electronic materials. *Proença* sets portions of several Provençal poems, chosen to convey 'the flowering and sudden death of a liberal society, finally wiped out by...the ruthless Albigensian Crusade'. Here the style of word-setting is such as to make aural comprehension difficult whatever the language; but a text and translation in the programme book, like vernacular surtitles in the opera-house, are sufficient to resolve the problems of both audibility and linguistic unfamiliarity. This unconcern for the possibility of a direct aural response to a text is found in a great deal of

[11] *Inner Light 2* (1977), one of a series of three works progressing from a small ensemble (with tape) to orchestra (with synthesizer), uses both.

'advanced' music written since 1945, and Buller can hardly be blamed for finding verbal distortion an aesthetic necessity. It does, however, raise the question whether there might be a fundamental mismatch between verbal material and its manner of setting. If words are merely a peg on which to hang self-sufficient music there is no great problem, but Buller's music conveys a passionate involvement. A passage from the full score (Ex. 7.3), though scarcely legible in so great a reduction, will convey something of the complexity and freedom achieved within a regular (but purely notional) pulse, and of the composer's 'dysfunctional' approach to word-setting—an idiom that is capable of expressing both erotic fulfilment and (as here) bitter regret.[12]

Buller's late twentieth-century radicalism is quite exceptional in an English composer of his generation. It is more to be expected of Davies and Birtwistle, both eight years his junior and in the first flush of youth when *Le marteau sans maître* hit the world in 1955. But they too would be of little account were it not for a personal development that in many respects has discarded the orthodoxy that first inspired them. What they have both retained from the post-war avant-garde is a predominantly atonal, rhythmically asymmetrical, coloristically exotic idiom, often enhanced by but not wholly dependent on improvisatory and electronic elements.

Davies has emerged as the more outwardly conventional of the two, cultivating the standard instrumental forms of symphony and concerto and capable of simplifying his idiom without compromising his integrity. At the first St Magnus Festival in 1977 his opera *The Martyrdom of St Magnus* was produced in the cathedral at Kirkwall, and the annual celebrations have been the primary focus of his activities ever since.

Davies's best music has a muscular litheness associated with an essentially contrapuntal idiom. His scores look relatively uncluttered, and he has turned away from the obscurantism that occasionally marred his earlier work. Each composition is perceived as an intellectual and technical problem—and Davies has been generous with explanatory notes. Thus we are told that the *Sinfonia concertante* (1982–3), for wind quintet and string orchestra with timpani, was his 'first attempt at a form related to the concerto'; the timpani were added 'mainly for the sake of their dramatic power'. The opera scores, from *Taverner* onwards, may give an account of the genesis of and philosophy behind the work as well as a synopsis. The operas written for the St Magnus festival are shorter and less complex than

---

[12] This portion of text is from a poem by Guiraut Riquier, who wrote in exile after the crusade; it follows an instrumental section depicting, in shamelessly Romantic fashion, the destructiveness of the war. '[I really should stop singing,] for song should be concerned with joyful things; and sorrow so constrains me that grief overwhelms me': the text as set continues with the words 'I was born too late' and ends with an orthodox prayer to the Blessed Virgin Mary. The string notation indicates a sustained chord embodying every note of the chromatic scale from top to bottom, the constituent notes being gradually removed until the end of the piece.

Ex. 7.3

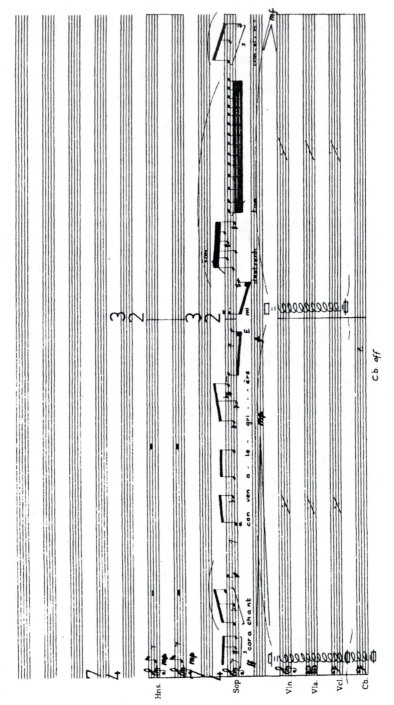

continued

Ex. 7.3. continued

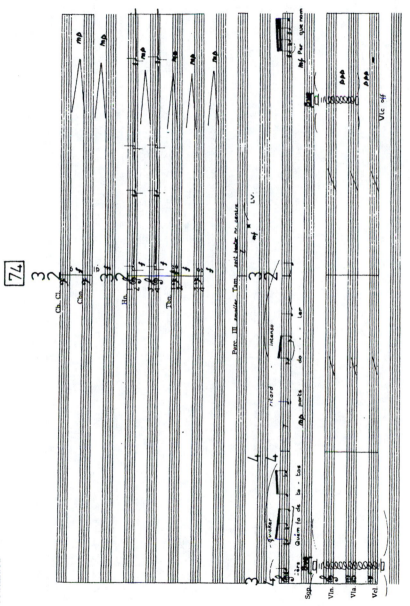

Ex. 7.3. continued

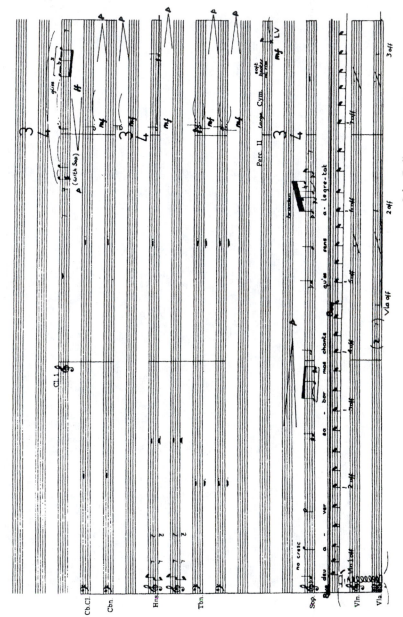

John Buller, *Proença* (New York, 1977), pp. 110–11

Taverner, as one might expect. *The Martyrdom of St Magnus* is skilfully constructed as a series of short scenes, while *The Two Fiddlers* (1978), *Cinderella* (1980), and several music-theatre works were written for local children. *The Lighthouse*, written for the Edinburgh Festival, 1980, is a short and powerful chamber opera on the subject of the mysterious disappearance of three lighthousemen in 1900. *Resurrection*, given in Darmstadt in 1987, is also in a prologue and one act but employs a diverse instrumentarium comprising a 'rock group', 'Salvation Army band', and a pit-orchestra of wind, keyboards, strings, and a vast array of percussion, together with an 'electronic vocal quartet' in addition to singers and dancers on the stage.

Resurrection, conceived as early as 1963, is somewhat exceptional in Davies's later output, though it is a salutary warning against premature judgement on the course of his work as a whole.[13] But the major effort in a huge workload since 1978 has been in the composition of (by 1996) six symphonies and numerous concertos, the latter mostly for soloists from the Scottish Chamber Orchestra. The symphonies are large-scale, austere compositions, predominantly contrapuntal in procedure though never slavishly so. The first (1978) takes as its starting-point the opening notes of the plainsong hymn 'Ave maris stella', a favourite theme previously projected through a distorting prism in an instrumental sextet of that title (1975). Here the intervals are unchanged to begin with except for inversion and octave-displacement (see Ex. 7.4), but they give rise to note-sequences which grow out of the chant in complex but organic ways. The second and third symphonies, which are scarcely less lapidary, explore the orchestral resource still more imaginatively, and while an underlying Nordic pessimism seems never far away, there are glimpses of a lighter-textured world, as for example in the altogether delightful theme of the third movement of the second symphony (Ex. 7.5), where the derivation is again from a chant, this time the antiphon 'Nativitas tua Dei Genitrix Virgo'.[14] The fourth symphony (1989) was written for the smaller forces of the Scottish Chamber Orchestra, but it is for all that a weighty full-length work in four movements, inspired this time by the plainsong antiphon 'Adorna thalamum tuum'. The fifth (1994) is a shorter one-movement work with evident analogies to Sibelius's seventh, while the sixth (1996) reverts to a four-movement plan.[15]

The fourth symphony makes a natural counterpart to the ten Strathclyde Concertos, where the restricted orchestral palette is balanced by virtuoso display. Even so, the versatility expected of the rank-and-file is considerable:

---

[13] There is a useful article on the scenario and libretto of *Resurrection* by J. Warnaby, 'Maxwell Davies's "Resurrection": Origins, Themes, Symbolism', *Tempo*, 191 (Dec. 1994), 6–13.

[14] For a discussion of its transformations, based on sketches in the Brit. Lib. Add. MS 71334, see R. E. McGregor, 'The Maxwell Davies Sketch Material in the British Library', *Tempo*, 196 (Apr. 1996), 9–19, esp. 13–15.

[15] For the fifth symphony, given at the Proms in 1994, see J. Beecroft, 'Maxwell Davies's Fifth Symphony', *Tempo*, 191 (Dec. 1994), 2–5.

Ex. 7.4

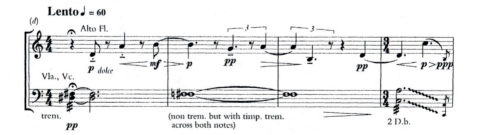

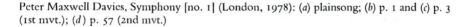

Peter Maxwell Davies, Symphony [no. 1] (London, 1978): (*a*) plainsong; (*b*) p. 1 and (*c*) p. 3 (1st mvt.); (*d*) p. 57 (2nd mvt.)

Ex. 7.5

Allegro molto, leggiero ♩ = 144

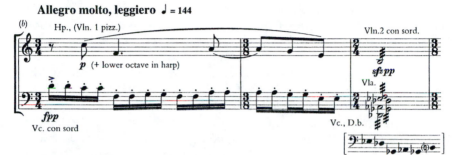

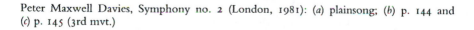

Peter Maxwell Davies, Symphony no. 2 (London, 1981): (*a*) plainsong; (*b*) p. 144 and (*c*) p. 145 (3rd mvt.)

piccolo, alto flute, bass clarinet, and double bassoon are all required, for example, in the eighth concerto, for bassoon (1993). The most remarkable feature of this work—which is by no means a predominantly light-hearted affair—is the accompanied cadenza with which the third movement begins, rising from the depths against a series of two-note chords beginning with a sepulchral tenth on the lowest notes of the bass clarinet and double bassoon. The concerto for piccolo (1997, written for the Royal Philharmonic Orchestra and its Scottish-born piccolo-player Stewart McIlwham) has a sustained lyricism rarely associated with this instrument.

A certain dourness is in fact never far away in Davies, even in a work so colourful as 'Orkney Wedding and Sunrise' for orchestra and solo bagpipe (1985: 'From practical experience it is recommended that the piper be auditioned before engagement', remarks the composer wrily). Rhythm-ically, too, despite the neatness of the designs on paper, the casual listener will be more aware of discontinuity than continuity. Orchestral textures are marked by oddities of balance (in the woodwind, for example, or when an independent double-bass line is pitted against inherently stronger cellos) and by extremes of high and low, soft and loud; vocal writing, solo or choral, is technically demanding and occasionally idealistic. Even when intentionally witty (as in the enchanting and vulgar *Miss Donnithorne's Maggot*, a piece of music-theatre in song-cycle form for soprano and instrumental ensemble), his music tends to make its point allusively. But behind the seeming disjunctions in musical time and space lies a strong compositional discipline that justifies the listener's perseverance and lends coherence to an astonish-ingly large and varied output.

Like Davies, Birtwistle emerged from a period of experiment and occa-sional frustration in the 1960s and early 1970s into one of artistic maturity and confidence. The fruits of that confidence are to be found above all in his three major operas, *The Mask of Orpheus* (1986), *Gawain* (1991), and *The Second Mrs Kong* (1995). But here it must be borne in mind that *The Mask of Orpheus* was originally commissioned by Covent Garden as long ago as 1971 and its first two acts composed in 1973–5; only in 1983, when the prospect of performance at the Coliseum became certain, was the third act written, the whole being eventually produced there in 1986.[16] It bears the marks not so much of its protracted genesis as of adherence to an over-complex theatricality, rich with obscure symbolism, once fashionable but inimical to dramatic cogency. Birtwistle's later operas have remained highly sym-bolic, but they are more approachable in purely theatrical terms.

The scenario and libretto of *The Mask of Orpheus* are by Peter Zinovieff, himself a composer and theorist of electro-acoustic music. Study of the

---

[16] M. Hall, *Harrison Birtwistle* (London, 1984), 171, gives the dates. He has some useful commentary on the opera, pp. 69–73, 114–42, 170–1 (catalogue entry): but the book was completed two years before the first performance and may require corrections of detail.

printed libretto is more than usually essential for the understanding of this opera: the published full score omits many details of the *mise-en-scène* as well as of much of the electro-acoustic element.[17] But although such features of the scenario as multi-level action, triplicated characterization, and reversed time seem complicated, the underlying conception is quite simple. The first act represents the wedding of Orpheus and Euridice and the funeral of Euridice, the second Orpheus' descent into Hades (perceived as a dream), and the third his destruction, primarily at the hands of the Maenads. The centrepiece of the whole opera is a seventeen-stanza aria by Orpheus, corresponding in its dramatic centrality and weight to Monteverdi's 'Possente spirto'. In purely musical terms, in fact, the opera proceeds as a succession of recitatives and arias, interspersed with choruses and dances or mimes, the latter to pre-recorded music. The real difficulty of the opera, apart from the practicalities involved in staging it, lies in attaching an enduring value to symbolic repetitions and distortions expressed in the inevitably clumsy mechanisms of the theatre, and it is perhaps significant that it has since (1996) been successfully given in concert performance.

Between the completion of *The Mask of Orpheus* and *Gawain* came *Yan Tan Tethera* (1984), a piece of music-theatre taking north-country methods of counting sheep as its starting-point. Here the element of ritualistic repetition so characteristic of Birtwistle seems unduly obsessive. The same problem recurred in *Gawain* in its original version, though this was remedied by the curtailing of Gawain's journey (at the beginning of Act II) in the 1993 revival. In any case *Gawain* is Birtwistle's most accessible opera, clear in plot if not always in diction,[18] its ritualism well suited to the world of Arthurian mythology and its more horrifying elements given a comic flavour by their sheer theatricality (the Green Knight's severed head, singing as he holds it in his arms, is a good old-fashioned *coup de théâtre*). The fivefold masque of the seasons (winter to winter) at the end of Act I, repetitive though it is, is an effective way of indicating the passing of the 'year and a day' of the Green Knight's ultimatum; during it Gawain is washed and armed for the fight, and the appropriate seasonal Marian antiphons are sung by the bishop and a choir of clerics. Gawain's journey, and his three-times attempted seduction, are further rituals. When Gawain finally returns as anti-hero, stained by deceit but spared by the Knight, it is as though nothing has changed—except for the self-knowledge gained by Gawain himself.

---

[17] This was to have been devised by Zinovieff, but in the event the prerecorded material was produced at IRCAM in Paris by Barry Anderson and the composer. Hall, 132–3.

[18] At the 1993 revival the complete text was shown in surtitles, surely an admission of communicative failure, at least on the basic level of aural comprehension, for a work in the audience's mother tongue. The same problem in *The Second Mrs Kong* is discussed by R. Adlington in his article 'Harrison Birtwistle's Recent Music', *Tempo*, 196 (Apr. 1996), 2–8.

Birtwistle's mature music, while stemming ultimately from the same constructivist impulses as that of Davies, has in the end taken a different direction. It can be overwhelmingly dense in texture and obsessively persistent in its pursuit of a temporal goal. In *Silbury Air*, for a chamber ensemble of wind, percussion, and strings (1977), a prefixed 'pulse labyrinth' enables the composer to negotiate a route through a series of metrical changes by choosing from a limited number of instances in which the bar-length, but not the metre, is identical. 'Three times Birtwistle sets out to find his way out of the labyrinth only to find himself at his starting point. When he does discover the exit, . . . it is purely by chance'[19]—a contrived chance, no doubt. One is reminded of those mysterious bronze-age labyrinthine carvings (e.g. at Rocky Valley near Tintagel, Cornwall), contemporary perhaps with the prehistoric Silbury Hill after which the work is named. But over and above the rhythmic constraints lies a strong melodic element, apparently free and even centred on a single gravitational note (E, which is also the tonal focus of *The Mask of Orpheus* and Birtwistle's other 'Orphic' works).

Davies and Birtwistle have been aptly dubbed 'twin peaks'.[20] In both, a strong intellectual foundation has been made to yield truly novel inventions in which old-fashioned compositional choice still plays a commanding role. If Davies is a master of clarity and intricacy, Birtwistle presents a more monolithic face to the world. But however purely abstruse some of their earlier work may seem, they have both regained in their maturity a powerful lyricism that already ensures the emotional response without which a fuller technical understanding would be pointless.

The Younger Avant-Garde

A smallish group of composers born since 1940 has pursued a consistently modernist agenda. Prominent amongst them are Brian Ferneyhough (b. 1943) and Michael Finnissy (b. 1946). Ferneyhough has spent much of his life in Europe and America; but unlike (say) Fricker or Bernard Rands (b. 1935—an older modernist who now lives in America)[21] he has remained an icon in his native country, a symbol of ultra-complexity and as such representative of one avenue (possibly an *impasse*) down which the vanguard has travelled. Amongst his followers and pupils in this country are Chris Dench (b. 1953), Roger Redgate (b. 1958), Richard Barrett (b. 1959), and Andrew Toovey (b. 1962). Ferneyhough's own complexity sometimes

[19] Hall, *Birtwistle*, 108–9.
[20] *BMBH*. vi. 319.
[21] Rands taught at York University in the 1970s and 1980s and established a following there. He and his pupil Roger Marsh (b. 1958) founded the music-theatre group CLAP; this was succeeded in 1981 by Northern Music Theatre, founded by Graham Treacher and Vic Hoyland. But Rands as a composer has failed to maintain a consistent personality.

appears self-defeating, the minutiae of the notation being impossible of strict realization by merely human performers. Computer-assisted processes are one answer to that, and Ferneyhough has used them in some of his compositions, and freer notations (involving an improvisatory element) in others; but like Birtwistle he has never forsaken the path of strict (if not necessarily total) control, and in as recent a work as *On Stellar Magnitudes* (1994) there is no sign of slackening rigour.[22]

Much of Finnissy's music is similarly complex, though he has been open to a far wider range of musical and cultural influences. During the 1970s, he wrote a number of music-theatre pieces including a set of eight *Mysteries* (1972–9), and he has incorporated ethnic and 'folk' elements in some of his music, not to mention 'arrangements' or impressions of Strauss, Verdi, Gershwin, and even Obrecht. A further strand is reflected in his appointment in 1968 as Lecturer at the London School of Contemporary Dance and an association with several dance companies. A formidable pianist, he has cultivated an air of improvisatory showmanship in his style that is quite distinct from the more solemn emanations of some contemporary avant-gardistes. There is a strong link with Messiaen's freely comprehensive pianism and its openness to practically any source of inspiration, even though the actual sources are rather different. Another influence seems to be that of Percy Grainger. Some of the shorter piano pieces are quite enchanting: *Kemp's Morris* (1979), for instance, requires the pianist to tie a ring of morris-bells to each hand, colouring the music from its deceptively simple, slightly jazzy, opening until at the end the piece dissolves into a peal of bells and nothing else. *English Country-tunes* (1977) is a more uncompromising treatment of eight tunes in a 45-minute work of almost unremitting complexity.[23] His output also includes seven piano concertos—two solo, the rest with varying ensembles including one with voice—and indeed a large array of scores for a wide variety of media.

Roger Smalley (b. 1943) at one time seemed a potential leader of the younger avant-garde. As a pupil of Stockhausen in Cologne (1965–6) and performer of his piano music, he absorbed the improvisatory and electronic elements then current, forming with Tim Souster in Cambridge the group Intermodulation (1970–6). But in 1976 Smalley went to the University of Western Australia at Perth, and since then his music has developed in different ways.

---

[22] See the review by R. Freeman, with examples: 'Retuning the Skies—Ferneyhough's "On Stellar Magnitudes"', *Tempo*, 191 (Dec. 1994), 34–7.

[23] In his notes to his recording of *Kemp's Morris* (on NMC D002), Finnissy explains that its nine sections represent the actor Will Kemp's reputed nine days of morris-dancing between London and Norwich; 'the music alludes to, without ever directly quoting, the twenty-sixth melody in Playford's "English Dancing Master" (1651)—sometimes called "The Cherping of the Larke" or "Muscadin"'. He has also recorded his *English Country-tunes* (KTC 1091, with an informative note by Jonathan Cross).

Nicola LeFanu (b. 1947) and Nigel Osborne (b. 1948) are two others who have fairly consistently pursued a 'modernist' agenda, though Osborne's recent politically motivated *Sarajevo* (1994), a tripartite music-theatre work, is evidently a more eclectic piece.[24] LeFanu is unusual, for a modernist, in her assiduous cultivation of the vocal ensemble; her instrumental works exhibit the textural delicacy that the vocal medium requires, but may seem insubstantial on that account. *Deva* (1979), for solo cello and chamber ensemble (alto flute, clarinet, bassoon, horn, violin, viola, and double bass), has a somewhat wispy quality, with its cautious chord-sequences and high-pitched susurrations. Nevertheless it is formally satisfying, with a cadenza at mid-point to reinforce its carefully controlled symmetry.

Osborne's work is generally more ambitious, though his larger experiments, which include the operas *Hell's Angels* (1986) and *The Electrification of the Soviet Union* (Glyndebourne, 1987), have not been uniformly successful. But the song-cycle *I am Goya* (1977), for bass-baritone, flute, oboe, violin, and piano, is a masterly evocation of a dream-like world, and there are a number of impressive orchestral works, including three concertos and two *Sinfonie*.

Younger Pragmatists (1)

Of the composers mentioned in the previous section, only Ferneyhough has maintained a strong commitment to predetermined complexity. Despite the fact that he has a loyal following, it would be difficult for any composer born since 1945 not to be 'pragmatic' in the sense of being willing to explore both constructionist and non-constructionist methods. Nor is it easy to define and to distinguish between modernism and postmodernism: few composers of any stature have been willing to discard all that can be learned from the seminal years of the post-war avant-garde. Even minimalism took its cue from certain of its nihilistic elements while transforming them, in music of any value, into something new and positive.[25]

It is clear, however, that already in Robin Holloway (b. 1943) and John Tavener (b. 1944) attempts were being made to clear the undergrowth without turning back to a pre-modern paradise. Tavener, still a prolific composer, has made an oriental-Christian (Greek Orthodox) mysticism the central focus of his work and has simplified the idiom drastically. His recent

---

[24] It is discussed, not very enthusiastically, by S. Sweeney-Turner in *Tempo*, 191 (Dec. 1994), 30–1.

[25] I do not consider 'minimalism' as a movement in English music, partly because its most systematic proponents have been American, and partly because it can take so many different forms. English composers who might be classed as minimalists usually have some better claim on our attention. For example the fallout from the Cardew circle (see Ch. 6) has included composers of the stature of Gavin Bryars (b. 1943) and Dave Smith (b. 1949). Michael Nyman (b. 1944) in a huge output has found a creative outlet in film-music, and Steve Martland (b. 1958) is a younger man for whom repetitive techniques are but one element in a comprehensive technical armoury.

large-scale work *The Apocalypse* (premiered at the Proms in August 1994) is based on a pedal D for virtually the whole of its two-hour length; its numbing slowness is arguably justified by the cataclysmic effect of the climax when it finally comes, but one is entitled to ask whether the assault on the psyche is brought about by hypomusical disturbances of the acoustic medium rather than by musical mechanisms as generally understood. However, this is perhaps an exceptional case: Tavener is also capable of exquisite work on a small scale, which makes a balanced assessment of his oeuvre as a whole difficult to achieve for the present.

While it would certainly not do to underestimate Tavener nor to ignore his place in a cultural milieu that embraces Arvo Pärt and Henryk Górecki, the real prophet in England of a postmodern aesthetic is Robin Holloway. Holloway's eclecticism seems to have stemmed from a conscious decision to accept his musical antecedents (the German Romantics, Debussy, mainstream twentieth-century music) as a positive element in his style rather than as so much lumber to be discarded. In other words, the pluralism inherent in late twentieth-century musical education was to be put to compositional use. Earlier composers, from Tchaikovsky onwards, had resorted to pastiche; but Holloway's intention is not so much pastiche as assimilation. Whether the results have consistently justified the attitude is another matter. From the first *Concerto for Orchestra* (1966–9) onwards, critics have been disconcerted by the sudden appearance of overt reminiscences, in this case of Brahms. In the orchestral *Scenes from Schumann* (1969–70), the indebtedness to a handful of Schumann's songs is made explicit. Unfortunately, it then becomes hard to distinguish between Holloway's aesthetic of recomposition and that of (say) Stravinsky in *Pulcinella* or *The Fairy's Kiss*; perhaps the composer would not claim that there was any real difference, but in that case it is hard to see why we need more of the same sort of thing. But *Scenes from Schumann* is clearly experimental, a gateway to a more integrated eclecticism such as we find in the *Second Concerto for Orchestra* (1979). Even so, the problem of the composer's own personality remains, just as it does for the postmodern architect. The analogy with architecture is important, for there the postmodern philosophy is predicated on the desirability of assimilating a new building into its external surroundings as well as ensuring its convenience for the intended user. It does not need to be spelt out how this thinking can be applied to music, but the balance between individuality and pastiche (as distinct from an organic relation with the past that characterized a slower rate of evolution) remains an issue. Holloway's *Idyll* for small orchestra (1981), while refreshingly luminous in texture, still operates in a kind of tonal no-man's-land that makes its conclusion seem not so much surprising as pointless.

It might be thought that vocal music would offer the opportunity for a more spontaneous use of reminiscence, but even in Holloway's songs the match between past and present is often imperfect. On the other hand, the opera *Clarissa* (1975), which had to wait until 1990 for a production, has been dismissed, rather unfairly, as simply 'dated'.[26] Like the songs, it attempts a rapprochement between Romanticism and freewheeling modernism, and it may just be that it has achieved this more successfully than other works of its period. Holloway's more recent music, which includes his orchestral works *Seascape and Harvest* (1985–6) and *Wagner Nights* (1989), shows no signs of a retreat from his instinctive preferences. It is easy to be amused, especially by the latter, but one wonders whether the whole idiomatic stance is not intrinsically obsolescent.

Oliver Knussen (b. 1952) exercises a more homogeneous form of pragmatism, influenced in many ways by that of the later Britten, though his earliest studies were with John Lambert (1926–95), an influential teacher at the Royal College of Music and elsewhere. Immensely precocious, Knussen conducted his first symphony with the London Symphony Orchestra at the age of 15; his capriccio *Fire*, for flute and string trio, was commissioned for the Aldeburgh Festival in 1969. His superb command of instrumental colour and his liking for extra-musical themes, including fantasy, suggest a parallel with Ravel; the two one-act 'fantasy operas' *Where the Wild Things Are* and *Higglety Pigglety Pop*, based on the illustrated children's books by Maurice Sendak and occupying him respectively from 1979 to 1983 and from 1984 to 1990, have a clear link with *L'Enfant et les sortilèges*. Their prolonged gestation suggests a composer not easily satisfied, despite the apparent spontaneity of his music: the third symphony was composed between 1973 and 1979, and the early *Pantomime* (1968) for wind quintet and string quartet, was revised in 1978 under the title *Processionals*. The operas apart, he has written less extensively for the voice, but *Océan de terre* for soprano and chamber orchestra (1972–3, revised in 1976 for the Fires of London) gave scope to his penchant for vivid musical imagery; the *Whitman Settings* (1991) are unusual in being for voice and piano.

It is not easy to define Knussen's style, which certainly embraces an element of reminiscence, deliberate or otherwise. But it is better integrated than Holloway's, and less dense than that of many others who have hovered above the marches of tonality and atonality. A recent horn concerto (1996) exhibited no lessening of his instrumental mastery. If his music as a whole seems somewhat lacking in gravitas, it is refreshingly free of turgidity, and his ability to entertain without patronizing is a precious quality.

Michael Berkeley (b. 1948), Lennox Berkeley's eldest son, took longer to find his voice but has in the end developed a tougher idiom. His oratorio *Or shall we die?* (1983) may have sunk under the weight of its anti-nuclear message (except, perhaps, for the aria *For Mrs Tomoyasu*, which has been

---

[26] *BHMB*, vi. 388: 'its sheer datedness is bound to preclude further productions'.

made available separately), but it was in the early 1980s that Berkeley was beginning to forge a more durable style in works like the chamber symphony (1980) and second string quartet (1984). His opera *Baa-baa Black Sheep* (1993), based on a story by Kipling, has a greater emotional impact than one would have thought possible, even if like the oratorio it is stronger in gesture than in properly musical argument. What one can safely say is that in a large and varied output, partly occasional, partly idealistic, there is a complex personality that sees each new work as an opportunity for further exploration.[27]

This first group of 'younger pragmatists', whose work is by and large still linked to traditional norms of rhythmic structure and tonal ambience (even if 'tonality' as such is avoided or kept on a long leash), might include in addition such names as Colin Matthews (b. 1946), Paul Patterson (b. 1947), John Casken (b. 1949), and Dominic Muldowney (b. 1952). Otherwise they have little in common beyond their underlying seriousness of approach. Matthews, an expert on Mahler as well as a composer, emerged comparatively late, but from 1984, starting with a colourful yet well-disciplined cello concerto, he has developed a consistent yet broadly varied idiom in a series of mainly instrumental works. His elder brother David (b. 1943), also a scholar, has again concentrated on instrumental music, with, for example, four symphonies to his credit so far; in style he is perhaps less exploratory, but he is equally a master of the modern orchestra, and it is difficult to predict how a later generation will view the relative merits of this remarkable pair.

Patterson owes his place in this group to a return, in the 1980s, to a quasi-tonal idiom following a period of experiment with indeterminacy. Both he and Casken have affinities with east European postmodernism, the latter exemplifying it in his opera *Golem* (1989). Muldowney, who has been kept busy since 1981 as Birtwistle's successor as Musical Director of the National Theatre, has perhaps achieved less than might at one time have been predicted. Yet his trombone concerto (1996), the latest in a series of such works,[28] has proved to be truly eclectic and even populist within a well-established framework: drawing on the BACH motif and on the signature tune of a once popular radio programme, it manages to make a crazily Hindemithian fugue of its first movement and stops short at nothing in its exploitation of the trombone's sonorous and even visual potential.

Two more instinctively populist composers may be mentioned here. Stephen Oliver (1950–92) achieved a substantial operatic oeuvre in his short life—around forty stage works of all kinds, though the total includes

[27] Berkeley's revitalization of the Cheltenham Festival, of which he became Artistic Director in 1995, is itself a major achievement.

[28] For saxophone (1984), violin (1989), percussion (1991), oboe (1992), and trumpet (1993). Muldowney's earlier work tended to be more self-consciously avant-garde.

several short pieces, one of them an eight-minute work for unaccompanied baritone (*Cadenus Observ'd*, 1974). His first full-length opera, *The Duchess of Malfi*, was written for the Oxford University Opera Club in 1971 (and revised in 1978); his last, *Timon of Athens*, was produced by English National Opera in 1991. Too little of his music is available for study to permit a proper assessment, but it is certain that he had immense facility in an easily assimilable style; at the same time he was alive to current fashions, and was able to draw on almost any technique, popular or otherwise, to further his ends.

Martin Butler, born a decade later, has had the advantage of a more complete immersion in the contemporary rapprochement between 'serious' and 'popular' modernism. His anti-heroic opera *Craig's Progress*, with a libretto by Stephen Pruslin, was produced at the appropriately named Meltdown Festival in June 1994 ('Meltdown' was started under George Benjamin's direction in 1993). One reviewer, at least, was not very impressed by its 'overstated references and maudlin humour'.[29] Yet Butler is a promising exponent of the new accessibility, above all perhaps in a series of showy orchestral works that includes the striking Latin-Americanized *O Rio* (1991). It is impossible, however, to foresee how this breezy idiom will develop in his hands.

Younger Pragmatists (2)

A second, and for present purposes final, group of composers consists of those who so far at least have maintained stronger links with the kind of modernism that has been the defining feature of the post-war avant-garde: it would include at any rate James Dillon (b. 1950), Simon Bainbridge (b. 1952), Robert Saxton (b. 1953), John Woolrich (b. 1954), Mark-Anthony Turnage (b. 1960), and George Benjamin (b. 1960).[30] Dillon at least has been linked to the 'new complexity', and some of his music looks on paper as forbidding as any. But it is less exacting, rhythmically, than some, and there is a strongly expressionistic quality in two works of the mid-1980s that might be regarded as typical: *Überschreiten*, for chamber orchestra, and *Windows and Canopies*, for chamber ensemble. Notational complexity in these is more concerned with sound-production than with rhythm; a 'breathing' quality is attained by crescendos and diminuendos on long-held notes, slowly progressing glissandi, and ornamental figurations that do not disturb the underlying pulse. Even the short piano piece *Birl*, fiendishly difficult to play and certainly complex in its own fashion, is

---

[29] Ian Pace in *Tempo*, 190 (Sept. 1994), 28–9. Benedict Mason's (b. 1954) 'football opera' *Playing Away*, premièred appropriately enough in Munich, 1994, is clearly of the same generic type: it is discussed more sympathetically, in the context of Mason's other work, by John Warnaby in the same issue, pp. 30–2.

[30] Composers born since 1960 will not be individually discussed here.

repetitively rather than unpredictably so. Much the same comments apply to Bainbridge, who has written a series of orchestral and other instrumental works since the viola concerto of 1976. For a time the influence of American minimalism came to the fore, but this has receded again in favour of a more expressionistic idiom.

Robert Saxton has adopted more conventional norms of texture and continuity; always precise in his understanding of instrumental balance, and favouring a clear-cut rhythmic profile, he has extended his range from a series of works for relatively modest forces (with or without the voice) in the 1970s to embrace a thoroughly idiomatic use of orchestral resource in the 1980s and since. Woolrich and Turnage seem to belong rather with Dillon and Bainbridge, though they continue to develop in ways that make them hard to classify. Woolrich studied at Lancaster in the late 1970s with Edward Cowie (b. 1943), himself a distinguished and fastidious composer. Much of Woolrich's own music is indebted to earlier models in ways that range from direct quotation to mere formal analogy; in this he is perhaps a successor to Holloway. But he has not relinquished a firm grasp of idiomatic integrity, and his recent oboe concerto (1996) demonstrates above all a fine feeling for melodic line in a broadly atonal context. Turnage has leavened the lump of modernism with elements of jazz, popular music, and 'gospel song';[31] but compared with (say) Martin Butler there is a core of idiomatic toughness, even in a work as extrovert as the saxophone concerto (1993).

Finally George Benjamin (b. 1960), like the older and much lamented Bill Hopkins (1943–81), has been decisively influenced by his early studies in France, in this case with Messiaen and later, more independently, at IRCAM. The outcome has been a decidedly modernist but not an inflexible approach to communication. His early nature-piece for orchestra, *Ringed by the Flat Horizon* (1979–80), was an immediate success at its Proms première in 1980; yet the composer knew that he could not stop at that point, and while he has since then again written for large orchestra (*Sudden Time*, 1990–3), the essence of his personality is more readily apparent in his smaller-scale works. His *Antara* (1987), for sixteen players and electronic keyboards, is a masterly synthesis of the two media—one of the few, perhaps, in which the electronic resources are not disadvantaged by their more conventional company. *Upon Silence* (1990), a setting of Yeat's 'Long Legged Fly', is a study in minuteness. Originally written for mezzo-soprano and five viols (the appropriately named Fretwork consort), but subsequently arranged for a modern string ensemble, it possesses an engaging intricacy and an absorbing quietude. Benjamin has not been too prolific for his own good, and he remains one of the most interesting of his generation.

---

[31] His opera *Greek* (1988), a setting of the play by Steven Berkoff, has been likened to a Brecht–Weill collaboration. *BHMB*, vi. 386.

While it is manifestly premature to pigeonhole composers as young as Turnage and Benjamin, the observation is even more valid for their junior contemporaries, of whom there are a great many. Rarely, in fact, has there been such a plethora of ambitious and talented young men and women engaged in serious composition. Some of the circumstances surrounding its continued cultivation during the half-century since the Second World War will now be examined.

Summary, 1945–1997

Perhaps the most striking feature of this period as a whole is the record of actual achievement when compared with the almost continuous jeremiad that constitutes its perception of itself. It is difficult not to draw a political analogy: here are fifty years of relative peace and rising prosperity, accompanied by an unending lament over social and economic conditions, the cold war, the proliferation of murderous weaponry, and environmental issues. Peace and prosperity are directly linked to artistic vitality, so it is not surprising that there has been a persistent subsidiary theme complaining of underfunding of the arts. A contrasting theme, that of 'wastage' (especially in the opera-house) has been loudly though intermittently stated by governments, politicians, and letter-writers. More specifically musical complaints have been of modernism and incomprehensibility on the one hand, and of the unadventurousness of audiences on the other. None of these protestations has been without foundation, but our adversarial traditions have often led to their exaggeration, while journalistic methods are such as to extract the maximum gloom from any given situation, so that the headline 'Rising factory output stifles rate cut hopes' (*The Times*, 3 Sept. 1996) is almost a paradigm of the epoch.

These comments do not apply only to England, or indeed to Britain as a whole, of course, and the same is true of the more immediate picture of contemporary music, and the circumstances that have sustained or threatened it according to the point of view. Even so, it is difficult completely to suppress a note of patriotic satisfaction. Perhaps the most surprising aspect is the continued strength of England's traditional institutions: its great orchestras, its concert-giving societies and festivals, and its opera companies. These have continued to commission and perform new British music, so that symphonies, concertos, and operas have been written throughout the period by the most advanced composers as well as by the more conservative. Beside this there have been numerous opportunities for smaller-scale, often experimental work, while the BBC, at least on radio, has played an essential role at all levels.

It would be idle to suppose that every novelty has been of great intrinsic value or to discount the undercurrent of more conservative music; nor can one safely predict which composers and which works will ultimately achieve canonic status. But it may be worth while to reflect a little further on the dialectic between advanced musical thought and the traditional outlets for its expression. (Again, the situation is not confined to Britain.) At one extreme are the conventional orchestras and opera companies, kept in being by the continued demand for their classical (or 'canonic') repertories, including a relatively small number of twentieth-century classics but consisting mostly of late eighteenth- and nineteenth-century works; they are sustained by competition with foreign orchestras and opera companies fulfilling similar roles; and they are supported by a burgeoning recording industry, itself catering mainly for conservative tastes,[32] and by governments not entirely oblivious of national reputation. Encouraged, again, by the BBC, new works are regularly commissioned, partly out of duty, but increasingly out of conviction, to give them a chance in the context of a 'normal' concert-programme or an otherwise 'safe' opera-season. A growing involvement with the European vanguard (for example by the BBC Symphony Orchestra under Boulez, 1971–5) has enabled performers to cope better with the demands of modern British music and to treat it with increased understanding and sympathy. By the 1980s it had become commonplace for the annual Proms to commission a fair number of demanding new orchestral works and even to repeat some of them in subsequent seasons, often to enthusiastic audiences. Meanwhile English National Opera, Covent Garden, and latterly Glyndebourne, evolved a pattern that includes the regular production of challenging new theatre-works: there are failures as well as successes, but the latter are signal achievements.

We have seen in specific instances how composers have reacted to the challenge of writing for traditional media. An orchestral work need not be in a classical form, but the symphony and concerto have been surprisingly resilient in the hands of English composers from Vaughan Williams in his old age to (say) Oliver Knussen or John Woolrich. Those of Maxwell Davies effectively took up the challenge laid down by Tippett, though he had begun his first symphony well before the appearance of Tippett's fourth in 1977. But symphonic form was already a highly malleable concept, while in the concerto new levels of virtuosity, honed by contact with European and American standards (as required in works by, for example, Berio or Elliott Carter), came to be exploited. Orchestration in the conventional sense was replaced by an approach which, if not entirely novel, could be said to be related to three European paradigms, singly or in combination: a chamber-like usage deriving ultimately from Mahler; a dense but usually

---

[32] The role and development of the recording industry in this period is a subject in itself. Technological developments, culminating in the CD, have led not only to improved sound-quality and user-convenience but also to the growth of small companies catering for specialist interests, including the interest in contemporary music.

'layered' sound-world, often using a minutely divided string-section and calling for glissandi, microtones, and novel methods of sound-production (cf. Ligeti, Penderecki); and an exotic use of colour related to the methods of Messiaen and Boulez. Naturally the result was affected by compositional method: predetermination of various kinds, the free use of a tonal or atonal framework, or indeterminacy. Finally, electro-acoustic resources could be brought into play.

These last have played a decisive role in the direction taken by modern music, both in large-scale forms, including opera, and in chamber ensembles. They have less often been used alone, though there are works for tape by Birtwistle, Harvey, Trevor Wishart (b. 1946), and others. Electronic sound as a creative medium was revolutionized first by the development of magnetic tape, and secondly by the invention (in the 1950s) of the electronic sound-synthesizer. Sounds generated from the latter have usually been recorded and then made available as a definitive contribution to (or version of) the 'score', though volume-control and balance-control are available to the operator and are sometimes prescribed in ensemble works. But the direct use of a synthesizer is more flexible and 'human'; its disadvantage is that it is comparatively cumbersome and expensive to use in live performances. Computerized sound-synthesis has given composers a vastly greater formal control over the electronic medium: complex formulae can be used to process the raw material, making of it, if desired, a fully predetermined element. At the other end of the scale, straightforward amplification has played a significant role.[33] English exploitation has eventually achieved independence from the Continental pioneering work of Varèse, Pousseur, Stockhausen, and Boulez.[34]

Ensemble music, often with voice, and with or without the electronic medium, has (together with solo instrumental music) been the predominant arena for experiment. Wishart's *Vox* (1979–86) is an ambitious five-movement work for amplified vocal quartet and electronic resources;[35] many others have been written for soprano and instrumental ensemble, drawing on vocal talents such as those of Jane Manning and Mary Thomas. (An exponential rise in the standard of English singing—in terms of accuracy and focus—has benefited both early and modern music.) Specialist ensembles,

---

[33] e.g. in works as diverse as Giles Swayne's (b. 1946) *Cry* (1979), for twenty-eight amplified voices, Tippett's *The Ice-Break* (see above), and Turnage's saxophone concerto (1993). Stockhausen's *Stimmung* (1968) for six amplified voices was a key influence on English composers: the British group Singcircle has specialized in performing it and works like Wishart's *Anticredos* (1979).

[34] Many English composers have used the studio for electronic music at Cologne, run by West German Radio and made famous by Stockhausen, and IRCAM (Institut de Recherche et de Coordination Acoustique/Musique), set up by Boulez in Paris as part of the Pompidou Centre. Harvey went to both, and at Sussex University set up what was for some time the most comprehensive centre for English students.

[35] It is described, with a reproduction from the score, in *BHMB*, vi. 446–50.

such as the Nash Ensemble and the Park Lane Group, have enabled experiment to flourish, while the Fires of London and the English Music Theatre Company (1975, previously the English Opera Group) have provided a focus for new dramatic and semi-dramatic music. In this way a very large repertory of non-standardized work, fertilized by American and Continental ideas, has sprung up, while traditional chamber media (including piano-accompanied song) have for most composers become less important (though the Arditti Quartet's championship of the immensely difficult string quartets of Brian Ferneyhough provides a notable exception). Finally, the exuberant folly of the Meltdown Festival, not to mention the occasional Prom commission, has offered a platform for wholly experimental, often extravagantly scored, new works.

In these ways the 1990s seem a world away from the prim 1950s and the cautiously outward-looking 1960s. The renewed search for authenticity in the performance of early music and the discovery of ethnic musics have invigorated both the composition and the performance of new music, while the cultural rapprochement of serious and popular amongst the young has promoted a degree of cross-fertilization unthinkable previously (even though the genres remain obstinately apart). The tolerance of critics and audiences to new and experimental music is much greater; a direct appeal to the rootless young (including the young in spirit) has circumvented the resistance of the stuffed-shirt and blue-rinse element (vital though this is for patronage) and the armchair inertia of the lower middle classes. A new and heartening feature is the uncliquish support given by composers to each other, not merely through long-established channels like the Society for the Promotion of New Music but by constructive published criticism. While older composers have generally preferred to write about themselves, if at all, Robin Holloway, Michael Finnissy, and Oliver Knussen amongst others have been well prepared to evaluate and promote their colleagues' music. A new generation of specialist critics and commentators, including Paul Griffiths, Paul Driver, Stephen Walsh, Richard Toop (a powerful advocate of the 'new complexity'), Malcolm Miller, Keith Potter, Jim Samson, and Calum MacDonald, has swept away many of the old barriers. A further interesting phenomenon is that of the composer- and/or performer-librettist: Stephen Pruslin, Michael Nyman, and Peter Zinovieff spring to mind.

That composers should often teach is axiomatic, but the growth of university departments as centres of composition-teaching is a post-war development. At Cambridge Robin Orr, a minor Scottish composer, was succeeded in 1976 by Alexander Goehr, while the faculty there has also included Robin Holloway and Hugh Wood. At Oxford, Edmund Rubbra, Kenneth Leighton, and Robert Sherlaw Johnson have been successively Fellows of Worcester College and University Lecturers in Music. Jonathan Harvey, now succeeded by Martin Butler, exerted a profound influence at

Sussex; composer-professors elsewhere have included Raymond Warren at Bristol, John Casken at Manchester, and Sebastian Forbes at Surrey, while Nigel Osborne followed Leighton in the Reid Chair at Edinburgh in 1990. University departments are not always an ideal milieu, either for teacher-composers or for their pupils; composers are often too weighed down by administrative and teaching duties (the latter not always of the most imme-diately relevant kind), while for students of composition the professional ambience of a music college, with its greater opportunities for performance, discussion, and alternative teaching, is lacking. In fact, ambitious university students almost invariably seek further tuition outside their institution, often abroad. But at the same time universities can nowadays provide electronic studios, with advanced instruction in theory and analysis, often at greater depth than elsewhere and at postgraduate level, quite apart from the more general benefits of a university course in music. Finally in this context is the fact that the enormous recent expansion in the number of universities (many of them former polytechnics) has led to a wide variety of approach to practical topics including composition, while the emphasis on composi-tion in the General Certificate of Secondary Education is likely to lead to the earlier recognition of unsuspected talent.

It is thus hardly surprising that the production and reception of adven-turous new music, largely freed from earlier restrictions and inhibitions based on social and musical prejudices, should flourish where it had been a weakly plant. It has been claimed[36] that in 1995 the BBC broadcast music by no fewer than three hundred living British composers—an astonishing total even when account is taken of writers of conservative and light popular music. It certainly would not be difficult to draw up a list of a hundred serious British modernists born since 1930, mostly happily still alive. All but half a dozen or so firmly established figures (Goehr, Birtwistle, Davies, Maw, and Harvey are certainly amongst them) must be seen as still con-tending for the inevitably limited accolade of classic status. That modernism should be the chosen battleground need cause no surprise. If it is true that the classics of literature are the writers who take pains to develop the language in order to cope with their semantic requirements, and that those who thereafter merely imitate them are of less account, then it follows that only those seen to be extending or refining the musical language, provided that this is necessary for their expressive purposes, are likely to achieve permanence. In a true artist the search for originality will be instinctive; in a lesser figure it may well be an artificial stance. Only time, in most cases, will make the difference clear.

[36] By John Birt, Director General of the BBC, at a conference in Edinburgh in Aug. 1996.

8

FOLK MUSIC AND POPULAR MUSIC

THE subject of this chapter is easier to describe than to define. Beside
the national body of centrally developed art-music, its style the outcome of a narrowly focused tradition of imitation and innovation, stands a
mass of material that lies outside the main stream, related to but not
dependent on it, rather as regional dialects may be related to a central
standardized language. A regional character is indeed an important facet of
what has come to be called folk music, though this does not preclude the
transmission of melodies and melody-types across regional and even
national boundaries. Just as important is its cultivation and preservation in
a stratum of society that exists independently of the 'higher' civilization that
surrounds it, though this again does not preclude the transference of
material across the social boundaries, whatever its origin. But notwithstanding the potential for regional and social migration, it seems important to
maintain a distinction between folk music, rural or urban, and the commercially produced variety that we think of as 'popular'. Even here the distinction is blurred by the fact that so much 'true' folk music seems to have
originated in the commercial enterprises of towns and cities, for example in
the production of single-sheet ballads to be sung to existing well-known
tunes. In such cases, the rural and urban proletariat have adopted the
material as their own, developing and interpreting it in their own way;
conversely, music originating in or already thoroughly assimilated by these
populations may for one reason or another quite suddenly achieve wide
circulation at all social levels. But there is still a large quantity of material,
more particularly from the eighteenth century onwards, that never had any
function beyond that of trivialized light entertainment.

The term 'folk music' is actually quite recent, and like the slightly older
'folk song' and other such combinations is the product of a somewhat
romanticized view of the people, or 'folk', a word that in modern
English (unlike the German *Volk*) carries archaic and sentimental conno-
tations of a kind beloved of Victorian and Edwardian social idealists. Earlier

investigators, beginning with those whose interest was primarily in poetry, had been more concerned with the recovery of the 'ancient'; other terms applied to the same overlapping series of ideas were 'popular', 'national', and 'traditional', together with what were thought of as 'balladry' and 'minstrelsy'. It will be instructive to look at some of these in turn.

In Thomas Percy's *Reliques of Ancient English Poetry* (1765), for example, the term 'ancient' obviously has a rather special sense. Percy was aware of poetry older than any in his collection, if only that of Chaucer; though in fact the study of Old English ('Anglo-Saxon') verse had already been in progress for well over a century. What his usage conveyed to his readers was a vaguer remoteness defined essentially by mysteriousness of origin: his poems were certainly older than the manuscripts he used, or so he thought, but who could say how much older?

It was Percy's tiresomely pedantic adversary Joseph Ritson (1752–1803) who introduced the specifically musical dimension into this interpretation of the 'ancient':[1] his *Ancient Songs and Ballads* (1790), though primarily an edition of poems, includes in its preliminary dissertations a discussion of 'our ancient songs and vulgar music', and includes musical quotations from a manuscript of his own and from one other in the British Museum.[2] John Stafford Smith (1750–1836) was a more formidable antiquary, and his *Musica antiqua* (1812) includes music from English sources as early as the twelfth century; he was less interested, however, in the 'traditional', and his enquiry builds on the more strictly historical enterprises of Burney and Hawkins.

What Percy and Ritson had hit on was a genuine vein of non-learned poetry of a type that antiquarians were coming to think of as 'ballads' *par excellence*: narrative poems in strophic form to be sung to familiar tunes. The printed street ballads that had begun to appear in large quantities from around 1550 onwards encouraged the application of the term to comparable manuscript poems, and, eventually, to sung strophic narrative verse preserved in the oral tradition.[3] So was born the 'ballad' industry, exemplified by the mammoth work of F. J. Child on the literary side and, in the rounding up of the associated melodies, the even more monumental

---

[1] The concept of 'ancient music' had been in use throughout the 18th c. to denote the art–music of earlier times (though not, in practice, music from before the late 16th c.). In a 'traditional' context it had been anticipated by the Welsh: John Parry published his *Antient British Music; or, A Collection of Tunes . . . Retained by the Cambro-Britons* in 1742. See further Weber, *The Rise of Musical Classics*, 30 and *passim*, and below, n. 7.

[2] Ritson owned what are now Brit. Lib. Add. 5665 (the 'Ritson' MS) and 5666; he used the latter and Roy. App. 58 for his musical illustrations. His *Ancient Songs and Ballads* 'is dated in 1790, though not published till two years after; though actually printed in 1787' (note to Advertisement of 2nd edn., 1829; a third edn., by W. C. Hazlitt, appeared in 1877).

[3] This scholarly usage overlaps with, but is distinct from, that of the popular composed ballad in the tradition established (to the best of my knowledge) by J. F. Lampe in 1731: see Ch. 1 n. 107.

achievement of B. H. Bronson.[4] Child was interested mainly in the oral and manuscript traditions; the printed ballads were investigated and published by numerous scholars in the late nineteenth and early twentieth centuries, and their musical companion was finally published in 1966 by C. M. Simpson.[5]

Meanwhile the range of what could be considered 'popular' had been enormously extended by William Chappell (1809–88), whose *Popular Music of the Olden Time* (1855–9, incorporating his earlier published work) draws on both written and oral tradition. While his approach was essentially antiquarian, he tried to present his material in such a way as to make it readily performable (with harmonizations and arrangements by G. A. Macfarren), and to relate it to surviving popular tradition.[6] The investigation of 'ancient' music through the testimony of its living practitioners had been pioneered in Wales by Parry and Jones, in Ireland by Bunting and Petrie, and in Scotland by the publisher James Johnson, aided by the indefatigable Robert Burns.[7] The further popularization of their materials by the composition of new poems, and by adaptations for polite use, by Burns and Scott, and by Thomas Moore in Ireland, provides a further strand in the historiography of 'folk' or 'national' music in the British Isles.[8]

Apart from Chappell and John Broadwood, another early pioneer, the collection of songs and dance-tunes from the living tradition began in earnest only in the late nineteenth century as far as England is concerned.

[4] F. J. Child, *The English and Scottish Popular Ballads*, 10 pts. (Cambridge, Mass., 1882–98); also in 5 vols., ed. G. L. Kittredge (Boston, 1882–98, and reprints); B. H. Bronson, *The Traditional Tunes of the Child Ballads*, 4 vols. (Princeton, 1959–72).

[5] See below, n. 33.

[6] W. Chappell, *Popular Music of the Olden Time*, 2 vols. (London, 1859; originally in parts, 1855–9); 2nd edn. by H. E. Wooldridge, *Old English Popular Music* (London and New York, 1893); see Bibliography for fuller details. Wooldridge's edn. is more 'scholarly' and is limited to evidence from no later than Renaissance times, but Chappell's original is nowadays more highly valued for the sake of its 'traditional' information.

[7] For Parry see n. 1. Edward Jones's *Musical and Poetical Relicks of the Welsh Bards* was first published in London in 1784, and in a 2nd edn. in 1794, and was followed by *The Bardic Museum* (London, 1802), and by *Hên Ganiadau Cymru: Cambro-British Melodies* in 1820. Edward Bunting's *A General Collection of the Ancient Irish Music* (London, 1796) was followed by the similarly entitled *A General Collection of the Ancient Music of Ireland . . . Vol. 1st* [sic] (London, [1809]), and by *The Ancient Music of Ireland* (Dublin, 1840); his MS materials were published as *The Bunting Collection of Irish Folk Music and Songs*, ed. D. J. O'Sullivan, 6 vols. (Dublin, 1927–39 = *JIFSS* 22, 23, 25, 26, 27, 28–9). *The Petrie Collection of the Ancient Music of Ireland* (Dublin, 1855) was repr. Farnborough, 1967, together with 48 pages of a planned 2nd vol. The Edinburgh music-engraver James Johnson (*c.*1750–1811) published *The Scots Musical Museum*, largely the work of Burns, in 6 vols. (Edinburgh, 1787–1803); it was repr. in 1839 and 1853, with notes by W. Stenhouse, 4 vols., and in 1962 (repr. of Stenhouse).

[8] It is sometimes difficult to distinguish between the traditional, the adapted, and the wholly new in the printed poems of Burns and Scott (e.g. in *The Scots Musical Museum* and in Scott's *Minstrelsy of the Scottish Border*, 3 vols., Kelso, 1802). Moore's *Selection of Irish Melodies*, with new words to tunes collected by Bunting, was originally publ. in 10 pts. and a supplement in London, 1808–34. The concept of 'national' song can be traced back to the early 18th c. and in particular to Allan Ramsay and his collections of 'substitute' poems from 1718 on: see D. Johnson, *Music and Society in Lowland Scotland in the Eighteenth Century* (London, 1972), 131–2.

It may be said to have come of age with the foundation of the Folk-Song Society in 1898, and from that point the mythology of the 'folk music' movement became common currency, with its assumptions as to the origin and maintenance of folk music in rural isolation, the primacy (if not indeed the exclusive validity) of the oral tradition, the legitimacy of pure melody alone, and the notion of a remote antiquity guaranteed by modal form. Although the dance and its tunes were also investigated, the main interest has always been in the direction of song.[9]

All these assumptions have long since been convincingly challenged. To begin with, there is undoubtedly an urban folk music readily distinguishable from commercial popular music,[10] and this, rather than the rural variety, has maintained its vitality to the present day. Nor was Sharp's theory of cultural isolation wholly credible as a context even for rural folk music. On the other hand, it is hardly sufficient to posit, with A. L. Lloyd,[11] a purely economic explanation for the existence and survival of folk song. Folk singers in general certainly come from the poorer strata of society, but the more important factor is that they belong to a cohesive community distinct from that of the wider 'civilized' world. This community may be rural or urban, geographically static or on the move, domestic or work-related; but folk music, however it originates and whatever form it takes, is essentially the property of the community, not of a single musician—even though such a musician may nevertheless enjoy it in private, transmit it to another community, or dictate it to a collector for posterity.

The community thus postulated is not wholly isolated from the society around it but lives in a delicate symbiosis with it, taking advantage of its amenities when it can afford to do so, giving as well as taking, but always maintaining its identity. It may consist, for example, of industrial workers and their families, gypsies, mariners, or settled villagers, but always of men and women whom birth and circumstances have bonded together and who have no reason to disrupt it. When such communities break up or are transformed out of recognition, their music generally dies with them. While this can happen to any community, the transformation of village life in modern times seems to have entailed the irrevocable loss of some at least of its musical traditions.

An exclusive concern with oral transmission and unharmonized melody has been conclusively shown to be unduly limiting. There is a wealth of

---

[9] For the main outlines of the folk-song revival in England see below, pp. 513–15. The issues of origins, social context, and musical character are discussed *inter alia* in C. J. Sharp, *English Folk-Song: Some Conclusions* (London, 1907), A.L. Lloyd, *Folk Song in England* (London, 1967), and F. Howes, *Folk Music of Britain—and Beyond* (London, 1970).

[10] Under this heading I include (though not strictly 'urban') such things as sailors' shanties and miners' songs: see e.g. C. J. Sharp, *English Folk-Chanteys* (London, 1914), and A. L. Lloyd, *Come All Ye Bold Miners* (London, 1952).

[11] *Folk Song in England*, 11, 17.

written and even printed music that is clearly distinct from centralized art-music both in style and in the circumstances of its origin, and most of it is harmonized or implies the existence of harmony. If its relevance to folk music is questioned, the answer must be that it fulfils all the necessary conditions. If it does not always match the criteria laid down by an earlier generation of specialists, its idioms nevertheless betray a striking independence from those of professionally trained musicians. This does not mean that it is necessarily incompetent or amateurish: on the contrary, it may well possess its own sophistication, and a finesse that justifies a highly developed connoisseurship.

The linguistic analogy may be pressed a little further here, since the liveliest traditions of folk music often coincide with linguistic particularity. This is most obviously true of Scotland, of which more is said below, but it is valid for England as well, even though educational philosophy has often (and surely wrongly) discouraged the retention of regional dialects. The important point, however, is that it is possible to cultivate both a 'dialect' and a 'standard language'; and the same is true of music, both in performance and as regards its appreciation. Thus the communal symbiosis mentioned above has its counterpart in a musical two-way traffic that excludes neither the gentry from the sphere of folk music nor its most gifted practitioners from a profitable exposure to art-music.

Finally one may question the presumption of the early collectors that they were involved in rescuing from oblivion an ancient repertory that was just on the point of disappearing for ever. It is certainly true that a proportion of the music recovered is of some antiquity in the sense that its stylistic implications are those shared by the art-music of an earlier period than the late nineteenth century. It is also true that many a melody would have been lost in the form in which it was collected had it not then been recorded in writing. But the hypothesis overlooks both the resilience of the essential melodic stock and the variability of orally transmitted music. From this point of view, any performance of a song is a valid expression only of that one performance. A melody may therefore be old in one sense but entirely new in another. Folk music is nothing if it is not a living, vibrant, art. Some researchers are content to explore and record its contemporary vibrancy without attempting to deal with a possible past; but for a historian there is a legitimate challenge in trying to recreate some sense of that living present as it once existed.

Popular Music to 1700

So far as purely musical evidence is concerned, it seems unrealistic for this period to distinguish clearly between 'folk' and 'popular' music as we have defined them. After that we can begin to do so, with the aid of written sources, on the grounds of style and, at least in some cases, of presumed local origin. Here the Scottish experience is of some help and will be introduced in order to throw light on questions for which the English evidence alone would not provide a sufficient answer. First, however, some consideration of earlier music warranting the designation 'popular' is desirable.

It must be admitted in the first place that the term 'popular' is itself highly ambiguous and has often been applied uncritically: it need after all imply only frequent repetition and ready recognition within a restricted circle, and nothing like the mass appeal usually meant by the word today. At the same time, while admitting that the concept of 'folk music' is difficult to apply before 1700, one can be certain that something like it has always existed in societies in which a centrally focused civilization has been achieved. English literary evidence shows that regional music-making was often remote from standard norms, and a substantial body of narrative verse provides at least indirect evidence of a musical subculture. Some English romances were evidently sung to their first audiences: the text of *King Horn* (*c.*1250) is unambiguous in this respect. The very fact that the poem is in English testifies to its non-courtly ambience (the nobility of the period spoke French), and the roughness of its metre and language, together with the considerable variation in the extant manuscripts, testify both to a freely declamatory delivery and to the oral transmission of the text.[12] Admittedly not all English narrative verse of this and later periods carries such implications, but a reasonable case can be made out for the persistence of sung romance in both courtly and non-courtly circles. This long-standing medieval practice can be linked to the sung balladry of the sixteenth and later centuries, somewhat tenuously it is true, by the 'ballad' literature of the fifteenth century, which is often 'folk-like' in its simplicity and repetiveness and is normally also regarded as a sung genre.[13]

On the other hand, such medieval lyrical poetry as deserves the epithet 'popular' is less easy to attach to a 'folk' culture as we have defined it. We know for certain that some poems were indeed popular songs, either from their intrinsic nature or from their quotation in sermons or their adaptation to sacred purposes.[14] What we cannot tell so easily is the social climate

[12] The poem begins: 'Alle beon hi blithe / That to my song lithe! / A song ich shall you singe / Of Murry the King.' (*Middle English Verse Romances*, ed. D. B. Sands (Exeter, 1986), 17). My scepticism in Vol. I, p. 30, is in need of qualification.

[13] Some 'folk' ballads, like some carols, survive in printed booklets from the early 16th c.: for example *Adam Bell, Clim of the Clough, and William of Cloudesly*, printed by Wynkyn de Worde in 1505 and in at least eleven later edns. (STC 1805.7 seqq.). These are to be distinguished from the earliest broadsheet songs, of which three fragmentary examples published by the Rastells, father and son, are now known, all with simple three-part polyphony. See J. Milsom, 'Songs and Society in Early Tudor London', *Early Music History*, 16 (1997), 235–93.

[14] Cf. J. A. W. Bennett, *Middle English Literature*, ed. and completed by D. Gray (Oxford, 1986), where most of the relevant fragments are discussed and quoted, 365–6, and elsewhere in the same chapter, 364–406. For the Red Book of Ossory and its named tunes see Vol. I, p. 104.

which gave them birth: sophisticated courtiers and clerics must often have launched attractive and memorable ditties upon the world.

The same observations apply to the musical remains, be they complete pieces or fragments, such as the tenors of polyphonic compositions. In the former category the 'Sumer' canon has become popular in our own day, but there is no clear evidence that it was so in its own.[15] For all its simple charm, it is a work of some sophistication, and it survives in only a single manuscript. But it may have been intended to evoke genuinely popular polyphony, perhaps of the sort of which Gerald of Wales at an earlier date had given a description.[16] The same may be said of much other thirteenth-century English polyphony, despite its avowedly sacred character.

The secular melodies that underpin a number of English fourteenth-century motets are similarly ambiguous as evidence of popular song. Most of them have French texts or incipits: some of them may have been popular in France, if that is where they came from, but they would not have been appreciated in England outside aristocratic circles. However, as noted above, one may legitimately speak of popularity within such a circle, and the simple melodic charm of a song like 'Mariounete douce' must have been hard to resist.[17] Much more lively (when suitably accelerated) is the bawdy 'Trop est fol', also in a modified virelai form, and for this we are fortunate in having a reasonably complete verbal text (Ex. 8.1).[18] But we cannot say much more than that it is simple and vigorous: the circumstances of its invention are beyond conjecture.

A few such tenors have an English text or incipit: the haunting 'Dou way Robin' is one, the enigmatic 'Wynter' another; yet others have no title at all, but seem by their nature to be pre-existent and popular.[19] There are similar things in the French motet repertory of the late thirteenth and early fourteenth centuries (though normally here the parent motet is also secular), and again the original ambience is hard to pin down. We know that refrain-songs were enjoyed by both the urban and the rural young;[20] perhaps this is the tip of the iceberg of their repertory, and perhaps also the English popular tradition drew some of its strength from that of France at this time.[21] It

[15] Cf. Vol. I, pp. 53–7, 61 (Ex. 19).

[16] *Descriptio Kambriae* (*Opera*, ed. J. S. Dimock, vi. 189–90); cf. Vol. I, pp. 32–3.

[17] Cf. Vol. I, pp. 76, 77 (Ex. 31); two settings complete in *Motets of English Provenance*, ed. F. Ll. Harrison (Monaco, 1980 = PMFC 15), nos. 5, 6.

[18] Ibid. no. 17; text and translation on p. 187.

[19] For 'Dou way' see Vol. I, pp. 74, 75 (Ex. 30); 'Wynter', from one of a series of motets in the fragmentary Tours MS 925, is given, with its completeable companions, in PMFC 17; others are the tenors of PMFC 15, nos. 5 (no text) and 6 ('Hey hure lure'), and of the conductus 'Volez oyer le castoy' (PMFC 17, no. 68).

[20] C. Page, 'Johannes de Grocheio on Secular Music: A Corrected Text and a New Translation', *Plainsong and Medieval Music*, 2 (1993), 17–41: see pp. 24, 26 (concerning the *cantilena rotunda* or *rotundella*), 26–7 (on the *ductia*).

[21] There are innumerable *refrains* extant from 13th-c. France, both with and without music, but their relevance to a popular tradition is not always clear.

Ex. 8.1

'Trop avet fet qui foll[e] que vus demeurez tant,
et tu le fras ke sage de fer le maintenant.'

Par un dymayne une matyn,
la plus belle q'unkes vi

A ly pris companie; son mari se repent,
mes il ne quidoit mye ke jeo l'amasse tant.

'Trop est fol': reconstructed from the motet 'Triumphat hodie' in Oxford, Bod. Lib., New College 362, fo. 85ᵛ, and London, Brit. Lib., Add. 24198, fo. 1ᵛ

Translation. He is too foolish who asks me to look after his wife so much, especially as the night draws us rather far from company. 'Lord! to be saddled with a husband! oh why are you not a lover?' 'You shouldn't have lingered so long; you had better do it straight away.' On a Sunday morning I took for company the prettiest girl I ever saw; her husband regrets it, but he never realized I loved her so much.

would be surprising, for example, if the forces that led to the founding of Oxford University, and the constant influx and interchange of young people that this involved, did not also lead to a vigorous exchange of easily assimilated musical traditions.

One of the best-known manifestations of such a tradition is the *carole* (later in English the 'carol'), the popular communal dance-song of young people throughout western Europe. This was a refrain-song, the verses sung by a leader and the chorus sung dancing in a line or circle. Church moralists denounced it furiously, partly because it was often danced in churchyards (a churchyard being an obvious open space in the tightly packed medieval town), partly no doubt because of its highly repetitive nature and hence hallucinatory potential.[22] In any case, it provided a good opportunity for the young of both sexes to meet and enjoy each others' company, and there has never in any age been a shortage of those ready to condemn that.

[22] 'Ductia vero est cantilena levis . . . quae in choreis [i.e. 'in caroles'] a iuvenibus et puellis decantatur': Page, 'Johannes de Grocheio', 26; id., *The Owl and the Nightingale* (London, 1989), 113–15.

If we knew more about the music of the *carole* we could say something of its cultural placement, so to speak; but we know virtually nothing, and from England not a single certifiable tune. In the fifteenth century in this country, the 'carol' emerges as a moderately sophisticated polyphonic form, usually but not always with sacred words, sometimes in Latin or a mixture of Latin and English, and retaining the original pattern of alternating refrain and stanzas. We possess the words alone of many more poems that are evidently in carol form, and most of these were probably also sung, perhaps to monodic tunes simply accompanied on an instrument if at all. Some of them are by no means seemly in content, and again the word 'popular' springs to the lips; yet still we can only conjecture as to the range of their intended or actual appeal.[23]

The carol apart, the fifteenth century affords a good deal of verse in a 'low register', not excluding the narrative ballad, much of it qualifying as presumptive popular song. The literature also abounds in references to popular music-making and the dance. These traditions continued into the sixteenth century, and it is only then that an unambiguous body of musical material emerges. Here again—at the risk of tedious repetition—one must insist on the vagueness of the idea of the 'popular' and the impossibility of identifying genuine 'folk' traditions. A good deal of popular music in sixteenth-century England seems to have been aristocratic in origin, and much of it may always have been restricted to the upper classes: the nobility, and the newly wealthy and newly educated burgesses and merchants. Much of it, too, was of foreign, especially Italian, origin. We may think of some of it as percolating gradually downwards in society, to the point at which the Elizabethan dramatists (for example) could count on the recognition of their allusions by the groundlings; but from the musical sources alone the extent of this percolation must remain a matter for conjecture.

The surviving popular music of Tudor times consists partly of simple harmonized music and partly of tunes used as the basis of sophisticated works of art. Some of these latter prove in turn to be derived from older materials whose legacy is a simple harmonic framework capable of generating further songs ('Greensleeves', 'Quodlings Delight'); and yet others survive in settings so simple that it is hard to decide whether one is justified in extracting and isolating the tune. At other times composers seem to have tried not merely to set a tune or tunes but to evoke something of their original social context, as for example in Byrd's wonderful medley 'The Barelye Breake'.

---

[23] R. L. Greene, *The Early English Carols* (2nd edn., Oxford, 1977), prints all extant English texts in carol form. His introduction (pp. xxi–clxxii) is a masterly study of the background and of the issues raised by the texts. For the few surviving monophonic tunes see *Mediæval Carols*, ed. J. Stevens (MB 4; 2nd edn., London, 1958), 110–11.

A good early example of a tune that can be extracted from its learned context is the 'Western Wind' melody used as the basis of Masses by Taverner, Sheppard, and Tye.[24] These Masses—the first and virtually the only ones in England to be based on a secular tune—are our sole sources of information about it. A musical manuscript of the time has a somewhat similar but more ornate melody set to the following poignant quatrain:

> Westron wynde, when wyll thow blow?
> The smalle rayne downe can rayne.
> Cryst, yf my love wer in my armys,
> And I yn my bed agayne![25]

These words can indeed be fitted to the melody used in the Masses, and it has usually been assumed that they originally belonged to it (see Ex. 8.2). While this is a perfectly reasonable inference, it does not follow that these were the original or only possible words; it is perhaps more significant that they are in the commonest of the various 'ballad' metres (that is, metres used in stanzaic narrative poetry); the optional repetition of the second half of the tune caters admirably for the six-line stanzas occasionally to be found in such poems.

The middle Tudor period—covering the reigns of Henry VIII, Edward VI, and Mary I—has left us a certain amount of simple harmonized music

Ex. 8.2

'Westron wynde': tune from Taverner's Mass *The Western Wind* (cf. EECM xxxv. 37–90); words from London, Brit. Lib., Roy. App. 58, fo. 5[r]

---

[24] Cf. Vol. I, pp. 230–3.
[25] Brit. Lib., Roy. App. 58, fo. 5r; J. Stevens, *Music and Poetry at the Early Tudor Court* (London, 1961), 130. Lloyd draws attention to a modern parallel, *Folk Song in England*, 113–14.

that may have become well known outside courtly circles. There are brief airs extant that are associated by their titles with poems by Wyatt (his 'Heaven and earth') and Henry Howard, earl of Surrey ('If care do cause men cry' and 'In winter's just return').[26] Surrey's poems are lengthy efforts in the so-called 'poulter's measure', paired lines of twelve and fourteen syllables respectively, equivalent to the quatrains in 'short metre' (6.6.8.6) of hymnologists.[27] The music of 'If care do cause men cry' (Ex. 8.3) was apparently adapted, with an extension, for use with Thomas Sternhold's paraphrase of Ps. 78—an even longer poem than Surrey's, incidentally (the Tudor tolerance of excessive musical repetition may be seen in Tye's *Actes of the Apostles* and some other examples of biblical paraphrase). When Sternhold's paraphrases were revised and incorporated into the standard 'Old Version' of the psalms they were given new tunes, for their metres were different from those of the Continental paraphrases which Hopkins, Whittingham, and others took as their models; but Sternhold may have originally devised them to be fitted to harmonized tunes already in existence as settings of courtly lyric. In either context these tunes would have enjoyed wider

Ex. 8.3

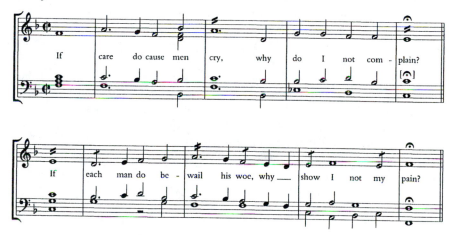

'If care do cause men cry': music from London, Public Record Office, MS E 36/170, p. 110 (first section); words from Tottel's *Songes and Sonettes* (London, 1557), spelling modernized

---

[26] For 'Heaven and earth' see my *English Keyboard Music Before the Nineteenth Century* (London, 1973), 110–11, 135; for 'If care', see my edn. of *Tudor Keyboard Music c.1520–1580* (MB 66; London, 1995), App. 2 and references on pp. 198–9; both of these, and 'In winter's just return', after Roy. App. 58, in J. M. Ward, 'The Lute Music of Royal Appendix 58', *JAMS* 13 (1960), 120.

[27] 'Heaven and earth', on the other hand, is in quatrains of 10-syllable lines. The first word should be scanned as disyllabic.

circulation, as is shown by the four very different surviving versions of 'Heaven and Earth'.

The same is true of the various pieces based on harmonic grounds—dumps, hornpipes, and the like—though not necessarily in the exact forms in which they survive. Raphe Bowles, who scribbled down seven or eight pieces in lute tablature in 1558[28] (including a version of 'If care'), gives the harmonic sequences known from Italian sources as *passamezzo* and *romanesca* (though the latter, which Bowles has in duple time, was always in triple time and called 'Aria di romanesca' in Italy). The *passamezzo* came to be known as the *passamezzo antico* (in England 'passingmeasures pavan') in contrast to the *passamezzo moderno* (the English 'quadran pavan' or 'quadro'), a major-key formula which likewise spawned its own tunes, amongst them 'John come kiss me now', used as the basis of variations by Byrd and by John Tomkins.[29] The English were perhaps technically wrong in thinking of these sequences as pavans (they were used not only in simple forms but gave rise to some of the most elaborate instrumental writing of the period); but it is true that, together with the pavan and galliard and the French *basse danse commun* with *recoupe* and *tourdion*, they transformed the old-style *basse danse/bassadanza* and associated dances into something that could be assimilated much more easily, because of its simple and predictable metrical structure, and hence of potentially far greater popularity. In fact the new Italian types of song and dance, based on metrical regularity, treble–bass polarity, and simple triadic harmony, quickly penetrated both France and England, transforming the idioms of popular and serious music alike.

Many of the tunes used in Elizabethan and Jacobean keyboard and lute music—ranging from single harmonized statements to elaborate variation-sets—seem inseparable from a harmonic foundation, even when this is in some way non-standard. 'Will you walk the woods so wild', for example, is based on a primitive harmonic scheme sometimes described as having dual tonality (Ex. 8.4), though in reality the F-chords are subordinate to the G-chords, the latter gaining predominance from their use at the end of the tune.[30] This opposition of chords a tone apart (stated or implied) is frequent in both English and Scottish folk music, and may well have descended from an older pre-history of simple triadic harmony.

[28] Brit. Lib., MS Stowe 389, fos. 120–3.

[29] For three further pieces on *Romanesca* ('Gaillarde Romanesque', etc.) see [A. Le Roy], *A briefe and easye instru[c]tion* (London, 1568), fos. 31ᵛ, 32ᵛ–33ʳ; for a version of Greensleeves, based on the same ground, see Vol. I, pp. 339, 340 (Ex. 128), and references there given; for the *passamezzo antico*, ibid. 342, 343 (Ex. 130). There is a very primitive version for the lute of the *passamezzo moderno* in Brit. Lib., Add. 60577 (the 'Winchester' MS), fo. 190, entitled 'La galantyne'; it may be an accompaniment only, but the musical text is in any case very corrupt. A. L. Lloyd mentions several other tunes based on the *passamezzo moderno* (*Folk Song in England*, 176).

[30] Cf. Exx. 8.6 and 8.7 below. The remaining words are unknown, except in the corrupt version of Ravenscroft's *Pammelia* (1609), reprinted in Chappell, *Popular Music of the Olden Time*, 66.

Ex. 8.4

'Will you walk the woods so wild': tune and harmonic foundation adapted from keyboard
setting by Byrd (cf. MB 28, pp. 141–4)

It is less easy to assimilate the tune of the well-known 'Walsingham'
ballad to ready-made harmony, though its curious lurch into the major
mode at the end is difficult to understand without the harmonic support it
always gets in the numerous extant settings (mainly for lute or keyboard).
Byrd's eloquent opening statement may be placed beside a conjectural form
of the tune with minimal supporting harmony (Ex. 8.5).[31]

Many 'monophonic' tunes scribbled down in the sixteenth and seventeenth centuries by amateurs may be isolated voice-parts of simple polyphonic songs. But sometimes a song of this kind has persuasive credentials as
a self-standing melody. One of those in the 'Shanne' commonplace book,
an early seventeenth-century survey of Methley in Yorkshire with miscellaneous additions, is of particular interest. The Shanne family were recusants, and this tune, headed 'The Queristers song of yorke in praise of

[31] Caldwell, *English Keyboard Music*, 87–8. The reference there to 'a Pepysian manuscript' is incorrect:
the text 'As I went to Walsingham / To the shrine with speed' is found in the Pepys collection of printed
ballads (ed. H. E. Rollins, 8 vols., Cambridge, Mass., 1929–32), and is evidently later. The sources of the
poem attributed to Walter Ralegh, 'As you came from the holy land / Of Walsingham', are: T. Deloney,
The Garden of Good-Will (1628, etc.); Oxford, Bod. Lib., Rawl. poet. 85, fo. 123[r] (subscribed 'Sir W.R.');
Huntington Lib. MS 198; and Bishop Percy's folio MS, now Brit. Lib., Add. 27879 (ed. J. W. Hales and
F. J. Furnivall (London, 1867–8), iii. 471; the MS also contains another Walsingham ballad, 'Gentle
heardsman tell to me', ibid. iii. 526). Cf. Percy's *Reliques*, ed. H. B. Wheatley, 3 vols. (London, 1876–7),
ii. 101 seqq. (and ii. 89 for 'Gentle heardsman'); A. C. Latham, *The Poems of Sir Walter Ralegh* (2nd edn.,
London, 1951), 120, adding a reference to the 1628 edn. of Deloney (STC 6553.5). Byrd's title 'Have
with yow to Walsingame' is unique, and his first statement implies a line-by-line dialogue in the first
stanza.

Ex. 8.5

Walsingham: (*a*) from Byrd's setting (MB 27, p. 29); (*b*) adapted to words attributed to Sir Walter Ralegh (Oxford, Bod. Lib., Rawl. poet. 85, fo. 123ʳ)

heaven', was used for 'Jerusalem my happie home', a poem with a strong recusant flavour (though also used by Protestants in a somewhat different form). Like the 'Walsingham' poems, this is in ballad metre. The tune could have been sung to a lute accompaniment now lost (it is difficult to envisage polyphonic voice-parts), but its wide leaps, together with the IV–V–I cadence, give the impression of a self-sufficient tune that also conveys within itself any necessary harmonic implications (Ex. 8.6). Its age is unknown, but a late sixteenth-century origin is most probable.[32]

---

[32] London, Brit. Lib., Add. 38599, fo. 133v. See further C. M. Simpson, *The British Broadside Ballad and its Music* (New Brunswick, NJ, 1966), 533–6, where it is cited under 'O man in desperation' (to

Ex. 8.6

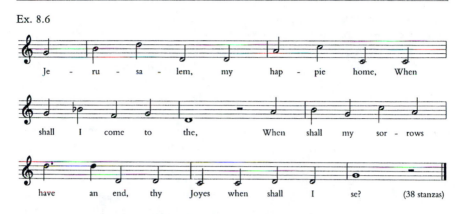

Je - ru - sa - lem, my hap - pie home, When
shall I come to the, When shall my sor - rows
have an end, thy Joyes when shall I se? (38 stanzas)

'Jerusalem my happie home': London, Brit Lib., Add. 38599, fo. 133ᵛ

Ravenscroft's collections *Pammelia* (1609), *Deuteromelia* (1609), and *Melismata* (1611) contain a wealth of potentially popular material in the form of rounds and other simple polyphony, mostly for equal voices. In some cases at least, genuine pre-existing popular material has been used. But it is always difficult to be certain of the 'original' form of a tune, particularly if the surviving setting is of some elaboration. English and Scottish seventeenth-century lute sources, however, often present their melodies with a harmonic support pared down to the essentials (if that); in such cases, it seems best not to attempt to restore a hypothetical melodic 'original', but to be content with a simple instrumental arrangement of the tune, devised, it may be, for a young lady to strum to herself and her friends in the family home, this being as authentic a form of it as one is ever likely to arrive at.

The 'broadside' or single-sheet ballads of the later sixteenth and seventeenth centuries were hardly ever printed with music, at least before the late seventeenth century, though the tunes were often named and in many cases are known.[33] The modern 'ballad' industry has tended to look down on these examples of popular poetry and to contrast them with those collected by oral tradition, linking this latter with the manuscript ballads copied in the fifteenth, sixteenth, and (in the case of the 'Percy' folio) even seventeenth

which my attention was drawn by John Stevens). It is possible that the 'tune' is an inner part, as suggested there, or even a bass, but the analogy may be rather with melodies such as 'The Boar's Head'. The C4 clef in Shanne's MS is highly improbable: G3 (= C1), or C3 with one flat, are more likely. The former has been assumed here, and the piece transcribed, with additional barlines and rests, in G2. Two other pieces from the MS are given in *NOBC*, nos. 42, 43.

[33] Simpson, *The British Broadside Ballad*, is a collection of 540 tunes; see also J. M. Ward, 'Apropos the British Broadside Ballad and its Music', *JAMS* 20 (1967), 28–86; id., 'Music for *A Handefull of pleasant delites*', *JAMS* 10 (1957), 151–80 (broadside ballad with music on plate facing p. 168); L. Shepard, *The Broadside Ballad: A Study in Origins and Meaning* (London, 1962).

centuries, and with ballads printed in booklet form from *c.*1500 to 1600 or later. Yet there is no clear-cut distinction, and the single-sheet ballads often draw upon the traditions found in the manuscripts and printed booklets. (Indeed, that is one of the main reasons for inferring that the manuscript and booklet ballads were also sung.) The main distinction lies between topical and politically charged balladry and that which is based on the distortion of history into myth, one of the main determinants of folk culture once myth-making has been relegated to the sidelines of literature; yet even this is not a hard-and-fast distinction, and the romantic conception of the ballad tends to obscure the political relevance such poems may once have had. The musical historian's attention, of course, must focus on poetry actually preserved with its tunes, and this too tends to overemphasize the romantic aspect, since the majority of extant tunes derive from the oral traditions of the late eighteenth and the nineteenth centuries.

After the great days of the Elizabethan and Jacobean virginalists and lutenists, popular music is found more and more in simple settings or even unaccompanied. We should not be deceived, however, by the un-accompanied presentation of the tunes in collections such as Playford's *English Dancing Master*, for some of them are demonstrably reduced from harmonized music by named composers.[34] Nor need we assume that 'country dancing' was itself invariably done to unharmonized fiddle-playing, though that was no doubt one of the possibilities. *The English Dancing Master* has often been treated quite uncritically as a repository of 'folk tunes', all the more authentic for being unharmonized; it can more realistically be thought of as a monument to the immense variety of materials that an enterprising publisher and his heirs might press into service to fill popular demand. Playford was in fact the first English publisher to cater for such a need, and in this and other prints he identified a market comparable to, though different in its requirements from, that satisfied by the printers of popular literature. And if Playford's tastes were too catholic to allow one to deduce from his publications specific repertories of folk song and dance, he was the founder of a publishing industry which in the eighteenth century does at last provide supporting evidence for the nature of these elusive traditions.

The Scottish Traditions

The 'folk' tradition of lowland Scotland has already been mentioned; and while it cannot be dealt with here in any detail, it deserves attention as a paradigm of what such a tradition might mean, and also (in the present context) because some of its features are shared with that of northern England. Indeed the repertory of 'border ballads' is a warning against too

---

[34] See *The Complete Country Dance Tunes from Playford's Dancing Master (1651–ca. 1728)*, ed. J. Barlow (London, 1985); facs. of 1651 edn. by M. Dean-Smith (London, 1957). Barlow prints 535 tunes in all.

rigid a distinction, and we should also remember that the Scots linguistic area was originally one with that of northern England. It was only in the later Middle Ages that a linguistic separation occurred, and that the Scots tongue, still cultivated today, came to represent a distinctive national cultural identity.[35] This is not to imply that the use of Scots is confined to 'folk' music and literature, or that in modern times the use of Scots is essential to its authenticity. We shall not be far wrong, however, in assuming that pre-modern Scottish folk song is primarily Scots in its verbal aspect, whatever the orthography in which the words have been transmitted to posterity. There is also a strong admixture of Gaelic tradition in what has come down to us as lowland Scots; the Gaelic language was once far more widespread than it was in (say) 1800, let alone today, and some part at least of the musical idiom may be accounted as representative of the Gaelic past.

We first encounter that idiom in a number of seventeenth-century sources of instrumental settings of songs and dances—settings for such instruments as the lute, mandora, harpsichord, violin, viola da braccio, and lyra viol.[36] There are also a few vocal sources, such as William Stirling's *cantus* partbook, 1639,[37] and John Forbes's printed *Songs and Fancies* (1662, with later editions in 1666 and 1682). Forbes's publication is also nominally a *cantus* partbook, though it is odd that in none of its three editions have any of its companions survived. Perhaps they were not published; but we cannot for that reason take its melodies at face-value as folk tunes, even though in a few cases (as with the Stirling book) they give the impression of being just that.

The instrumental books are more helpful, since they are complete in themselves and include tunes which, whether harmonized or not, have all the characteristics of a regional and self-standing idiom. These include the use of gapped scales (pentatonic or hexatonic) and endings on notes other than the modal finalis (a feature which must be clearly distinguished from the actual use of modes other than major and minor). At the same time these books usually also include imported music of various kinds, and even the demonstrably Scottish material often relies on standard European techniques such as the use of a simple (implied or stated) harmonic framework and of the varied reprise.

[35] For a careful discussion of this emotive issue see *The Oxford Companion to the English Language*, s.v. 'Scots', 'Scottish English'.

[36] These include the 'Skene' MS for mandora (Edinburgh, Nat. Lib. of Scotland, Advocates' Lib., 5.2.15, *c.*1620; transcribed, not quite fully or accurately, in W. Dauney, *Ancient Scotish Melodies*, Edinburgh, 1838); the 'Rowallan' lute MS (Edinburgh, University Lib., Laing III 487: contents listed by Dauney, 138–9); and the 'Straloch' lute MS (partial transcript of 1847 from an early 17th-c. original, NLS, Adv. 5.2.18). For these and others see M. Spring, 'The Lute in England and Scotland after the Golden Age', D.Phil. thesis (University of Oxford, 1987). There is a useful list of MSS, 1680–1840, in Johnson, *Music and Society*, 209–11.

[37] Edinburgh, NLS, Adv. 5.2.14; cf. *Music in Scotland 1500–1700*, ed. K. Elliott (MB 15; London, 1957, no. 73.

The use of a standard (or very simple) harmonic framework is very common and links the Scottish tradition with that of Elizabethan (and indeed European sixteenth-century) popular song. One of the earliest examples of the 'Scottish' genre in English sources is a 'Scotish Gigg' found in two seventeenth-century keyboard manuscripts. The ground on which it is based (*GFGG*) is close to that of 'The woods so wild' (see Ex. 4.4 above), and the Scottish element lies in the brisk, wide-stepping dance-melody (Ex. 8.7).[38] The melodic idiom, in turn, resembles that of a dance in the Skene manuscript called 'Who learned you to dance and to towdle', though this implies at least three bass pitches (Ex. 8.8).[39] But the pattern of the *Gigg* recurs in one of the best-known of all early dance tunes, *Tulloch-gorum* (Ex. 8.9).[40] The title, incidentally, is Gaelic, meaning 'blue hill': the tune obviously predates the poem 'Let Whig and Tory all agree' by the Revd John Skinner of Langside (1721–1807), which is usually associated with it.

Ex. 8.7

Scotish Gigg: New York, Pub. Lib., Drexel 5612, p. 2

---

[38] New York, Pub. Lib., Drexel 5612, p. 2 (also Paris, Bibl. nat., Rés. 1186, fo. 17r); ed. H. Gervers, *English Court and Country Dances of the Early Baroque* (Corpus of Early Keyboard Music, 44; Neuhausen, 1982, no. 1).

[39] Dauney 237 (no. 51).

[40] After M. A. Allburger, *Scottish Fiddlers and their Music* (London, 1983), p. 36; she cites a MS of 1734 written by David Young for the duke of Perth but does not give a precise reference.

Ex. 8.8

(followed by 2 more statements)

'Who learned you to dance and to towdle': (*a*) after W. Dauney, *Ancient Scotish Melodies* (Edinburgh, 1838), p. 257; (*b*) a possible ground

Ex. 8.9

(followed by 8 variations)

Tullochgorum: MS of 1734 as given by M. Allburger, *Scottish Fiddlers and their Music* (London, 1983), p. 36

Another tune based on a harmonic pattern is that of 'John Anderson my jo', first found in the Skene manuscript (Ex. 8.10).[41] This is based on the *passamezzo antico*, though later versions of the tune, such as that found in Agnes Hume's book of 1704,[42] halve the values and reduce it to a form of

[41] After Dauney, 219 (no. 7). The words (as given by Percy, but restored by Wheatley) are presumably roughly contemporary; there are of course later versions, including one by Burns. Percy's view that the poem, with those of *Greensleeves* and *Maggie Lauder*, was intended to satirize Catholic practice and burlesques a Latin hymn, cannot be sustained. There is a much more robust 18th-c. poem printed in *The Oxford Book of Scottish Verse*, ed. J. MacQueen and T. Scott (London, 1966), 418.

[42] Allburger, 34; Edinburgh, NLS, Adv. 5.2.17.

Ex. 8.10

(1 variation follows)

'Johne Andersoune my jo': Dauney, *Ancient Scotish Melodies*, p. 219; words from Thomas Percy, *Reliques of Ancient English Poetry*, ed. H. B. Wheatley (London, 1876–7), ii. 132 (first of two stanzas)

romanesca. The latter is also the basis of *Greensleeves*, which also turns up in Scottish sources (Ex. 8.11).[43]

[43] It is not clear how the three stanzas of Herd's version would have fitted a binary structure with repeats; in any case it is unlikely to have been sung in precisely this form, so the remainder of the text is omitted. For a full account of the tune and its associated texts from the early 1580s onwards see J. M. Ward, '"And Who but Ladie Greensleeues?"', in Caldwell, J., Olleson, E., and Wollenberg, S. (eds.), *The Well Enchanting Skill: Music, Poetry, and Drama in the Culture of the Renaissance* (Oxford, 1990), 181–211. See Vol. I, 339–40, for one late 16th-c. setting. Ex. 8.10 is from Margaret Sinkler's violin MS

Ex. 8.11

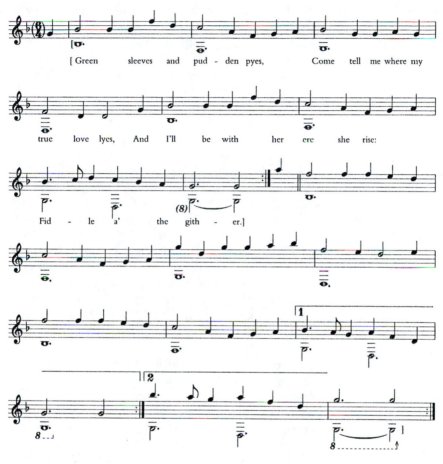

'Grien slievs and pudding pys': Edinburgh, National Library of Scotland, MS 3296, fo. 63, after Allburger, *Scottish Fiddlers*, p. 35: beginning of text from *Songs from David Herd's Manuscripts*, ed. H. Hecht (Edinburgh, 1904), p. 177

These examples also serve to illustrate the interdependence of song and dance in the Scottish folk tradition: tunes whose names suggest an origin in song are requisitioned as instrumental dances, while such dances (whether originally vocal or not) are later given words to make them into songs. The Italianate violin superseded its medieval ancestors during the seventeenth

(Edinburgh, NLS, 3296, fo. 63ʳ) as given by Allburger, 35, but with original values restored and bass outline added. The words implied by the title are added from *Songs from David Herd's Manuscripts*, ed. H. Hecht (Edinburgh, 1904), 177.

century and became the folk–dance instrument *par excellence*, supplanting for instance the border pipes.[44] It was not necessarily heard alone: violin and 'bass' (really a Baroque cello) was a common combination. 'Fiddle' music, as it was still called, became immensely popular and reached its apogee with Niel Gow, who with his son Nathaniel published several collections of reels and similar material, and there are numerous manuscript collections from the eighteenth and nineteenth centuries. The tradition continues, not only in lowland Scotland but also (for example) in Shetland and Northern Ireland, though it is threatened increasingly by other forms of popular music-making.

The antiquarian movement (as it originally was) to recover songs from oral tradition began in the late eighteenth century and immediately shed new light on the range of the Scottish folk repertory. But a good deal of distinctively Scottish song has reached us from before then, both in the form of instrumental collections and in the commercially opportunist vocal publications of William Thomson (*Orpheus Caledonius*, London, 1725; second edition, with a second volume, 1733) and his successors.[45] Some at least of these songs must have reached their editors from the oral tradition, if only indirectly; others were literate, composed music from the outset, usually to pre-existing literary texts, which is not necessarily to exclude them altogether from the sphere of genuine folk music. But the antiquarian collectors of the later eighteenth century were more interested in narrative ballads and reflective lyrics, sung usually (it would appear) by older people for whom they were distant memories and who had lost touch with the original performing context. James Johnson's *Scots Musical Museum* came out in six volumes between 1787 and 1803: his principal purveyor of materials was Robert Burns, who collected and edited a vast body of poems and tunes as well as writing and rewriting many lyrics himself.[46] The *Museum* is thus itself something of an archeological site, not to be approached uncritically; and its figured basses (by Stephen Clarke) are a feeble attempt to make the songs available for general use, unrelated to the oral tradition itself. Nevertheless, it is a formidable repository and can be supplemented by materials such as the 'Brown' manuscripts (recording the singing of Mrs Brown of Falkland, Aberdeenshire, at the close of the eighteenth century)[47] and the later

[44] For border (or 'lowland') pipes and the Northumbrian small pipes see A. Baines, *Woodwind Instruments and their History* (3rd edn., London, 1968), 348–53; see also *NGD* s.v. 'Bagpipe'.

[45] The earliest English publication devoted exclusively to 'Scotch' tunes was issued by Henry Playford in 1700. The words of thirty out of fifty songs in Thomson's 1725 volume were taken from Allan Ramsay's *Tea-table Miscellany* (vol. i, 1723); Ramsay then arranged for a rival musical edn. to be published in Edinburgh (c.1726), but Thomson again pillaged vols. i and ii of the *Miscellany* in 1733. Johnson, *Music and Society*, 140–1.

[46] Cf. above, n. 7; Johnson, 147–9.

[47] Edinburgh, Univ. Lib., Laing XIII.473 (words); Harvard Univ. Lib., MS 25242.12 (melodies). Mrs Brown was no country lass but a 'professor's daughter' (Lloyd, *Folk Song in England*, 21). The Laing MS is

publications of G. R. Kinloch (*Ancient Scottish Ballads*, 1827), William Motherwell (*Minstrelsy, Ancient and Modern*, 1827), and others. As a result we are better informed about the Scottish tradition of folk song and balladry around 1800 than for any other part of the British Isles.

Folk Music in Rural England since 1700

England made a very late start in the collection of musical materials from oral tradition, and it is therefore difficult to say anything positive about English rural folk music before the middle of the nineteenth century. The published popular music of the eighteenth century continues the tradition of the seventeenth: it often professes by means of its titles, and by its words if there are any, some kind of regional (often Scottish) origin, but it has been packaged for polite use. There actually seems to be a decline in the number of surviving manuscript books compiled by or for the young ladies of local great houses, in which one might have hoped to find (as in Scotland) specimens of the favourite tunes of the region.[48] Published popular song, mostly in single-sheet form, is even more obviously cosmopolitan in flavour; if it exhibits any kind of non-standard idiom in words or in music, it is almost certain to be bogus.

With the exception of the local written music of church and chapel, to be discussed below, therefore, there is little that can be said of the eighteenth century. There were no enthusiasts comparable to Bunting in Ireland, Scott and Burns in Scotland, or Parry and Jones in Wales, questionable as some of their published material was and even though they saw their researches in 'national' rather than 'regional' terms. That was also the basis of Chappell's work in the 1830s and subsequently: he drew largely on the written materials (so much more plentiful than those of Ireland, Scotland, or Wales) of the sixteenth, seventeenth, and eighteenth centuries to illustrate 'the popular music of the olden time'. The first experimental issue of sixteen tunes taken down from dictation by the Revd John Broadwood of Lyne (1798–1864) in 1843 was therefore a novel departure.[49] It also quite

'a faithful transcript of Popular Ballads, written from oral recitation by [her nephew] Mr R. Scott, Professor of Greek in King's College, Aberdeen [as attested by] Robert Jamieson, July 29, 1799': cf. J. Kinsley, *The Oxford Book of Ballads* (Oxford, 1969), 695.

[48] Notable, however, is the recently discovered set of eight vols. written by Jane Austen and preserved at the family home in Alton, Hampshire. It is not clear as yet whether any of the contents could legitimately be described as 'folk'. A catalogue by D. McCulloch and I. Gammie is in preparation. Two volumes copied by Branwell and Anne Brontë are preserved at Haworth Parsonage, Yorks. (MSS Bonnell 56, 133); facs. edn. Clarabricken, 1980.

[49] *Old English Songs of Sussex and Surrey* (London, 1843). A still earlier pioneer was John Bell of Newcastle, who published only poems (*Rhymes of the Northern Bards*, Newcastle, 1812); but his unpublished papers include tunes (Newcastle, Soc. of Antiquaries; see Lloyd, *Folk Song in England*, 211), some of which may have found their way into J. C. Bruce and J. Stokoe's *Northumbrian Minstrelsy* (Newcastle upon Tyne, 1882). For the carol publications of Gilbert and Sandys see below.

unexpectedly revealed the persistence of 'modal' inflections in this orally preserved music, a phenomenon which came to be regarded as a mark of authenticity and an indication of considerable antiquity. While the uncritical presumption of antiquity does in fact raise difficult issues, the modal character of so many orally transmitted tunes is certainly something that requires explanation.

John Broadwood's enthusiasm was shared by his niece Lucy (1858–1929), who expanded his work in her *Sussex Songs* (1889), and who published *English County Songs* with J. A. Fuller-Maitland in 1893. The other major contributor before 1900 was the Revd S. Baring-Gould (1834–1924); with the Revd H. F. Shephard he published *Songs and Ballads of the West* in four volumes (London, 1889–92 and later editions). The only other significant publication at this period was Bruce and Stokoe's *Northumbrian Minstrelsy* (1882), which includes pipe-tunes as well as songs. Unfortunately, it cannot compare with the wealth of materials already by then available from north of the border, and the melodies seem to have little regional individuality.

After 1900 the collection of 'folk' melodies in southern England achieved astonishing results in terms of quantity. The Folk-Song Society was founded in 1898, and Cecil Sharp became the movement's crusader,[50] collecting tunes on his own account and collaborating with and inspiring such men as Vaughan Williams, G. B. Gardiner, H. E. D. Hammond, and George Butterworth; later E. J. Moeran, Percy Grainger, A. L. Lloyd, Margaret Dean-Smith, and Sharp's disciple Maud Karpeles became prominent figures in the movement. Karpeles edited Sharp's manuscripts with devoted care, and more recently those of Vaughan Williams, Gardiner, Hammond, and Grainger have received similar treatment.[51] Many of their findings had been published in the *Journal of the Folk-Song Society*, but for general consumption the songs were mostly selected according to the county in which they had been collected and given a piano accompaniment, as well as being drawn on for use in hymn-books, carol-books, and school songbooks. As a result they were welcomed enthusiastically but often without critical discernment, and access to what the collectors actually heard and notated, with their records of when, where, and by whom, is an essential starting-point for study.

The significance of the earlier investigators' regional arrangement by county has been questioned on the grounds that many tunes have proved

---

[50] Sharp was also a pioneer in the collection of English folk dances, of which he noted down some 200 tunes. He founded the English Folk Dance Society in 1911; it and the Folk-Song Society were amalgamated as the English Folk Dance and Song Society in 1932. Similarly the two journals (*JFSS*, 1899–1931; *JEFDS*, 1914–15, 1927–31) were amalgamated (*JEFDSS*, 1932–64, subsequently *FMJ*, 1965–).

[51] For Karpeles's editing of Sharp see below, n. 53; the Sharp archive is housed in Clare College, Cambridge. Cf. *Folk Songs Collected by Ralph Vaughan Williams*, ed. R. Palmer (London, 1983: MSS in Brit. Lib., Add. 54187–91, 59535, 59536, and 57294 D and F); F. Purslow (ed.), *English Folk Songs from the Hammond and Gardiner MSS*, 3 vols. (London, 1965–72); P. Grainger, *Seven Lincolnshire Folk Songs*; *Twenty-one Lincolnshire Folk Songs*; *More Folk Songs from Lincolnshire*; each ed. P. O'Shaughnessy (London, 1966, 1968, 1971).

to have had a wider currency. Yet as a matter of history the tunes were collected somewhere, and another way of looking at the matter is to see current scholarship as insufficiently interested in the still greater localization of the material and its social context. The difficulty lies in the latter half of this exhortation, for while times and places were meticulously recorded, the collection of the tunes was usually divorced from any real social occasion. The collectors themselves had a strong sense of having rescued a vast body of material in the nick of time by taking it down from the lips of elderly people; and while the undertaking yielded results far beyond those originally anticipated, the previous history of the songs and the circumstances of their performance in earlier times can only be inferred, if at all, from other types of evidence.

One further development was Sharp's belief that the folk music of southern Appalachia might well preserve features of British melody as it had been prior to the migrations there in the seventeenth and eighteenth centuries. Plausible as this is, it introduces an element of conjecture into the equation and removes the melodic stock still further from its local roots. Sharp's views were formed by Child's use of Appalachian sources for his collection of 'English and Scottish' ballads, and his researches subsequently enabled Bronson to supply for it both otherwise unknown melodies and alternative versions of surviving tunes.[52]

When we turn to the songs recorded by the nineteenth- and twentieth-century collectors our first impression will be of a wide variety of style and register, irrespective of locality. Alongside a great many commonplace verses and melodies are found smaller (but still impressive) numbers of really beautiful tunes, recorded frequently in a variety of different versions of a greater or lesser degree of perfection. Published collections frequently obscure the situation by selecting only the more obviously satisfying songs in the 'best' of their versions, sometimes with editorial emendation and often with piano accompaniment. This can be rectified by the study of the collectors' transcriptions in their original form, either in posthumous works of *pietas* or (where available) in the manuscripts themselves. Even Karpeles's edition of Cecil Sharp's English materials[53] includes only about one-third of the nearly 3,300 tunes originally noted down, omitting dance tunes, singing-games, 'chanteys', versions offering only slight variants, and others judged to be of only marginal interest or doubtful relevance. And even this calculation excludes nearly 1,700 tunes from southern Appalachia, which had been comprehensively dealt with in print by Sharp himself.[54] This valuable record is thus limited to little more than a fifth of the total haul.

[52] Cf. above, n. 4.

[53] *Cecil Sharp's Collection of English Folk Songs*, ed. M. Karpeles (London, 1974).

[54] C. Sharp with O. D. Campbell, *English Folk-Songs from the Southern Appalachian Mountains*, 2 vols. (London, 1917; 2nd edn., 1932; 3rd edn. by M. Karpeles in 1 vol., 1960).

The Karpeles edition is nevertheless of great use for setting the repertory into a broader context. Sharp collected his English materials before and after the Great War, between 1903 and 1923, and in Appalachia from 1916 to 1918; by far the bulk of the English tunes were collected by 1914. He wrote out the tunes, normally without the aid of a phonograph, at any convenient pitch (which we are told was not necessarily that at which they were sung to him); in Karpeles's edition they are often transposed so that different versions of the same tune can be compared. It is less clear how the words of lengthy songs were recorded,[55] and in most cases which tune-variants corresponded to which stanzas. But Sharp did not 'doctor' the texts, and while his methods precluded a scientifically precise record of the tunes as sung, one may be sure that his instinctive musicianship has preserved for us a quite reasonably authentic, if somewhat idealized, form of each song. One may compare his approach with that of Grainger, who tried to represent every vocal inflection and metrical anomaly as he heard them; the result gives the impression of a wild and untamed idiom, but the same would have been true (apart from the regularity imposed by the harmonic foundation) if it had been applied to art-song. Grainger's methodology resembles that of the earliest notators of plainchant, and has its own validity; but it may obscure for the unwary the musical essence of each song.

Karpeles's modal analysis, which demonstrates an overall majority of major—mode tunes, is useful as far as it goes, but does not refer to such aspects of modality as range, melodic formulae, or intermediate cadential points. The two latter, together with the rhythm of the songs, are often responsible for an idiom that may seem startlingly at variance with that of plainchant and other long-established European types of melody. This is even more true of Scottish folk song, but it is far from being a negligible factor in the English. Cadential and formulaic peculiarities occur even in major-mode melodies and in 'variable-seventh' melodies with major mode (see Exx. 8.12 and 8.13, a version of 'Waly waly' and one of 'Johnny Doyle').[56] Purely Mixolydian (or Hypomixolydian) melodies are, after major-mode, the commonest type, and Dorian (or Hypodorian) the next, while a subset of these, with variable third, equates the two. Even the seventh and/or the subfinalis may alternate between flat and sharp, with or without a similar alternation in the third: we may trace these modal varieties through a number of versions of 'As I walked through the meadows' (Ex. 8.14).[57] As for the Dorian itself, it may be illustrated by a fine

---

[55] In the case of Vaughan Williams they were sometimes completed from printed broadsides. So much for the purity of oral tradition.

[56] Sharp, ed. Karpeles, nos. 35B, 82A. The allocation of words to notes in the second stanza of Ex. 8.13 is conjectural.

[57] Ibid., nos. 95C, A, D, E. Numerous variants of the erotic 'As I walked' motif, usually to some form of this tune, are known: cf. Lloyd, *Folk Song in England*, 198, 207–8, 209–10, 216; for 96C cf. also p. 226.

Ex. 8.12

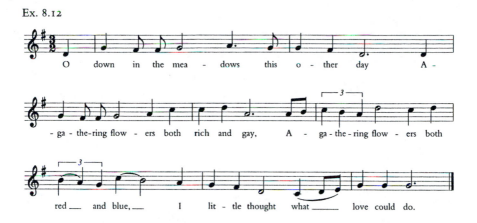

O down in the mea - dows this o - ther day A -
- ga - the-ring flow - ers both rich and gay, A - ga - the - ring flow - ers both
red __ and blue, __ I lit - tle thought what ____ love could do.

'O down in the meadows': *Cecil Sharp's Collection of English Folk Songs*, ed. M. Karpeles (London, 1974), no. 35B

version of the ballad known as 'The drowned lover', with a localized text otherwise sung to related major and Mixolydian tunes (Ex. 8.15).[58]

These few examples will illustrate both the difficulties of modal classification and the frequency with which related versions of a tune fall into different modal categories. Indeed the finalis as such is a somewhat misleading criterion for tune-type, though it has the merit of objectivity when combined with range and scale-form to indicate a mode or submodal category.[59] But form and metre are also often interchangeable and yet important for our perception of tune-type. Simple triple and duple metre are common, as is compound duple, but there are also tunes with metrical irregularities which are evidently structural, even though other versions of the 'same' tune may not have them. As for form, ABBA is a common type, illustrated in one way or another in all of the examples just quoted, and paralleled verbally in Exx. 8.11 and 8.12. The subtlety often lies in the way such a scheme is modified, not to speak of the reuse of short segments of melody in formally distinct units.

[58] Ibid. no. 57A, sung at Bridgwater; Stokes Bay, however, is on the Solent at Gosport, Hampshire (my thanks to Stephen Banfield for this).

[59] Even so, the question of the modally insignificant final note arises. 'The first nowell' has been absurdly described as being in the Phrygian mode, whereas it is plainly Ionian (i.e. modern major), but ending on the third note of the scale. Here the matter is resolved by inspection of the predominant melodic formulae. (The editors of *NOBC* believe the tune to be a conflation of a melodic tenor and the upper parts of a lost 'gallery' setting: see their pp. 482–3 and their reconstruction on pp. 480–1.) Aeolian with intermittently sharpened sixth and/or seventh (i.e. modern minor) is also modally ambiguous, being equally analysable as Dorian (with sharpened sixth only) or as Mixolydian/Ionian with flattened 3rd.

Ex. 8.13

(hypoionian with variable subfinalis)

1. There ___ was all things of some young, girl What
2. One ___ morn - ing quite ear - - ly All

I have heard them say, There ___ was nev - er no - one to
in the month of May, Her ___ mo - ther did step to

pi - ty her Nor not to hear her mourns, There ___ was
her bed - room And un - to her did say, Saying ___ we'll

ne - ver no - one to pi - ty her Nor not to hear her
send ___ to John - ny Dial if you think we're not too

mourns, So she thought it in her own ___ heart Her
late; For ___ her my heart a - break - - ing For the

(1)

ve - ry heart must break.
loss of John - ny Dial.

(1) Possibly B was sung here, or at least intended.

'There was all things of some young girl': Sharp, ed. Karpeles, no. 82A

It is not at all difficult to find cause to admire a carefully picked handful of songs, but it is harder to assess the historical and social significance of the entire repertory. Sharp's singers, like those of other collectors, were mostly elderly, and in some cases are specifically said to have learned their songs in their youth from an old man or woman of that time. The traditional view is that this method of transmission was commonplace and in all probability was carried forward through several generations, so guaranteeing the antiquity of many of the songs. As we have seen, however, this evades the issue

Ex. 8.14

(1) Nearly always sung clearly F♯, sometimes neutral, but never F♮ (Sharp's note).

continued

of performing context and puts an unduly high premium on the concept of the unaccompanied, aurally transmitted artefact.

The rural folk song repertory as preserved by the collectors is like a many-layered palimpsest of which only the topmost stratum is visible. Research into the history and typology of the songs must start with as accurate a version of their recorded forms as can be attained; their comparison may

Ex. 8.14, continued

(1) One stanza only given, conflating stanzas 2 and 3 of (a) and (b) above.

(1) one stanza only given, corresponding more or less to the 3rd stanza of (a) and (b) above.

'As I walked through the meadows', four versions (Sharp, ed. Karpeles), nos. 95C, A, D, E: (a) 'Young William the ploughboy' (first of four stanzas); (b) 'Now the winter is gone' (first of seven stanzas); (c) 'Where are you going to, my pretty maid'; (d) 'Can I accomp'ny you, my fair pretty maid'

then suggest a lineage at least for some of them. While much of the repertory raises a presumption of antiquity and while many songs (either as to their words or their tunes or both) can be traced back to the printed popular material of earlier times, there is a large element of imprecision as regards their origin, their distribution, and their reception in rural

Ex. 8.15

'As I was walking down in Stokes Bay': Sharp, ed. Karpeles, no. 57A (first of five stanzas)

communities. There are also difficult questions as to the relation between oral and written transmission, between the words and music of the songs, and between song and purely instrumental dance.

But while the orally collected repertory inevitably raises such questions, there is in addition a body of written music from the eighteenth and nineteenth centuries which, while often of no great melodic distinction or regional 'flavour', can nevertheless be firmly attached to the activities of a rural community. We have noted the dearth of secular tune-books that might have preserved local traditions, but there is a good quantity surviving of the repertory of church musicians from provincial towns and villages: settings of metrical psalms and hymns to old and new tunes, more elaborate hymns and carols, and even short cantata- or anthem-like compositions. Much of this music is in manuscript, but there are examples of regional church music printed either locally or in London, some of it quite elaborate. There is also a considerable amount of extant 'local' material from the Dissenting traditions.

This is a repertory that has little or nothing in common with the 'folk music' of the collectors, yet which is clearly at variance with the generally accepted canons of art-music. Some kinds of psalmody preserve the old tradition of placing the tune in the tenor in a four-part harmonization; but the results are very unlike those of a musician such as Ravenscroft. Consecutive fifths and octaves abound, incomplete triads are frequent, upper parts lack obvious direction. In the so-called 'fuguing tunes', brief imitative episodes are interspersed, and usually abandoned once the contrapuntal going gets tough.[60] It is easy to be dismissive, but our appreciation is hampered by our remoteness from the performing tradition. One must imagine strong, if rough, voices, regional pronunciation, and an enviable security: for if one thing is clear from the literary evidence, it is the seriousness and quasi-professionalism of rural church musicians, aided as they were by a comprehensive if informal apprenticeship. Indeed these qualities can still be met with today, but the older repertories have long ceased to be cultivated.

Tunes still familiar may turn out to have unexpected origins. The York-shire song 'On Ilkla Moor baht 'at' is found as one of a very large number of harmonized hymn-tunes by Thomas Clark (1775–1859) and first published in his *Set of Psalm and Hymn Tunes* (London, 1805). Clark was a cordwainer of Canterbury, a Methodist whose enterprise has all the hallmarks of a genuine folk culture; his vigorous setting has long been associated with Nahum Tate's 'While shepherds watched their flocks by night', though he himself intended it for Philip Doddridge's 'Grace! 'tis a charming sound'.[61]

Clark's piece is typical of huge numbers of four-part hymn-tunes that vary from very plain settings, with the tune in the tenor, to ambitious pieces with short fugal and/or antiphonal sections. An associated idiom was derived from continuo song, while the most elaborate compositions of all are miniature cantatas or homespun anthems, perhaps in two or more sections and with independent instrumental 'symphonies'. In church-gallery manuscripts the instrumentation is usually left vague and the scoring is highly adaptable, but there are also published collections in which the instrumentation may be surprisingly full and detailed. Another tune which has become associated with 'While shepherds watched' is a fully scored setting of Ps. 47 (Old Version), 'Ye people all with one accord', from John Foster's *2nd Collection of Sacred Music* (York, *c.*1820). Foster came from a village near Sheffield, and his collection reflects the patronage of local music-making by two Methodist industrial families in the area.[62]

The influence of the Dissenting bodies—Methodists, Baptists, and Con-gregationalists—was crucial in encouraging these activities, since Anglican parishes often attempted little more than metrical psalmody. The Dissenters' hymn-books contain much of the best religious poetry of the eighteenth and early nineteenth centuries, and its settings varied widely in style and competence. Handel's three tunes for Methodist hymns—including the still popular 'Rejoice, the Lord is king'—are exceptionally well crafted,[63] but they also demonstrate a feeling for congregational melody which was shared

---

[60] Cf. Ch. 2 above, pp. 166–8, and the references in nn. 131–3.
[61] *NOBC*, no. 46 V (p. 138, and notes on p. 144).
[62] Ibid., no. 46 VII (pp. 140–2, and notes on pp. 144–5). The original scoring was for choir, organ or piano, strings, flute, 2 oboes, 2 horns, trumpet, and drum.
[63] See Ch. 1, p. 85, and Ex. 1.16

by many lesser figures. At other times, however, genuine congregational potential was marred by over-elaborate setting or simply by poor harmony, often rectified editorially in the versions current today.

The local church-gallery books preserve what is in many ways the most characteristic and beguiling sector of this repertory, that of Christmas carols.[64] Research into this began in the early nineteenth century in the work of two Cornish antiquarians, Davies Gilbert and William Sandys, who drew on local materials for their publications of 1822 and 1833 respectively. Gilbert's eight tunes were presented with their original basses, rough-and-ready as these were. Sandys's larger collection of eighteen tunes was less rigorous but is still valuable; both, however, can be supplemented by the surviving manuscript materials on which they relied.[65] Later carol-books such as those of Husk and Stainer, while retaining folk tunes from these and other sources, brought their harmonies into line with currently approved methods, and sophisticated carol-arrangements have become a familiar feature of the modern Christmas. However, enthusiasts such as Ralph Dunstan added to the stock of local materials in 1920s and 1930s, even if their presentation was sometimes maddeningly wayward, and in recent years a very definite movement for the recovery of earlier performing styles has got under way.[66]

The activities of church-gallery musicians have become familiar from fictionalized accounts such as those of Thomas Hardy, whose *Under the Greenwood Tree* depicts the institution in decline and whose description of the players' replacement by a harmonium in the 1840s has considerable poignancy. More precise documentation on gallery choirs and orchestras has been supplied by Macdermott, and by Langwill and Boston, from parish records throughout the country,[67] together with a description of surviving barrel-organs, which provide invaluable information on the contemporary repertory and on the performance of metrical psalms and hymns. When all the evidence has been sifted—and much still remains to be done—a fuller

[64] The modern use of the term 'carol' to denote a Christmas song in stanzaic form—not necessarily with a refrain—seems to have arisen in the early 16th c.

[65] These include the 'Hutchens' MS in Truro, Cornwall County Record Office, DG 92; another MS, made for Gilbert in 1825 by John Davey of St Just-in-Penwith (1770–1845), seems to have disappeared (a book of carol texts, copied by Davey in 1795, is now Brit. Lib. Add. 52421). *NOBC*, 681.

[66] *NOBC* has uncovered earlier versions of numerous familiar carols, has added a copious stock of largely unfamiliar tunes from rural sources, and is exhaustively documented. The folk carol from the oral tradition, also extensively used in *NOBC*, is discussed by Lloyd, *Folk Music in England*, 114–34. R. Dunstan's *Christmas Carols* (London, 1923), *A Second Book of Christmas Carols* (London, 1925), and *A Cornish Song Book* (London, 1929) all draw on MS materials, most of them no longer traceable.

[67] Cf. Ch. 2 n. 131. Apart from Hardy, there are noteworthy descriptions of 19th-c. rural music in George Eliot's *Silas Marner* (1861), and at the beginning of *Amos Barton* (from *Scenes of Clerical Life*, 1858). There is some pleasing anecdotal evidence in K. H. Macdermott, *Sussex Church Music in the Past* (2nd edn., Chichester, 1923). It should be remembered that while church musicians frequently occupied a west-end gallery, this was not invariably the case.

picture will emerge of an important element in rural music-making in the century 1750–1850.

Industrial and Urban Folk Song

Industrial and urban song are not necessarily the same thing: under the former heading we may include the songs of agrarian workers, mariners, navvies, and coal-miners, none of whom work in towns. In the early years of the industrial revolution a good deal of work was still being carried on in villagers' cottages. Nor should we over-emphasize the distinction between town and country. Some of the material just discussed emanated from cathedral cities, which like market-towns had always enjoyed a close relationship with the rural life surrounding them. The distinction becomes more significant with the rise of the big manufacturing towns of the midlands and the north: Birmingham, Manchester, Liverpool, Leeds, Newcastle, and many others. The growth of London, too, transformed its appearance and social life, and the same may be said of Bristol, which like London, Newcastle, and Liverpool (and eventually Manchester) was also a major port. The agrarian revolution of 1750–1850 and the industrial revolution together dictated a massive flight to the towns, where subsequent population growth became intense and living conditions for the working classes deteriorated markedly. With enclosure and a shift in favour of animal husbandry, on the other hand, farming became less labour-intensive and the rural population that remained grew more prosperous.

It might seem that under the prevailing conditions a thriving folk-song tradition in the towns could not possibly have existed. In conditions of long hours, squalid housing, and child labour, this is to a certain extent true. But earlier traditions of work-song were nevertheless kept alive, notably in the context of the mining and textile industries. Political protest movements also spawned a new repertory of song that gradually became common property. A good example of the latter is the song known as 'John of Greenfield' (variously spelt), an early nineteenth-century weaver's song: its title derives from a somewhat earlier ballad from which the tune was taken. (The tune itself was recovered by Frank Kidson from the oral tradition in Cheshire, though it seems unduly cheerful for the subject.) A shortened version of the words is given in Lancashire dialect in a narrow (if unscientific) transcription by Elizabeth Gaskell in chapter 4 of *Mary Barton* (1848), where the 'air' is described as 'a kind of droning recitative, depending much on expression and feeling'. The context of this performance, though clearly not of a 'first-generation' kind, is not without interest: the young female singer, from whom it has been requested by an older woman in her working-class home, follows it with 'the grand supplication "Lord remember David"'; Mary Barton is held spellbound, while 'A far more correct musician than Mary might have paused with equal admiration of the really scientific knowledge with which the poor depressed-looking needle-woman used her superb and flexile voice'. The author then reminds us that Mrs Knyvett (Deborah Travis, second wife of William Knyvett, himself a singer, composer, and conductor) was 'once an Oldham factory girl'.[68]

Here again is evidence of that cross-fertilizing between folk music and its sophisticated sister that we have noted earlier. Coal-mining was no less productive of song than weaving, though here too we are at a disadvantage as regards the tunes, which in most cases have been collected much more recently. There is, however, an earlier strand of melody extant from the northern coalfields, some of it collected by John Bell (see above); and several compilations of fiddle and bagpipe tunes from the region were published in the early nineteenth century.[69] Their sometimes curious contours can be illustrated by a version of the tune associated with an early nineteenth-century song, 'The bonny pit-laddie', which shows the sharpened fourth and 'non-tonic' ending (here on the subfinalis) characteristic of some pipe-tunes (Ex. 8.16).[70] The mining-village culture long retained something of the ethos of its rural counterpart, with songs embracing the usual range of lyric subject-matter and with sword-dances for morris-dances. The element of industrial protest was an additional feature, and it has contributed to the vitality of the tradition up to modern times.

Sea shanties are a different genre again, true work-songs, in which simple choruses are sung as the labour is performed and are of psychological help in getting it done. They are the only ones of their kind about which anything very much is known, though similar songs must often have lightened the tedium and the hardship of agricultural labour, collective or solitary (ploughboys' songs, for example), road-and railroad-building, and other heavy labour-intensive industries. Shanties are attested in Britain at least from 1548, when they are mentioned in a poem called *The Complaynt of Scotland* along with much other interesting material pertaining to folk and popular music.[71] But their emergence into the light of day was delayed, partly by the rule of silence on ships of the Royal Navy, until the early nineteenth century, when they began to take their classic form of brief solo

[68] For the tune see Lloyd, *Folk Song in England*, 324. The words were 'written by Joseph Lees, a Glodwick (near Oldham) weaver and ballad-maker, who created a number of "John o' Grinfilt" ballads and many other songs in the early part of the nineteenth century': *Mary Barton*, ed. E. Wright (Oxford, 1987), 478, q.v. also for information about Mrs Knyvett. Cf. E. Elbourne, *Music and Tradition in Early Industrial Lancashire 1780–1840* (Woodbridge, 1980)

[69] Lloyd, *Folk Song in England*, 333: he gives a comprehensive account, pp. 331–407, of songs from the coalfields and from other industries, illustrated mostly with tunes collected in the 1950s and 1960s; see also his collection *Come All Ye Bold Miners*.

[70] Lloyd, *Folk Song in England*, 43 (source not noted).

[71] *The Complaynt of Scotland*, ed. J. A. H. Murray (EETS; London, 1872); cf. *NGD* s.v. 'Shanty'; Lloyd, *Folk Song in England*, 288–9 and, more generally, 286–315. Dunstan (*Cornish Song Book*, 75) gives a purported Ox-Driver's Song as well as several shanties in his own arrangements.

Ex. 8.16

'The bonny pit-laddie': A. L. Lloyd, *Folk Song in England* (London, 1967), p. 43

verses, often embodying a primitive narrative, and a short (single or double) choral refrain. They were collected (on dry land) by Sharp and others in the early twentieth century, and much scholarship has been expended on the precise function to which they pertained. Their potentially international character makes some of them only doubtfully English in the strict sense, but such features as a triadic form of melody suggestive of pre-set harmony (as in 'What shall we do with a drunken sailor') or a 'bitonal' structure relate some of them to earlier paradigms, as in this fascinating example of a sequentially repetitive 'one-pull' shanty (Ex. 8.17).[72]

Sailors sang songs other than shanties, of course, and they were the subject of many more land-based ones. Few topics, morever, were more vigorously quarried by commercially motivated balladeers, of whom Charles Dibdin is the best known (though William Shield had stronger nautical associations). But the element of *multum in parvo* makes the shanty a peculiarly interesting genre. The same is true of the street cries whose melodies (real or bogus) are enshrined in the elaborate contrapuntal fantasies of Dering and others (see Vol. I, p. 394). Here the idea of a melody is more important than the actual notes: indeed the reality is often closer to a cantillation or a shout (as in some shanties) than to anything that could be notated precisely.

Lullabies, nursery-songs, and children's game-songs also usually have the merit of brevity. It is doubtful whether the lullaby really counts as a genre,

[72] Lloyd, *Folk Song in England*, 302, from C. J. Sharp, Novello's School Series, Bk. 262, 15. The singer was John Short of Watchet.

Ex. 8.17

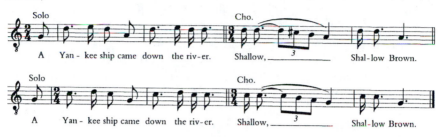

'A Yankee ship came down the river' (*Shallow Brown*): Lloyd, *Folk Song in England*, p. 302 (first of numerous stanzas)

since any sad or soothing song could be pressed into service—though the presence of the 'lullay' motif in many carols of the Nativity, both medieval and modern, suggests that it may once have been a widespread refrain. Nursery rhymes and songs are again of very diverse origin, adapted by mothers and nannies from various sources, their tunes often so distorted by childish imitation that very little sense of melody remains. Children's game-songs are different, since they are the product of the children themselves and transmitted amongst them—the counterpart of adult work-songs, in fact. Like shanties, their words and tunes are of the simplest, relying much on schematic repetition and sometimes degenerating into mere shouting.

It has been possible to mention folk dances only in passing in this survey; in any case their tunes were often, perhaps normally, either used for songs or adapted from songs, or indeed sung while being danced to. In addition to the 'classical' forms of fiddle- and pipe-tune should be added the later development of ensemble marches, polkas, and other measures, the repertory of brass bands and more heterogeneous groups that in the late nineteenth and early twentieth centuries provided the music for local regattas, miners' galas, garden parties, Sunday School treats, and the like. The music must often have been drawn from centralized repertories of light popular music, but it could also bear the marks of local authorship or arrangement and of collective improvisation in the performance.[73]

Popular Music since 1700

In the main body of this book we have considered the popular music of earlier times as no more than one extreme of a unified musical culture. In

---

[73] Dunstan, *Cornish Song Book*, contains several examples of this sort of thing, including versions of the Helston 'Furry Dance', which can be traced to a song printed in 1848 (p. 82). His collection was not intended as a work of scholarship, but it suggests some interesting lines of enquiry.

the earlier part of this chapter we have considered it in relation to the development of a regional musical culture distinct from that of the centre. In these contexts the year 1700 marks no clear dividing line. For long after 1700, music simple to sing or play or easy to assimilate, or both, continued to be composed by the recognized masters of the art. Indeed one might say of a great deal of eighteenth-century music that it is of its nature easy to assimilate. If Italian opera or the symphonies of J. C. Bach were not popular in the sense of being widely admired at all social levels, it was not for strictly musical reasons but because of social convention. More accessible theatres than the King's covered a wide range, and concerts of a less socially exclusive type than those at which Bach's symphonies were performed existed, for example in London's pleasure gardens, to purvey to the middle and lower urban classes a great deal of standard concert repertory and song of all kinds.

However, the trend was towards a socially differentiated type of music. The 'Scotch songs' fashionable in the late seventeenth and early eighteenth centuries, and the homely balladry of Leveridge, Carey, Dibdin, and Shield (for example) were destined to appeal to classes for whom the further development of opera beyond the comedies of Hook or Arnold and of concerted music beyond that of (say) Arne or Hook (again) presented an obstacle to their understanding and receptivity. These composers and perhaps one or two others represent the oldest layer in the popular song-books of the later nineteenth and early twentieth centuries, such as Hatton's *Songs of England* (1873) or *The Singer's Pocket Portfolio of 101 Favourite Songs*.[74] To their songs are added such things as 'The Death of Nelson' by Braham, songs from the operas of Balfe, Benedict, and Wallace, Horn's 'Cherry Ripe', undemanding pieces by George Baker ('I'm leaving thee in sorrow, Annie'), and others of the mid-nineteenth century, Hatton's own 'To Anthea', and, as the twentieth century is approached, the first American importations from Stephen Foster (1826–64). This agreeable mixture of the simple and the slightly pretentious is characteristic; and some of the most straightforward songs, whether truly anonymous or not—songs ranging from 'The Vicar of Bray' to Foster's 'Way down upon the Swanee River' become almost folk songs, the property not of a localized community but of a whole layer of society for which communal music-making is still a genuine relaxation, generally in the context of the local pub, the club, the church 'social', or the municipal dance.

These last two songs represent the very common type with solo stanzas and a choral refrain in which the community can join: yet others could be

---

[74] Hatton's collection is undated, but the publisher, Boosey & Co., issued similar collections of Welsh, Scottish, and Irish songs, of which the Welsh and Irish have prefaces dated 1873. *The Singer's Pocket Portfolio* was published by Bayley & Ferguson in London and Glasgow; it too is undated (and seems not to be in the British Library), but a date around 1900 cannot be far wrong.

sung in choral unison throughout, whether originally so intended or not. The composition of unison songs, for both school and adult use, became an end in itself—unison hymns are an example of it—and folk-song enthusiasts attempted to popularize their discoveries by including them, often with new or bowdlerized words, in hymn-books, carol-books, and school song-books.[75] The production of such books continues unabated, though the older repertory has become faded and its newer replacements (with the exception of a few really fine hymn-tunes) have degenerated into lazy formulaic imitations of contemporary 'pop'. It is tempting to regard the Edwardian period and that of the Great War—the era of 'Land of Hope and Glory', of 'Jerusalem', and 'I vow to thee, my country'[76]—as the last in the production of genuinely popular tunes written or, in the case of Elgar and Holst, adapted for massed community singing.

But the canonized repertory of eighteenth-century popular song was also the ancestor of that much bigger phenomenon of music intended for passive enjoyment by large numbers. As we have seen, simple well-written songs, however homely, remained part of a common musical culture in the early nineteenth century. But as the century progressed, a new element crept in: that of writing down, so to speak, in order to capture the widest possible market at a time of unprecedented demographic opportunity. It should be emphasized that this did not necessarily or even primarily entail an appeal to the lower classes exclusively. In addition to the growth of Music Hall and Variety, with their comic songs, ballet, acrobatics, and pantomime, there were brought into existence a more blatantly sentimental type of song for the middle-class drawing room, less demanding types of musical theatre, and a more democratic type of dance-music with a broader appeal than either its aristocratic or its more rustic ancestors. This is not so much a social as a musical phenomenon: the creation of a style sufficiently commonplace to serve as entertainment or background listening for all classes. Nor is it a peculiarly English phenomenon: it belongs rather to Western culture as a whole, its earliest and strongest manifestations being in Vienna and Paris and much of its later strength being drawn from North America.

Some of this music has been alluded to in earlier chapters as part of the wider picture, while on another level the repertory rubs shoulders with what we have characterized as folk song or folk dance. But it deserves at least

[75] For *The English Hymnal*, to which Vaughan Williams and others contributed several notable tunes for unison singing, see Ch. 4.

[76] 'Land of Hope and Glory', to words set by Arthur Benson to the Trio of *Pomp and Circumstance* March no. 1 (1902), was incorporated into Elgar's *Coronation Ode* in that year and soon made into a solo song for Clara Butt (J. N. Moore, *Edward Elgar*, 365–7). 'Jerusalem' was composed in 1916 for a patriotic concert (Dibble, *C. Hubert H. Parry*, 483–4); the later 'England' (to words from *Richard II*) was less successful. 'I vow to thee', from 'Jupiter' in *The Planets* (composed 1914–16), is an adaptation to a poem Sir Cecil Spring Rice (M. Short, *Gustav Holst*, 197).

brief consideration for its own sake. The lyrical song or ballad is paramount here, and the composition of its words as important as the music for the achievement of its objective. The sentimental or 'drawing-room' ballad is one type, and an immensely profitable one for its publishers before the days of sound-recording. Low as it had sunk by 1914, however, and irrespective of its origin in the theatre or otherwise, it was far from having plumbed the depths. Since then the increasing vapidity of words, melody, and harmony have been compensated for by more and more elaborate forms of accompaniment, whether of the sentimental strings, jazz big band, or modern pop-group style. Recording, film, and broadcasting have accelerated this development, which habitually reaches its nadir in the entries (British and otherwise) for the annual Eurovision Song Contest.[77]

Comic song is another subgenre, flourishing in turn in Music Hall, pantomime, operetta, and musical comedy, in radio and television shows, and in films. Indeed its outlets have been very similar to those of sentimental song, except that it has generally lacked drawing-room appeal. Nor is it in vogue amongst the young of today. Patriotic song was popular during the two World Wars, often combining sentimentality, humour, and patriotism in one. 'How bright everything seems' (Ex. 8.18) reflects job-prospects in the wake of the Depression. Such prelapsarian ditties have evolved little, in strictly musical terms, since the days of Sullivan.

Ex. 8.18

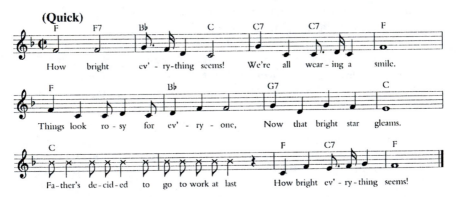

'How bright everything seems': retrieved from contemporary recording

---

[77] The specific categories of jazz and 'pop' style are referred to below. Published songs of all kinds normally include only a straightforward keyboard accompaniment, usually with chordal indications for a guitarist; and many rhythmic nuances remain unnotated.

Popular musical theatre, and later film and television, provided the background for most of these developments. Sullivan's light operas were—just—within the boundaries of the 'legitimate' theatrical culture of their day. (There was already in existence a 'non-legitimate' theatre of pantomimes, burlesques, and what-not, but the pretence of drama in these—except for pantomime, which turned into a Christmas entertainment for children—disappeared when they were subsumed by music hall and variety).[78] But by 1900 a new type of light musical theatre, known variously as operetta or musical comedy, had come into being. The operettas of the late nineteenth and early twentieth centuries in general lacked the musical sparkle and verbal spice of their models in Johann Strauss the younger (1825–99), Franz von Suppé (1819–80), and Jacques Offenbach (1819–80); nor did English composers maintain the tradition as successfully as Franz Léhar (1870–1948) and other Europeans before 1939, though Edward German (1862–1936) looked at one time as though he might do so. Musical comedy, with 'book', 'lyrics', and music, was a more sentimental genre, in its heyday before the Great War. There was a revival after the war, when Ivor Novello (1893–1951, Welsh on his father's side) came into prominence.[79] But it was then and after the Second World War that the American form of 'musical', as it came to be known, with music by such composers as Jerome Kern (1885–1945), Cole Porter (1893–1964), and Richard Rodgers (1902–79), began to exert a considerable influence, bringing to the genre (in addition to the spectacular element for which the impresario was responsible) their characteristic jazz-inspired idiom and its encouragement of a 'crooning' vocal style.[80] The commercially most successful British composers of musicals since the Second World War have been Lionel Bart (b. 1930) and Andrew Lloyd Webber (b. 1948), who has also become his own impresario. It is beside the point to criticize the conventional and at times second-hand nature of Lloyd Webber's ideas; in fact he is a more thoughtful composer than many, reflecting the serious as well as the populist strand in his musical heritage.

This is hardly the place for a technical discussion of such genres as pantomime, variety, cabaret, and revue. The first two are rarely musically inventive in their own right; the others have been so in varying degrees. The satirical element in these is usually considered to be less pungent than in their Continental counterparts. Characteristic of the gentle-mannered English approach in the 1950s and 1960s were the revues ('At the Drop of a Hat'

---

[78] See Ch. 4.

[79] Novello had written the popular song 'Keep the home fires burning' during the 1914–18 war. For the principal contributors before then, see Ch. 4.

[80] Subsequently the work of Leonard Bernstein (1918–90) and Stephen Sondheim (b. 1930: also writer of the lyrics for Bernstein's *West Side Story*) has been enormously popular in Britain.

and 'At the Drop of Another Hat') produced and performed by the writer and singer Michael Flanders and the composer and pianist Donald Swann (1923–94). While the verbal humour of the songs and their linking commentary was fairly harmless, it gained considerable point from its association with musical parody, in which Swann excelled. The sharper television 'satire' of the 1960s embraced little in the way of musical novelty (jazzy big-band songs for female singers were a long-standing feature of radio revue), except for the imaginative jazz pianism of Dudley Moore (b. 1935).

An important aspect of the music of the popular theatre and related genres, since 1945 at least, has been its abandonment of traditional orchestration in favour of smaller bands led by the piano. This in turn has given way to ensembles of the jazz and 'rock' type, including the use of electronic instruments; even without these, amplification from the pit (and often from the stage as well) has become the rule rather than the exception. Precisely the same trend has affected the music of the related genres in film, sound-recording, radio, and television, where the microphone is a sine qua non in any case.

Early films, lacking a soundtrack, relied on live instrumental music to disguise their silence (or rather the whirr of the projector). This was already a stock-in-trade of pantomime, variety, and the circus as an accompaniment to dramatic action, ballet, or acrobatics, so the principle behind it was not new, though the problems of synchronization were more severe. Improvised music on the piano or organ was more flexible than composed orchestral music, but the latter was preferred whenever possible, and with the introduction of the soundtrack it became a normal accompaniment. For sentimental films, whether original or based on a stage 'musical', songs were added, the whole thing being capped by a 'theme song' at the beginning and end. Serious composers such as Arthur Bliss (*Things to Come*, 1935), Vaughan Williams (nearly a dozen scores, including *Scott of the Antarctic*, 1947–8), William Walton (over a dozen including *The First of the Few*, 1942, and *Henry V*, 1944), Benjamin Frankel (whose hundred or so scores include some sparkling Ealing Comedy music), Malcolm Arnold, and Richard Rodney Bennett (b. 1936) have probably found their widest audiences in the cinema. Television drama of all kinds has called for both theme-music and incidental music, the two being subtly intermingled in the work of such masters as Geoffrey Burgon (b. 1941: a serious composer whose introduction to mass audiences was through his music for the serialized spy novels of John Le Carré) and the American-born Carl Davis, the BBC's standby for costume drama. Films depicting a violent and sordid underworld have succeeded in harnessing a music of concomitant brutality.

Popular dance has succumbed to a comparable evolution. During the nineteenth century the polite and the rustic (the latter, for example, in the form of the country dance) were merged in such dances as the waltz and the quadrille, both imported from Paris, later the polka and the galop. The scoring depended on the resources available, varying from a full orchestra to a few strings with piano, a 'Palm Court' type of ensemble appropriate for a fashionable *thé dansant*. By the Edwardian era the waltz had degenerated into a languid crawl (Ex. 8.19),[81] anticipating the style that would (with the aid of saxophones and soft percussion) come to be known as smoochy. Innumerable dance fashions have succeeded in the twentieth century, but for the young and the would-be young they were revolutionized first by jazz and then by rock or pop.

Jazz and pop[82] were American importations, and while enormously influential in Britain (and in Europe generally) have always seemed an alien stock. Jazz in all its many permutations (Dixieland, ragtime, blues, 'classical' jazz, swing, bebop, and their 'modern' successors) is based essentially on regular periodicity and diatonic harmony enlivened by melodic irregularities (including rhythmic shifts and non–diatonic intervals) and harmonic chromaticism. Jazz is properly improvised as a series of solo breaks over a pre-set harmonic sequence, interspersed with instrumental 'choruses'; in a jazz song, the voice will enter only after a copious exploration of these elements. The idiom is essentially an Afro-American development based on the spiritual and other inherited resources of the Negro slave population. Rock-and-roll has been defined as 'A commercial amalgam of the styles of American White country music and Black rhythm and blues, the forerunner and shaper of the popular music of the 1960s and 1970s that has simply become known as "pop".'[83] Its lazier approach to chordal progression, embracing, for example, wholesale triadic shifts up or down a step, and heavier accentuation of a regular pulse, are its predominant characteristics as compared with jazz, with which it otherwise has much in common. The improvisational and ornamental element is often strong, with virtuoso (electric) guitar and percussion-playing a commonplace. Its British exponents—Tommy Steele, Cliff Richard, The Beatles, The Rolling Stones, The Sex Pistols, and The Damned, for instance—have enjoyed a higher profile than British jazz musicians, mainly because of their appeal to the classless young. They themselves began as young men (and, more recently, women), and in the case of the Beatles we can observe their emergence from a genuine urban folk culture based on collective musicianship and raw poetic imagination into the pressurized world of mass entertainment. As one group or individual ages and disintegrates, another takes its

---

[81] *The Druid's Prayer* by Gordon Davson (London, 1909); published also for small orchestra, and arranged as a song, 'By the Druid's Altar'.

[82] As will be clear, I use these terms in a wide generic sense. 'Pop' is unsatisfactory, being a by no means unprecedented abbreviation of 'popular'; but 'rock' (short for 'rock-and-roll') has a more limited application in normal use.

[83] P. Gammond in *The New Oxford Companion to Music*, ed. D. Arnold, 2 vols. (Oxford, 1983). But cf. the admirable brief entry on 'Rock' in M. Kennedy, *The Oxford Dictionary of Music* (2nd edn., 1994).

Ex. 8.19

Gordon Davson, *The Druid's Prayer* (London, 1909), pp. 2–3

(or his or her) place; the music becomes more violent and outrageous, in common with the culture that supports it, but it maintains a certain integrity in its refusal to compromise.

A gentler type of popular music persists but has been marginalized. Outdoor music for brass band or military band[84] (not to mention bands of drums and bugles or even fifes) has a continuous history since the later nineteenth century, its repertory based on the marches of J. P. Sousa (1854–1932) and his British imitators. The music is (or at any rate was) rarely notated in full score, and its arrangement was very much a matter of local custom (as we have already observed). But at its best it is meticulously prepared and has given rise to its competitive offshoot in the brass and military band movement centred on industrial firms and local clubs. Increasingly sophisticated music (from that of Elgar and Holst onwards) has contributed to the repertory, so that as in the film a rapprochement has come about between straightforward light entertainment and more ambitiously crafted work.

The same is true of light orchestral music. Elgar is well known for his contribution to that repertory in such trifles as *Salut d'amour* (1889), and in the five *Pomp and Circumstance* marches (1902–30). He also wrote a *Coronation March* (in 3/4 time) for George V in 1911, a genre to which William Walton's *Crown Imperial* (1937) and *Orb and Sceptre* (1953) also belong. Light orchestral music was a speciality of Eric Coates (1886–1957), best remembered now for his march for the film *The Dambusters* (1955).

Light orchestral music is hardly composed at all nowadays except as incidental music in films and television; and even then it is the preferred idiom in only a minority of cases. The undemanding but decently crafted music of the middle classes—the orchestral music of Coates, the piano music of Billy Mayerl (1902–59), the repertories of the string orchestras of A. P. Mantovani (1905–80, Italian-born) and Alberto Semprini (1908–90: also a pianist), of the BBC Light and Concert Orchestras, and of hotel and seaside pavilion orchestras such as those of the Grand Hotel at Eastbourne and of Max Jaffa in Scarborough—has been squeezed out between the pressures of pop and of 'serious' modern music, its place taken by the even less demanding amenities of fireside television.

Conclusions

These developments are as much a product of social change as of aesthetic preference. But it seems even more necessary to associate folk and popular

---

[84] Military bands employ woodwind as well as brass instruments; either may nowadays include percussion. See T. Herbert (ed.) *The Brass Band Movement in the 19th and 20th Centuries* (Buckingham, 1991). There is a useful survey of 19th-c. band music in *BHMB*, v. 135–43, and a comprehensive one by N. Temperley, ibid., v. 109–34, of ballroom and drawing-room music in the same period.

music with its social circumstances than it is in the case of 'high' art, for which one can claim a reasonable self-sufficiency irrespective of its origins. It is not only that such studies can illuminate the music for us, making it more 'interesting' and 'relevant'; they can properly enhance the genre of social history *per se*, which often deals with literature and the fine arts with depth and understanding but rarely more than superficially with music if at all. Even 'social' histories of music rarely bring the music itself to bear on the discussion; it can perhaps be taken for granted as background knowledge, but the fact is that in neither case is the 'soundscape' as such painted in.[85]

What is self-evidently true of urban popular music is equally so of rural music, though here there are problems both of definition and of the availability of relevant material. Moreover there is a mismatch between what we know of musical distribution and the natural units of rural society. Tunes, we know, travelled widely, even across the oceans. The logical basis for social study is the parish, a geographical unit that has maintained its stability for a millennium (and possibly for much longer, if one may assume that parishes were formed on the plan of existing blocks of agricultural land), and which is still often visible on our maps in the form of civil parishes even where the ecclesiastical boundaries have been modified. Although its villages and its farmsteads may have moved, grown, or disappeared over the centuries, the parish almost always retains its visible focus in the local church. It retained its integrity through the processes of manorial creation, monastic settlement, and emparkment, and indeed the records of the invading gentry and clergy could probably tell us a good deal about the local life into which they entered, even at a musical level in some cases.[86] To seek the re-creation of our past rural musical life (let alone the music itself) in this way presents a severe challenge, but it is only in isolated cases (as for example with the Hardy-inspired work at Puddletown in Dorset) that it has even been recognized as a desideratum. Such an investigation may indeed lead us away from the concept of folk music as such towards a less biased view of musical activity in rural society generally. This would be no bad thing, and, together with more comprehensive studies than have yet been attempted of music in our towns and cities, would set us further on the road towards a genuine 'History of Music in England'.

---

[85] I borrow the term 'soundscape' from R. Strohm, whose *Music in Medieval Bruges* (Oxford, 1985) is a model of its kind. For some studies of local English musical history see Chap. 9, p. 547, n. 9.

[86] For the possible pre-history and the continuity of the parish system see e.g. C. Taylor, *Village and Farmstead* (London, 1983). W. G. Hoskins, *Local History in England* (3rd edn., London, 1984) is an excellent introduction for the non-professional investigator.

9

ENGLAND AND ITS MUSIC

AT the end of a lengthy narrative it seems appropriate to consider again its basic premises; to ask whether they are borne out by the evidence laid before the reader, and to offer some conclusions about the nature and relevance of what has been described.

Foremost among these premises is that there is such a thing as English music, the music of the English people as distinct both from that of other nations and from that of the larger entities to which the English belong or have at one time belonged. A second is that the music of a nation or people acquires a self-sustaining impetus that enables it to retain its individuality over a long period embracing profound historical and social changes. The music itself has self-evidently evolved in ways that are at least as far-reaching; but it is an underlying presumption that a connecting thread, a characteristic reaction to changing conditions and to musical fashion elsewhere, has determined its course throughout.

There is a more fundamental issue, irrespective of national character, that has affected the way in which the material has been presented. This is not a 'History of Music in England', because it is concerned with the consequences of artistic influence and emulation as much as with the outcome of external circumstances. These have their importance, particularly as they impinge on the employment and patronage of composers, but they affect the general nature of the product rather than the details that make it interesting and give it lasting relevance. This therefore is largely a history of music in response to other music; but more needs to be said both about what that entails and about the social context itself.

English Music and the European Context

That England, musically speaking, is an offshoot of western Europe need not be doubted. Its secular element in Anglo-Saxon times was derived from its Germanic conquerors, including those of Scandinavia. In the Church, its materials came from the great tradition of Roman chant. The Norman Conquest, and later the arrival of the Plantagenets, strengthened an already existing predisposition to look to France for guidance, and in due course the

French tradition of polyphonic music made its way over here, together with that of secular song and the use of the French language. That did not prevent the growth of a distinctively English style (described in Vol. I) in the period 1250–1350, but this was a graft on to foreign stock—a view that has been challenged, but which can be substantiated in its broad outline—rather than the product of isolated endeavour. From 1350, initially in the functional forms of sacred music, a more clearly insular idiom arose; but French influences, and in due course Italian ones too, continued to be absorbed, and before long English compositions began to be exported abroad. In the era of John Dunstable and Leonel Power the reputation of English music in France, the Netherlands, and Italy was at its height, despite the rise of a non-French royal dynasty and the resumption of the Hundred Years War. The latter led to brief and inglorious hegemony over part of France, but neither political upheavals, nor even the dissensions afforded by rival papacies, could seriously reduce the international movement of men and ideas in the early fifteenth century. Indeed the calling of Councils to resolve religious schism facilitated rather than hindered the travels of musicians to countries not their own, and their clerical status (in most cases) amounted to a passport for free movement, however strained the relations between nations and between ecclesiastical dispensations.

There are signs in the early sixteenth century of a renewed role for English musicians abroad and for the welcome of foreigners to England, but the Reformation, in Europe as well as in England, challenged the old assumptions. Sympathetic foreign regimes afforded a refuge for dissenters (Protestant in the reign of Mary, Catholic thereafter), while new alliances channelled musical traffic in new directions. Even so, England continued to benefit from the settlement of Italian musicians, many of whom were Jewish, in the time of Henry VIII; Italianate music was in high favour in Elizabethan times, and must be set beside the forging of links with the Protestant Netherlands and Germany. These provided the opportunity for a further wave of English musical export, but Catholic dissent had its musical consequences too: Peter Philips and John Bull left England permanently, and Richard Dering for a long period before his return to serve in the chapel of Henrietta Maria, consort of Charles I. Italy and the Catholic Netherlands between them accounted for a good part of the musical collections of Edward Paston and Francis Tregian, recusants of whom the latter compiled, in the Fitzwilliam Virginal Book, the most famous of all manuscript anthologies of music.

The Catholic sympathies of the Stuart monarchs and their consorts (even Anne of Denmark, James I's wife, was a Catholic, though an undemonstrative one) contributed to a flood of European visitors in the seventeenth century. The court music of James I and Charles I pursued Baroque innovation with a decidedly English accent, but after the interregnum

Charles II, brought up in France, encouraged a more extrovert style, initially of French inspiration but soon overlaid by a predominantly Italian idiom. This was strengthened by the arrival and permanent settlement of G. B. Draghi and Nicola Matteis, as well as by the evident preferences of a series of English-born composers including Locke, Humfrey, Purcell, and Blow.

After 1685 the growth of political (and to a certain extent religious) freedom and the development of a capitalist economy could only encourage the free movement of music and musicians across the English Channel. Unfortunately, the inventiveness of English-born composers declined after Purcell's early death, and it is tempting to regard this as a failure to live up to the general level of the late Baroque in Europe. But that is too simplistic an assumption: Handel, an ever-present challenge and one of the two greatest masters of the early eighteenth century, would have been hard to emulate under any circumstances. The tendency of the times was towards normalization, so that Corelli, whose music is normal to a fault, became the approved model for many composers even in preference to Handel. English composers such as Maurice Greene, Thomas Arne, William Boyce, and John Stanley are best thought of as the English representatives of the European movement that also produced Hasse, Graun, Jommelli, and J. C. Bach, with countless others as good and a few of a more individual stamp such as Gluck and C. P. E. Bach.

The most significant contribution from abroad in the eighteenth century, including that of Handel himself, lay in the provision of Italian operas. Otherwise composers came primarily as virtuosi, even though like Geminiani and Giardini their music might be excellent in itself. The English were usually content to play second fiddle to foreign virtuosi, a trend that continued in the nineteenth century and is not unconnected with their lacklustre contribution to an increasingly standardized repertory of recognized classics. At the level of solo performance, English composers, with few exceptions, neither achieved the technical skill to rival the foreigners nor, consequently, were able to contribute to the genres of display pieces that they cultivated. Thus Viotti and Moscheles, to name only two, had a clear advantage as violinist- and pianist-composers in the early nineteenth century.

The insular nature of musical education had much to do with this. While the music of foreign visitors from Haydn to Wagner, together with a vast amount by European composers who never touched these shores, was welcomed and enjoyed, English composers lacked the training that would have enabled them to write more imaginatively in the genres that now dominated the repertory, symphonic music and opera. They were unable to handle the symphonic medium with flair, or to exploit fully the possibilities of enlarged forces and the constantly improving standards of orchestral playing. These were being fostered in English orchestras by foreign players and conductors, while great singing in the theatres was provided more and more by visitors from abroad or by singers trained abroad. So English composers failed to penetrate the established canon, and had to be content with an individual and thoroughly worthwhile contribution to genres such as church music and song, which flourished independently of it.

In the late nineteenth and early twentieth centuries English composers can be said to have rejoined the European mainstream. While access to European music has increased still further since then, English music has maintained its place alongside it, even if programme-planners remain cautious. Some of it at least has gained a foothold internationally. A continuing resistance on the part of audiences is as much a resistance to any new music (especially if it is perceived as experimental or iconoclastic) as to English music. Opera has been slower to emerge from insularity, but it too has achieved full recognition since 1945. All this is partly a result of better educational opportunities, including study with European composers and better funding for the arts generally, and partly because the spirit of emulation has been directed further afield. In the nineteenth century the most favoured European models were provided by the oratorios of Mendelssohn, Spohr, and Gounod, even though the public at large (and to their credit a number of composers) set their sights far higher. In the second half of the twentieth century, by contrast, the stimulation has been provided by, for example, Shostakovich, Hans Werner Henze, Messiaen, Boulez, Stockhausen, Ligeti, and Penderecki, and latterly by Alfred Shnitke and Arvo Pärt. In between, Brahms, Hindemith, and Webern in turn have offered seemingly viable methodologies, while very little in the modern French and German pantheon has remained wholly uninfluential. If at times the outcome has seemed chaotic, a syncretist tendency has been offset by the powerful individuality of a substantial number of English composers.

England has also played its part in the broadening sphere of influence of western art-music. Its earliest impact on American music was in the lesser forms of Dissenting and parochial psalmody, where the Bostonian William Billings (1746–1800) became the leading figure. But the Boston- (and later German-) educated Horatio Parker (1863–1919) was amongst those who inherited the English choral tradition and built on it in an individual way, notably in his oratorio *Hora novissima* (1893), published in London and heard at the Three Choirs Festival (Worcester) in 1899. One cannot really claim that the later development of American music owes much to England in particular—its roots lie as much in the Hispanic and Germanic traditions, together with its absorption of the Negro element in spirituals, jazz, and art-music alike. But one can at least point to the American preservation of a tradition of ambitious Anglican church music, fostered by the emigration of T. Tertius Noble (1867–1953) to Massachusetts and of Healey Willan (1880–1968) and Bernard Naylor (1907–86) to Canada. The British Empire

as a whole may have seemed at one time to have more potential than proved
to be the case: the distinction of much modern music from the 'Old
Commonwealth' postdates independence and owes little to developments
in England, while Samuel Coleridge-Taylor (1875–1912) is a unique example from that period of a black composer from anglophone Africa to have
sustained a reputation as a composer of serious music.

But England, or at any rate London, has for the whole of the present
century, and more especially since the end of the Second World War, been a
highly important trading-post for the modern extension of Western musical
ideals, particularly to the Far East and to Israel. A number of factors, moreover, have contributed to England's welcome to non-Western musics: the
more open attitude since the 1950s to non-Western culture and religion, a
fascination with the transcendental—to which classical Indian music especially has seemed to offer the prospect of an initiation—and the growth of
scholarship. Political sympathy, too, plays its part in the appreciation of
traditions undervalued by authorities in the countries concerned, as with
those of China and Tibet.

England and its Immediate Neighbours

It is a moot point how far such generalizations about England apply equally
to Britain as a whole, or to Britain and Ireland together. Scotland, Wales,
and Ireland each have their own long-established traditions, though not
necessarily in isolation from those of England or wholly unified in themselves. The purely Celtic element is in principle distinct from the English,
although its influence on the latter is easily detected in the English-language
folk song of these countries as well as in the art-music of many otherwise
Anglo-orientated composers.

The 'English' factor in Irish music may stem from even before the
Norman Conquest of Ireland: a short piece of two-part polyphony, found
also in a now destroyed fragment from Chartres, was included in an early
twelfth-century Irish Benedictine Gradual seemingly copied from a
Winchester exemplar.[1] Two years after the Conquest, in 1172, it was
decided to adopt the Salisbury Use in the Irish Church. Two fourteenth-
century Graduals from Dublin provide the only fully notated copies of the
Easter Sepulchre drama from Britain or Ireland; another Dublin source of
similar date is a 'proser' of Salisbury Use.[2] In Elizabethan times the hold on
Ireland was strengthened: the foundation of Trinity College in Dublin
offered a local resource for the higher education of well-to-do Protestants,
and Dublin Castle became the focus of the social elite. After the upheavals of

---

[1] See Vol. I, p. 18. Facs. in *EBM*, iii, pl. 64. The editor suggests (p. lxxxv) that the MS was copied for
the use of Malchus, first bishop of Waterford (cons. 1096), previously a monk of Winchester.
[2] Cambridge, Univ. Lib., Add. MS 710. See Vol. I, pp. 11, 63.

the seventeenth century, a pattern of civilized living ensured for the Anglo-Irish population an international diet of concerts, opera, and oratorio exceeded only in London. But this provided little opportunity for native Irish talent, and no indigenous composers of distinction emerged. After the Union of England and Ireland in 1801, the situation changed somewhat. Despite an increasingly vice-regal attitude on the part of the Lords Lieutenant, the official patronage of music declined; it became less of a passport to social acceptance and more the preserve of genuine enthusiasts. The new order, moreover, encouraged the spread of English values to other cities. In these circumstances, which included the continuing strength of the Protestant cathedral choir schools and the foundation of the Irish Academy of Music (1848; Royal from 1872), Irish composers of the calibre of Balfe, Wallace, and Stanford appeared, even though all of them were to establish their names in London and beyond. Hamilton Harty, a northern Irishman, was also a resourceful composer, but it was as a conductor that his reputation became finally established. The most conspicuously talented Irish composer of modern times is Gerald Barry (b. 1952), whose highly assertive music is mostly unaffected by specifically national elements and has been performed throughout Ireland as well as in London and many other parts of the world.

The Scottish picture is in some ways similar to the Irish, though for political and geographical reasons the ties are closer. Uncertainty over the origins of the 'insular' element in the thirteenth-century repertory of St Andrews makes it impossible to ignore in a study of English music.[3] In the early sixteenth century, the 'Carver' (or 'Carvor') choirbook demonstrates both English and French affinities, as does that of the eponymous composer himself,[4] while the slightly younger Robert Johnson, a composer of both Catholic and Protestant music preserved in English sources, fled to England when he came under suspicion of heresy in Scotland. There is a good deal in common in the development of metrical psalmody and associated genres in England and Scotland, though their traditions later diverged. The strength and independence of Scottish music are well illustrated in the eighteenth century: Edinburgh became a lively musical centre, acting as a magnet for European musicians and providing a repertory largely independent of that of London. Local composition in the Lowlands, as elsewhere in Scotland, was, however, essentially a contribution to what we have defined in the previous chapter as 'folk music'; it both influenced the course of popular music in England through the cult of 'Scotch song' and deserves study as a paradigm for the lost traditions of northern England.

The development of Scottish art-music was partly a product of the late nineteenth-century movement towards musical nationalism, parallel to that

---

[3] See Vol. I, pp. 26–9; to the literature cited there should be added M. E. Everist, 'From Paris to St Andrews: the Origins of W1', *JAMS* 43 (1990), 1–4

[4] Vol. I, pp. 245–6.

of Stanford and Harty in Ireland. Hamish MacCunn (1868–1916) and John McEwen (1868–1948) deserve mention here, though like Stanford and their compatriot Mackenzie they spent much of their lives in London. Mac-Cunn's music as a whole, despite its emphasis on Scottish subject-matter, now seems rather bland, though colourful orchestration redeems his early overtures *Cior Mhor* and *The Land of the Fountain and the Flood*, first given in London in 1885 and 1887 respectively. McEwen was only a minor composer, more significant as a pedagogue; but he was in his way more original than MacCunn, despite being closer to the European mainstream. He became Professor of Composition at the Royal Academy of Music in 1898, and was Principal there from 1924 to 1936 in succession to Mackenzie.[5] Robin Orr (b. 1909), the best-known Scots composer of his generation, similarly pursued most of his career in England, including a lengthy period at Cambridge culminating in his professorship there from 1965 to 1976.

Latterly Scottish composers have played a more significant role, both internationally and throughout Britain. Thea Musgrave (b. 1928) is an outstanding composer, much of whose music lacks overtly Scottish associations. From the 1960s, after a period of experimental serialism, she developed an individual manner based on a free atonality and often involving an improvisatory element. The music of Iain Hamilton (b. 1922), a more thorough-going serialist, is dourer and still closer to the central European agenda of the mid-century. From 1961 to 1981 he lived in America. A number of English composers have settled in Scotland. Peter Maxwell Davies has kept a foot in both camps; Kenneth Leighton, Edward Harper (b. 1941), and more recently Nigel Osborne have taken up teaching posts at Edinburgh University. Harper's music has remained comparatively little known in England, but his relative freedom from the orthodoxies of his generation has given it a potentially much wider appeal. Something has already been said of James Dillon (b. 1950), a thorough-going modernist.[6] The most promising of the younger Scots composers are Judith Weir (b. 1954 in Cambridge) and James MacMillan (b. 1959), whose music in both cases can be uncompromisingly dissonant but is engagingly colourful and free of structural pedantry. MacMillan in particular has maintained a distinctly Scottish—and socially responsive—personality without in any way weakening his broader appeal or the underlying toughness of his idiom.

Outside its folk music—trustworthily recorded only in comparatively recent times—the work of Welsh composers has tended to merge still more closely with that of their English counterparts and to be bound up with English opportunities for performance. Arwel Hughes (1909–88) wrote two operas to Welsh texts, and a number of other Welsh-inspired works; but

[5] Mackenzie's music has been briefly considered in Ch. 4.
[6] See Ch. 7.

Welsh National Opera, which premièred his operas, has been more ambitious of achieving excellence in an international repertory (latterly in the original languages) than in promoting native products. Grace Williams (1906–77) was devoted to her country's musical traditions and is often thought of as a proponent of musical nationalism; yet this forms only one element of her artistic persona, and she deserves to be remembered for more than her *Penillion* for orchestra (1955), striking though that is, as well as being a landmark in her stylistic development. There is very little that is distinctively national in the work of Alun Hoddinott (b. 1929) or William Mathias (1934–92), though Hoddinott's first opera, *The Beach of Falesá*, was another WNO creation (1974, following Grace Williams's *The Parlour* in 1960). Hoddinott's large output includes a great deal of orchestral and chamber music, much of it written in an uncompromising though for the most part tonally orientated idiom. Mathias has contributed to the modern Anglican liturgy as well as writing some very effective larger-scale choral works, a fact that has tended to obscure the existence of some noteworthy orchestral music. His opera *The Servants* was produced in Cardiff in 1980.

In modern times the administration of the arts in Britain has probably contributed to the submergence of its individual national traditions in serious music, despite their earlier history of separate development. The BBC has so far retained its UK-wide remit, while conservatory training and the teaching of music in the universities have followed the English model. The Arts Council, originally of Great Britain, has since been divided: at the moment there are separate bodies for each country of the United Kingdom, and the funding of higher education is similarly divided; yet the administrations work very similarly in each case. Whether it is desirable or possible for a national identity in serious music to be maintained in present-day circumstances is a difficult question. It is possible that the decline of the European orthodoxies—be they of German or French origin—will usher in an era of greater national distinctiveness in European music generally, whatever political developments may be in store. On the whole the art can only be well served by regional diversity, whether at the serious or at the popular level.

London and the Provinces

A similar question arises concerning the relation of London to the regions. London was always bound to be the musical centre of England, even though it failed to gain the ecclesiastical primacy and did not become a permanent capital until the time of Edward the Confessor, who rebuilt Westminster Abbey and made its palace the seat of government. From then onwards London, including Westminster, was the focus of all the most significant developments. The Royal Household, while essentially itinerant until the reign of Edward VI, was based at Westminster and to a lesser extent at other royal residences such as Windsor, Greenwich, and (from the time of Henry VIII) Hampton Court. The most important body of musicians in the late Middle Ages was the Royal Household Chapel, whose members supplied much of the secular entertainment of the court as well as composing the most elaborate sacred music of their time, much of which found its way to outlying institutions (Eton, Cambridge, Oxford, and some of the provincial cathedrals).[7] As the political, trading, and social capital of England, London never lost its predominance, which could only increase as it encroached on the countryside that originally separated its elements and expanded into the surrounding territory. Royal residences, churches, theatres, and concert halls, together with lesser venues such as taverns and private houses, all played their part in making its music the most varied and forward-looking in the country. London also became, from Tudor times onwards, the major centre of music printing and publishing.

Provincial music-making has therefore tended to be a specialized concern. Few composers of any distinction have remained associated with a particular locality, whether adoptive or that of their birth, in such a way as make them its musical mouthpiece, so to speak. In the eighteenth century Charles Avison at Newcastle and Thomas Chilcot at Bath were somewhat exceptional in achieving both personal eminence and complete identification with their community. In modern times there has been Britten at Aldeburgh (and Maxwell Davies at Kirkwall, though we are here thinking primarily of England itself); but Britten's musical personality, like that of any truly great composer, transcended the associations, real enough, that accounted for much of his inspiration and provided the working conditions on which he depended. Modern technologies of music distribution and of personal communication, moreover, have reduced the relevance of domicile as a factor in a composer's character and the breadth of his or her appeal.

But while the provincial composers of earlier times were usually nothing more than minor local worthies, they were nevertheless an important element in the regional cultivation of music. The earliest important centres were the cathedral cities, together with a few towns housing important abbeys and parish churches. Some of these maintained their own town or city waits, and these musicians, with other bodies of minstrels, were trained through a system of apprenticeship. Until the Reformation, the Church provided an elementary musical training throughout the kingdom as part of its educational mission. In the more privileged places this was extended to a level of training that enabled boys to participate in elaborate polyphony; and it was these children from whom the ranks of our medieval composers were drawn, a career that frequently drew them to the royal service in London.

---

[7] For a recent series of informative articles see the May 1997 issue of *Early Music* (vol. 25/2), entitled 'Music in and around Tudor London'. A study by David Skinner of music in medieval Arundel is forthcoming.

But many—like Taverner in Tattershall, Oxford, and Boston in turn—remained to ensure if possible the maintenance of the musical traditions in the provinces.

Oxford and Cambridge, together with the colleges of Eton and Winchester and a large number of collegiate churches up and down the country, had a musical importance that either was severely reduced or completely disappeared at the Reformation. And while the most substantial of the foundations that enabled church music to flourish were endowed by royalty, the wealthy nobility and gentry, or by ecclesiastical dignitaries, it should not be forgotten how much the ordinary laity contributed, by their personal bequests or through the guilds to which they belonged, at least to a modest level of liturgical music-making.

The Reformation was no less than a disaster for the provincial creation and performance of music in England. Not only the sacred music, but also much of the secular music patronized by local magnates, monasteries, and other religious communities, and by individual ecclesiastics, came to an end as a result of religious change. There was, it is true, an element of continuity. Most of the aristocracy and gentry (other than Catholics in secret) no longer perceived any necessity for a private chapel establishment, but they sometimes maintained professional musicians to provide their entertainment and teach their children. Provincial cathedral musicians—like Francis Pilkington in Chester in the early seventeenth century—enjoyed contacts with local gentry, as can be seen from the dedicatory letters of their publications.

During the seventeenth and eighteenth centuries the patronage of music by provincial magnates tended to become less ambitious. The elaborate establishment of James Brydges at Cannons, complete with its chapel music, was unusual, although well-to-do families continued to support local musical activity in various ways. However, a more modest but communally more rewarding pattern arose as amateur orchestras and ensembles, led by one or more local professionals, were formed in cathedral and market-towns up and down the country. Members of the Wainwright family fostered music in Manchester and Liverpool for several decades, as did those of the Valentine family at Leicester over a much longer period. Joseph Gibbs (1699–1788) was active in Ipswich and elsewhere in Suffolk for many years, and F. E. Fisher (who may have been of German origin, however) pursued his career in several east Anglian towns including Cambridge. Thomas Ebdon (1738–1811) was organist at Durham Cathedral from 1763 until his death and contributed to the conducting of the Newcastle subscription concerts; and Joseph Garth, presumably related to the composer John Garth, was in charge of the Gentlemen's Subscription Concerts in Durham itself. In Doncaster Edward Miller was the local organist and enabler.[8]

[8] See e.g. M. Medforth, 'The Valentines of Leicester', MT 122 (1981), 812–18; F. Knight, Cambridge Music (Cambridge, 1980). Recent work by P. Holman on Colchester has revealed an extensive

In some of the larger towns annual festivals or seasons grew up. Foremost was the 'three choirs' festival at Worcester, Gloucester, and Hereford in turn (from around 1715); others were at Leeds (established in 1767), Birmingham (1768), Norwich (1770), and Sheffield (1786). Bath enjoyed extended 'seasons' for the well-to-do, in which concerts played an important part; there and in Oxford, Norwich, Manchester, and Newcastle, the music-making was usually controlled by amateurs, though with the support of professional players.[9] In the later eighteenth century women choralists began to replace the boys of the local cathedrals in the oratorio per-formances that formed the principal attraction at the local festivals.

The rapid growth of places like Birmingham, Leeds, Manchester, and Newcastle in the nineteenth century, and the rise of other manufacturing towns, led to the emulation of London's amenities in the arts, not least music, in the provinces. Town halls and concert halls, often equipped with a large organ, provided a venue for choral and orchestral music, and in due course fully professional orchestras, starting with the Hallé at Manchester in 1858, were formed. Despite the difficulties associated with their funding, England's provincial orchestras have flourished; local talent has been fed by conservatories at Manchester and Birmingham (and by smaller institutions elsewhere), and local choral societies have developed high standards. Unfor-tunately, the optimism that led to the building of opera-houses in many cities did not lead to the permanent establishment of opera companies; only Leeds, where the Grand Theatre and Opera House was built in 1878, is nowadays home to a permanent company, Opera North.

Professional music in the regions, though it has made use of local performing talent, has not since the middle of the nineteenth century been associated with provincial composition. At best a quite minor figure, such as the Lancastrian Thomas Pitfield (b. 1903), has enjoyed a well-deserved local reputation. Pitfield, a man of varied artistic talents, studied at the Royal Manchester College of Music in the 1920s, and taught there from 1947 until 1973, by which time the College had become the Royal Northern School of Music. But the political centralization of England, like that of France, means that for major composers a national identity is bound to subsume a local one. The question nowadays, in fact, is whether a

---

involvement by amateurs such as the Revd. Thomas Twining (1735–1804), Rector of St Mary's, violinist, and composer. Miller's references to the local music are to be found in his *History and Antiquities of Doncaster* (Doncaster, 1804). William Herschel, the future Astronomer Royal, whose early musical career was centred on Durham, Newcastle, and Leeds (where he became director of the subscription concerts), was also a visitor to Doncaster. See *BHMB*, iv. 317, 458.

[9] See A. Boden, *Gloucester, Hereford, Worcester*; T. Fawcett, *Music in Eighteenth-Century Norwich and Norfolk*; S. Wollenberg, 'Music in 18th-Century Oxford'; Burchell, *Polite or Commercial Concerts?*. At Bath, apart from Chilcot, the principal professionals were Thomas Linley sen. (see Ch. 2) and Herschel, who moved there in 1766 after a very brief appointment at Halifax and who succeeded Linley as director of the Bath orchestra in 1776.

national identity can be maintained in the context of an international reputation.

We have seen in the previous chapter how difficult it is to pin down the local element in the makeup of folk song. Regional amateur music-making flourishes, for example in the big choral societies and in the context of competitive music festivals, brass band competitions, and the like. But the repertory has virtually no local affiliations, and in this respect too, therefore, the music of England seems to lack regional diversity. Modern communications, and an educational system that has aimed at (and usually succeeded in) delivering a highly standardized curriculum, have ultimately weakened the significance of the local voice.

Education and Scholarship

The character of a national music depends largely on its systems of education. Prior to the Reformation, musical education in England followed European patterns. It was largely, and exclusively insofar as it depended on the writing of music, the province of the Church. In the monastic churches and secular cathedrals, in collegiate and parish churches, boys and young men were taught the chant, both by rote and, from the later Middle Ages at least, from written notation by means of solmization. From the fifteenth century in the larger establishments they were taught to improvise polyphonic parts to a given plainsong ('descant'), to play the organ and clavichord if they were sufficiently talented, and to read from mensural notation or 'pricksong'. By the early sixteenth century the standards of singing and reading music expected of both boys and men were phenomenally high; and if these accomplishments were not as widespread as has sometimes been assumed, they must have been attained in a good many of the better-endowed establishments.

Beside this church-orientated system was that of apprenticeship to a minstrel, generally through the guild of which he was a member. Here the teaching was almost entirely by rote, and repertories of secular ensemble music must have been the outcome of communal improvisation. We know very little about the earlier history of musical apprenticeship, but it is important, because it was the principal means of providing musical tuition, apart from that given by the church, until the early nineteenth century.[10] After the Reformation, as we have seen, the choir schools occupied a proportionately much less important position than before, and while the most favoured establishments—the Chapel Royal, Westminster Abbey, St Paul's, St George's, Windsor, and a few places outside London—maintained

---

[10] Ehrlich, *The Music Profession in Britain since the Eighteenth Century*, cites in full articles of apprenticeship dated 1860 (pp. 239–40); and organists were still being 'articled' to their mentors in the first half of the 20th c.

high standards, others will not have been able to do so. As the status of secular musicians increased, however, the apprenticeship system embraced an increasing range of skills, including the reading and writing of music and the mastery of newer and more difficult instruments. Individual tuition outside this system was provided for young people and servants in well-to-do families, but that was mainly for the sake of its amateur cultivation.

It is important therefore to recognize both the merits and the limitations of this long-lasting dual system and its effect on both composition and standards of performance. Before the Reformation, in England as elsewhere, it explains the predominance of sacred music in the surviving written repertories and the fact that almost all written secular music is the product of composers trained, and in most cases employed, in an ecclesiastical context. After the Reformation church music was simplified in style (though the best of it exhibits a new sensitivity to verbal declamation and musical nuance); and while a great deal of secular and instrumental music continued to exhibit ecclesiastical features (for example, the setting of cantus firmi), we also begin to find repertories, in particular of instrumental dances, that are independent of it. These perhaps came originally from Italy, which had supplied the English court with musicians and had earlier developed a musical literacy outside the Church. Indeed the title accorded to these newcomers, musicians rather than minstrels, testifies to their enhanced standing and prefigures the more general application of the term to performers, singers as well as players. However that may be, English composers were quick to build on this novelty, and by the early seventeenth century there were a number of court composers who owed little or nothing to training through the Church.

The place of written theory and instructional literature needs some comment here. Medieval writing of a simple and practical nature, whether in Latin or in English, was produced for the convenience of a teacher, not his pupils. Leonel Power's vernacular treatise on improvised descant is just such an example, copied out by a member, possibly the precentor, of an Augustinian abbey.[11] We possess in John Tucke's compilation the musical notebook of an early sixteenth-century schoolmaster, an Oxford-educated Bachelor of Music who taught first at the school attached to the collegiate church at Higham Ferrers and after that at the grammar school of Gloucester Abbey.[12] Printed literature on music in England (other than two brief summaries of speculative music in books published by Caxton) post-dates the Reformation. Simplified rules for sight-singing were attached to some editions of the metrical psalter with tunes from the 1560s onwards. Morley's *Plaine and Easie Introduction* (1597) is a landmark, but it is difficult to assess its

---

[11] See Vol. I, p. 172.
[12] See R. Woodley, *John Tucke: A Case Study in Early Tudor Music Theory* (Oxford, 1993).

impact. Few if any will have learnt to sing or to compose simply by reading it; the interlocutors in Morley's dialogue are adult seekers after knowledge whose grasp of musical practicalities appears to be minimal and who are made to appear too obtuse ever to have any prospect of success as composers. Thomas Tomkins bought a copy, but he was already a fully trained composer and annotated it solely to amplify Morley's points. Yet it was reprinted in 1608, six years after Morley's death, and was followed by other books containing the rudiments of music and the elements of composition; there were also a number of instrumental tutors from the later sixteenth century onwards.[13]

Even the most practical of books, however, could only be supplementary to individual tuition, however much an author might claim for them. It may well be that their readiest market was amongst amateurs for whom such tuition was a luxury, and this was a market that rapidly increased from the second half of the seventeenth century. But still the choir schools and the apprenticeship system, together with the practical experience which came with them, were the primary means by which professional musicians were taught. (It should always be borne in mind that a term of apprenticeship could follow on from a choir- school education.) These served England well until the end of the seventeenth century, but they were less effective in the eighteenth, partly because of the decline of standards (and expectations) in the cathedrals and partly because they were ill fitted to foster the cult of the the virtuoso singer and player. England came to be dominated by foreign virtuosi, as we have seen, and even in the burgeoning orchestras the best players were often foreigners. Attempts to initiate a conservatory on the Italian model came to nothing, and it was not until 1822 that an Academy of Music was founded.

Even then, things were slow to improve, despite the best efforts of dedicated teachers like Cipriani Potter and George Macfarren. It was not until later in the century, when the Royal College of Music was founded, that a comprehensive system of practical musical education at the tertiary level came into being; and the competitive spirit engendered by the new foundation saw to it that the Academy quickly raised its own standards, at the same time putting the emphasis on tuition at the tertiary rather than the secondary level. The junior departments at both institutions (and later at others) catered for younger aspirants, but their opportunities had improved elsewhere too.

Before the middle of the nineteenth century, primary education outside the choir schools, and secondary education generally, made little or no provision for music. A few Charity Schools taught singing to poorer children in a religious context. The grammar schools were intended to

[13] See Vol. I, pp. 500–1, and, for the later 17th c., pp. 542–5, 553–4, 560.

equip their pupils with the means for reading an Arts course at one of the two universities, though some taught a wider range of subjects of practical application. Indeed the advance of non–university learning in the sixteenth and seventeenth centuries is remarkable, and must be mainly attributed to enlightened teaching in the grammar schools. But musical instruction seems to have been rare, perhaps because the profession was considered ungentlemanly. Where it was given, it was for the sake of the pursuit and understanding of music at an amateur level, and cannot have led by itself to instrumental or vocal fluency, let alone to the practice of composition. Possibly in a few schools, such as Christ's Hospital, the Charterhouse School, and Alleyn's College at Dulwich, at each of which an organist was employed, more was achieved. But by the eighteenth century a substantial barricade had been erected between the means by which professional standing could be obtained and the normal course of education. The speculative study of music, and the scientific investigation of its materials, were another matter. The former arose out of its study in the medieval and Tudor universities, and the latter went hand in hand with the scientific spirit that resulted in the foundation of the Royal Society.

It was rare for professional musicians to penetrate the social barrier erected by the well–born and by those who had received the benefits (if they were that) of a university education. Charles Burney was somewhat exceptional in being a composer of merit, a keyboard player, and in due course a learned historian of music who could count on the respect of his intellectual peers. He had been apprenticed to Arne in 1744 at the age of 18, a drudgery from which he was rescued only after a payment of £300. He was saved by his intelligence, his wit, and ultimately by his willingness to sacrifice the highest standards in his practical career to the pursuit of learning in his subject. In the next century William Crotch was able to combine the careers of composer and learned commentator, becoming the first Principal of the Royal Academy and Professor at Oxford, while Henry Bishop abandoned the theatre before accepting the chair at Oxford in his turn.

There was, it is true, a level of tolerance for those who, like Greene, Boyce, and Arnold, combined active professionalism with self-evident taste and learning, and the Oxford and Cambridge doctorates acknowledged the place of composition in the academic scheme of things; yet the ability to transcend engrained prejudice was rare, and the idea that the universities might themselves play a part in the professional development of a musician was far in the future. The composer-professors of the seventeenth and eighteenth centuries, most of whom were also college organists, simply pursued their own interests through their control of practical music. The universities were willing enough to make a fuss of composers who had made the grade by their own efforts, just as the nobility were willing to patronize

Italian opera; but that was a very different matter from active involvement in their education.

Of course social stratification and the prejudice that went with it were still more acute in pre-Revolutionary Europe, and the universities were even less relevant there to the education of musicians; but the institutional and private patronage of music was far stronger, and the discussion of aesthetic issues frequently brought practitioners and *savants* on to common ground. However that may be, few English composers, and still fewer performers, had been to a university or even a secondary school before the second half of the nineteenth century (though it should be remembered that in those days a choir-school education might last until the age of 16 or 17). One of the reforms at Oxford and Cambridge in the later nineteenth century was the restriction on granting musical degrees to those who had graduated as BA, and the addition of an examination to the presentation of an exercise. The BA itself had to be in another subject or group of subjects, which ensured a wider general education for those who took this route. However, the fuller involvement of the universities in the preparation for a career in music is a post-Second World War development, following the introduction of courses devoted entirely to it. Even so, only a minority of professional musicians have taken this path, which normally has to be supplemented by conservatory-based training in any case.

The role of the universities in a practical musical education has always been ambivalent and will doubtless remain so. Just as significant, however, is the part they have played in forming an educated audience and a corps of intelligent commentators, a process that is largely independent of formal studies in music but rather the product of new listening experiences combined with an exposure to intellectual discipline in the formative years of an undergraduate career. The universities play no essential part here, either, but they have conspicuously helped to raise the level of critical discourse and to guarantee the intellectual respectability of the subject.

The development of musicology (a term that has unfortunately come to stay), that is to say the disciplined study for its own sake of music in its historical, analytical, and philosphical aspects, clearly overlaps with more intuitive, though at its best incisive and well-informed, critical judgement. Musicology thus defined is far older than its pursuit in universities, but it has burgeoned in an academic context since 1945. It seems to be characteristic of the modern English university system that it is able to embrace a variety of approaches to musical study without any compromise of intellectual integrity and without the danger of lapsing into irrelevance. Its achievement since the late nineteenth century is to have encouraged the composition and understanding of music as a unified ideal, and in doing so to have created a context for the furtherance of English music in particular.

The pursuit of music in schools has advanced, too, from the singing–class movement of the nineteenth century to the fostering of a wider appreciation and its inclusion in an examination-orientated curriculum. Hand in hand with this has gone the Anglican public-school chapel revival and the wider provision of instrumental tuition in state schools as well as in the private sector. These developments have led to a wider musical literacy in the population as a whole, and to a broader base for the recruitment of audiences, composers, and performers. Latterly bridges have been built between 'serious' and 'pop' musical cultures on the foundations of this broader base: many, young and old, display enthusiasm for both.

English Music

It remains to explore, in the light of these comments on the country's external and internal relations and on its educational traditions, the issue of Englishness in music.

National histories of music are a comparatively recent development, dating from the end of the nineteenth century. They are both the result of an understandable patriotism and a pragmatic method of reducing the scope of a narrative without sacrificing a lengthy chronological span. Their historiography has sometimes been based on a survey of the primary material, the music itself, and sometimes on the study of archives and what they can tell us of the circumstances under which music was produced and consumed. They are supplemented by numerous works dealing with specific topics or periods in the national history, and by single chapters in books of larger scope. Social histories, on the other hand, whether based on a complete or a partial chronology, speak more for how music has affected society than for how society has affected music.

Rarely, however, so far as England at any rate is concerned, is there any attempt to justify the endeavour on the grounds of an inherent relationship between the political geography and the national musical character. Even Walker in his *History of Music in England*, where a number of stylistic features, such as the occurrence of 'false relations' in sixteenth- and seventeenth-century music, are adduced, does not attempt a single unified picture. His image is rather of a culture characterized by alternations of peaks and troughs; if there are continuities, they are in the minor arts of folk song and of hymn-tune writing, and in the peripheral (but revealing) addiction to examinations and professional qualifications.

It is certainly clear that one cannot seriously maintain the idea of national characteristics of style over a long period of profound changes. It may, however, be possible to pursue the question in terms of a characteristic response to circumstances, even at the risk of making generalizations open to various kinds of objection.

One of the enduring features of English music, it seems to me, is its tendency to adopt technical developments only after they have been tried and tested elsewhere, but then to put them to new and interesting uses. The argument hardly applies to liturgical chant, which was imposed by authority and of which the nucleus was supposed to remain unaltered, and the sense in which it might be applicable to other types of medieval song, sacred and secular, is difficult to unravel in the light of the available evidence. However, it can be substantiated for medieval polyphony in general, despite some apparent anomalies. The earliest source of practical polyphony anywhere is the early eleventh-century Winchester troper, but it is likely, to the extent that it actually represents English composition, that the style is a development of a simpler Continental note-against-note idiom. The 'insular' element in the St Andrews manuscript, though quite possibly Scottish rather than English, may also be a local refinement on Continental innovations of some time previously (rather than, as previously thought, an innovatory further development of Notre-Dame style). English motet-composition of the later thirteenth and early fourteenth century would be unthinkable without a Parisian prototype, but in building on this it has developed a new and readily recognizable idiom.

It is true that from time to time a demonstrably English innovation seems to cast doubt on this thesis. One such is the the cantus-firmus Mass cycle in the early fifteenth century. It can hardly be doubted that the first such examples are by Leonel Power, John Dunstable, and their English contemporaries. But it is worth examining that particular instance in more detail. The cantus-firmus Mass is really the application of the principles of the medieval motet to the movements of the Mass, and the English, who had indeed been slow to adopt the structures and rhythmic idiom of the French *ars nova* motet, began to transfer these techniques to the Mass in the late fourteenth century, at first in single movements and then in pairs of movements (Gloria and Credo) similarly constructed over the same cantus firmus. When the idea arose of extending this to the complete Ordinary of the Mass, it became desirable to avoid a succession of exactly 'cloned' movements, so to speak, and various ways were introduced of modifying the formal outlines while retaining the unifying cantus firmus. Although Continental composers seem to have got the idea from the English (further modifying it in their own fashion), the latter were not thrusting a ready-made innovation forward but merely exploiting in their own way the technical principle of the long-note cantus firmus.

Another aspect of late medieval English music is its concern for ritual propriety. While it no longer seems appropriate to be satisfied with the notion that this repertory was conceived for the 'liturgy' in the abstract, but rather to look for the specific forms of patronage that called it into being, the demands of a magnate or the statutes of an institution were clearly best satisfied by a response that demonstrated a proper subservience to long-established principles. Polyphony was a kind of glossed chant (even if composed independently of it or based on material drawn from another context), not an art-work intended to excite admiration for its own sake. This is a rather different attitude from the one which prevailed on the Continent from the time of Dufay onwards, and it accounts for the conservatism of much later fifteenth-century English music.

Tinctoris had lamented this conservatism, while praising the originality, as he saw it, of earlier English music. But even this originality, celebrated by the Burgundian court poet Martin le Franc as 'la contenance angloise', was more a nationally identifiable strain whereby the harshnesses of the late fourteenth-century idiom had been smoothed out than a radically new technique.

We can detect over and over again the Continental sources of English methods and the novel ways in which they were exploited. The dance idioms and variation techniques of the sixteenth century came from Italy and found their highest expression in the music of the virginalists; the madrigal also came from Italy and grew a small but distinctive English pendant; lute song had French as well as Italian antecedents; the Latin sacred music of Tallis and Byrd was indebted to Netherlandish models (in addition to earlier English ones), and the English service-music of Byrd, Gibbons, and Tomkins came from the same stock. The innovations of the Italian Baroque were slow to take root, and their adoption before the middle of the seventeenth century has a decidedly experimental flavour; in the music of Purcell, however, who was able to draw on later Italian models and to benefit from the earlier English experiments, the entire idiomatic range was thoroughly assimilated and given a personal flavour. It is hard to generalize about the seventeenth century, because so much of its music was genuinely innovatory: the court of Charles I provided employment for William Lawes, one of the most original of all English composers. But the pattern of careful assimilation and considered reaction remains. The eighteenth century is a period of retraction analogous to the later fifteenth, but a response to Viennese classicism can be detected, for example, in Storace, the younger Linley, Samuel Wesley, Pinto, Attwood, and Crotch, all of whom varied it in their own way.

No one could claim that this group of composers was able to offer a brilliant re-creation analogous to that of the Elizabethans or the later Stuart composers. In the earlier Victorian period, too, English composers, for reasons implicit in the account given of their educational and professional opportunities, failed to get a grip on European Romanticism and employ it for their own ends. It makes a striking contrast to the achievements of nineteenth-century English literature, and the answer to the conundrum probably lies in the lower status accorded to music in this period. At the end of the century, however, English composers regained their significance, not as innovators but as beneficiaries of innovations that they could turn to their own use. First Parry and Stanford, and then above all Elgar, capitalized on German Romanticism and made something personal of it. Elgar's overture *Froissart* (1890) is a key work—more so in some ways even than the *Enigma* variations of 1899—because of its technical self-confidence and orchestral mastery. Elgar was in due course to draw on Wagner and Strauss in addition to the substratum of Schumann, Brahms, and Dvořák on which he and his contemporaries had largely relied.[14]

English composers younger than Elgar largely turned their back on the German tradition, preferring instead the French as well as a return to their own earlier roots. In fact it is the heady combination of Tudor and modern French that gives Vaughan Williams's music much of its characteristic flavour. Debussy, Ravel, and the pre-war Stravinsky (whose Russian nationalism was very much overlaid with French sophistication) now provided the models, not only for Vaughan Williams but for others, like John Ireland, who were relatively unaffected by the Tudor revival. They were not the only influences but they provided the foundation for the individualism that arose from them.

Holst, Vaughan Williams's greatest contemporary, needs special mention because he stretched the limits of stylistic assimilation to breaking point. It takes a special kind of genius to marry sturdy English melodiousness with Straussian orchestral opulence and Stravinskian rhythmic bite, as he does in the 'Jupiter' movement of *The Planets*. The well-deserved popularity of this extraordinary work has tended to obscure its utter originality—an originality of conception and in the use to which the materials are put, however, as much as one of pure invention. The wordless female chorus of 'Neptune' has a clear precedent in Debussy, but the way in which it is deployed to convey the unearthly singularity of that distant planet and its 'mystical' eponym is unique to Holst.

The non-German, or indeed anti-German, precedents have often gained the upper hand in the twentieth century. Stravinsky and the French, including Messiaen and Boulez, have predominated, but there has also been the direct influence of jazz, of modern Russian music, and of Italian opera. Britten, for example, drew on Rossini and Puccini in his approach to operatic composition in preference to the Wagnerian ideal. But these very examples also illustrate a new propensity, that of emulating the Stravinskian attitude to the past. This is not so much a delayed reaction as a deliberate return, a reuse of 'classical' models for present purposes. But yet again,

---

[14] I am not convinced that *Froissart* owes very much beyond some slight thematic resemblances to the prelude to *Die Meistersinger* (see Moore, *Edward Elgar*, 145); in spirit and form it differs profoundly. But one could reasonably add the influence of Schumann in his heroic mood to that of Parry adduced above (Ch. 4).

English neoclassicism—in, for example, certain works of Bliss, Walton, Britten, and Tippett—is less stark than the Stravinskian protoptype: it is a reinterpretation of neoclassicism as well as of the Classical models themselves.

It is harder to make sense of any notion of Englishness in the late twentieth century, partly because the materials available to composers have become more varied and less cohesive—there is less obviously a canon of European masterpieces, and the course of idiomatic development is less clear—and partly because the English have themselves been arguably at least as innovative in primary terms as composers from anywhere else in the world. Hitherto, we have argued, English innovation has rested on a bedrock of European precedent. Since Birtwistle and Maxwell Davies that has no longer been the case. But the position has not been completely reversed, because it does not seem that aspiring young composers from abroad yet flock in their droves to learn from English masters or in English institutions. Whether there may be a small number who do so is another matter, but even so it would be hard to name a single foreign composer of distinction who has learnt the craft from England. And that is the crux of the matter. English composers have always been free to ignore all or some of what they have learnt abroad or from foreign composers, though they have generally retained a good deal, consciously or otherwise. But though their music has often been admired, as well as ignored and unfairly denigrated, it has only rarely been influential.

The present situation therefore represents a change of emphasis rather than a radical reversion. With the successive musical hegemonies of Italy, Germany, and France at an end, classicism itself is called into question, since the alternative traditions—those of eastern Europe or America, for example—are less well established. Hence there is no clear set of guidelines for an aspiring composer, while at the same time there seems to be no disposition amongst English composers to offer an alternative. If the outcome seems like anarchy, it is a price that has to be paid for the present crisis in 'western' culture.

There are, however, signs that the crisis may be approaching a resolution in a way that could not have been foretold forty years ago. Throughout the century serious composers have drawn on popular idioms, but almost always in a spirit of irony, or at any rate to make a dramatic point. Vaughan Williams and Walton, for example, have done so, and more recently Maxwell Davies; while amongst English composers Constant Lambert is almost unique in having used jazz as a positive, non-ironic element in his style. But jazz has proved to be a less universal idiom than might have been anticipated, and in some of its manifestations is not popular at all. Since the 1960s, however, the simpler processes of a genuinely popular music have created a challenge that cannot be ignored. In the world of postmodern serious music the truly popular can be incorporated without irony, and many modern British composers have made use of its surface characteristics.

It is possible therefore that the English, with their traditional respect for sound craftsmanship based on established practice, may come to view the popular as the new classicism and build creatively on it. It is difficult to imagine serious English composers (as opposed to the mostly uninventive purveyors of mass entertainment) at the cutting edge of an idiom associated above all with brash exhibitionism. But in recent years the work of composers like Gavin Bryars, Dominic Muldowney, Michael Finnissy, Steve Martland, and Martin Butler has tended to cast aside the artificial barrier between the serious and the popular, and, while never achieving (or seeking to achieve) the truly demagogic, has offered a new rapprochement.

In the longer term, some such rapprochement is clearly desirable. Modern popular music, and its widespread enjoyment amongst the young of all classes, demands it. Since the 1960s, moreover, English society has become more mobile, and class distinctions have been redrawn, not entirely on economic lines. There is a wider appetite for the established classics, and a way will have to be found of satisfying it, for example by making opera more genuinely accessible. English (and indeed other British) composers are poised to play their part by responding to commissions with work of broad appeal. Many recent Prom commissions have done just that, and it is one of the most heartening aspects of the late twentieth century that this biggest of all music festivals has witnessed a trend towards accessibility in the new music of the host country.

The twentieth-century classics, to which England has contributed a healthy share, will live on, but the conditions of cultural mandarinism which created them are coming to an end, and in the incipient millennium it can be expected that English composers will adapt, as they always have, to the society whose needs they must satisfy.

Bibliography

T HE Bibliography is organized on the same lines as in Volume I. It lists all cited material, except for unedited primary sources of music and literature and for tangential works, together with other items of value and relevance. It is not claimed to be complete as regards the latter; to a certain extent it is designedly selective, though it will doubtless prove incomplete in ways not intended.

The 'General' Bibliography is a revised version of that in Volume I. Otherwise material from Volume I is not repeated here, even if cited in Chapter 8; first citations there are in any case complete. Sections II A and B do not include facsimiles or reprints without added value; where facsimiles are included the term 'ed.' usually means 'with an introduction by'. Section III lists 'folk' or 'traditional' material collected since 1800 or shortly before, including some from elsewhere in the British Isles, under the name of the collector or primary editor. Material overlooked in section II of the Bibliography in Volume I, or which has appeared since its publication, is given in a separate Appendix below. Items appearing in the List of Abbreviations are not repeated here. The arrangement is therefore as follows:

I. General   A. Works of Reference
                    B. Historical and Critical Works
II. For Volume II A. Scholarly Editions of Music
                    B. Scholarly Editions of Texts
                    C. Books and Articles
III.   Collections of Folk Song and Dance
Appendix   Arranged as in Section II

I.   GENERAL

A.   Works of Reference

ARKWRIGHT, G. E. P., *Catalogue of Music in the Library of Christ Church, Oxford,* 2 vols. (London, 1915–23).

CROSBY, B., *A Catalogue of Durham Cathedral Music Manuscripts* (Oxford, 1986).

DAWE, D., *Organists of the City of London 1666–1850: A Record of One Thousand Organists with an Annotated Index* (for the Author, 1983).

DIXON, W. E., *A Catalogue of Ancient Choral Services and Anthems . . . in the Cathedral Church of Ely* (Cambridge, 1861).

EITNER, R., *Biographisch-bibliographisches Quellen-Lexicon,* 10 vols. (Leipzig, 1900–4).

FELLOWES, E. H., *The Catalogue of Manuscripts in the Library of St. Michael's College, Tenbury* (Paris, 1934).

FENLON, I., *Catalogue of the Printed Music and Music Manuscripts before 1801 in the Music Library of the University of Birmingham Barber Institute of Fine Arts* (London, 1976).

FORD, W. K., *Music in England Before 1800: A Select Bibliography* (London, 1967).

FULLER MAITLAND, J. A., and MANN, A. H., *Catalogue of Music in the Fitzwilliam Museum, Cambridge* (London, 1893).

GRIFFITHS, D., *A Catalogue of Music Manuscripts in York Minster Library* (York, 1981).

—— 'The Music in York Minster', *MT* 123 (1982), 633–7.

Handbook of British Chronology, ed. E. B. Fryde, D.E. Greenway, S. Porter, and I. Roy (Royal Historical Society Guides and Handbooks, no. 2; 3rd edn., London, 1986).

HARMAN, A., *A Catalogue of the Printed Music and Books on Music in Durham Cathedral Library* (London, 1968).

HAYES, G., *King's Music* (London, 1937).

HIGHFILL, P. H., *et al.*, *A Biographical Dictionary of Actors, Actresses, Musicians, Dancers, Managers, and Other Stage Personnel in London, 1600–1800* (Carbondale, Ill., 1973–).

HUGHES, DOM A., *Catalogue of the Musical Manuscripts at Peterhouse* (Cambridge, 1953).

HUGHES-HUGHES, A., *A Catalogue of Manuscript Music in the British Museum*, 3 vols. (London, 1906–9).

HUMPHRIES, C., and SMITH, W. C., *Music Publishing in the British Isles from the Beginning until the Middle of the Nineteenth Century* (2nd edn., Oxford, 1970).

JAMES, M. R., *A Descriptive Catalogue of the Manuscripts in the Library of Corpus Christi College, Cambridge*, 2 vols. (Cambridge, 1912).

JULIAN, J., *A Dictionary of Hymnology* (2nd edn., London, 1907; repr. New York, 1957).

KIDSON, F., *British Music Publishers, Printers and Engravers . . . from Queen Elizabeth's Reign to George the Fourth's* (London, [1900]).

KING, A. H., *Printed Music in the British Museum* (London, 1979).

The King's Musick, ed. H. C. de Lafontaine (London, 1909).

LOEWENBERG, A., *Annals of Opera 1597–1940* (Cambridge, 1943).

MILLER, L., and COHEN, A., *Music in the Royal Society of London 1660–1806* (Detroit Studies in Music Bibliography, 56; Detroit, 1987).

MOULD, C., *The Musical Manuscripts of St. George's Chapel, Windsor Castle* (Windsor, 1973).

The Old Cheque-Book, or Book of Remembrance, of the Chapel Royal, from 1561 to 1744, ed. E. F. Rimbault (London, 1872).

SHAW, W., *The Succession of Organists of the Chapel Royal and the Cathedrals of England and Wales from c.1538* (Oxford, 1991).

SIMPSON, A., 'A Short-Title List of Printed English Instrumental Tutors up to 1800, Held in British Libraries', *RMARC* 6 (1966), 24–50.

SQUIRE, W. B., *Catalogue of Printed Music in the Library of the Royal College of Music, London* (London and Leipzig, 1909).

—— *Catalogue of Printed Music Published between 1487 and 1800 and now in the British Museum*, 2 vols. (London and Leipzig, 1912).

—— *Catalogue of the King's Music Library*, 3 vols. (London, 1927–9).

WARNER, T. E., *An Annotated Bibliography of Woodwind Instruction Books, 1600–1830* (Detroit, 1967).

WILLETTS, P. J., *Handlist of Manuscripts Acquired* [by the British Museum] *1908–1967* (London, 1970).

B. Historical and Critical Works

ATKINS, SIR I., *The Early Occupants of the Office of Organist and Master of the Choristers of the Cathedral Church of Christ and the Blessed Virgin Mary, Worcester* (London, 1918).

AVISON, CHARLES, *Essay on Musical Expression* (2nd edn., London, 1753).

BLOM, E., Music in England (2nd edn., Harmondsworth, 1948).

BUKOFZER, M. F., *Music in the Baroque Era* (New York, 1947).

BUMPUS, J. S., *A History of English Cathedral Music 1549–1889*, 2 vols. (London [1889]; 2nd edn., 1908).

—— *The Organists and Composers of St Paul's Cathedral* (London, 1891).

BURNEY, C., *A General History of Music*, 4 vols. (London, 1776–89, repr. 1789; ed. F. Mercer, 2 vols., New York, 1935).

CALDWELL, J., *English Keyboard Music Before the Nineteenth Century* (Oxford, 1973).

The Cambridge Guide to the Arts in Britain, ed. B. Ford, 9 vols. (Cambridge, 1988–).

CHAPPELL, W., *Popular Music of the Olden Time*, 17 parts or 2 vols. (London [1855–9]; reissued as *The Ballad Literature and Popular Music of the Olden Time*, 2 vols., London [1859]; 2nd edn. by H. E. Wooldridge, *Old English Popular Music*, 2 vols., London and New York, 1893; repr. of 1st edn. with Introduction by F. W. Sternfeld, New York, 1965; repr. of 2nd edn. in 1 vol., with Suppl. by F. Kidson [first publ. 1891], New York, 1961).

CLUTTON, C., and NILAND, A., *The British Organ* (London, 1963).

COLLES, H. C., *Voice and Verse: A Study in English Song* (London, 1928).

COOPER, B., 'Englische Musiktheorie im 17. und 18. Jahrhundert', in *Geschichte der Musiktheorie*, ix (Darmstadt, 1986), 141–314.

DAVEY, H., *History of English Music* (London, 1985; 2nd edn., 1921).

FELLOWES, E. H., *Organists and Masters of the Choristers of St George's Chapel in Windsor Castle* (London [1939]).

—— *English Cathedral Music* (London, 1941; 5th edn., rev. J. A. Westrup, 1969).

GALPIN, F. W., *Old English Instruments of Music* (London, 1910; 4th edn., rev. R. T. Dart, New York, 1965).

GOUK, P., 'Music in the Natural Philosophy of the Early Royal Society', Ph.D. diss. (London, Warburg Institute, 1982).

HAWKINS, SIR J., *A General History of the Science and Practice of Music*, 5 vols. (London, 1776; 2nd edn., 1853; 1875; 2nd edn. repr., with an Introduction by C. L. Cudworth, 1963; 3rd edn. repr. 1969).

HUSK, W. H., *An Account of the Musical Celebrations on St. Cecilia's Day in the Sixteenth, Seventeenth and Eighteenth Centuries* (London, 1857).

KNIGHT, F. *Cambridge Music* (Cambridge, 1980).

LASOCKI, D. R. G., 'Professional Recorder Players in England, 1540–1740', 2 vols., Ph.D. diss. (University of Iowa, 1983).

LONG, K. R., *The Music of the English Church* (London, 1971).

McGuinness, R., *English Court Odes 1660–1820* (Oxford, 1971).

Mackerness, E. D., *A Social History of English Music* (London, 1966).

Mellers, W., *Harmonious Meeting: A Study of the Relationship between English Music, Poetry and Theatre, c.1600–1900* (London, 1965).

Mellor, A., *A Record of the Music and Musicians at Eton College* (Windsor [1929]).

Milhous, J., 'Opera Finances in London, 1674–1738', *JAMS* 37 (1984), 567–92.

Music Survey: New Series 1949–52, ed. D. Mitchell and H. Keller, 3 vols. in 1 (London, 1981).

Neighbarger, R. L., 'Music for London Shakespeare Productions, 1660–1830', Ph.D. diss. (University of Michigan, 1988).

Olleson, E. (ed.), *Modern Musical Scholarship* (Boston, Henley, and London, 1978).

Pine, E., *The Westminster Abbey Singers* (London, 1953).

Procter, F., Rev. Frere, W. H., *A New History of the Book of Common Prayer* (London, 1901; 3rd impr., 1905).

Robertson, D. H., *Sarum Close* (London, 1938; 2nd edn., Bath, 1969).

Routh, F., *Early English Organ Music from the Middle Ages to 1837* (London, 1973).

Strunk, O., *Source Readings in Music History* (New York, 1950; repr. in 5 vols., London, 1965).

Sundry Sorts of Music Books: Essays on the British Library Collections. Presented to O.W. Neighour on his 70th Birthday, ed. C. Banks, A. Searle, and M. Turner (London, 1993).

Temperley, N., *The Music of the English Parish Church*, 2 vols. (Cambridge, 1979).

Walker, E., *A History of Music in England* (Oxford, 1907; 3rd edn., rev. J. A. Westrup, 1952).

White, E. W., *The Rise of English Opera* (London, 1951).

—— *A History of English Opera* (London, 1983).

Williams, C. F. A., *Degrees in Music* (London [1893]).

Wilson, M., *The English Chamber Organ* (Oxford, 1968).

Wilson, R. M., *Anglican Chant and Chanting in England, Scotland, and America 1660–1820* Oxford, 1996).

Young, P., *A History of British Music* (London, 1967).

II.   FOR VOLUME II

A.   Scholarly Editions of Music

Alcock, John [the elder], *Four Voluntaries*, ed. P. Marr (London: Hinrichsen, 1961).

Anon., *Sonata in D minor for Violin and Continuo*, ed. H. McLean (MC 103; Oxford: Oxford University Press, 1987).

Anon., *Voluntaries in A minor and G minor*, ed. W. Emery (London: Novello, 1961).

Arne, Thomas Augustine, *Alfred*, ed. A. Scott (MB 47; London: Stainer and Bell, 1981).

—— *Comus*, ed. J. Herbage (MB 3; London: Stainer and Bell, 1951).

—— *Concerto 1 [–6]*, ed. R. Langley (MC 81–6; London: Oxford University Press, 1981).

—— *Eight Keyboard Sonatas* (facs.), ed. G. Beechey and T. Dart (London: Stainer and Bell, 1969).

—— *Eight Keyboard Sonatas*, ed. C. Hogwood (London: Faber, 1983).

—— *The Judgment of Paris*, ed. I. Spink (MB 42; London: Stainer and Bell, 1978).

—— *Overture 'The Guardian Outwitted'*, ed. G. Beechey (MC 11; London: Oxford University Press, 1973).

—— *Sonata in E major for Violin and Basso Continuo*, ed. J. A. Parkinson (MC 80; London: Oxford University Press, 1978).

—— *Symphony No.1 [–4]*, ed. R. Platt (MC 1–4; London: Oxford University Press, 1973).

ARNOLD, SAMUEL, *The Castle of Andalusia* (facs.), ed. R. Hoskins (MLE, C/5; London: Stainer and Bell, 1991).

BABELL, WILLIAM, *Sonata in F minor* and *Sonata in G minor*, ed. M. Tilmouth (London: Oxford University Press, 1963).

—— *Sonata 2 in C minor* and *Sonata 11 in G minor*, ed. G. Pratt (MC 51–2; London: Oxford University Press, 1978).

BARSANTI, FRANCESCO, *Two Sonatas for Treble Recorder and Continuo*, ed. G. Beechey (MC 9; London: Oxford University Press, 1973).

Beatles Complete, ed. R. Connolly (London: Music Sales, 1983).

The Beggar's Opera, ed. J. Barlow (Oxford: Oxford University Press, 1990).

BENNETT, JOHN, *Six Voluntaries for Organ*, ed. H. D. Johnstone (London and Sevenoaks: Novello, 1988).

—— *Voluntaries IX and X*, ed. H. D. Johnstone (London: Novello, 1966).

—— see also *Ten Eighteenth-Century Voluntaries*.

BENNETT, WILLIAM STERNDALE, *Piano and Chamber Music*, ed. G. Bush (MB 37; London: Stainer and Bell, 1972).

—— *Works for Pianoforte Solo* (facs.), ed. N. Temperley, 2 vols. (LPS 17–18; New York and London: Garland, 1985).

—— see also *The Overture in England*

BERNERS, LORD, *Collected Music for Solo Piano*, ed. P. Dickinson (London: Chester, 1982).

—— *Collected Vocal Music*, ed. P. Dickinson (London: Chester, 1982).

BISHOP, HENRY: see *The Overture in England*.

BOYCE, WILLIAM, *Overtures* [from MS sources], ed. G. Finzi (MB 13; London: Stainer and Bell, 1957).

—— *The Shepherd's Lottery* (facs.), ed. R. J. Bruce (MLE, C/4; London: Stainer and Bell, 1990).

—— *Solomon: A Serenata*, ed. I. Bartlett (MB 68; London: Stainer and Bell, 1996).

—— *Ten Voluntaries for the Organ or Harpsichord* (facs.), ed. J. Caldwell (London: Oxford University Press, 1972).

—— *Three Birthday Odes for Prince George, 1749 or 1750, 1751, 1752* (facs.), ed. R. J. Bruce (MLE, F/4; London: Stainer and Bell, 1989).

—— *Twelve Overtures* [1770], ed. R. Platt, 12 vols. (London: Oxford University Press, 1970).

—— see also Greene, Maurice.

BRIDGE, FRANK, *Five Early Songs*, ed. P. Hindmarsh (London: Thames, 1982).

—— *Three Songs*, ed. P. Hindmarsh (London: Thames, 1982).

CAMIDGE, MATTHEW, *Concerto No. 2 in G minor* [for organ solo], ed. F. Jackson (London: Novello, 1966).

CHILCOT, THOMAS, *Concerto in A major, Opus 2 No. 2; Concerto in F Major, Op. 2 No. 5*, ed. R. Langley (MC 22–3; London: Oxford University Press, 1975).

—— *Six Suites of Lessons for the Harpsichord or Spinet (1734)*, ed. D. Moroney (Le Pupitre, 60; Paris: Heugel, 1981).

CLEMENTI, MUZIO, *Works for Pianoforte Solo* (facs.), ed. N. Temperley, 5 vols. (LPS 1–5; New York and London: Garland, 1984–7).

A Collection of Favourite Lessons for Young Practitioners on the Harpsichord [A. Hummel, *c*.1765] (facs.), ed. G. Beechey (London: Oxford University Press, 1981).

COGAN, PHILIPS, *Complete Works for Piano Solo* (facs.), ed. E. Barry (New York and London: Garland, 1984).

The Complete Country Dance Tunes from Playford's Dancing Master (1651–ca. 1728), ed. J. Barlow (London, 1985).

Continental Composers in London, 1766–1810 (facs.), ed. N. Temperley (LPS 6; New York and London: Garland, 1985).

Continental Composers in London, 1810–1850 (facs.), ed. N. Temperley (LPS 15; New York and London: Garland, 1985).

CRAMER, JOHN BAPTIST, *Studio per il Piano Forte; Sonatas; Pieces for Pianoforte Solo* (facs.), ed. N. Temperley, 3 vols. (LPS 9–11; New York and London: Garland, 1985).

DELIUS, FREDERICK, *Complete Works*, ed. T. Beecham, 34 vols. (London: Boosey and Hawkes, 1951–93).

—— *Eventyr* [corr. repr. of Augener edn., 1921, 1923, by R. Threlfall] (London: Stainer and Bell [1976]).

—— *Four Posthumous Songs* (Vienna: Universal, 1981).

—— *Requiem* (corr. reissue, London: Boosey and Hawkes, 1986).

—— *A Song Before Sunrise (Study Score)* [corr. repr. of Augener edn., 1918 etc., by R. Threlfall] (London: Stainer and Bell [1984]).

DIBDIN, CHARLES, *The Touchstone or Harlequin Traveller* (facs.), ed. A. D. Shapiro (MLE, D/1; London: Stainer and Bell, 1990).

DUPUIS, THOMAS SANDERS: see *Three Voluntaries of the Later Eighteenth Century.*

D'URFEY, THOMAS (ed. and author): see *Wit and Mirth.*

Early Victorian Composers, 1830–1860 (facs.), ed. N. Temperley (LPS 16; New York and London: Garland, 1985).

The Edwardian Song Book, ed. M. R. Turner and A. Miall (London: Methuen, 1982).

Eighteenth-Century Violin Sonatas, ed. L. Salter, 2 vols. (London, 1975).

ELGAR, EDWARD: *Elgar Complete Edition*, ed. J. N. Moore and C. Kent (Borough Green: Novello 1981–).

The English Glee, ed. P. Young (Oxford: Oxford University Press, 1990).

English Organ Music: An Anthology from Four Centuries in Ten Volumes, ed. R. Langley (London: Novello, 1987–8).

English Romantic Partsongs, ed. P. Hillier (Oxford: Oxford University Press, 1986).

English Songs 1800–1860, ed. G. Bush and N. Temperley (MB 43; London: Stainer and Bell, 1979).

FESTING, MICHAEL CHRISTIAN, *Concerto Op. 3 No. 11 in E minor*, ed. R. Platt (MC 6; London: Oxford University Press, 1973).

—— *Two Sonatas for Violin and Basso Continuo*, ed. G. Beechey (MC 24; London: Oxford University Press, 1975).

FIELD, JOHN, *Complete Works for Piano Solo* (facs.), ed. N. Temperley, 2 vols. (LPS 12–13; New York and London: Garland, 1985–6).

—— *Piano Concertos 1–3*, ed. F. Merrick (MB 17; London: Stainer and Bell, 1961).

FINGER, GODFREY, *Pastorelle and Sonata for Three Treble Recorders*, ed. R. Platt (MC 48; London: Oxford University Press, 1978).

FISHER, F. E., *Trio Sonata 7 in G Minor, Op. 2 No. 1*; *Trio Sonata 10 in B flat Major, Op. 2 No. 4*, ed. R. Platt (MC 49–50; London: Oxford University Press, 1980).

The Glee, ed. P. Young (Oxford: Oxford University Press, 1990). A large number of single works were issued in a uniform format by Novello & Co. in the 19th c. under the title 'The Glee Hive'.

GOODWIN, Starling: see *An RCO Miscellany*.

GRAINGER, PERCY, *Thirteen Folksongs*, ed. D. Tall, 2 vols. (London: Thames, 1981–2).

GREENE, MAURICE, *A Collection of Lessons for the Harpsichord* (facs.), ed. D. Moroney (London: Stainer and Bell, 1977).

—— *Florimel* (facs.), ed. H. D. Johnstone (MLE, C/6; London: Stainer and Bell, 1995).

—— *Four Voluntaries for Organ or Harpsichord*, ed. F. Routh (London: Hinrichsen, 1960).

—— *Ode on St Cecilia's Day; Anthem: Hearken unto Me, ye Holy Children*, ed. H. D. Johnstone (MB 58; London: Stainer and Bell, 1991).

—— *Three Voluntaries for Organ or Harpsichord*, ed. G. Phillips (London: Hinrichsen, 1958).

—— *Twelve Voluntaries for Organ or Harpsichord by William Boyce or Maurice Greene*, ed. P. Williams (New York: Galaxy, 1969). Certainly by Greene, not Boyce.

—— *Voluntaries and Suites for Organ and Harpsichord*, ed. G. Beechey (RRMBE 19; Madison: A-R Editions, 1975).

—— see also *An RCO Miscellany*.

GURNEY, IVOR, *Five Elizabethan Songs* [1920, separately] (reissued London: Boosey and Hawkes, 1983).

—— *Ludlow and Teme* [1923, version with piano], ed. M. Pilkington (London: Stainer and Bell, 1982).

—— *Ten Songs*: 5 posthumous collections of, viz. *Twenty Songs*, ed. M. Scott, 2 vols. (Oxford: Oxford University Press, 1938); *A Third Volume of Ten Songs*, ed. M. Scott (ibid. 1952); *A Fourth Volume of Ten Songs*, ed. H. Ferguson (ibid. 1959); *A Fifth Volume of Ten Songs*, ed. M. Hurd (ibid. 1980).

—— *The Western Playland* [1926, version with piano], ed. M. Pilkington (London: Stainer and Bell, 1982).

HANDEL, GEORGE FRIDERIC: the two collected edns. are (1) *G.F. Händels Werke*, ed. F. Chrysander (Leipzig, 1858–94, 1902), and (2) *Hallische Händel-Ausgabe*, ed. M. Schneider, R. Steglich, and others (Kassel, 1955–). Individual volumes from these are not listed here.

—— *Complete Sonatas for Flute and Basso Continuo*, ed. D. Lasocki and P. Holman (London: Faber, 1983).

HANDEL, GEORGE FRIDERIC: *The Complete Sonatas for Treble Recorder and Basso Continuo*, ed. D. Lasocki and W. Bergmann (London: Faber, 1979).

—— *Complete Sonatas for Violin and Basso Continuo*, ed. T. Best and P. Holman (London: Faber, 1983).

—— *Concerto in F Major; Concerto in A Major*, ed. T. Best (MC 104–5; London: Oxford University Press, 1984).

—— *Fantasia and Sonata for Violin and Basso Continuo*, ed. R. Howat (MC 26; London: Oxford University Press, 1976).

—— *Fugue in E major*, ed. H. D. Johnstone (London: Novello, 1974).

—— *The Harpsichord Pieces from the Aylesford Collection*, ed. C. Kite (London: European Music Archive, 1983).

—— *Klaviersuiten I–VIII*, ed. A. Hicks (Munich: Henle, 1983).

—— *Klavierwerke I*, ed. P. Williams, 2 vols. (Vienna: Schott/Universal, 1991).

—— *Six Concertos for the Harpsichord or Organ (Walsh's Transcriptions, 1738)*, ed. W. Gudger (RRMBE 39; Madison: A-R Editions, 1981).

—— *Six Fugues or Voluntarys*, ed. G. Phillips (London: Hinrichsen, 1960).

—— *Six Fugues or Voluntarys*, ed. H. D. Johnstone (Oxford: Oxford University Press, 1986).

—— *Sonata in D Minor for Violin and Basso Continuo*, ed. R. Howat (MC 25; London: Oxford University Press, 1975).

—— *The Three Authentic Sonatas for Oboe and Basso Continuo*, ed. D. Lasocki (London: Faber, 1979).

—— *Trio Sonata in C Major for Two Violins and Basso Continuo*, ed. M. Gilmore (MC 89; Oxford: Oxford University Press, 1986).

—— *Twenty Overtures in Authentic Keyboard Arrangements*, ed. T. Best, 3 vols. (London and Sevenoaks: Novello, 1985–6).

—— (attrib.), *Four Voluntaries for the Organ or Harpsichord*, ed. F. Routh (London: Hinrichsen, 1961).

—— (attrib.), *Serenata 'There in Blissful Shades'*, ed. F. B. Zimmerman (MC 58; London: Oxford University Press, 1982).

HEBDEN, JOHN, *Sonata 1 in D Major for Flute and Basso Continuo*, ed. J. Barlow (MC 74; London: Oxford University Press, 1979).

HINE, WILLIAM: see *Ten Eighteenth-Century Voluntaries*.

HOLST, GUSTAV, *Collected Facsimile Edition* (London: Faber, 1974–).

—— *The Mystic Trumpeter*, ed. C. Matthews (London: Novello, 1989).

—— *Twelve Humbert Wolfe Songs*, ed. I. Holst (Great Yarmouth: Galliard, 1970).

HOOK, JAMES, *Concerto Opus 20 No. 2*, ed. R. Langley (MC 59; Oxford: Oxford University Press, 1986).

HOWELLS, HERBERT, *Concerto for String Orchestra*, ed. G. Easterbrook (Borough Green: Novello, 1985).

—— *Sonata No. 1 in E Major for Violin and Piano, Op. 18*, ed. C. Palmer (London: Boosey and Hawkes, 1986).

HUMPHRIES, JOHN, *Concerto in D Major, Opus 2 No. 12*, ed. R. Platt (MC 35; London: Oxford University Press, 1978).

—— *Concerto in D Minor, Opus 3 No. 10*, ed. R. Platt (MC 36; London: Oxford University Press, 1977).

JAMES, JOHN, *Two Trumpet Voluntaries*, ed. H. D. Johnstone (London: Oxford University Press, 1975).

—— see also *An RCO Miscellany*.

JONES, RICHARD, *Suite 1 [–4] for Violin and Basso Continuo*, ed. G. Beechey (MC 27–30; London: Oxford University Press, 1974).

KEEBLE, JOHN: see *Three Voluntaries of the Later Eighteenth Century*.

LAMPE, J. F., *Pyramus and Thisbe* (facs.) ed. R. Fiske (MLE, C/3; London: Stainer and Bell, 1988).

Late Georgian Composers, 1766–1838 (facs.), ed. N. Temperley (New York and London: Garland, 1985).

LINLEY, THOMAS [the younger], *Shakespeare Ode*, ed. G. Beechey (MB 30; London: Stainer and Bell, 1970).

—— *Two Madrigals*, ed. G. Beechey (London: Novello, 1978).

LOEILLET, J. B. ['de Gant'], *Two Sonatas* [for two flutes], ed. G. Beechey (MC 7; London: Oxford University Press, 1973).

MACFARREN, GEORGE: see *The Overture in England*.

MUDGE, RICHARD, *Concerto 2 in D Minor*, ed. R. Platt (MC 97; London: Oxford University Press, 1981).

NARES, JAMES, *Il Principio [1760]* (facs.), ed. R. Langley (London: Oxford University Press, 1981).

—— *Six Fugues with Introductory Voluntaries for the Organ or Harpsichord* (facs.), ed. R. Langley (London: Oxford University Press [1974]).

O'KEEFE, JOHN, and SHIELD, WILLIAM, *The Poor Soldier*, ed. W. Brasner and W. Osborne (Madison: A-R Editions, 1978).

O Tuneful Voice: 25 Classical English Songs, ed. T. Roberts (Oxford: Oxford University Press, 1992).

The Overture in England: Eight Overtures, 1800–1840: Bishop, Potter, Thomson, Macfarren, Sterndale Bennett (facs.), ed. N. Temperley with M. Greenbaum (The Symphony, 1720–1840, E/vi; New York and London: Garland, 1984).

PARRY, HUBERT, *Songs*, ed. G. Bush (MB 49; London: Stainer and Bell, 1982).

Pills to Purge Melancholy: see *Wit and Mirth*.

PINTO, GEORGE FREDERICK, *Complete Works for Pianoforte Solo* (facs.), ed. N. Temperley (LPS 14 (1); New York and London: Garland, 1985).

—— *Sonata in E flat Minor*, ed. N. Temperley (London: Stainer and Bell, 1963).

—— *Two Canzonets*, ed. N. Temperley (London: Novello, 1965).

POTTER, PHILIP CIPRIANI HAMBLY, *Selected Works* [for pianoforte solo] (facs.), ed. N. Temperley (LPS 14 (2); New York and London: Garland, 1985).

—— see also *The Overture in England*.

PRELLEUR, PETER: see *An RCO Miscellany*.

An RCO Miscellany: Eight Organ Voluntaries by John James, John Stanley, Peter Prelleur, Starling Goodwin and Others from a Mid-Eighteenth Century Manuscript now in the Library of the Royal College of Organists, ed. H. D. Johnstone (Eastwood: Basil Ramsey [1980]).

ROBINSON, JOHN, *Voluntary in A Minor*, ed. S. Jeans (London: Novello, 1966).

ROSEINGRAVE, THOMAS, *Compositions for Organ and Harpsichord*, ed. D. Stevens (University Park, Pa. and London, 1964).

ROSEINGRAVE, THOMAS, *Sonata 2 in D Major, for Flute and Basso Continuo*, ed. J. Barlow (MC 54; London: Oxford University Press, 1978).

—— *Two Sonatas for Flute and Basso Continuo*, ed. R. Platt (MC 21; London: Oxford University Press, 1975).

—— *Ten Organ Pieces*, ed. P. Williams (London: Stainer and Bell, 1961).

SAMMARTINI, GIOVANNI BATTISTA, *Concerto in G Major, Op. 6 No. 1*, ed. B. Cooper (MC 46; London: Oxford University Press, 1976).

SCHETKY, J. G. C., *Three Duets for Two Violoncellos*, ed. G. Beechey (MC 47; London: Oxford University Press, 1976).

SCHIKHARDT, JOHANN CHRISTIAN, *Sonata in D Major Op. 5 No. 2*, ed. B. Cooper (MC 39; London: Oxford University Press, 1978).

—— *Sonata in A Minor Opus 17 No. 3*, ed. R. Platt (MC 40; London: Oxford University Press, 1976).

A Selection of Four-Hand Duets (facs.), ed. N. Temperley (LPS 19; New York and London: Garland, 1986).

SHERARD, JAMES, *Twelve Trio Sonatas, Op. 2* (facs.), ed. M. Gilmore (Oxford: Oxford University Press, 1986).

Songs 1860–1900, ed. G. Bush (MB 56; London: Stainer and Bell, 1989).

STANFORD, CHARLES VILLIERS, *Songs*, ed. G. Bush (MB 52; London: Stainer and Bell, 1986).

STANLEY, JOHN, *Complete Works for Flute and Basso Continuo, Set 1 [–4] (Eight Solos Opus 1)*, ed. J. Caldwell (MC 15–18; London: Oxford University Press, 1974). (Continued as *Solo 9 [–14]*: see below.)

—— *Six Concertos Op. 2*, ed. J. Caldwell (MC 106; Oxford: Oxford University Press, 1987).

—— *Six Concertos for Organ, Harpsichord or Fortepiano (Opus X)* (facs.), ed. G. Gifford (Oxford: Oxford University Press, 1986).

—— *Solo 9 [–14]*, ed. J. Caldwell (London: Oxford University Press, 1978).

—— *Thirty Organ Voluntaries Op. 5–7*, ed. G. Phillips (London: Hinrichsen, 1967).

—— *Voluntaries for the Organ* (facs.), ed. D. Vaughan (London: Oxford University Press, 1957).

—— see also *An RCO Miscellany*.

STORACE, STEPHEN, *No Song, no Supper*, ed. R. Fiske (MB 16; London: Stainer and Bell, 1959).

SULLIVAN, ARTHUR, *Songs*, i, ed. A. Borthwick and R. Wilson (London: Stainer and Bell, 1986).

The Symphony 1720–1840, ed. B. S. Brook, 60 vols. (New York: Garland, 1979–86). The majority of the relevant works are in series E; titles and/or cross-references to composers are given in this Bibliography.

Ten 18th Century English Voluntaries, ed. R. Peek (St. Louis, Mo.: Concordia, 1965). An edn. of *A Collection of Voluntaries* (*c.*1770).

Ten Eighteenth-Century Voluntaries, ed. G. Beechey (RRMBE 6; Madison: A-R Editions, 1969).

THOMSON, JOHN: see *The Overture in England*.

WALOND, WILLIAM, *Three Cornet Voluntaries*, ed. G. Phillips (London: Hinrichsen, 1961).

—— *Three Voluntaries*, ed. G. Phillips (London: Hinrichsen, 1962).

—— see also *Ten Eighteenth-Century Voluntaries.*

WARLOCK, PETER, *Peter Warlock Collected Edition*, ed. F. Tomlinson, 8 vols. (n.p.: Thames, 1982–93).

—— *The Curlew*, ed. F. Tomlinson (London: Stainer and Bell, 1973).

—— *Thirteen Songs*, ed. P. Pears (Great Yarmouth: Galliard, 1970).

WEIDEMAN, CHARLES FREDERICK, *Sonata 2 in E Minor for Flute and Basso Continuo*, ed. J. Barlow (MC 71; London: Oxford University Press, 1980).

—— *Sonata 5 in D Major for Flute and Basso Continuo*, ed. J. Barlow (MC 72; London: Oxford University Press, 1980).

WESLEY, CHARLES, *Concerto No. 4 in C*, ed. G. Finzi (London: Hinrichsen, 1956).

—— see also *The Wesleys.*

WESLEY, SAMUEL, *Confitebor tibi, Domine*, ed. J. Marsh (MB 41; London: Stainer and Bell, 1978).

—— *Duet for organ*, ed. W. Emery (London: Novello, 1964).

—— *Fourteen Short Pieces for Organ*, ed. R. Langley (London: Oxford University Press, 1981).

—— *Six Voluntaries and Fugues for Organ*, ed. R. Langley (London: Oxford University Press, 1981).

—— *Symphony 2 in D Major*, ed. R. Platt (MC 53; London: Oxford University Press, 1976).

—— *Symphony 5 in A Major*, ed. R. Platt (MC 13; London: Oxford University Press, 1974).

—— *Trio in F Major for Two Flutes and Pianoforte*, ed. H. Cobbe (MC 12; London: Oxford University Press, 1973).

—— *Twelve Short Pieces*, ed. G. Phillips (London: Hinrichsen, 1957).

—— *Two Motets*, ed. J. Marsh (n.p.: Novello, 1974).

—— see also *The Wesleys.*

WESLEY, SAMUEL SEBASTIAN, *Anthems*, ed. P. Horton, 2 vols. (MB 57, 63; London: Stainer and Bell, 1990–93).

—— see also *The Wesleys.*

The Wesleys [organ pieces by], ed. G. Phillips, 2 vols. (London: Hinrichsen, 1960–61).

Wit and Mirth: Or, Pills to Purge Melancholy [ed. and largely written by T. D'Urfey], ed. C. L. Day, 6 vols. in 3 (New York: Folklore Library Publishers, 1959). Facs. of 1876 repr. of a mixed set of *Songs Compleat, Pleasant and Divertive* (for vols. i, iii, iv, v, London 1719) and *Wit and Mirth* (for vols. ii, vi, London 1719–20).

Works for Two Pianos (facs.), ed. N. Temperley (New York and London: Garland, 1986).

B. Scholarly Editions of Texts

BAX, ARNOLD, *Dermot O'Byrne: Selected Poems of Arnold Bax*, ed. L. Foreman (London, 1979).

BURNEY, CHARLES, *Dr Burney's Musical Tours in Europe*, ed. P. A. Scholes, 2 vols. (London, 1959).

—— *The Letters of Dr Charles Burney*, ed. A. Ribeiro, 4 vols. (Oxford, 1991–).

BURNEY, CHARLES, *Music, Men and Manners in France and Italy, 1770*, ed. H. E. Poole [from the same materials as Scholes, vol. 1] (London, 1969).
—— see also *Memoirs of Dr Charles Burney*.

CHORLEY, H. F., *Thiry Years' Musical Recollections*, 2 vols. [London, 1862] (repr. New York, 1984, with new index in vol. ii).

COKE, THOMAS, *Vice-Chamberlain Coke's Theatrical Papers 1706–1715*, ed. J. Milhous and R. D. Hume (Carbondale and Edwardsville, Ill., 1982).

CROTCH, WILLIAM, *Elements of Musical Composition* [London, 1812; 2nd edn., 1830] (facs. of 2nd edn.), ed. B. Rainbow (Aberystwyth, 1991).

DAY, ALFRED, *A Treatise on Harmony* [London, 1845] (fac. of Part II, and of Ch. 14 and the Appendix in Macfarren's edn. of 1885, in F. Jacobi, *Die Entwicklung der Musiktheorie*: see sect. *C* below).

D'URFEY, THOMAS, *The Songs of Thomas D'Urfey*, ed. C. L. Day (Cambridge, Mass., 1932).

ELGAR, EDWARD, *Elgar and his Publishers: Letters of a Creative Life*, ed. J. N. Moore (Oxford, 1987).
—— *The Windflower Letters: Correspondence with Alice Caroline Stuart Wortley and her Family*, ed. J. N. Moore (Oxford, 1989).

GEMINIANI, FRANCESCO, *The Art of Playing on the Violin* [1751] (facs.), ed. D. Boyden (London, 1952).

GURNEY, IVOR, *Collected Poems*, ed. P. J. Kavanagh (Oxford, 1982).
—— *War Letters*, ed. R. K. R. Thornton (Manchester, 1983).

The Librettos of Handel's Operas: A Collection of Seventy-One Librettos Documenting Handel's Operatic Career (facs.), ed. E. T. Harris, 13 vols. (New York and London, 1989).

Memoirs of Dr Charles Burney 1726–1769, ed. S. Klíma, G. Bowers, and K. S. Grant (Lincoln, Nebr. and London, 1988).

The Mirror of Music, 1844–1944 [selections from *MT*], ed. P. A. Scholes, 2 vols. (London, 1947).

NORTH, ROGER, *Roger North on Music*, ed. J. Wilson (London, 1959).
—— *The Musicall Grammarian 1728*, ed. M. Chan and J. C. Kassler (Cambridge, 1990).

SHAW, BERNARD, *Shaw's Music*, ed. D. H. Laurence, 3 vols. (London, 1981).

SMYTH, ETHEL, *The Memoirs of Ethel Smyth*, ed. R. Crichton (Harmondsworth, 1987).

STEVENS, R. J. S., *The Recollections of R. J. S. Stevens*, ed. M. Argent (London, 1992).

VAUGHAN WILLIAMS, U., and HOLST, I. (ed.), *Heirs and Rebels: Letters to Each Other and Occasional Writings on Music by Ralph Vaughan Williams and Gustav Holst* (London, 1959).

WOODFORDE, JAMES, *The Diary of a Country Parson*, ed. J. Beresford, 5 vols. (Oxford, 1924–31; repr. Norwich, 1996).

C. Books and Articles

Note. A 'Cumulative List of Accepted Dissertations and Theses to 1991' with 'Supplement 1', compiled by I. Bartlett and B. Sarnaker, was published in *RMARC* 25 (1992); a 'Supplement 2' appeared in vol. 27 (1994). It is arranged by subject-matter and is virtually complete for theses submitted to British and Irish universities. Section II, 'The British Isles', covers pp. 33–52 and 141–4 of vol. 25, and 106–8 of vol. 27; some of the items in Section III, 'General Subjects', are also relevant. American theses on British music can be extracted from *Doctoral Dissertations in Musicology* [*DDM*], ed. C. Adkins and A. Dickinson (7th North American/2nd International edn., American Musicological Society/International Musicological Society, 1984; *DDM*, Feb. 1984–Apr. 1995 (2nd ser., 2nd cumulative edn., AMS/IMS, 1996); now available as DDM-Online at http://www.indiana.edu/ddm (Project Director T. J. Mathiesen), with retrospective conversion in progress and frequent updates. Theses are listed below only if they have been used in writing the present work.

ABRAHAM, G., 'Our First Hundred Years', *PRMA* 100 (1973–4), pp. v–xi.

ADLINGTON, R., 'Harrison Birtwistle's Recent Music', *Tempo*, 196 (Apr. 1996), 2–8.

ALEXANDER, P. F., 'A Study of the Origins of "Curlew River"', *ML* 69 (1988), 229–43.

ALLBURGER, M. A., *Scottish Fiddlers and their Music* (London, 1983).

ANDERSON, R., 'Elgar and Some Apostolic Problems', *MT* 125 (1984), 13–16.

——— *Elgar* (London, 1993).

APLIN, J., 'Aldous Huxley and Music in the 1920s', *ML* 64 (1983), 25–36.

ATKINSON, M. E., 'The Orchestral Anthem in England, 1700–1775', DMA thesis (University of Illinois at Champaign-Urbana, 1991).

BANFIELD, S., 'Bax as a Song Composer', *MT* 124 (1983), 666–9.

——— *Sensibility and English Song* (Cambridge, 1985).

BANKS, P. (ed.), *The Making of 'Peter Grimes'*, 2 vols. (Woodbridge, 1996).

BARRETT, W. A., *English Glee and Madrigal Writers* (London, 1877).

——— *English Glees and Part-Songs* (London, 1886).

BARTLETT, I., and BRUCE, R. J., 'William Boyce's "Solomon"', *ML* 61 (1980), 28–49.

BEECHEY, G., 'Thomas Linley, 1756–78, and his Vocal Music', *MT* 119 (1978), 669–71.

BEECROFT, J., 'Maxwell Davies's Fifth Symphony', *Tempo*, 191 (Dec. 194), 2–5.

BEEDELL, A. V., *The Decline of the English Musician, 1788–1888: A Family of English Musicians in Ireland, England, Mauritius, and Australia* (Oxford, 1992).

BEEKS, G., 'Handel's Chandos Anthems: The "Extra" Movements', *MT* 119 (1978), 621–3.

——— 'Handel's Chandos Anthems: More "Extra" Movements', *ML* 62 (1981), 155–61.

BENNETT, A., 'Broadsides on the Trial of Queen Caroline: A Glimpse at Popular Song in 1820', *PRMA* 107 (1980–1), 71–85.

BEST, T., 'Handel's Chamber Music: Sources, Chronology and Authenticity', *Early Music*, 12 (1985), 476–99.

BIDDLECOMBE, G., *English Opera from 1834 to 1864 with Particular Reference to the Works of Michael Balfe* (New York and London, 1994).

BLAKE, A., *The Land without Music* (Manchester, 1997).

BODEN, A., *Gloucester, Hereford, Worcester. Three Choirs: A History of the Festival* (Stroud, 1992).

BOWEN, M., *Michael Tippett* (London, 1982).

BOYD, M., 'English Secular Cantatas in the Eighteenth Century', *MR* 30 (1969), 85–97.

BOYDEN, D., 'A Postscript to "Geminiani and the First Violin Tutor"', *AcM* 32 (1960), 40–7.

—— *The History of Violin Playing from its Origins to 1761* (London, 1965; 3rd impr., 1974, repr. Oxford, 1990).

BRETT, P. (ed.), *Benjamin Britten: 'Peter Grimes'* (Cambridge, 1983).

BRITTEN, B., 'Introduction', in E. Crozier (ed.), *Benjamin Britten: Peter Grimes* (London, 1946: Sadler's Wells Opera Books, No. 3), an important source-book reprinted in P. Brett (ed.), *Benjamin Britten: 'Peter Grimes'* (Cambridge, 1983).

The Britten Companion, ed. C. Palmer (London, 1984).

A Britten Source Book, comp. J. Evans, P. Reed, and P. Wilson (rev. edn., Aldeburgh, 1987).

BROCK, D., 'A Note on F. E. Bache, 1833–58', *MT* 124 (1983), 673–5.

BROWN, B. L., 'The Harpsichord Music of Handel's Younger English Contemporaries: A Reassessment', D.Phil. thesis (University of Manchester, 1965–6).

BRUCE, R. J., 'William Boyce: Some Manuscript Recoveries', *ML* 55 (1974), 437–43.

BUDDS, M., 'Music at the Court of Queen Victoria: A Study of Music in the Life of the Queen and her Participation in the Musical Life of her Time', 3 vols., Ph.D. diss. (University of Iowa, 1987).

BURCHELL, J., *Polite or Commercial Concerts? Concert Management and Orchestral Repertoire in Edinburgh, Bath, Oxford, Manchester, and Newcastle, 1730–1799* (New York and London, 1996).

BURDEN, M., 'The British Masque 1690–1800', Ph.D. diss. (University of Edinburgh, 1991).

—— 'The Independent Masque in Britain in the Eighteenth Century: A Catalogue', *RMARC* 28 (1995), 59–159.

BURN, A., 'The Music of Howard Ferguson', *MT* 124 (1983), 480–2.

BURROWS, D., 'Sources for Oxford Handel Performances in the First Half of the Eighteenth Century', *ML* 61 (1980), 177–85.

—— 'The Composition and First Performance of Handel's "Alexander's Feast"', *ML* 64 (1983), 206–11.

—— 'The "Granville" and "Smith" Collections of Handel Manuscripts', in *Sundry Sorts of Music Books* (London, 1993), 231–47.

BURTON, A., 'The Recent Music of Edward Cowie', *MT* 123 (1982), 99–103.

BUTTON, S., *The Guitar in England 1800–1924* (New York and London, 1989 [repr. of Ph.D. thesis, University of Surrey, 1984]).

BYARD, H., *The Bristol Madrigal Society* (Bristol, 1966).

CARERI, E., *Francesco Geminiani* (Oxford, 1993).

CARLEY, L., *Delius: A Life in Letters* (London, 1983).

CARPENTER, H., *Benjamin Britten: A Biography* (London, 1992).

CHAN, M., and KASSLER, J. C., *Roger North's The Musicall Grammarian and Theory of Sounds: Digests of the Manuscripts; with an Analytical Index of the 1726 and 1728 Theory of Sounds by J. D. Hine* (Kensington, NSW, 1988).

CHAPMAN, C., 'A 1727 Pantomine: *The Rape of Proserpine*', *MT* 122 (1981), 807–11.

CHARLTON, P., *John Stainer and the Musical Life of Victorian Britain* (Newton Abbot, 1984).

CHRYSANDER, F., *Georg Friedrich Händel*, 3 vols. (Leipzig, 1858–67).

CLEMENTS, A., 'John Casken', *MT* 123 (1982), 21–3.

—— 'Harrison Birtwistle: A Progress Report at 50', *MT* 125 (1984), 136–9.

COBBE, H., 'The Royal Musical Association 1874–1901', *PRMA* 110 (1983–4), 111–17.

COLE, H., *Malcolm Arnold: An Introduction to his Music* (London and Boston, 1989).

COLLINS, B., *Peter Warlock: The Composer* (Aldershot, 1996).

COOK, D. F., 'The Life and Works of Johann Christoph Pepusch (1667–1752), with Special Reference to his Dramatic Works and Cantatas', Ph.D. thesis (University of London, 1983).

COOPER, B., 'New Light on John Stanley's Organ Music', *PRMA* 101 (1974–5), 101–6.

—— 'Keyboard Sources in Hereford', *RMARC* 16 (1980), 135–9.

—— *English Solo Keyboard Music of the Middle and Late Baroque* (New York and London, 1989 [repr. of thesis, Oxford 1974]).

COOVER, J., *Music at Auction: Puttick and Simpson (of London), 1794–1971* (Detroit Studies in Music Bibliography, 60; Warren, Mich., 1988).

COPLEY, I. A., *The Music of Peter Warlock: A Critical Survey* (London, 1979).

COX, G., *A History of Music Education in England 1872–1928* (Aldershot, 1993).

CRAGGS, S. R., *William Walton: A Thematic Catalogue of his Musical Works. With a Critical Appreciation by Michael Kennedy* (London, 1977).

—— 'Felix White: A Centenary Note', *MT* 125 (1984), 207–8.

—— *Arthur Bliss: A Bio-Bibliography* (New York and London, 1988).

CUDWORTH, C. L., 'The English Organ Concerto', *The Score*, 8 (Sept. 1953), 51–60.

—— 'Boyce and Arne: The Generation of 1710', *ML* 41 (1960), 136–45.

DAUB, P. E., 'Music at the Court of George II (r. 1727–1760)', Ph.D diss. (Cornell University, 1985).

DAUBNEY, B. B. (ed.), *Aspects of British Song: A Miscellany of Essays* (Upminster, 1992).

DAVIE, C. T., *Catalogue of the Finzi Collection in St Andrews University Library* (St Andrews, 1982).

DAWE, D., 'New Light on William Boyce', *MT* 109 (1968), 802–7.

DAWES, F., 'The Music of Philip Hart (*ca.* 1676–1749), *PRMA* 94 (1967–8), 63–75.

DEAN, W., *Handel's Dramatic Oratorios and Masques* (London, 1959).

—— *Handel and the Opera Seria* (Berkeley and Los Angeles, 1969).

—— 'Handel's Atalanta', in *Sundry Sorts of Music Books* (London, 1993), 215–31.

—— and Knapp, J. M., *Handel's Operas 1704–1726* (Oxford, 1987).

DEARNLEY, C., *English Church Music 1650–1750 in Royal Chapel, Cathedral and Parish Church* (London, 1970).

DE-LA-NOY, M., *Elgar the Man* (London, 1983).

DEUTSCH, O. E., *Handel: A Documentary Biography* (London, 1955).

DIBBLE, J., *C. Hubert H. Parry: His Life and Music* (Oxford, 1992).

DICKINSON, P., 'Lord Berners, 1883–1950', *MT* 124 (1983), 669–72.

DICKINSON, P., *The Music of Lennox Berkeley* (London, 1988).

DREYER, M., 'Herbert Howells at 90: The Cello Fantasia and its Orchestral Predecessors', *MT* 123 (1982), 668–71.

DRIVER, P., '"The Mask of Time"', *Tempo*, 149 (June 1984), 39–44.

DRUMMOND, P., 'The Royal Society of Musicians in the Eighteenth Century', *ML* 59 (1978), 268–89.

DUNCAN, R., *Working with Britten* (London, 1981).

EDWARDS, O., 'English String Concertos before 1800', *PRMA* 95 (1968–9), 1–13.

EHRLICH, C., *The Music Profession in Britain since the Eighteenth Century: A Social History* (Oxford, 1985).

—— *Harmonious Alliance: A History of the Performing Right Society* (Oxford and New York, 1989).

—— *The Piano: A History* (2nd edn., Oxford, 1989).

—— *First Philharmonic: A History of the Royal Philharmonic Society* (Oxford, 1995).

ELBOURNE, E., *Music and Tradition in Early Industrial Lancashire 1780–1840* (Woodbridge and Totowa, NJ, 1980).

ELKIN, ROBERT, *Queen's Hall 1893–1941* (London [1944]).

—— *The Old Concert Rooms of London* (London, 1955).

ELLIS, D., 'Thomas Pitfield at 80', *MT* 124 (1983), 230.

ELLSWORTH, E. M., 'The Piano Concerto in London Concert Life between 1801 and 1850', Ph.D. diss. (University of Cincinnati, 1991).

EVANS, P., *The Music of Benjamin Britten* (2nd edn., London, 1989; reissued with additions, Oxford, 1996).

FALLOWS, D., 'Musicology in Great Britain, 1979–1982', *AcM* 55 (1983), 244–53.

FAWCETT, T., *Music in Eighteenth-Century Norwich and Norfolk* (Norwich, 1979).

FENBY, E., *Delius as I Knew Him* (London, 1936).

FISKE, R., 'The "Macbeth" Music', *ML* 45 (1964), 114–25.

—— *English Theatre Music in the Eighteenth Century* (London, 1973; 2nd edn., Oxford, 1986).

FOREMAN, L., 'Bax and the Ballet', *PRMA* 104 (1977–8), 11–19.

—— *Arthur Bliss: Catalogue of the Complete Works* (Sevenoaks, 1980).

—— *Bax: A Composer and his Times* (2nd edn., Aldershot, 1988).

—— *From Parry to Britten: British Composers in Letters 1900–1945* (London, 1987).

—— *Music in England 1885–1920* (London, 1994).

FREEMAN, R., 'Retuning the Skies—Ferneyhough's "On Stellar Magnitudes"', *Tempo*, 191 (Dec. 1994), 34–7.

FROGLEY, A., 'H. G. Wells and Vaughan Williams's *A London Symphony*: Politics and Culture in Fin-de-siècle England', in *Sundry Sorts of Music Books* (London, 1993), 299–308.

FROST, T., 'The Cantatas of John Stanley', *ML* 53 (1972), 284–92.

GATENS, W. J., 'Fundamentals of Musical Criticism in the Writings of Edmund Gurney and his Contemporaries', *ML* 63 (1982), 17–30.

—— *Victorian Cathedral Music in Theory and Practice* (Cambridge, 1986).

GIBSON, E., 'Owen Swiney and the Italian Opera in London', *MT* 125 (1984), 82–6.

—— *The Royal Academy of Music 1719–1728* (New York and London, 1989).

—— 'Italian Opera in London, 1750–1775: Management and Finances', *Early Music*, 18 (1990), 47–59.

GILLESPIE, N., 'The Text of Stanley's "Teraminta"', *ML* 64 (1983), 218–24.

GIRDHAM, J., *English Opera in Late Eighteenth-Century London: Stephen Storace at Drury Lane* (Oxford, 1997).

GOEHR, A., 'Richard Hall: A Memoir and a Tribute', *MT* 124 (1983), 677–8.

GOOCH, B. N. S., and THATCHER, D. S., *Musical Settings of Late Victorian and Modern British Literature: A Catalogue* (New York and London, 1976).

—— *Musical Settings of British Romantic Literature*, 2 vols. (New York and London, 1982).

GOODALL, R., *Eighteenth-Century English Secular Cantatas* (New York and London, 1989).

GRANT, K. S., *Dr Burney as Critic and Historian* (Ann Arbor, 1983).

GRAY, C., *Peter Warlock: A Memoir of Philip Heseltine* (London, 1934).

GREENE, R., 'A Musico-Historical Outline of Holst's "Egdon Heath"', *ML* 73 (1992), 244–67.

—— *Gustav Holst and a Rhetoric of Musical Character: Language and Method in Selected Orchestral Works* (New York and London, 1994).

GRIFFITHS, P., 'Bill Hopkins: A Provisional Catalogue of Compositions and Writings', *MT* 122 (1981), 600–1.

—— *Maxwell Davies* (London, 1982).

Gustav Holst (1874–1934): A Centenary Documentation, ed. M. Short (London, 1974).

HALL, B., *The Proms, and the Men who Made Them* (London, 1981).

HALL, M., *Harrison Birtwistle* (London, 1984).

A Handbook for Studies in 18th-Century English Music, ed. M. Burden and I. Cholij, 11 vols. (Edinburgh, 1987–).

HARLEY, J., 'Music at the English Court in the Eighteenth and Nineteenth Centuries', *ML* 50 (1969), 332–51.

—— *British Harpsichord Music*, 2 vols. (Aldershot, 1992–4).

HARRIES, M. and S., *A Pilgrim Soul: The Life and Works of Elisabeth Lutyens* (London, 1989).

HARRIS, E. T., *Handel and the Pastoral Tradition* (London, 1980).

HARRIS, R. L., 'Robert Sherlaw Johnson at 50', *MT* 123 (1982), 326–9.

—— 'Bernard Rands at 50', *MT* 126 (1985), 532–4.

HEARTZ, D., 'Thomas Attwood's Lessons in Composition with Mozart', *PRMA* 100 (1973–4), 175–84.

HEIGHES, S. J., *The Life and Works of William and Philip Hayes* (New York and London, 1995).

HERBERT, T. (ed.), *The Brass Band Movement in the 19th and 20th Centuries* (Buckingham and Bristol, Pa., 1991).

HICKMAN, R., 'The Censored Publication of *The Art of Playing on the Violin*, or Geminiani Unshaken', *Early Music*, 9 (1983), 73–6.

HINDLEY, C., 'Platonic Elements in "Death in Venice"', *ML* 73 (1992), 407–29.

HINDMARSH, P., *Frank Bridge: A Thematic Catalogue* (London, 1983).

HINNELLS, D., *An Extraordinary Performance: Hubert Foss, Music Publishing, and the Oxford University Press* (Oxford, 1998).

HOGWOOD, C., 'Thomas Tudway's History of Music', in *Music in Eighteenth-Century England*, ed. C. Hogwood and R. Luckett (Cambridge, 1983), 19–47.

HOGWOOD, C., and Luckett, R. (eds.), *Music in Eighteenth-Century England: Essays in Memory of Charles Cudworth* (Cambridge, 1983).

HOLST, I., *Gustav Holst: A Biography* (London, 1938; 2nd edn., 1969).

—— *The Music of Gustav Holst* (London, 1951; 3rd edn., 1975; with *Holst's Music Reconsidered*, Oxford, 1987).

—— *A Thematic Catalogue of Gustav Holst's Music* (London, 1974).

—— (comp.), *Gustav Holst, 1874–1934: A Guide to his Centenary* (Cambridge, 1974).

HOSKINS, R. H. B., 'Dr Samuel Arnold: An Historical Assessment', Ph.D. diss. (University of Auckland, 1981).

—— 'The Pantomimes and Ballets of Samuel Arnold', *Studies in Music* (University of Western Australia), 19 (1985), 80–93.

HOWARD, P. (ed.), *Benjamin Britten: 'The Turn of the Screw'* (Cambridge, 1985).

HOWES, F., *The Music of William Walton* (London, 1965; 2nd edn., 1974).

—— *The English Musical Renaissance* (London, 1966).

—— *Oxford Concerts: A Jubilee Record* (Oxford, 1969).

—— *Folk Music of Britain—and Beyond* (London, 1970).

HUDSON, F., 'A Revised and Extended Catalogue of the Works of Charles Villiers Stanford (1852–1924)', *MR* 37 (1976), 106–29.

HUME, R. D., 'Covent Garden Theatre in 1732', *MT* 123 (1982), 823–6; followed by articles by A. Saint, C. Chapman, and L. Langley, to mark the 250th anniversary of the theatre, pp. 826–38.

—— 'Handel and Opera Management in London in the 1730s', *ML* 67 (1986), 347–62.

HURD, M., *The Ordeal of Ivor Gurney* (London, 1978).

—— *Vincent Novello—and Company* (London, 1981).

—— *Rutland Boughton and the Glastonbury Festivals* (Oxford, 1993).

HUTCHINGS, A., *The Baroque Concerto* (London, 1961).

HYDE, D., *New-found Voices: Women in Nineteenth-Century English Music* (London, 1984).

IRVING, H., 'William Crotch on "The Creation"', *ML* 75 (1994), 548–60.

JACOBI, E. R., *Die Entwicklung der Musiktheorie in England nach der Zeit von Jean-Philippe Rameau* (Strasbourg, 1960).

JACOBS, A., *Arthur Sullivan: A Victorian Musician* (Oxford, 1984; 2nd edn., Aldershot, 1992).

JOHNSON, D., *Music and Society in Lowland Scotland in the Eighteenth Century* (London, 1972).

JOHNSTONE, H. D., 'An Unknown Book of Organ Voluntaries', *MT* 108 (1967), 1003–7.

—— 'The Life and Work of Maurice Greene (1696–1755)', 2 vols., D.Phil. thesis (University of Oxford, 1968).

—— 'The Genesis of Boyce's "Cathedral Music"', *ML* 56 (1975), 26–40.

—— 'The RCO Manuscript Re-examined', *MT* 126 (1985), 237–9.

—— 'More on Dr. Hoadly's "Poems Set to Music by Dr. Greene"', *Studies in Bibliography*, 50 (1997), 262–71.

KASSLER, J. C., *The Science of Music in Britain, 1714–1830: A Catalogue of Writings, Lectures and Inventions*, 2 vols. (New York and London, 1979).
—— 'The Royal Institution Music Lectures, 1800–1831: A Preliminary Study', *RMARC* 19 (1983–1–30.

KEMP, I., 'Rhythm in Tippett's Early Music', *PRMA* 105 (1978–79), 142–53.
—— *Tippett: The Composer and his Music* (London, 1984).

KENNEDY, M., *The Works of Ralph Vaughan Williams* (London, 1964; 2nd edn., 1980, substituting a short catalogue for the original full one [see *A Catalogue*, below]).
—— *Portrait of Elgar* (London, 1968; 3rd edn., Oxford, 1987).
—— 'The Unknown Vaughan Williams', *PRMA* 99 (1972–3), 31–41.
—— *Britten* (London, 1981).
—— *A Catalogue of the Works of Ralph Vaughan Williams* (2nd edn., Oxford, 1996).
—— *The Hallé 1858–1983: A History of the Orchestra* (Manchester, 1982).
—— *Portrait of Walton* (Oxford, 1989).

KENT, C., 'A View of Elgar's Methods of Composition through the Sketches of the Symphony No. 2 in E♭ (Op. 63)', *PRMA* 103 (1976–7), 41–60.
—— 'Elgar's Third Symphony: The Sketches Reconsidered', *MT* 123 (1982), 532–7.
—— 'John Marsh and the Organ: Introducing an RCO Manuscript', *RCO Journal*, 1 (1993), 27–45.

KENYON, N., *The BBC Symphony Orchestra: The First Fifty Years, 1930–1980* (London, 1981).

KIDD, R. R., 'The Sonata for Keyboard with Violin Accompaniment in England', Ph.D. diss. (Yale University, 1967).
—— 'The Emergence of Chamber Music with Obligato Keyboard in England', *AcM* 44 (1972), 122–44.

KLEIN, H., *Thirty Years of Musical Life in London 1870–1900* (London, 1903).

KLÍMA, S. V., 'Dussek in England', *ML* 41 (1960), 146–9.

KURZHALS-REUTER, A., *Die Oratorien Felix Mendelssohn Bartholdys: Untersuchungen zur Quellenlage, Entstehung, Gestaltung und Überlieferung* (Tutzing, 1978).

LANGLEY, L., 'The Life and Death of the Harmonicon: An Analysis', *RMARC* 22 (1989), 137–63.

LANGLEY, R., 'John Field and the Genesis of a Style', *MT* 123 (1982), 92–9.

LANGWILL, L. G., and Boston, N., *Church and Chamber Barrel Organs* (2nd edn., Edinburgh, 1970).

LARSSON, R. B., 'Charles Avison's "Stiles in Musical Expression"', *ML* 63 (1982), 261–75.

LARUE, J., 'British Music Paper, 1770–1820: Some Distinctive Characteristics', *Monthly Musical Record*, 87 (1957), 177–80.

LASOCKI, D., 'The French Hautboy in England, 1673–1730', *Early Music*, 16 (1988), 339–57.

LEPPERT, R., *Music and Image: Domesticity, Ideology, and Socio-cultural Formation in Eighteenth-century England* (Cambridge, 1988).

LINDGREN, L., 'Ariosti's London Years', 1716–29', *ML* 62 (1981), 331–51.
—— 'Musicians and Librettists in the Correspondence of Gio. Giacomo Zamboni (Oxford, Bodleian Library, MSS Rawlinson Letters 116–138)', *RMARC* 24 (1991), 1–194.

LINDGREN, L., 'Another Critic Named Samber', in *Festa Musicologica: Essays in Honor of George J. Buelow*, ed. T. J. Mathiesen and B. V. Riviera (Stuyvesant, NY, 1995), 407–34.

LLOYD, A. L., *Folk Song in England* (London, 1967).

LLOYD, S., *H. Balfour Gardiner* (Cambridge, 1984).

LOVELL, P., '"Ancient" Music in Eighteenth-Century England', *ML* 60 (1979), 401–15.

LOWE, R., *Frederick Delius 1862–1934: A Catalogue of the Music Archive of the Delius Trust* (London, 1974).

—— *A Descriptive Catalogue with Checklists of the Letters and Related Documents in the Delius Collection of the Grainger Museum, University of Melbourne, Australia* (London, 1981).

LOWENS, I., 'The *Touch-stone*: A Neglected View of London Opera', *MQ* 45 (1959), 325–42.

LYNAN, P., 'The English Keyboard Concerto in the Eighteenth Century', 2 vols., D.Phil. thesis (University of Oxford, 1997).

LYSONS, D., *et al.*, *Origin and Progress of the Meeting of the Three Choirs of Gloucester, Worcester & Hereford, and of the Charity Connected with it* (Gloucester, 1895).

McCULLOCH, D., 'Royal Composers', *MT* 122 (1981), 525–9.

MACDERMOTT, K. H., *Sussex Church Music in the Past* (2nd edn., Chichester, 1923).

—— *The Old Church Gallery Minstrels* (London, 1948).

MacDONALD, M., *The Symphonies of Havergal Brian*, 3 vols. (London, 1974–83).

McGRADY, R., 'The Music of Constant Lambert', *ML* 51 (1970), 242–58.

McGREGOR, R. E., 'The Maxwell Davies Sketch Material in the British Library' *Tempo*, 196 (Apr. 1996), 9–19.

McNEILL, R., 'Moeran's Unfinished Symphony', *MT* 121 (1980), 771–7; see also ibid. 122 (1981), 230.

McVEIGH, S. W., 'Felice Giardini: A Violinist in Late Eighteenth-Century London', *ML* 64 (1983), 162–72.

—— 'Music and Lock Hospital in the 18th Century', *MT* 129 (1988), 235–40; see also ibid. 385.

—— *The Violinist in London's Concert Life 1750–1784* (New York and London, 1989).

—— 'The Professional Concert and Rival Subscription Series in London, 1783–1793', *RMARC* 22 (1989), 1–135.

—— *Concert Life in London from Mozart to Haydn* (Cambridge, 1993).

MARK, C., *Early Benjamin Britten: A Study of Stylistic and Technical Evolution* (New York and London, 1995).

MASLEN, K., 'Dr. Hoadly's "Poems Set to Music by Dr. Greene"', *Studies in Bibliography*, 48 (1995), 85–94.

MATTHEWS, B., 'Handel and the Royal Society of Musicians', *MT* 125 (1984), 79–82.

—— *The Royal Society of Musicians of Great Britain: List of Members 1738–1984* (London, 1985).

MATTHEWS, C., 'Some Unknown Holst', *MT* 125 (1984), 269–72.

MATTHEWS, D., *Michael Tippett: An Introductory Study* (London, 1980).

MEDFORTH, M., 'The Valentines of Leicester: A Reappraisal of an 18th-Century Musical Family', *MT* 122 (1981), 812–18.

MEE, J. H., *The Oldest Music Room in Europe: A Record of Eighteenth-Century Enterprise at Oxford* (London and New York, 1911).

MELLERS, W., *Twilight of the Gods: The Beatles in Retrospect* (London, 1973).

—— *Vaughan Williams and the Vision of Albion* (London, 1989).

MILHOUS, J., and HUME, R. D., 'J. F. Lampe and English Opera at the Little Haymarket in 1732–3', *ML* 78 (1997), 502–31.

MILSOM, J., 'Songs and Society in Early Tudor London', *Early Music History*, 16 (1997), 235–93.

MITCHELL, D., *Britten and Auden in the Thirties: The Year 1936* (London, 1981).

—— (ed.), *Benjamin Britten: 'Death in Venice'* (Cambridge, 1987).

—— and Keller, H. (eds.), *Benjamin Britten: A Commentary on his Works from a Group of Specialists* (London, 1952).

MOORE, J. N., *Edward Elgar: A Creative Life* (Oxford, 1984).

MORONI, F., 'Keyboard Ensembles in Britain: Piano Trios, Quartets, Quintets and their Antecedents', D.Phil. thesis (University of Oxford, 1966).

NETTEL, R., *Music in the Five Towns 1840–1914* (Oxford, 1944).

—— *The Orchestra in England: A Social History* (London, 1948).

NEWBOULD, B., '"Never done before": Elgar's Other Enigma', *ML* 77 (1996), 228–41.

NIELSEN, N. K., 'Handel's Organ Concertos Reconsidered', *Dansk aarbog for musikforskning* (1963), 3–26.

NORMAN, J., *The Organs of Britain: An Appreciation and Gazeteer* (Newton Abbot, 1984).

NORMAN, P., 'More Wesley Organ Duets?', *MT* 125 (1984), 287–9.

NORRIS, G., *Stanford, the Cambridge Jubilee and Tchaikovsky* (Newton Abbot, 1980).

NORTHCOTT, B., 'In Search of Walton', *MT* 123 (1982), 179–84.

—— 'On—and From—Goehr', *MT* 123 (1982), 541–4.

—— (ed.), *The Music of Alexander Goehr* (London, 1980).

NOSKE, F., 'Sound and Sentiment: The Function of Music in the Gothic Novel', *ML* 62 (1981), 162–75.

PAGE, J. K., 'The Hautboy in London's Musical Life, 1730–1770', *Early Music*, 16 (1988), 358–71.

PALMER, C., 'Constant Lambert—A Postscript', *ML* 52 (1971), 173–6.

—— *Herbert Howells: A Study* (Sevenoaks, 1978).

PARKINSON, J. A., *Victorian Music Publishers: An Annotated List* (Detroit Studies in Bibliography, 64; Warren, Mich., 1990).

—— 'A Knot of Weipperts', in *Sundry Sorts of Music Books* (London, 1993), 174–81.

PAULTON, A., *Walton: A Discography* (London, 1981).

PEARCE, C. W., *Notes on English Organs . . . from the MS of Henry Leffler* (London, 1911).

—— *The Evolution of the Pedal Organ* (London, 1927).

Peter Maxwell Davies: Studies from Two Decades [repr. from articles in *Tempo*, 1964–78], ed. Stephen Pruslin (London, 1979).

PICKERING, J. M., *Music in the British Isles 1700–1800: A Bibliography of Literature* (Edinburgh, 1990).

PILKINGTON, M., *Gurney, Ireland, Quilter and Warlock* (English Solo Song: Guides to the Repertoire, [i]; London, 1989).

PIRIE, P. J., *The English Musical Renaissance* (London, 1979).

POHL, C. F., *Mozart und Haydn in London*, 2 vols. (Vienna, 1867).

PONSONBY, R., and KENT, R., *The Oxford University Opera Club: A Short History, 1925–1950* (Oxford [1950]).

PONT, G., 'Handel's Overtures for Harpsichord or Organ: An Unrecognized Genre', *Early Music*, 9 (1983), 309–22.

PRICE, C., MILHOUS, J., and HUME, R. D., *The Impresario's Ten Commandments: Continental Recruitment for Italian Opera in London 1763–64* (RMA Monographs, 6; London, 1992).

—— MILHOUS, J., and HUME, R. D., *Italian Opera in Late Eighteenth-Century London: The King's Theatre, Haymarket, 1778–1791* (Oxford, 1995).

PRITCHARD, B. W., 'The Music Festival and the Choral Society in England in the 18th and 19th Centuries: A Social History', Ph.D. thesis (University of Birmingham, 1968).

—— 'Some Festival Programmes of the Eighteenth and Nineteenth Centuries, 3: Liverpool and Manchester', *RMARC* 7 ([1967]), 1–25, with addenda to '2: Cambridge and Oxford', communicated by G. Beechey, ibid. 26–7 [see Reid].

—— and D. J. REID, '. . . 4: Birmingham, Derby, Newcastle upon Tyne and York', ibid. 8 (1970), 1–22; 'Addenda and Corrigenda to 1: Salisbury and Winchester', communicated by B. Matthews, ibid. 23–33 [see Reid].

PUFFETT, D., 'In the Garden of Fand: Arnold Bax and the "Celtic Twilight"', in *Art Nouveau Jugenstil und Musik* [Festschrift W. Schuh] (Zurich and Freiburg im Breisgau, 1980), 193–210.

RAINBOW, B., *The Land Without Music* (London, 1967).

—— *The Choral Revival in the Anglican Church 1839–1872* (New York, 1970).

—— *John Curwen: A Short Critical Biography* (Sevenoaks, 1980).

—— 'Singing for their Supper', *MT* 125 (1984), 227–9.

REED, W. H., 'Elgar's Third Symphony', *The Listener*, 14, no. 346 (28 Aug. 1935), Supplement of 16 extensive facs. of the sketches.

—— *Elgar* (London, 1939; repr. with additions, 1943).

REID, D. J., 'Some Festival Programmes of the Eighteenth and Nineteenth Centuries, 1: Salisbury and Winchester', *RMARC* 5 (1965), 51–79.

—— '. . . 2: Cambridge and Oxford', ibid. 6 (1966), 3–22; 'Addenda to 1: Salisbury and Winchester', communicated by A. D. Walker, ibid. 23 [see Pritchard for remaining articles and further addenda].

RENNERT, J., *William Crotch* (London, 1975).

RIGBY, C., *Sir Charles Hallé: A Portrait for Today* (Manchester, 1952).

RISHTON, T., 'William Smethergell, Organist', *MT* 124 (1983), 381–4.

RITCHLEY, L. I., 'The Untimely Death of Samuel Wesley; Or, The Perils of Plagiarism', *ML* 60 (1979), 45–59.

ROE, S., 'J. C. BACH, 1735–1782: Towards a New Biography', *MT* 123 (1982), 23–6.

—— 'J. C. Bach's Vauxhall Songs: A New Discovery', *MT* 124 (1983), 675–6.

RUSSELL, D., *Popular Music in England, 1840–1914: A Social History* (Manchester, 1987).

SAINT, A., et al., A History of the Royal Opera House Covent Garden (1732–1982) (London, 1982).

SAMUEL, H. E., 'John Sigismond Cousser in London and Dublin', ML 61 (1980), 158–71.

SCHOELCHER, V., The Life of Handel (London, 1857).

SCHOLES, P. A., God Save the Queen: The History and Romance of the World's First National Anthem (London, 1954).

SCHUELLER, H. M., 'The Quarrel of the Ancients and Moderns', ML 41 (1960), 313–30.

SEARLE, M. V., John Ireland: The Man and his Music (Tunbridge Wells, 1979).

SELF, G., The Music of E. J. Moeran (n.p., 1986).

SHAPIRO, A. H., ' "Drama of an Infinitely Superior Nature": Handel's Early English Oratorios and the Religious Sublime', ML 74 (1993), 215–45.

SHARP, C. J., English Folk-Song: Some Conclusions (London, 1907).

SHEAD, R., Constant Lambert (London, 1973).

SHORT, M., Gustav Holst: The Man and his Music (Oxford and New York, 1990).

SILBIGER, A., 'Scarlatti Borrowings in Handel's Grand Concertos', MT 125 (1984), 93–5.

SMITH, J. B., Frederick Delius and Edvard Munch: Their Friendship and their Correspondence (Rickmansworth, 1983).

SMITH, R., 'Intellectual Contexts of Handel's English Oratorios', in Music in Eighteenth-Century England (Cambridge, 1983), 115–33.

—— 'The Achievements of Charles Jennens (1700–1773)', ML 70 (1989), 161–890.

—— Handel's Oratorios and Eighteenth-Century Thought (Cambridge, 1995).

SMITH, W. C., Handel: A Descriptive Catalogue of the Early Editions (London, 1960; 2nd edn., Oxford, 1970).

—— and HUMPHRIES, C., A Bibliography of the Musical Works Published by the Firm of John Walsh during the Years 1721–1766 (London, 1968).

SMITHER, H., The Oratorio in the Classical Era (Oxford, 1987).

SOMFAI, LASZLO, 'The London Revision of Haydn's Instrumental Style', PRMA 100 (1973–4), 159–74.

STRADLING, R., and Hughes, M., The English Musical Renaissance 1860–1940: Construction and Deconstruction (London, 1993).

STROHM, R., Essays on Handel and Italian Opera (Cambridge, 1985).

TEMPERLEY, N., 'Instrumental Music in England, 1800–1850', Ph.D. diss. (University of Cambridge, 1959).

—— 'Raymond and Agnes', MT 107 (1966), 307–10.

—— 'The Origins of the Fuging Tune, RMARC 17 (1981), 1–32.

—— Haydn: The Creation (Cambridge, 1991).

—— 'The Lock Hospital Chapel and its Music', JRMA 118 (1993), 44–72.

—— (ed.), The Lost Chord: Essays on Victorian Music (Bloomington and Indianapolis, 1989).

TERRY, C. S., John Christian Bach (London, 1929; 2nd edn., rev. H. C. Robbins Landon, Oxford, 1967).

THRELFALL, R., 'Delius: A Fresh Glance at Two Famous Scores', *MT* 125 (1984), 315–19.

THRELFALL, R., *A Catalogue of the Compositions of Frederick Delius* (London, 1977); *Frederick Delius: A Supplementary Catalogue* (ibid. 1986).

TILMOUTH, M., 'The Beginnings of Provincial Concert Life in England', in *Music in Eighteenth-Century England* (Cambridge, 1983), 1–17.

TIMMS, C., 'Handelian and Other Librettos in Birmingham Central Library', *ML* 65 (1984), 141–67.

TORTOLANO, W., *Samuel Coleridge-Taylor: Anglo Black Composer 1875–1912* (Metuchen, NJ, 1977).

TREND, M., *The Music Makers: The English Musical Renaissance from Elgar to Britten* (London, 1985).

TRETHOWAN, W. H., 'Ivor Gurney's Mental Illness', *ML* 42 (1981), 300–9.

TROWELL, B., 'Elgar's Marginalia', *MT* 125 (1984), 139–43.

—— 'Acis, Galatea and Polyphemus: A "*Serenata a tre voci*"?', in *Music and Theatre: Essays in Honour of Winton Dean*, ed. N. Fortune (Cambridge, 1987), 31–93.

—— 'Elgar's Songs as "Contrafacta": Some Lost or Unknown Songs and Song-Texts Recovered', in *Sundry Sorts of Music Books* (London, 1993), 282–98.

—— 'Elgar's Use of Literature', in R. Monk (ed.), *Edward Elgar: Music and Literature* (Aldershot, 1993), 182–326.

TURBET, R., 'The Fall and Rise of William Byrd, 1623–1901', in *Sundry Sorts of Music Books* (London, 1993), 119–28.

—— 'An Affair of Honour: "Tudor Church Music", the Ousting of Richard Terry, and a Trust Vindicated', *ML* 76 (1995), 593–600.

VAUGHAN WILLIAMS, U., 'Ralph Vaughan Williams and his Choice of Words for Music', *PRMA* 99 (1972–3), 81–9.

—— *R.V.W.: A Biography of Ralph Vaughan Williams* (London, 1964; repr. with corrections, Oxford, 1984).

WAINWRIGHT, D., 'John Broadwood, the Harpsichord and the Piano', *MT* 123 (1982), 675–8.

WARBURTON, E., 'J. C. Bach's Operas', *PRMA* 92 (1965–6), 95–105.

WARNABY, J., 'Maxwell Davies's "Resurrection": Origins, Themes, Symbolism', *Tempo*, 191 (Dec. 1994), 6–13.

WEBER, WILLIAM, 'Intellectual Bases of the Handelian Tradition, 1759–1800', *PRMA* 108 (1981–2), 100–14.

—— *The Rise of Musical Classics in Eighteenth-Century England* (Oxford, 1992).

WHITE, E. W., *Tippett and his Operas* (London, 1979).

—— (ed.), *Benjamin Britten: His Life and Operas* (London, 1983).

WHITTALL, A., 'The Study of Britten: Triadic Harmony and Tonal Structure', *PRMA* 106 (1979–80), 27–41.

—— *The Music of Britten and Tippett: Studies in Themes and Techniques* (Cambridge, 1982; 2nd edn., Cambridge, 1990).

—— 'The Signs of Genre: Britten's Version of Pastoral', in *Sundry Sorts of Music Books* (London, 1993), 363–74.

WILLIAMS, A. G., 'The Life and Works of John Stanley (1712–86)', 2 vols., Ph.D. thesis (University of Reading, 1977).

—— 'Stanley, Smith and "Teraminta"', *ML* 60 (1979), 312–15.

WILLIAMS, P. F., 'English Organ Music and the English Organ under the First Four Georges', Ph.D. thesis (University of Cambridge, 1962–3).

WILSON, J., 'John Stanley: Some Opus Numbers and Editions', *ML* 39 (1958), 359–62.

WOLLENBERG, S. L. F., 'Music in 18th-Century Oxford', *PRMA* 108 (1981–2), 69–99.

—— 'Music and Musicians', in *The History of the University of Oxford*, v: *The Eighteenth Century*, ed. L. S. Sutherland and L. G. Mitchell (Oxford, 1986), 865–87.

YOUNG, P. M., *George Grove 1820–1900: A Biography* (London, 1980).

ZON, B., 'Plainchant in the Roman Catholic Church in England, 1737–1834', D.Phil. thesis (University of Oxford, 1993).

—— *The English Plainchant Revival* (Oxford, 1998).

III. COLLECTIONS OF FOLK SONG AND DANCE

Collections made since about 1800 are listed under the name of the collector or primary editor. The modern literature on folk song and popular music, insofar as it concerns the period covered by this volume, is incorporated into section II.C above. Some items from lowland Scotland, Ireland, and Wales are included. An asterisk indicates a collection with no music.

BARING-GOULD, S., *English Minstrelsie: A National Monument of English Song*, 8 vols. (Edinburgh [1895]).

—— and Sheppard, H. F., *Songs and Ballads of the West Country*, 4 vols. (London, 1889–92; 2nd edn., 1891–5; 3rd edn., rev., 1905; 4th edn., rev., n.d.)

BARRETT, W. A., *English Folk Songs* (London, 1891).

*BELL, J., *Rhymes of the Northern Bards* (Newcastle, 1812).

*BELL, R., *Ancient Poems, Ballads and Songs of the Peasantry of England* (London, 1857).

BOULTON, H., and SOMERVELL, A., *Songs of the Four Nations* (London, 1892).

BROADWOOD, J., *Old English Songs of Sussex and Surrey* (London, 1843).

BROADWOOD, L., *English Traditional Songs and Ballads* (London, 1905).

—— and FULLER-MAITLAND, J. A., *English County Songs* (London, 1893).

—— see also Reynardson and Birch.

BRONSON, B. H., *The Traditional Tunes of the Child Ballads*, 4 vols. (Princeton, 1959–72).

BROWN, C., *The Songs of Scotland* (London and New York [1873]).

BRUCE, J. C., and STOKOE, J., *Northumbrian Minstrelsy* (Newcastle upon Tyne, 1882; repr. 1965).

BUNTING, E., *A General Collection of the Ancient Irish Music* (London, 1796).

—— *A General Collection of the Ancient Music of Ireland...*, Vol. 1st [*sic*] (London, [1809]).

—— *The Ancient Music of Ireland* (Dublin, 1840).

The Bunting Collection of Irish Folk Music and Songs, ed. D. J. O'Sullivan, 6 vols. (Dublin, 1927–39 = *Journal of the Irish Folk Song Society*, 22, 23, 26, 27, 28–9).

BUTTERWORTH, G., *Folk Songs from Sussex* (London, 1913).

CAREY, C., *Ten English Folk Songs* (London, 1915).

CHAPPELL, W., *A Collection of National English Airs* (London, 1839 [–40]).

—— see also Sect. I.B above.

*CHILD, F. J., *The English and Scottish Popular Ballads*, 10 parts (Cambridge, Mass., 1882–98; 5-vol. edn. by G. L. Kittredge, Boston, 1882–98; shortened edn. by H. C. Sargent and G. L. Kittredge, 1904; repr. in 3 vols., 1957; repr. New York, 1965).

CHRISTIE, W., *Traditional Ballad Airs* (Edinburgh, 1876).

COPPER, B., *Songs and Southern Breezes* (London, 1973).

DAUNEY, W., *Ancient Scotish Melodies, from a Manuscript of the Reign of King James VI. With an Introductory Enquiry Illustrative of the History of Music in Scotland* (Edinburgh, 1838).

DUNSTAN, R., *Christmas Carols* (London, 1923).

—— *A Second Book of Christmas Carols* (London, 1925).

—— *A Cornish Song Book* (London, 1929).

FOXWORTHY, T., *Forty Long Miles: Twenty-three English Folk Songs from the Collection of Janet Heatly Blunt* (London, 1976).

GARDINER, G. B., *Folk Songs from Hampshire* (London, 1909; repr. in Sharp *et al.*, 1961).

—— see also Purslow.

GRAINGER, P., *Seven Lincolnshire Folk Songs*, ed. P. O'Shaughnessy (London, 1966).

—— *Twenty-one Lincolnshire Folk Songs*, ed. P. O'Shaughnessy (London, 1968).

—— *More Folk Songs from Lincolnshire*, ed. P. O'Shaughnessy (London, 1971).

HAMER, F., *Green Groves* (London, 1973).

HAMMOND, H. E. D., *Folk Songs from Dorset* (London, 1908; repr. in Sharp *et al.*, 1961).

—— see also Purslow.

HATTON, J. L, *The Songs of England* (London and New York [1873]).

HUNTER, J., *The Fiddle Music of Scotland* (Edinburgh, 1979).

JOHNSON, J., *The Scots Musical Museum*, 6 vols. (Edinburgh, 1787–1803); ed. W. Stenhouse, 4 vols. (Edinburgh and London, 1853; repr. 1962).

JONES, E., *Musical and Poetical Relicks of the Welsh Bards* (London, 1784; 2nd edn., 1794).

—— *The Bardic Museum* (London, 1802).

—— *Hên Ganaidau Cymru: Cambro-British Melodies* (London, 1820).

JOYCE, P. W., *Old Irish Folk Music and Songs: A Collection of 842 Irish Airs and Songs Hitherto Unpublished* (London and Dublin, 1909).

KARPELES, M., *The Crystal Spring* (London, 1975).

KENNEDY, P., *Folk-Songs of Britain and Ireland* (London, 1975).

KIDSON, F., *Traditional Tunes* (Oxford, 1981, repr. 1970).

KINSLEY, J., *The Oxford Book of Ballads* (Oxford, 1969).

LLOYD, A. L., *Come All Ye Bold Miners: Ballads and Songs of the Coalfields* (London, 1952).

MERRICK, W. P., *Folk Songs from Sussex* (London, 1912, repr. in Sharp *et al.*, 1961).

MOERAN, E. J., *Six Folk Songs from Norfolk* (London, 1924).

—— *Six Suffolk Folk Songs* (London, 1932).

MOLLOY, J. L., *The Songs of Ireland* (London and New York [1873]).

MOORE, T., *A Selection of Irish Melodies*, 10 parts and Supplement (London, 1808–34). There are numerous later edns.; see also Stanford, C. V.

MOTHERWELL, W., *Minstrelsy Ancient and Modern, with an Historical Introduction, and Notes* (Glasgow, 1827; 2nd edn., Paisley, 1873).

PALMER, R., *Songs of the Midlands* (Wakefield, 1972).

—— *The Valiant Sailor* (Cambridge, 1973).

The Petrie Collection of the Ancient Music of Ireland (Dublin, 1855; repr. Farnborough, 1967, with 48 pp. of the planned 2nd vol.).

PURSLOW, F., *English Folk Songs from the Hammond and Gardiner MSS*, 3 vols. (London, 1965–72: the 3 vols. are called *Marrow Bones* (1965), *The Wanton Seed* (1968), and *The Constant Lovers* (1972).

REYNARDSON, H. F. B., and Birch, H. E., *Sussex Songs* (London, 1889). Based on Broadwood, J. (1843), with additional material supplied by L. Broadwood.

RICHARDS, B., *The Songs of Wales* (London and New York [1873]).

SHARP, C. J., *Country Dance Tunes*, 4 vols. (London, 1909–22).

—— *English Folk Carols* (London, 1911).

—— *The Sword Dances of Northern England*, 2 vols. each of dance notations and of piano arrangements (London, 1911–13; 2nd edn., ed. M. Karpeles, 1950–1).

—— *English Folk-Chanteys* (London, 1914).

—— *English Folk Songs* (London, 1920; repr. 1959 as 'Centenary Edition').

—— *Cecil Sharp's Collection of English Folk Songs*, ed. M. Karpeles, 2 vols. (London, 1974).

—— and CAMPBELL, O. D., *English Folk-Songs from the Southern Appalachian Mountains*, 2 vols. (London, 1917; 2nd edn., 1932; 3rd edn. by M. Karpeles, 1960).

—— and MARSON, C. L., *Folk Songs from Somerset* (Taunton, 1904–19; repr. in Sharp *et al.*, 1961).

—— *et al.*, *English County Songs* (London, 1961: reprs. of various vols. of *Folk Songs of England*, 1904 foll.).

SHEPARD, L., *The Broadside Ballad: A Study in Origins and Meaning* (London, 1962).

SIMPSON, C. M., *The British Broadside Ballad and its Music* (New Brunswick, NJ, 1966).

STANFORD, C. V., *The Irish Melodies of Thomas Moore* (London and New York, 1895).

TERRY, R. R., *The Shanty Book* (London, 1921–6).

VAUGHAN WILLIAMS, R., *Folk Songs from the Eastern Counties* (London, 1908, repr. Sharp *et al.*, 1961).

—— *Eight Traditional Carols* (London, 1919).

—— *A Yacre of Land*, ed. I. Holst and U. Vaughan Williams (London, 1961).

—— *Folk Songs Collected by Ralph Vaughan Williams*, ed. R. Palmer (London, 1983).

—— and LEATHER, E. M., *Twelve Carols from Herefordshire* (London, 1920).

—— and LLOYD, A. L., *The Penguin Book of English Folk Songs* (London, 1959).

WHITTAKER, W. G., *North Countrie Ballads, Songs and Pipe Tunes* (London, 1921).

Wilson's Edition of the Songs of Scotland, 2 vols. (London [1842]).

APPENDIX. ADDENDA TO VOLUME I

A.   Modern Editions of Music

Berkeley Castle, Select Roll 55: Motets and Sequences from the Early Fourteenth Century, ed. A. Wathey (Newton Abbot: Antico, 1991).

BLOW, JOHN, *Anthems III: Anthems with Strings,* ed. B. Wood (MB 64; London: Stainer and Bell, 1993).

The Bodleian Year-Books Mass: An Anonymous Three-voice Mass of the Early Sixteenth Century, ed. N. Sandon (Newton Abbot: Antico, 1991).

COPRARIO, JOHN, *The Two-, Three-and Four-Part Consort Music,* ed. R. Charteris (London and Bermuda: Fretwork, 1991).

COX, RICHARD, *Missa sine nomine,* ed. N. Sandon (Newton Abbot: Antico, 1989).

DOWLAND, JOHN, *Lachrimae (1604): A Reproduction of the Copy Owned by Robert Spencer,* ed. W. Edwards *et al.* (Newbury: Severinus Press, 1992).

English Song 1600–1675: Facsimiles of Twenty-Six Manuscripts and an Edition of the Texts, ed. E. B. Jorgens, 12 vols. (New York: Garland, 1986).

FERRABOSCO, Alfonso the younger, *Four-Part Fantasias for Viols,* ed. A. Ashbee and B. Bellingham (MB 62; London: Stainer and Bell, 1992).

Five Sequences for the Virgin Mary, ed. M. Bent (London: Oxford University Press, 1973).

JENKINS, JOHN, *Consort Music of Three Parts,* ed. A. Ashbee (MB 70; London: Stainer and Bell, 1997).

—— *The Lyra Viol Consorts,* ed. F. Traficante (RRMBE 67–8; Madison: A-R Editions, 1992).

LAWES, WILLIAM, *Fantasia-Suites,* ed. D. Pinto (MB 60; London: Stainer and Bell, 1991).

LUPO, THOMAS, *The Six-Part Consort Music,* ed. R. Charteris (London and Bermuda: Fretwork, 1993).

MICO, RICHARD, *Consort Music,* ed. A. Hanley (MB 65; London: Stainer and Bell, 1994).

—— *The Four-part Consort Music,* ed. R. Tyler (London and Bermuda: Fretwork, 1992).

MORLEY, THOMAS, *English Anthems; Liturgical Music,* ed. J. Morehen (EECM 38; London: Stainer and Bell, 1991).

Music for Elizabethan Lutes, ed. J. M. Ward, 2 vols. (Oxford: Oxford University Press, 1992).

PARSONS, ROBERT, *Latin Sacred Music,* ed. P. Doe (EECM 40; London: Stainer and Bell, 1994).

PHILIPS, PETER, *Cantiones Sacrae Octonis Vocibus (1613),* ed. J. Steele (MB 61; London: Stainer and Bell, 1992).

—— *Cantiones Sacrae Quinis Vocibus,* ed. J. Steele (Dunedin: University of Otago Press, 1992).

—— *Fifteen Motets for Solo Voice and Continuo,* ed. L. Pike (Newton Abbot: Antico, 1991).

PLUMMER, JOHN, *Missa sine nomine,* ed. N. Sandon (Newton Abbot: Antico, 1990).

Priscilla Bunbury's Virginal Book, ed. V. Brookes (Albany: PRB Productions, 1993).

TOMKINS, THOMAS, *Consort Music*, ed. J. Irving (MB 59; London: Stainer and Bell, 1991).

—— *Musica Deo Sacra*, vols. v, vi, ed. B. Rose (EECM 37, 39; London: Stainer and Bell, 1991–2).

Tudor Keyboard Music c. 1520–1580, ed. J. Caldwell (MB 66; London: Stainer and Bell, 1995).

Two Songs for Christmas, ed. M. Bent (London: Oxford University Press, 1974).

WARD, JOHN, *Consort Music of Five and Six Parts*, ed. I. Payne (MB 67; London: Stainer and Bell, 1995).

WILDER, PHILIP van, *Collected Works, Parts I and II*, ed. J. A. Bernstein (Masters and Monuments of the Renaissance, 4; New York: The Broude Trust, 1991).

WILSON, JOHN, *Thirty Preludes in All (24) Keys for the Lute*, ed. M. Spring (Utrecht: The Diapason Press, 1992).

B.   *Modern Editions of Literature*

COPRARIO, GIOVANNI, *Rules How to Compose* [*c.*1610] (facs.), ed. M. F. Bukofzer (Los Angeles, 1952).

A Handefull of Pleasant Delites, ed. H. E. Rollins (Cambridge, Mass., 1924).

Three Rastell Plays: Four Elements, Calisto and Melebea, Gentleness and Nobility, ed. R. Axton (Cambridge, and Totowa, NJ, 1979).

C.   *Books and Articles*

BENT, M., 'Pycard's Double Canon: Evidence of Revision', in *Sundry Sorts of Music Books* (London, 1993), 10–26.

—— and HOWLETT, D.: '*Subtiliter alternare*: The Yoxford Motet *O amicus/ Precursoris*', in *Studies in Medieval Music: Festschrift for Ernest H. Sanders*, ed. P. M. Lefferts and B. Seirup (New York, 1990 = *Current Musicology*, 45–7), 43–83.

BOWERS, R., 'The Cultivation and Promotion of Music in the Household and Orbit of Thomas Wolsey', in S. J. Gunn and P. G. Lindley (eds.), *Cardinal Wolsey, Church, State, and Art* (Cambridge, 1991).

BRENNAN, M. G., 'Sir Charles Somerset's Music Books (1622)', *ML* 74 (1993), 501–18.

BRETT, P., 'Pitch and Transposition in the Paston Manuscripts', in *Sundry Sorts of Music Books* (London, 1993), 89–118.

BROWN, A., '"The Woods so Wild": Notes on a Byrd Text', in *Sundry Sorts of Music Books* (London, 1993), 54–66.

BULLOCK-DAVIES, C., *Menstrellorum Multitudo: Minstrels at a Royal Feast* (Cardiff, 1978).

—— *A Register of Royal and Baronial Domestic Minstrels 1272–1327* (Woodbridge, 1986).

Byrd Studies, ed. A. Brown and R. Turbet (Cambridge, 1992).

CALDWELL, J., 'Music in the Faculty of Arts', in *The History of the University of Oxford*, iii: *The Collegiate University*, ed. J. McConica (Oxford, 1986), 201–12.

CHARTERIS, R., 'Newly Discovered Sources of Music by Henry Purcell', *ML* 75 (1994), 16–32.

COOPER, B., 'Problems in the Transmission of Blow's Organ Music', *ML* 75 (1994), 522–47.

CUTTS, J. P., *Roger Smith, His Booke: Bishop Smith's Part-Song Books in Carlisle Cathedral Library* (n.p.: American Institute of Musicology, 1972).

ELLIOTT, J. R., Jr., 'Invisible Evidence: Finding Musicians in the Archives of the Inns of Court, 1446–1642', *RMARC* 26 (1993), 45–57.

EVERIST, M. E., 'From Paris to St Andrews: The Origins of W 1', *JAMS* 43 (1990), 1–42.

FALLOWS, D., 'The Drexel Fragments of Early Tudor Song', *RMARC* 26 (1993), 5–18.

—— 'Henry VIII as a Composer', in *Sundry Sorts of Music Books* (London, 1993), 27–39.

FENLON, I., 'Michael Honywood's Music Books', in *Sundry Sorts of Music Books* (London, 1993), 183–200.

—— and Milsom, J., '"Ruled Paper Imprinted": Music Paper and Patents in Sixteenth-Century England', *JAMS* 37 (1984), 139–63.

FLANAGAN, D. T., 'Polyphonic Settings of the Lamentations of Jeremiah by Sixteenth-Century English Composers', 2 vols., Ph.D. diss. (Cornell University, 1990).

FORD, R., 'Bevins, Father and Son', *MR* 43 (1982), 104–8.

GOUK, P. 'Music', *Seventeenth-Century Oxford* (=*History of the University of Oxford*, iv), ed. N. Tyacke (Oxford, 1997), 621–40.

HAMESSLEY, L., 'The Tenbury and Ellesmere Partbooks: New Findings on Manuscript Compilation and Exchange, and the Reception of the Italian Madrigal in Elizabethan England', *ML* 73 (1992), 177–221.

HARPER, J., *The Forms and Orders of Western Liturgy from the Tenth to the Eighteenth Century* (Oxford, 1991).

HARRISON, F. Ll., 'Music at Oxford before 1500', in *The History of the University of Oxford*, ii: *Late Medieval Oxford*, ed. J. I. Catto and R. Evans (Oxford, 1992), 347–71.

HOLMAN, C. W., 'John Day's "Certaine Notes" (1560–1565)', 2 vols., Ph.D. diss. (University of Kansas, 1991).

HOLMAN, P., *Four and Twenty Fiddlers: The Violin at the English Court 1540–1690* (Oxford, 1993).

—— *Henry Purcell* (Oxford, 1994).

HULSE, L., 'The Musical Patronage of Robert Cecil, First Earl of Salisbury (1563–1612)', *JRMA* 116 (1991), 24–40.

—— 'Matthew Locke: Three Newly Discovered Songs for the Restoration Stage', *ML* 75 (1994), 200–13.

IRVING, JOHN, 'Morley's Keyboard Music', *ML* 75 (1994), 333–43.

KAY, D., *Melodious Tears: The English Funeral Elegy from Spenser to Milton* (Oxford, 1990).

KERMAN, J., 'The Missa "Puer natus est nobis" by Thomas Tallis', in *Sundry Sorts of Music Books* (London, 1993), 40–53.

KIRKMAN, A., 'The Transmission of English Mass Cycles in the Mid to Late Fifteenth Century: A Case Study in Context', *ML* 75 (1994), 180–99.

KISBY, F., 'Music and Musicians of Early Tudor Westminster', *Early Music*, 23 (1995), 223–40.

LEAVER, R. A., *'Goostly Psalmes and Spirituall Songs': English and Dutch Metrical Psalms from Coverdale to Utenhove* (Oxford, 1991).

LOSSEFF, N., *The Best Concords: Polyphonic Music in Thirteenth-Century Britain* (New York and London, 1994).

MATEER, D., 'The Compilation of the Gyffard Partbooks', *RMARC* 26 (1993), 19–43.

—— 'The "Gyffard" Partbooks: Composers, Owners, Date and Provenance', *RMARC* 28 (1995), 21–50.

MEMED, O., *Seventeenth-Century English Keyboard Music: Benjamin Cosyn* (New York and London, 1993).

MILSOM, J., 'English Texted Chant before Merbecke', *Plainsong and Medieval Music* 1 (1992), 77–92.

—— 'The Nonsuch Music Library', in *Sundry Sorts of Music Books* (London, 1993), 146–82.

—— 'Songs and Society in Early Tudor London', *Early Music History* 16 (1997), 235–93.

MOREHEN, J., 'The Southwell Minster Tenor Part-Book in the Library of St Michael's College, Tenbury (MS. 1382)', *ML* 50 (1969), 352–64.

MORONEY, D., '"Bounds and Compasses": The Range of Byrd's Keyboards', in *Sundry Sorts of Music Books* (London, 1993), 67–88.

Music in the Medieval English Liturgy, ed. S. Rankin and D. Hiley (Oxford, 1993).

ORME, N., *English Schools in the Middle Ages* (London, 1973).

PAYNE, I., 'The Musical Establishment at Trinity College, Cambridge, 1546–1644', *Proceedings of the Cambridge Antiquarian Society*, 74 (1985), 53–69.

—— *The Provision and Practice of Sacred Music at Cambridge Colleges and Selected Cathedrals c.1547–c.1646: A Comparative Study of the Archival Evidence* (New York and London, 1993).

PHILLIPS, P., *English Sacred Music 1549–1649* (Oxford, 1991).

PRESTON, M. J., *A Complete Concordance to the Songs of the Early Tudor Court* (Compendia, 4; Leeds, 1972).

RUFF, L. M., and Wilson, D. A., 'The Madrigal, the Lute Song and Elizabethan Politics', *Past and Present*, 44 (1969), 3–51.

—— 'Allusion to the Essex Downfall in Lute Song Lyrics', *LSJ* 12 (1970), 31–6.

SCHOLES, P. A., *The Puritans and Music in England and New England* (London, 1934).

SHAW, W., *The Services of John Blow* (Croydon, 1988).

SKINNER, D., '"At the mynde of Nycholas Ludford": New Light on Ludford from the Churchwardens' Accounts of St Margaret's, Westminster', *Early Music*, 22 (1994), 393–410.

—— 'Nicholas Ludford (c.1490–1557): A Biography and Critical Edition of the Votive Antiphons with a Study of the Collegiate Foundations of Westminster and Arundel', D.Phil. thesis (University of Oxford, 1996).

SPINK, I., *Restoration Cathedral Music, 1660–1714* (Oxford, 1995).

STEVENS, J., '*Angelus ad virginem*: The History of a Medieval Song', in *Medieval Studies for J. A. W. Bennett*, ed. P. L. Heyworth (Oxford, 1981), 297–328.

WALLS, P., *Music in the English Courtly Masque 1604–1640* (Oxford, 1996).

WATHEY, A., 'The Marriage of Edward III and the Transmission of French Motets to England', *JAMS* 45 (1992), 1–29.

WESTFALL, S. R., *Patrons and Performance: Early Tudor Household Revels* (Oxford, 1990).

WICKHAM, G., *Early English Stages 1300–1660*, 3 vols. (London, 1963–72).

WILLETTS, P., 'Sir Nicholas Le Strange and John Jenkins', *ML* 42 (1961), 30–43.

——'Benjamin Cosyn: Sources and Circumstance', in *Sundry Sorts of Music Books* (London, 1993), 129–45.

WOODLEY, R., *John Tucke: A Case Study in Early Tudor Music Theory* (Oxford, 1993).

Index